MOMENTS *of* TRUTH

Four Creators of Modern Medicine

MOMENTS
of TRUTH

THOMAS DORMANDY

WILEY

Published in 2003 by   John Wiley & Sons, Ltd, The Atrium, Southern Gate
Chichester, West Sussex, PO19 8SQ, England

Phone   (+44) 1243 779777

Email (for orders and customer service enquiries): cs-books@wiley.co.uk
Visit our Home Page on www.wiley.co.uk or www.wiley.com

Other Wiley Editorial Offices

John Wiley & Sons, Inc. 111 River Street, Hoboken, NJ 07030, USA

Jossey-Bass, 989 Market Street, San Francisco, CA 94103–1741, USA

Wiley-VCH Verlag GmbH, Boschstr. 12, D-69,469 Weinheim, Germany

John Wiley & Sons Australia, Ltd, 33 Park Road, Milton, Queensland, 4064, Australia

John Wiley & Sons (Asia) Pte Ltd, 2 Clementi Loop #02–01, Jin Xing Distripark, Singapore
129809

John Wiley & Sons Canada Ltd, 22 Worcester Road, Etobicoke, Ontario, Canada, M9W 1L1

Wiley also publishes its books in a variety of electronic formats. Some content that appears
in print may not be available in electronic books.

British Library Cataloguing in Publication Data

A catalogue record for this book is available from the British Library

ISBN 0-470-86321-8

Typeset in $10\frac{1}{2}/13\frac{1}{2}$pt Photina by Mathematical Composition Setters Ltd, Salisbury, Wiltshire.
Printed and bound in Great Britain by T.J. International Ltd, Padstow, Cornwall.
This book is printed on acid-free paper responsibly manufactured from sustainable forestry
in which at least two trees are planted for each one used for paper production.

To Liz, as always, and to Simon and Charlotte,
Richard and Ruth, and to Michael and Letty,
with love

Contents

CONTENTS

Acknowledgements

Without Liz, Michael and Letty there would be no book.

I am grateful to many others who have helped me. Howard and Margaret Chapman have been a wonderful support. My brother John has given me more help than he will admit or even perhaps realises. Among other kindnesses, he has re-analysed statistically some of Lister's early results. Adam Storring has guided me along the trail of Crazy Horse and Sitting Bull. Bill Newsom gave me many hints and much valuable information on Semmelweis. Mihály Boros, an inspired translator among many other accomplishments, sent me important original material. Ian Douglas-Wilson has been a superb adviser on style and content. Sally M. Smith has been a most perceptive and helpful editor.

I also owe a debt of gratitude to two people, both now dead. First my mother, Clara Dormandy, had been planning to write a biography of Semmelweis for 40 years. I cannot pretend that her papers included much previously unavailable information, but they did contain many human insights and personal assessments. I hope I have made judicious use of those. Second, as a medical student I had the temerity to ask Dr Jean-Claude Masset who that fellow Laennec was. He was outraged. 'If you were studying to be a writer, you would not have to ask me who that fellow Shakespeare was. If you were preparing for a career as a composer, you would not have to ask me who that fellow Mozart was. But as an ignorant medical student ...' Over a period of some months he then nearly overwhelmed me with Laennec lore, correcting in minor details even his friend Rouxeau. Spiritually Laennec has been my companion ever since.

The courtesy and helpfulness of the staff of the Libraries of the Royal Society of Medicine and the Wellcome Medical Historical Museum are a source of continual wonderment to me.

I am grateful to the Science Photo Library for permission to reproduce the prints at the beginning of each part.

London, 2003

INTRODUCTION

Professions like to claim long and impressive pedigrees. Princely dynasties too, especially those of obscure or plebeian origin, liked to trace their lineage to Julius Caesar or King Solomon. These were innocent conceits. So are most professional ancestries. Yet there was usually a decade or a century when modern professions turned into what makes them recognisable today. Only the time of transformation was rarely the one that is traditionally commemorated.

Traditionally, doctors in the West have looked back to the island of Cos where, 2500 years ago, Hippocrates dispensed words and perhaps deeds of medical wisdom. He was a nebulous historical figure. His name means a driver of horses, but little else is known about him. The Hippocratic writings are a collection of old texts of mixed and uncertain origin. His most famous aphorism, 'Art is long, opportunity is fleeting, experiment is uncertain and judgement is difficult', is usually misquoted or given in its corrupt Latin form.[1] He also formulated a code of conduct and an oath. They are noble precepts, but as hard to obey in practice as the Ten Commandments.

Sometimes the profession is traced back even further, to the semi-divine figure of Aesculapius (or Asklepios). The son of Apollo and the nymph Coronis, he dwelt on the slopes, if not on the very summit, of Mount Olympus. He had many shrines in the Hellenic world. They were usually situated near healing springs in salubrious surroundings, not unlike some of the more expensive sanatoria and health farms 2000 years later. Pilgrims in search of health slept in the temple grounds because the god performed his cures during sleep. His professional attendants sometimes supervised lengthy courses of treatment. Those who were healed were asked to hang up votive tablets recording their names, ailments and the manner of their cure. Hundreds of such tablets survive. They are interesting, but impossible to interpret in modern pathological terms. Yet Aesculapian attributes are still widely used as medical symbols. Most common is the healing staff with a snake, the ancient symbol of wisdom, curled round it. It is often confused with Mercury's *caduceus*, which has two snakes wrapped round it in a double helix, anticipating the DNA molecule. Two snakes are presumably wiser than one.[2]

There is of course no doubt that concepts of health and disease—and of death as the outcome of certain diseases—have exercised the minds of men and women since before the beginning of written history.[3] 'Medicine men' flourished in the earliest civilisations; they still do in primitive societies.[4] They wrestle with evil spirits, ward off death, tend the sick and comfort the dying. Or so they claim; and they are believed by their followers. Their exploits remain an important division of archaeology, anthropology, comparative religion and related disciplines. As atavistic images they are also of some interest to doctors. Ancient medicine too is a recognised though usually somewhat arid branch of historical scholarship. It is arid because so much of it remains incomprehensible or highly speculative. Is it right to call it medicine at all?

Texts on medical history often begin with dramatic images of prehistoric skulls showing trephine holes. Some at least of the victims must have survived, since the edges of the holes show evidence of new bone formation. They can be regarded as deliberate and perhaps successful surgical interventions, even as the beginning of keyhole surgery.[5] Some recognisably modern illnesses—tuberculosis of the spine, gallstones and rickets among them—are undoubtedly of ancient origin. The term medicine itself dates back to antiquity: *medicus* is what Galen and Celsus styled themselves. However, these are word games.

Moving forward in time, the learned monks who taught in the famous medical school of Salerno in Southern Italy in the twelfth and thirteenth centuries are usually credited with reinventing medicine after the Dark Ages. The school was supposedly founded by a Greek philosopher, a Latin teacher, a Jewish rabbi and an Arab sage. The legend is figuratively true. Situated at cultural crossroads, the establishment benefited from its geographical location. Rapacious Norman dukes promoted tourism and the influx of students and scholars.[6] Though usually poor, robed and absent-minded academics added a certain *ton* to their otherwise rowdy court. With a few amendments, the monks' most famous literary product, the *Regimen sanitatis salernitatum*, a guide to healthy living from youth to old age in chiming verse, still makes common sense. It existed in more than 200 Latin versions during the Middle Ages and was translated into several European vernaculars. But that was the beginning of home doctoring, not of medicine as a profession and a specialised field of expertise.

Despite the odd absence of a Christian priest from among the legendary founders, the Salernian tradition, soon to be copied elsewhere, was devoutly Christian as well as classical. There was no contradiction. Physical as well as spiritual healing had been among Christ's divine Acts. According to venerable sources, St Luke the Evangelist was a doctor as well as an artist. Not only artists' guilds but also hospitals were named after him. In Renaissance Italy in times of peril the two professions petitioned together for his intercession. Their pleas were often answered. The early Medici were proud of the medical ancestry implied by their name.[7] Nevertheless, it was still not medicine as the term is generally understood today.

The Renaissance and Baroque produced the first medical figures whose individual lives, achievements and writings are documented and dusted down from time to time. Paracelsus, Ambroise Paré, Sylvius, Sir Thomas Browne and a few others have all had their dedicated biographers; and their names acquire a vaguely familiar ring to most medical students during their pupillage.[8] A few of their sayings survive and continue to be quoted, though they are almost always distorted, turned inside out or out of context.[9] The melancholy skeleton that adorns the first page of Vesalius's anatomical masterpiece is reproduced in

most modern textbooks of anatomy, as well as on the dust covers of thrillers of a particularly gruesome kind.[10]

William Harvey has become the secular patron saint of English physicians. In unconscious tribute to him, doctors with a naturally tidy mind learn to affect his famously illegible hand.[11] John Hunter is his nearest surgical counterpart.[12] Harveian orators of the Royal College of Physicians of London and Hunterian professors of the Royal College of Surgeons of England search their works for a suitable quotation with which to introduce their oration or memorial lecture.[13] Yet none of these historical figures, not even Harvey who was a successful practitioner as well as an inspired experimental scientist, were recognisably practising medicine as the word is used today. Many advanced the basic sciences, but their personal discoveries were quickly developed and transformed and are now barely recognisable as individual creative acts.[14] This is not to belittle their achievement: they were great men. But were they doctors?

Moving on a century, neither Jenner nor Withering would be allowed to carry out their experiments today; but over the centuries their enterprise has saved millions of young lives.[15] Thomas Sydenham gave an excellent description of rashes and fevers. His was probably a brilliant mind, although it is impossible to be certain since, outside a few short passages, most of what he wrote makes no sense to the modern medical reader.[16] But did any of these people ever examine their patients?

The story of the Chinese emperor asking for guidance about his painful feet and addressing his letter to 'Monsieur Boerhaave, doctor, Europe' is no legend, but its real significance is not that the fame of a particular Dutch physician in the early eighteenth century had circled the globe.[17] Star quality travelled even then. Of course, the anecdote does testify to Boerhaave's reputation as the most astute diagnostician of his age. The Chinese emperor is not the only witness. In his rooms in Leyden Boerhaave received petitions begging for his advice not only from China but also and more regularly from Vienna, Lisbon, Madrid, Paris, Berlin and even Moscow. The King of France wanted to know how to deal with his piles on horseback. The Queen of Spain wanted a cure for her barrenness. Nevertheless, this is no more than gossip. What is significant is that, despite being celebrated today as the father of *bedside* teaching,[18] Boerhaave regarded such enquiries as perfectly reasonable. Like the medical newspaper sages of today, provided that a fee was forthcoming he answered his correspondents at length. Some of his advice was sound. Most of it was harmless. Actually seeing patients was optional, even at times suspect. Examining them was almost improper, at best a form of cheating. At worst, it meant sinking to the level of itinerant surgeons, an inferior breed.[19]

When a physical examination was carried out by a learned physician, it rarely ventured beyond inspection of the tongue, fingering of the pulse and prolonged gazing at a sample of urine. Thousands of genre paintings showing such a scene survive from the seventeenth and eighteenth centuries. The social settings range from the aristocratic to the poverty stricken, but the patients are usually comely young women. What probably exercised their minds was the possibility of pregnancy.[20] While there is no proof of this, some things never change. But others do. Medical diagnosis then was the art of interpreting symptoms; that is, the patient's own complaints, doubts, fears and hopes. It was not significantly different from the skill of a lawyer or a priest. Physical signs, let alone objective tests, were not part of the professional repertory.[21] Boerhaave's introduction of the clinical thermometer, an unwieldy instrument but an instrument nevertheless, was widely deplored rather than hailed as a breakthrough. He himself justified it as a tool for scientific research, the study of variations in body temperature in different ambient temperatures, not as a diagnostic aid.[22]

Not only would modern patients and doctors find it difficult to recognise the activities of these ancestral figures as medical practice, medicine itself, as propounded by these figures, would also remain incomprehensible. Many of the ailments they treated seem to have virtually disappeared. Where are all the painful feet labelled 'gout'? Others have drastically changed. Conversely, the ancients seem to have been unaware of the most common illnesses that doctors see today. Or were they? One cannot be sure. What did all these imprecise words like 'irritation', 'phlegmasme', 'vapours', 'deregulation', 'ill-humour' and a hundred others signify in modern pathological or clinical terms? What did adjectives like 'acrimonious', 'peccant', 'fulgurant', 'lymphatic', 'indurated', 'boastful', 'petulant' and many others mean when applied to a cough, a headache or a bout of diarrhoea?

The four humours (and a variable number of temperaments), for centuries the framework of medical theory, are all familiar *words* today; but their meaning has become transformed. Politicians tend to be *sanguine*, but they are not all bloody. The English have a reputation of being *phlegmatic*, but they do not all suffer from a productive cough. There is no mention of the common cold or hayfever as recognisable ailments in any ancient medical text. Did they exist under the guise of some ponderous Latin name? Or are viruses and pollens among the blessings of the technological age? Many pontificate, but nobody knows.

The commonest remedies employed as recently as the eighteenth century—clysters, leeches, cupping, sudorification, magnetic exposures—would perplex the most assiduous medical student today. What did prescriptions of mind-boggling complexity, often containing snake venom, fox livers, tortoise meat, slugs, snails, grilled mice, macerated earthworms, white she-asses' milk, maidenhair, wormwood and a thousand similar ingredients actually mean, let alone do?[23] Did they, as was claimed and taught, 'sweeten the blood'? Or 'make the humours of the brain less acrimonious'? Or 'filter the lymph of noxious principles'? Or 'purify the black bile'? Perhaps; but if so, how did one know? And when did this interesting, often lucrative and sometimes probably effective while today wholly incomprehensible hocus-pocus suddenly become medicine as the word is used and understood today?

Putting dates to such transformations is always arguable, but anyone doing the rounds of the Paris hospitals and healing parlours about the year 1800 could see both the safely traditional and the defiantly new. The old was not necessarily bad. At the Salpetrière, one of the city's great hospitals, the immortal Philippe Pinel, the doctor who removed the chains of the mentally ill, was in most other respects an upholder of the traditional. His inspiration was not Hippocrates but the great botanist and classifier Linné. To him every disease was a well-defined natural and philosophical as well as a nosological entity (like species of plants and animals), with an anatomically localised though often invisible seat in the body and fitting into a classification so complex and so remote from everyday experience that it defeats his admiring modern biographers.

The old was surviving at less exalted levels too. Even after a century of Reason and Enlightenment and after the shorter but bloodier upheavals of the Terror, Paris was dotted with 'electromagnetic healing parlours' where disciples of Monsieur Mesmer treated every ailment with 'animal magnetism'. His grateful patients included not only France's former queen, but also the first Mme Danton.[24] With less precise but no less impressive paraphernalia, 'hypnotic', 'astrological', 'alchemical', 'Egyptian', 'Chinese' and similar health emporia flourished in elegant *hôtels* as well as in foul-smelling courtyards. Robespierre secretly but regularly consulted the reincarnation of the Great Oracle of Delphi in the rue de Bac about his probably migrainous headaches. (The terminally effective cure was probably not among the recommendations.)

All this was in a long and more or less honourable tradition. Yet, at the same time at the Charité, another of Paris's great hospitals, the commanding figure of Jean Nicholas Corvisart and his team of young doctors were constructing an entirely new practical discipline. Their medicine was based on such recognisably modern concepts as physical examination aimed at detecting specific physical signs. Physical signs were visible and audible facts, not figments of a wishful imagination. They were associated with identifiable diseases. Identifiable diseases corresponded to demonstrable pathological processes. Successfully or not, treatment was now aimed at dealing with these processes as well as superficially with symptoms. It was an explosive new development, as revolutionary as the proclamation of the new trinity, *liberté*, *fraternité* and *egalité*, was in politics.

Of course Corvisart had forerunners, most notably the Austrian innkeeper's son Leopold Auenbrugger, and soon his teaching would spread.[25] However, from the moment one of his pupils, René-Théophile-Hyacinthe Laennec, applied his stethoscope to a young woman's chest, medicine would never be the same again. Or rather, it suddenly became medicine that would be recognised as such by modern doctors and patients alike. This may sound wilfully provocative at a time when doctors have given up using the stethoscope except as a professional trade mark, indispensable in television soap operas but 'killing tubes' in bedside practice.[26] What is true of the stethoscope is also true of physical examination in general. Few doctors examine their patients from top to bottom any more as Corvisart and Laennec undoubtedly did and as medical students are still half-heartedly enjoined to do. But laboratory tests, X-rays and other imaging techniques, as well as complex electrical records, are only physical signs one step removed from the bedside, not essentially different from the results of looking, feeling and listening. All aim at establishing objective facts as distinct from the patient's account and the doctor's 'intuition'. Corvisart, Laennec and other pioneers of modern medicine would warmly approve of their use, with one proviso. The idea that these wondrously accurate new signs have to be elicited and interpreted by doctors and machines miles removed from the patient would strike them as profoundly dangerous. And in this they would be perfectly right.

A similar though slightly slower transformation had begun a little later in hospitals. It has been said that soldiers in the Crimean War were more likely to die after being admitted to Florence Nightingale's legendary field hospital in Scoutari than by participating in the charge of the Light Brigade. Though factually probably correct, the comparison is of course a statistical outrage. Most of those admitted to Florence Nightingale's field hospital were already dying from infected wounds, blood loss, exposure, malnutrition or, most commonly, a combination of all four. Their chances of survival in the field hospital were significantly better than if they had been left to rot on the battlefield (as tens of thousands were). Yet hospitals, even the best, had long been regarded as dangerous places. Their role was partly inherited from the leprosaria of the Middle Ages: it was to keep the sick from passing on their terrible diseases or at least to keep them out of sight. That mission was soon to be partially revived by the tuberculosis sanatoria. They existed as much to protect the healthy as to cure the sick.[27]

In no branch of hospital medicine were the fear and danger greater and the eventual change more dramatic than in obstetrics. In other specialities most patients were admitted with severe injuries, virulent infections, advanced degenerative diseases or malignancies. They expected to die and their expectations were generally fulfilled. But there was no 'natural' reason why healthy young women giving birth to normal babies should perish—and perish after indescribable suffering. Nor indeed did they in remote villages and nomadic encampments on the Steppes barely touched by civilisation. Yet at the time Ignác Semmelweis took up his post as *aspirant* in 1843 in the immensely prestigious lying-in hospital of the Allgemeines Krankenhaus in Vienna, one in four expectant mothers admitted for delivery never left the building alive.[28] The devastation of childbed fever can barely be comprehended today. Not one of the tens of thousands of nativities adorning the walls of the world's great museums even hint at its horror. Nevertheless, over the centuries when many of these pictures were painted, nativity and death were inextricably linked. The virtual disappearance of the disease transformed not only obstetrics but every aspect of hospital practice.

Modern surgery emerged a little later. When it did, anaesthesia and antisepsis made the past unrecognisable. One without the other would have had little impact. The two together transformed the profession from highly skilled butchery into an art and a science equal to the new medicine.

Antisepsis was the product of lateral thinking and Quaker tenacity.[29] Joseph (later Sir Joseph and even later Lord) Lister was not only a surgeon and scientist but also an 'eminent Victorian', as representative of his country and period as the four characters mocked and memorialised by Lytton Strachey.[30] He alone of the four individuals described in the present work lived long enough to undergo a common (though by no means invariable) age-related transformation. From bold innovator he turned into a slightly petulant enemy of many 'new-fangled' notions. For this he was sometimes taken to task (insofar as a medical lord could be taken to task for anything); but he was of course often right.

Lister's inspiration, microbiology, itself produced a firework display of individual discoveries unparalleled in the history of the natural sciences.[31] Advances in anatomy, physiology, biochemistry and pathology usually take a generation or two to have an effect on clinical practice. Vesalius and a few other anatomists purged anatomy of its Galenic misconceptions. Harvey's recognition of the significance of the venous valves, a piercing insight into the obvious, was a physiological milestone.[32] Leeuvenhoek's microscope revealed a new dimension of the living world.[33] Father Mendel's modest experiments with sweet peas created a new science.[34] But none of these discoveries changed the life expectancy of their generation or even the next; and their immediate impact on human suffering was negligible. Microbiology was different and unique.

The discoveries of Pasteur, Koch, Behring, Roux, Ross and Reed transformed every branch of medicine and surgery within their lifetimes. Pasteur, though not a doctor himself, not only founded a new science, he also saved the life of a peasant boy from Alsace who had been bitten by a rabid dog. Had Walter Reed lived a little longer, he would have seen vast killing swamps transformed into some of the most beautiful (and profitable) regions of the world.[35] He and his fellow 'microbe hunters' also brought the century of individual medical heroes to an end.[36] Looking back from 1899 and speaking of science as a whole, Alfred Russell Wallace called it 'the wonderful century'.[37] Turns of centuries tend to impair otherwise quite intelligent people's sanity, but this was no exaggeration. Of course, a reservation must be added. The end of individual medical heroes did not mean the end of medical progress.[38]

Even accepting that over a period of 100 years, give or take a decade, modern medicine was created by a comparatively few recognisable individuals, a selection of four must surely be arbitrary. Perhaps. But an age of great individual achievements calls for an approach different from what is appropriate to great communal changes. The lives of generals, however thrilling, rarely shed much light on the cataclysmic realities of their wars. Conversely, Wallace's wonderful century is best illuminated by individual lives. Even in sound and searching general histories, characters like Laennec, Semmelweis, Lister and Reed tend to become names with dates among other names with dates. Yet their personal backgrounds and characters mattered as much as their dramatic inspirations. Their blunders, often accurately reflecting the beliefs of their times, were as significant as their moments of truth.

They all made mistakes. Laennec, Bayle and Bichat possessed perhaps the most penetrating minds ever applied to medical problems, yet their refusal to recognise *la phthisie* as contagious not only killed them in their prime. In the light of later discoveries it was also unbelievably obtuse.[39] Semmelweis's intemperate defence of his doctrine was arrogant as well as counter-productive. It was a rebellion against seemingly invincible complacency, the most exasperating of adversaries. And his ideas eventually prevailed. Many would still regard Reed's human experiments as indefensible. Perhaps they were; they would not be tolerated today, at least not openly. Even Lister was not all whiskers and atrocious puns. The contradictions also apply to the supporting players, some of them as interesting as the principals.

Individual case histories can also illustrate an important general truth. The practical benefit of medical discoveries depends on their reception as much as on their intrinsic merit. Doctors have always been killers as well as healers.[40] The killing has rarely been intentional. It should not be seen purely in terms of mistakes, negligence, callousness or the 'god syndrome'. There has never been a period when 'good' medicine and 'bad' medicine were separable with absolute certainty; and 'bad' medicine has always been killing medicine.

The dilemmas that doctors face tend to crystallise around new developments. When the new development contradicts the lessons of long experience it is usually best ignored. But not always. At some point ignorance becomes culpable—but where is that point? This has never been an easy question to answer. The administration of pure oxygen to premature babies is now known to be dangerous: though it may save the baby's life immediately after birth, it is likely to lead to progressive and irreversible blindness later.[41] But when did failure to recognise this become negligence? After the first paper suggesting a seemingly far-fetched connection was published in a relatively obscure journal? Or after a controlled trial showing that 1000 babies had gone blind as the result of the treatment?

Nowadays doctors tend to be praised for 'keeping abreast of advances'. Indeed, elaborate and expensive schemes are devised by politicians to ensure that this happens. Nevertheless, not every new advance, especially when supported by massive advertising, is a blessing. Bumbling family doctors who failed to recommend a much-vaunted 'complication-free' new sedative called thalidomide to expectant mothers in the 1950s saved thousands of yet unborn infants from stillbirth or deformities.[42] Today such practitioners might fail their re-assessment for not being up to date. Never was this dilemma more acute than during the founding century of modern medicine. It was always personal and individual. No general history can convey this.

The acceptance or rejection of a new medical doctrine or discovery often depends on historical circumstances quite unrelated to medicine. Medicine does not evolve in a social, political and cultural vacuum. Auenbrugger's brilliant innovation of percussion had no chance of being hailed as a revolutionary advance in Vienna under the bonhomous but anxiety-ridden reign of Francis II.[43] It quickly swept the board in France under the aegis of a young Corsican adventurer who had already upset every apple cart. Vienna in 1800 was the citadel of reaction in medicine as in politics. Paris in the same year witnessed an explosion of youth. Sixty years later, Lister benefited from living in an age that used to be regarded as stuffy but in truth was bubbling with invention and more ready to engage in fundamental and contentious rethinking than any period since.

The response of individual medical heroes to historical constraints also varied.[44] Auenbrugger was a good-natured Austrian who found solace for his rejection in *Kuchen mit Schlag* and musical evenings often featuring the latest works of Herr Haydn.[45] Semmelweis was a temperamental Hungarian who, facing an even more reactionary atmosphere, went into a huff and did not publish his insight into puerperal fever for eight years. He has been criticised for this by later medical historians and the criticism is understandable. Yet it ignores the historical background and his preaching by word of mouth and by example. Of course, his enemies were not all devils. Nor was he a paragon of virtue. But he was right and he stuck by his beloved doctrine. He was a hero, though his lack of communication skills caused avoidable suffering and deaths.

Sometimes in synoptic histories spectacular discoveries obscure more significant but less dramatic developments. In some respects and certainly for patients living at the time, Laennec's battle with Broussais over the dangers of massive blood-letting was more important than his discovery of the stethoscope. Massive blood-letting had been a trusted remedy for centuries. It was being opposed by Laennec in the spirit of new 'scientific medicine'. To many of his colleagues the very sound of this had an ominous ring. It was rumoured that a strange character, black-bearded and hollow-cheeked, carrying a sheaf of papers, was haunting the wards of Parisian hospitals and adding up the numbers of blood-lettings and the deaths and survivals arising from them. The devil himself, perhaps, in one of his guises. Where would it all end? What had the humanist pursuit of medicine to do with columns of figures? Today, the question would be the reverse but equally misleading. Thousands of physicians had to make an agonising choice. Broussais was wrong, but 'his nonsense suited their nonsense'.[46] Among caring practitioners who continued to bleed people to death was Dr James Clark, then resident in Rome. Young John Keats happened to be one of his patients.[47]

The selection of the four individuals through whom the great century of individual medical discoveries is here surveyed was not entirely arbitrary. They are a French physician, a Hungarian obstetrician, an English surgeon and an American army pathologist. Their lives span the century. They were partly at least the products of their different national cultures. Coincidentally, they also represent the four main branches of medicine. Compared to other medical heroes, they may not have been the 'greatest'. What does the term mean in this context anyway? Among the 'great' of the century generally, they are surely the least chronicled. Compared to politicians, poets, writers, artists, musicians, actors, scientists, economists and of course the ancestral figures of the professional chroniclers themselves (mostly rather boring), they are virtually unknown.[48] Yet their moments of truth transformed the lives of millions and their impact continues to be felt.

PART I

LAENNEC AND THE STETHOSCOPE

René-Théophile-Hyacinthe Laennec (1781–1826)

Portrait reproduced by permission of Science Photo Library

CHAPTER ONE

CHILD OF BRITTANY

The French Revolution is often represented as a series of events that happened mostly in Paris and its immediate environs. There is some truth in this. Many parts of France remained extraordinarily calm. From there the local population cast disapproving glances at the excesses of the capital, the habitat of a fickle mob of rootless layabouts. They accepted the republican reforms. They contributed to the call to arms when *La Patrie* was in danger. It was as good a way as any to get rid of local hotheads. But they aspired to no historic role in shaping the nation's destiny, let alone the future of mankind.

Often this was the achievement of a sensible local *maire* or even a level-headed *comte*, more concerned with keeping the peasantry in their traditional state of grumbling discontent than with high ideological issues. But elsewhere ancient Catholic and royalist sentiments were stirred. Why it happened in some provinces and not in others remains a mystery.[1] There were regions in France both richer and poorer than the Vendée. Neither the Church nor the Bourbon kings had been especially kind to it. Nor indeed were the local aristocracy or bishops the fomenters of the uprising. The leaders of the royalists were farmers, gamekeepers, fishermen and local *curés*. The republican army, on the other hand, was led by a *ci-devant* marquis and the ambitious bastard son of Louis XV.[2] The rebellion coalesced only because the danger was not recognised in time in Paris. It had no clear aim except to get rid of the *scorpions* sent by the big city to suck the life-blood out of the countryside.

However, once a royalist army had assembled, it had to be given an objective.

The Vendée itself had no large towns; Nantes on the southern edge of Brittany was the nearest lootable target. Thanks largely to its excellent natural harbour at the mouth of the Loire, the city had become one of the richest in France. Like Bristol in England, it prospered from a triangular trade in West Indian sugar and West African 'ebony'.[3] During wars with England (and often during ostensibly peaceful remissions) patriotic piracy added to its coffers. The local *parlement* was influential, articulate and staunchly though moderately republican. Nevertheless, it was unprepared for a siege by armed royalist peasants and would certainly have fallen prey to them had the peasants' most gifted leader, Jacques Cathelineau, not been the victim of a stray bullet as his men were crossing the Loire.

After briefly entering and looting the city, the peasant army withdrew in disorder. Even so the casualties were high, though not comparable to those of the republican reprisals.[4] The surviving wounded were conveyed to the Hôtel Dieu, which had been renamed a year earlier Temple de l'Humanité. There Dr Guillaume Laennec, surgeon and recently elected rector of the university, was cleaning and cauterising the wounds and operating and amputating around the clock.[5] At his home in the Place Bouffay, his wife, sons and nephews had been set to prepare dressings. His elder nephew carried the baskets of fresh bandages to the hospital and later recalled holding the tourniquet during amputations. It was his introduction to medicine.

The nephew's full name was René-Théophile-Hyacinthe Laennec, but he was always known by his middle name. He was born on 17 February 1781 in the ancient city of Quimper. Though commercially insignificant compared to Nantes or the busy naval port of Brest, it had been the capital of the legendary King Gradlon and the seat of the counts and bishops of Cornouaille.[6] Like all the Laennecs, Théo (only his father addressed him as Théophile) would always think of himself as a Breton first and a Frenchman second.[7] The house of his birth at

the end of the rue de Quai only survives in old engravings. Built of granite, it looked out over the garden of the Hôpital Sainte-Catherine. The grounds, like much of the countryside, were dotted with mysterious prehistoric stones. They were guardians of an ancient faith, seemingly extinct but whose spirits still lingered. On the other side was the city's small inland port where, between tides, fishing boats rested on the mudbanks. They still do.

While both the Laennecs and Théo's mother's family, the Guesdons, had distant aristocratic connections, they were representatives of the Third Estate: teachers, preachers, judges, academics and doctors. Among their ancestors were the poet François de Malherbe and the eminent historian the Abbé Bougeant. Elie Fréron, editor of *L'Année litéraire* and 'intimate enemy' of Voltaire, was a kinsman. So was the Capuchin friar Roscoff, a pioneer of Breton philology. With such a background Théo inevitably became a poet—even something of a literary prodigy—before his interest in medicine. Later he would be acknowledged as a prose writer of exceptional clarity. 'C'est la bêtise mais c'est composé bien' was Broussais's verdict on one of his papers. Many of his private letters survive and are delightful.[8]

His father, Théophile Marie Laennec, had his share of the family gifts. He was a lawyer and the composer of popular madrigals, and his letters to his son are well written (and immensely long). Unfortunately, they would rarely be accompanied by anything more substantial than advice, and that advice was often inane. Théophile Marie was a *phantaisiste*, a weaver of ambitious dreams rather than a performer of sensible deeds. From his son's biographers he has had a universally bad press. Yet he took risks during the Terror in speaking up for his imprisoned aristocratic clients, which few of his *confrères* did. Even in moments of exasperation, his sons would address him with affection.

A year after Théo's arrival his mother gave birth to a second son, Michaud, and two years later to a girl, Marie-Anne. Soon after that she herself died from a nameless illness, perhaps tuberculosis.[9] Laennec *père*, left a widower at 39, had no difficulty in disposing of his three children. This was not uncommon in Brittany as elsewhere in France when young children were left motherless. Théo and Michaud were informally adopted by their uncle Guillaume of Nantes and his kindly wife, a native of the pretty town of Vitré. The two boys became brothers to their younger cousin, Christophe, and later to two more, Ambroise and Mériadec. They also became co-owners of the family dog Mirza and the elderly parakeet Jacquot. It was a happy home.

The boys were bright. As a day pupil at the College of the Oratorians, Théo had more than his fair share of fevers, coughs and sore throats, but he shone academically.[10] He was a 'natural Latinist' and he had an aptitude for Breton. (But Nantes was outside Breton-speaking Brittany and he had little chance to practise his native tongue.) Several of his youthful literary efforts survive, including a fable, composed at the age of 10 in well-turned alexandrines in the manner of La Fontaine. It is elegant, like young Mozart's first minuets. Théo's later translations of Horace and Virgil are extraordinarily accomplished.[11] But the boy's interest in the natural world was also growing, fostered by his uncle and aunt to whom *nos deux de Quimper* were like their own children. Most of the summer holidays were spent at a smallholding owned by Madame Laennec's family about 15 miles outside the city. Situated at the confluence of two lazy streams, the Cens and the Erde, the area is still idyllic. It is here that Théo's exploration of the natural world began. He would never tire of it.

Boyhood was overtaken by history. Soon after the royalist siege, the revolution both in Nantes and in Paris began to move beyond the moderate republicanism of Dr Laennec. On 14 November 1793, in front of the Laennec house, a wooden platform was erected supporting the guillotine, the invention of a kindly doctor.[12] Its first victim was an old peasant from Retz, convicted for adulterating flour. The town council's original intention had been to take the structure down between rare executions.

This soon proved impossible. Not only were the executions multiplying, no workmen would do the job. The town council had also ordered the platform to be sluiced down after each beheading. This too remained a pious wish. It was easier to paint the whole edifice a dark red: then the pools of blood could be left to dry. The flies rose in swarms as the blade piercingly descended. The approaching noise of the carts, the chanting of the victims, the raucous abuse of the patriots milling around the scaffold, the screams of many as they were being strapped to the plank, and the cheers of the crowd as another head dripping with blood was held up for viewing became part of the background of daily life of the Laennec home.[13] Not to watch was deemed unpatriotic, and the family's maid and cook had to take turns at the window.

By the summer the situation was unbearable and Madame Laennec and the children were planning to move. A few days earlier the *representant-en-mission* of the Committee of Public Safety in Paris, Jean-Baptiste Carrier, arrived. His instructions were 'to cleanse the cesspit of treason' that Nantes had become. At the Hôtel-de-Ville he was greeted by the clerk to the town council, a cousin of Madame Laennec. Would the *representant-en-mission* honour the clerk's kinsman, the famous Docteur Laennec, with his presence at a festive dinner to celebrate his arrival? He certainly would.

Carrier was a monster, not of the fastidious and incorruptible variety of his chief Robespierre, but a degenerate, eminently corruptible sadist. Consuming bottle after bottle of the local red wine, slobbering, shouting and posturing at the Laennecs' dinner table, he boasted that he intended to 'exterminate' like vermin a third or even half of the brigands who made up the population of the cesspit, children and women as well as men. The Laennecs listened horror-struck. Only Madame Laennec's 80-year-old mother dared to raise her voice in protest. She was quickly removed. Nevertheless, the dinner party saved the family's lives. At the end of the meal Carrier became maudlin and administered the 'revolutionary blessing', one of Robespierre's metaphysical *jeux d'esprit*, to the five boys. Then he officially retained the services of Dr Laennec as his personal medical adviser. He was, he explained, a martyr to his liver and occasionally his spleen, and Dr Laennec's elixirs were known even in Paris.

Next day the butchery began. First came the recruitment of squads of *marats*, the dregs of the town's criminal population, to act as 'revolutionary constables'.[14] Their zeal in rounding up suspects and their families—anybody, in fact, who had been denounced as harbouring counter-revolutionary or religious sentiments—would be rewarded by having their victims' clothing and personal possessions distributed among them. The prisons were soon full and hospitals and schools were requisitioned as additional centres of detention. However, the simplest way to deal with the overcrowding was to transport suspects wholesale to the guillotine. After beheading 16 young women between the ages of 12 and 17, Michel Sénéchal, the executioner, went mad and had to be put in chains. He died the next day. There was a rush of applicants to take his place. The youngest counter-revolutionary to lose her head was a girl aged seven. Because her neck was too slender to be severed by a single blow, the blade had to be rehoisted and released three times.

Nevertheless, even working from dawn to dusk the guillotine was too slow. At one point Carrier, anticipating the twentieth century, summoned two chemists from the university (one brought to him from prison). Could they suggest a way of 'fumigating' the prisons with some agent that would finish off the inmates without going through time-wasting trials and executions? The chemists had no solution, and Carrier hit on the idea of what he playfully referred to in his letter to the Committee of Public Safety as *deportations vérticales*. With their hands and feet tied, the condemned counter-revolutionaries, men, women and children, were crowded on to flat-bottomed barges with holes below the water line, temporarily sealed. The barges were pushed out into the middle of the Loire to catch the current. The seals were then removed, the executioners with their loot of clothing jumping into boats alongside the barges. At first Carrier seemed concerned that the spectacle might cause unrest among the population and the *noyades* were carried out at night. However, when nobody dared to protest they became a daytime event. About 4000 are thought to have perished in this way.[15] After a reign of terror lasting three months, having just issued an order for schoolchildren to attend the executions as part of their revolutionary education, Carrier was recalled to Paris.

Throughout these events, Théo, Michaud and Christophe Laennec continued their schooling. Death was part of a middle-class childhood and their immediate family survived. But Théo's attitude to politics was marked for life. He came to despise the paraphernalia of power, whether revolutionary, imperial, pontifical or royal. His life would be shaped by people, not by heroes. On the other hand, even before his involvement with the Congregation in Paris, he never lost his faith in a mystical universe greater than humans could perceive. *Le bon Dieu* does not figure much in Théo's boyhood letters, but he is never mocked.

There was another legacy. Throughout his formative youth, while man-made institutions rose dizzily and then crumbled, family ties became closer. They would remain a certainty in a world that was otherwise unpredictable and often dangerous. Beyond the immediate family, there was the soil, the language and the past of Brittany. It was extraordinarily rich in magicians, spirits and demons, but also in saints.[16] They continued to be a source of spiritual strength.

Of course, there was a romantic side to this. Chateaubriand of the flowing locks was a much-admired contemporary as well as a Breton compatriot. The misty cult of Ossian had already crossed the Channel and was beginning to sweep through France and Europe.[17] There were popular Celtic writers in Brittany too, among them Gregoire de Rostrenen, de La Tour, and, above all, Le Brigant, a personal friend of Laennec *père*. (Breton to Le Brigant was the most ancient of all languages and the original tongue of the Homeric epics as well as of the Old Testament.)

Nevertheless, the Laennecs were also heirs to the Age of Reason and unsentimental in their everyday responses. At this level Théo could not fail to be impressed by the special status accorded to his uncle even by political enemies. What secured this respect was not power, title or wealth. Guillaume Laennec was revered because of his reputation as a doctor.

On 8 June 1794 Nantes, like Paris though on a more modest scale, celebrated the Festival of the Supreme Being. There were flowers, garlands, flags and republican emblems in every window. Floats and *tableaux vivants* had never been more popular. They featured such well-known early Jacobins as Brutus the Elder, Cornelia, mother of the Gracchi, Vercingetorix the Gaul, William Tell, Jean-Jacques Rousseau and George Washington (but not yet Astérix), as well as muses, nymphs and symbolic apparitions in patriotic poses and varying degrees of undress.

Prominent families like the Laennecs were expected to participate. Théo, Michaud and Christophe were duly attired in military uniforms with swords. The crowning ceremony on the Place de la Liberté did not perhaps attain the surpassing bathos of the corresponding event on Paris's Champs de Mars, but it too boasted a giant pyre on which symbols of throne and altar were consumed by flames. Enthroned on another mound bedecked with flowers and personified by a well-known prostitute, Sagesse, the new divinity, was crowned by the *citoyen-président* of the local Committee of Public Safety, a former Oratorian.[18] The boys raised and rattled their swords at the moments prescribed by the new rites. All ended their day in the cathedral, renamed Temple de la Nation at a revolutionary mass. It was the last ceremonial manifestation of the Terror. A month later Robespierre, Saint-Just and their closest associates in Paris went (or were dragged) to the guillotine after their defeat in the Convention. Carrier was returned to Nantes to be tried and to follow his victims to the guillotine. Contemporary accounts describe him as facing death in a 'mad rage alternating with whimpering fright'. More likely, he was in the terminal stages of *delirium tremens*.

Some time during that summer Théo decided to follow his uncle into the medical profession. Jealous perhaps of his brother's influence, his father protested. He had recently remarried a wealthy lady of high aristocratic provenance and he had 'plans', he wrote, for his son to go into the public service or commerce. Laennec *père* always had plans. Théo's letters were always politely but firmly resistant. In the summer of 1797 he followed them up with a visit to Quimper. He walked most of the way, across some of Brittany's (and France's) most lovely countryside. He was warmly received and took at once to the town and its surroundings. He and Michaud were heirs to his mother's extended family, notable for generations in the affairs of Cornouaille. The Guesdins were to remain dear to him. His stepmother too was welcoming. Eventually his father gave his grudging consent to Théo's wishes, but difficulties remained.

In a moment of inspired madness the Convention in Paris had abolished all universities in France. They were seen as the breeding grounds of privilege and superstition. The condemned institutions included the ancient university of Nantes. They were to be replaced by establishments more in tune with the free, fraternal and egalitarian present and future. Somehow that never happened. The Directory, which took over the functions of the Committee of Public Safety after the fall of Robespierre, was probably France's most corrupt and frivolous regime ever.[19] Still at war with half of Europe, the Treasury empty, constantly threatened both by the Royalist right and the Jacobin left, universities were low on the agenda of the senior Director, *ci-devant* vicomte, former Jacobin, regicide, womaniser and pillar of corruption Paul Barras.

Fortunately for Théo and a few other young men with similar aspirations, a handful of surviving teachers of the old medical school began to organise private courses. Some were men of distinction who had miraculously escaped Carrier's bloody rampage. Darbefeuille taught physiology, Bacqua anatomy, Jean Le Meignen, director of the Jardin Botanique, gave memorable demonstrations of the life of plants. Botany was still regarded as one of the foundations of medicine. Later the former Abbé Fizeau from the old Dominican college gave a course in zoology. Guillaume Laennec himself was an inspired teacher of clinical medicine and surgery. But studies did not entirely fill Théo's life. A few tender lyrical 'rhymes' (but no letters) addressed to a young lady called Nisa survive from 1798 and 1799. Nothing else is known about the recipient, except that she died in her twenties. Then there was another war-like episode.

Profiting from the feebleness of the Directory, and incited from a safe distance across the Channel by the late King's younger brother, the Comte d'Artois, there was another royalist uprising in the Vendée.[20] The rebels were called *chouanes*. They were desperate and their rebellion was badly timed. The days of corrupt and incompetent regimes in Paris were numbered. Historical divides rarely follow calendar dates, but they did in France as the eighteenth century turned into the nineteenth. If 1789 marked the end of the divine right of kings, the coup of 18 Brumaire of Year VIII of the revolutionary calendar (9 November 1799) inaugurated a new brand of dictatorship.[21] General Bonaparte's assumption of the office of First Consul for four years was speedily followed by his election to the office of First Consul for Life. Then came his coronation as Emperor of the French.[22] Each advance was overwhelmingly endorsed by a plebiscite.[23]

The first few months of the Consulate were critical. Few on the morrow of 18 Brumaire regarded the new regime as anything but another stopgap before something sensible and permanent emerged. However, the 31-year-old First Consul was no shooting star. A man of unbounded ambition, surprising charm when he chose to turn it on and considerable ruthlessness, he won over, bribed or conciliated where he could but crushed plots and opposition in the time-honoured and by and large effective style of Corsican bandits.[24] During the last months of the old century the *chouans*, under the leadership of Georges Cadoudal, scored a few victories and even occupied Nantes for a day. But Bonaparte quickly assembled an army of 60,000 and placed it under the command of Brune, a former sansculotte and bosom friend of Marat. Anxious to earn a living at last, Théo signed up and used his uncle's influence to be nominated 'surgeon, third class'. Happily, by the time he reached the army the war was over. The *chouans* were thoroughly beaten. Cadoudal escaped to plot another day, but eventually did it once too often and was captured and guillotined.[25]

To entertain his friends by the campfire, Théo composed a tragi-comic 'epic' called *Guèrre des Vénètes*.[26] Written in the manner of an imaginary ancient Celtic bard, 'Poème de Cardoe, Barde de Condivic, Antérieur de Homer, Traduit de la langue celtique par le Docteur Cenneal, professeur des langues primitives', the last name an easy anagram on his own, it satirised war, conquest and military glory. Even celtomania did not escape. Le Brigant appeared in the dedication in 24 imaginary languages, all of course derived from Celtic, as 'The Robber'. Though not a great work of literature, it is sharp and witty. It also provides an early glimpse into the author's character. That would often seem self-contradictory. His love for Brittany and for Breton culture was deep and genuine, but the more he cherished something, the more intolerant he became of its cheapening and profanation. He disliked excess of any kind. He also had a horror of the theatrical and the phoney. At times this would hinder his professional advancement. Bombast in speech, dress and behaviour was the common coinage of the Revolution, circuses often acting as substitutes for bread. The fantastical costumes, grandiose titles, golden eagles, plumes, bees, diamond-studded decorations and laurel wreaths would reach their apogee under Napoleon. Laennec could never hide his distaste for them. Nor, as a rule, did he even try.

The war over, it was time for Théo to immerse himself in medical studies. Despite the efforts of Uncle Guillaume and his colleagues in Nantes, this could be done only in Paris. Laennec *père*, under the benign influence perhaps of his second wife, sent a modest sum to both his sons to speed them on their way. On 20 April 1801, after a tearful farewell to the Guillaume Laennecs, Théo departed on the coach for Paris.

CHAPTER TWO

PARIS

Paris had rid itself of the Farmers General's hated tollgates during the Revolution, but in its general layout was still much as it had been in the days of the Valois kings.[27] Beyond the Bastille and the Temple in the east lay fields, farms, orchards and market gardens. In the west the Champs Elysées traversed woodlands, formerly a royal hunting preserve, criss-crossed by narrow paths. The Champs de Mars was a large empty space, bearing the unappetising detritus of popular republican *fêtes*. The expensive and elegant faubourgs had barely begun to develop and distance themselves from the mediaeval heart of the city.

Much of that heart was still a huddle of closely packed tenements separated by alleyways, noisy, busy, crowded and dangerous. Rubbish lay about in the gutters until it was carried away by torrents of rainwater. Street lighting had been erratic when Voltaire had visited the city decades ago; under the Directory it had virtually ceased. The few lanterns in front of important public buildings only deepened the surrounding gloom. For all the fine architecture of past centuries and a few elegant *hôtels* looking inwards to their courtyards, the houses had a bedraggled look. Some of the grandest had become untenanted and were occupied by squatters. The paintwork was peeling. Bare brick showed through the plasterwork. For ten years nothing had been maintained or repaired. The public gardens were unkempt: the old plane trees looked wounded and sickly. On street corners the remains of blood-curdling posters flapped in the wind.

Yet even bedraggled, Paris to contemporary eyes was huge and exciting. It boasted a population of 600,000.[28] The Revolution had been against the 'aristos', not against wealth. Class stratification persisted, only it was vertical. Rich and poor—many had made a fortune out of the Revolution and would make another fortune out of the Napoleonic slaughter—entered the same houses by the same doors. The rich typically mounted a short, broad staircase to a spacious apartment on the ground floor. It had its private staircase to the wine cellar and ice cave. Its glass doors opened on to quiet formal gardens, with orange trees in pots, a tinkling fountain and playful lead amoretti. The poor climbed up progressively narrower and more rickety stairs until they reached their often leaky garrets.[29]

Michaud had preceded Théo by a few weeks and for a time they shared furnished lodgings on the top floor of a tenement in the Place Saint Michel. When sheets and linen arrived from Quimper, they moved to even higher and cheaper unfurnished rooms in the rue Saint-Hyacinthe, the heart of the Latin Quarter. Ever since the Middle Ages this district had been kind to impecunious students and hungry scholars. At the scrubbed wooden tables of Le Père Martin in the rue Saint-Jacques one could get a nutritious *potage du jour* for a few sous. Guests brought their own bread and dunked it in the soup. Another few sous bought the famished and affluent a generous portion of meat. When even a few sous were lacking, one could usually count on the open-handedness of a few fellow Bretons: the younger Fizeau of Nantes, Janais of Brest or Bruté de Rémur of Quimper. They would remain Théo's closest friends for the rest of his life. Having settled in, he could set out to try to find his way in the labyrinth of Parisian medicine.

Like everything else in the disorganised state, the universities had received the quick and decisive attention of the First Consul and his new Council of State.[30] Medical education in particular had to be re-established and re-organised. Bonaparte's own experience as a general had convinced him that doctors were an essential facility in war. Wars there would undoubtedly be, therefore doctors would have to be trained in the requisite numbers. There would in fact be two ways to gain a medical qualification. The Ecole Spéciale de Santé was to be the successor of the former Faculté de Médicine and would produce competent, run-of-the-mill practitioners. Anybody with some kind of a school certificate and a few declensions in Latin could enter. Tuition was free. For poor boys from the provinces, especially for the sons or orphans of war veterans, state scholarships would be available. However, élitism was inbred in French public life, seemingly timelessly. The Revolution had changed nothing in that respect. This was in tune with Bonaparte's personal outlook. The Ecole Pratique was to be separate and reserved for high flyers. Entry was to be by a stiff competitive examination. Graduates would later proudly claim to be former *Praticiens*. It is from their ranks that Bonaparte planned to recruit his future professors and top army surgeons.[31]

For some months at least Théo had no such ambition. His sojourn in Paris was to be temporary, an unwelcome necessity. Compared to Quimper or even Nantes, the capital was filthy, expensive and hysterical. People were rude, always in a hurry. Only a madman would prefer it to the scented hush of the Breton countryside. All the Laennecs (like most French people even today) were country folk at heart. Théo would start to lose weight and appetite and begin to suffer from attacks of 'asthma' as soon as he entered Paris. Michaud too could hardly wait to complete his legal training. He would leave as soon as he was qualified. What changed Théo's mind was meeting a few people who, he quickly discovered, were transforming medicine as he had known it and as he had been taught in Nantes. Their personal influence, combined with the intellectual challenge, was irresistible.

Leading the medical revolution was Citizen Jean Nicholas Corvisart, head of the medical service at the Hôpital de la Charité. This had become the most rigorous but also the most sought-after training ground for young doctors. To his staff and students *le patron* was cold, sarcastic and often unreasonably demanding. Laennec, a more transparent and a greater man, never liked him. Nevertheless, 'without Corvisart,' he wrote toward the end of his life, 'I would have become a country doctor in Brittany.'

The Corvisarts were an old but impoverished family with a dilapidated château in the Ardennes and a somewhat obscure coat of arms.[32] In 1783, probably for reasons of economy, the eight-year-old Jean-Nicholas, one of eleven siblings, was farmed out to an uncle, a country *curé* in Vimille near Boulogne-sur-Mer. The uncle entrusted the boy's education to the local church school, the Collège Saint-Barbe. There Jean-Nicholas was an outstandingly lazy and troublesome student (though good at outdoor activities). On several occasions he was nearly expelled. He was no more amenable to paternal threats, diatribes and admonitions as a law student in Paris. The law was fossilised, a laughing stock. His professors were imbeciles. But in Paris he made his first forays into medicine, sneaking into lectures and working as a hospital orderly. He was captivated by the aura of authority of the leading medical figures and bowled over by the skill of surgeons like Desault and Rouvière.

Unlike the law, which seemed immovable, medicine was in ferment. It was also associated with power. There was a Bonaparte streak in the young Corvisart, the same iron will to reach the top that animated the hungry Corsican artillery officer at about the same time.[33] When the former announced that he was abandoning the law for medicine, he was duly disinherited (mostly it seems of debts) and never returned to the family seat. (None of his family would visit him in his solitary last years.) But for the first time in his life he applied himself to his studies. He had a capacious mind, a phenomenal memory and, when so inclined, a prodigious capacity for work. He carried no ideological luggage. Despite his sharp tongue and the fiercely competitive setting, he succeeded with apparent ease.

His academic success—he quickly acquired a legendary reputation as a winner of prizes—was remarkable since he never made a secret of his contempt for traditional medicine. In the highest echelons of the profession and at the city's most prestigious hospitals, the discipline was still treated as a complex theoretical science. To its protagonists it had a certain abstract beauty. To young people like Corvisart it seemed a disaster, 'as useless as the law'. (That remark, much publicised by his ill-wishers, did not endear him to either profession.) Medicine, he would often say, was not a theoretical science: 'If your inclinations are theoretical, you should become a philosopher or a theologian.' However, in forging ahead he was a pragmatist. To demolish the old, it had to be mastered. This he did.

Winning prizes still depended on memorising a stupendous array of symptoms and their intricate inter-relations. In 1763 François Boissier de Sauvages, professor first of botany and then of medicine at the university of Montpellier, had published his *magnum opus* based on the work of the immortal Linné of Sweden. It classified all diseases—or rather, all *symptoms* of diseases—first into 10 major 'classes', then each class into 'orders'. Each of the 658 orders was then subdivided into 'genera' (*genres*) and these into 'species' (*espèces*). The net result was a grand blueprint of all ailments, major and minor, acute and chronic, a total of 24,000 explicitly defined *identités* based entirely on their symptomatology. (Linné would have arrived at a similar edifice of monumental nonsense had he decided to start his classification of plants according to the colouring of their flowers.) Of course diseases—that is, symptoms—tended to appear not in isolation but in 'groupings' (*groupements nosologiques*). Items from the master list of 24,000 therefore could be—indeed had to be—combined and recombined in an almost infinite number of permutations. To be conversant with those and their supposed anatomical seat or seats in the body was deemed essential for attaining competence in the practice of medicine.[34] At least, it was deemed essential for passing competitive examinations.

Corvisart would later entertain his august patients by declaiming long lists of mind-boggling *combinaisons* that had to be committed to memory and regurgitated across the examination table. Of course he exaggerated, but the system did not need much exaggeration. It was as abstruse as any medieval scholastic *summa*. How the 'network' (*réseaux*) of symptoms might or might not relate to physical signs, let alone pathological processes, was not even considered. On the other hand, symptomatic medicine was closely linked to the arcane science of *materia medica*. Every symptomatic *entité* had, by definition (and by God's grace), a specific remedy, though some still awaited discovery. To the ambitious and industrious this provided scope for pushing back the frontiers of knowledge (an expression already beloved by academics). The known remedies constituted a precious body of botanical, zoological and chemical lore, culled mainly from ancient Latin and Greek textso with a sprinkling from the Arabic and Persian. Familiarity with these would enable future practitioners to compose awe-inspiring prescriptions.

Many such prescriptions survive in old textbooks. They would be impossible to reconstruct today, but frequent injunctions to take the products quickly and without inhaling, accompanied by copious libations of water or wine, suggest that they must have smelt and tasted vile. Their heavy metal content—mercury was an almost invariable ingredient—would render apoplectic a modern health and safety officer. They could not but induce nausea and vomiting. Whether they had any other effect can no longer be established.

When more dramatic treatment was required, the choice lay largely between purgation and blood-letting. The choice of purgatives (many with specific indications) was the subject of several textbooks. Some forms, generically known as *les grandes laxatives*, were exceedingly violent. Patients were advised to stay indoors and solitary for the duration of their anticipated action. When still ineffective, they could be supplemented with heroic enemas. Blood-letting was often massive. In extremis the two treatments would be combined. Not many people survived. If they did, they often lived to a ripe old age.[35]

As the foundations of *materia medica*, exotic plants and animals loomed large in the curriculum. Some had to be imported from far-away lands. Their outrageous price added to their efficacy. Anatomy was also required, but consisted mainly of the minute study of the small and unimportant bones in which both human and animal skeletons abound. In the early 1790s the future Baron de Cuvier, the man who would transform and rationalise these disciplines, was still tutoring the son of Count d'Hérley at the count's château near Caen and collecting fossils on the beach.[36]

Despite his cleverness and hard work, it is unlikely that 20 or even 10 years earlier Corvisart would have become a winner of prizes. His correspondence and even his first published articles were scathing about the syllabus and contemptuous of leaders of the profession. 'How, pray tell me, do his [Dr Jeanneret's] patients survive?' he asked his friend Jacques-Louis Moreau.[37] The question was of course rhetorical, but it referred to one of the capital's fashionable physicians. 'I am told he purges them all to death. Yet his equipage drips with gold and Chinese lacquer. Oh Molière, you should be alive today!'

Fortunately for the questioner and like-minded young men, in the 1780s old certainties were crumbling in academe as in other fields. In Paris mesmerism and all kinds of diabolical practices were the rage. Quackery was flourishing as it had not done since the first Medici queen. Nor was this surprising. Despite all the mumbo jumbo, traditional medicine was widely perceived to be useless. Worse, it killed more often than it cured. Young Corvisart and his friends were not alone in thinking that the classification of symptoms in isolation from physical signs and pathologies was meaningless. Translated into practice, such doctrines could be lethal. Traditional therapeutics also needed to be swept away.

Even so, Corvisart's arrogance was astounding. After qualifying with high honours, his future in the capital still depended on being appointed to the staff of one of the city's public hospitals. One had recently been founded by the ambitious wife of the king's financial wizard, the Swiss banker Jacques Necker.[38] Madame Necker prided herself on being thoroughly modern, a true intellectual. She approached young Corvisart with an offer of a post. Corvisart replied that he was prepared to accept, but under no circumstances would he wear a wig on his ward rounds. Madame Necker did not like her protégés to set conditions. She also liked them to be properly attired. The offer was withdrawn.

Nevertheless, another opportunity soon arose. Corvisart had impressed not only Desault, the surgical chief at the Charité, but also Father Potentian, the non-medical director. The institution was, like most Paris hospitals, a religious foundation. Corvisart had never pretended to be devout. He was not a believer in healing saints. But who would intercede for his patients? A few years earlier such unorthodoxy would have barred him from an appointment. But the year was 1788, ten months to go to the storming of the Bastille. Father Potentian himself would soon shed his soutane and don a tricorne with a cocarde.[39] When chief of medicine Desbois de Rochefort died, Corvisart was appointed to replace him without even a show of competition.

Around 1800, taking advantage of a temporary lull in hostilities following the Treaty of Lunéville, Corvisart toured medical centres in the Netherlands, Austria and perhaps Italy.[40] None seemed to him superior to Paris; but in Vienna he was impressed by the privately circulated *Aphorisms* of Maximilian Stoll.[41] Stoll had been the first native Austrian to hold the chair of medicine in the university and had clearly been a man of ideas.[42] Naturally, one had to be selective in accepting them. Corvisart wisely ignored the professor's theories about gastric poisons being the universal cause of ill-health, just as he treated Franz-Joseph Gall's fashionable 'phrenological' doctrines with scepticism.[43] However, Stoll had been interested in a new method of examining patients. He had not practised the method himself—his aristocratic clientèle would not have taken to it kindly—but some of his colleagues, working in the city's poorer quarters, had found it diverting, even at times useful. It had been described 30 years earlier by a doctor, well-liked and still on the staff of the city's Spanish hospital (for the military), but not otherwise known for his academic attainments. Corvisart was keen to try any new device for eliciting physical signs as opposed to speculating about transcendental systems of health and metaphysical truths. He tried it and found it amazing.

The man who had invented this new method was the son of a Graz innkeeper, and he himself told the story of his invention. As a boy, Leopold Auenbrugger had watched with fascination his father tapping casks in the wine cellar. This was a skilled procedure that taught him to distinguish the musical sounds of air, solids and liquid inside a resonant container. After qualifying as a doctor, he was inspired to apply the method to the diagnosis of diseases of the chest. This was more than a fleeting inspiration. He laboured for years correlating the sounds elicited by percussion with the underlying pathology, both in patients and in dead bodies. Once mastered, the technique was so simple that it could be used to follow changes in the chest—the accumulation of fluid, the collapse of lobes of the lungs, shifts in the position of the heart—by monitoring them daily, even hourly.[44]

Of course, there were pitfalls. Individual variations could only be overcome by comparing the two sides of the chest: it was rare for both lungs to be equally affected. However, this depended on tapping over corresponding points. It was no use tapping over a rib on the right and an intercostal space on the left. By turning the patient into different positions, it was also possible to distinguish between fluid that was encapsulated and immovable from fluid that gravitated freely in the pleural cavity. All this required a detailed knowledge of the surface markings of the organs inside the chest of the living. Auenbrugger carefully mapped them out. It was an impressive achievement at a time when eliciting physical signs was regarded by many as bordering on the salacious

Eventually he summarised his discoveries in a short book.[45] It was the medical equivalent of the storming of the Bastille; or it would have been if the medical Bastille had fallen. In fact, as Auenbrugger himself had predicted, the book was largely ignored. For a time his teaching became a popular cabaret turn. The ritual of placing a piece of wood on selected parts of an actress's curvaceous body and eliciting imaginary information hidden under her skin proved uproarious if somewhat risqué fun.[46]

Auenbrugger continued his tapping but accepted the fate of his *inventum novum* stoically. He married into the nobility, sired two gifted daughters, and was ennobled by Leopold II for his services to music rather than to medicine. He was not a composer himself but did write successful operatic libretti, including one for Mozart's rival, the court composer Salieri.[47] Its success easily surpassed that of *The Marriage of Figaro*. After his accolade he signed himself Edler von Auenbrugg. Perhaps his stoicism accounted for his long and contented life. He died dozing quietly in his armchair in 1808, aged 89, undisturbed by the cannonade of Napoleon's approaching army that drove poor Beethoven, only a mile or two away, to a frenzy.[48]

There is no record that Auenbrugger and Corvisart ever met, but Corvisart certainly did the older man proud. He not only immediately adopted percussion as a diagnostic aid, but undertook to translate Auenbrugger's work into French.[49] When the translation was eventually published, it was four times the size of the original. It contained a detailed account of Corvisart's own observations and interpretations, especially those relating to the heart.[50] For once, an increase in bulk did not mean a shrinkage in content. Corvisart could justly have claimed to be the co-author at least, but he never did.[51]

Around Corvisart and his newly founded *Journal de Médicine, Chirurgie et Pharmacie* there gathered a contumacious but bright group of young doctors. Laennec, starting his studies in 1801, had a few months to come under the spell of one of those consumptive geniuses who somehow crammed a lifetime's creative achievement into a few years.[52] At 32 Marie-François-Xavier Bichat, the son of a doctor from the Jura, was already subject to painful fits of coughing and severe haemorrhages. At times he was so weak that he could barely mount the steps leading to his rooms.[53] In one of his letters to his father Laennec described him as 'ghost-like ... his eyes are sunken, his skin is transparent, his voice is husky, sometimes barely more than a painful whisper.'

But what a ghost! A few months before his death he would still spend most of the daylight hours over his dissections or visiting patients; and during sleepless nights he produced page after page of manuscript, some of the seminal works of modern medical science. He had begun his medical studies in Lyon, but in 1791 he had moved to Paris for much the same reasons as compelled young Laennec to move there a decade later. In Paris he became the prize pupil of Desault, surgeon in chief of the Hôtel Dieu, Paris's oldest and largest hospital.[54] (It would soon be renamed Grand Hospice de l'Humanité, but the change would not last long. Napoleon was happy to restore hospitals to God's care.)

Desault was a charismatic teacher but was too busy to commit his thoughts to paper.[55] After his death Bichat collected, edited and completed the master's jottings. Then he proceeded to publish his own works. He also founded a medical research society with Dupuytren and Henri Husson, which Corvisart and Pinel soon joined. It was dedicated not to spreading the wisdom of the ages but to questioning it. Bichat conducted a private course in anatomy at his home as well as filling the post of chief demonstrator of physiology at the Hôtel Dieu. He had a large private practice, but he never accepted a fee. His original works, *Sur les membranes et leurs rapports généraux d'organisation*, *Traitée des membranes*, *Anatomie générale* (which remained incomplete) and the tremendous *Recherches physiologiques sur la vie et la mort* were published within 30 months. He was reputed never to have had a day's holiday and he had virtually no private life. He worked as if he knew that his days were numbered: indeed, like other consumptive geniuses, he almost certainly did. But perhaps—at the same time—he was secretly sustained by what would soon be known as the *spes phthisica*, the false hope of the tuberculous.

The immediate cause of Bichat's death remains uncertain. Descending the steps of his home in the rue des Chanoinesses he was probably seized by a lung haemorrhage. He collapsed and may have suffered a head injury. He died a few hours later. He had been the medical adviser of some of the most powerful personages of revolutionary Paris; but there was not enough money in his rooms to pay for the funeral. The cost was defrayed by his friends. Corvisart was sparing to the point of stinginess with expressions of admiration for his juniors, but he persuaded the First Consul to erect a plaque in Bichat's memory.[56]

Old medical books that were once widely read and quoted are rarely consulted by later generations. However important they are historically, they are inevitably out of date. The content of many is incomprehensible and their style is often painfully convoluted. But for purposes of synoptic histories, still valued for providing literary polish, a tag usually gets attached to their authors. These are supposed to encapsulate the authors' achievement and explain their contemporary reputation. Since Boerhaave did not discover anything in particular, he is simply 'the Batavian Hippocrates'.[57] Morgagni is the 'founder of morbid anatomy'. In the same vein one is supposed to describe Bichat as the 'father of histology'. This is more than usually meaningless. Histology is essentially a microscopic science, and, though Bichat was a meticulous dissector, he was not a notable microscopist.[58] He was also, like Laennec, Corvisart, Bayle and others in their circle, primarily a clinician. He devoted at least half his time to the care of patients.

Nevertheless, there is, as sometimes happens, a grain of truth in the label. Whereas Morgagni was concerned with organs— the liver, the heart, the brain and so on—Bichat's work drew attention to diseases of certain tissues or systems widely distributed in the body. They included the vessels, the lymphatic channels, the nerve fibres, the synovial membranes of joints, the lining of the gut and what today would be called 'connective tissue'. Just as chemistry is the science of a comparatively small number of elements entering into the formation of an almost infinite variety of compounds, the body can be conceived (according to Bichat) as being constructed of widely distributed tissues that share a similar structure and function. Of course he did not deny the existence and importance of organs, but he was the first to emphasise their common as well as their distinctive features. His concept proved exceedingly fruitful, and remains so.[59]

Even more remarkable perhaps—his discoveries were 'in the air' and would probably have been made sooner or later by someone else—his epigrammatic style still makes his works a pleasure and a provocation to read. Like other masters of French scientific prose, he could turn a trite tautology into a lambent truth, or at least a wondrously resonant phrase. 'La vie est l'ensemble des fonctions qui resistent la mort,' begins his treatise on life and death. This is *it* at last, the elusive encapsulation of the mystery. But what exactly does it mean? It does not really matter. Other masters of French scientific prose are known to have spent weeks polishing such sentences. Bichat seems to have poured them out without effort. There was no time to do anything else. To Laennec his materialism was flawed, but his personality left an indelible impression. And his ideas influenced not only Claude Bernard, an uncle at least if not the father of modern physiology, but also Schopenhauer and Auguste Comte, materialist philosopher and inventor of the term 'sociology'.

On Bichat's death, his closest friend, colleague and, above all, rival is said to have exclaimed: 'Je respire'. That does not shed a pleasant light on Guillaume Dupuytren, and the great surgeon's most recent sympathetic biographer pours cold water on the story.[60] True or not, it shows how the man was perceived by some at least of his contemporaries. He was four years older than Laennec, the handsome and cantankerous descendant of a long line of barber surgeons of the Limoges region. Little is known about his childhood with certainty: stories about his struggles

and deprivations as well as his own account of being kidnapped not once but twice were probably exaggerated. Arriving in Paris to study medicine, he immediately attracted Corvisart's attention. He was hard-working and, if he lacked the perceptive eye and sharp mind of a Bichat, he made up for it by his determination to succeed. And succeed he would as a surgeon.

In France, though not yet in the rest of Europe, it was a propitious moment to make such a resolution. The advance of surgery had already begun. Ambroise Paré was a distant forerunner of Dupuytren's.[61] A royal order in 1725 freed surgeons from their traditional association with barbers. In 1751, much to the dismay of the physicians of the Paris Faculté, Maréchal and Gigot obtained Louis XV's approval to found an Académie Royale de Chirurgie. Nevertheless, it was the Revolution and the Napoleonic Empire that established surgeons as a profession equal in status to physicians. The two regimes of course had different agendas. The Revolution was against all privileges and social distinctions. To Marat the Faculté, the professional organisation of physicians that had had the impudence to censure him when he was still in practice (or malpractice), was a band of thieves and brigands. Danton too railed against 'the conspiracy of dressed-up monkeys'. Robespierre had faith only in what was not yet called 'alternative medicine'. A decree issued by the Convention on 2 March 1791 expressly proclaimed the 'freedom to practise medicine and surgery for anyone who so desires'. And not only to practise. Anyone could call themselves a doctor or a surgeon if they were so inclined. For ten years the healing profession in France was wholly unregulated, the only such episode in modern history.[62] It should have been accompanied by a dramatic rise in mortality and morbidity. Nothing untoward happened.

Fortunately for the professions, Bonaparte had no truck with such beguilingly principles. A clutch of registering bodies, faculties and colleges were quickly deemed essential for the protection of the public and re-established under the Consulate. On the other hand, the First Consul and later Emperor probably felt a certain admiration for 'mes braves chirurgiens'. Men like François Percy, Jean-Dominique Larrey and René Dufriche-Desgenette were not only *braves*, they were also military assets. Percy was the first surgeon to operate regularly on the battlefield.[63] He was wounded more than once and was much admired by the grenadiers. Larrey's horse-drawn, two-wheeled *ambulances volantes* became a legend not only among the French but among their enemies as well.[64] Count István Szécheny, who took part in the Battle of Leipzig, wrote to his father that he had never seen such bravery. To his amazement, the *ambulances* picked up wounded Austrians as well as French while the fighting was still going on. He was, he assured his father, not delirious. When the chief of the French army medical service, Dufriche-Desgenette, was captured during the retreat from Moscow, the Czar gave him his freedom and offered him a decoration for having devoted as much care to Russian prisoners as he had to the wounded French.[65] Napoleon gave all three, as well as Corvisart, baronies after Austerlitz and remembered them individually in his will on St. Helena.[66]

Dupuytren did not fancy the military life. He applied for and received exemption from conscription on the ground that he was indispensable looking after victims of distant battles in Paris. Instead, he seized every opportunity to shine as an original research worker. It was the flavour of the revolutionary decade and the early Napoleonic years. He felt the more impelled to make his mark since, even as a second and later first assistant in the department of surgery at the Hôtel Dieu, his scope for shining as a clinician was limited. His chief, Pélletan, Desault's successor, did not like him. Pélletan was a mediocre surgeon but no fool, and he may have resented his assistant habitually referring to him as *le fossil*.

To Dupuytren competitors always seemed to be lurking in the wings, waiting and conspiring to pounce and take his place. The Revolution and Bonaparte had opened the way to the rapid advancement of the young and unprivileged. If every private in the Emperor's army carried a field marshal's baton in his

43

knapsack, every trainee doctor could cherish the ambition of becoming a professor. The difficulty was that aspirant professors always vastly outnumbered university chairs. Dupuytren was a clumsy and laborious writer. He was also impatient. This meant that he was continually appealing to Laennec, Bichat, Bayle and others for 'collaboration'. However, he could not bear the idea of sharing in the glory of what they had jointly achieved.

Laennec, newly arrived in Paris, was at first flattered by the interest shown in him by someone who was already chief of anatomy at the Hôtel Dieu. Then he became suspicious and later repelled as he realised that his 'gracious and generous colleague' was ruthlessly exploiting him and his friends. (That kind of thing did not happen in Brittany.) They had at least one public row. The rights and wrongs of such contretemps are difficult enough to establish at the time; after two centuries the task is impossible. But there is no doubt that Dupuytren was feared and distrusted as a colleague. Later he would be grudgingly admired, though he was rarely loved.

Yet once he was in command and could turn his energy to the much-needed reorganisation of a ward, a service, a hospital or even a profession, he achieved wonders with his persistence and bullying.[67] When required, he could also be subtle and emollient. Visiting England after his rise to European fame, he charmed Sir Astley Cooper, not an easy target.[68] He was to survive Laennec by nine years and would end his career as surgeon to the last kings of France, a baron and a not entirely happy role model to generations of less gifted practitioners of his craft.

Neither Bichat nor Dupuytren, nor even Corvisart, made such a deep impression on Laennec as Gaspard-Laurent Bayle. Bayle was a grave and taciturn Provençal, 'une espèce rare mais précieuse', in Edouard Rist's charming phrase.[69] Laennec, seven years younger, was immediately drawn to him. Though hailing from opposite corners of France, their family background was similar. Bayle's ancestors had been soldiers, priests and advocates before the Parliament of Aix, devout but not bigoted, reformists but not revolutionary. Gaspard-Laurent himself was at first destined for the church, entering the seminary of Digne. After a year he did not feel the calling strongly enough to take holy orders. He nevertheless remained deeply religious.

The Revolution too intervened. At 19 Bayle was elected to the General Assembly of the Basses-Alpes, as divided in its loyalties as were the Vendée and eastern Brittany. The Convention in Paris felt it necessary to dispatch there two *representants-en-mission* to root out enemies of the people. While neither Barras nor Fréron was in Carrier's class of depravity, their lukewarm private sentiments made them the more determined to prove themselves inflexible enforcers of the Convention's will. Expecting a cowed Assembly—a government force of 1000 was only a day behind and their reputation for ferocity had preceded them—they appeared before it waiting to be assured of the region's unshakeable loyalty. Instead, they were harangued by young Bayle 'with smouldering passion', telling them to work for the welfare of the people rather than trying to please the 'clowns' in Paris. Stunned, Barras and Fréron withdrew, but not before ordering the local militia to arrest Bayle and transport him to Lyon. Forewarned by his friends, Bayle escaped to an uncle in Montpellier. There, more to distract attention from himself than because he felt a burning interest in the subject, he enrolled as a medical student. Once enrolled, his interest was aroused.

As a medical school Montpellier was in decline, a victim of its own high achievement and reputation in past centuries. Nothing was allowed to change. Improvements were impossible. Like other young and ambitious medical students, Bayle travelled to Paris as soon as it was safe for him to do so. He made an impression not so much with his clinical skill as with his intelligence and integrity. In the turbulent and treacherous world of Parisian medicine, here was a young man who said what he thought and whom a chief could trust. Some found his austerity forbidding. Many thought him remote, even haughty. None ever questioned his honesty.

Then as now, doctoral theses were 'defended' in public. Bayle defended his on 9 October 1802. It attracted a crowded auditorium, not just medical students, the usual audience, but also grizzled old academics. There was even a sprinkling of fashionable young ladies, an unusual sight on such occasions. (Women were not barred from public examination since the Revolution as they were elsewhere in Europe.) The candidate was known to be saintly, but he was also 'insanely handsome'. 'Tachygraphie', a kind of primitive shorthand, was one of Laennec's accomplishments, and he kept notes of the exchange between the candidate and the examiners.

Philippe Pinel, physician in charge of the Salpetrière, presided. At once he plunged into questioning Bayle about the nature of variola (smallpox). Pinel himself had classified the disease into two main 'types', further dividing them into subgroups. He regarded these as distinct illnesses. Bayle replied that he had performed numerous post-mortem examinations on smallpox victims and had found no evidence of such divisions and subdivisions. Nor, when properly interpreted, did the writings of other investigators (including the great Jenner) support Pinel's elaborate system. This struck at the root of Pinel's approach to medicine: he was an impassioned classifier. He was, fortunately for Bayle, also a great man.[70]

Did the candidate not think that recognition of different types of a disease was essential for the right treatment of patients? Yes, Bayle replied, when such types actually existed: not when they were figments of the unenlightened imagination. There must have been a tense moment or two, impossible to convey by a tachygrapher. Then Pinel said that it was important for medical science to recognise different viewpoints provided that they all aimed at uncovering the truth. He did not agree with the viewpoints expressed by M. Bayle, but the candidate's case in his thesis had been well argued. The president, moreover, had great respect for the candidate's moral as well as intellectual qualities, which were well known.[71] Other examiners took their cue from the president. Bayle's thesis was not only admitted but was also thought worthy of being printed at public expense.

By then Bayle was recognised as Corvisart's right-hand man. He accompanied the First Consul and later Emperor when his chief could not (or did not want to) go. But he was essentially a pathologist rather than a clinician, perhaps the greatest of his age.

His post-mortems would have been crowded with students had he allowed more than a dozen or so to attend at a time. 'This is not the opera house,' he protested, 'it is necessary for you to see what my hands are doing as well as to listen.' But of course they *were* performances, even if not operatic ones. None of Bayle's post-mortems was routine, though he worked at great speed. The clinical history of the subject was first reviewed and the post-mortem was planned to focus on the essentials. Eyewitnesses commented on the assurance with which, with a few deft strokes of the scalpel, he exposed the seats of the illnesses and the cause of death. Master surgeons can make complex and delicate operations seem simple. The same is true of morbid anatomists at their best. Bayle must have been of that breed. He would point out the salient features of the pathology to the students present and show how they fitted into the canonical framework; or did not. Sometimes the findings were unexpected. This too was noted and earmarked for further study.

Laennec, who was not a voracious reader of old texts, described Bayle's knowledge of the pathological literature as 'all-embracing', yet he was continually questioning established doctrine. Nothing was taken for granted because the great Morgagni had said so or because it was stated in some long-revered textbook. The whole of medicine based on a solid pathological basis was opening up, virtually a new art and science. And it was not merely pathology, though the careful dissection of bodies and the correlation of pathological and clinical findings were recognised as the most powerful new tool. 'Passionately dedicated to our art, eager for new revelations, we want all fields of human knowledge to contribute,' Bichat had written in his *Discours préliminaire* of the new Societé d'Emulation. Disciplines as varied as philosophy, ethics, chemistry, physics and natural history (but not, significantly, theology) were to be mined.

> We are convinced that medical theory will be enriched by a wide general knowledge of which medicine is only one application ... There are no 'ancillary' sciences ... They are all 'essential' because medicine must become at once their product and their complement.

What was crucial was that these sciences should be based on observation and experimentation, not on 'authority'. What mattered, in other words, was the verifiable. In medicine, weighed down by tradition, unquestioning faith in the wisdom of the past and sometimes a genuine but unscientific humanism, this was a novel concept. Bayle and Laennec were far from being rationalists but, where medicine was concerned, both were believers in the rigorous pursuit of the truth. It was a beginning. In retrospect at least, it was the birth of modern medicine as a science.

CHAPTER THREE

MATTERS TEMPORAL AND SPIRITUAL

One topic above all exercised medical minds. *La phthisie* was known as an ancient disease, the term itself of Hippocratic origin, meaning decline or wasting away.[72] In England it was better known as 'consumption' or 'hectic fever', but both in England and on the Continent it went by other names as well.[73] Or perhaps the other names represented different diseases. Nobody knew. In 1689 Richard Morton, a London physician, published a book entitled *Phthisiologia* in which he referred to the lesions in the lungs and elsewhere as 'tubercles'. The book was a success and the name caught on. But was *la phthisie* in fact tuberculosis of the lungs? It was one of the questions that needed to be answered and there were many more. In 1779 the famous London surgeon Percival Pott had described cases of 'palsy of the lower limbs due to curvature of the spine'. This he showed was due to the wedge-shaped collapse of one or several vertebrae. Three years later he suggested that the disease that had gnawed away at the bones was similar or even identical to Morton's tubercles.[74] If that was so, phthisis or tuberculosis was truly as old as humanity: hunchbacks had existed in ancient Egypt.[75] Others believed that the common swelling of lymph nodes in the neck, often leading to suppurating abscesses, discharging sinuses and horrific scarring, known as 'scrofula' or the 'king's evil', was another form of the same illness.[76]

In the closing years of the eighteenth century the subject acquired a new urgency. The disease had, for reasons unknown, suddenly become devastatingly common. Of course there had been famous sufferers before. In France *la phthisie* had killed the painter Antoine Watteau in 1721 at the age of 36. He was out of fashion in Laennec's day, but a few connoisseurs regarded him as a master waiting to be rediscovered.[77] In his last days, mute and exhausted with tuberculous laryngitis, he was still clutching his brushes and painting imaginary pictures in the air.[78] The immortal Molière had had severe, sometimes incapacitating bleeding from the lungs—already known as haemoptyses—for some years before he collapsed at Versailles during a production of his *Le malade imaginaire*. Despite the King's urgings to repair to his room and rest, he insisted on continuing. But soon he was seized with an all too unimaginary fit of coughing and died just off stage.[79] Many believed that the illness had also killed Madame de Pompadour, Louis XV's mistress and a discriminating and lavish patron of the arts. It may have been the cause of her bouts of abdominal pain and her sterility.[80]

La phthisie had been suspected in some female members of the Laennec family too. Not only Madame Laennec, Théo's mother, but several of her sisters and aunts had died young. Did mothers transmit the affliction to their children? Perhaps. Unlike Théo, who had always been thin and subject to colds, coughs and digestive upsets, Michaud Laennec had been fit as a schoolboy. Now, after only a year or two in Paris, he was pale and losing weight. Many families had similar tales to tell. It was said that on the English side of the Channel the picture was even more grim. Before being dispatched to Nantes, the Laennec boys had spent a year after their mother's death in the care of a kindly uncle, the Reverend Michel-Jean Laennec, parish priest in Eliant in Cornouaille. On the outbreak of the Revolution the uncle had fled to England and had settled in Southampton. The Laennec brothers learnt in Paris that he had died there of consumption within two years. Why was the illness becoming so widespread? Nobody knew the answer, though theories abounded. They still do.[81]

Bichat, Bayle, Laennec and their friends were confident that the careful eliciting of physical signs in life and meticulous dissection after death would soon dispel the uncertainties. Auenbrugger's percussion as perfected by Corvisart was helpful. So, on rare occasion, was direct auscultation, using the ear to listen to sounds arising in organs inside the body such as the lungs or the heart. In the post-mortem room Bayle and Laennec were tireless collecting material for new monographs on the subject. There was no shortage of bodies, though a question mark hung over that too. Both Bayle and Laennec resolutely dismissed the idea that the handling of cadavers, sometimes only a few hours after death, was in any way dangerous. Both men were exceptionally intelligent. Nevertheless, once they had set their minds against the idea of contagion, evidence that seems inescapable in retrospect counted for nothing.

Yet if they *were* wrong, they were a danger not only to themselves. Cuts and puncture wounds were an inevitable feature of autopsies. Bayle regularly developed purulent sores on his hands and enlarged glands in his armpit. So had Bichat for at least two years before he died. So had Jean-Pierre Armanard, another promising young doctor, friend and tireless dissector. He had wasted away in a matter of months in 1802 and died at the age of 26. So had his brother, still a medical student. The local lesions were often accompanied by shivering and sweats, clearly suggesting a general systemic illness. This too was dismissed as of no significance. However, all these young men spent as much time in the wards as they did in the post-mortem room. They looked after infants and children as well as adults and the old. All were firm believers in the physical examination of their patients. They regularly handled open wounds. The idea that they might actually be transmitting disease seemed to them an absurdity.

Disbelief in contagion was no eccentricity. It was shared by most of the medical fraternity of Paris. In England too (and a little less consistently in Germany and Scandinavia), professional opinion was wedded to the idea of the 'tuberculous diathesis', an inborn tendency to develop the disease. It was a sad predicament, deserving of pity and prayers, but nothing much else could be done about it. Symptoms could sometimes be alleviated, but a cure was virtually impossible. Nor, of course, could the affliction be prevented.

By contrast in Mediterranean countries, including the South of France, the illness was regarded as highly contagious and strenuous efforts were made to avoid its spread by contact.[82] During a concert tour the celebrated violinist and composer Niccolò Paganini suffered a relapse of his tuberculosis in Naples. As soon as his landlord guessed the nature of his high-pitched cough, he turned the artist out into the street, hurling his travelling cases after him, including his treasured Guarneri. The violin survived, the violinist did not. The prospect of having his and his friend John Severn's possessions burnt after his death added to the despair of John Keats' last weeks in Rome. In the same city Chateaubriand had much difficulty in finding accommodation for his friend Madame de Beaumont when it transpired that she might be suffering from the dread disease. His contacts in the Vatican eventually found a secluded villa for her, though there were no takers when he tried to raise funds by selling her carriage. It had to be publicly burnt. A few decades later the already mortally sick Chopin and George Sand had to flee Majorca when the nature of his illness became known.

By 1800 in many Mediterranean countries the law required notification of the disease. In Lucca failure of notification was punishable (in theory at least) with death. In Spain the law stipulated that all objects known to have been in the possession of a person who had died of phthisis should be confined to the flames like heretics. Of course, the division was only roughly North versus South. In Vienna, Prague and other cities of the Habsburg Empire, where Italian influence had always been strong, contact with the illness was much feared. On the other hand, the inhabitants of Nice on the Riviera seemed to consider themselves immune. Or perhaps the risk was worth taking. The

indecently profitable influx of the debilitated rich from northern climes had already begun.

Bayle and Laennec were familiar with the fears of their southern compatriots. Bayle's own uncle and aunt from Aix-en-Provence were reluctant to stay with him in Paris and did not press him to visit them at home. They had three small children. He had earlier written to his parents telling them that he suspected that he was suffering from 'mild phthisis'. Some years later he would return to his native province to die, but not to stay with his family. Both men poured scorn on what Chateaubriand had aptly (in their opinion) described as a 'Gothic superstition' and 'mediaeval practices'. Laennec wrote:

> Many facts prove that phthisis is not contagious though it is possible that under exceptional circumstances it may become so ... Woollen garments used by consumptives which are burned in some countries after the patient's death are never even washed in France. It seems to me that they have never communicated the disease to anyone.[83]

Of course, garments did not cough; patients did. Laennec's view is hard to understand, but it was not unique. John Keats devotedly nursed his younger brother Tom during the latter's final illness, sleeping in the same room, sometimes in the same bed, only to re-enact the illness himself shortly after Tom's death. Looking after Michaud, Laennec seemed determined to follow a similar path.

Frequent ill-health added misery and sometimes desperation to the hardships of Laennec's first years in Paris. This was not for lack of academic success. Both Michaud and Théo were winning praises and prizes. Théo was generally acknowledged to be the brightest student of his year. Uncharacteristically, Corvisart referred to his 'luminous mind'. Bayle admired him. He was disliked by Dupuytren, but also respected. He regularly contributed to the *Journal*. By the time he was ready to submit and defend his *Thèse*, he had published several significant papers.

One demonstrated the difference between inflammation of the abdominal organs and inflammation of the peritoneum, the fine connective-tissue sheath that envelops them. People could die of general peritonitis with pus and inflammatory exudate covering that sheath without the interior of the organs being diseased. In some cases—but not all—it was possible to find a 'primary focus' in the abdomen.

One of the cases Laennec had studied in detail was a mother who had died of childbed fever. In this terrible illness the primary focus was clearly the womb. Within a few days of delivery it had become a purulent, necrotic mass. From here the infection had spread upwards and outwards. The result was peritonitis. The suffering must have been terrible. Because the inflammatory exudate was white and viscous, faintly resembling clotted milk, some obstetricians believed that the disease was actually caused by 'milk retention'. Laennec argued forcefully against such an idea; but the real explanation would not come for another 50 years.[84] Laennec also guessed that some forms of general peritonitis were tuberculous in origin.

In another paper he described three cases of hydatid cyst of the liver and rightly suggested that these were caused by living parasites. One patient had died after the cyst had ruptured following a comparatively slight injury. The inside of her abdomen was dotted with small 'daughter cysts'. Laennec could not quite unravel the eccentric life cycle of the dog tapeworm (*Echinococcus granulosus*), but he was convinced that some stages of the cycle required a 'host' other than a human. The dog was certainly implicated, but so perhaps were sheep and cattle. Laennec's actual descriptions of the lesions were always clear. He gave a graphic account of the double lining of the cysts and of the clear hydatid fluid inside them. It contained thousands of tiny hooklets.[85]

His interest in parasitology continued for some years. He later described the glandular structure of the prostate. The organ had been known to Galen, but it was Laennec who suggested that it made an important contribution to seminal fluid. The serous

pouches or *bursae* of the shoulder region also engaged his attention. He guessed correctly that their inflammation could be one of the causes of the painful condition still known as a frozen shoulder.

None of these discoveries changed the face of medicine, but they were remarkable for a man still in his early twenties, writing his *Thèse*. Unfortunately, they raised no money. The two brothers sometimes starved. Soon after their arrival in Paris Michaud was forced to sell a cherished medallion bequeathed to him by his mother. It must have been a painful parting, but heating their garret was a more pressing problem. When Michaud's cough became troublesome, laudanum too had to take precedence over bread. This was the more outrageous since Laennec *père* was now a wealthy man. At least he lived in great style. Not only was his second wife rich, another source of his wealth was the estate of his first wife, of which he was a trustee. This should have provided funds for the education of their two sons and a dowry for their daughter.

His sons begged him for financial support. His brother Guillaume, a poor man by comparison, upbraided him for his parsimony. Laennec *père* always answered at length and with affection, but took no notice of his sons' and brother's pleas. His actions and attitude remain mystifying. He was immensely proud of his progeny. Michaud was as successful in his law examinations as Théo was in medicine. The father wrote to them effusive, affectionate, congratulatory and sometimes humorous letters. In fact, he had conceived the idea of entering the state service himself at some exalted level and of moving to Paris. To achieve this he repeatedly asked his sons to put in a good word for him with 'your influential friends ... I hear that you number important ministers and politicians among your acquaintances.' In vain did Théo and Michaud try to convince him that shaking hands with a minister at a prize-giving ceremony did not entail having influence in 'government circles'.

Their father was also writing odes in honour of the country's saviour, 'our beloved General Bonaparte' and later 'Napoleon, emperor and sun of our lives'.[86] These he had printed in Quimper,

signed 'Laennec, a grateful father' and sent to 'men of influence' in Paris. They included some of the boys' teachers. 'Who is the Laennec who sends me sonnets from Brittany?' Corvisart wanted to know. Théo was too upright not to acknowledge the relationship. 'Tell him to stop,' Corvisart snapped. Letters from Quimper were always full of advice. Parcels sometimes arrived containing books on Breton grammar, sometimes slim volumes of Breton poetry. There were newspaper cuttings reporting the dazzling success of the two young Laennecs in the capital. It was not difficult to guess where the news items had originated. Friends travelling to Paris from Quimper would sometimes arrive laden with a cheese or a bag of apples. The only thing Laennec *père* refused to send was money. Yet even from a distance he must have exerted a certain charm. Theo's and Michaud's letters to 'chèr Papa' remained exasperated but solicitous.

Some penniless students seemed to survive by moonlighting as waiters, lackeys or providers of musical entertainment. After Robespierre's fall Paris plunged into an orgy of parties, soirées, masked balls, dances, romps and galas. Most were riotous street affairs, but some surpassed in splendour or at least in ostentation the formal *fêtes* and *jours* of pre-revolutionary society. There was always need for occasional staff to handle the trays and tureens, often bearing the coat of arms of unfortunates who had lost more than the family silver during the Terror. Other budding academics were good at scrounging. To defraud the philistine was becoming the competitive sport of the Quartier. The ritual would be affectionately depicted by Mürger and set to music by Puccini. A few students found a benevolent patron or more often a patroness whose drawing room and sometimes boudoir they would adorn. The salons were re-opening, more fiercely competing for conversational talent than ever. 'Incroyable!' and 'merveilleux!' echoed under the arches of the Palais Royale. The theatres were packed and always in need of 'extras', either on the stage or in the audience. Cheers and raucous laughter paid for by the minute, modest forerunners of television's canned applause, were among the new century's first inventions. Sometimes the demand was for boos and stampedes, and they too could be provided.

There were other possible sources of income. Under the Directory and the first years of the Consulate Paris was still a lawless city. The screams of mugged citizens did not figure among the 'Cris de Paris', a popular subject on cards, plates and engravings, but they were not uncommon. Rich bourgeois and bourgeoises paid beefy young men to act as bodyguards. But neither Théo nor Michaud was beefy. They were also inept scroungers. While both could be charming, mindless chatter was not their forte. Anyway, they needed time for their studies. For occasional relaxation Théo would play the flute, Michaud the violin. Théo would also immerse himself in Breton literature. He also kept up with his Latin and Greek. Languages would remain a lifelong passion.

By the end of the century tuberculosis would acquire the reputation of being a great aphrodisiac. 'Cousining' in the grim municipal sanatoria of England was the forbidden pleasure and comfort of young inmates. Orgiastic parties among those dying *de luxe* in Davos became legendary. The *fin-de-siècle* Bohemia of Aubrey Beardsley (the original perhaps of Shaw's Louis Dubedat) was riddled with sex and consumption. But the image—it was never much more—was a later accretion.

Of female company there is no hint in any of Théo or Michaud's letters. Perhaps they were too reticent to write about conquests or *petites amies*. More probably they had nothing to write about. Michaud's painful cough and Théo's 'asthma' often kept them awake at night. When, after many years, Théo was revisiting Brittany for the first time, he was so thin that some of his relatives barely recognised him. Only one development gave him spiritual if not physical solace.

It was Bayle who, in the summer of 1801, first invited his friend to 27 rue Saint-Guillaume to meet the Abbé Jean-Baptiste Delpuits. This former Jesuit had remained in Paris as a refractory priest and, sheltered by his flock, had survived the Terror. Most churches in

Paris had been closed or reassigned to practical and patriotic uses under the Convention, but in a bricked-off side chapel of the Church of Saint Sulpice and in private houses, Delpuits continued to celebrate mass. Appearing in public for the first time a few days after the bloody events of Thermidor, he prayed for the souls of Robespierre and Saint-Just: 'No soul is entirely lost to the mercy of God.' Soon men, women and children were once again seen going to church, though they still risked mockery. Priests and nuns, those that is who had survived, could walk the streets again in their habits. Even the Jesuits were tacitly tolerated.

On 2 February 1802, the Feast of Purification, six young men, including Bayle and Laennec, attended a meeting at Delpuits's house. After prayers and a brief address by the priest, they vowed to devote themselves to the glorification of God and His church and to the witnessing of the Catholic faith. They adopted the name 'Sancta Maria auxilium Christianorum,' soon to be known as the 'Congrégation'.[87]

When did Laennec become a committed Catholic? The family had produced a number of priests, but on the whole they inclined towards Voltairian scepticism. Guillaume Laennec was not a churchgoer, though his wife was. A cousin of Madame Guillaume Laennec was a Carmelite nun who had died on the guillotine. Her memory was revered. Laennec *père* in Quimper was not known for his piety nor for leading a virtuous Christian life, but he wrote to his sons frequently and at length about the importance of 'true religion'. It is not clear what he meant by this and his homilies probably made little impression.

While anticlericalism was endemic in Brittany, an irreligious Breton was almost a self-contradiction.[88] The province always had more saints than the rest of France put together, even if most of those prayed to in the villages were not listed in the canonical register in Rome.[89] But it was not only Brittany. As had happened before and was to happen again, what the church had lost in temporal power during the Revolution it had gained in spiritual stature. Neither intellectually nor morally could a man like Delpuits be dismissed as a fool, a fraud or a fanatic. This was the other side of the coin of orgiastic merrymaking. Within a year the Congrégation was to count among its members some of the most illustrious names in French history: Sully, Rohan, Richelieu, Forbon, Montmorency. This was not perhaps surprising. The aristocracy in France had always been staunchly Catholic or at least Gallican. More unexpected was the rising number of professional men among its members. Doctors had rarely been distinguished by their religious fervour. Louis XV had apostrophised them as godless scoundrels. (He was surely an expert.) Now they flocked to join.

Among established practitioners there was Régis de Buisson, a cousin of Bichat's and a successful doctor in the Cité; Louis Fizeau, a former artillery officer in the Vendéan army and soon to become professor of pathology at the Charité; and Jean Maisonneuve, a well-known surgeon and future professor of surgery. Among Laennec's contemporaries destined for a distinguished medical career were Bruté de Rémur, Jacques Varannes, Jean Legoupil and Savary de Brûlons. The last, on obtaining first prize in the final examinations, was invited to an official dinner by Quinette, minister of education and a regicide.[90] As it was a day of fasting Savary put in a brief appearance, only to decline food and drink and to refuse to shake hands with his host. Despite the rapprochement between Church and State in the following decade, he had to wait for the Bourbon Restoration before obtaining a university chair.

The rise of the Congrégation coincided with moves towards the Concordat. Both Bonaparte and the Vatican had something to gain from an accommodation. Bonaparte could not hope for the permanent pacification of the Vendée, Savoie and the newly occupied Belgian provinces without reopening the churches and letting the *curés* back into the primary schools. The Vatican, despite its denunciation of the Revolution, was prepared to make concessions. Pius VII, elected to St Peter's throne in 1800, was a simple and holy monk who hated the Revolution, but his more worldly-wise advisers pointed to the unalterable fact that France now controlled most of Northern Italy. First cousins and a favourite aunt of the Holy Father were among the subjects of the Antichrist. Papal agents were secretly dispatched to Paris. Negotiations proceeded fast and satisfactorily.

They were concluded by July 1801. Bonaparte's maternal uncle, Monsignor Fesch, was created a cardinal. In April 1802 the Concordat was announced. A new episcopate would be instituted to include a proportion of the bishops who had sworn an oath of allegiance to the godless constitution. Like the 'peace-priests' of Communist Eastern Europe 150 years later, they were a grisly lot but, hopefully, they would not live for ever. The Church accepted the seizure of Church lands and the payment of clerical salaries by the state. Catholicism was to be described as 'the religion of the great majority of citizens' rather than as the religion of state. Its practice was to be free and public 'provided it conformed to police regulations'. The Revolutionary calendar was abolished, together with the wonderfully poetic names of the months. No more Thermidor, Prérial, Fructidor or Brumaire; a great loss to the vocabulary but a conciliatory gesture.

Neither side meant what it said. The proverbial ink was hardly dry on the official document when Bonaparte issued a series of 'Organic Articles', distorting some of the key provisions of the agreement.[91] That was what organic meant in Napoleonic parlance. And the pope was in no hurry to consecrate the bishops nominated by the First Consul. Such grave matters had to be implemented *sub specie aeternitatis*. The episcopate of the *ancien régime* who had lost their sees retained the loyalty and affection of the faithful, forming a kind of unofficial *petite Eglise*. Among them was the bishop of Nantes, an old friend of the Guillaume Laennecs.

On the face of it, the Concordat was a triumph for Bonaparte and Gallicanism. In the long run, its legacy was more equivocal.[92] Nevertheless, for a time the differences were patched up. Symbolically, an official national *fête* was created for the day of the Assumption. By a happy coincidence it turned out to be Bonaparte's birthday. By another fortunate accident it transpired

to be the feast day of a previously virtually unknown martyr, Saint Napoléon. To guild the transition from First Consul to Emperor, the Pope travelled from Rome to Paris.

The coronation in Paris's Notre Dame on 2 December 1804 was both stage-managed and commemorated by the former pageant master of the Terror, Jacques-Louis David. The commemoration was immensely accomplished but as fraudulent as were all of David's historical tableaux. The new Emperor's mother, the wonderful Letitia, now styled Madame Mère, refused to attend this 'blasphemous charade'. This did not stop David from painting her in. The Pope, though a kindly man, did not sit on his throne blessing the proceedings with a beatific smile. He was mortified when Charlemagne's newly discovered successor snatched the crown from his hands and placed it first on his own head and then on Josephine's. The Emperor of the French would not owe his elevation to a Tuscan peasant.

However, Corvisart, present in the congregation, was impressed —or as impressed as he ever was by any display of wealth and power. He had been recommended to Josephine by Madame Lannes and Josephine had recommended him to the First Consul. He was, in Josephine's words, 'a funny sort of a doctor. He does not believe in drugs and potions. He does not think much of enemas. He thinks we eat too much. He does not really believe in medicine at all.' He was, in short, a man after Bonaparte's heart. After their first meeting he would be in constant attendance on the First Consul and later Emperor. He became what would be the closest to a friend Napoleon ever had.[93]

Independently of the Coronation and the Concordat, the Catholic revival had taken wing. It was inevitably led by Bretons. Lamennais of St Malo—'le sacristan' as he was dubbed for his stunted appearance and scarecrow attire—was incubating his revolutionary blueprint for the Church Militant, *Réflexions sur l'état de l'église en France pendant le 18ième siècle et sur sa situation actuelle.*[94] Implausibly on the face of it, the revival was to be based not on a strong and independent Gallican church but on an alliance between the Pope and the French people. The idea never worked in practice, but during his stay in the French capital for the coronation, the then incumbent of St Peter's throne gave an audience to some of the country's leading Catholics as well as a few young converts. In the German Chapel near Saint Sulpice he received Bayle and Laennec. 'Pius medicus, res miranda' (pious doctor, wondrous thing) he exclaimed, before giving the two doctors his pontifical blessing.

Chateaubriand of Combourg had already published his master-piece, *Le Génie du christianisme*.[95] The book was a wonderfully eloquent apologia for Christianity, not on theological grounds— that, the author wrote, could be left to others better qualified than a poet—but as the inspiration behind the world's greatest works of art and literature. (The world to Chateaubriand meant of course France and a few non-French-speaking countries clustering around it.) Ten years later Laennec was to question the writer: 'What about science, Monsieur le Vicomte? Did Christianity produce the greatest science as well as the greatest art and literature?' The Vicomte hummed and hawed. Regrettably, most regrettably, he knew few scientists of any eminence and science was a closed book to him. 'And medicine?' Laennec pressed him. 'Yes, medicine certainly. And you, my dear Laennec, are here to prove it.'[96]

Coincidentally with Laennec's religious crisis—if it was a crisis rather than a gradual evolution—his politics also changed. It was not something in which he had ever taken much interest; nor would he in the future. But one could not live in France during the Revolution, the Empire and the Bourbon Restoration without responding to political events. Like most moderate republicans, Laennec at first welcomed the advent of Bonaparte. The consulate promised order and stability. Order and stability was clearly what the overwhelming majority of Frenchmen and even more of French women wanted. The idea of an empire was less shocking in France than it was to Bonaparte's republican admirers abroad.[97] However, a seemingly minor event made a deep and disturbing impression on him.

Early in March 1804, Drake, British minister in Munich, was induced by an ex-Jacobin *agent provocateur* to provide a comparatively small sum of money to finance a royalist *coup* in France. Drake was an ambitious fool. A direct descendant (he claimed) of the Elizabethan pirate and navigator, he fancied himself as the answer to His Majesty George III's prayers. A knighthood bestowed on him (not necessarily on board ship) might give an upward swing to both their careers. He provided the French agent with information that seemed to connect the plot with the imminent arrival in France of 'a Bourbon Prince'. The plot was 'discovered'. The *Moniteur*, France's official newspaper, thundered in indignation. Pitt had no wish to provoke a quarrel with France at that particular moment. Drake was sacked and the matter seemed to be at an end.

Unfortunately, a totally innocent young prince—the Duc d'Enghien, the last of the Condés—was living in Baden, not far from the French border.[98] Bonaparte decided to 'send a message' to royalist sympathisers. The Prince was seized on foreign soil, carried off to the fortress of Vincennes and shot at dawn on 21 March 1804. In the popular French press the news unleashed a torrent of patriotic prose. Everybody seemed to be congratulating the First Consul on frustrating the dastardly schemes of the enemy. Nevertheless most of Europe, and not merely royalists and reactionaries, was deeply shocked. The Czar, though heavily implicated himself in the murder of his monstrous father, expressed his abhorrence. The Pope was shocked. So was a silent but significant minority in France. In Talleyrand's famous phrase, the murder was worse than a crime: it was a mistake.

It may seem odd that, within a few years of the judicial carnage of the Terror, the shooting of a single prince should provoke such revulsion. But it was as a restorer of normality, not as a vengeful *condottiere*, that Bonaparte had been welcomed by the French. Ironically, the *Code Civile*, what was to be the written foundation of the newly instituted rule of law and still the foundation of the French legal system, was published on the day of the execution. The two events were incompatible. Bonaparte's apotheosis was still to come, but for some the imperial image was tarnished forever. They included Laennec. He would never tiptoe around the subject. Winks, nudges and deep dramatic sighs were not his style. His lack of enthusiasm for Bonaparte, soon to be Napoleon, would in no way affect the meteoric rise of the Corsican adventurer, but it did not help the career of the insignificant young doctor from Brittany.

CHAPTER FOUR

Humdrum Practice

Five months before the beanfeast in Notre Dame, Laennec successfully defended his *Thèse* before the examining board of the University. Corvisart presided. Entitled 'Propositions sur la doctrine d'Hippocrate relativement à la médicine pratique', the work was a beautifully written exposition of the Hippocratic doctrine—as interpreted by Laennec. Fortunately, it chimed in with Corvisart's own ideas. Practice must be based on careful observation, not on pre-conceived doctrines. Unnecessary mystification must be avoided. Patients must be treated with kindness, but must not be deliberately misled.

At a practical level, the candidate dismissed both universalist systems and complicated classifications. He was particularly dismissive of the then fashionable division of fever into no less than eight different 'types': inflammatory, bilious, mucous, putrid, pestiferous, adenonervous, verminous and catarrhal. These had no basis in Hippocratic writings. They had none in reality either. While the causes of fever were many, the feverish response was the same. What was more helpful was to observe the fever over a period of time, to see if it was hectic or continuous. If hectic, what was the pattern of the fluctuations? This was pure Laennec: Hippocrates never made such a suggestion. All Hippocrates suggested was that the course of the fever should not be ignored. Another of Laennec's remarks was prophetic: 'Fever is not always harmful. Curing the fever sometimes makes the disease worse.'[99]

If the contents of the thesis did not always conform to the title, Corvisart and his two fellow examiners, Baudlecocque and Noyer (both chosen by Corvisart), were not inclined to quibble. This was clearly and thankfully the new medicine based on facts and observation. It was the end of 'scholasticism' and 'obscurantism'.

Though Laennec was an excellent Latinist—he would later deliver some of his lectures in Latin to make them comprehensible to foreign visitors—the thesis was in French.[100] Only the dedication was in elegant Ciceronian convolutions. To Corvisart? To some other powerful academic? To the all-inspiring figure of the First Consul, perhaps? That was the accepted custom. But Laennec's dedication was to his Uncle Guillaume:

> Optimo, dilecto patruo, secondo patri, Guilhelmo Francisco Laennec, doctori medico monspeliensi, exercituum olim medico, nosocomiorum nannentensium primario medico, ob educationem a pueritia institutam, optima in studio medico consilia, et omnis generis beneficia, theses hasce inaugurales dicat et vovet gratus et amantissimus R.H.T. Laennec.

The liberal sprinkling of superlatives was well deserved and appreciated in Nantes.

By 1805 a certain amount of private practice, mainly among fellow Bretons, was at last beginning to make Laennec's day-to-day existence less precarious. He was elected associate of the newly founded Societé de l'Ecole de Médicine. This carried a small salary and, more importantly, gave him free access to the *Journal*. From now on he would contribute editorial and general review articles as well as original papers. He was also beginning to be known as a literary stylist. Revolutions are notoriously prolix and the one in France was no exception. Now, after years of ungrammatical and often hysterical rhetoric, the wonderfully precise language of Racine, Descartes and de la Rochefoucauld was coming back into fashion. Those ambitious to see their names in print but incapable of constructing a sentence (who included at least one professor of anatomy) approached Laennec. Would he act as an 'editor', in effect a ghost? Laennec disliked this kind of work, but it was well paid and he did not always refuse.

At Bayle's invitation he also gave his first course of lectures in pathological anatomy at the Ecole de Médicine. This was notable because one of his students—Jean-Baptiste Guépin of Nantes, who later became chief of medicine in Angers—was an assiduous attender and took detailed notes of each lecture. He also appended brief, critical comments about the manner of delivery: 'hesitant to start with, but increasingly eloquent' or 'a passionate and powerful peroration'.[101] Laennec used these lectures—one a week for fifty weeks a year—to elaborate and clarify his thoughts. It was in one of them that he first stated categorically that *la phthisie* was pulmonary tuberculosis, and that pulmonary tuberculosis was the most important and most common but not the only site of tuberculous infection. These were notions that had been floating about but had never been clearly formulated. Many other ideas first mooted in a lecture would later emerge in print. The pay, as for all teaching work then as now, was derisory, but their success added to Laennec's growing reputation.

Towards the end of 1803 Michaud had completed his legal studies and had departed for Beauvais as a trainee on the staff of M. de Belderbuch, newly appointed prefect of the Département de l'Oise. Laennec could now afford more respectable lodgings, first to be shared with Jacques Varanne of Nantes and then on his own. He eventually moved to 5 rue du Jardinet, near the Ecole de Médicine. The street was named after the gardens of the nearby Collège de Vendôme, one of the oldest teaching institutions in Paris. It was pulled down in the 1870s to make way for the eastern extension of the Boulevard St Germain; only the Cour de Rohan, where the street ended, still exists. In Laennec's day this was a quiet, respectable, almost provincial neighbourhood, the home of many doctors, including Bayle, Dubois and Tenon. Laennec's landlady, Madame Harel, was of course a Bretonne, ready to adjust the rent to suit the purse of her tenants.

In the autumn, following the defence of his thesis and award of his doctorate, Laennec took his first holiday since his arrival in the capital. The record of these three weeks, lovingly preserved by Madame Laennec after her husband's death, slightly changes the picture that one forms of the man. From his early Paris years he emerges as an intensely serious and almost frighteningly brilliant young academic, totally honest but also a little priggish. His slight, thin, nervous physical frame gave him the appearance of a starving seminarist rather than of a slightly bohemian medical student.

Many of Théo and Michaud's letters home, both to Laennec *père* and to Uncle Guillaume, survive, and a fair selection (though not all) have been published. They contain accounts of occasional dinner parties, musical soirées and receptions, always at the homes of high clerics, respected professional men or conservative hostesses. Nowhere is there a whiff of tomfoolery, let alone dissipation, part of medical student life everywhere in all ages. Travellers to Paris during these years, the last of the Directory and the first of the Consulate, were scandalised by the city's debauchery. For Parisians living through it, it was to be in retrospect what the 'swinging sixties' would be for another generation in another century. None of this is evident from the correspondence of the two brothers.

Many of Théo's letters contain expressions of lofty aspirations. What he wants from life is not success or power but the knowledge of serving his fellow men. He loves medicine because it provides scope, more perhaps than any other calling, for helping the helpless. These are noble sentiments and they are always felicitously expressed. The licence and excesses of the post-revolutionary years were clearly only part of the scene; this was also the beginning of the romantic age. Similar stirrings were expressed by many other young men, not only in France but all over Europe. (Often they would be set to music.) Théo's thoughts and language are still wholly commendable, and yet in private correspondence the sustained high-mindedness is slightly unnerving.

The letters and papers relating to Laennec's three weeks in Couvrelle tell a more relaxed story. While the holiday was neither dramatic nor extravagant, a more human person suddenly emerges. He chose to accept the invitation of his maternal cousin, Madame de Pompéry, because he badly needed a break and the Soissonnais was nearer than going home to Brittany. From visits to Quimper in his boyhood, he also remembered the lady as a person of great charm. In her day Madame de Pompéry's mother, Madame de la Potterie, had been the leading intellectual hostess of Cornouaille. She possessed an excellent two-keyboard harpsichord, the only one in Quimper, and an extensive library. Laennec *père* described her as the sun around whom the cultural life of the city revolved. (He himself was of course a leading planet.) Expelled from her town house during the Revolution, she settled happily into the village life of Le Brigant. It was there that Laennec met the family. One daughter later married an exceedingly rich nobleman from the North of France, M. de Pompéry. How and where the couple had met and how the Pompéry seat near Soissons had survived the Revolution virtually unscathed are not known. Laennec described the château as a

magnificent Louis XIV building, with a large light grey slated roof, surrounded by a moat and flanked by two elegant wings. One wing contained the stables, the other the orangerie. A splendid wrought iron gate opens onto the forecourt. An old church behind the château raises its gothic bell-tower above the roof. Behind it one glimpses vineyards and rolling, wooded countryside.[102]

A state coach from the château met Laennec in Soissons. It was a balmy September day. The landscape reminded him of Lower Brittany, though of course it was richer, more luscious. Brittany was poor. The Soissonnais was one of the gardens of France, with vineyards rather than orchards. The villages looked more prosperous, the churches more imposing. Perhaps it was just the quiet and the fresh air, so unlike the noise and evil-smelling bustle of Paris, which brought back happy childhood memories. On arrival Laennec was greeted by the stately figure of the major domo, M. Perival. A footman was summoned to carry his modest luggage and escort him to his bedroom. His name was already inscribed on a framed slate on the door. Here the Revolution might never have happened.

The room was spacious, spotlessly clean and yet pleasantly lived-in. A fine porcelain washbasin and pitcher had been placed on a *bonheur-du-jour*. Fresh flowers stood in a vase. From the window he glimpsed a group of young people playing a ball game in the park. Sounds of a harpsichord skilfully played reached him from another part of the building. He recognised a piece by Corette.

> Having disposed of my bags, my guide escorted me to the drawing room. 'Here we are,' he said. I had expected to meet Monsieur or Madame de Pompéry, but there was only a young woman there whom I had not met before. She was reading. She seemed more embarrassed by my sudden appearance, still in my travelling costume, than I was myself. Then I guessed that she must be Madame de Pompéry's godchild, Jacquette Guichard from Brest, the widow of a certain Monsieur Argou. Madame de Pompéry had mentioned her in her letter: apparently she now lived with them as one of the family. She was, she wrote, charming and cultivated though perhaps a trifle *timide*. Her husband had died during the Revolution, I do not know how. So I knew about her. But I had expected somebody older. She was shy like a convent girl. The book she had been reading was a volume of religious *pensées*. But she quickly regained her composure and invited me to sit in one of the *fauteuilles*. I must be hungry after the journey. She would call for food and wine. Her dear godmother would be with us presently.[103]

It was his first encounter with the woman whom, 19 years later, he would marry.

Laennec had a writer's touch conveying mood and atmosphere. His three weeks in Couvrelle were among his happiest. The weather was mild and the trees were turning gloriously autumnal. In the mornings he would join members of the family and friends on long walks over the fields or in the woods. Sometimes there were rabbit shoots. The house was full of friends of the younger de Pompérys, some of them of Laennec's age. A few were gifted musicians and in the evenings they sometimes improvised concerts. Gluck had been the great favourite of the late lamented Queen Marie Antoinette; he was still the favourite at Couvrelle. Jacquette tinkled on the clavichord, Laennec played the flute. *The Dance of the Blessed Spirits* could never have sounded more blessed.

Or there were games, charades, competitions creating *tableaux vivants*. Laennec recreated David's *The Oath of the Horatii*. (The men were allowed to wear tunics.) It was a great success. For another occasion he composed an ode, some 200 lines long, comparing the Soissonnais with Paradise. It was impossible to choose between the two. His parodies of the classics, both Latin and French, were much appreciated. Monsieur de Pompéry maintained that he had not laughed so heartily since the 'detestable revolution'. Detestable but barely mentioned. For the sixteenth birthday of Antoine, the youngest of the de Pompérys, the guest composed a drinking song. It rhymed *vin* with *chien*. As a reward, he was presented with a choice bottle of the local growth.

One Sunday in church Laennec tried his hand at the organ. 'It sounded a little congested; but Monsieur Phillion [the *curé*] assured me that it showed promise. I duly promised not to try again.' For another solemn occasion he wrote an edifying religious hymn set to a revolutionary air by Gossec. It was probably acceptable when sung. He played chess with Monsieur de Pompéry and allowed him to win. Making elaborate bouquets of artificial flowers from paper and material was a long-established pastime. *Decoupomanie*, sticking cut-outs inside glass globes and then pouring in plaster of Paris, was a more recent craze. To everybody's delight, Laennec was hopelessly clumsy. However, he did hold long *causeries* with Madame de Pompéry in Breton. She spoke it as her native tongue and was delighted to discover that her cousin was another enthusiast. 'What a relief after all the boring Greek and Latin!' she exclaimed after one of their sessions.

Almost every day brought another pleasant surprise. His 'asthma' never troubled him. After the morning walks or rabbit shoots he felt ravenous. He slept 'like a babe'. All that is missing from the diaries, letters and carefully preserved manuscripts (even of bits of word games played after dinner) is any mention of Jacquette. Nor were any notes or letters from her to him or from him to her in the pile of documents perused by Rouxeau when lovingly researching his biography.[104] The probable reason is that it was she who sorted out his papers after his death. They undoubtedly corresponded—there are several references in Laennec's letters to his father to news received from 'Madame Argou'—but she clearly valued their posthumous privacy. Nevertheless, the little that does survive reveals a different Laennec from the grave, ascetic, often ailing doctor that he had become in Paris. It harks back to the irreverent versifier and popular guest that he had been in his youth in Brittany.

He tore himself away with a heavy heart, but his practice was growing and could not be left unattended. For a few years Bayle and he acted as locums for each other. As their practices were getting big, this had become impossible. While initially Laennec's patients were mainly acquaintances, friends and friends' friends from Nantes, soon his waiting room—shortly to become a suite of several rooms—was overflowing. There was of course no appointment system, and patients who had come from far away sometimes had to wait 24 hours or more to see him. Accommodation of sorts and food were provided. Urgent home visits at any time of the day or night had to be fitted in and interrupted the flow. Laennec's father wrote:

> All the talk in Brittany is about the phenomenal success of the young Breton doctor in Paris. Yes, you, my dear

Théophile. Apparently he has taken a grand carriage and has a coachman. No doctor is busier than he. It is the talk of all Finistère and the Côte du Nord.[105]

In January 1807 Bayle married Mademoiselle Moutard-Martin and moved to the Faubourg St Germain. Laennec took over his house in the same street, 'four lovely spacious rooms opening into each other but also connected by an airy corridor'. Even the new apartment soon proved too small to accommodate his whole practice. He annexed first two and then three rooms of the neighbouring building, a disused oratory. He engaged a cook, the faithful Angélique, who would stay with him until his return to Brittany. In his will she would be left a generous pension.

Whatever accounted for his success in practice, it was not a smooth or ingratiating manner. The de Chateaubriands were at that time living in the Vallée aux Loups near Sceaux, the vicomte consoling himself for his disappointments in public life by exchanging magnolia cuttings with the ex-Empress Josephine. In her *Cahiers Rouges* Madame de Chateaubriand was to give a vivid account of their encounter with Laennec. A year earlier her husband had met Monsieur Aristide de Loupineau, 'an eminent man of letters'.[106] At the time of their meeting Monsieur de Loupineau was already suffering from palpitations, shortness of breath, headaches, giddiness and chest pains. These were diagnosed by his doctor, the elderly Brochard, as manifestations of a growing aortic aneurysm. The prognosis was poor and a few months later Monsieur de Loupineau died. Madame de Chateaubriand wrote:

On our way home from the funeral, my husband experienced the first symptoms of what he took to be an ailment identical with the one that had killed Monsieur de Loupineau. He took to his bed, refused his food, and abandoned the book on which he was working. Instead he immersed himself in composing his Will ... As he lost no weight and his colour remained unchanged, I was convinced that he only suffered from a nervous complaint.

This did not prevent me from worrying. Even if he was not gravely ill to start with, he soon would be from not eating, sleeping hardly at all and from nervous agitation. I never stopped begging him to see Monsieur Laennec, a Breton doctor in Paris in whom my friend, Madame Duras, had unshakeable faith. But Monsieur de Chateaubriand insisted that it was too late to consult anyone: he was doomed and resigned to die. Happily, one day we entertained Madame de Lévis, who absolutely insisted that he should avail himself of her carriage and at once go to Paris with her and consult Dr Laennec. He gave in and they left; but such was my disquiet that, within a few minutes, I followed in my own carriage. I arrived at Monsieur Laennec's consulting room a few moments after my husband and Madame de Lévis. I hid until the end of the consultation. This took some time although there were many patients waiting. As I learnt later, Monsieur de Chateaubriand did not minimise his ailments. Nor was he expecting miracles. As a Christian, he could face the truth. He did not need comforting. Doctor Laennec examined him at length. He was extremely meticulous. He seemed deeply concerned. During the examination he said nothing. He asked my husband to save his questions till later. At the end of the examination he told my husband that there was nothing whatever wrong with him. Monsieur de Chateaubriand once again listed all his sufferings, but in vain. Nothing would make Doctor Laennec retract his opinion. He would not prescribe anything. He bade Monsieur de Chateaubriand to take his hat and go for a walk. 'But,' said my husband, 'what about leeches?' 'If you want to have leeches, you can have leeches,' Doctor Laennec answered, 'but I advise you to have nothing.' Then the doctor descended the steps and I made myself known to him. I asked him what was wrong with my husband. He said 'nothing at all'. He told me what I have described here, bade me goodbye and went into another room to see another patient. He would accept no

payment since, he said, he had done nothing. Anyway, the de Chateaubriands were virtual neighbours of his uncle in Brittany. A few minutes later I heard my husband coming down the steps singing a jaunty tune. I did not reveal myself but went straight home. Monsieur de Chateaubriand arrived some hours later in good humour. I asked him what Dr Laennec had said. 'Ah,' said my husband, 'the doctor said that my condition was so advanced that even leeches would have no effect.'[107]

Yet numerous stories, no less credible, testify to Laennec's devotion to patients who were seriously ill. Rouxeau describes the case of an elderly woman who was dying of heart disease and in almost constant pain. She had been rich before the Revolution but had lost her fortune as well as her husband during the Terror. Laennec visited her every day and often stayed overnight. He never charged her anything. Medical fees in general were low except for the comparatively few princes of the profession. Men like Corvisart could charge a fortune but often, like Laennec, charged nothing. The Emperor paid him a yearly retainer of 10,000 francs, more than the average Paris craftsman, shopkeeper or indeed general medical practitioner would earn in a lifetime. Laennec was beginning to approach that status.

In 1806, at the recommendation of an ordained Breton aristocrat, the Count de Queleu, he become physician-in-ordinary to Cardinal Fesch, the Emperor's uncle (and Archbishop of Lyon *in absentia*). For this he received an annual retainer of 2000 francs. However, it was a costly honour. Son Altesse et Eminentissime expected his personal physician to present himself at the Hotel Hocquart, the cardinal's sumptuous residence in Paris, in court dress complete with ceremonial sword, driven in a carriage and attended by a liveried flunkey.[108] He was, like his nephew, a dedicated hypochondriac and, apart from weekly regular visits, he would also summon his doctor when he suspected the communion wine to be poisoned. (Revolution or no

Revolution, nobody expected vicomtes from Brittany or cardinals to wait in a queue.)

What Laennec wanted above all was a senior appointment as professor or *chèf de médicine* in one of the large public hospitals in Paris where he could continue his teaching and research. This eluded him with a regularity that was deeply depressing. Between 1805 and 1810 he applied for three senior appointments at the Hôtel Dieu, two at the Charité, one at the Salpetrière and one at the Saint Louis. They all went to others. Some of the successful candidates were both younger and less deserving (on paper at any rate). Most painful was his failure to be elevated to the Chair of Hippocratic Medicine of Rare Diseases, a bizarre-sounding but prestigious post. His wide range of publications and especially his *Thèse* made him the obvious choice. After endless delays, intercessions and intrigues, however, the chair was abolished. What had gone wrong? Laennec agonised over the question. The chair, like most similar appointment, was in the hands of Bouvier, a colourless bureaucrat in the Ministry of Education but a tool of powerful forces within the profession. And within the profession Laennec was unpopular. It was not entirely surprising.

Since becoming one of the chief editorial contributors to the *Journal*, he had written frequent reviews of books and articles on current medical topics. Reading them today, one cannot but cringe (or marvel) at his uncompromising severity. Today reviews in professional journals tend to be anodyne. The publications themselves, of course, are mostly uncontentious. They are written by people eminent in their fields. They sell because medical students and academic libraries buy them. Few aim at being readable; even fewer are read. All this tends to blunt criticism. This was clearly not so in Laennec's Paris. He undoubtedly read what he was about to criticise. To check some of Gall's statements, he carried out a series of dissections himself. He was therefore well equipped to exercise his critical faculties, which were acute. He was especially scathing about universal systems. While these had had their heyday in the previous century, many were still wafting about. Their attraction is easy to understand.

They simplified matters that were in reality dauntingly complex. They offered rules of thumb for making difficult therapeutic decisions. John Brown was such a systematiser and became one of Laennec's literary targets.

The author of four heavy volumes amounting to a total of 3200 pages cannot be lightly dismissed, but one's sympathies remain with Laennec. Brown, known in his lifetime as the Scottish Paracelsus, was a pupil (though later an enemy) of William Cullen of Edinburgh. Cullen was one of the most influential medical writers of the age.[109] Brown carried Cullen's doctrines to their logical (or illogical) conclusion. All diseases were manifestations of the same basic disorder. They could masquerade in many guises, but this must not deceive doctors. What doctors had to do was to unmask the masquerade. Health (and disease) were basically a question of irritability (or what Brown called 'excitability'). All sicknesses stemmed from a disturbance of this function. They were either 'sthenic' or 'asthenic', depending on whether they derived from over- or under-excitement. On a universal numerical scale, comparable to that of a clinical thermometer, illnesses could be ranged from zero (lethal asthenic under-stimulation) to 80 (fatal sthenic over-stimulation). The mid-point, 40, represented the healthy balance. Quantified in this way, the management of illnesses became simple. What was needed was the administration of sedatives or stimulants to re-establish the lost equilibrium. Sedatives were mainly opium derivatives, though they came in a great variety of concoctions. Stimulants were mainly alcohol, but they too were dressed up in a variety of garbs. Blood-letting was a pivotal regulator.

Even today, such systems are seductive. Accept their premise and they become logical. There was also, in their astonishing success, an element of wish fulfilment. Experts can be stupendously gullible when they are being persuaded to accept a doctrine that they have long been wanting and waiting for. Fortunately for the pursuit of truth—not always for the pursuers—there are usually exceptions. In medicine Laennec was one. Intuitively perhaps, his patients appreciated this more than his colleagues. The sthenic—asthenic scale and similar universal systems were exceedingly persuasive: 3200 pages could not all be nonsense. But they could. Pulmonary phthisis and cancer of the stomach were *not* the same disease, except perhaps on a remote metaphysical plane. Laennec was blunt. Brown deserved credit for his industry. He deserved credit for his inventiveness. He deserved no credit for explaining the facts. Gall's clear identification of the bump for music in the brain, 'astonishingly developed in song-birds', was a charming conceit, but Laennec, the reviewer, had looked for such bumps himself and never found any trace of them. If he did not find them, they did not exist.

To make his scepticism more wounding, it was often expressed in epigrammatic French. He was an incorruptible stylist. He hated imprecision and questioned every unnecessary neologism. 'Why invent a new name for something clearly described and defined by Hippocrates?' This was a rhetorical question addressed to Bluvois, obstetrician to the Queen of Naples. Language mattered, French as well as Breton. Laennec was also insistent on proper attributions, especially when they involved his friends, dead or alive. While Napoleon's star shone brightly, Corvisart was above criticism. He had resigned from his chair at the Charité, but only to be able to devote himself fully to the well-being of his exalted patient. His was still the most influential voice in academe. Did he relish being told by his erstwhile pupil that his ideas of the origins of localised swellings in the legs were but a recapitulation of the ideas already expressed (and with greater precision) by the late Bichat? Was Boyer, surgeon in chief to their Imperial Majesties, indebted for having his limping sentences corrected by the *Journal*'s young editorial writer?

Laennec was intelligent enough to realise what he was doing. He did not stop writing, but after a time he stopped applying for senior teaching posts and chairs. In 1807 a rumour was being bandied about, especially in Brittany, that he was to be appointed Physician to the Imperial Pages. Who started the rumour is not known. In a letter to his father Laennec angrily

denied it. It was a non-post and it went to Chaptal, a nonentity. Laennec's only public appointment during the Empire was to become physician to the Société Philanthropique, a highly regarded charitable organisation that maintained clinics for the destitute. The role was unpaid but prestigious and Laennec devoted a great deal of time to it.

If he was disappointed, he was sustained by his faith. In 1806 he became Vice President of the Congrégation. A year later, in the company of two friends and colleagues, Récamier and Maisonneuve, he went on a pilgrimage to Luzarches, not far from Paris. The shrine, dedicated to Saints Cosmas and Damian, two Arabic physicians martyred in Sicily in 302 under Diocletian, was—and still is—a lovely, tiny Romanesque church in the middle of fields. Its ceiling has been blackened by the smoke of tens of thousands of candles. So much hope. So much faith. It was a kind of a transposed Breton *pardon*.

1808 was a year of bitter family feuds. For the past five years Laennec *père* had been living on a princely scale, dividing his splendiferous hospitality between his town house in Quimper and the house of his wife's family, the Hôtel Saint-Bedan in Saint-Brieuc. He was unabashed by the fact that he was spending his second wife's fortune and the legacy left in trust for their children by his first wife. These 'debts'—and many others that he had accumulated from creditors blinded by his seigneurial lifestyle—would be repaid when he at last obtained a public appointment, to which he felt himself virtually predestined. As a lawyer it would probably be the post of Procureur to the Département or at least official Avocat to the Court in Brest. He did not exclude the possibility that he would be summoned to Paris to fill a vacancy on the staff of the Conseil d'Etat. His experience of the world, but especially of Breton affairs and traditions, would be invaluable to the Emperor. (In this particular folly he was not alone. All 'ethnic minorities' in France—the Provençales, the Catalans, the Basques of Navarre as well as the Bretons—expected the sympathy of a kindred soul from

Napoleon. He too, after all, was a Corsican who had never learnt to speak French properly. All were to be disappointed. Napoleon was no more tolerant of minority cultures than the Georgian Stalin or Austrian Hitler would be 100 years later.)

All schemes of Laennec *père* suddenly collapsed in the summer of 1808. His second wife applied for the separation of properties—in effect the separation of his debts from what remained of the Saint-Bedan fortune—and the three children of the first marriage were notified that they would be held responsible for their father's unpaid liabilities. This would in fact have spelt ruin not only to Théo and Michaud but also to their unmarried younger sister, Marie-Anne. Michaud was urgently summoned home, ostensibly to rest after a severe attack of haemoptysis but in fact to sort out the chaos. This proved an almost superhuman task. Laennec *père*, though always charming and solicitous about his children's health, refused to give an account of his tutelage of his first wife's legacy. Nor did he cooperate in any other way in matters financial.

In desperation, the two younger Laennecs took the matter to court. Quimper society watched events unfold with unconcealed relish. Everyone was kept fully in the picture by the local press. Eventually, in October 1809, the Family Tribunal found in favour of the second Madame Laennec. She promptly departed for Saint-Brieuc. It also ordered Laennec *père* to pay into the court a huge sum to cover his debts. When this proved impossible, he was declared unfit to conduct his own financial affairs, let alone to act as a trustee; and his remaining property was transferred to his children. At the same time, he lost his official position as Councillor to the Court and was left with a pittance of a pension. Michaud's official salary was modest and it was left to Théo to liquidate his father's debts. He was grieved to have to sell the family house in Quimper, but at least he managed to hold on to that of his mother's family in Kerlouarnec. Nevertheless, it was Michaud who paid the heaviest price.

Since Théo could not leave Paris without ruining his practice, it had been the younger brother who had carried the burden of the legal battle. Totally exhausted, he fell ill in the autumn of 1809. In addition to a cough and pulmonary bleeds, he developed severe diarrhoea. His painfully inflamed throat prevented him from taking any but the lightest of liquid nourishment. This, as the older brother knew, was an ominous late development. It was irreversible. Half-blind and drenched in sweat, Michaud tried to sort out the still mountainous legal papers. At least he and his grief-stricken father were reconciled. After a day of whispered exchanges of love and esteem, the son died in his father's arms on 5 January 1810.

Théo blamed himself. Perhaps he could have done more to relieve Michaud of the legal chores, though he could not have done anything to change the course of the illness. Perhaps he was casting a glance into his own future. More and more tuberculous brothers and sisters were doing that all over Europe. It was not a happy prospect.

The strain of these events is reflected in the first extant portrait of Laennec. It is dated 1811 and signed Dubois. The painter was Laennec's patient, tuberculous like his sitter. Then as now, artists usually paid their doctors in kind. The work was well received and hung in the Salon the following autumn. It shows Laennec as pale, with the sunken eyes and prominent cheekbones of the consumptive. His eyes are brooding, his hair is delicate. His clothes are dark. It was probably about this time that he decided that before long he would have to retire to Brittany and that he would never be fit to marry.

CHAPTER FIVE

EMPIRE'S END

A banquet in the spring of 1812 in the city of Dresden, capital of the Kingdom of Saxony, saw the greatest gathering of European monarchs ever assembled under one roof. All came to pay homage to Napoleon, Emperor of the French. Counting heads, Metternich, Austrian ambassador at the time, concluded that all of Europe's kings and reigning princes were there with the exception of the Turkish Sultan, the King of England, the Pope and the Czar.

Some were members of the Bonaparte clan. Jerome of Westphalia, Louis of the Netherlands, Joseph of Spain and Joaquim Murat of Naples were brothers or brother-in-law. One, Bernadotte, now Charles XIV of Sweden, was a former marshal of France. The Emperor of Austria and Apostolic King of Hungary, the two titles united in the person of Francis I of Habsburg-Lorraine, was an ally and father-in-law. Eugene, Vice-Roy of Italy, was a stepson. The King of Prussia ('he wouldn't make sergeant in the French army'), the King of Bavaria ('an imbecile') and the ostensible host, the King of Saxony ('a blockhead'), were barely more than French satraps.[110]

All were tottering under the weight of their bemedalled uniforms. Their names and lengthy titles and those of their tiara-wearing consorts were sonorously intoned by Maret, chief imperial butler. The line-up took an hour and a half. Metternich thought that some of those present looked distinctly sheepish. Probably many felt humiliated, though none had dared to stay away. Then came *Sa majesté, l'Imperatrice des Français*, the former Habsburg Princess Marie Louise. There was then a pause lasting—Metternich dutifully timed it on his diamond-encrusted Bréguet—four and a half minutes. Then the simple announcement: *L'Empereur*. And in he strutted in his plain green uniform, with only the star of the Légion d'Honneur on his jacket.

It was the pinnacle of Napoleon's career. Around the city was encamped the greatest army Europe had ever seen. Napoleon's envoy, Narbonne, was still negotiating with the Czar: hope lingered that war with Russia could be avoided. It fizzled out within a few days, as Napoleon had planned. The Czar had politely assured Narbonne that he did not underestimate the power and unbroken record of victories of the *Grande Armée*. 'But,' he added, pointing to the map on the wall, 'distance would be a problem.' And so it proved.

The electrifying news that the army had taken Moscow and that the Emperor was now in residence in the Kremlin hit Paris on 14 September. There were celebrations, a ball in the Tuilleries and a public *fête* in the Place de la Concorde (formerly the Place de la Revolution). After that the news began to turn disquieting. Or rather, the lack of news. The benighted Czar was in no hurry to sue for peace. Emissaries from St Petersburg had still not arrived. Then there were disturbing rumours that timber-built Moscow was in the grip of a conflagration. And most unsettling, the weather was turning chilly. After 25 October the advance, or what *Moniteur* still referred to as an advance, was resumed— but moving backward.[111] It was to be the greatest military catastrophe in European history before 1943. Its horrors have been documented in the memoirs of a few survivors and described in one of the monumental novels of the century. It was to be represented in paint by the young Meissonier four years after the event and memorialised in music by Tchaikovsky. His overture, complete with cannon shot and national anthem, remains one of the evergreens of the al fresco orchestral repertory.[112]

Until the famous 29th Dispatch, released on November 22, a few days after the carnage of the crossing of the Beresina, Paris was kept in the dark. Even with all the 'victories' played up to the full and the famous (or notorious) final sentence, 'His Majesty's health has never been better', the news when the Dispatch arrived was shattering. The few stark facts that were revealed hinted at the magnitude of the disaster. 'Lack of transport for the artillery' meant that more than 600,000 horses had been lost. In fact, there was virtually no artillery left. The weather was 'unusually severe' even for Russia.[113] 'Food has to be carefully husbanded.' Properly interpreted, tens of thousands were freezing and starving to death every week. Bands of Cossacks continued to harass what remained of the army.

On 7 December Napoleon appointed the hapless Murat to command it.[114] The Emperor himself and few intimates, including his valet, the Mamelouk Rustem, departed in three coaches. Paris was 1300 miles away, most of the intervening territory hostile. Travelling under the pseudonym Count Gérard de Reynéval, the Emperor and his one final companion, Caulaincourt, covered the distance in coach and sledge in under two weeks. They arrived at the Tuilleries just before midnight on 18 December, in a postmaster's poste-chaise requisitioned at Meaux. It was freezing cold. The bewildered guard at first would not let them in. The travellers kicked their heels for ten minutes before they were identified by the wife of the concierge.

The débâcle had a more immediate effect on France's allies than on France itself. On paper Napoleon was still master of Germany, the Netherlands and much of Italy and Spain. He still had large forces at his command on the Vistula and the Elbe. He could, at a stretch, withdraw 100,000 men from Spain and Portugal. There was no whisper of a challenge to his rule at home. But he himself was not entirely fooled. He would soon have to fight for his survival. The much-humiliated king of Prussia, already in secret negotiations with the Czar, was about to declare war on him. His father-in-law, the Emperor of Austria, was dithering as usual. Russia itself was thoroughly exhausted but almost inexhaustible. The Czar, not entirely happy about leaving all the military glory to his somnolent commander,

Kutuzov, was impatient to cover his own dashing person with martial laurels.[115]

In Paris the weight of the tragedy took some time to sink in. News of the tens of thousands of dead, wounded and captured trickled back slowly.[116] The few exhausted survivors who had made their way home found themselves caught up in a season of balls and lavish receptions. They were deliberate attempts to boost morale. 'I felt I was dancing on tombs,' de Fézensac wrote on the concluding page of his campaign diary.[117] But dance he did. Napoleon raised a fresh army, calling up boys under military age, retired veterans and even sailors from his ships to swell his battalions. By April 1813 he had 200,000 men in the field. The industries of France, working against the clock, had restored much of his artillery and restocked his supplies. Only his cavalry was left without horses. If there were to be another advance on Berlin and Vienna, it would be slower than in the past. This particular difficulty did not arise.

Despite the upbeat communiqués, two days after his arrival back Napoleon summoned Corvisart. What did 'mon vieux charlatan' think of recent events? Corvisart professed to be delighted to see His Majesty in robust health and high spirits. He offered to check his patient's heart and lungs. But that was not what the Emperor had in mind. Over the next few months matters could go either way. If the fates were against him, he could face ending up a prisoner of war. He almost did so in Russia. For such an eventuality he wanted Corvisart to supply him with a small vial of instant and painless poison. Corvisart refused: 'My job, Sire, is to save lives, not to take them.' For once, Napoleon did not press him. Now running to fat and still stuffing himself with bonbons, the Emperor was not really the suicidal type. Corvisart knew him as a man, not as a hero. The man needed moral support. Whether he deserved it or not, he got it from his doctor.

As France was preparing for further disasters, Laennec too was passing through a phase of physical ill-health and spiritual low.

The two always tended to go together. None of his cousins or other close family had gone to Russia, but two old friends, the surgeon Nicoleau and the physician Françinet, had enlisted. There was no news from either of them.[118] The Concordat had proved unworkable. The Pope was a prisoner in Savona in Northern Italy. Cardinal Fesch had quarrelled with his nephew and had departed for Rome. Because of their official position, Corvisart and Bayle had always been sober and circumspect in their assessment of the international situation. Now Corvisart was unnaturally upbeat and Bayle deeply gloomy.[119] Soon the need for a new army confirmed everybody's worst fears. The ultra-cautious—or ultra-wise—began to hoard food.

Early in 1813 Napoleon took the offensive. For a few months it seemed that his genius—or lucky star—had not deserted him. He won victories over the Russians at Lützen and Bautzen. Then he faltered and unaccountably accepted an armistice.[120] There was a memorable meeting with Metternich near Dresden. The Emperor boasted that his military strength was now fully restored. The Russian débâcle was history. Metternich was a master at needling his opponents. 'I have seen your soldiers. They are children. And when these infants have been wiped out, you're left with nothing.' Metternich's instruction from the Emperor Francis was to arrange a peace treaty. There was the awkward matter of Marie Louise, Napoleon's wife and Francis's daughter. However, an accommodation was not what Metternich himself had in mind. France, he insisted, must relinquish all its German and East European conquests. The interview ended in one of the famed Napoleonic rages. Metternich watched the Emperor hurl his tricorne into a corner. Metternich did not stir. On the floor in the corner the hat remained.

On 12 August Austria too declared war on France. An undecisive battle near Dresden was followed by the Battle of the Nations near Leipzig. While Napoleon's army was not annihilated, he had not won the victory he needed. His withdrawal was a masterly exercise in defensive manoeuvring. In a series of useless battles he continued to inflict losses on the enemy. Had he sued for peace as they approached the Rhine, France's natural frontier, relinquishing his European acquisitions, he might still have remained Emperor and France would have been spared much suffering. It was not in his nature to do so. The enemy crossed the Rhine in the last days of 1813. Foreign troops were on French soil again, for the first time since their ignominious attempt at an invasion in 1792.[121] The news created panic.

To Laennec the year had already been one of anxiety. His Aunt Desirée, Uncle Guillaume's wife and the nearest he had to a mother, died in the autumn. He grieved for her but could not attend the funeral. His most immediate concern was Couvrelle. When he visited the château in September, the de Pompérys were making preparations to leave. So were many others of the local gentry and the wealthier burghers of Soissons. What would happen to Jacquette? Once again, there is a gap in documentation. The de Pompérys no doubt pressed her to accompany them; indeed, they probably pressed both her and Laennec. For some reason she would not go. Yet the fearsome reputation of the Cossacks had preceded them. By the end of January 1814 the panic had engulfed Paris. Coaches laden with trunks, furniture and the family canary were leaving the city. For the first time since he set up in practice, Laennec's waiting rooms were empty. As if to make up for their emptiness, the hospitals were filling up with the wounded soldiers of many nations. The French had been enlisted from all provinces and were of all ages. They arrived from the front in endless convoys of waggons, worn out, at the end of their strength. Many had died on the way. The living were dirty, cold and hungry. They had brought typhus in their knapsacks.

During the Napoleonic wars epidemics after lost campaigns had been familiar in Milan, Vienna, Prague, Berlin and Smolensk. Now it was Paris. The Val-de-Grâce and the Gros-Caillou, the city's two military hospitals, were soon overcrowded. Beds and then sacks of straw were crammed into the Hôtel Dieu, the Saint-Louis, the Bicêtre and the Salpetrière. Many of the medical staff of the hospitals were with the Army or had left

Paris. Some had gone down with typhus themselves. Laennec, working at all hours at the Salpetrière, soon discovered that among the sick and wounded were conscripts from Brittany. Most of these young peasants from Cornouaille, Tregorrois, Léon and the Vannetais spoke no language other than their own.[122] They felt isolated and desperately homesick. When Laennec addressed them in their own tongue, they cried. He obtained permission from Landerneau, the medical superintendent and himself a Breton, to concentrate all Breton conscripts in one ward. He also found a few young Breton doctors and medical students to help him: Marion de Procé, brother-in-law of Christophe Laennec, Bernard Pellerin, Jean de Guislain and Louis Le Ray.

Laennec now virtually lived at the hospital, only returning home for a few hours to reassure Angélique. And he spent two or three hours every day in the Breton ward. Marion de Procé was soon down with typhus himself. He would eventually pull through, but only just. Le Ray had to accompany his parents to Brittany. Pellerin stayed on and wrote about the experience some years later: 'Laennec was so thin and weak that I was expecting him to collapse under the strain any minute. But he carried on and was always cheerful with his patients.' It was the seemingly superhuman energy that consumptives could summon in an emergency. Laennec himself sent a scribbled note to Christophe in Nantes:

> You must be worried about us in Paris but there is no need to. I spend much of my time with young Breton conscripts in the hospital and am well. All the dialects are spoken here, so I have been obliged to return to my studies of Celtic. If you were familiar with the language and if you were here, I would give you a demonstration ... To cheer up your father I shall add a few lines in the dialect of Léon.[123]

Some months later the Bishop of Quimper, Monseigneur Dombideau de Cruseilhes, wrote to thank him for saving 'many lives of the young men of Finistèrre under your care. God will reward you, Doctor Laennec.' Laennec's answer, written after the emergency, has been preserved:

Monseigneur, I was touched by the kindness which you have shown me. It gives me great satisfaction that you praise the help I have tried to give to my unfortunate compatriots ... What I did was really very little but I did all that I could. Young sick conscripts, already worn out with fatigue and hunger before being struck down by disease, were hastily piled into hospitals. Some of the wards were unhealthy even before they became overcrowded. Under those circumstances it is difficult to be useful, especially when one has to add to these misfortunes the lack of nourishment, medicine and dressings, as well as an insufficient number of doctors, nurses, surgeons and orderlies. All this was aggravated by the chaotic organisation and the fear of worse to come.

In this misfortune my young Breton brothers, some only thirteen or fourteen, were even more to be pitied than the other patients. Isolated in wards where they could not make themselves understood either by staff or by fellow patients, many lapsed into a deep depression. After a few days they refused any help or indeed to utter a sound. My colleagues found them more difficult to understand than the Germans and even the Russians, since Bretons generally make no use of sign language. To others they often appear slow and even half-witted. When I addressed the first one in Breton, he embraced and kissed me and then broke down in sobs. Those whom I was then able to assemble in my ward were perhaps a little less unhappy. I lost only about one in five or six, a mortality that would be fearful under other circumstances but which was better than the overall mortality of one in three among French-speaking and foreign patients.

I would have liked to obtain for my patients the spiritual help they needed but it was impossible to find a Breton-speaking priest left in Paris. But your deacon, Monsieur le Floc'h, visited my sick as well as other Bretons in other hospitals, and, though he did not speak Breton, his visits did much for the morale of my patients. He gave them encouragement which I translated into Breton and he administered to them the Sacrament.[124]

Early in March he heard from Couvrelle. The château had been occupied by Cossacks who had lived up to their reputation for looting, drinking and raping. Jacquette spent several days locked in the loft in a state of panic but, from what one can deduce from one surviving letter, she escaped serious harm. But for some years she suffered from 'alarm reactions', with palpitations and constricting pain in the chest. Laennec diagnosed them as *angine*. The rest of France accepted the invaders as passively as it had borne Napoleon's rule. Epinal surrendered to fifty Cossacks, Rheims to a platoon, Chaumont to a single horseman. The Legislative Body, a spineless assembly, voted by an overwhelming majority for an address of unprecedented lamentation, asking the Emperor to 'abandon the ambitious and useless schemes which, for twenty years, had been so fatal to France and all the people of Europe.' (It took the idiots some time to voice their concern, as Fouché, Duc d'Otranto, commented.)

In March Napoleon negotiated for the last time with the Allies but could still not bring himself to abandon past conquests. With a small army of 60,000 he continued to manoeuvre brilliantly, inflicting pinpricks on the advancing invaders. On 29 March Marie Louise and the King of Rome, accompanied by Corvisart, left Paris.[125] Napoleon commanded all higher officers of state to do likewise. Few did. On 31 March Paris capitulated, its garrison moving to Fontainebleau. In the South Wellington's troops, entering France from Spain, advanced on Toulouse and occupied Bordeaux. On 6 April Napoleon abdicated unconditionally. A week later the Comte d'Artois, as lieutenant-general for his brother Louis XVIII, entered Paris in triumph.[126]

Some admired Napoleon for his skilful last-ditch resistance. To Laennec it seemed yet another odious demonstration of a dictatorship that cared only for itself, nothing for the suffering of ordinary people. He wrote to Christophe when at last Napoleon seemed to have gone,

> This revolution is noteworthy for its moderation and calm. Paris, with 180,000 foreigners within its walls or on the outskirts, is as tranquil as in peacetime. The ordinary citizens are like spectators of events in which they have no part ... In the salons, the cafés and in the streets, people discuss the new constitution without getting too heated about it. The senators have taken good care of themselves as usual: most of them have left for their country seats. An insignificant nonentity, Jussieu, was left to read their loyal address to the King whenever the King should arrive. This is awaited with some impatience: it is generally assumed that everything will then be arranged quietly and amicably. Monsieur [the Comte d'Artois] was received with jubilation by a vast crowd yesterday. I found myself near his route by accident. I never in my life heard such an ovation ... 'Long live Henri IV,' the crowd shouted as the prince's coach came into sight ... He was clearly moved. We can only hope that, after so many storms, errors, and unbelievable suffering, we have come to a new order and peace.[127]

It was not to be, though for a few months the prospects seemed good. Louis XVIII, when he did arrive, appeared to be an amiable character, obese and gouty but not without dignity. A glimmer of intelligence too perhaps. He promised to forget and forgive. To Laennec's liking, he sometimes carried the forgetting too far. Both he and his brother forgot to attend the memorial mass for Georges Cadoudal who had died for their cause. The King then created Brune, the butcher of the Vendée, a Chevalier de Saint Louis; and he appointed the vile Turreau, inventor of the 'Vendée columns' of evil memory, to escort the daughter of Louis XVI on her pilgrimage to the 'Faithful Province'.[128] During the winter

Laennec, with his practice slow to pick up, preserved his serenity by immersing himself in medical writing. He wrote several long chapters for the new *Dictionnaire des Sciences Médicales*, including two on 'Dégéneration' and 'Dégénerescence'.[129] As the summer approached, he prepared to revisit Brittany for the first time in many years.

He set out on the last day of July. It was a memorable homecoming, the beginning, it seemed to Laennec, of a new and happy chapter in his life. As the coach neared Le Mans,

> I felt as full of laughter as a child ... the blue of the sky, the grey slate roofs of the houses, the shape of the church steeples, the pattern of the fields, everything seemed familiar and indescribably beautiful.

He visited an old aunt, Madame Flauçet, in Minniac.

> She was as charming and welcoming as only the old and poor can be. She gave me a miniature 'to remember her by', the only treasure she possessed. Why cannot the rich be so generous?[130]

On 20 August he arrived in Quimper, happy to be reunited with his father. Laennec *père* seemed to have changed not at all: he was as affectionate, witty and full of fantastical plans as ever. Would his son like to listen to his latest composition in Breton? His son, of course, could think of nothing that would give him greater pleasure. A few days later Laennec met Madame de Pompéry, who could not bring herself to return to Couvrelle. 'It is too, too lovely here, especially at harvest time.' As indeed it was. She had heard from her husband who had returned and had reported that the château had been thoroughly looted and the park made to resemble a land after an earthquake, but that the damage was not irreparable.

Then Laennec set out to visit his mother's family estate in Kerlouarnec. It was beautiful, at least to his eyes, though in a state of near-terminal neglect. The noble Louis XIII manor house near Ploaré still stood, but only just. Cows and horses were stabled in one wing. The family Louboutin, appointed by Laennec *père* many years earlier to act as guardians, lived in the other. Some of the walls had disappeared. The stuccoed roof of the entrance hall had collapsed. The park was a wilderness. The land seemed in no better shape: most of the fields were lying idle. Laennec did not mind, however. It was, he felt, the challenge he needed. He would spend the rest of his life restoring the estate until it was the fairest in Brittany. He was now a moderately wealthy man and might become more so over the next year or two. He set about taking stock and making plans.

He managed to recover some acres that had been colonised by neighbours without ruffling too many feathers. He made a generous offer to buy part of Kergiomigou moor. With Kerlouarnec it would make a manageable estate with good access to the royal road to Quimper. The avenue leading there opened out at the foot of a hill. An ancient stone cross stood on the top. It provided a superb view towards Ploriez and Le Juch. This was rugged country; and when Laennec explored it, much of it was untenanted.[131] When he offered the local farmers to buy some of it for real money, they were astounded. Unemployment was high, labour cheap. Laennec made plans of how the estate should be repaired, planted, drained and reconstructed. Some of his aides-mémoires are 20 or 30 pages long, with carefully drawn maps for planting, livestock, possible market gardens.

Between Chevalier Island and Combrit he discovered the salt marsh of Cosquer, stretching north, white and shimmering. It was grand but forbidding. Large areas were covered with seaweed and dotted with a few stunted willows. Wild ponies grazed on the scant grass. He observed birds he had never seen before. Old peasant women were collecting strange shellfish, the *chiforegel*, not found anywhere else in Brittany. He learnt that twice a year the equinoctial tide completely separated the marsh from the mainland. He made plans to buy this area, which would adjoin the land he already owned. In Combrit he explored and admired the small sixteenth-century church with its squat dome flanked by two turrets.[132]

Despite such exertions Laennec's health remained good, as it usually did in the country. He liked the people and they liked him. Life in Paris seemed infinitely remote. He determined to return to Brittany as soon as possible and settle for good, as soon as he could wind up his affairs in the capital. He arrived back there, to the rue du Jardinet, full of hope. It was October 1814.

In Paris the talk was all politics and gossip: what the King said to Metternich, what Metternich said to the Czar, what the Czar said to the ex-Empress Josephine, what the Empress Josephine said to the Duke of Wellington, what the Duke of Wellington said to his mistress and what the Duke of Wellington's mistress said to the fishmonger in the rue de Boulle. But enthusiasm for the Restoration was beginning to fray. Talleyrand, the Bourbons' most valuable asset, had his hands full manipulating the rest of Europe at the Congress that had assembled in Vienna. At home the old system of 'government from above' with no chief minister and no effective ministry was revived sooner than even pessimists had expected. Baron Louis, the king's finance minister, put the budget into shape, but only by retaining all the old and unpopular taxes and introducing even more unpopular new ones.

This might have been less of an affront if flagrantly expensive and useless schemes had not been introduced at the same time to placate the returning émigrés. The incompetent and tactless Dupont at the ministry of war retired many of the imperial officers and put others on half pay, while promoting hundreds of former exiles who had never seen a battlefield. He recreated the old household guards and crammed them with royalists. They were ostentatious and arrogant. Many of the empty but costly court ceremonies were revived. The veterans of the old imperial army were seething.

Laennec's health began to deteriorate as soon as he was back in Paris. 'My only thoughts are of a return soon to Brittany,' he wrote to Uncle Guillaume. Then the least expected happened.

On 5 March 1815 *Moniteur* carried the memorable headline: 'The beast has escaped.' There followed the statement: 'He has been declared an outlaw [shades of Robespierre] and is being hunted down.' The beast had in fact slipped away from his island kingdom of Elba and had landed with 1050 men in Fréjus on the Riviera four days earlier.[133] A week later the beast had been promoted to 'the Usurper', who had so far escaped his pursuers and had unaccountably reached Grenoble.[134] A news item also reported that Marshal Ney had been dispatched with an army. He had vowed to bring back the beast/usurper in a cage.[135] Another slight change in style marked the news four days later when *Moniteur* reported that Marshal Ney and his 'regiment' had apparently deserted and had actually joined the army of 'Buonaparte' south of Lyon. Entry of that army in Lyon saw the transformation of Buonaparte into Bonaparte and in Dijon from Bonaparte into the former Emperor Napoleon. The 'former' was dropped when Napoleon reached Fontainebleau. At midnight on 19 March Louis XVIII and an escort of a few horsemen took the road to Lille.[136] On 21 March *Moniteur* exulted: 'His Majesty the Emperor had returned to the Tuilleries yesterday amid the indescribable jubilation of all the people of Paris.' The jubilation would last 100 days.

One can hardly blame Laennec *père* if he felt despair. In February he had composed a Breton song, 'Buez ha bennos d'ar Roue' (Life and greetings to the King) to be sung to the tune of a popular gavotte, and sent it to Paris. Sadly, one of his ill-wishers, perhaps a disgruntled creditor, unearthed an old edition of *Moniteur* that carried an address from Brittany, congratulating the Convention on sentencing the King—the present tenant's brother—to death. Prominent among the signatories was Marie-Théophile Laennec. Despite his promise to hold no grudges, on that occasion Louis XVIII was roused and dismissed the culprit from his post as counsellor to the Préfecture. Laennec *père* appealed on the grounds that the report in *Moniteur* had been based on a fake. By the time his appeal reached Paris, Napoleon was back in the Tuilleries. Undaunted, Laennec *père* submitted another appeal, extolling his impeccably Bonapartist credentials. It reached Paris a few days after Waterloo. There were many such cases in France. The second arrival of the Bourbons after Napoleon's final defeat was more discreet than the first but also more vengeful.[137] Fortunately for Laennec *père*, his wife in St Brieuc was a kindly and gregarious person who welcomed him back. The solitary life did not suit her. His surviving son would pay him a generous allowance for the rest of his life.

The next year started badly for Laennec. The new tax levied by the Bourbons on all citizens as a 'war contribution' hit some more than others. It hit Laennec severely. He refused to appeal. He would simply have to postpone his planned return to Brittany by a year or two. Uncle Guillaume was dismissed from his chair in Nantes at the age of 68 as a former Jacobin; he was nearly deported. While Laennec's private practice was picking up, his health was troubling him again. On 11 May Bayle died. It had been expected but it left a void. Laennec knew that they had shared not only medical opinions and a religious faith but also a disease. It is impossible to believe that he did not know that it would kill him too. Corvisart had retired from public life.[138] Other friends had left Paris, Maisonneuve to settle in Nantes, Bruté for America. There had been a brief and happy reunion with Cardinal Fesch during the Hundred Days, but now the Cardinal too had departed for Rome for good. The prospect of a public hospital appointment seemed to have receded for ever. Now all Laennec wanted was to earn enough capital to restore the estate in Brittany and to retire there. He no longer applied for posts; the rejections had become humiliations.

It was at that moment that an old patient, Charles-Louis Becquey, was appointed under-secretary of state at the ministry of interior. Poor-law administration, including hospitals, came under his jurisdiction. The two men met in the street by accident. Becquey wanted to know how matters stood at the Salpetrière. The last he had heard Laennec was setting up a Breton ward. Laennec explained that he had been on the staff there only during the emergency. He had departed without even a thank-you from the medical superintendent. He had no hospital appointment and he was too old now to apply. 'What about the vacancy at the Necker?' Becquey wanted to know. 'How many applicants do you have?' Laennec asked. 'About 20.' Laennec explained that he had applied for about as many posts unsuccessfully over the past eight years. Besides, the Necker was far from his home. It was small. He was not fit. But Becquey insisted that he must apply. Laennec did not want to seem ungracious. Of course senior teaching posts were not in Becquey's gift, but he had the final say. After a week's hesitation, a day after the closing date, Laennec put in an application.

'I applied when I discovered that the Necker had a lovely garden with some beautiful old chestnut trees,' he wrote to his cousin, Mériadec, 'and the nursing is done by the Sisters of Charity. They are the best. The wards of the unit where the vacancy is are named after my favourite saints, Saint Joseph, Saint Suzanne and Saint Vincent.' They must have smiled. On 16 September 1816 he was notified that he had been appointed.

CHAPTER SIX

THE MOMENT OF TRUTH

To many during the next 30 years Paris became a promised land. Most of the reasons had nothing to do with medicine. It was the time of the Holy Alliance, a repressive and reactionary period in much of Europe.[139] Paris attracted young poets, writers, composers, philosophers and even bushily bearded economists as well as doctors and medical students.

Not that the Bourbon Restoration was intentionally liberal or permissive. Some of its clerical legislation outraged even Laennec. The Panthéon was purged of the heretical remains of Voltaire and Rousseau. Secondary education was placed under the supervision of bishops. A high but incompetent ecclesiastic, Monsignor Frayssinous, was made grand master of the University. The profanation of the consecrated host became punishable by death. In fact, little of the draconian legislation was enforced. The police and censors were always less eager to please —or lazier—in France than they were in the lands ruled by the Habsburgs or the Romanovs. 'Surtout, pas trop de zèle' was the advice given by Talleyrand to new recruits to the civil service. The injunction filtered down to the police, especially to those charged with keeping an eye on foreigners and other undesirables. The agricultural depression had swelled the number of the force but not their efficiency. They were busy doing little. Their indolence kept France in the vanguard of European civilisation.

In Paris the Revolution could never be quite undone.[140] An unofficial alternative establishment remained influential though not in power, a fact that foreign commentators rarely grasped.

Its broadsheets always outsold the servile official press. Bohemia was about to be born on the Left Bank. It would become the stronghold of the creative, the disrespectful and the dispossessed, invincible because it had no material assets. (It would also become the stronghold of tuberculosis.) However, medical reasons too drew to Paris doctors from the rest of Europe and even from across the Atlantic.[141]

Revolution and Empire had transformed the teaching of medicine in France. In other countries it was still a haphazard and often stupefying apprenticeship, sometimes little more than shadowing a few charismatic teachers and memorising a selection of hallowed texts. When in the 1830s James (later Sir James) Paget entered Bart's (as St Bartholomew's Hospital, the most ancient of England's medical schools, was already known),

> there was little or no personal guidance, teaching or direction of new students. The demonstrators had a few private pupils whom they 'ground' for the College examinations, the surgeons had a few apprentices to whom they occasionally imparted a few 'tricks of the trade'; but no one was responsible for the students as a whole. For the most part they guided themselves or one another to evil or to good, to various degrees of work or idleness ... The deadhouse (it was never called by any other name) was a miserable kind of shed, stone-floored, damp, smelly and dirty where all stood round the table on which the [post-mortem] examinations were made. These were usually carried out in the roughest and least instructive way, and, unless one of the physicians happened to turn up, nothing was carefully looked at, nothing was taught. Pathology in any proper sense was hardly considered.[142]

The contrast with a post-mortem conducted at the Charité by Bayle or at the Necker by Laennec could hardly have been greater. It is true that what today would be called morbid anatomy had long been something of a speciality in Paris, but it also epitomised a fundamentally different approach to medicine.

Money came into it, as it does into most things. None of the senior teaching staff at Bart's whom Paget encountered as a medical student was paid. Nor would any have dreamt of demanding a salary either from the Treasury or from London University. The latter in fact did not yet exist.[143] Laennec, as head of the department at the Necker and later as professor at the Collège de France, received a salary from the state that was sufficient to live on without relying on private practice, coaching or some other source of income. More importantly, it was his reputation as a teacher on which his *renommé* in society and among his colleagues depended.

Medical training in Paris was a serious matter, not the hobby of a few enthusiasts. In the 1820s Laennec would sometimes give the same lecture twice in succession, once in French for up to 100 French-speaking students and once in Latin for an even greater number of foreigners from Germany, England, the United States, Italy and Scandinavia. His *Grandes Cliniques* were attended by a select concourse of postgraduates and sometimes went on for four or five hours. Every case was discussed in depth and every postgraduate took his turn to percuss the chest and later to listen to the heart sounds. Halfway through there was an intermission for refreshments and *causerie*.

Insistence on the importance of physical signs was another fundamental difference between Paris and medical schools elsewhere. It was the foundation of accurate diagnosis, in the same way as familiarity with esoteric laboratory tests would be the hallmark of the up-to-date physician 100 years later. It signified the evolution of medicine from the mumbo jumbo of past ages— essentially the times before the Revolution—into a scientific discipline. Doctors as a breed could be recognised in most countries by their professional attire, their frequent use of Greek and Latin tags, their masterful personality and their often spectacular greed; but there was no way of distinguishing a good from a bad doctor in London, Prague, Vienna or Rome. But when Laennec (or even his arch-enemy Broussais) finished with the physical examination of a patient, his knowledge of what was happening inside that patient was patently greater than that of a layman or a charlatan.

For a few decades the diagnostic virtuosity of France's leading doctors (on a par with the virtuosity of Monsieur Chopin at the keyboard or Signor Paganini on the violin) was tacitly admired by the younger generation even in Vienna. In the stronghold of European reaction it was of course dangerous to give expression to such sentiments. The elderly professors who were now the majority of the once avant-garde Vienna medical school continued to regard themselves as the Olympian peak of the profession. But many of their juniors, especially those from the more remote regions of the Habsburg Empire, would walk if necessary to Paris to attend the lectures of Laennec, Cayol, Piorry and Dupuytren and catch up on the latest developments. They knew that it was the French Corvisart who had brought to fruition the discovery of the neglected Viennese, Auenbrugger. In Vienna the discoverer was still regarded as an amiable buffoon, now safely dead. They had also heard of new diagnostic methods discovered by the godless French. Among the young Austrians who came to listen and learn and who spoke between themselves a strange non-Austrian dialect were Josef Skoda and Carl Rokitansky.[144]

One snag remained, recognised even by the French innovators. Diagnosis is rarely the only reason that people consult doctors; often it is not even the main one. Some patients also want to get better. Neither Bayle nor Laennec ever denied that their treatment lagged behind their understanding of illnesses. It was this that, in Laennec's last years, would inflame his dispute with Broussais. To Broussais and his acolytes treatment was paramount. To Corvisart, Bayle and Laennec masterly inactivity was better than the risk of active harm. Real advances in treatment could only come from grasping the causes of illnesses. And that would undoubtedly come—eventually.

Of course, Paris had many charms besides clinical expertise and dedicated teaching. The Revolution and the Napoleonic decade made people aware of the glories of youth and the wonders of the new. It was this that frightened the rulers of old Europe, not any specific revolutionary or Bonapartist doctrine. What made the Holy Alliance holy was faith in the sanctity of tradition. Change was inherently bad, to be deplored and, whenever possible, to be nipped in the bud. It was particularly harmful in the young in whom the insane craving for novelty was untempered by the wisdom of experience (or the limitations of decrepitude). The young, moreover, had a lifetime to put their crazy ideas into practice—or so they imagined until and unless they were firmly told not to. This was true not only in politics. It applied to cultural and social activities too. It applied with special force to medicine.

This is hard to imagine at a time when no television news programme is complete without a white-coated miracle man (or woman) selling a health-related breakthrough as if it were a washing powder or a dog biscuit. In the lands of the Holy Alliance this would have been exceedingly dangerous. Medicine was respected as a more or less honourable profession, but medical *research* was the pursuit of revolutionaries. The human body did not change. God did not change. Birth, health, disease and death did not change. So why medicine? Of course medicine had advanced from time to time in the past. Harvey, an undoubtedly clever man, had demonstrated the circulation of the blood. Jenner had discovered vaccination. Leeuvenhoek had rejoiced in his little animalcules under the microscope. But most of these advances could be regarded as developments in the natural sciences rather than in medicine. They did not as a rule impinge on ordinary practice. Harvey himself did not envisage that his little tome on the movement of the blood and the heart would change the treatment of patients. And indeed, its only immediate effect was to revolutionise the art of embalming. Jenner did see vaccination as a useful practical measure, though he shied away from its wider implications. The cavortings of Leeuvenhoek's animalcules under the microscope were innocent fun.

Pre-revolutionary medicine was a static art, though speculative minds could indulge in fanciful new classifications and philosophical ruminations about the nature of disease. Did it

exist? Was it a figment of the imagination? Such questions were harmless—or almost harmless. They kept the speculators, often rich aristocrats bored to distraction in their splendid but remote châteaux, out of mischief. Elegant literary descriptions of maladies, old and new, a genre now wholly extinct, was also permissible.

Inevitably, a few muddle-headed individuals tried to bring about some fundamental practical change. That sometimes threatened to undermine the teachings of the Holy Church. It often ignored the authority of the all-wise State. As the likes of Auenbrugger and Gall soon discovered, such individuals remained solitary and sometimes pathetic voices. Nor were they even voices for long. They fell silent or were speedily silenced. For better or for worse, clinical research as part of medical practice and medical practice based on verifiable facts were revolutionary concepts. A bloody political revolution had been necessary to invent them. To be more precise, they were the inventions of the generation of Corvisart, Bichat, Bayle, Laennec and Dupuytren, and that generation had invented them in the foul-smelling hospitals of revolutionary Paris. The change even in Paris was not universal, but there it was irreversible. It is not surprising, then, that the young flocked to the French capital from all the corners of Europe. Nor is it surprising that Laennec's great discovery—his moment of truth—became almost at once a European and indeed a worldwide sensation.

Several versions exist of what planted the idea of the stethoscope in Laennec's mind.[145] Was his 'remembrance of a well-known acoustical phenomenon' stimulated by remembering a childhood game, listening to approaching footsteps by pressing one's ear to the ground?[146] Or had he been watching street urchins 'transmitting secret messages' in the garden of the Louvre? The method was simple but brilliant. Laennec himself was to describe it; he never claimed to be its physical inventor.

Take a long wooden pole. A felled poplar would do admirably. Scratch the cut surface at one end with a pin. The sound cannot be heard even by your friends standing next to you. But it will be heard with crystal clarity by another, pressing his ear to the other cut end at a distance of ten yards or more.

All or none of the stories may be true. Divine inspiration can strike in many ways.

Auscultation as such was not new. It had always been 'immediate'; that is, performed by the application of the ear directly to a part of the patient's body. It had been described in one of the Hippocratic texts. In particular, the text mentioned that a 'weird knocking noise' could sometimes be heard by pressing one's ear to the chest of a child over the region of the heart. It was a useful manoeuvre to check that the little patient was still alive. (But not *very* useful: one could sometimes hear the noise continue for some hours in fresh cadavers.) There was also the fearfully energetic manoeuvre of Hippocratic 'succussion'. To Auenbrugger's chagrin, it had sometimes been confused with percussion. Holding patients by their shoulders and shaking them vigorously, the sound of fluid splashing about in the pleural space could sometimes be heard.[147] Unsurprisingly, the method was never popular either with doctors or with patients. Both Corvisart and Bayle had deplored it, but they had both used direct or immediate auscultation from time to time. Even that was rarely illuminating. Laennec wrote later that it was

> as uncomfortable for the doctor as it was for the patient. A natural sense of modesty made it virtually impracticable in hospitals ... It was unsuitable where most women were concerned. With some the size of their breasts was an insurmountable obstacle.[148]

Nor, of course, did doctors know what they were listening for. This is still a prerequisite of success.

How Laennec was led to mediate auscultation he described in an oft-quoted passage:

> I was consulted in 1816 by a young lady who presented the general symptoms of heart disease. Because of her

stoutness, the application of the hand to her chest and percussion gave poor results. The age and sex of the patient forbid the application of the method I have just described [direct auscultation]. I then remembered a well-known phcnomcnon of acoustics, thc transmission of a sound by a beam of wood over a long distance ... I thought that I might make use of this fact in this particular case. I took some shccts of papcr and rolled thcm up vcry tightly. I applicd one end of the paper cylinder to the precordial region [where the tip of the heart lies nearest to the chest wall and some heart sounds are most clearly heard]. I placed my ear to the other end. I was as surprised as I was gratified. I could hear the beating of the heart more clearly than I had ever done before. It was far more distinct than when I applied my ear to the chest directly. It occurred to me that this could become a useful method, applicable not only to the study of heart beats but also to that of all movements that might produce sounds in the chest. It might, for example, help in the investigation of breathing, voice production, wheezing and even pleural and pericardial effusions.[149]

It might indeed. It was a methodological discovery that would transform both the science and the practice of medicine. Laennec called the method *auscultation* but added *mediate* to indicate that a tube was mediating between the patient's body and the observer's ear. One might have thought that a 'mediated' sound would be more difficult to pick up and interpret than an unmediated one, but the opposite was true. The group of students around him at once set about making their own 'stethoscopes'. It was laughably simple. All that was needed was a roll of paper.

Among the students were two cousins. Ambroise Laennec had recently successfully defended his *Thèse* on epidemics, but had stayed on for postgraduate study at the Necker. Mériadec was still an undergraduate. Both knew that they would never forget the day. But it was not necessary to be a Laennec to hear the sounds: the magic worked even for the most dim-witted. And its potential was immediately obvious. Of course the *râles*, the *soufles*, the *bruits* and the *crépitations* meant little to anyone. They had never been heard before. Nevertheless, they knew that would soon change. The sounds were similar and yet different in different patients. The heartbeat was a clearly heard lubb-dubb, lubb-dubb, not just 'a weird knocking noise'. The breath sounds were the sounds of breathing. Were they normal? They would soon know.

Moments of truth are rarely recorded by a crowd of paparazzi. Did the teaching round end with students stripped to the waist and listening in wordless excitement to each other's hearts and lungs? Medical students are a blasé lot, not easy to enthuse. But 'yes' is surely a good guess.

The next echelon to take up the invention were Laennec's circle of friends and colleagues, many of them inevitably Bretons: Récamier, Fizeau, François-Marie Beauregard (a former naval doctor from Quimperlé), Dalbant, Follet (from Quimper) and Adolphe Toulmouche (from Nantes). The last, who acted as Laennec's assistant for a year, left a description of his chief about the time of his discovery:

Laennec arrived every morning at eight o'clock in a hired cab. His dress was always the same: black knee breeches, black coat, white cravat. On a gold watch chain he carried a cross and a medallion. He also wore a wide-brimmed black hat and in the winter a black overcoat. He was thin, pale and quietly spoken but had great presence. First he always went round the wards on his own or with one of the Sisters of Charity. He talked to each patient and then examined them. Then he talked to them again. At ten o'clock the students were allowed to enter and each was instructed to examine a patient and to make notes of his findings. Laennec spoke little but read the notes carefully. His greatest compliment was: 'oui, ça va'. Anything poor or even mediocre was at once returned. It would have to be

done again. But he was prepared to discuss or even to argue a point with a student, something neither Corvisart nor Bayle ever did. Broussais of course never listened to anybody but himself. Laennec would sometimes return to a patient and verify what a student had said. More than once I heard him say that the student was right. Sometimes his tone was gently mocking but he never ridiculed anybody. Abuse and sarcasm were wholly alien to him. The only occasion when I saw him in a temper was when he thought that one of his students had handled a patient roughly. 'In order to interrogate nature it is not necessary to torture a patient ... You must not ask a patient to cough unless it is absolutely necessary: it often causes pain ... Never cause suffering to the dying, however anxious you are to hear a rare sound.'[150]

Two or three times a week Laennec proceeded to the autopsy room. Before starting the post-mortem he would announce what he expected to find. He did not often make a mistake. If he did, he set about trying to find out the cause of his error. He rarely finished at the hospital before three o'clock. He then started on his round of home visits and returned for consultations in the rue du Jardinet in the mid-afternoon. It was a demanding routine for someone far from robust. He lived simply, looked after by Angélique. She was devoted to him. Her only grievance was that he picked at his food 'like a bird'. He rarely went out to the theatre or opera. Friends occasionally came to see him. Fizeau sometimes accompanied his flute on the fortepiano. His discovery of mediate auscultation revived his interest in carpentry. In his workroom he was making dozens of model stethoscopes. It remains a mystery how he found time to write his great work. Its first edition was published in 1819 and it was at once recognised as a landmark.

Although the *Traité de l'auscultation mediate et des maladies des poumons et du coeur* is dedicated to the Paris Faculty, the

Introduction makes it clear that the author disliked most of the still fashionable 'systems', whether Broussais's 'aetiologist' or Pinel's 'nosological'. They were, in his opinion, at best scaffoldings. In the present state of ignorance, health and disease were too complicated for any 'unifying' concept. The next 130 pages of the book are devoted to 'traditional' methods of examining the chest, including Auenbrugger's percussion as developed by Corvisart. Then come the chapters describing his own 'mediate auscultation'. They are a unique instance of a new and complete diagnostic system with all the essentials in and nothing essential left out, emerging in about 100 pages of print. Not many of Laennec's actual observations could be improved today. Not one of his interpretations needs to be apologised for as 'historical'. That all the material was collected by one individual in less than three years staggers belief. A summary can do the work little justice, but has to be attempted.

First, Laennec describes the normal breath sounds as heard through the stethoscope, those of children as well of adults. There is even a paragraph about the newborn. Then comes the description of an astonishing range of abnormal sounds— bronchophony, rhonchi, pectoriloquy, egophony (a sound resembling the bleating of a goat), the tinkle (like grains of sand falling into a porcelain cup), the boom, crepitations, the cavernous rattle, the puff, the echo, the coarse rubbing of the inflamed pleura—all vividly characterised, almost as recognisable from the page as they are when heard. Some of these abnormalities are common though others are rare: even with a plentiful supply of untreated pulmonary tuberculosis, for example, Laennec could not have heard more than half a dozen examples. He suggests a method of auscultation that might help deaf-mutes. He mentions that he has auscultated several species of animals. He does not believe that the sounds that can be elicited in most mammals will prove significantly different from those audible in humans.

The next sections are descriptions of the underlying pathologies, constantly referring back to the first part and explaining the physical origin of the sounds heard in the living. He describes the normal lung structure (apologising for going over familiar ground), the windpipe dividing near the midline into two main bronchi, the branching bronchial tree dividing into ever-smaller bronchioles and ending in trillions of microscopic air sacs in which the vital gas exchange between blood and air (the release of carbon dioxide and the uptake of oxygen) takes place.[151] The structure of the bronchi and bronchioles is described, pointing out the increasing elasticity of the tubes as their diameter diminishes. There are no microscopic descriptions, but the writer is clearly aware that the normal brush border of the bronchioles and bronchi, millions of little hairs or *ciliae* moving in a wave motion like grass in the wind, can propel phlegm upwards. This provides the basis of the description of a wide range of abnormalities, some never described before. In this category one was to prove of particular importance, though Laennec is not always credited with its discovery.

Even before Laennec, but especially throughout the tuberculous century, haemoptysis, or the coughing up of blood, became almost universally regarded as the cardinal, even a 'diagnostic' sign of tuberculosis. One evening during the winter of 1818, as John Keats tucked himself into bed after a windy coach ride from Westminster to Hampstead, he coughed. To his horror he tasted blood. 'Bring me a candle, Brown,' he asked his friend and fellow lodger, John Arbuthnot Brown. Brown later recorded the sequel:

> After I handed him the candle and he examined the blood on his shirt, he looked into my face with a calm countenance I can never forget ... 'This is arterial blood, Brown, I cannot be deceived by its colour. It is my death warrant.'[152]

Hundreds of thousands would come to share Keats' experience over the next 100 years. To them and to their families, coughing up blood became a death sentence. While the suffering might be prolonged for years, the end was not in question. The majority of those experiencing it were young people in their teens or early twenties. Doctors would rarely contradict them. Paradoxically, it was Laennec, the greatest medical figure in the history of tuberculosis before Koch, who established the fallacy of this belief. In his book he pointed out that tuberculosis was *not* the only common cause of coughing up blood in young people.

Among the alternative conditions he described for the first time the most important was bronchiectasis, the abnormal dilatation of small or large segment of the bronchi. The reason or reasons for this happening are still not entirely clear,[153] but the end result was clearly established and described by Laennec. The dilated segments are in fact paralysed and cannot propel inhaled foreign material or phlegm upward to be eliminated by clearing one's throat or by coughing. The stagnant pool becomes the focus of infection and the delicate and specialised inner lining of the bronchus is soon destroyed.[154] There may be ulceration. When bronchiectatic ulcers erode a blood vessel, they bleed just as tuberculous ulcers do. It took the best part of 150 years for the importance of this to be recognised. Today in Western Europe and the Americas bronchiectasis is a far more common cause of haemoptysis than is pulmonary tuberculosis. Some cases of tuberculosis that 'miraculously' recovered during the tuberculous century may have been misdiagnosed cases of bronchiectasis.

Laennec also noted the frequency of enlarged lymph nodes around the branching point of the trachea and around the entry of the main bronchi into the lungs and described the various forms this can take. He guessed—rightly—that in life these nodes might act as filters of inhaled air. 'White stone dust', found mainly in country folk, he thought was comparatively harmless, but the black variety, present in those living in towns long before cigarettes and car exhausts, was almost always associated with diseased lungs.

Laennec's account of tuberculous lesions and their progression has never been bettered, though it has frequently been overloaded with unnecessary detail. He described how tubercles develop from minute semi-transparent grey granules, resembling millet seeds;[155] how these grow and coalesce into yellowish and opaque 'tubercles'; and how small tubercles aggregate into ugly grey masses. His insight into the next steps anticipated the work of immunologists several generations later. Sooner or later the solid masses begin to liquefy at the centre and the liquefaction spreads outward. The change in consistency is like that from hard to soft cheese. Laennec meticulously attributes the 'excellent descriptive term *caseation*' to Matthew Bailley.[156] However, the description of the next step is pure Laennec: not even his friend Bayle in his much-admired book on phthisis gave such an accurate description of it. The softened mass grows, presses on a bronchus and eventually ulcerates through and empties its semi-liquid contents into it. This leaves a cavity with a ragged, inflamed lining. The tuberculous material in the bronchus may be coughed up, but it may also be aspirated towards the periphery, setting up new lesions. In either case, the cavity itself does not heal. 'It is largely the pull of the surrounding normal lung which keeps it open,' Laennec suggests, a remark that points uncannily to the future and to the artificial pneumothorax.[157] Indeed, the cavity tends to grow since the disease process continues in its wall.

There was hardly a stage in this complex process that Laennec did not explore and explain—and usually explain correctly. Though he was always careful to attribute priority to Bayle in many areas, he was a long way ahead of his dead colleague. In contrast to Bayle, who had detected various distinct types of tuberculous lesions, Laennec saw their continuity and outlined how one stage could merge into another: 'There is no more difference between miliary tubercles and large ulcerating lesions than there is between unripe and ripe fruit. The first develops into the second.' In contrast to Bayle, Laennec also realised that 'ossification'—that is, the deposition of calcium and the stone-like hardening of a tuberculous lesion—was the occasional end result of the disease rather than a specific type. He also identified the illness in other organs: the kidneys, the intestines, the bones, the joints, the pelvic organs. He admitted that the route by which the infection spread was not clear to him—'this needs much further research'—but he insisted that they were the same disease. This particularly contentious statement would not be vindicated until Koch's work 80 years later.

Laennec dismissed almost in passing Broussais's view that tuberculosis was merely the end result of any inflammation of the lung and that it all began with inflammation of the stomach: 'There is simply no evidence to support this statement.' Like Bayle, he had seen only comparatively few cancers of the lung— the condition may have been rare at this time—but unlike Bayle, he clearly distinguished between tuberculosis and cancer. He described pleurisy, the inflammation of the pleural envelopes of the lungs, both tuberculous and other kinds. This was almost always a result of inflammation of the underlying lung tissue. In tuberculosis it was an ominous development. When the pleurae became inflamed, fluid accumulated between the two layers. Often the fluid turned into pus, a condition known as empyaema. Laennec was weary of surgical intervention in any chronic inflammation, but an empyaema was like an abscess anywhere. Surgical drainage offered the only hope of recovery, perhaps of a permanent cure. Nevertheless, treated or not, the outlook was poor.

Among the fruits of percussion and mediate auscultation were the discovery and correct interpretation of the condition known as a pneumothorax. It meant the entry of air into the pleural 'space'; that is, between the two layers of the closed pleural sac. This could happen from the outside through a wound in the chest wall, though it could also happen from the inside when an airspace or cavity burst through the inner pleural layer. Laennec even suggested, once again correctly, that sometimes a minute hole in the pleura could act not merely as a hole but also as a valve, allowing air to enter but not to escape. The pressure inside the pleural space would then increase, the heart and great vessels would be pushed aside as if by a balloon, and death would be inevitable. The condition, still on occasions a life-threatening emergency, would later be called a 'pressure pneumothorax'.

Ironically, Laennec's book mentioned extensive scarring of the liver only in a footnote, tentatively attributing it to chronic alcoholism rather than to tuberculosis. Alcoholic or 'Laennec's' cirrhosis subsequently became the only disease eponymously linked to his name and familiar to doctors today. He also understood that asthma was not always a manifestation of heart disease, as was widely believed at the time. (It had been Corvisart who had pointed out that various kinds of breathlessness were more commonly the result of a diseased heart than of diseased lungs.) Laennec suggested that asthma could also result from bronchial malfunction. Once again, the stethoscope proved invaluable. It revealed that the typical asthmatic wheeze was due to spasm of the bronchi and that, unlike the 'asthma' of heart disease, it occurred in expiration but not in inspiration. It was due, Laennec correctly explained, to the fact that the bronchial tree, which dilated to allow fresh air to enter the lungs, was unable to contract to encourage used air to escape.

These are almost random examples of his insights. Every pathological change—the consolidation of formerly air-filled lung segments, the paralysis of diseased bronchi, the accumulation of fluid and air in cavities—was not only described but carefully and almost always accurately related to the sounds elicited by the stethoscope.

The third part of Laennec's treatise dealt with heart disease and was less original than the pulmonary section. This was partly because diseases of the lungs, especially tuberculosis, were then far more common, but also because in this field Laennec had been anticipated by Corvisart. Nevertheless, auscultation transformed the 'pathology of the living'. The famous 'murmurs' between the lubb and the dubb (or replacing one or the other) made their first appearance in print. Laennec guessed that they indicated some obstruction or irregularity in the flow of the blood from one heart chamber into the other or from the heart chambers into the great vessels. He did not clearly distinguish between the consequences of the abnormal narrowing of the valvular openings ('stenosis') and their abnormal dilatation ('incompetence'), but he was aware that either could impair cardiac efficiency and lead to heart failure. On the other hand, he recognised the rasp of pericarditis, the two inflamed layers of the pericardial sac rubbing against each other instead of gliding elegantly and soundlessly, and he gave a brilliant description of the dull sound on percussion and the faintness of the heart sounds that result from the accumulation of fluid in the sac. (He coined the term 'hydrocardia', widely used for a century to describe the condition.)

Laennec's style was dry, precise and impersonal, though sometimes he allowed himself a slightly polemic note. He dismissed Bouillaud's view that every ailment of the heart was a variation of 'endocarditis' as 'almost as ridiculous as Monsieur Broussais's idea that all diseases are sequels of gastroenteritis'. In only one paragraph does one get a glimpse of Laennec's elitist outlook on life, of his contempt for ignorance and his dislike of the pretentious. About the then common habit of deducing from the pulse complicated pathologies he remarks:

> The practice is better suited to those who are mediocre by nature or by education, sometimes both. Among physicians, as in all other classes of society, such people always represent the majority.

While the remark was (and is) of course true, it gives one an idea of why the author was not every doctor's favourite uncle.

Few people read Laennec's book today. The methods he described have been superseded by techniques infinitely more precise and sometimes infinitely more misleading. Nevertheless, the *Traité* remains one of those mysterious creations that defy explanation, like the ceiling of the Sistine Chapel or a Schubert song. In its own time it was recognised as both the manifesto and the summation of the diagnostic revolution. Within two years it was translated into English. The translator was John Forbes, a pupil of Laennec's. He was an excellent linguist and a good doctor, but not much of a prophet. In his Preface he wrote:

> I am sure that Monsieur Laennec's ingenious instrument will never come into general use in this country ... not only

because its beneficial application requires a great deal of trouble and skill but also because its whole character will remain utterly foreign to the English mind. To Englishmen there will always be something ludicrous in the image of the great physician listening to the patient's chest through a long tube as if the disease was a living thing in communication with him ... Besides, there is about this method a sort of commitment to the actual physical examination of the patient which is wholly alien to English medicine, more attuned to calm and cautious philosophical musings.[158]

Perhaps it is unfair to recall Forbes' limitations as a clairvoyant. He could hardly have foreseen that the descendant of Laennec's 'long tube' would become not merely a diagnostic aid but the badge of office, the prayer bead, the crutch, the fetish, the executive toy, the mating call and the status symbol of a profession in every kind of its pictorial representation and, strange to behold, even in real life.[159]

Besides its diagnostic value, there were several reasons for the triumphant spread of the invention. Laennec was a good amateur carpenter and engraver, and by the time he first published and illustrated his discovery, he had made several improvements on his original roll of paper. He noticed at once that, however tightly a tube of paper was rolled and gummed together, a central hollow conduit always remained. He was quick to realise that this was in fact a happy accident, that as a hearing aid it made the instrument much superior to a solid rod. He experimented with different kinds of material: ebony, cedar wood, malacca cane, limewood, glass, various metals, hardened skin rolled into a tube, even Mériadec's old oboe. He experimented with various lengths and thicknesses, changing the total diameter, the diameter of the central conduit and their proportions. He discovered the enhancement afforded by a cupped end. He eventually settled for a cylinder of light beech about a foot long, pierced through the centre and composed of two adjustable parts and detachable cups.[160]

Although early in 1818 Laennec still thought that publication was premature, his hand was forced by an allusion to the instrument in the *Annales politiques, morales et litéraires* and by a complimentary reference to it by his friend Portal, Madame de Stael's doctor, in the *Journal Universel des Sciences Médicales*. He therefore presented it to the Académie de Médicine on his thirty-seventh birthday, 17 February 1818. While there was much interest, the Académie, cautious as ever, appointed a five-man commission to study and to report on it. Laennec's friend Morlaix foresaw that the commission would take ten years to make up its mind (by which time half of its members would be dead), but in fact, prodded by Récamier, it reported back within a few months. It was full of praise. The lay press picked up the news. The *Journal de l'Ouest* suggested that the new tube would make it a simple matter for anyone to make a correct diagnosis of all diseases of the lungs and heart. Rejoice, doctors would become superfluous. By then at least 100 instruments of various designs were in use in Paris and a few outside. They were easy to manufacture and easy to personalise. Uncle Guillaume was presented with a fancy ebony one by his sons and wrote excitedly to his nephew. The invention, he suggested, marked a new beginning in medicine and the start of fame and fortune for the inventor. In fact, to Laennec the moment seemed more like an end than a beginning.

He was utterly exhausted. On 6 August 1818 he had written the last line of his book. The manuscript was 2434 pages long, in print it would be 878 pages. Next day he handed it to his publishers, MM Brosson et Chaude, his neighbours in the rue Pierre Sarazin.[161] Since July he had turned away all new patients. The last he saw was Madame de Chateaubriand, who had been having haemoptyses and feared that she had tuberculosis. Laennec made the diagnosis of bronchiectasis and reassured her. He was right: she would outlive him by more than 20 years.[162] Then he handed over his case notes to his friend Cayol. On 7 August, accompanied by Mériadec, he left for Rennes and Quimper. They did not even stop to see his father at

St Brieuc. The journey in the cabriolet sapped his last strength. On arrival in Douarnerez he collapsed in the house of his friend Jérome de Grivart de Kerstrad. He was unable to get up for several days and seriously doubted if he ever would.

Gradually, the mild Breton summer, the murmur of the sea and the familiar smells and sounds worked their usual miracle.[163] Mériadec could return to Nantes. Laennec started on his rambles and then continued his journey to Pont l'Abbé. Over the next two months he explored his estate and other farms and lands adjoining it. He supervised the pruning of trees, the trimming of hedges, the felling of trees. He inspected the farms in Lan-Vale and Cosquer that he had already purchased and visited others he hoped one day to buy. It was this that made him return to Paris again and again. It would become a pattern. He wanted to earn the money he needed to fulfil his dreams in Brittany. On this occasion he also wanted to be about for the launch of his book.

Staff at the Necker welcomed him back. To the Sisters of Charity he was a saint. A room had been set aside for him to retire for short rests. It never lacked a bowl of fruit of the season and fresh flowers. The book made headline news even in the lay press. Not all the headlines were complimentary: Laennec did not expect that. His approach to medicine was too uncompromising to please everybody. The *Gazette de Santé* deplored 'the exploitation of unscrupulous empiricism' (whatever that meant). The *Nouvel Journal de Médicine* devoted ten pages to explaining why the book did not deserve the éclat it had received. None of this could stop the advance of the new invention. As happens sometimes, a few perceptive lay observers grasped the significance of a medical discovery even better than the doctors. Chateaubriand, reviewing the notable events of 1819, wrote:

By means of a tube applied to the outer parts of the body, our learned compatriot Laennec has succeeded, by the nature of sounds generated in the chest, to clarify the mechanism of many of the main complaints afflicting the heart and the lungs. This great and wonderful discovery will mark a new era in the history of medicine. If only a machine could be invented to tell us more of what is happening in the mind, how wonderful it might be! But perhaps this is a dangerous thought. Dr Laennec has opened a new chapter in the study of diseases of the chest and heart.[164]

Within a few years and in a variety of incarnations, the stethoscope would be everywhere. By the early 1820s Cayol, Récamier, Winslow, Quesneu, Le Roux, de Mussy, Fizeau, Louis and Charpy were using it in the Paris hospitals. Broussais himself became an expert while firing off fusillades of hate at the inventor. Ambroise Laennec established it in Nantes, Toulemouche in Rennes, Rieu in Paimboeuf, Beaugendre in Quimperlé, Rault in Saint Brieuc and Murvel in Lyon. When Lejumeau de Kergaradée expressed his enthusiasm in a series of articles in the *Bibliothèque Médicale*, he could not have known that the instrument would bring him immortality. Ten years later he was the first to diagnose pregnancy when he applied his stethoscope to the abdomen of a woman and heard the first faint heart sounds of a foetus. The instrument quickly conquered the young in England and Scotland. James Clark, future royal physician, devoted a short book to it. The 25-year-old Thomas Hodgkin visited Paris and learnt the use of it from the inventor.[165] It was praised in Edinburgh by Andrew Duncan. The treatise got an enthusiastic reception in Spain, Holland, Germany, Russia, Poland and the United States.

Little is known about the sojourn of the young Czech-born Austrian, Josef Skoda, in Paris. The future patron of Semmelweis and ornament of the Vienna medical school was still a person of no importance, and he has had no worthy biographer to ferret out the formative events of his apprentice years. But the two stethoscopes that he would flourish and show off to his classes in later life—one for the heart and one for the lungs—he always claimed to have purchased in Paris under the impact of a lecture demonstration by the great Laennec himself. Did Skoda actually speak to his French hero? He would never give a straight

answer. What is certain is that many of the doctors who flocked to Paris to meet the inventor of the wonderful new instrument in person were to be disappointed.

Whenever he could, Laennec would now be back in Brittany, walking his dogs, Kiss and Moustache, or riding on horseback along the beaches and in the fields, planning his future in Douarnerez. This was the world he loved, a world regulated by tradition. He had made friends not only with the du Fretay, the distantly related local gentry, and with the parish priest, the saintly Abbé Guezengar, but also with the Floc'hays, the Caradecs, the Scordias, the Celtons, the Kervoalens, farmers and fishermen and their families. He spoke to them in their own language and they turned to him for advice on matters medical and occasionally non-medical. In some way, not perhaps unique, his physical frailty gave his opinions a special gravity. He never asserted anything he was not sure about. He was trusted. His 'clients' sometimes paid him in fish and lobsters of mythical proportions.

On Sundays he went to mass at the church of Saint Herlé. It was (and is) an unpretentious building, but it is embellished with ancient gargoyles, not all of them unfriendly, Breton inscriptions and some exquisite woodwork. Laennec sat at the *prie-Dieu* carved with his name. After mass, rosary in hand, he would join the procession around the square in front of the church. Occasionally, when the rain was too heavy or the squalls from the West too violent, he would set to work with his files and lathe, making stethoscopes with ever-increasing attention to detail. Villard, the village joiner, had taught him some of the finer points of the craft. The two dogs were always ready for a well-rewarded session of auscultation. But then it was time to set off for Paris. Major improvements needed to be done to the estate and the manor house had to be renovated. All this cost money.

CHAPTER SEVEN

THE LAST BATTLES

In Paris, despite his absences, Laennec had become a celebrity. With regret he had resigned from the Necker on being appointed head of medicine and professor at the Charité. This time he did not have to apply: Corvisart's old post, still the most prestigious in Paris, was pressed on him by Villèle, the King's favourite and first minister. Though Laennec sedulously avoided making capital of his religious and political affiliations—he had resigned from the Congregation when it became too shrill for his taste—during the last years of Louis XVIII's reign and the first of Charles X's many of his friends came to occupy positions of influence. Monseigneur de Quelen, Bishop of Samostate, a friend, patient and admirer, was consecrated archbishop of Paris. Chateaubriand was minister of foreign affairs.[166] Laennec was elected member of the Académie de Médicine, made a knight of the Légion d'Honneur, appointed professor at the Collège de France and invited to become physician to the Duchesse de Berry.[167] The stethoscope was hailed everywhere.

Nevertheless, much of Laennec's professional life during his last years was taken up by an increasingly bitter and personal battle with Broussais. The two men and their approach to medicine differed in almost every respect; but, ironically, their last ferocious clash had nothing to do with either the stethoscope or tuberculosis. Indeed, to understand their dispute—almost a brawl on the part of Broussais—it is necessary to digress to look briefly not only at Broussais as a person, but also at one of the most fiercely fought-over medical controversies of the century.

Born in St Malo in 1772, François Joseph Victor Broussais was a Breton like Laennec, while in almost every other respect his opposite. His childhood was disturbed by the revolutionary wars, his youth was tragic. His parents were massacred by royalist rebels in 1794. He himself only narrowly escaped, hiding in the hayloft. After few desultory years of medical training, he knocked about as a ship's surgeon under the command of the legendary (or notorious) St Malo privateer Robert Surcouf. Within a few years he managed to accumulate sufficient means to move to Paris and pursue a more formal course of medicine. In 1799 he successfully defended his thesis on gastric inflammation and joined the army. He was bold, brave, brutal and a braggart and participated in every Napoleonic campaign from Egypt to the Danube. In 1814, after Napoleon's first abdication, he became professor of medicine at the Val de Grâce, Paris's main military hospital.

He was a brilliant lecturer, though in the tradition of political demagogues like Mirabeau and Danton rather than in the more cerebral style of Pinel or Corvisart. He loathed Corvisart, Bayle and Laennec as representatives of a defeatist and degenerate approach to medicine as well as personally. They were murderers. This was not meant metaphorically; nothing about Broussais was metaphorical. Perhaps the murders were by default, but they were murders nevertheless.

His own teaching was embodied in two books, *Traitée des Phlegmasies chroniques* and *Examen de la Doctrine Médicale généralement adoptée*.[168] They were written in clipped short sentences like orders of battle. Their message was enticingly simple: diseases are not distinct entities but diverse manifestations of essentially the same abnormality. Indeed, they are not 'abnormalities' in the true sense of the word but exaggerations of a normal function. In Broussais's view this normal function was the 'digestive activity' of the lining of the stomach and the intestines. Those who contradicted him were contemptuously labelled the 'ontological' school. The term implied they assumed that diseases did actually *exist*. To Broussais therapeutic principles were equally simple. Effective treatment had to aim at weakening the patient in order to make the noxious over-activity of the gastrointestinal lining less virulent. This meant heroic blood-letting and a near-starvation diet. As effectively chief medical officer to the army, his position was unassailable. He could also count on the vocal support of army-trained doctors. He used his position to launch personal attacks of a viciousness exceptional even when verbal duellists did not mince their words.

It is tempting to dismiss Broussais's doctrine and campaign as the ravings of a lunatic; and indeed, Laennec's replies never lost their quiet dignity. (Inevitably, this enraged Broussais even more.) Yet Broussais deserves more than passing mention, though not for his discredited notions of pathology.

In a sense, the revelations of Corvisart, Bayle, Bichat and Laennec and their disciples left an uncomfortable gap. So long as illnesses could be defined in terms of such universal doctrines of warring humours, unbalanced irritations, restless temperaments or even gastrointestinal inflammation, there was a basis for treating them in an 'appropriate' way. As the work of the new school of medical scientists uncovered the multiplicity and complexity of diseases, it exposed the hopelessness of such therapies. But there was nothing to replace them. Laennec was aware of this. After the sparkling exposition of the natural history of tuberculosis and other ailments of the heart and lungs, the statement that most of these afflictions sometimes got better of their own accord, but that not much could be done to promote such a happy outcome, sounded a little lame. This was not for lack of trying. Both Bayle and Laennec were constantly searching for therapies that were both rational in terms of pathology and effective.

Laennec was impressed by the apparent rarity of tuberculosis in Cournouaille. (It would not last much beyond his lifetime: by the middle of the century tuberculosis was widespread among the fisher folk in Brittany.) He also recalled the invariable improvement he himself experienced when returning home. Could it be something in the moist, scented air of the region that was health-giving? Try the experiment. Soon after his appointment to the Charité, Laennec arranged at his own expense for waggon-loads of wet seaweed to be transported from Douarnerez to Paris. As soon as the seaweed arrived, 'still smelling of the sea', it was spread out on the floor of his wards. This was repeated with further consignment every second or third day. Many patients declared themselves improved. Some felt 'transformed'. They were deeply grateful. Nevertheless, the physical signs did not change. Mortality remained the same.

Laennec was a harsh critic of his own as well as of other people's inventions. He was not convinced. Facts were more important than impressions. After a period of six months he discontinued the regime. To Broussais such faintheartedness would have been unforgivable. Anything was better than shaking one's head in despair and admitting that all treatment was hopeless. That was not the spirit that had carried the Napoleonic eagles to Moscow and the Pyramids. Nor was it an attitude appropriate to the healing arts. It was the more reprehensible since a tested and 'incontrovertibly effective' treatment was at hand.

Doctors have bled patients for every imaginable ailment and simply to keep them fit for thousands of years.[169] Hippocrates himself (or one of the writings attributed to him) commended it when a sickness was caused by an imbalance of humours (which was usual) and especially when the illness seemed 'strong' and the patient was still vigorous. From Greece the method passed to Rome and to the Islamic world. Avicenna, the learned Persian physician, was scathing about the Byzantine habit of bleeding from the same side as the seat of the trouble when the cure was clearly conditional on bleeding from the opposite side, but of the benefits of blood-letting he was in no doubt. Venesection was enthusiastically propagated by the School of Salerno, declined during the Renaissance but became immensely popular again in the seventeenth century. Numerous accounts survive retailing the miracles achieved by the method. 'There is no remedy in the world which works so many wonderful cures,' enthused Guy Patin, dean of the Faculty of Medicine of Paris in 1654 and the most influential medical teacher of his day. 'Parisians take little exercise, drink and eat too much and become very plethoric ... In them copious blood-letting must precede any other form of treatment.'[170] One of his patients, attacked by 'rude and violent rheumatism', was bled 64 times before he was cured. Another who developed 'pleurisy by overheating himself playing tennis' required 13 large bleeds before he was restored to good health. Eventually even his tennis improved. Patin bled his own wife 12 times on consecutive days for congestion in the chest, his son 20 times and himself 7 times for a chest cold. While he may have been particularly enthusiastic, on a more modest scale the practice was universal.

Elaborate systems were developed to determine exactly how much blood should be taken, how frequently and from which site in different ailments. Bleeding bowls of expensively engraved Venetian glass or cheap tin-glazed earthenware, depending on the family's wealth and social status, were an essential ingredient of every well-regulated household. A wide range of special techniques were developed in addition to the simple opening of a superficial vein with a lancet. 'Cupping' consisted of applying a glass cup to the skin with an edge slightly raised and heating it with a candle until the relative vacuum inside raised a large blood blister. The blister was lanced, the blood let out and the cup applied elsewhere. A Viennese doctor produced a widely used spring-loaded lancet, called *Schnapper* in German, 'phleam' in English. However, most popular and developed to the highest degree of perfection was the application of leeches.

Hirudo medicinalis, the slug-like creature used for blood-letting, is about 5 cm long when empty but grows to 15 cm or more after feeding. It has five stomachs on each side and a row of teeth that puncture the victim's skin (leaving a mark similar to the Mercedes car badge). After sucking for half an hour it fills up with about 15 ml of blood but causes further bleeding into the tissues of three or four times that volume.[171] It then detaches itself and drops off. (It can be re-used after the blood has been let out by slitting the stomach open.) All this may sound comparatively simple, but the craft required considerable skill and not a little luck.[172]

In contrast to simple venesection, leeches had a well-marked local as well as a general effect and it was in the relief of local inflammatory swellings and engorgements that they excelled. They could be introduced into the anal canal and rectum using a special kind of perforated chair, not only to relieve haemorrhoidal congestion but also for the relief of other abdominal inflammatory conditions like hepatitis, suppressed menstruation and puerperal fever. Anal leeches sometimes relieved prostatic and bladder pain and painful retention of urine. Techniques were developed for applying leeches to the eye, inside the nostrils and, most effectively, to the larynx. In tuberculous laryngitis it was sometimes the only remedy that stilled the cough and pain and allowed the patient a night's rest. Applications to the vagina and the cervix uteri had a wide range of somewhat obscure gynaecological indications. None of these procedures was without risk. Even anchored to the operator's finger by a silk thread passed through the leech's head, the creature occasionally got detached in the throat or in the rectum. A leech in the stomach, lung or the bowel was no laughing matter. Nevertheless, the potential benefits outweighed the dangers.[173]

Broussais and his acolytes were not the only propagators of leechcraft, but also its most fervent practitioners. In the early years of the nineteenth century the collection and selling of leeches was a way of earning a pittance for a few poor families living near marshes.[174] (Small children, apparently favoured by leeches over the old, were sent in among the reeds, and the slugs were quickly detached and placed into a jar before they could gorge themselves.) This soon changed. France was originally a leech-exporting country. By 1830 more than five million leeches were imported every year from Germany, Scandinavia, Poland, Russia, Turkey and even India. Large leech farms were established where cattle and donkeys driven round in circles could be used to feed the bloodsuckers and bring them home. Hiruduculture became big business, more profitable than breeding oysters.

Leeches were Broussais's favoured method of bleeding: he would sometimes apply as many as 50 over 24 hours. They were uniquely effective in toning down gastroenteric inflammation, to him the root cause of all ills. Some of his patients ended up so weakened that they could not move and had to be fed for days or weeks. Nevertheless, it was worth it. If they recovered, they were cured. If they died, they would have died anyway.[175]

To Laennec Broussais's approach to medicine was deplorable and his blood-letting particularly obnoxious. Laennec's inaugural lecture at the Collège de France on 2 December 1822 was devoted to methods in medicine. He praised observation, analysis of facts, scientific study as conceived and propagated by Morgagni, Bichat, Corvisart, Bayle and Dupuytren. He deplored 'unitary' theories. He did not mention Broussais by name, but he condemned a latter-day 'follower of Paracelsus' who was a vain, deceitful, ignorant, aggressive demagogue, a 'phrase-monger' and a bully. The person was not hard to identify.

When the *Archives Générales* published the lecture, Broussais became 'nearly insane with rage'. He too had his journal, the *Annales de la Médicine physiologiques*, and he (in his own words) tore Laennec to shreds. He suggested that Laennec and Bayle had allowed many of their patients to die needlessly so that they could prove their vaporous theories at post-mortems. The post-mortems themselves were of course fraudulent from beginning to end. Laennec was then taken to task for allowing the influx of foreigners into his service and letting them kill French men and women with their crude methods. His predilection for the sea climate was patently lunatic. Even his manner of dressing was pernicious. Broussais's rages were frightening to behold, and many people were more than a little frightened. Politics once again played a part. By some Laennec was seen as a creature of the Bourbon Restoration, and the Bourbons were getting more unpopular by the day. Broussais represented past Napoleonic glory.[176] Laennec found that some of his closest colleagues were becoming somewhat more guarded in their expressions of devotion and friendship. 'Distancing oneself' was once again becoming a French virtue.

The battle of the leeches would be eventually resolved neither by Laennec nor by Broussais but by an unassuming young doctor who had spent his early medical career in Russia and who, in the 1820s, was still barely known in Paris. After his Russian years, mostly in the service of French diplomats, Pierre Charles Alexander Louis returned to his native country to 'relearn medicine'.[177] His past studies, he maintained, had taught him nothing. Medicine should be an exact science, not necessarily infallible but based on facts. Questions like 'Are leeches any use in chest pain?' should not be a matter of guesswork, and the answer should not be determined by which party shouted loudest or had the ear of the Minister.

At some point in his career Louis would utter the memorable statement: 'J'ai la haine des à peu près'. However, as a fresh arrival in Paris in 1820 he was lucky to meet up with an old schoolfriend, François Chomel. Chomel was now an influential physician at the Hôtel Dieu and gave him *une petite chambre d'entresol* in a remote wing of the hospital. There Louis spent six years crunching numbers. More precisely, he spent all the time left to him after haunting the wards of Paris hospitals, counting the number of patients who had been treated with blood-letting, estimating the amount of blood taken from them, making a note of the outcome and trying to compare the results with the outcome of various illnesses in those who, for some reason or other, had had no blood-letting. He counted everything that could be counted: leeches, volumes of blood, ages, days of survival.

Statistics are not necessarily dull. In England, 50 years after Louis, founders of the statistical method like Francis Galton, William Farr, Thomas Huxley or John Graunt could make it almost exciting. Louis never could. Today his publications are unreadable. His figures are paltry. His conclusions are questionable. Yet in his day they provoked both admiration and outrage. The latter was, as usual, more vocal. 'Il n'y a en médicine ni que des individues,' Cruveilher pronounced (to be echoed down the centuries by a chorus of statistical sceptics). But to many doctors a rigorous mathematical approach—statistics was not yet a meaningful term—was one they had been waiting for.

Louis was appointed physician to the Hôpital de la Pitié, not one of Paris's most famous hospitals but a respectable base. Some of the most promising of the younger physicians in the city joined his Societé médicale de l'Observation.[178] More surprisingly, he became a popular society doctor, married the daughter of the Marquis de Montferral, and his doctrine acquired an international following.[179] Of course, he could not silence Broussais from one day to the next, nor were his mathematical proofs totally convincing even in his lifetime. But they confounded many of Broussais's followers. Percentages and probabilities were new and shadowy concepts that they could neither understand nor effectively silence. Any dispassionate observer would sooner or later conclude that the massive blood-letting that Laennec had deplored did more harm than good. It did not need statistical proof. Nevertheless, it was not common sense but the newly fashionable jargon of numbers that would eventually put an end to it.[180]

By the early 1820s Laennec was no longer in the front line of the battle. Soon it was a private matter that would occupy his mind. When in 1819 he had departed for Brittany he had sold his house. Most of his furniture was subsequently dispatched to Kerlouarnec. On his return he settled first in the Hôtel du Bon-Lafontaine (run by a descendant of the fabulist) and then moved into a large and rather sumptuous rented apartment at 23 rue du Cherche-Midi. This could accommodate Mériadec as well as himself, but it needed a full-time housekeeper. He wrote to Christophe that he had made arrangements for the household to be run by a 'distant relative', a Madame Argou, 'whom I have known well for twenty-odd years'. It is the first one hears about Jacquette since she had consulted him professionally for her panic attacks in 1815. However, the two must have remained in touch.

Couvrelle itself had passed into the hands of the Lobau family in 1822, after the death within a year of both Monsieur and Madame de Pompéry. Charles, their eldest son, had moved to Quimper to be near the home of his wife's family. Marie had married the Marquis de Locmaria and lived in some state in St Germain. The younger son, Antoine, had moved into another family château in Salsogne.[181] It was convenient, perhaps necessary, for Jacquette to move to Paris. 'Thanks to Madame Argou now running my household, I am free to devote more of my time to my work and studies,' Laennec wrote.

In 1824 they both set out for a holiday in Brittany. Jacquette met the family, who took to her at once. Laennec *père* was particularly enchanted: a jewel of our race (meaning of course Bretons). Brittany had been her childhood home too, though she did not speak the language. Not since his first visit to Couvrelle did Laennec so enjoy himself. The sojourn was interrupted only by an urgent summons to go to Bordeaux. He was offered 10,000 francs for a consultation at the bedside of a Spanish nobleman and another 50,000 if the patient recovered. The offer was too tempting to refuse, especially as he had set his eyes on some more land and further renovations. He left Jacquette with Christophe in Nantes. Having examined the patient in Bordeaux, he demonstrated with his magic listening tube why he did not think that the man had a cavity in his lung. (There were plenty around for comparison.) He advised simple rest and almost at once the patient started to get better. He also gave a demonstration of his instrument at the Hôpital St-André to a gathering of doctors who had come from far and wide in the South West.[182]

Laennec was getting annoyed about the gossip surrounding his domestic arrangements. Jacquette was now 45 and infinitely respectable but, known for his piety and rectitude, he was an irresistible target. A few weeks after his return to Paris he made up his mind and broke the news to Christophe:

My good friends, I truly never thought I would marry. Nevertheless, I am. On my return I had a few days' leisure and thought how much more agreeable my journey would have been had I made it with my wife rather than with my friend. One thought led to another ... At first she said 'no' but later 'yes'. My father thinks that it is a very good idea which is the only reason why I think it might not be ... but between now and Christmas you will have a new cousin by marriage.[183]

The marriage took place on 16 December 1824 at the Mairie of the VI *arondissement* and then at Saint Sulpice. Cayol and Récamier, by now both professors, were witnesses. Laennec *père* and his wife came from St Brieuc, the former slipping a Breton poem composed by himself in honour of the event into the bride's bouquet. It was a happy occasion and it was followed by a few months of happiness. The couple moved to 17 rue Saint-Maur, close to the present Hôpital Laennec. In the spring of 1825 Jacquette announced that she was pregnant.

After numerous delays and the overturning troublesome objections, the Département des Ponts et Chaussées in Brest approved Laennec's plans for draining the Cosquer marshes. About the same time he had a letter from Fauriel, the noted philologist and originator of the systematic study of Celtic folklore. Fauriel had the words of a number of old Breton songs but not the tunes. Sainte-Beuve, almost a doctor himself before he became a luminary of the French literary establishment, wrote in his *Portraits Contemporains*:

> Would you believe it, the only man who could help Fauriel in his quest was the great and famous Doctor Laennec. He knew all the tunes: they were the never-to-be forgotten melodies of his childhood. Despite being the most sought-after physician in Paris and in far from perfect health, he visited Fauriel and brought his flute. Picture the doctor as a Lycidas, delighted when many of the half-forgotten words Fauriel recited to him brought back the notes to his mind. *Numeros memini si verba tenerem* [I remember the notes if I can get hold of the words, a common enough experience].

Smile as you picture the touching scene, worthy of the two great hearts and minds, in their simplicity recalling more serene times.[184]

In April 1826 the second enlarged edition of the *Traité de'Auscultation Mediate* went to press. This gave Laennec pleasure because he had been able to correct a few mistakes and misspellings. He had also added further observations: 'My new publishers are as courteous and helpful as the old ones were negligent and villainous.'

However, the period of happiness did not last. In April Jacquette developed a fever and had a miscarriage. In the same month Laennec himself developed a cold and for the first time admitted to Mériadec that he might be suffering from tuberculosis. He called in Récamier, the pupil he most trusted, not as a friend but as a doctor. Récamier examined, percussed and auscultated him as thoroughly as Laennec had taught him. Repeatedly he asked the patient to cough, clear his throat, stop breathing, cross his hands in front of his chest. It was Laennec who had shown how the last manoeuvre would lift the shoulder blades off the rib cage and allow the examiner to listen to the apices of the lungs. It was also Laennec who had demonstrated that tuberculosis most often started in the upper lobes.

The flexible-tubed stethoscope had not yet been invented: the patient could hear only the sounds of percussion, not those of mediate auscultation. But percussion was revealing enough. And, as the patient would have done himself when examining a colleague, Récamier kept up a running commentary of the sounds audible to him through the new instrument. They were unmistakable, exactly as Laennec had described them. There were the rales, the crepitations, the pleural rub, the coalescing areas of bronchial breathing, the signs of consolidation, on both sides. Above all, there was the loud *bruit de pot felé* (the sound of the cracked pot) over the right apex, indicating a large cavity communicating with a major bronchus.

Laennec had also given clear accounts of the prognosis associated with these signs. Once again, as the patient himself had taught him to do, Récamier summarised his conclusions briefly but without prevarication. The 'case' was one of severe bilateral tuberculosis, more advanced on the right than on the left. Though the apices were most severely affected, the process had extended into the right middle and even into the lower lobes. The pleurae were 'touched' on both sides, though there was as yet only a slight accumulation of fluid. The disease was beyond any prospect of spontaneous arrest or regression. There was no curative treatment.

He ended his summary in exactly the way his teacher had taught him to do and as he had seen that teacher do many times. He took the patient's right hand between his own hands. No prospect did not mean no hope. A poor prognosis must not engender loss of faith. Hope and faith in divine mercy must never cease. The ways of Providence were far beyond the efforts of a physician to predict. But, so far as human guesswork could go, the patient would be dead within a year. 'Never use synonyms for dying,' Laennec had instructed his pupils many times. 'Remember that death is part of life. Transmit your faith to your patients.' Nor, the patient must remember, did a lack of cure mean a lack of treatment; the very reverse. Récamier would always be at the patient's side to relieve his symptoms. There was no need for physical suffering. There would be no loss of dignity. And last: would the patient like to join him in a brief prayer? Few patients ever turned down the offer and Laennec certainly did not. But could Jacquette join them? She did, wordlessly. After a few seconds, instead of a prayer of supplication, Récamier intoned: *Te Deum laudamus*.

There was now much to do. Donning ceremonial sword and court dress, Laennec paid a formal farewell visit to the Duchesse de Berry. She invested him with the Cross of St Michael. He bid his *adieux* to his colleagues at the Charité, the Faculty and the Collège de France. On 30 May he descended the stairs of his house on

Jacquette's arm and climbed into his carriage, bound for Brittany for the last time.

During the journey he suffered from sharp pains in the chest, fever and diarrhoea. He had a painful tooth extracted at Rennes. Pus streamed out of the socket. Was it perhaps a hopeful sign, pointing to the maxillary sinus rather than the lungs as the cause of his illness? It was the first of those self-deceptions that, over the next century, would become a hallmark of terminal tuberculosis. Laennec was delighted, as always, to recognise the familiar landmarks, the chapel of Saint-Croix, the newly planted orchard, the white façade of the manor. Tenant farmers, servants and friends welcomed him at the end of the avenue of poplars leading to the gates. He made the last journey on foot, though with difficulty.

His letters to Mériadec over the next weeks give a detailed and composed account of his fluctuating symptoms, the resignation but also the occasional flashes of hope. He was nursed by Jacquette and there was a constant stream of visitors. He revised his will, leaving a few mementoes and his medical books to Mériadec, his Breton books and manuscripts to the Celtic Library at Quimper, but otherwise the bulk of his property to his wife. On days when he felt slightly better he was taken round the grounds in a light cart as far as the little fountain of spouting dolphins that he had restored himself. With Jacquette he visited the chapel at Saint-Croix. At the door he got out of his cart and entered on foot. 'Let us kneel and pray, Madame.' They did.

Ambroise and Christophe arrived in 23 June. Ambroise listened to his chest with his stethoscope and realised that the situation was terminal. He gave a detailed account of his findings to Mériadec. Laennec wrote his last letter to his father:

> May the Merciful God before whom I shall soon appear, bestow upon you, my dear father, his blessings. Forgive my impatience and my frequent misbehaviour. For two months I have tried to purge my soul and, by God's grace, I feel that I would rather appear before him now than at any other moment.[185]

In reality the end in tuberculosis was rarely the graceful fading away that it became in romantic fiction and on the operatic stage but, thanks to the blessing of opium, it was often a comparatively quiet departure. On 13 August Laennec awoke from his doze, removed his rings and laid them on the bedside table. 'I know that for anybody else this is such an unpleasant task,' he whispered. He died a few hours later.

The next day Jacques Kervoalen, one of the tenant farmers, and Guillaume Le Berre, the village carpenter, carried the news to Monsieur du Fretay, mayor of Ploaré. As witnesses they appended crosses to the official notification. Neither could write. A black flag was hoisted on the spire of the town hall. Two days later the doctor was buried in what was then the new cemetery, halfway on the road to Douarnerez. It was and remains the resting place of peasants and fishermen. It is open to all the winds from the sea and it is well cared for by the villagers. The Laennec grave lies at the foot of the Calvary, a curved block of grey granite of Keranton, now golden with lichen. It is inscribed:

ICI REPOSENT
RENE-THEOPHILE-HYACINTHE
LAENNEC
Médecin de S.A.R. Madame
la Duchesse de Berry
Lecteur et Professeur Royal en Médicine
au Collège de France
Membre de l'Académie Royale de Médicine
Chevalier de la Légion d'Honneur
né à Quimper en 1781
mort à Kerlouarnec le 13 Août 1826
et Dame JAQ. GUICHARD
son épouse
née à Brest en 1779
Morte à Kerlouarnec le 3 Août 1847
Priez pour eux

PART II

SEMMELWEIS AND CHILDBED FEVER

Ignác Philipp Semmelweis (1818–1865)

Portrait reproduced by permission of Science Photo Library

CHAPTER ONE

ROOTS

Returning from Paris to Vienna with their newly acquired stethoscopes in their rucksacks, their heads buzzing with heart sounds and respiratory murmurs, young doctors like Josef Skoda and Carl Rokitansky travelled 1000 miles along one of the highways of Europe. If they had continued their journey for another 40 miles, they would have found themselves off the beaten track. Even today the strip of land known as the Burgenland between Austria and Hungary is something of a backwater. By-passed by the old Landstrasse, it is still by-passed by motorways and railway lines. It has no famous cathedral and no three-star restaurant. It is quietly rolling countryside of great beauty, like the slow movement of a Haydn symphony.[1] The region can even boast a Haydnesque joke: a lake that in the summer sometimes disappears.[2] The water leaves behind a forest of reeds, puddles and one of Europe's great bird sanctuaries.[3] After a few days the lake reappears. The neat villages on its shores cluster round onion-domed churches. In front of the churches a painted statue of the kindly St John of Nepomuk often welcomes worshippers. Among them there are still families called Semmelweis. It is an odd sort of a name, not known anywhere else in Europe.[4]

Laennec was 37—he had just discovered his famous instrument—when Ignác Semmelweis was born, the second of the pioneering doctors who make up the present gallery of four. The year was 1818. Semmelweis's place of birth was Buda, the hilly part of today's Budapest, but his roots were here, in the Burgenland. In the village of Sieggraben (Szikra meaning 'spark' in Hungarian), about 20 miles south of Eisenstadt, the regional capital, the parish register mentions the first two attested ancestors. Here, 'am 16. September 1692 ist der Erbare Jenggesöll Jörg Semmelweis mit der Tugendsamen Jungfrau Kunygundt Copuliert worden'. But the name is mentioned even earlier, towards the end of the sixteenth century, among the independent winegrowers of the region. In 1776 one of Georg Semmelweis's grandsons, Johann, is listed among the *cives* of Eisenstadt, clearly a man of substance. It was his eldest son, Josef, who in 1802 moved himself and his family to Buda.[5]

The exact reasons for the move, which was to make Ignác Semmelweis Hungarian by birth as well as by sentiment, are not known, though the first great European drift from country to town had already begun. Vienna was nearer, but it was the grand imperial metropolis where all manner of bureaucratic restrictions blighted the prospect of new businesses. Bratislava (Pressburg to Austrians and Pozsony to Hungarians), even closer, was slowly declining in the shadow of Vienna. Buda had not yet recovered from 150 years of Turkish rule,[6] but it was once again Hungary's capital. Situated on a hill on the western side of the Danube, its position was naturally commanding. The river itself had grown in width and majesty since leaving Austria. A pontoon bridge connected Buda with the small but thriving town of Pest. Pest was already the home of the country's only university. Since 1770 the university even boasted a medical faculty.[7]

Language was not yet the spurious ethnic marker it was to become a century later. The country's leading poets were beginning to reinvigorate the Magyar tongue, but even fervent patriots like Count Stephen Szechenyi, leader of the political reform movement, spoke German as their first language. The language of government, of the Diet (until 1835), of the university and even of secondary schools was Latin. At the time of the March 1848 uprising Buda and Pest had two newspapers, both German. 'Race' in the malign sense of the next century counted for even less. Alexander Petöfi, the most Magyar of poets, never denied that his father was a Serbian innkeeper called Petrovich. The great patriot Kossuth's mother was a Slovak who never learnt to speak Hungarian. Of the 13 Hungarian generals executed by the Austrians after the defeat of the Hungarian Liberation Struggle of 1848–49, nine had German, Polish or Serbian names and only half spoke Magyar like natives. Though Ignác Semmelweis himself was to be occasionally described as Austrian after his death, even his Burgenland-born parents regarded themselves as Magyars.

Stiff but not unattractive portraits in oils exist of both Joseph Semmelweis and his wife, Theresa, née Müller, the daughter of a well-to-do coachmaker of Bavarian origin. Indeed, the proud parents even had a likeness in their bedroom of their promising second son, Ignác, aged about 14, painted by Leonard Landau, a competent local artist. (Their eldest son had died of scarlet fever a few years earlier.) Joseph was by then the proprietor of a flourishing grocery shop, a *civis* of Buda and the registered owner of several houses. The family themselves lived over the shop on the first floor of a two-storey rented building, today's Semmelweis Museum. Besides the shop, the ground floor housed a popular tavern and a coach house. What now seem somewhat cramped quarters under the roof provided accommodation for a maid, a cook, a manservant and two apprentices.

It was in this house that Ignazius—Ignác in Hungarian, commonly abbreviated to Náci by family and friends—was born on 1 July 1818, the fifth of ten children. Seven survived infancy and childhood. The district itself, mostly slightly dilapidated but friendly one-storey buildings, occupying the low ground between Castle and Gellert Hills, was deemed to be a blot on the image of Budapest, the emerging and glamorous metropolis of the 1930s, a favourite haunt of the then Prince of Wales. It was pulled down to make way for an exceedingly dull park. Only a few houses adjoining today's Semmelweis Museum and two graceful Baroque churches survive.[8]

The Semmelweis house was not an aristocratic mansion as today's appearance might suggest. As in former times, the aristocracy had their town houses on Castle Hill, usually one of their many residences and usually the one least inhabited.[9] What was styled the royal palace, a barrack-like pile of bricks without its later cupola and the more recently excavated medieval accretions, had been visited by reigning monarchs only three times over the previous century. They never stayed for more than a week. In the absence of the king the palace housed the court of the Palatine, an unofficially hereditary office held by successive members of the 'Hungarian' branch of the Habsburgs. In the year in which Semmelweis was born the holder was the Archduke Joseph, one of the more enlightened members of his house. He even learnt a few words of Hungarian to enable him to communicate with his coachman. This was acclaimed by his subjects as showing signs of burning patriotism.[10] The Semmelweis house was not even the home of rich bourgeois. The families who had done indecently well out of the Napoleonic wars had moved into a row of pompous edifices on the left bank of the Danube. Most of these would collapse during the great flood of 1836 (now commemorated on the walls of the Franciscan church). Yet even today the house where Semmelweis spent his childhood has a friendly, un-museum-like feel, with a spacious courtyard where large delivery vans could unload and turn and where carthorses could be fed, watered and sponged. In Semmelweis's day it must surely have accommodated a sandpit and a swing. He was always to recall his boyhood with affection.

Apart from such occasional references, little is known about Semmelweis's youth. Between the ages of nine and fifteen he attended the college of the Order of the Piarists. Unlike other ecclesiastical establishments that loyally supported Vienna's Germanising aspirations, the Pious Fathers were traditionally reformist and nationalist. Their school was the breeding ground of the leaders of Hungary's national revival. Semmelweis in particular had several distinguished Hungarian scholars among his teachers, including the geographer Brassay and the Latinist Heilsiedler. The order had been founded to provide shelter and education for the street urchins of sixteenth-century Rome. The establishment was still, in name if no longer in practice, a free school.[11] The fathers prided themselves on fostering piety and academic excellence rather than on providing sprigs of the upper and rising middle classes with a serviceable stock of Virgilian tags. Ignác won several prizes, though never the school's coveted Founder's Medal. When, many years later, he returned to Buda from Vienna, it was to him a homecoming, not an exile.

After school he completed two years of 'philosophical studies' at the University of Pest, a requisite for any further academic career. (Then as now, disciplines with 'studies' attached to their name seem to have been rather nebulous in content.) In 1837, in conformity with his father's wishes, he travelled to Vienna and entered the university's faculty of law. He would be training to become a military judge, a profession that, according to Josef Semmelweis, combined the two noblest of professions. His son disagreed.

According to a contemporary anecdote, later propagated by Hebra, one morning he was smuggled into the foul-smelling anatomy theatre of the Medical School in the Schwarzpanierstrasse. It was a gloomy edifice that had once served as a rifle manufactory. His guides were medical students and their girlfriends, naturally disguised as boys. They came to attend one of the grand dissections presided over by the celebrated Professor Hofrat Baron Joseph von Berres. This was a popular scrape that did not seem to constitute an immediate threat to the Emperor, his all-wise chancellor or the Holy Roman church. It was therefore tolerated by the police. The more ghoulish might even take a peep themselves. Semmelweis watched the solemn entrance of the professor and his acolytes and the cadaver being lifted dripping from its malodorous vat onto the marble slab of the dissecting table. The actual dissection was done by the nimble fingers of the prosectors, a specialised breed of technicians. Their performance was accompanied by von Berres's often bitingly sarcastic running commentary. (A few years later Rokitansky would create a furore when he insisted on performing his own autopsies.) The professor had a captive audience. The young interloper duly turned green, to the giggling delight of his hosts; but the experience apparently changed his mind. His transfer from the law to medicine seems to have caused no anguish to his parents. He himself never regretted it.

None of the teachers whose names had made Vienna one of the medical centres of Europe during the eighteenth century was alive in 1836,[12] but the medical school still enjoyed a nearly unrivalled reputation.[13] This was not undeserved, though the staff neatly divided into a small group of charismatic teachers who earned the institution its international fame and a crowd of worthy plodders who deplored the publicity seeking of their younger colleagues, though they were prepared to bask in their reflected glory. All those in the first category had travelled widely; above all, they had all been to Paris. There they had absorbed an exciting body of new knowledge.

More importantly, they had absorbed some of the city's sceptical, subversive atmosphere. Not only prospective physicians but also pathologists and even budding surgeons and obstetricians had returned with at least one stethoscope. Laennec's revolutionary new invention, the key to the physical examination of patients, was becoming their badge. In academic circles it was still unsafe to brandish them about too provocatively, but some were beginning to be made locally. They were not hard to construct and the Viennese were accomplished craftsmen. (Sadly, instruments made of pretty hard-paste porcelain proved ornamental rather than practical.)

Quietly leading the new wave was Carl Rokitansky. Born in 1804, he was of Czech origin—none of the leading lights of the Vienna Medical School was Viennese and only a minority was Austrian—and would become one of the century's great exponents of the art and science of morbid anatomy.[14] This branch of medicine looked back to the Italian master, Giovanni Battista Morgagni, as its founding father and was wedded to the idea that the causes and seats of all diseases (and ultimately perhaps their treatment and cure) could be uncovered by the diligent dissection and examination of dead bodies.[15] By the time Rokitansky took up the speciality, this examination included the microscopic study of cells and tissues removed from the dead, though not yet the examination of biopsies from the living.[16] By the end of his career he is said to have personally performed 44,000 post-mortem examinations, a record (if true) never surpassed before or since.

Like his younger rival, Rudolf Virchow, he firmly opposed such mystical concepts as vital energy and other transcendental influences on health and disease. (He would not tolerate a crucifix in the dissection room, though a chapel to comfort the bereaved was attached to the mortuary.) On the other hand, he was prone, as were and are many scientists who pride themselves on their rigorously rational approach to the living world, to construct grandiose but rather vague unifying concepts of disease. In Rokitansky's case this tendency took the form of the doctrine of 'Krasis', which attributed all ailments to an imbalance of the constituents of blood plasma. A clever idea, it was later comprehensively demolished by Virchow.[17] The setback did not significantly dent Rokitansky's international reputation.[18]

Unlike clinicians, daily exposed to the proof and consequences of their diagnostic blunders, morbid anatomists, dealing at the time only with dead bodies, could rarely if ever be disproved and this tended to endow them with an air of omniscience. Their pronouncements were accepted by their clinical colleagues like pontifical utterances if not supernatural revelations.[19] Rokitansky was in many ways a prototype. His literary output was colossal. His brilliantly illustrated *Handbuch der pathologischen Anatomie*— three tomes requiring the strength of a weightlifter to shift—was published by the time he was 45, and by the time he retired his collected papers filled several shelves in university libraries. Coming from humble Protestant stock, he was austere in his private life, resisting for many years all attempts to move his department from an unheated peasant house and former inn on the outskirts of Vienna to a more impressive building in the university quarter.[20] Honours were heaped on him late in life, including the title of 'Freiherr' with the coveted 'von'. His teaching made a great and lasting impression on young Semmelweis. Indeed, it was ultimately responsible for the young man's familiarity with post-mortem appearances, which in turn led to his moment of truth.

Josef Skoda was only a year younger than Rokitansky and his name is still eponymously linked to a physical sign in medicine.[21] He too was born in what is today the Czech Republic, the son of a blacksmith. It was an industrious family. One of the physician's nephews, Frantisek Skoda, later founded the Habsburg Empire's great armaments factory. The factory still makes motor cars today. Unwilling to join the family workshop, Josef walked to Vienna when he was 15 and supported himself as a private tutor while he completed his medical studies. He then travelled to Paris.

In many ways the moment of his return and entry into the profession determined his future. The poverty of diagnostic aids —no X-rays, no electrical records and laboratory tests virtually confined to gazing at and occasionally tasting the patient's urine—would be paralysing to doctors today. It is also hard to explain. Doctors had practised what was recognisably medicine for at least 2000 years, yet none, it seems, had tumbled to the fact that eliciting the sounds of a diseased chest (and other body cavities) by percussion and auscultation can yield extraordinarily detailed information about what is happening inside it. Even when Skoda arrived back from Paris, the discoveries of Auenbrugger, Laennec and Corvisart were ignored by the city's medical establishment.[22] Skoda himself, unprepossessing to look at, extremely short-sighted, carelessly attired, indifferent to professional etiquette and devoid of social graces, had a hard struggle before a lucky break brought him to the attention of the Emperor's personal physician, Baron Ludwig von Türkheim. After a stint as a police surgeon, he was called almost by accident to the bedside of a visiting and terminally ill princeling who had been unsuccessfully treated by a bevy of court physicians for 'liver trouble'.[23] After prolonged palpation, percussion and even applying his new-fangled 'listening tube' to his Serene Highness's chest, all regarded by his medical brethren as both ill-mannered and lacking in professional gravitas, the young man diagnosed an aortic aneurysm. Court physicians Professors von Hildebrand and Schiffner professed themselves unconvinced. Skoda was dismissed. The princeling died within a week. Von Türkheim ordered a post-mortem examination. Skoda's diagnosis was confirmed by Rokitansky on the autopsy table.[24]

It was a portent. Skoda claimed to be a disciple of the great French clinician-pathologists around Corvisart, but this was not quite accurate. To Bichat, Bayle and Laennec treatment mattered, even if they were limited by their commitment to base therapy on reason and observed facts. Skoda was one of the new breed of scientific physicians to whom a correct diagnosis was all. It was an intellectual challenge. It was what made medicine—indeed life—interesting. Later in his career pupils flocked to his department from all over Europe and many left admiring descriptions of the chubby little man with the pebble glasses spending half an hour or more percussing and listening to his patient's chest, bellowing at the unfortunate to breathe, stop breathing, cough, croak, keep still, turn over, until, at the end of the performance, he would sketch on a piece of paper the exact extent of the disease, briefly summarise its character and prognosis and then proceed to the next bed. The trivial task of prescribing treatment—'Ach, das ist ja alles eins' was his usual comment—was left to one of his juniors. A few days or weeks later he and his retinue would turn up in Professor Rokitansky's autopsy room and, more often than not, he would note with quiet satisfaction the confirmation of his diagnosis. Despite his uncouthness—or perhaps because it offended everybody else at Court—he became a favourite of the Empress-Queen Elizabeth, who would trust nobody else. He died in 1881, aged 76. Semmelweis admired his luminous intellect, but never subscribed to his therapeutic nihilism.

The third and youngest member of the mould-breaking trio who both befriended and impressed young Semmelweis was Ferdinand

Hebra. Like Skoda and Rokitansky, he had his roots in what is today the Czech Republic: he was born in Brno in 1816. His family background too was similar, that of small shopkeepers, artisans and lowly government officials. (The last were the backbone of the Habsburg Monarchy's elephantine bureaucracy.) But Hebra's personality was gay, easy-going and debonair. Instead of a beard or imperial whiskers, he sported a natty little moustache and was not averse to practical jokes.

He may have chosen dermatology as his field of activity for reasons not perhaps dissimilar from those that propel some young doctors today in a similar direction. There were few nocturnal emergencies in diseases of the skin, and if the ailments rarely got dramatically better in response to treatment, nor did they often turn suddenly lethal.[25] This allowed Hebra to preside over a happy family home—Rokitansky and Skoda had virtually no private life—in addition to writing numerous short and elegant essays on what is still the body's most visible but also one of its most mysterious organs.[26] He was also a good judge of character and medical competence, choosing his younger colleague in preference to a galaxy of famous names to deliver his wife's first two children, a boy followed by a girl. Both, fortunately, were born after May 1847.[27]

One other Viennese doctor's teaching made a deep impression on the young Semmelweis (the two could never have met in the flesh). Lucas Johann Boër (1721–1835) was not a Young Turk but a late survivor of the first golden age of the Vienna School of Medicine. Beginning his career as a general practitioner in charge of Vienna's municipal orphanage, in 1778 he attracted the attention of the Emperor Joseph II.[28] At the Emperor's expense the young doctor was sent on a study tour of western Europe, including London and Dublin. On his return was appointed obstetrician to the imperial family and later professor of obstetrics at the university. He remained an ardent admirer of his reforming benefactor and the sentiment was reciprocated. The two men shared such sensible but revolutionary ideas as natural childbirth and the sparing use of blood-letting and purgation. Boër attended Joseph's two wives and later his lady friends and mistresses.[29]

His last service to his master ended tragically. He was called to deliver the Emperor's last platonic love, the Archduchess Elizabeth, wife of the Archduke Francis, the Emperor's nephew and heir. Against the Emperor's wishes, the young woman had earlier visited her uncle by marriage on his sickbed and was so horrified by his appearance that she fainted. She then went into premature labour. It proved a difficult delivery. Reluctantly Boër used forceps. All seemed well and the archduchess was delivered of a healthy baby archduchess. A day later she developed a fever and severe abdominal pain; 36 hours after that she lapsed into coma. Within 48 hours she was dead and so was the baby. In his university clinic Boër had by then reduced the incidence of puerperal fever to below 1 per cent, and special care was inevitably taken to avoid the complications in the case of a future empress. Nevertheless, the disease was one to which no mother seemed immune. The Emperor survived his beloved Elise by less than three days.

Joseph II had been one of those freak reforming geniuses who provide intermittent relief in the otherwise dreary annals of the later House of Habsburg. An enlightened despot, 'the French revolution compressed into one individual',[30] he refused to be crowned King of Hungary because the ceremony entailed an oath to uphold the country's ancient and unworkable constitution. He loosened the link between the dynasty and the church. He freed Protestants and Jews of their legal disabilities. He emancipated the serfs (though they remained saddled with the *robot* or labour rent for another 50 years). He planned to codify the rights of illegitimate offspring.[31] He interfered with and by and large improved every aspect of the governance of his empire. What he lacked was his mother's emollient charm, her capacity to win over or at least to pacify his opponents. His isolation was his weakness and eventually the undoing of most of his reforms. An 'imperial Jacobin' remained a self-contradiction and he died convinced that all his labours had been in vain. This was not quite true. Some of his achievements endured, especially those relating to the church and to non-Catholics. Nevertheless, after the terrors and tribulations of the French Revolutionary and Napoleonic Wars, his decade of flirtation with reform was remembered with a shudder by the next generation of Habsburgs and their courtiers. Never again.

Inevitably perhaps, a somewhat similar fate befell his favourite obstetrician.[32] Boër was a sceptic, an admirer of Jean-Jacques Rousseau and in obstetric practice an advocate of masterly inactivity. It was his misfortune that his old age coincided with what was developing into one of the most interventionist phases of European midwifery. Such trends are as irrational and as difficult to rationalise in retrospect as fashions in women's hats, but at the time they are irresistible. Around 1800 watchful prayer was still the obstetrician's guiding principle. By the 1820s at the slightest indication—and sometimes even without any discernible indication—out would come the new obstetric forceps from their beautifully embossed cases.[33] They were, to be fair, handsome instruments, with their elegant silver handles and double-curved blades, still an aesthete's joy. With their help labour was often quick. Of course, without anaesthesia it was not easy to dull the agony of the mother as the unyielding metal pressed against her bruised tissues. No less unyielding (but still easily concealed) statistics tended to show that a few days after the triumphant manoeuvre an unusually high proportion of the mothers would be delirious not with joy but with childbed fever. However, for a time this was considered an unavoidable price to pay for the display of technical virtuosity ('always in the mother's best interest' of course, as Klein would testify to the first imperial commission to investigate his department). Osiander of Göttingen prided himself on using forceps in 40 per cent of all deliveries and Gramont of Lyon used it in 38 per cent.

Boër, whose corresponding figure was 0.4 per cent, was now widely apostrophised as a fuddy-duddy. And it was not only forceps delivery: he was staunchly opposed to any operative intervention and to the massive use of any medicine except opium. What was particularly difficult to swallow was that his general caution, and what was perceived as his incorrigible laziness, had reduced the incidence of puerperal fever in his department to the lowest figure in living memory. There was then no compulsory retiring age for university professors, but in 1822, at the age of 70, he was obliquely accused of obstinacy in refusing to take advantage of significant advances in his speciality, of not allowing student midwives to take part in dissections and, most significantly perhaps, of forbidding his junior doctors to participate in post-mortems while on obstetric duty.[34] Despite the sycophantic wording of the unsigned memorandum, reprinted in Vienna's *Medizinische Wochenschrift,* he was forced to retire and his least able pupil, and the probable secret instigator of the plot to remove him, Johann Klein of the Salzburg obstetric hospital, was appointed as his successor.

Boër lived on for another 13 years and his *Textbook of Obstetrics,* a work of astonishing modernity, reached a third edition in 1834. It was to become Semmelweis's trusted work of reference and may have been partly responsible for drawing him towards obstetrics. The new reign of Klein was marked by one immediate and dramatic change: mortality figures from puerperal fever leapt from 0.5 to 7 per cent.

CHAPTER TWO

VIENNA

Universities and medical schools do not function in a vacuum. Vienna was the capital of an empire that in Semmelweis's day sprawled from Switzerland in the west to Turkey and the Ukraine in the east. What empire? Oddly perhaps, the political construct never acquired a settled name. Its constituent parts were bound together by neither geography nor nationality. Even the constitution of the parts varied. Later they were sometimes described as the lands of the Danube valley, but in Semmelweis's time they still included much of northern Italy, Polish Galicia, Bosnia, Bukovina and Bohemia, apart from the Austrian 'homelands' (not all of them in Austria) and the theoretically independent Kingdom of Hungary. Some of those were a long way from the Danube.

The imperial title originally referred to the crown of the Holy Roman Empire, which, with a brief interval (1740–45), had been passing from one Habsburg to the next since the sixteenth century. On the death of the Emperor Charles VI (Charles III as King of Hungary) in 1740, the Electors would not elect his daughter and only child, Maria Theresa, to succeed him.[35] For four years the only title she could rightly claim was Queen of Hungary, though her empire was certainly not the Hungarian Empire. She became Empress only by marriage to the greedy and randy Francis Stephen of Lotharingia (or Lorraine), who, as Francis I, was duly elected Holy Roman Emperor. In 1807 Napoleon demanded that Francis II, the grandson of Francis I and of Maria Theresa, relinquish the title so that he could refashion Germany in the Bonaparte mould. In time-honoured Habsburg fashion, Francis complied but reinvented himself as Francis I, Emperor of Austria. This too was something of a confidence trick. At best the empire was the empire of the House of Austria, not the Austrian Empire.[36]

In other countries dynasties were episodes in the history of a people. In the Habsburg Empire people were unwelcome complications in the history of the dynasty. In times past the dynasty could claim to have discharged many missions. In the sixteenth century it defended Europe against the Turks—or caused it to be defended by its allies.[37] In the seventeenth century it put a stop to Louis XIV's overweening ambitions to unify Europe under French tutelage. In the eighteenth century it patronised some of the ideas of the Enlightenment. By the beginning of the nineteenth century its only mission was to maintain its members in grandeur. Habsburg creativeness had had its last flicker with Boër's patron, Joseph II. After a brief interlude— Joseph's younger brother, Leopold II, reigned for only two years (1790–92)—he was succeeded by his nephew, Francis II (later Francis I as Emperor of Austria and Apostolic King of Hungary).

The new Emperor was a man of mediocre character and less than mediocre intelligence. Battered in youth by his clever uncle and in manhood by his formidable son-in-law, Napoleon,[38] after Napoleon's defeat in 1815 stubborn resistance to any change either in domestic or in foreign policy became his obsession. Comparatively benign provided that the status quo was not threatened, he would have made an admirable constitutional monarch in the British tradition. Unfortunately, thanks to his predecessors Maria Theresa and Joseph II, the Emperor of Austria had the means to make his will felt throughout the Empire. Francis had no will and left his bureaucracy without direction.[39] Or rather, he relied increasingly on his Foreign Minister and later Chancellor, Clemens Prince von Metternich, to govern in his name.

Metternich had emerged as a saviour in 1809, at the age of 36, at a time when Napoleon threatened the very existence of Austria. He had dominated the Congress of Vienna after Napoleon's fall in 1815. He continued to represent, even to personify, the Habsburg Empire until 1848. He was a German from the Rhineland, western European in upbringing and outlook and a belated rationalist.[40] He has often been portrayed as a rigid and hidebound upholder of the status quo. This is unfair. He delighted in constructing abstract systems of politics and remained convinced, as had been most abstract thinkers of the Age of Reason, of his infallibility. His diplomacy did in fact transform a ramshackle state with no obvious *raison d'être* into a European necessity, or what was perceived by the other powers of Europe as a necessity.[41] He was also fertile in new schemes and clever ideas of how the empire could be made viable and even prosperous as well as necessary.

Unfortunately, unlike Richelieu (with whom he was often compared in his lifetime) or Bismarck, he lacked the brutality to translate his scintillating *jeux d'esprit* into reality. For some decades after the slaughter and turmoil of the Napoleonic wars, he was also probably in tune with European sentiment. Most people wanted repose. This suited Metternich's natural inclination for procrastination. His misfortune was to outlive the post-Napoleonic generation. He was also handicapped by the fact that he could count on his Emperor's support only so long as any political change or manifestation of the *Zeitgeist* was mercilessly suppressed. Since 'political change' included any tampering with the traditional order of succession, on Francis's death in 1835 his eldest son duly succeeded him.[42] The new Emperor, Ferdinand (Ferdinand I as Emperor of Austria and Ferdinand V as King of Hungary),[43] who resided in the Hofburg and Schönbrunn during Semmelweis's stay in Vienna, was known as *der Trottel* (nincompoop) by his beloved Viennese. He was an imbecile, his character best expressed by his only sensible remark: 'I'm the Emperor and I want noodles.'[44]

Whoever occupied the throne, the Empire was a quintessential police state: even members of the imperial family had their correspondence read and censored. Every fifth Viennese adult was said to be a part-time police informer. In its defence, Habsburg tyranny was mitigated by traditional Austrian *Schlamperei* as well as by economic prosperity. (The latter was of course selective, favouring the towns and the high aristocracy, but these had always been the pillars of Habsburg rule.) There was one more benefit. Excluded from exercising any political influence, the modestly comfortable middle classes—and that included families like the Semmelweises of Buda—turned inward and created an intimate, pious and deliberately unambitious lifestyle. It was firmly based on 'traditional' family values, which, after much ridicule (like Victorian England), acquired a nostalgic appeal.

The Biedermeyer age was not a great artistic period, like the Florentine Renaissance or the French *fin de siècle*, but it possessed a modest charm.[45] It was comfortable rather than luxurious. It was sustained by solid rather than elegant craftsmanship. It was inspired by nature in its more placid moods. Storms, witches, cruel knights, rampaging beasts and natural cataclysms were never more popular—but only on the page, on canvas or on the clavier. Indoor flowers and curiously unchanging green plants requiring daily dusting became the emblems of the happy home.[46] Philosophy with its questioning, subversive overtones was suspect. Poetry was abundant but, unless turned into a *Lied*, painfully insipid.

All this mediocrity was redeemed by the blossoming of the least ideological of art forms. By the time Semmelweis arrived in Vienna, Schubert had been dead for ten years,[47] but this was still Schubert's city. His fame was beginning to spread from a small circle of friends to a wider audience; and his *Sehnsuchtswaltzer* was whistled in the streets as well as swooned over in the salons. He was not the only one. Schumann, Mendelssohn and Liszt did not live there but were frequent visitors. Chopin spent some of his happiest days in the city as houseguest of the doctor who had looked after the late Herr van Beethoven. There was lighter fare too. Lanner and the elder Johann Strauss had introduced the daring and seductive *Dreitakt* to polite society during the Congress of Vienna. ('Le Congrès ne marche pas, mais il danse,' was

Gentz's famous comment.) Semmelweis's stay coincided with the emergence of the younger Johann, 'Jeany' as he was known to all the *Mädl*. As a medical student and young doctor, the Hungarian was an enthusiastic dancer, and there is at least one reference in his letters home to 'my beloved fiddle'. The first performances of the *Gunstwerber Walzer* and the *Herzenslust Polka*, debuts of the amazing son and heir of the old *Walzerkönig*, would not have passed him by.

Of course, there was another side to this jollity. The Biedermeyer lifestyle was not cruel, but it firmly excluded anybody who offended against its ground rules. And whether the offence was wilful or due to misfortune, the way back in was difficult. Emil Gruber's *Vademecum*, which Semmelweis purchased on his arrival in the great city and which he carried around with him as, distinctly overawed, he explored the famous sights, informed its readers that the Inner City was surrounded by no less than 32 *Aussenbezirken* (suburbs); that it had over 9000 houses, many of them three- or four-storeyed; that it could boast 32 aristocratic palaces; that the houses and palaces were inhabited by 400,000 people 'noted for their cultivation, exquisite manners and captivating charm'; that the university had 2100 enrolled students; and that 700 registered fiacres plied their trade in the streets both by day and by night.[48]

What this invaluable tome did not mention was that the Kaiserstadt also provided a livelihood to 25,000 *registered* prostitutes and that it had about 1000 brothels catering for all tastes, some of them *de grand luxe* but many well within the means of an impecunious composer, piano teacher or medical student. There was a need for such amenities. Herr and Frau Bieder Meyer (like Herr Wieck in Dresden, Robert Schumann's future and unwilling father-in-law) would never entrust their daughters to young men of no fixed income and of uncertain prospects, however clever, charming and gifted. To live in settled sin with a partner, let alone several partners, would quickly lead to an irrevocable expulsion from Paradise. So what were young men of modest means to do? Fortunately, there was the ubiquitous and compliant 'other world', tacitly allowed if not necessarily approved of by Herr and Frau Bieder Meyer: it was indeed one of the not-so-secret prides and toasts of Vienna.

Unfortunately, safe sex was a mortal sin in a devoutly Catholic country and therefore expensive as well as complicated. Unsurprisingly, illegitimate births accounted for more than two-thirds of all *registered* births, and three-quarters of those admitted to the university lying-in hospital where Semmelweis was to discover the truth about puerperal fever were unmarried mothers. More fatefully, syphilis was rampant and difficult to detect, and it was incurable. This was the background to the mental illness that would strike down Robert Schumann 17 years after his marriage to his beloved Clara and Semmelweis 20-odd years after his carefree student days in Vienna.[49] Of course, in many cases the interval between infection and death was shorter—about eight to ten years in the case of Schubert—but then the immediate cause of death was almost certainly medical poisoning by an assortment of mercurial medicaments rather than the pallid spirochete itself.[50]

By the early 1840s there was also an unmistakable whiff of political and social change in the air: whether it was a whiff of menace or of hope depended on the whiffer's political affiliations. Perhaps it was sheer boredom, a more potent historical force than historians like to admit. Even in the Hofburg there was a dim realisation that progress—or at least a change of some kind—was an essential ingredient of history, and that sooner or later a system dedicated to its denial was bound to collapse.[51]

Semmelweis did not keep a diary and only a few, unrevealing letters home survive, but he shared lodgings in Vienna's cheerful student quarter in the Alser with an older friend and colleague from Pest, Ludwig von Markusovszky. Von Markusovszky, Marko to his Hungarian friends (who were many), would later recall their student days. While the two were obviously different in temperament, the older man already showing signs of the skilful medical politician he would later become, the pen portrait is vivid and credible:

> He [Semmelweis] was vigorous, kind and cheerful, sometimes even boisterous, but easily roused to anger if something offended his sense of justice and sometimes difficult to calm down. But even as a student he was too big-hearted to nurse grudges for long and he was entirely without malice or sides ... He had a big appetite and was a little portly even in his twenties but very nimble on his feet, a good dancer of the Czardas and the Ländler and a hard worker. He made up for his receding hairline by a luxuriant Magyar moustache of which he was very proud. He was exceedingly popular with the ladies ... more so than I ever was ... The ladies were also exceedingly popular with him. In short, he was a jolly companion, you could not wish for a better one.[52]

Of course, there was another and more serious side to him: at least his older friends—Skoda, Rokitansky, Hebra and the forensic scientist Jakob Kolletschka—all thought highly of him professionally. There was also his doctoral dissertation, a remarkable document despite the constraints of the genre. Written in literate, even poetic Latin, a testimony to the erudition of the Pious Fathers in Buda, *De vita plantarum genere* ('About the propagation of plants') is far removed from his later medical interests.[53] It is in fact a tribute to Valentin Jaquin, his professor of botany and a distinguished early classifier of the Alpine flora. In his Introduction the candidate expresses his awe at the prodigality of Nature, far surpassing the imagination of even the greatest artist or poet:

> To try and understand it all would be a futile labour of vanity and will always remain so. And yet man will not rest in his search for answers and explanations ... And most deeply, to find the link between matter and driving force, perhaps the same in different guises.[54]

Beyond the Baroque phrases there was clearly a superior intelligence at work: the message harks back to Greek philosophers like Heraclitus and Empedocles and looks forward to the twentieth century. The dissertation closes with ten theses that the candidate proposed to 'defend' in front of the faculty:

I. *Botanicae studium pro medico practico summi momenti*. (The study of plants must be the practising doctor's chief driving force.)

II. *Non dantur morbi intermittentes*. (There are no 'intermittent' diseases; a swipe against the then fashionable doctrine that tended to link all of a lifetime's diseases into a single but intermittent process.)

III. *Causam hydropis melius principiis mechanicis explicabis*. (Oedema is best explained by mechanical principles.)

IV. *Sine Opio et Mercurio nollem esse medicus*. (I would not like to be a doctor without opium and mercury.)

V. *Omnis medicus sit psychologus*. (Every doctor must be a psychologist.)

VI. *Fons floritionis medicinae modernae in Anatomia Pathologica quaerendus est*. (Morbid anatomy is the fount of the flowering of modern medicine.)

VII. *Viget in omnibus corporibus nisus conservationis*. (Self-preservation is alive in every living body.)

VIII. *Prognosis non de aegri, verum de Medici sorte decernit*. (Prognosis often foretells the fate of the doctor rather than of the patient.)

IX. *Nullum datur signum morbi pathognomicum*. (There is no sure single sign that indicates one particular illness.)

X. *Nullum venenum in manu Medici*. (Nothing is poison in a doctor's hand.)[55]

Only the last calls for additional comment: the candidate who was about to defend it would spend his professional life trying to disprove it. But that was in the future. On 4 April 1844 he successfully defended his thesis in front of the examining body of the faculty. It was an illustrious line-up, including Skoda, Josef Hyrtl, a great anatomist as well as a noted musician—his father was oboist in Haydn's orchestra in Eszterháza—surgeon Franz Schuh, Ludwig Türck, the first to use a form of laryngoscope, and Ernst Feuchtersleben, a noted poet (some of his verses were set to music by Brahms), as well as a pioneer psychiatrist. Skoda opened the proceedings by asking the candidate whether he intended to be a doctor or a poet. 'It would have confused me,' Semmelweis wrote to his parents, 'without the twinkle behind his thick spectacles. Later he [Skoda] told me that he thought my dissertation was more poetry than science but "none the worse for it".' Türck asked him if he intended to stay in Vienna. ' "For a time," I answered him. "But then I shall go back to Ofen [Buda in German]. That is my home and a better place." "Well, you cannot argue with a Hungarian," Türck commented not unkindly.'[56]

A few days after the examination he received his embossed invitation to the graduation ceremony. A day before the solemn proceedings news came from Buda that his mother was seriously ill. He rushed home, a two-day journey though he did it in one, without notifying the university. His absence, creating a few moments of awkward silence when his name was called, was noted 'mit Bedauern' by the official scribe. It was a trivial incident though not perhaps uncharacteristic. In clinical practice Semmelweis would always remain unhurried and meticulous, almost pedantic, but in private life he was often impetuous and impatient. (*Punch* had not yet invented the 'bedside manner' that he patently lacked.) His friends forgave him, ascribing his occasional curtness to his Magyar temperament. His enemies would sometimes use it as a stick.

Frau Theresa died a few days after his arrival home. Though she had been suffering from a heart complaint for some years, her passing was a blow. It was she who had held the family together. Her husband and the children—six of the latter were assembled around the grave—were desolate.[57] Ignác's younger brother, Paul, now an ordained priest living in Bratislava, gave the funeral oration; or would have done had he not broken down in tears.[58] A week later Semmelweis returned to Vienna and, on the last day of April, having tendered his abject apologies to the Rector Magnificus and obtained a personal testimonial from Rokitansky about his trustworthiness, he was duly presented with his medical diploma.

It seems that for a time he toyed with the idea of taking up general practice. He liked dealing with people on an intimate long-term basis and his patients had great faith in him. This might seem an anodyne statement impossible to verify; but both in Vienna and later in Pest he would always be his colleagues' first choice when the services of a gynaecologist or an accoucheur were needed in their own families. (This is still as good a measure as any of a medical man or woman's worth as a doctor as distinct from a medical scientist or a surgical technician.) In the event he was persuaded by Skoda, Hebra and Rokitansky that his vocation lay in some special field of investigation, requiring a sharp and enquiring mind, and that he should stay in Vienna. This would mean years of unpaid or poorly paid work and uncertain prospects. Without substantial private means, it ruled out settling down and starting a family for at least another five years.

After a walking holiday with 'my dear and wise friend Marko' (von Markusovszky) in the tranquillity of the lake district of Salzkammergut, Semmelweis decided to take the plunge. There still remained the choice of a speciality. Skoda had hoped that his young protégé could join him in his newly created department of chest medicine, but all the established posts were filled or 'reserved' for years ahead. (Skoda did not yet possess the clout that would conjure up supernumerary vacancies at his whispered word into the ear of the Empress.) Johann Klein, professor of obstetrics, was, despite his humble origins—his father was a village carpenter in Styria—a fashionable figure both in the medical world and in aristocratic circles. He was considered sound rather than brilliant, a good Catholic, a family man and a patriot for whichever Habsburg Emperor might be residing in the Hofburg. He was also a man of effusive Viennese charm: 'He never speaks ill of anybody except behind their backs,' Semmelweis's friend Franz von Arneth wrote of him later.[59] There were other attractions. Klein's son-in-law, Johann Chiari, was already first assistant in his father-in-law's clinic.[60] He was only a year older than Semmelweis and the two were close friends. This was probably the decisive consideration. In August 1844, after two months of book-bashing, Semmelweis passed his examination for the degree of Master of Midwifery and applied for the post of aspirant in Klein's clinic. It is not known what the competition was, but he was appointed.

To be an aspirant in a university clinic was the lowest rung on the academic ladder. While the job was unpaid, if the holder performed to the professor's satisfaction he would be promoted to assistant in a year or two when the term of the current holder, Gustav Breit, had run out. In some keenly sought-after departments the unpaid stint lasted longer, but Klein's clinic was not one of them. By modern standards it was huge, eight intercommunicating wards of twenty beds each, occupying a crevice in the vast and sprawling Allgemeines Krankenhaus between the fever hospital and the surgical department. It had been built about ten years earlier to modern specifications. Each ward had ten windows about two metres above ground. This was considered sufficient to prevent patients jumping out into the courtyard three floors below and damaging the old plane trees there. It was also sufficient to ensure that the windows would never actually be opened. Ventilation was obtained by the intercommunicating doors being left open. The infants slept with their mothers. The lavatories at the end of each ward were open to prevent infanticide, though surrounded by a grill to prevent users from being molested.

A medical staff of four was assigned to look after the patients and to staff the delivery ward and operating theatre. This included the professor, whose attendance was erratic. Klein had one of the largest private practices in Vienna. On the other hand, 20 to 30 medical students assisted the doctors and about half that number of unpaid foreign postgraduates. They had came to gain experience in what was the largest obstetric unit in Europe. The official daily routine of the aspirant would start at eight o'clock with preparation for the round of the first assistant and for the more stately progression of the professor and his *Schlepp* later in the day.

By then and by special arrangement, Semmelweis had already spent an hour or two in Rokitansky's laboratory and dissection room. He was to refer to this in a brief but poignant passage in his book published years later. Hurrying from dissecting room to the wards, 'how often must I have carried infection and death to my patients'.[61] Later in the day he would assist at deliveries and operations. He was on emergency duty at night on take days three times a week. (His tiny room next to the lying-in ward, barely more than a broom cupboard, could hardly have afforded him much sleep even when he was not needed on the wards.) There were no statutory holidays from a post in a university clinic: time off depended on the whim and goodwill of the professor. In Klein's case the whims were there but the goodwill was usually lacking. (But in Austria religious feast days were numerous and strictly observed: it was one field where Joseph II's efforts to modernise the country had dismally failed.) Yet somehow Semmelweis found time to study for the surgical specialist examination, and in December 1844 he obtained the separate surgical doctorate.

He may have considered changing his speciality, though he was deterred by the horrors he had witnessed in the celebrated Professor Lauthof's department. Rokitansky summed it up a few years later as: 'Diagnosis, Operation, Death, Dissection.'[62] On Breit's appointment to a post in Graz in July 1846, Semmelweis was promoted to provisional assistant, third in the departmental pecking order. The appointment would have to be regularly renewed; but it was—or seemed to be—a beginning.

Apart from the clinical work, there were many problems in obstetrics to occupy the aspirant's and later the assistant's mind. There was the painful mastitis of the lactating breast, the 'impetigo' of new-born infants, the babies' 'summer diarrhoea' and the indications for the use of a forceps. But one problem above all was to obsess Semmelweis more and more with every passing week. It would continue to engage not only his mind but also his deepest emotions for the rest of his life.

CHAPTER THREE

CHILDBED FEVER

Outbreaks of puerperal or childbed fever had been recognised and occasionally described since the seventeenth century. Epidemics—or what were generally referred to as epidemics—had swept through Leipzig in 1652 and 1665, Copenhagen in 1672 and Frankfurt in 1732.[63] There were several major outbreaks at the Hôtel Dieu in Paris as well as in Rouen and Caen in the early years of the eighteenth century. The disease occasionally struck British lying-in hospitals: Alexander Gordon of Aberdeen wrote of one in which 'none who were seized with it survived' and mentioned another, lasting 32 months in a London lying-in hospital in the 1750s, in which 'almost all who contracted the fever died'.[64] As for the nature of the illness, Charles Meigs, professor of obstetrics and diseases of women at Jefferson College in Philadelphia, warned his students in 1848:

> There is a word of fear that I shall pronounce when I utter the name Puerperal Fever; for there is almost no acute illness that is more terrible than this—no, not even smallpox ... There is something unbearable in the tormented death of a woman who had recently given birth to her child ... It is a sort of desecration. And the suffering is indescribable.[65]

Forty years later Jacques-Francois-Edouard Hervieux wrote:

> Epidemic puerperal fever is to women what war is to men. Like war, it cuts down the healthiest, bravest, and most

essential part of the population; like war, its victims are in the prime of their lives.[66]

The illness most commonly started two or three days after delivery, though in premature rupture of the membranes it could start even before delivery. Very rarely it occurred outside pregnancy, and one such occasion later served Semmelweis as a pointer to the true aetiology of the disease. He was assisting Chiari in the removal of a benign tumour, probably a fibroid, extruding from the uterine cervix of a middle-aged woman.[67] Chiari performed the enucleation with his usual dexterity and received the plaudits of the students around the operating table as well as the congratulations of his friend and assistant. Two days later the patient started a fever, three days later she was raving, four days later she was dead. What had killed her was plainly 'childbed fever', but without the childbed. The anomaly was explained by both Chiari and Semmelweis in terms of the 'dense miasma' that had come to pervade the entire clinic. Neither of them truly believed it. 'What was this miasma nobody could see, hear or smell?' Semmelweis wrote later. 'It was a terrible figment.'[68]

Whatever the cause, death was often dreadfully swift and appallingly distressing. A woman could be delivered on Monday, happy and well with her newborn baby on Tuesday, feverish and ill by Wednesday evening, delirious and in agony with peritonitis on Thursday, and dead on Friday. 'You see, gentlemen,' Meigs wrote,

> you must not be surprised or astonished when, after leaving your patient at ten o'clock in the evening happy and smiling, you find her at six in the morning a prey to the most unspeakable disorder of the nervous system, the circulation and the respiration.[69]

By and large, the earlier after delivery the fever struck, the faster and the more certain was the outcome. The infection, once it gained entry to the uterus, could spread to the pelvic tissues and general peritoneal cavity within hours. Arteries and veins thrombosed. Deprived of their blood supply, tissues necrosed. Dead tissue provided the ideal culture medium for pus-forming organisms. The immediate cause of death was either general septicaemia—that is, blood poisoning—or peritonitis, or a combination of the two. Death from general septicaemia was slightly more merciful because it often quickly led to coma. Those dying of peritonitis suffered not only pain, unresponsive sometimes even to opium, but also unspeakable terror. Alexander Gordon spoke with obvious feeling of the

> torture of puerperal peritonitis, so excruciating that I would call it anybody's worst nightmare and patients prayed to die quickly ... Then suddenly and mercifully the pain and rigidity would cease and the patient became preternaturally calm. This was often greeted with relief by the family but it was usually the harbinger of death within an hour or less.[70]

William Leishman, in his classic *System of Midwifery*, described the course of the illness in slightly more dispassionate clinical terms:

> The belly swells and becomes tense and drumlike ... so that the patient can now no longer bear even the pressure of the bedclothes ... Low muttering delirium sets in ... Hiccups, picking of the bedcloths, loud delirium and fits or coma are the common immediate precursors of death.[71]

It is a measure of the terror the disease inspired that, when it first attracted Semmelweis's interest, several monographs devoted to it were already in circulation in Vienna and a stream of learned papers clamoured for attention. Besides the terror, such a plethora of words, many of them fiercely polemical, also reflected the ignorance that continued to surround aetiology— that is, causation—and management. Most textbooks broadly divided the 'causative factors' into external and internal, though they differed sharply in the relative emphasis they laid on the two groups. External influences were generally favoured in

German-speaking countries and included not only such relatively comprehensible terms as the weather, moisture and the 'general atmosphere', but also mysterious influences under such headings as miasmas and 'cosmic' and 'telluric' emanations. These had the merit not only of sounding impressive: they were also inescapable, or at least beyond the bounds of responsibility of mere earthlings. Klein in his first submission to the Imperial Commission of Enquiry into the Prevalence of Childbed Fever in the First Obstetric Clinic of the Allgemeines Krankenhaus spoke 'at length and learnedly about the possible sources of telluric radiations, akin but not identical with lunar influences'. The unnamed scribe of the report was clearly unable to grasp the details of the discourse, or at least was unable commit its mental nebulae to paper.

In the category of 'internal factors' many explanations confused cause and effect. A popular belief was that the fever was partly at least the result of 'lochial suppression'. Lochia is the term given to the normal discharge from the womb during the first week or two after delivery and in puerperal fever this was usually scanty. This was the result of the infection, not the cause of it. Nevertheless, most textbooks devoted whole chapters to it and complicated prescriptions, often containing 50 or more ingredients, some unknown or incomprehensible today, designed as 'lochial stimulants', were a recognised remedy.

Another cart-before-the-horse explanation, especially popular in Vienna, was the abnormal accumulation of milk inside the body due to some mysterious blockage of the glandular canals in the breast. There was, as Laennec had pointed out in 1801, no anatomical or other evidence for this.[72] Whatever the dirty white precipitate was, it was not milk, clotted or otherwise. Yet in Albert von Mouralt's three-volume textbook, first published in 1828 and widely used in Semmelweis's day, separate and lengthy chapters were devoted to 'milk meningitis', 'milk pneumonia' and 'milk peritonitis', all allegedly distinct variants of puerperal fever.[73] The conditions were not only described but also illustrated with artistic engravings. Obviously with hindsight—but Laennec and presumably others had clearly recognised this 25 years earlier—what von Mouralt and his disciples saw was pus, not 'altered milk'. (Medical self-deception can conquer everything. In 1928 the layer of tuberculous pus that floated on top of most bottled milk delivered to the houses of Edinburgh was described by the city's medical officer of health as 'wholesome cream from our world-famous healthy Scottish cows'.) For some years the milk hypothesis was embraced with ardour by Klein, perhaps because it was another pointer to the tragic 'untreatability' of the disease.

Similar misconceptions fuelled Rokitansky's elaborate explanation based on blood Krasis. He suggested that the fibrin and fibrinous deposits found at necropsy had been the cause rather than the result of the inflammation. Other obstetricians believed in obscurely predisposing 'gastro-bilious conditions', whatever that meant; and French obstetricians, like Etienne de Candolle of Strasbourg, muttered darkly about the liver and an excess of green bile. Long before modern psychobabble and notions of psychosomatic diseases, most obstetric textbooks gave due prominence to such powerful 'contributory aetiological factors' as fear and shame, especially in unwed mothers.

This is not to say that practical observations and inspired guesswork did not on occasion point in the direction of the truth long before Semmelweis. No great medical discovery is entirely without antecedents and, however tentative, they deserve to be remembered. In his popular textbook, *A Treatise on the Management of Pregnant and Lying-in Women and the Means of Curing, More Especially Preventing, the Principal Disorders to Which They Are Liable*, Dr Charles White of Manchester was on the right track when in 1773 he attributed puerperal fever to 'putrid and excrementous matter' passing from the lower intestine of pregnant mothers to the womb.[74] Even if he guessed wrongly about the source and route of the infection, his doctrine led him to advocate loose-fitting comfortable clothing, open windows, clean air and correct posture for the passage of stools and lochia. This was in sharp contrast to what he described as the

> common practice both in England and in many countries on
> the Continent of Europe ... where women in labour are
> confined in a small, unventilated room, filled with their
> friends [to give them moral support] ... A large fire brings
> the temperature to an almost unendurable height and
> further discomfort is produced by an attendant pouring
> into the woman in labour numerous warm alcoholic drinks
> to diminish her pains if too strong and to increase them if too
> weak.[75]

The delivery over, the woman would be covered with
additional blankets, the bed curtains would be pinned together
around her and every crevice that might let in fresh air would
be sealed. The diet of warm liquors would be continued to the
exclusion of everything else. Among the poor living in cellars
White described even worse conditions, with dampness, dirt and
vermin aggravating the heat. Garrets were no better, for the
patients there were subjected to 'the putrid miasmata of all the
families living below'.

Once the disease had developed, White's treatment was
surprisingly modern. He had the patient placed in a semi-
recumbent position and ordered mild antiseptic douches. He
stipulated that women in fever should be given separate rooms
for the safety of other patients as much as for their own comfort.
As soon as they recovered (or succumbed), the room would be
thoroughly cleansed, the bedding and curtains would be washed
and the floor would be wiped with vinegar. The 'healthfulness of
the room would be increased if it were stoved with brimstone'.
But, though in many ways admirable, White did not even
mention the possibility that the source of the infection might
be the hands of those attending the woman in labour, and
he continued to be an advocate of bleeding and purgation as
'preventive measures' for most disorders of pregnancy.

According to A. Hirsch's massive text of geographical
pathology, the idea that puerperal fever could be carried by

doctors or midwives from one woman in labour to another was first suggested by Denman in the second edition of his *Introduction to the Practice of Midwifery* in 1788,[76] though no later textbook refers to this. Conclusive—or what should have been conclusive but was not—evidence of contagion spreading from mother to mother by a birth attendant was first published by Alexander Gordon of Aberdeen in 1795.

Gordon, the son of a tenant farmer, studied medicine in Aberdeen, Edinburgh and probably Leyden, and served as a naval surgeon from 1780 to 1785. He then started practice in Aberdeen. Puerperal fever had apparently been unknown there until 1789 when a severe outbreak began on Christmas Day and lasted, with intermissions, for over two years. At first the fever was thought to be no more than the common ailment known as 'Weed', for which the accepted and effective remedy was the regular imbibing of cordials; but Gordon, who had seen an epidemic of puerperal fever in London, soon recognised it for what it was. By making careful and detailed notes—a model epidemiological study—he made the crucial observation that the disease was confined to the practice of a minority of midwives and doctors. To his distress he found that he himself was among those who had at times carried the infection from one woman to another. By the end of two years he concluded that evidence that the fever was spread by birth attendants was irrefutable:

> The disease seized only such women who were visited or delivered by a practitioner or midwife who had previously attended patients with the disease. Every new patient attended by these was later seized by the disease.[77]

Gordon also showed that the dread fever was sometimes linked to erysipelas, a then common skin infection.[78] Sadly, he also came to the conclusion that the only possible treatment was massive bleeding and purging. This, he lamented, was 'repugnant to popular opinion' and, coupled with his honest but devastating admission of having spread the infection himself, popular repugnance sealed his career in the town. Hurt by the 'ungenerous treatment' he received from the women of Aberdeen, he left the city to rejoin the Navy. There he contracted pulmonary tuberculosis within a year, was invalided out and died young.[79]

Modern historical research has unearthed other accounts similar to Gordon's, though not quite so detailed and conclusive. Describing an epidemic, Dr Armstrong of Sunderland noted 'that in whatever place the fever occurred, it was principally limited to one accoucheur in that place'.[80] Starting in the spring of 1824, cases of both erysipelas and puerperal fever began to appear together. At first only a few, the epidemic quickly reached a peak in the spring of 1814 'when cases of puerperal fever began to appear thirty-six to forty-eight hours after delivery' and 'nearly all the cases were fatal'. Armstrong also noticed that 'while many cases occurred in some villages, other adjoining villages were totally free'.

John Roberton of Manchester found in 1831, when he described a somewhat similar epidemic, that the first 16 cases— all of whom died—were confined to the practice of one midwife and none occurred in the practice of the other 24.[81] In the same year Edward Blackmore reported an epidemic in Plymouth in which one practitioner had 18 cases in rapid succession while the other practitioner in the town had none.[82] Thomas West, a surgeon apothecary, described an epidemic that started with a few cases of both puerperal fever and erysipelas in the spring of 1813 and reached a terrible peak a year later. Here too the fever generally started 36 to 48 hours after delivery (that is, early) and nearly all the cases were fatal. None of the neighbouring villages was affected and the epidemic abated as suddenly and as mysteriously as it had started.[83]

Robert Lee, a successful London obstetrician and textbook writer, had no doubt that the fever occurred mainly in institutions.[84] William Campbell of Edinburgh described how

in October 1821, I assisted at the dissection of a woman who died of puerperal fever after an abortion. I removed the pelvic viscera and carried them in my pocket to show them to my classroom. The same evening I attended a delivery of a poor woman in Canongate without changing my clothes. She died. Next morning, without changing my clothes, I went to assist my pupil engaged with a woman in Bridwell. She also died.[85]

By the 1830s, it was fairly widely suspected in England—less so on the Continent—that puerperal fever could occasionally be spread by the birth attendant and that the danger could be mitigated, though not eliminated, by frequent and complete changes of clothing. 'That the fever may occur spontaneously, I admit,' James Blundell wrote in 1834,

> that its infectious character may be plausibly disputed I do not deny ... but in my own family I had rather that those I esteemed most be delivered in a stable with nobody at the manger-side than that they should receive the best help in the fairest apartment but exposed to the vapours of the pitiless disease.[86]

Robert Collins, Master of Dublin's famous Rotunda Hospital, probably gave the best account before Semmelweis of practical measures that could be effective. When he entered the hospital in 1829, puerperal fever was raging. Conditions in fact must have been not dissimilar to those prevailing in Klein's clinic when Semmelweis assumed the post as first assistant. In desperation Collins had all the rooms in the hospital evacuated in turn and filled them with nascent chlorine gas for 48 hours with all the openings sealed. The walls and floors were treated with chloride of lime in the form of a paste. The woodwork was painted and the walls and ceilings washed down with fresh lime. Blankets and other articles of bedding were treated with dry heat in a stove. The epidemic was controlled and there were no more cases of puerperal fever for five years. None of this was published, 'lest details of the terrible epidemic, which might indeed recur, might cause alarm'. Also, Collins had no clear idea of what he had accomplished and was probably worried that the expenses incurred by his drastic measures might be censured by the hospital authorities as extravagant. The event was excavated from the records eight years later.[87]

The 'forerunner' of Semmelweis most often mentioned in medical history books is the doctor, poet, wit and man of letters Oliver Wendell Holmes. In the summer of 1842, at the age of 33, he attended a meeting of the Boston Society for Medical Improvement where Dr Condie, the senior member of the Philadelphia group of physicians, begged leave to report on cases of puerperal fever in the practices of some doctors.

> This particularly insidious and malign disease has been found to occur alike in the middle-aged and the young, the robust and the delicate, in those afforded every attention and the destitute, in those who were confined for the first time and those who had had many children, and after the most rapid as well as after the most protracted labours.[88]

Dr Condie did not believe that the fever was contagious, but he noted the extraordinary circumstance that 'the disease was confined to the practice of a single physician, a Fellow of this College, extensively engaged in obstetric practice'. The person he was referring to was a Dr Rutter, by all accounts a competent doctor, as skilled in obstetrics as any in Philadelphia. During the 1840s he found that, for no apparent reason, every woman he delivered developed puerperal fever. Many of them (about 75 percent, in fact) died. The effect on his reputation and practice can be imagined and Dr Condie hastened to express his sympathy. Much distressed, Dr Rutter stopped practising and quarantined himself. He shaved his head and face. He changed his clothing and all his equipment, down to the pencil he carried for making notes. 'Yet the puerperal fever still followed him wherever he went, till, worn out and dispirited, he left Philadelphia.'[89]

Sitting in the audience, Holmes's curiosity was aroused and he decided to study the matter for himself. The result was his famous paper, 'The Contagiousness of Puerperal Fever', which he presented to the Boston Society for Medical Improvement on 13 February 1843. He was a relatively obscure young doctor who freely admitted that he had hardly seen a case of puerperal fever. The ones he had seen he had not studied in any depth. His conclusions were based entirely on a careful reading of the literature (in four languages). He was a voracious peruser of print and he marshalled his material with skill. In addition to Dr Rutter, he cited the case of a village practitioner, a Dr Jackson. Dr Jackson too suffered a spate of successive deliveries followed by puerperal fever. Women who had booked for their delivery now removed themselves from within his reach; many sent for physicians residing over 50 miles away. These women all did well. Jackson's patients continued to die.

Another, a Dr Storer of Boston, seems partly to have anticipated some of Semmelweis's discoveries by a few years, though he never himself published his findings. Following an experience similar to that of Dr Jackson, being dogged by puerperal fever in his patients, he decided to wash his hands routinely after each delivery with a solution of chloride of lime. He then attended seven women in succession, none of whom developed puerperal fever.[90]

Most remarkable perhaps was Holmes's perception of the dangers of contact with the post-mortem room:

> It seems proper to allude to the dangerous and often fatal effects which have followed wounds received in the post-mortem examination of patients who had died of puerperal fever ... A moment's reflection will show that the number of bodies who have perished from puerperal fever is vastly lower than those who have succumbed to other fatal diseases such as typhus, or pneumonia ... The conclusion is irresistible that a most fearful morbid poison is often generated in the course of the disease which lingers on after death.

Holmes may have thought that his conclusion was irresistible, but nothing is more resistible in clinical practice than the obvious. Indeed, his ideas did not even arouse a storm of protest, as some later writers seem to imply. He was simply ignored. Reviews of the literature in themselves and speculations based on other people's experience, however persuasive in themselves, tend to be brushed aside by those in actual practice. The reaction is often justified. Reviews can be selective and as misleading as selective quotations from the Bible. Holmes had quoted from the experience of physicians in London, Dublin and Paris, while he had admitted that he had had virtually none himself. His only comment to arouse fury was the suggestion that any physician who found that he had a series of three or more cases of puerperal fever when others had none should conclude that he was a carrier of contagion and conduct himself accordingly. This, coming from a tyro, was an outrage.

Holmes went on to cultivate and adorn other fields.[91] In 1845 he was appointed Parkman Professor of Anatomy and Physiology in the Medical School of Harvard University—'a settee rather than a Chair'—but he did publish one even more provocative paper on puerperal fever eight years later. Disgusted by the fact that, despite his warnings and the 'obvious' truth of his earlier utterances, the illness continued unchecked in several institutions and practices, he expressed the opinion that

> the time has come when the existence of a *private pestilence* in the practice of a single physician should be looked upon not as a misfortune but as a crime; and in the knowledge of such occurrences, the duties of the practitioner to his profession should give way to his paramount obligation to society.[92]

His use of the word 'crime' was too much for Charles Meigs, who, at the age of 51, was an experienced and careful obstetrician with a large practice and a popular teacher. He regarded Holmes as a bumptious pen-pusher and took deep offence at the suggestion that he or any of his colleagues should be labelled common criminals. To his dying day he would deny that puerperal fever was a contagious disease, and in old age his reputation suffered as a result. But Holmes did not pursue the matter either. By the time he published his last paper, his success as a wit and man of letters had established him as a medical thinker rather than as a clinical doer, and his advanced views had no impact on obstetric practice. He died in 1894, aged 85, honoured for his literary accomplishments rather than for his prophetic clinical insights.

None of these papers, even those published in the 1830s and 1840s, were in journals widely read on the Continent of Europe. Transactions of a learned society in Boston would certainly not be daily fare in Vienna. Nor, of course, were the papers more than interesting 'case reports'—and interesting only in retrospect. None of the literature in German and Latin that *was* accessible in Vienna referred to them. Even in England and Ireland Gordon was soon forgotten (or remembered for the wrong reason as an advocate of blood-letting) and Oliver Wendell Holmes was not rediscovered for another 30 years.

Semmelweis was meticulous in acknowledging intellectual debts: whatever his weaknesses, a concern with 'primacy' was not among them. Indeed, any hint of support from earlier observers would have been welcome. None of the precursor papers mentioned here was ever mentioned by him. Apart from White's textbook, which had been translated into German and which he may have read, he was almost certainly unaware of them. He did nevertheless hope to travel and, perhaps under the lingering influence of Boër, he planned to visit England and Ireland. During his period of unemployment he even started to learn English. Nothing ever came of these plans: he never ventured beyond the frontiers of the Habsburg Monarchy.

CHAPTER FOUR

QUEST

The reasons for calling Klein's department the *First* Obstetric Clinic dated back to the late 1830s. On Boër's forced retirement, the Imperial Ministry of Education, which exercised tight control over all university hospitals, decided to split the old lying-in hospital in the Allgemeines Krankenhaus into two. One division was to be mainly staffed by doctors and would concentrate on training medical students and postgraduates. The other would have a medical professor, but would be concerned with training midwives. No reason was given for the split and no certain reason is known today.

The move may have been prompted by spite. Throughout his active life Boër had passionately opposed such a division, arguing, not unreasonably, that so far as he could see the delivery of a baby by a midwife was not a procedure fundamentally different from the delivery of a baby by an obstetrician. The Vienna Medical School under Maria Theresa and Joseph II had pioneered the specialist training of midwives and was almost a century ahead (in this respect as in many others) of most medical centres in Europe.[93] Boër feared that splitting the service into two would create two tiers of care and would leave the midwives' division trailing behind. This, he argued, would damage the midwives' professional status. Since the vast majority of births in the empire were conducted by midwives, this could have dire consequences.

Klein of course supported the division, provided that his department was to be named the First Clinic (*Erste Abteilung*)— the subject of a lengthy memorandum from him—and provided that it would be the one concerned with training doctors and medical students. (He had a low opinion of midwives.) He also stipulated that his division should be accommodated in new and up-to-date premises, while the midwives' division should remain in what Klein described as Boër's 'serviceable but somewhat obsolete accommodation'. Despite these disadvantages, one of Klein's former assistants in Salzburg, Theodore Bartsch, a somewhat withdrawn scholarly individual whose main interest was in Byzantine church architecture, readily accepted the second professorship. Klein also insisted—once again successfully—that the 'Secret Department' (*Geheime Division*, about 12 beds) reserved for paying patients, should remain entirely under his control.

The document outlining the organisational reform was dated 1840, but nothing was ever done in a hurry in Vienna and the divisions were not actually separated until four years later. Within a month of young Semmelweis taking up his appointment as aspirant, however, his that is, Klein's—clinic moved into its new wards, while Bartsch was assigned Boër's old beds. In fact, the two divisions remained adjacent, sharing an anteroom. However, the training of midwives and doctors was formally divorced. The effect was stunning—and one of the decisive influences in Semmelweis's life—but was the very opposite to what Boër had feared and Klein had perhaps hoped.

Even before the formal separation, mortality from puerperal fever was high in both clinics compared to what it had been under Boër: in Klein's half it was on the average 6.56 per cent and in Bartsch's half 5.58 per cent. Within six month of the separation the mortality in Bartsch's second clinic, as it was now called, now entirely staffed by midwives, had sunk to 3.38 per cent. Over the same period mortality in Klein's first clinic had risen to a catastrophic 9.92 per cent. But even that was catastrophic only compared to the past, not the future. Within another year the mortality rate in childbirth (almost entirely accounted for by puerperal fever) sank to just under 3 per cent in the midwives' division and rose to a nearly unbelievable 18 per cent in the doctors' division. This was almost as high as the peak mortality in the Paris Maternité during the epidemic of the early 1820s, still widely referred to in textbooks as the worst disaster in modern obstetric history.[94]

This was not a development that could be kept under wraps and soon it was the talk of Vienna. Though the actual figures were only published by Semmelweis much later, in the public mind lack of precise information exaggerated rather than camouflaged the truth. Not that it needed exaggeration. The unvarnished facts were that women admitted to the lying-in hospital over the 24-hour periods starting on Mondays, Wednesdays and Fridays at 4 p.m. had a one-in-thirty chance of never leaving the hospital alive, a sad but 'acceptable' figure, whereas of women admitted on Tuesday, Thursdays, Saturdays and Sundays (the last day added to the 'doctors' rota' at the ministry's insistence), one in six and later one in five died a horrible death.

If the search for the cause and mechanism of childbed fever was intense even before the 1840s, it now became a sensational issue exercising lay as well as medical minds. Childbirth was, after all, not an esoteric event incomprehensible to ordinary folk. Even if most women admitted to the Krankenhaus were 'common people', and indeed many were known to be fallen women 'off the street', a tenfold difference in mortality between two adjacent divisions was an intolerable provocation.

Semmelweis, who was now part of the team looking after the first clinic, felt deeply and personally involved. It drove him to distraction. Nowhere has his search for an explanation been better described (without any retrospective self-pity) than in the book he published almost ten years later, and it is impossible not to quote from it at some length. To the most widely touted theory that the fever was the result of adverse cosmic-atmospheric-telluric conditions, he replied:

Now if the atmospheric-cosmic-telluric conditions of the City of Vienna were so malignly disposed as to cause a deadly illness in women in childbirth, how does it happen that these atmospheric-cosmic-telluric conditions over such a long period have carried off mothers in the first clinic while mothers in the same city, indeed in the same building and next door to the second clinic, have mostly been spared? Surely if the terrible illness in the first clinic is due to some mysterious 'external epidemic', then the same 'epidemic' would have to affect the second clinic too. Since mothers are admitted to the two clinics on alternate days, such an epidemic would also have to operate only every second day ... But even if one did accept such a manifest absurdity, it would not explain the different mortality. The 'epidemic' influences would have to work on the prospective mother either before her admission or during her stay. If before, it would have to affect those seeking admission to the first clinic as well as those admitted to the second clinic. If the pernicious 'epidemic' began after admission, then again there could be no difference in mortality between two clinics which are so close to each other that they share an anteroom. These and similar considerations forced on me the unshakeable conviction that outside 'epidemic' influences could not cause a devastation in one but not in the other clinic.[95]

These were not sentiments that would endear Semmelweis to Klein, but there is no evidence that at this stage the professor had conceived his later intense antipathy for his assistant. The professor himself could not be blamed: that was obvious. In confidence he could—and did—proudly point out that among his private patients mortality from puerperal fever was less than 1 per cent. The Fürstin Liechtenstein and the Countess Harrach had no reason to fear consulting him. Yet the situation in the Krankenhaus was getting desperate. Women would go to any lengths to escape from being admitted to the dreaded first clinic. When the days of the admission rota were secretly changed and the fact became known, harrowing scenes were enacted in the corridors. Women in the first stage of labour would run screaming from the building. Others were writhing in agony on the floor but refused to be carried into the wards. Family, friends and hospital staff were locked in fisticuffs.

This was not something that the ministry could ignore, especially since it had been largely responsible for splitting the old lying-in hospital in the first place. The minister, Baron Landolf, a recent Metternich appointee and not averse to blackening the record of his immediate predecessor, summoned the vice-director of the University Medical Faculty, Feuchtersleben, effectively the executive head of all university clinics in Vienna, for urgent consultation.

Feuchtersleben confessed himself to be as baffled as was everybody else. Of course, had the statistics moved in the opposite direction, as Boër had predicted, the explanation would have been simple. Any number of reasons could have been held to account for the difference. It was well known that, instead of learning their craft on dead bodies, as did the doctors and medical students, midwives were constrained by imperial decree dating back to the reign of the Empress Maria Theresa, to learn and practise on so-called phantoms. Some of these, it is true, were wonderfully executed coloured wax or porcelain models (as distinct from ordinary painted leather ones) of the female genitalia at different stages of pregnancy and in labour,[96] but they could not be expected to instil the same superior skills that bodies—dead, admittedly, but still usually in quite early stages of decomposition—allowed medical students and doctors to acquire.

Another reason one might have expected the midwives' clinic to lag behind that of the doctors' was the strict banishment of all women from the post-mortem room. Professor Rokitansky never tired from saying—and he had no more admiring a disciple than Semmelweis—that a thorough understanding of pathology was the key to good clinical practice, and that a thorough understanding could be gained only from the diligent dissection of dead bodies. Klein himself was lukewarm about this (as he was about most modern claptrap) and he never went near the mortuary, but both Chiari and Semmelweis urged students and postgraduates to check their clinical knowledge in the post-mortem room as often as possible and not only to watch the pathologist at work but also to participate in the autopsy. All this made sense—except that 'sense' (as so often in medicine) was starkly contradicted by the facts. It was not Bartsch's underprivileged second clinic that turned out disastrous figures but Klein's privileged first.

An examining commission was quickly assembled by the imperial ministry, as weird as such instant assemblages usually are. There was only one obstetrician among the members, a retired professor from Laibach with time on his hands. The rest were two civil servants from the Ministry of Agriculture, Count Thurn, much loved for his charitable work among the prostitutes of Vienna but with no medical background or knowledge of obstetrics whatever, a pathologist, a general practitioner from Linz and a canon of St Stephen's Cathedral, representing the Cardinal Archbishop of Vienna. They walked round the wards, interviewed a few mothers, watched a young woman in the last stages of puerperal fever ('a disturbing experience') and, above all, listened to Professor Klein's 'lucid exposition of the known facts relating to this terrible disease'.

The commission then quickly produced the answer; indeed, it produced not one answer but several. This, in such situations, is a sure sign of intellectual bankruptcy. First among its findings was that the 'epidemic' was largely the fault of the foreign students. These had been admitted in rather greater numbers to Professor Klein's clinic than had perhaps been wise. The commission did of course appreciate the renown that the clinic had achieved all over Europe, it was a reflection of Professor Klein's international stature,[97] but some of the foreign doctors the commission had encountered (or, if not actually encountered, glimpsed lurking in the background) seemed very rough fellows indeed. Their kind should not be allowed to practise on the delicate women of Vienna, however far fallen they were. The commission recommended that their number should be reduced to a maximum of 24. It also endorsed the concern of Canon Gasthammer. The Canon had noted that, whereas midwives were strictly supervised by the chief midwife in observing the rules of baptism at various stages of labour, including the proper wording when two heads of conjoined twins presented simultaneously, the doctors and especially, once again, foreign visitors, were often remiss in this duty.[98] Professor Klein himself expressed dismay at this revelation and undertook to remedy the deficiency.

The epidemic raged on. It was now almost impossible to persuade women to enter the hospital. Why should they? The vast majority of births in Vienna, as elsewhere in the Empire, took place at home. The difficulty this might create for a teaching hospital had been appreciated by Anton Stoerck, a great figure of the First Viennese School of Medicine and founder of the University Obstetric Service. The answer was the bait dangled in front of prospective mothers by the Theresianum Foundling Hospital attached to the Krankenhaus. In return for offering themselves for teaching purposes and later for acting as wet nurses for a period of two or three months, women giving birth to their children in the University Obstetric Clinic could by right hand over their babies to the care of the Foundling Hospital. This initially was a great draw: the only alternatives in many cases— the abandonment of the newborn or infanticide—were criminal offences that could carry the death penalty. Nevertheless, the draw only functioned if it did not threaten the mother's life even more than the law.

There was one tenuous escape route: the so-called *Gassengeburte* or street births. If labour began on the way to the hospital (as shown by the freshness of the state of the umbilical cord) and the mother was brought in from the street with the baby already born, then the birth qualified as a hospital delivery. It quickly emerged—one more puzzle in the terrible mystery of the epidemic—that these street births were relatively immune to puerperal fever. They were also comparatively easy to simulate. What had to be done was to have the baby born at home, have a carriage waiting, drive post-haste to the Krankenhaus and then pretend that the baby had emerged on the way, effectively 'in the street'. The ruse did not go undiscovered: statistics quickly showed that on four days of the week (but not on the other three when admission was to the midwives' clinic) the percentage of *Gassengeburte* rose from 4 to 35 per cent.

Semmelweis was not concerned with such irregularities, but the comparatively low death rate among those giving birth outside the hospital was yet another riddle:

> Surely these street births occurred under more unfavourable conditions than those on our delivery beds. Or should have done! Whatever happens in hospital, it must surely be less harmful than to get up immediately after labour and descend from God knows how many floors to a carriage and to travel helter-skelter in every sort of weather over wretched pavements to the hospital and there to mount again two flights of steps.[99]

Yet facts and figures could not be denied, not at least by a man burdened with Semmelweis's troublesome conscience. There were other pointers to somewhere, if only one could divine where.

> Slow progress in labour occurred as a rule only in *primiparae* [those who were giving birth for the first time] ... And it was these blooming girls, full of health and hope, whose period of cervical dilatation was prolonged, who were most likely to become ill either during labour or immediately afterwards and die of rapidly progressive puerperal fever. And to add to the mystery, again and again, none of this happened on the midwives' ward![100]

Instrumental or manual intervention in labour was another prognostic indicator. Failure of the placenta to separate spontaneously after birth is a rare complication that may require manual removal. It was recognised as an especially grave but mysterious predisposing cause to puerperal fever, aggravated perhaps by the massive blood loss suffered by the mother.[101]

Another piece of evidence, contradicting current teaching, was Semmelweis's own post-mortem findings in infants who had died either just before or just after their mothers:

> The anatomical findings in the bodies of these unfortunates were, apart from the genital organs, indistinguishable from those found in women who had died of childbed fever. It was the same disease! But how could it be called 'childbed' fever in these infants? Whatever killed the infants, it had nothing to do with 'childbed'. And infant mortality showed the same difference between the two clinics as was shown by maternal mortality.[102]

The 'childbed fever' of infants must surely silence the mindless chatter about puerperal fever being caused by fear, remorse, shame or modesty. The idea of fear as an aetiological factor was particularly ludicrous. 'Fear! Soldiers in battle are often afraid but they do not die of childbed fever.' But what use was arguing? The fever continued to devastate the first clinic and drove Semmelweis to distraction. There had to be an explanation, and it was neither cosmic-telluric radiation nor the alleged roughness of foreign students. Yet in one respect he knew that he was more fortunate than others who may—indeed must—have suffered similar anguish before him. The difference in both morbidity and mortality (that is, the incidence of the fever and deaths from it) between two clinics occupying the same floor of the same hospital, and looking after the same population of 'randomised' women, was the kind of 'controlled experiment' that would not be invented by medical statisticians for another 100 years but that, on grounds of common sense (which already existed), must surely lead him to the answer.

It did not. The manoeuvres prescribed and used in labour, the handling of the bed linen, the food served, the lavatories, the visiting hours, the transfer from delivery room to the wards, the bathing of the infants, the first feed—all were exactly the same in the two clinics. What about overcrowding? This had exercised the ministerial commission for a few minutes: somebody on the panel had heard of the potentially deleterious effect of hospital beds being too close to each other. It had been quickly established that bed occupancy was indeed significantly different in the two clinics. Unfortunately the difference was the wrong way round. It was the midwives' clinic that was habitually overcrowded and the doctors' clinic that had empty beds.

Still, it was a question of trying. Semmelweis had noticed that in the second clinic mothers were being delivered lying on their sides, in the so-called lateral position, one of Bartsch's few innovations, whereas in the first clinic students and doctors continued to use the more orthodox 'dorsal position'; that is, mothers sitting up supported by pillows. He ordered that henceforth all deliveries in the first clinic should be in the lateral position too. The change was resented as troublesome and irrational; and so it undoubtedly was. A running battle ensued between the provisional assistant and the rest of the staff. Klein eventually put a stop to the innovation: Semmelweis was too weary to argue, but not too weary to clutch at other straws. What about the priest? Or at least the priestly procession?

The hospital chapel was so situated that the priest going to the 'fever ward' —more brutally known as the 'death ward'—in the first clinic had to traverse all the other wards, whereas in the second clinic he could get to it directly from the stairwell. As prescribed by canon law (and hospital regulations, once again dating back to the reign of the Empress Maria Theresa), the priest had to proceed to the dying in all his vestments, surrounded by a cloud of incense and preceded by a ministrant charged with ringing a small silver handbell, a pious donation of the Archduchess Maria Ludovica of Blessed Memory. Though the staff tried their best to ensure that this should happen only once in 24 hours,

the speed with which the terrible fever could develop often led to the priest being recalled two or three times a day. You can picture the doleful impression the procession, and especially the moving sound of the little bell, made on the lying-in mothers. Let me confess that it made even me feel deeply uncomfortable to hear it ringing past my door: I knew that it meant that another unfortunate innocent young mother had arrived at death's door or was already dead.[103]

It is impossible to believe that Semmelweis seriously suspected the incense or the bell to be the cause of the fever, but the route to the 'dying ward' was undoubtedly different in the two clinics and no such difference could be ignored. Fortunately, Father Himmelroth of the Cistercian Order, the hospital chaplain, was a humane and understanding individual. Risking censure from his superiors, the bell at least was banished from the procession. It made no difference to the number of dying.

By now Klein was beginning to lose patience. Perhaps he was seriously worried about his provisional assistant's state of mind. Opportunely, his former assistant, Breit, turned up from Graz. Apparently he had had a serious disagreement with the hospital superintendent there and was asking for re-appointment as assistant in Vienna. This was irregular, but not unprecedented. It is even possible (though undocumented) that Klein had secretly informed Breit that the post would be available if he 'unexpectedly' returned. Semmelweis was only a provisional assistant: he could be tactfully demoted back to aspirant; tactfully and perhaps even beneficially. Nervous breakdowns and post-traumatic stress had not yet been invented, but the young Hungarian—not so very young any more by the standards of the age—was behaving oddly. What he needed was a holiday. In this at least Klein had the support of the man who, over the past few years, had become one of Semmelweis's closest friends and advisers.

Jakob Kolletschka was a studious Slovak from Bratislava, 43 when in 1846 he met Semmelweis. Slovaks were not one of the 'historic' nations of the Empire like the Magyars and the Poles; indeed, they were hardly recognised as a nation at all.[104] They were the predominant peasant population of northern Hungary, known to their Hungarian masters as *tóts*, but Bratislava was a Hungarian and Austrian city: the few Slovaks who migrated there from the countryside and became 'emancipated' quickly became Hungarianised or Austrianised. Kolletschka was something of a freak, the son of a lawyer who spoke his native Slovak as fluently as he spoke German and Hungarian. He had had a distinguished career as a medical student in Vienna and had become a Rokitansky protégé. His interest was in morbid anatomy, but in a new and specialised branch: forensic science. This had been pioneered in some Dutch universities, though it had not in the past been recognised as a discipline in its own right in Vienna.

Kolletschka was the right man to bring this about. He was knowledgeable and industrious, but he established his eminence with astonishing tact. Fortunately for him, Rokitansky was a great enough man to foster the careers of his gifted juniors, not a universal attribute of university professors. 'That Slovak peasant knows ten times more about strangulation than I do,' the older man was reported as saying, 'and what he does not know about rape is not worth knowing. You would hardly believe it looking at him.'

The first link that developed between Kolletschka and Semmelweis was that of being early birds. Both tended to turn up in Rokitansky's post-mortem room at the crack of dawn, Semmelweis because he had to rush back to the obstetric clinic for his routine duties, and Kolletschka because he was writing and illustrating a textbook, the first in German to be devoted to forensic medicine. Soon they became friends. Both hailed from 'backward provinces', both were bachelors dedicated to their work, and both were without social ambitions in the fashionable world of the city.

When Semmelweis was told about his demotion, it was Kolletschka who softened the blow. A mind intensely preoccupied with a seemingly insoluble problem, as Semmelweis's was, needed a proper airing. As an aspirant, Semmelweis would still have official access to the obstetric clinic; Klein had even promised that his salary—paltry enough as an assistant—would remain unchanged. As a further inducement (or perhaps kindness), he could have three weeks' paid holiday. Kolletschka was in no doubt that his friend needed just that. The speed and excellence of the new railway line from Vienna to Trieste was one of the prides of the Metternich regime. Trieste itself, the brash and booming imperial port, was of course of no cultural interest, but a branch line would take the traveller to the mainland embarkation point for Venice. And over the past ten years Venice had once again become a tourist attraction.[105]

Largely at Kolletschka's urging, Semmelweis set out for his first holiday in years with two colleagues, neither of them close friends. No letters of his from Venice survive, but he later described it as an 'enchanted city, its art works beyond compare ... The memory of Bellini's altarpiece [it is not clear which, perhaps the one in the Frari] still brings tears to my eyes.'[106] And, as so often in the past, his friend Kolletschka had been right: after three weeks he returned to Vienna with a reinvigorated mind.

While the events of the next few days remain undocumented, it is not unreasonable to suppose that as soon as he could he hurried to Rokitansky's laboratory at the usual early hour, partly to resume his dissections but mainly perhaps to report to Kolletschka. In an old German biographical film (a casualty of the war, one hopes), he is greeted on arrival by the old technician in charge of the bodies. 'Don't overdo the work again, Dr Semmelweis, or you'll end up like the good Professor Kolletschka,' the technician warns him.

'Why, how did he end up?' Semmelweis asks archly. 'He hasn't entered holy matrimony, I hope, while I've been away.'

'Oh no,' the technician replies. 'He died of cadaveric pyaemia. There's his post-mortem protocol still on professor's table.'[107]

CHAPTER FIVE

THE MOMENT OF TRUTH

Medical historians and Semmelweis's biographers differ in how much significance to attach to Kolletschka's post-mortem protocol, which Semmelweis perused with mingled despair and fascination. Are great scientific and medical discoveries really made in a matter of seconds? Perhaps, if the mind is ready to receive them. Despite all the disappointments, Semmelweis's progress towards an understanding of puerperal fever had already made advances. True, the advances had been mainly negative, disproving to his own satisfaction widely held ideas; but negative findings in medicine can be as important as positive ones. Nevertheless, even though he could exclude a number of popular misconceptions, when he arrived back from Venice he was no nearer to understanding the cause of puerperal fever than when he had entered Klein's department three years earlier. And there is his own testimony, retrospective but in Semmelweis's case no less credible, that Kolletschka's harrowing post-mortem notes acted as a revelation.

Kolletschka had died of pyaemia, a condition where globules of pus enter the circulation from a primary abscess and set up multiple—hundreds or even thousands—of secondary abscesses. (In bacteraemia and septicaemia, by definition, it is organisms or their toxins that circulate rather than globules of pus carrying the organisms in their millions; but the difference is essentially one of degree.) In Semmelweis's day and indeed until the advent of sulphonamides and penicillin, the progress of the disease was rapid and fatal. The brain, the lungs, the bones, the eyes, the abdominal and pelvic organs, all became colonised by globules of pus. New abscesses formed with devastating speed. Depending on the organism, the focal signs of infection were accompanied by general toxaemia: delirium, hallucinations, coma. Often the primary site remained small and inconspicuous. A tiny cut or pinprick could act as the portal of entry for the organism.

In Kolletschka's case it was a clumsy (or perhaps over-excited) student who nicked the professor's index finger. It was given little attention. Such accidents were an occupational hazard of both surgeons and pathologists. In the course of operating on an infected site (and before Lister all surgical sites were potentially infected) and even more in the course of post-mortem examinations, they were almost unavoidable. The vast majority needed no treatment (even if treatment had been available). The injury triggered off an immediate defence response by the body itself. This too could be obvious or microscopic. It effectively isolated the lesion and destroyed the invading organisms. (In Semmelweis's day such organisms were unheard of, though 'noxious particles' or 'ichor' were well recognised.) Healing would follow, leaving a tiny, often invisible scar.[108]

But very occasionally, depending partly on the resistance of the individual but more often on the virulence of the organism, there would be a slight redness and throbbing around the wound the next day and 24 to 48 hours later ominous red streaks would appear, coursing up the arm.[109] Then, in spite of everything that could be done—compresses, rest, blood-letting, purges, all kinds of weird and wonderful remedies—there would come the first spike of fever, followed by sweating, a racing pulse, deepening toxaemia with delirium, the laboured stertorous breathing of pneumonia, swelling of the limbs due to venous thrombosis, neck stiffness from inflamed meninges, agonising pain in the limbs from abscess formation in the bones, the distended exquisitely tender abdomen of peritonitis and, if death was still delayed, multiple visible abscesses erupting in all parts of the body. Though the reason for this was unknown in Semmelweis's day, it was widely recognised that the course of the illness was likely to be particularly severe and deadly after injuries received at post-mortem examinations.[110]

Semmelweis's mourning for his friend could not still his scientific brain. Peritonitis. Pneumonia. Meningitis. Osteomyelitis. Multiple abscesses. Delirium. Coma. Death. These were terribly familiar words. Surgical pyaemia. Cadaveric pyaemia. Childbed fever—no less truly a pyaemia. And the source of the last pyaemia was now crystal clear:

> The disease from which Kolletschka had died was that from which thousands of women in so-called child-bed fever had died and were still dying ... In Kolletschka's case, as in women after labour, the cause of death was not the wound as such but contamination of the wound with minute cadaveric particles. [This was as near to microbes as it was possible to get in the years before Pasteur.] Instead of these particles being overcome and eliminated locally, they had clearly made their way into the lymphatic vessels and bloodstream setting up lesions in distant parts. If this could happen through a minute cut in the finger, as had happened in the case of Kolletschka, how much more likely was it to happen through the raw, bleeding surfaces of the uterus, cervix and often the perineum. I had to face the question: could such deadly cadaveric particles be introduced into these sites by the examining hand of the doctor, coming straight from the morbid anatomical dissection room? I was compelled to answer: yes, yes, yes![111]

One telltale sign confirmed this: the lingering and unmistakable cadaveric smell clinging to the hands of doctors and medical students. It would not disappear after a cursory washing with water, not even after a desultory scrubbing of the hands with soap and brush. It was indeed a matter of pride to many medical students and young doctors to have the sweet cadaveric aroma wafting around them. A terrible thought; but how often had Semmelweis heard crude jokes about its aphrodisiac effects, allegedly more powerful with some girls than the most expensive masculine scent? Had he, in his more callow days, cracked such jokes himself? His own single suit certainly carried the smell around, as did some of his underwear. There was no secret about how the cadaveric particles got introduced into the parturient women's genitalia: no secret at all. Nor was it incomprehensible that it did not happen in the midwives' clinic. The two doctors in charge, Professor Bartsch and Franz von Arneth, almost never visited the post-mortem room; nor, of course, did midwives and student midwives. Nor was it surprising that Klein's private patients seemed to be immune: he had not been near a body for years. Nor was it inexplicable that women who gave birth in the filthy streets of Vienna and were not immediately examined on admission nevertheless did comparatively well. By contrast, instrumental deliveries and especially such traumatic interventions as the manual removal of the placenta would inevitably enlarge the exposed raw areas and would make the entry of the infectious material into the circulation more likely. All the pieces of the monstrous jigsaw were falling into place.

The knowledge of having stumbled across the truth, a simple and clear answer to a question that had exercised the minds of doctors for centuries, must have been overwhelming. So, surely, was the urge to act on it. The next practical step was obvious. The pungent, yellowish-green gas known as chlorine had been discovered by the Swedish chemist Scheele in 1774 and given its name by Davy in 1810.[112] The name was subsequently 'endorsed' in the *Transactions of the Royal Society* and Faraday succeeded in condensing the gas into a liquid 12 years later. Even before then, it had been used by Collins in fumigating the lying-in wards of the Rotunda in Dublin and by Morveau in France and Cruikshank in England for the purification of water. It was this comparatively well-established antiseptic with which Semmelweis decided to try to get rid of the 'cadaveric particles'. At the same time he wrote to Justus von Liebig, Germany's most eminent chemist, asking for his advice. Von Liebig's letter arrived ten days later: he assured Semmelweis that either *chlorina liquida*

or the much cheaper chlorinated lime would rapidly 'digest' most cadaveric material other than bone or cartilage.[113]

It was with this letter in his pocket that Semmelweis hurried off to the Hebra home to deliver Frau Hebra of her first baby. Before setting out, despite the urgency of the call, he changed his underwear and scrubbed his hands, arms, face and moustache. He soaked his hands and fingers in a chlorine solution. On arrival, he asked the happy but understandably worried prospective father to breathe in the air and make sure that it conveyed no cadaveric odour. For several minutes Hebra sniffed at him 'like a dog'. Even the cook (whose sense of smell was said to be unerring) was asked in to sniff. She did. There was no smell. Semmelweis was given the all-clear. Frau Hebra's labour was prolonged but uncomplicated, as was her puerperium.[114]

A few days later Breit was offered the chair of obstetrics at the University of Tübingen and departed at once. Semmelweis was reinstated as assistant, assuring Klein that he had found the answer to the prevention of childbed fever. Whether or not Klein believed him is uncertain. The fact that Semmelweis was reinstated without having to submit to another selection procedure suggests that the professor had at least an inkling that his troublesome junior, heavy cross though he was, was not entirely demented. Re-appointment enabled Semmelweis to introduce his prophylaxis to the first clinic early in May 1847. owls of chlorine solution, each with some clean sand at the bottom that could be used for scrubbing, were placed at the entrance of the clinic through which both doctors and students had to enter. Pinned to the wall were posters with the directions:

ALL STUDENTS AND DOCTORS WHO ENTER THE WARDS FOR THE PURPOSE OF MAKING AN EXAMINATION MUST WASH AND SCRUB THEIR FINGERS AND HANDS THOROUGHLY IN THE SOLUTION OF CHLORINATED LIME PLACED IN BASINS AT THE ENTRANCE TO THE WARDS. ONE DISINFECTION IS SUFFICIENT FOR ONE

VISIT BUT BETWEEN THE EXAMINATION OF EACH PATIENTS THE HANDS MUST BE WASHED WITH SOAP AND WATER.[115]

Semmelweis had himself tested the efficacy of the method using the only criterion available to him: his sense of smell. Fortunately, of all the traditional five senses at human command, olfaction is by far the most sensitive. Fortunately also, some of Semmelweis's enthusiasm may have rubbed off on his chief, for, wonder of wonders, Klein himself publicly submitted to the ritual.[116] (He made it clear, though, that he did so only to humour his excitable Hungarian assistant.) The proof was not long in coming. In May 1847 the mortality from puerperal fever in the first clinic was still 14.5 per cent. In June it was 2.38 per cent. In July it was 1.83 per cent. In August it was 1.2 per cent. For the first time since the two clinics had been separated, mortality in the first clinic was marginally lower than it was in the second clinic.

Even after August 1847 there were setbacks, however. In October 11 out of 12 women in a single row of beds, all examined on the same day, became suddenly ill with a virulent form of the fever. All the affected women died within the next five days. It was a terrible blow, since Semmelweis had himself supervised the observance of his prophylactic ritual, virtually encamped at the entrance to the wards. He was convinced that it had not been breached. Yet the poisonous substance had reached these women, despite the washing of hands between examinations. Nevertheless, the years of frustration had not been entirely wasted: at least Semmelweis now approached the problem logically. If cadaveric poison had not contaminated the unfortunate mothers, then a poison of a different kind must have done. No prolonged search was needed. The logical place to look was the first patient examined that morning, for, though she had herself escaped the fever, 11 women in the next 11 beds had contracted it and had died.

I then discovered to my horror, but also to my relief, that the parturient patient in the first bed had an advanced

medullary carcinoma of the uterus which afflicted her with a foul discharge. After examining this woman we washed our hands only with soap, not enough to destroy the ichor [the material in the discharge causing the disease]. It is necessary therefore to clean the hands with chlorine solution not only after dissection but also after contact with necrotic material in the living.[117]

Semmelweis's new orders, that everyone must wash their hands in an antiseptic solution after *each examination,* provoked a storm. He was accused of being obsessed with lunatic theories. A wealth of practical arguments were advanced, some in written memoranda to the professor. Washing in chlorinated water regularly was bad for the skin: in particular, it destroyed that sensitive touch that was essential in the performance of obstetrics. The chlorine lingering on the hands was 'demonstrably harmful' to the birth passages of the mother. The procedure took up so much time that none was available for the proper examination of the patients. Semmelweis took no notice of these, descending 'like a madman' on any luckless student who tried to examine a woman with the smell of 'necrotic material' clinging to his hands.[118]

Klein, it seems, sat on the fence. There was a faint air of political uncertainty about: his sensitive Viennese nose had registered it long before the barricades went up. Semmelweis's discovery was widely discussed in medical and university circles—a small world—and the younger professors seemed enthusiastic. Klein was 60, an age when careerists who owe their rise to conspiracy begin to suspect conspiracies around them. But, for whatever reason, he did not, during the autumn and winter of 1847, try to squash Semmelweis.[119] Yet there was one further setback.

In November puerperal fever flared up again in the first clinic: ten mothers died in November and eight in December. The tragedy was traced to its source relatively quickly. A pregnant woman with a discharging carious knee joint had been admitted on 12 November. Her genital tract was normal, hence the examining finger could not have carried the infection to other patients; but 'the exhalations of the diseased knee were so strong that the whole air of the ward was permeated with it'.[120] On 5 December the woman was discharged—having given birth to a healthy infant—and in January the number of deaths once again fell to one. Semmelweis decided that in future such cases must be isolated from the day of their admission.

At this point one is faced with the first of the questions that have puzzled Semmelweis's biographers since the pioneering studies of Alfred Hegar and Tibor de Győry.[121] Why, having made arguably the most important medical discovery since vaccination, did he not immediately publish his findings? One obvious reason must have been the very importance of the discovery. Understanding and seeing the way to the prevention of childbed fever was not an advance comparable to an ingenious new modification of the obstetric forceps or an improved unguent for the inflamed lactating breast. Its acceptance would save millions of young lives and prevent immeasurable suffering; its rejection would have the opposite effect. For a 29-year-old doctor, not even a *Dozent*, a slightly uncouth foreigner in one of Europe's couthest cities, this was not an easy message to encapsulate in an elegant short communication.

It is true that most great discoveries in medicine are laughably simple, but this is usually true only in retrospect. To suggest, in effect, that most of what had been written in weighty textbooks by venerable professors and in innumerable learned articles by experienced obstetricians about one of the most terrifying illnesses known to medicine had been nonsense was far from easy. Even less easy was it to suggest that a practice still widely followed by all these eminences was continuing to cause extreme suffering and frequent deaths. As events would show, and as Semmelweis probably sensed, his claim would provoke extreme reactions throughout Europe. He was no coward and the prospect of notoriety did not frighten him, but nor was the

prospect of fame a spur. There can be no doubt that he wanted his discovery to be accepted, but he wanted it accepted to save lives, not to win laurels. How best to set about making it palatable was far more difficult to decide than is sometimes implied by medical historians today.

This is not to say that he was lacking in ambition: no normal person embarks on a profession like medicine without hoping to achieve a position where he can fulfil his potential. Nor does it mean that his actions were necessarily wise and sensible. Neither wisdom nor common sense is a conspicuously Hungarian characteristic. But in different—that is, in normal— circumstances, the way in which he set out to propagate his discovery might have achieved its purpose.

In 1847 Vienna was still one of the great centres of medical knowledge. Like many such centres its actual performance was patchy, and Klein's reign had done nothing to advance the reputation of Viennese obstetrics. Nevertheless, the lying-in hospital within the Allgemeines Krankenhaus was still the largest obstetric teaching unit in Europe and Boër's textbook, the last edition about to be published posthumously, still gave it an aura of academic excellence. Skoda, Rokitansky, Hebra, Hyrtl and Feuchtersleben, though not obstetricians themselves, were other draws. The doctors who came to the city from other countries might be expected to spread the news of Semmelweis's discovery as certainly and as quickly as would printed articles; more so, perhaps. They knew the circumstances of their own hospitals and the personalities of their own professors. They could see for themselves that Semmelweis was neither a fantasist nor a fanatic. This was not yet the age of medical press conferences and television soundbites. Even in a television age, Semmelweis might not have had the irresistible urge to achieve five minutes' fame at the cost of causing much anguish and suffering.

In the summer of that year two newly qualified postgraduates from Heidelberg, Adolf Kussmaul and Edward Brunner, arrived in the city. Fifty years later the former, by then one of the leading clinical teachers of Europe, published his reminiscences,

Jugenderinnerungen eines alten Artzes.[122] He and his friend had spent six months in Vienna and Kussmaul was to look back on this period of his life as one of the happiest. For a few weeks after their arrival they found the medical school still in recess—only Hebra continued to give his already famous course of lectures in August—but they inspected the buildings and wards and marvelled at the clinical and post-mortem material available for teaching. In the obstetric clinics 3000 births took place every year. Rokitansky, still ensconced in his 'wholly inadequate morgue' miles away from the Krankenhaus, performed 'with amazing skill, speed and knowledge' nearly 1500 autopsies. Even in the summer there were other students about 'from every country in Europe, even Ireland and Russia, with whom one could exchange impressions and experiences'.

With the opening of the autumn semester the two Heidelbergers enrolled in Semmelweis's course in obstetric surgery. They found it 'wholly superior to anything they had so far witnessed'. When Semmelweis learnt that the two young men had acted as assistants to the great Naegele, one of the elder statesmen of European obstetrics, he managed to secure for them the much sought-after but not easily won permission to practise under supervision in the lying-in hospital for six weeks.[123] Kussmaul found Klein 'an ineffectual creature, indifferent to his duties as professor and clinician, of no help to his assistant and possessed of a strong and scarcely concealed prejudice against foreign students like us'. Semmelweis, on the other hand, 'could not have been kinder and more helpful':

> He was of more than medium height, broad and strongly built, his face with rather prominent Asiatic cheekbones [what Semmelweis's Hungarian friends described as characteristically Magyar], his forehead high and his hair rather thin for his age. He had strong, fleshy and dextrous hands and an astonishing capacity for work ... and he was kind to his patients and conscientious to an extreme degree. He was not at his best as a lecturer but when he talked to us

about his recent great discovery he became exceedingly passionate. Far from being secretive, he particularly wanted us to tell Professor Naegele about it and about his marvellous results.[124]

Apart from Kussmaul and Brunner, there were others from abroad who Semmelweis could reasonably hope would spread his gospel: F. H. C. Routh had come from London, Strendrichs from Amsterdam, Schwartz from Kiel and Wieger from Strasbourg. All observed the workings of his prophylaxis and the seemingly miraculous protection it gave against a disease that in their own hospitals they had come to accept as the manifestation of the wrath of God. They wrote letters home and promised to propagate his doctrine on their return.

On Semmelweis's home ground too the news of his discovery spread. His course of lectures in the first semester of the academic year 1847–48 was almost as well attended as the famous classes of Skoda and Rokitansky. He also had devoted friends among the younger members of the university who, exasperated though they were by his refusal to publish 'too precipitately' or to speak at medical meetings, decided to do his work for him. Franz von Arneth, Bartsch's assistant, spoke English well—his mother was Scottish—and wrote to Edinburgh's obstetric autocrat, Sir James Young Simpson. Skoda wrote to his friend and patron Nadherny in Prague, asking him, as president of the medical university, to introduce his 'young friend's happy and momentous discovery' to the obstetricians in the university. Nadherny complied, communicating the news to the Prague faculty in a circular memorandum. He then sent Skoda's letter to his son-in-law, Kiwisch von Rotterau, professor of obstetrics at Würzburg.

Most effectively perhaps, Hebra used his position as editor of the *Übertragungen der Kaiserlichen und Königlichen Gesellschaft der Ärzte zu Wien* to publish in January 1848 (without consulting Semmelweis) an extensive editorial:

The Editor of this Journal feels it his duty to communicate to the medical profession, in view of the prevalence of puerperal fever in all lying-in hospitals, the following observations made by Dr Semmelweis, Assistant in the First Obstetric Clinic in the Allgemeines Krankenhaus of this city. [No mention of Klein, whom Hebra disliked.] Dr Semmelweis has become thoroughly instructed in practical obstetrics over the past five years both at the bedside and at the dissecting table. For the last two years he has devoted special attention to the causes at the root of the prevailing epidemic of puerperal fever. On this subject he has left nothing untested and everything that could exercise an injurious influence was systematically eliminated ... These and other observations aroused in him the thought that perhaps in lying-in hospitals pregnant and parturient women might be inoculated by the *obstetrician himself* and that puerperal fever might be no more in most cases than a cadaveric wound infection. In order to test his opinion, he ordered that everyone in the First Clinic should wash their hands in an aqueous solution of chloride of lime (Chloratic calcis unc. 1 Aqua fontana lib. duas). The result was both surprising and gratifying: during the month of April and May before this rule was in force, there were eighteen deaths out of a hundred, whereas in the following months, up to November 26th, the percentage fell to 2.45.

This probably explains why in training schools for midwives mortality has been so much lower than in clinics devoted to the training of medical students and doctors. A well-known exception is the Paris Maternité where pupil midwives regularly undertake post-mortem examinations ... and where puerperal fever has been rampant.

Three distinct facts further confirm the above conclusions and indeed extend its scope. Dr Semmelweis believes that he has proof that:

1. Owing to the careless prophylactic washing of some students, several patients were lost in the month of September.

2. In the month of October, some patients were lost because a patient in labour with a foul-smelling medullary sarcoma [sic] of the uterus had been repeatedly examined and these examinations had not been followed by washing in chloride of lime.

3. Owing to a filthy discharge from an ulcer of the leg in one patient, several patients confined at the same time and in the same ward were infected.

Therefore, *the conveyance of a foul exudation from a living organism may be the main cause of puerperal fever* [Hebra's italics]. In publishing these experiences we invite directors of all lying-in institutions, some of whom have already been contacted by Dr Semmelweis, to contribute the results of their investigations either to support or to refute them.[125]

This and another Hebra editorial in April 1848 contained all the salient facts of Semmelweis's discovery. However remiss it may have been of Semmelweis not to try to publish his results in the form of a separate article under his own name—a course of action unthinkable without Klein's *imprimatur*—it cannot be seriously suggested that, even at this comparatively early stage, his findings were insufficiently publicised. Hebra's editorials were, admittedly, a somewhat unorthodox way of communicating a medical discovery of great importance, but the *Übertragungen* had a wide circulation and its editorial pronouncements carried authority.

To say that Semmelweis had only himself to blame for the neglect of his discoveries does him and his friends a grave injustice. The responses over the next year or two were mixed, ranging from the tragic to the enthusiastic and the hostile. To some extent these reflected the personalities and interests of the responders; but, even more, they were influenced by entirely non-medical events.

CHAPTER SIX

REVOLUTION

It is possible that historians of medicine and science sometimes focus on scientific and medical developments at the expense of the social and political setting. The delay in the wider recognition of Semmelweis's discovery was in large part the fortuitous result of its timing: 1848 and 1849 were not normal years in the history of Europe, and in Central Europe they were cataclysmic.

Although 13 March is the date commonly designated as the watershed in the history of the Habsburg Monarchy, the events of the day were not unheralded. There was a rebellion against Austrian rule in the Polish province of Galicia in 1846. The Hungarian Diet in Bratislava convened in 1847 'became drunk' on the rhetoric of Lajos Kossuth.[126] In the cafés of Vienna changes in the constitution, freedom of speech, the rights of man and Metternich's dismissal were discussed openly and indeed clamorously in a way that would have been unthinkable a few years earlier. The trigger, as on more than one occasion in the past, was the uprising in Paris in February against the uninspiring rule of King Louis Philippe.[127] Daumier's pear-shaped monarch abdicated and fled to England, opening the way to the Second French Republic.[128]

When the news reached Vienna, the students of the university and thousands of the city's unemployed proletariat took to the streets.[129] Without even a show of reluctance the concourse of archdukes and archduchesses in the Hofburg, clustering round *der Trottel* Ferdinand, decided to throw Metternich to the wolves. (Many disliked the all-powerful chancellor personally or thought him either 'too stubborn' or 'too soft'; and some of their imperial highnesses may even have been instrumental in stirring up trouble in the streets. If so, their action soon showed up the folly of mobilising the masses to decide a game of court intrigue.) Metternich obliged, resigned and quietly departed. Instead of stemming the revolution, his resignation brought down the old regime.

On 15 March the students of Pest too rose and demanded freedom and virtual independence for Hungary: universal suffrage, a responsible government, the end of the 'Hungarian Chancellery' in Vienna and of course freedom of speech and of the press. The *robot* should be abolished without compensation.[130] The Palatine, the Archduke Stephen (son of the Archduke Joseph), surrendered without even waiting for Vienna's approval and transferred his powers to a responsible government. It was to be headed by the radical and high-minded magnate, Count Louis Batthányi.[131] The court in Vienna murmured imprecations, but on 11 April Ferdinand confirmed the 'March Laws'. What persuaded him—or, rather, the flock of archdukes and archduchesses milling around him—was that the uprising in Pest was quickly followed by a revolution in Prague; and on 18 March Lombardy, the centre of Austria's military power, declared its secession from Austria and appealed to the King of Sardinia for help. A few days later Venice declared itself an independent republic.

A 'Central Committee of the Estates' met in Vienna in mid-April and demanded 'increased representation of the middle classes' (whatever that meant; semantics were not the Committee's forte) and a constitution. Metternich's successor, Kolovrat, was replaced by a Metternich clone, Fiquelmont, but within a few days he was driven from power by another student demonstration. He was succeeded by Pillersdorf, an elderly and notably ineffectual bureaucrat who in pre-March days had acquired an undeserved reputation as a liberal. He in turn was ousted by a fresh revolt that led to the publication of a 'Parliamentary Constitution for the Whole of the Empire'. This was espoused by the Court, though it flagrantly contradicted liberties already granted to Hungary, Croatia and Bohemia. In any case, the radicals wanted to make their own constitution. After more demonstrations, the April Constitution was withdrawn. Two days later, on 17 May, the Emperor and the Court fled to Innsbruck. They may or may not have been comforted there by the earlier arrival of the imperial accoucheur, Professor Johann Klein, of Vienna. Coincidentally perhaps, Professor Bartsch had also found urgent business to transact in his home in Styria. Since Dr von Arneth was busy visiting hospitals in France and England and the foreign postgraduates had all departed, during these turbulent days the lying-in hospital of the Allgemeines Krankenhaus was run by one medically qualified assistant, Dr Semmelweis.

The imperial family's flight was widely perceived as its final break with the Revolution and it thrust the moderate liberals back into the arms of the radicals. On 26 May a Committee of Public Safety was set up 'to supervise the activities' of the ministers left in Vienna. This could not have been too arduous a task. The number of ministers left in post in Vienna was three, two of them invalids. They planned to engage in no activity whatever. For a few weeks all government was at a blessed standstill.

What makes the events of 1848–49 so complex and the outcome in many ways so unexpected was the multiplicity of levels at which sectional interests clashed. The Habsburg Empire was overwhelmingly rural and its only immovable objects were the peasants. Their one wish everywhere was to get rid of the *robot* and other feudal dues. But the wish was unformulated and had to be exploded by a spark from the towns. The towns did so, but had their own agenda. In Hungary, paradoxically and uniquely, peasant discontent made the Hungarian lesser gentry revolutionary too. Threatened in their very existence, they were persuaded by Kossuth's magnificent oratory (and nothing much else) to lead the peasants from the front rather than trail behind. This transformed the Hungarian Liberation Struggle of 1848–49 into a historical rarity: a truly national uprising.

Even many of the great Hungarian magnates, usually the most dependable allies of the dynasty, felt betrayed when Vienna was unable to keep the peasantry and the lesser gentry in their timelessly allotted places. They had to seek allies elsewhere, and their *fronde* completed the revolutionary line-up. Though Semmelweis's own class, the modestly prosperous urban shop-keepers, traders and professional people, was the least involved, Semmelweis's brother, Paul, volunteered and served as a field padre in Kossuth's army; and Semmelweis's close Hungarian friends in Vienna were all ardent patriots and paraded in the streets under the national flag.[132]

But Kossuth had another weapon in his rhetorical armoury. His Hungarian nationalism at the time was firmly opposed to the nationalist aspirations of the Slovaks, the Croats, the Romanians and the Serbs, numerically the majority of the people living within the lands of the Crown of St Stephen. This backfired. The dynasty was ultimately saved by three incorrigible rebels who ignored the timid, confused and often contradictory signals issuing from Vienna (or in whatever provincial capital the archdukes and archduchesses happened to be congregating in deadly fear of their subjects) and acted on their own initiative. They all acted for their own purposes, but at least they all had a purpose and they knew how to achieve it.

The first of those was the Croatian *Ban* or governor, Joseph Jelačić. In defiance of half-hearted orders from Vienna to accommodate Magyar demands, however outrageous, he launched the first of those bloody ethnic wars that, with intermissions, have been a feature of Balkan history ever since.[133] At that stage his was still a united Slav movement. The Serbs were a brother nation and the Croats were sympathetically supported by their northern cousins, the Czechs.[134] The Magyars were the common enemy. This was a new development. Neither in the university nor in the circles around the Hofburg had ethnic differences ever been a divide. After 1848–49 relations between the people of the Monarchy would never be the same. (In later years in exile Kossuth tried to backtrack and preached the cause of a Greater Danubian Federation. It was too late.) In this new constellation it was no accident that it was the Prague obstetricians who would lead the campaign against Semmelweis's doctrine and decry his personal achievement. Militarily Jelačić was not notably successful, but to the new Hungarian government he was a serious distraction.

The second rebel who loftily ignored the vacillations of the Court and decided to do what he knew he could do best was the Austrian Commander-in-Chief in Italy, Field Marshal Count Johann Radetzky.[135] While a minister from the Court was timorously negotiating the unconditional surrender of all Austria's Italian possessions to almost anybody who would have them, Radetzky (who received unexpected volunteer reinforcements from Vienna) defeated the Italians at Custoza on 25 July and recovered Lombardy in a leisurely walkabout during August.[136] The final chapter in the 1848–49 Italian rebellion came with Radetzky's decisive victory at Novara over the Sardinian forces on 26 March 1849. The Republic of Venetia was defeated in an effortless aftermath in July.

The third rebel was Prince Windischgrätz, the Austrian commander in Prague. Prague had seen a succession of riots, uprisings and constitutional conferences since the initial revolt in March 1848. Encouraged by the April riots in Vienna, Czech radicals and nationalists once again took to the streets in June. This was not significantly different from earlier demonstrations. What was different was Windischgrätz's response. Denied his chance to shoot at the rabble in Vienna in March, he eagerly accepted the challenge of Prague. The demonstration was in fact a rather orderly one, mostly university students out for the fun of it. Windischgrätz decided to ignore 'the bleatings from Vienna'. A brief show of military force was enough: 'Prepare for a bloodbath and it will prove unnecessary.' The fusillade, leaving not more than a handful of dead, crushed the prospect of Bohemian statehood for 70 years. When the members of the dynasty next took to their heels, it would be safe for them to flee to Moravia and for the deposed Ferdinand later to take up residence in the castle of Prague.

In Vienna in the meantime a Constituent Assembly met, inaugurating the only democratic episode in the history of the Habsburg Empire. The Court returned in July and waited. The Constituent Assembly abolished most of the hereditary rights of landowners and the labour service of peasants and put through a number of measures once planned but never put into effect by Joseph II. But by now the archdukes and archduchesses had partially regained their nerve. While the Constituent Assembly deliberated, they secretly dispatched imperial troops to assist Jelačić in Hungary. This provoked the bloodiest uprising so far in Vienna. Kossuth's Hungarian army advanced gingerly towards the city to support the rebellion, then withdrew.[137]

The Court fled to Olomuc (Olmütz), though this time with some resolve to put an end to the mayhem and unseemly shouting in the streets. The man to do it for them was at hand. In November they appointed a new ministry under Prince Felix Schwarzenberg, an aristocrat known for his violence both in his private and in his public life. With his authority and with the help of Jelačić's Croat legions, Windischgrätz, Schwarzenberg's brother-in-law, subdued the rebellion in Vienna with comparatively little bloodshed. It was the end of Austria's constitutional episode. Ferdinand was persuaded to abdicated in favour of his 18-year-old nephew, the Archduke Francis Joseph.[138] The new Emperor, though wholly without ideas of his own, was dedicated to the survival of the dynasty. His mentality was that of a conscientious bureaucrat, but he had what his Viennese subjects called *Sitzfleisch* (dogged patience). He was to reign over the shrinking Habsburg domains for 68 years.[139]

One aspect of these revolutionary upheavals, too insignificant politically to interest non-medical historians, affected not only Semmelweis's discovery but the rest of his private life as well. The University of Vienna, like other universities in the Empire, had long been regarded by the dynasty as one of its proudest and most personal achievements. Maria Theresa and Joseph II took an intense interest in all university appointments; and even Francis I, an intellectual vacuum, cultivated a special link with his academic subjects. The institutions were imperial (or royal in the case of the University of Pest) in name and were governed by the King-Emperor and his ministers in the same way as were the army, the civil service and (after Joseph II) even the church. This had many advantages. A Van Swieten in Maria Theresa's day and a Baron Türkheim, 'our second Van Swieten' as Skoda dubbed him, in the late 1830s could promote advanced ideas and cut through red tape and the paraphernalia of democratic decision making. On the other hand, such exotic ideas as university autonomy or academic freedom were barely contemplated and never openly discussed.

A vice-director appointed by the Imperial Minister of Health (later of Education) controlled not only all university appointments, from professors to under-gardeners, but also the contents of lectures and examinations. In the words of Joseph Andreas von Stifft, Imperial Minister of Health for 33 years (1803–36) and a tireless codifier of the system, it was the duty of the vice-director 'to guard over all teaching and to make sure that it kept strictly to the approved syllabus as embodied in officially prescribed textbooks'. Or, in the lofty utterance of the Emperor Francis I when graciously addressing professors of his university in 1818: 'Keep to what is old. Honour what is old. What is old is good. I will not have any gripes' (in untranslatable Austrian: 'Das Alte is' immer gut. Ich will keine Grübeleien').[140]

A new era seemed to begin with the appointment of Baron Ludwig von Türkheim as vice-director. He was genuinely in the Van Swieten mould. Both Skoda and Rokitansky owed their appointments to him. But ideas of academic freedom or university autonomy were as alien to him as they had been to his predecessors. He was an intelligent and benevolent dictator who would never have tolerated any interference from vague and impractical academics. The matter was never tested, for he died in 1846. His immediate successor, Ernst Feuchtersleben, did his best to step into his shoes, but in the heady atmosphere of March 1848 this was no longer enough.

Now the very idea of a powerful administrator supervising and directing academic activities began to be questioned. The man who questioned it most vocally was Skoda. What he actually wanted (other than having his way and irritating the old guard) was never clear, but suddenly everything seemed within the grasp of the reformists. The university, not some jumped up vice-director, should have the final say in filling academic posts. Professors, not the vice-director, should decide what was being taught in the classes. At the end of the year Feuchtersleben resigned and the man appointed in his place was Skoda's choice. Anton Rosas, the professor of ophthalmology, seemed a colourless but hard-working bureaucrat who had carefully avoided committing himself to any policy whatever. Skoda confidently expected to 'guide' him.

However, by the beginning of 1849 the forces of reaction seemed to be in the ascendant and Rosas had no intention of losing his job. To Skoda's consternation he suddenly emerged as the spokesman of the traditionalists, an academic Schwarzenberg. The old discipline was to be re-imposed. It was time to put a stop to all the loose talk about academic autonomy. The new vice-director's dedication to the August House and its absolute rule may have been reinforced by the dark secrets of his own Hungarian origin and faintly revolutionary utterances in the past. He received the immediate support of all the conservative professors, still the silent and only temporarily silenced majority. Klein, returning from sick leave as the revolutionary ferment fizzled out, was prominent among them.

University professors do not erect barricades, fire guns or go waving flags under the windows of the Hofburg, at least they did not in the Vienna of the Habsburgs. Nevertheless, they had other means to bring about or to crush a revolution. Fought in committees, subcommittees, working parties, and (above all) at private gatherings and musical soirées with memoranda, minutes and humble submissions, their war was every bit as determined as the struggle of the political revolutionaries in the streets. It was also at times far more vicious. It had nothing to do with puerperal fever. The death of women entered into it not at all. The horrors of pyaemia were never mentioned. It was about power. But it was Semmelweis's misfortune to become the reformists' most handy live ammunition and the reactionaries' useful target.

In some respects he was a clever choice. His spectacular achievements in the lying-in hospital were by then widely known. They were also generally admired. The politically reactionary Klein, on the other hand, had not only failed to support Semmelweis but had tried, as soon as it was safe to do so, to get rid of him. The details of the struggle were as petty (and are still as tedious to dissect) as such academic infighting usually is. Nevertheless, to explain Semmelweis's seemingly inexplicable behaviour the main events have to be chronicled.

In January 1849, with the reform movement still apparently in the ascendant, Skoda delivered a much-heralded lecture in the Imperial Academy. In it he praised Semmelweis and his achievements. The praise was probably genuine—and it was well-deserved—but Skoda's aim had nothing to do with women in labour. At the end of his lecture he proposed that the Faculty (as distinct from the ministry or the vice-director who would normally have handled such matters) should appoint a committee to study the problem in the University Lying-in Hospital. It would then make recommendations to the Professorial Council of the University (which did not yet exist) as to whether the findings should be passed on to other hospitals and universities in the Empire. This was a flagrant encroachment on Klein's authority as well as a declaration of war on the vice-director.

Klein, who was present, did not protest. He bided his time. A month later, the revolutionary tide already ebbing, the ministry (which had not even been addressed) rejected Skoda's suggestion and declared themselves confident in Professor Klein's efficient handling of matters pertaining to his department. One result of such handling became evident a month later when, out of the blue, Semmelweis was informed that his tenure of the post of assistant had come to an end and had been terminated. The first part of the statement was strictly true; but there were no applicants for the post and Semmelweis's tenure would normally have been automatically extended for at least another two years. In his place a young specialist in internal medicine, Carl Baum, with no obstetric experience, had already been appointed.

Meekly or not, Semmelweis himself might have accepted the decision. He would continue in private practice for a time and he wanted to conduct some animal experiments for which the university had voted him a sum of money. But Skoda immediately counter-attacked. In a lengthy memorandum to the ministry, but circulated to all professors, he outlined the 'ground-breaking' innovations of Dr Semmelweis, pointed to the 'extraordinary favourable results already obtained not only in Vienna but also in other university clinics that had adopted Dr Semmelweis's methods'—he had already mentioned Kiel and Heidelberg—and suggested that 'it was the clear and unequivocal duty of the Faculty to inquire into the circumstances of how Dr Semmelweis's great discovery was being implemented and expanded by the university clinics'.[141] The memorandum was endorsed by seven other professors, including Rokitansky and the young and up-and-coming surgeon Dumreicher. While Klein was not mentioned by name, he was by implication the villain of the piece, a petty and jealous incompetent to whom the welfare of his patients mattered not at all.

The memorandum landed on the desk of Rosas, to whom Semmelweis's doctrine (as distinct from its role as Skoda's 'weapon') was probably a matter of complete indifference. On the other hand, the idea of the Faculty, as distinct from the ministry and its appointed vice director, pursuing any kind of inquiry about anything and even making decisions was anathema. Rosas decided to forward the memorandum to the minister with a damning commentary, quoting the revered and honourable Professor Klein's 'wholly justified' outrage. He also encouraged Klein to submit a counter-memorandum, signed not only by himself but also by other traditionalist professors. They protested against the 'unwarranted interference' of 'some university

professors' in university departments directed by other professors. Semmelweis was mentioned in passing as the subject of one interference, but the merits or demerits of his discovery were not discussed. All these memoranda gathered more marginal comments on their way to the minister, including one from an under-secretary by the name of Rudolf Weill. Weill suggested that a discovery as important as that outlined by Professor Skoda might be judged on its scientific merits rather than on grounds of politics or academic etiquette. It was clearly an outrageous suggestion and nothing more was heard of it or him.

By March 1849 the ministry was in total disarray. The minister, Weissenberg, was being replaced by the more 'reformist' figure of Count von Rathebon, a charming aristocrat said to be the best shot in Carinthia. It is not clear what happened to these various papers. After the statutory summer lull—no revolution was ever allowed to interfere with the *Ferien* in Austria—Skoda decided to go on the offensive again. In October 1849 he persuaded Semmelweis to submit an application for the title of *Dozent*. Among other benefits, this would give him access to the university clinic more or less independently of Klein. The submission coincided with the coming to power of Schwarzenberg's reactionary government and the final defeat of the uprising in Hungary. Semmelweis's application was rejected without explanation; and, coincidentally or not, the medical press carried attacks on his doctrine by Professor Scanzoni of Würzburg and by Professor Seyfert of Prague.

But Skoda could not be so easily deflected. He invited Semmelweis to give a series of lectures to the Vienna Medical Society. He also persuaded him to appeal against the rejection. The lectures, delivered in May, June and July 1850, were a success, despite the fact that Semmelweis was an indifferent speaker. They would later be printed in the *Wochenschrift* and were widely read.

In the meantime, Schwarzenberg had not only consolidated his position but had also shown himself as merciless with inefficient political reactionaries as he had been with muddle-headed reformists. His government has had a bad press from liberal-minded historians. It was undoubtedly repressive. It ignored the *Zeitgeist* and trampled on nationalist sentiments. It proclaimed no lofty programme and committed itself to no goals. But it was also the most efficient government the Habsburg Empire had had for 50 years or was to have again for the rest of its existence. Haller, the new Minister of Education, an ex-lawyer, had only contempt for his aristocratic predecessor and could see no reason why Semmelweis's original application had been rejected. He sensed personal intrigue and, like his chief Schwarzenberg, he disliked politicking. Whether or not he considered the merits of Semmelweis's discovery is uncertain; there is nothing to suggest that he did. But the man was clearly experienced enough to be a *Dozent*. He had expressed no disloyal sentiments. He was recommended by the only two professors in the university who were of European renown, Skoda and Rokitansky. Of Klein Haller had never heard. Of Rosas he thought little. After appending a few caustic remarks about his own officials he scribbled on the application: 'Approved'.

The next event is a mystery.[142] The diploma of *Dozent*, suitably curlicued, was a standard document and contained a sentence authorising the honorand to teach on living patients and on phantoms. In Semmelweis's diploma somebody on the way down from the minister crossed out 'on living patients' and inserted 'only' before the word 'phantoms'. It has proved impossible to establish who this was. Was it Klein, through whose hands the document must have passed, or some vindictive official in the ministry? Could it even have been a practical joke? It is not important, because the change was so blatantly malicious and contrary to custom that it would have been rectified on another appeal. That would undoubtedly have been Skoda's advice. But, equally certainly, for Semmelweis it was the last straw. Was he unduly sensitive? Perhaps. Most of his Viennese patrons and friends thought so and were shocked by his response. But none of them thought the less of him. He had been sorely tried. He had become a pawn in a political game. Whatever his reasoning or lack of it, it took him only a few minutes to make up his mind. He returned the diploma to the secretary of the university with a brief note declining the honour. Then he packed his modest belongings and returned to Pest.

What had he achieved during his two years in Vienna following his great discovery? Very little, even sympathetic biographers tend to suggest. But this is not so. By 1850 his findings were known in most obstetric centres in Europe. In at least one case they led to a personal tragedy.

Hermann Schwartz of Holstein had visited Vienna and reported back to his chief, Gustav Adolphus Michaelis, in Kiel. Puerperal fever was rife in the lying-in hospital there. Semmelweis's doctrine made sense. His prophylactic regime with chlorine washing was introduced and the results were as remarkable as they had been in Vienna. Michaelis's letter remains one of the most generous testimonials Semmelweis ever received: 'I have no doubt that you have made a great contribution to obstetrics, indeed mankind. I have already written to my friend, Levy of Copenhagen, advising him of your important discovery.'[143]

Nevertheless, Semmelweis had only a few weeks to derive pleasure from Michaelis's letter. A few months earlier the Kiel obstetrician had attended his favourite young cousin. He remembered visiting her straight after a demonstration to students in the Institute of Morbid Anatomy. The young cousin developed puerperal fever and died. The better the results with Semmelweis's prophylaxis, the more Michaelis became convinced that he had been the unwitting agent who had introduced the deadly poison into his patient. A few weeks after writing to Semmelweis, he threw himself in front of the Hamburg express.

In Copenhagen Professor Levy's reaction to Michaelis's letter was more typical. He could not understand why, if Dr Semmelweis's discovery was so momentous, it had not been published in the *Neue Zeitschrift für Geburtsheilkunde*. This did not stop him from trying the method. When in 1850 he published his next paper on puerperal fever, he listed washing his hands with chlorine as 'one of the reforms which I have introduced and which have significantly improved our rate of infection'. Of Semmelweis there was no mention.

In his book published ten years later Semmelweis refers to several correspondents whose letters to and from him do not survive. One of them was James Young Simpson of Edinburgh, not yet knighted but already famous.[144] He in fact wrote not to Semmelweis but to Semmelweis's friend, Franz von Arneth, who was in London on his west European study tour.[145] According to Semmelweis,

> the letter was filled with abuse: Simpson said that even without [von Arneth's] letter he was perfectly aware in what a lamentable condition midwifery in Germany, and especially in Vienna, remained; he knew for certain that the cause of the high mortality in the lying-in hospitals lay in the unbounded carelessness with which patients were treated; as, for example, when they put a healthy lying-in woman in the same bed in which another patient had just died, without changing the bed clothes and linen.[146]

This was almost certainly one of Semmelweis's misinterpretations, an example of why, even in his lifetime but even more after his death, he was accused of 'hypersensitivity'. Simpson was an autocrat and disinclined to be lectured by anyone, least of all by a foreign obstetrician. But conditions in most British lying-in hospitals at the time *were* better than they were in most continental countries, and chlorine disinfection was not unknown in Edinburgh. Simpson himself was aware that birth attendants could introduce infections. But when, a few weeks later, von Arneth himself lectured in Edinburgh, he was courteously received. A few months after that Simpson himself published an article in which he stressed the importance of Semmelweis's prophylaxis, mentioning Semmelweis by name.

F.H.C. Routh, a former postgraduate student in Vienna, also got a warm reception when he spoke before the Royal Medico-Chirurgical Society on 28 November 1848. His lecture was reprinted in the *Transactions* and an abstract of the communication and discussion was published in the *Lancet* on 9 December. In January Routh wrote to Semmelweis (in Latin), describing the occasion:

> In the assembly of English physicians I delivered a lecture in which I announced your discovery, securing great honour rightly due to you. Many of the most learned members expressed the view that the arguments were convincing. Webster, Copland and Murphy, all famous physicians, spoke extremely well of you.[147]

Tilanus of Amsterdam also wrote a complimentary letter; and another former postgraduate student, Friedrich Wieger of Strasbourg, did his best to introduce Semmelweis's discovery to France. Sadly, his article submitted to the *Union Médicale* was published under the column of 'Drôleries' with other bits of somewhat questionable humour about the Vienna Medical School. But Wieger later published his report in a separate pamphlet. Joseph Schmidt of the Charité hospital in Berlin was alerted to the discovery by another Semmelweis disciple, Ernst von Brücke, professor of physiology, and referred to it favourably in the *Annals* of the hospital. Unfortunately, he mentioned only cadaveric infection.

But 'hypersensitivity' did not need to colour Semmelweis's response of rage when it came to the attacks emanating from Prague. The Czech capital had been for centuries the second city of the Empire and one much favoured by several emperors.[148] Its medical school enjoyed a reputation second only to Vienna's. Its first professor of obstetrics, Antonin Jungman, had been appointed in 1808 at the age of 30 and was by the late 1840s something of a living legend; but not much more. His second in command, Franz William Kiwisch von Rotterau, later professor in Würzburg, possessed a brilliant mind—he had written several useful though essentially descriptive works on puerperal fever— but had an unpredictable temperament. He disliked Skoda, as did many Prague academics, and he was wounded by what he considered the patronising manner in which Semmelweis's discovery had been passed on to them.[149] Nevertheless, he hurried to Vienna to discuss the matter with Semmelweis personally.

For some reason the meeting was not a success. Kiwisch may have been self-important—he came from an aristocratic family and was already famous—and Semmelweis was never at his best dealing with celebrities. But Kiwisch's later attacks may have been directed against a Skoda protégé rather than against Semmelweis personally. The Prague school generically regarded the Vienna establishment as insufferably arrogant, perhaps with some justice. Vienna was certainly favoured by the imperial bureaucracy and family. (After the reign of Joseph II, who liked the Czechs, imperial and royal physicians were without exception professors in Vienna.) Rokitansky could be forgiven for his desertion: there was nobody like him in either Prague or Vienna. But to many in the Czech capital Skoda was a traitor. In any case, Kiwisch was prepared to give Semmelweis's method a trial; and he might have changed his mind had he not already been terminally ill. He died of tuberculosis a year later.[150]

Wilhelm Scanzoni, Kiwisch's successor first in Prague and then in Würzburg and later professor in Prague, was an altogether shadier character.[151] A noted charmer and womaniser and an accomplished lecturer, even admiring historians of the Prague Medical School have little to say for him as a doctor. His 'statistics' do not add up, let alone make sense, and for years he presided over a horrendous 25–28 per cent mortality from puerperal fever in his department when he could not have been ignorant of either its cause or its remedy. All that can be said in mitigation both for him and for his protégé, Bernhard Seyfert, is that it was impossible to be neutral about Semmelweis. The idea of pyaemia transmitted by a birth attendant was not a clever modification of an obstetric manoeuvre that could be adopted or ignored at whim. It was either a life-saving discovery or a damnable deceit. Scanzoni and Seyfert tried to play it both ways. For ten years, during most of Semmelweis's career in Pest, they never lost a chance to denigrate him; and as authors of popular textbooks and centres of the social whirl at international conferences, they had many opportunities. Then, at some date impossible to ascertain, they adopted Semmelweis's prophylaxis, and from then on claimed to be its inventors.[152]

The most charitable interpretation of Semmelweis's rejection in many places was his own emphasis on cadaveric infection. Despite the fact that he quickly realised that this was not the *only* source of puerperal pyaemia, it was almost certainly the main source in Vienna. In this respect, however, the Habsburg Empire was unusual. Since the early nineteenth century a ministerial order was in force that post-mortem examinations were to be performed on as many bodies as possible in teaching hospitals 'to ascertain and to clarify the causes of death'. After Rokitansky's appointment to Vienna, a further ministerial memorandum was circulated requesting that all 'interesting' specimens (or parts thereof) should be forwarded to the Imperial Institute of Morbid Anatomy in Vienna for future reference. As a result, more autopsies were performed in Habsburg lands than anywhere else in Europe (with the possible exception of Paris), not only by pathologists but also by clinicians. Indeed, the practice may have contributed to the reputation of the Vienna Medical School.[153] But in obstetric units in other parts of Europe, where post-mortem examinations were infrequent and performed exclusively by technicians under the remote supervision of a pathologist, the idea that contamination with cadaveric material might be a significant cause of puerperal fever, a common illness, seemed improbable.

CHAPTER SEVEN

PEST

The Pest to which Semmelweis returned in 1850 was still a city in shock, the capital of a country in deep mourning. It is possible that in time Windischgrätz's army would have ground down Kossuth's *honvéds* unaided. In the spring of 1849 there was no sign of that. Austrian forces everywhere were in retreat. Then 200,000 Russian troops crossed the Carpathians.[154] Six weeks later their commander, General Paskiewitz, could report to his master that 'Hungary lies prostrate at Your Majesty's feet'. Nicolas I was not in fact interested in Hungary, prostrate or otherwise. Nor were his Austrian allies interested in honouring the promises he had made to the Hungarian Commander in Chief. Thirteen generals of the *honvéd* army, former imperial officers, were shot or hanged.[155] Hungary's first constitutional Prime Minister, Count Louis Battyányi, who stayed in Buda confident that his conduct had been strictly constitutional, was shot.[156]

A reign of terror was unleashed by General Count Julius Haynau, Schwarzenberg's choice for teaching Hungary a lesson. Haynau was a sadist. In Italy Radetzky, no bleeding heart himself, had pensioned him off for his brutality. Thousands were sentenced to death and shot or hanged. Those who had fled with Kossuth were executed *in absentia*.[157] Tens of thousands were sent to Austrian fortress prisons. Seventy percent of those died of tuberculosis before the first amnesty in 1854. The rest of Kossuth's army, mainly peasant boys in their teens or early twenties, were enlisted in Austrian regiments. There was probably no family in the country, irrespective of class, who did not mourn a husband, brother or son—dead, imprisoned or fate unknown. Many of those left behind were under deliberately harassing police surveillance. Of the 18 professors in the Faculty of Medicine of the University of Pest, 12 (who had worked in field hospitals in Kossuth's army) were sacked. Some were banished from the capital. Others, including the young surgeon Janos Balassa, were imprisoned in Pest's 'New Building'.[158] Only those known for their unswerving loyalty to the dynasty or for their terminal decrepitude (or for both) were left in post. They included the professor of obstetrics, Birly, an ardent advocate of purgation for all ills. Of the Semmelweis family three brothers of Ignác, a lawyer, a shopkeeper and a market gardener, had gone into exile.

By the time Semmelweis arrived back Haynau himself had been sacked.[159] His reign was replaced by an ubiquitous police network. Presiding over it from Vienna was the Imperial Minister of the Interior, Alexander Bach. Bach was a gifted man of unbounded energy. He had started life as a revolutionary but had become disillusioned by the practical incompetence of street-corner orators. (He admired the organising genius of Kossuth.) Now his spies and officials were supervising schools, universities, theatres, registry offices, shops and the law courts.[160] Professional associations were banned from holding meetings. The permission of the chief of police was required for social gatherings of more than five or of more than two families (to include church weddings). It was usually granted on condition that a police official attended. His presence was not a prescription for conviviality. To avoid police surveillance, Semmelweis and his medical friends met on horseback in the woods of the Buda Hills. Somebody later dubbed them the *Faculté de Médecine à cheval*.[161]

Yet after the first shock of defeat, hope was never wholly extinguished. Ferenc Deák emerged from political retirement and preached passive resistance with astonishing success. 'Cogito ergo sum: ergo non cogito ergo non sum', as the country's leading novelist, Mór Jókai, summed up the attitude of many.

Deák knew that economic incompetence and defeat in foreign wars would eventually force the dynasty to negotiate. He also knew that, in dealing with the Habsburgs, one could confidently look forward to both.[162]

Semmelweis was welcomed by old friends like von Markusovszky and new ones like the surgeons Janos Balassa and Sándor Lumnitzer and the physician Frigyes Korányi.[163] The family house had been sold in 1847 and he had no private means, but he survived. Presumably he lived in rented accommodation and made a living from private practice. Despite the dire state of the country, the few letters surviving from this period show him extraordinarily relaxed. Police harassment infuriated him, but it infuriated everybody else too. In *Galgenhumor* Pest was at least the equal of Vienna. ('The situation is critical but not serious' dates from this period, not the First World War.) Significantly perhaps, the only surviving photograph of Semmelweis from the early 1850s shows him in Hungarian costume.

Then a vacancy arose in Pest's oldest general infirmary, the Rokus (St Roche's) Hospital.[164] With room for about 400 patients, a paid medical staff of three, an unpaid medical staff of two, no postgraduate students and no teaching, it was a far cry from Vienna's Allgemeines Krankenhaus. Semmelweis later recounted that on his first visit (before applying for the post of obstetrician), he found that the obstetric unit consisted of eight beds in the general surgical ward. In one of the beds lay the cold body of a woman who had died of childbed fever the evening before. In the next bed another woman was groaning in the death throes of the same illness. All the other six bed occupants suffered from some disease, in addition to being about to give birth. The surgeon in charge, who had also been looking after the obstetric and gynaecological beds, did his own post-mortem examinations. Being of a scientific cast of mind, he started most days with two or three autopsies.

Even the appointment to the unpaid post took time, since Semmelweis insisted that he should be in sole clinical charge of all obstetric and gynaecological patients. He also wanted these to be in a separate ward, even if the ward was only a disused corridor. Fortunately, the medical superintendent, Dr Torday, liked him. More surprisingly, he half-believed in his doctrine. (Less happily, he was also an advanced alcoholic.) The hospital budget was derisory and the work arduous. There was no competition.

Semmelweis eventually worked at the hospital for six years. After some initial resistance from elderly midwives, he forced through his chlorine prophylaxis. (In contrast to his fraught relations with university professors, he was always good at dealing with midwives. While he exasperated them, they trusted him.) Between 1851 and 1856, 933 women gave birth at the hospital under his care. Mortality from childbed fever fell from 8.4 to 0.85 per cent, lower than it had ever been in Vienna.

On 21 November 1854 Professor Birly suddenly died. Fifty years later Semmelweis's posthumous champion, Tibor de Györy, wrote the following characteristic paragraph:

> Never has a medical historian faced a more distasteful task than I have to face when penning the next few lines. After Birly's death in a secret ballot the Faculty of Medicine of the University Pest did *not* nominate in the first place as Birly's successor the pride of our country and one of mankind's greatest benefactors.[165]

Much as one may sympathise with de Györy's wounded patriotic pride, the vote was not unexpected. Even though Deák's prognostications were proving accurate and the dynasty was beginning to try to make amends for the butchery and oppression of the past, more than half of the professors of the Pest Medical School were still appointees of the early Bach years, replacing those who had disgraced themselves in 1848–49. They nominated in the first place Hofrat Carl Braun, one of Semmelweis's fiercest opponents in Vienna. Braun was known for his loyalty to the August House as well as for his staunch resistance to 'Herr Semmelweis's crackpot ideas'. (It was indeed surprising that Semmelweis rather than Franz Walla, Birly's assistant, was nominated in second place.)

The outcome sheds some light on the much-maligned Bach era. Neither Schwarzenberg nor Bach would tolerate criticism of the government. They regarded national sentiment, tradition, freedom of speech and patriotic honour as claptrap, at best dispensable impediments to the efficient running of a modern state. But they *did* try to make the Habsburg Monarchy, the most creaking political machine in Europe, efficient. One of the officials in the ministry of education, Under-secretary Helfert, misguidedly appended the marginal comment to the faculty's submission: 'Braun is the obvious choice even though he speaks no Hungarian.' This was the sort of remark that made Count Thun, Bach's Minister of Education, apoplectic. What use 'um Gottes Willen' would a professor be in a country whose language he did not speak? 'What about that Semmelweiss [sic]?' He was assured that, though a controversial figure in obstetrics, Semmelweis spoke Hungarian as a native. Indeed, he was a native. He was a patriot but not an anarchist. He had spent the years of the so-called Liberation Struggle in Vienna. He had never met Kossuth. That was that. A month later, on 18 July 1855, Count Thun's humble submission was approved and signed by the Emperor.[166]

In some respects Semmelweis's appointment to Birly's chair was a sign of recognition. It was also a huge challenge. The clinic was in a horrendous state. Birly was more an accountant than a doctor. For 25 years he had prided himself on his 'prudent economy'. In that field he had achieved wonders. Crowded in six rooms almost impossible to ventilate, on the top floor of an old tenement on the corner of what are today Kossuth Lajos and Semmelweis Streets, the evil reputation of his department had ensured that at least half the beds were permanently empty. Even the poorest women of the streets struggled against being admitted. The patients who occupied the beds were the 'overflow' from other hospitals transferred to the clinic despite their protestations. Nobody kept count, but Semmelweis estimated that at least a third of the women admitted never left the unit alive. Yet for some weeks he could not account for the mortality. Neither Birly nor any of his staff had attended post-mortem examinations, though the morgue was on the ground floor. Its smell was all-pervasive. Students were few. It also perplexed him that the onset of puerperal fever was usually a day or two later than in other obstetric units he had known.

A much resented lightning search for other possible sources led him to the truth. A few years earlier Birly had discovered a laundry firm that had offered to deal with the linen of the clinic at a fraction of the cost charged by the university cleaners. Semmelweis seized his opportunity. At the crack of dawn, soon after taking charge, he ambushed the 'clean laundry' being returned to the clinic. It was, as he himself described it, an 'indescribably foul-smelling mess' of dried blood, pus, lochia and other excreta. He doubted if a drop of water, let alone soap, had been expended on it. He sacked the cleaners, but carried one of their baskets in a hired carriage to the offices of the university. There he waited patiently for the arrival of the administrative director, Herr Beifreier. The change of cleaners was one improvement that was quickly accomplished. Others took a little longer.

The Congress of Paris that ended the Crimean War in 1856 incidentally exposed Austria's diplomatic isolation. Having chastened the Czar, Britain and France no longer regarded the Habsburg Empire as a necessity. On the other hand, they felt under an obligation to Count Cavour, Prime Minister of Piedmont, who had sent Sardinian and Piedmontese troops to help them.[167] Austria's international isolation was aggravated by an economic crisis, exactly as Deák had prognosticated. The Emperor made his first tentative moves towards reconciliation with his not-so-loyal Magyar subjects. This was still unofficial and took odd forms. One was a letter addressed to von Markusovszky from the Imperial Minister of the Interior in Vienna. During the years of oppression Marko had become the

Deák of the medical profession. Now he was informed that the minister no longer objected to the Hungarian Medical Society, once a flourishing professional body but in abeyance since 1849. Nor would the Minister object to a resumption of the publication of the *Orvosi Hetilap* (Hungarian Medical Weekly) under Professor von Markusovszky's 'temperate editorship'. Its censorship would be benign. Among the interesting case reports in the first resumed issue in February 1857 was one by Professor Semmelweis on a patient with a rare ovarian tumour.

A month later Semmelweis, now 38, met the 19-year-old Maria Weidenhofer, the pretty daughter of a prosperous haberdasher, Ignác Weidenhofer. Three months later their wedding took place in the homely setting of the church of the Holy Trinity in the Inner City. The ceremony was performed by Károly Semmelweis, the bridegroom's youngest brother, and was 'a happy occasion exceptionally well attended by friends and well-wishers'. The ban on social gatherings was forgotten though never officially lifted.

Fifty years after Semmelweis's death his widow was still alive and was interviewed by Semmelweis's first biographer, Fritz Schürer von Waldheim. Ironically perhaps, both she and Semmelweis's nephews and nieces had 'Hungarianised' their name to Szemerényi after the death of their wayward uncle. (The only Semmelweises left today are the ones still living in Burgenland.) By then Frau Szemerényi's reminiscences were no doubt coloured by the piety due to the memory of a great man. After a long period of embarrassed silence even in his own country, he was beginning to be referred to as the 'Saviour of Mothers'. Nevertheless, her recollections chimed in with other personal testimonies.

At the time of his marriage he was already almost completely bald and a little corpulent but quick and agile in his movement and fit looking. What struck everybody at once was his extraordinary kindness, especially to those in need, to the old and the sick. He could fly into a rage with colleagues and even assistants; but with patients he was infinitely caring and had all the time in the world. When our first two children died he grieved; but he hid his own sorrow to comfort me. He could be extraordinarily tender. Had he any weaknesses? Yes. He understood nothing about money, whether it was a matter that concerned his clinic or his home. We were always short of cash, though he looked after some of the richest people in town. We lived in my parents' house [in the Váci ucca where today is No.10] because we could never afford our own; and his suits always looked shabby and threadbare.[168]

Despite the loss of their two first children—one died a few hours after birth with hydrocephalus, the other at four months from peritonitis—the first two or three years of the marriage were probably Semmelweis's happiest since boyhood. He worked hard and complained much and bitterly about the meanness of the university authorities in providing for his department; but when in 1858 he was offered the chair of obstetrics in Zurich (still a small provincial town, though already on the road to financial grandeur) he declined.[169] Eventually the marriage was blessed with a girl, a boy and then another girl.[170]

However, Semmelweis—or, more important to him, his doctrine—continued to be the target of denigration from abroad, and he was aware that in many famous obstetric hospitals childbed fever continued to extract its terrible toll. It was probably Marko's taunts, that it was all his—that is, Semmelweis's—fault, since he refused to make his teaching easily accessible in print, that finally overcame his inhibitions. Once embarked on, the 500-odd pages of *Die Aetiologie, der Begriff und die Prophylaxis des Kindbettfiebers* took less than a year to complete. Dated 1861 on the title page, it was in fact published in 1860 by the well-established academic publishing house of Hartleben.

The *Aetiology* is both a terrible and a wonderful book. The first half is a personal account of the author's long and troubled pilgrimage from tormenting ignorance to sudden illumination, from inkling to certainty: in short, of his path to his moment of truth. It is verbose, repetitive, chaotic, self-centred, unrelenting —and totally riveting, a book of revelation rather than a scientific treatise. It is the writing of a man incapable of embroidering the truth and not even trying to hide his emotional involvement, his private outrage and his despair at his own incapacity to convince others of the facts. Men totally without side themselves are rarely convincing portraying timorous characters brimming over with caution, and readers may groan at Semmelweis's seeming puzzlement at the 'obtuseness' of elderly and eminent university professors when simple facts were explained to them 'in plain language'. Why did they not recognise the obvious? Why did they oppose him? They may also be repelled by his apparent conceit. Doctors and scientists may believe but do not usually state that their discoveries are 'the blinding and eternal truth'. Nevertheless, to Semmelweis his findings were exactly that and he wrote what he believed.

The second half of the book is a long polemic, a compendium of the letters he wrote and received, of the responses printed by his antagonists and occasional supporters. His contempt for the former—and they included men of such fame as Rudolf Virchow of Berlin as well as some of the most prestigious names in European obstetrics—was scathing. His praise for the latter was never over-generous. They were, after all, only ordinary people recognising the obvious and doing their job.

Having at long last published the book, and having sent it to 20 prominent obstetricians, physicians and pathologists with his compliments, Semmelweis waited for their reaction.[171] For practical purposes there was none. Marko published a detailed but perhaps too fulsome unsigned editorial review in three consecutive numbers of the *Hungarian Medical Weekly*, though other journals neither praised nor blamed. When reactions started to trickle in, they were almost uniformly hostile. In a medical yearbook of 1861 Joseph Späth nominated the inflammation of the fallopian tubes as the fundamental cause of puerperal fever.[172] This prompted the first of Semmelweis's *Offene*

Briefe or open letters. These appeared in German as supplements to the *Hungarian Medical Weekly* and must rank among the most extraordinary medical publications ever. The first set the tone, though comparatively mildly:

> The Herr Professor has given me the impression that his spirit has not yet been illuminated by the puerperal sun which arose in Vienna in the year 1847, although it has shone near him [a reference to his own discovery of the causation of puerperal fever and its prevention] ... This stubborn ignoring of my doctrine and persistence in errors has caused thousands and thousands of lying-in women and sucklings to die unnecessarily. All of them could have been saved ... I simply recall to your memory when happened in the First and Second Divisions of the Lying-in Hospital in Vienna between 1847 and 1851.

The writer then analysed the statistics of the Vienna Krankenhaus over a ten-year period after his own departure and arrived at the conclusion that 1824 patients, all young women in the bloom of their youth, had lost their lives from infections that could have been avoided. He then became personal again.

> In this massacre you, Herr Professor, have participated. The murders must cease, and with this object I shall keep watch and every man who dares spread dangerous errors regarding puerperal fever will find in me an implacable foe. For me there is no other means for putting an end to the mass murder than unsparingly to unmask the perpetrators.[173]

The second open letter was addressed to Wilhelm Scanzoni, Semmelweis's most persistent critic, whose attacks had recently taken the form of reviews he had caused to be signed by one of his assistants.

> Herr Hofrat will have learned from my recent letter to Professor Späth that I have resolved to put an end to the

mass murder and to attack unsparingly those who dare to spread errors regarding puerperal fever ... The greatest service rendered by my doctrine is that it shows how the unhappiness wrought by this terrible illness can be prevented with certainty. Your own teaching is achieving the opposite ... You say that special attention must be drawn to the fact that puerperal fever cases in your university did not occur in the practice of one doctor. This is not surprising since all who practise there are ignoramuses and you have sent all over Germany a considerable contingent of practitioners whom you have instructed in your homicidal practices.[174]

He concluded with surely the most scathing printed denunciation of one medical professor directed at another.

Your teaching, Herr Professor, is attested by thousands of dead bodies of young women slaughtered through your ignorance ... I have formed the unshakeable resolution to put an end to this murderous practice so far as it is in my power to do so ... I shall denounce you before God and the world as a murderer and the history of puerperal fever will justly remember you as a medical Nero.

Semmelweis sent a copy of his first two open letters to Eduard von Siebold, Professor of Obstetrics at Göttingen. They had met in Vienna and von Siebold had been a guest in the Semmelweis home. But in 1861 von Siebold had published an article in which he suggested that in Semmelweis's view cadaveric infection was the 'sole source of puerperal fever'. A third open letter to von Siebold struck a tone more of sorrow than of anger:

I know you, Herr Professor, as a man of kind disposition: I am convinced that it is not possible for you to do intentionally a thing disagreeable to any man. I therefore entreat you, Herr Hofrat, to acquire an intimate knowledge of the truth as set forth in my book.[175]

And more in this vein. At the same time Semmelweis published another vituperative epistle to Scanzoni, telling him that 'you have demonstrated, Herr Hofrat, that even in your new hospital provided with all the most modern facilities, a good deal of homicide can be perpetrated where there is the will'.[176]

A photograph taken of Semmelweis at the time—he was 43—shows a man already old. The bald dome of his head is fringed with sparse grey hair, the eyebrows and moustache are almost completely white, and the mouth and brow are set in a fixed expression of anger. One more open letter was addressed to 'all professors of obstetrics':

> If you do not instruct your students in my doctrine, then I will address myself to the helpless public directly. 'You, father of a family, do you know what you are doing when you summon an obstetrician? You are exposing your wife and unborn child to the danger of death. And if you do not wish to become a widower and if your children are not to lose their mother, then buy a single penny-worth of chloride of lime, dissolve it in water and do not allow your obstetrician to examine your wife until he has washed his hands in the chlorine solution in your presence. And do not allow the obstetrician to make an internal examination until you have convinced yourself that his hands have become slippery.[177]

Were these the utterances of a person in his right mind? With hindsight it is easy to see them as the first—or even as the second or third—stages of insanity. Benedek, Semmelweis's admiring biographer and himself an experienced neuropsychologist, speaks not yet of madness but of a 'grievously hurt mind'. It would be difficult to disagree with him. However, that 'hurt' was not groundless as it might be in the case of a mental illness. Almost 20 years after Semmelweis had recognised the aetiology of puerperal fever and a way to prevent it, 15 years after his doctrine appeared in print, and 4 or 5 years after the publication of his book, 35 out of 101 women died of childbed fever in

Dr Zipfel's lying-in hospital in Vienna. In Professor Karl Braun's first university clinic, where many years earlier Semmelweis had made his discovery, 113 women sickened with puerperal fever in the early autumn of 1861 and 48 died within a period of 45 days. In making their report to the ministry, both Zipfel and Braun denied the possibility of 'infection from decomposed animal matter' and insisted that the disease had resulted from 'malign miasmas' that had settled on their institutions. In Prague during 1861–62 5 per cent of women (and 3 percent of babies) and in Stockholm 8 per cent of women died of childbed fever. Almost all these deaths were avoidable. None of this could be kept secret. It might have been known locally but not generally 100 or even 50 years earlier. By the mid-nineteenth century not only individual travel but international meetings and conferences ensured that academic medicine had few secrets.

This had its advantages as well as drawbacks, and not all news was bad news. A temperament different from Semmelweis's might have drawn comfort from intermittent shafts of light. At the annual meeting of German physicians and scientists in Speyer in September 1861, Professor Wilhelm Lange of Heidelberg spoke with enthusiasm about his experience with Semmelweis's antiseptic regime. He was in no doubt that it accounted for the low (0.3 per cent) death rate from puerperal fever in his department. A few months later his paper was printed in the *Monatschrift für Geburtsheilkunde*. Ludwig Kugelman, a Hanover obstetrician, wrote: 'Talking to a colleague I burst out involuntarily when he mentioned your doctrine. "Ah, that man is a second Jenner! If only he was granted the same recognition!"[178] He enclosed, as a token of his admiration, a copy of Jenner's book dedicated by the Englishman to Professor Blumenbach, *magister Germaniae*. Semmelweis's answer has been lost, but Kugelman soon wrote again:

It has been given to few to have bestowed on mankind a gift that is true, lasting, and free; and almost without exception the world has repaid them with burning them on the stake or crucifying them. And yet I hope that you will not weary from proclaiming the truth until the final victory ... Remember that men often put self-interest above the truth, even deceiving themselves that what they do is right. But let me remind you, honoured colleague, that it is all too easy to be deafened by the shrill voices of your enemies. You do not hear about the many who are adopting your teaching. Let me as a proof, enclose a letter from our colleague, Hofrat Dommes.[179]

The enclosed letter contained a handsome tribute from Dommes, acknowledging all that he had learnt from Semmelweis's book. Nevertheless, these still seemed like solitary voices. They did not dispel the darkness that was closing in.

In his last years Semmelweis took an interest in gynaecology; and medical historians may wonder what he might have achieved in this field. His description of the prophylactic cleaning of the hands, at that time the most important source of infection in surgical operations, clearly anticipated antisepsis and even asepsis:

> The necessity for disinfecting the hands will always be present. To attain this objective it is necessary to oil the hands well before any contact with any decomposed or infective matter, so that their penetration into the pores of the skin is prevented. After that the hands must be washed with soap and then exposed to the action of a chemical agent capable of destroying the decomposed matter not yet removed: we employ for this matter chloride of lime and wash till the hands are slippery.[180]

Except for Semmelweis being unaware of the key role of living micro-organisms, this was an advance on Lister.[181]

But his tendency to moodiness was becoming worse. There were days when he hardly spoke to his assistants, lecturing in an almost unintelligible monotone and breaking now and then into an impassioned harangue against a variety of dark forces. He started to use coarse language in a way he had never done before. (His invective had often been biting but never crude.) He ate voraciously and put on weight. His wife and friends were getting worried. They were watching him closely. Once a genial guest at dinner parties, his behaviour became so erratic that time and gain he had to be escorted home. He was abrupt and dismissive of his wife. Only holding their baby daughter Antonia in his arms seemed to calm him. Hoping that he might improve with rest, the family went to a spa in the Bakony Hills in Transdanubia. There he was quiet, almost apathetic, 'like a good sick child' as his wife later described it. He was better for a time after their return.

On 15 June 1861 a faculty meeting was held to discuss the appointment of assistants. Semmelweis was asked for his views. He pulled from his pocket the text of the oath of midwives and recited it in ringing tones. He was escorted home by Balassa, von Markusovszky, Hirschler and another colleague. A few days later a professorial meeting was held at his home. They decided to take him to Vienna, to the well-known sanatorium of Dr Riedel. A telegram was sent to Hebra, asking him to meet the party at the station. Then, under the pretext of going on a short holiday to Baden bei Wien, Semmelweis, his wife (with Antonia in her arms), Semmelweis's assistant, Dr Báthory, and a male relative boarded the train. Hebra met them at the Ostbahnhof. There were happy embraces. Hebra expressed the wish to show Semmelweis his new department. Semmelweis agreed. On the way in the carriage he talked animatedly. Arriving at the hospital it was suggested that Semmelweis should take a rest. He had a short nap, then he wanted to rejoin his family. They had gone. What did they mean, 'gone'? They were all going on a family holiday. He was told that he must stay for a few days. A break was necessary. He protested. There was an affray. He was put into a straitjacket and locked in a cell. There he started to rave.

These are the last undoubted facts about the living Semmelweis. The rest is unclear. A day or two after admission an injury—perhaps sustained during the affray, perhaps self-inflicted—went septic. A week later he was suffering from fever, pain and delirium. Disseminated pyaemia was diagnosed. There was no consultation with a specialist, but he was seen once by the director of the institute, a Dr Mildner. There is no record of sedatives being prescribed or administered. It is uncertain whether or not a telegram was ever sent to his wife while he was alive. She had apparently tried to visit her husband on the day after his detention, but had been told that he was in a 'rage' and could not be visited. (There is no record of this.) She and her daughter then returned to Pest. She would always maintain that the next news she received was a telegram two and a half weeks later. It informed her with regret that her husband had died on 13 August.

Apart from the penultimate telegram, many questions remain unanswered. Why, in the first place, was he sent to Vienna without being seen in Pest by a neuropsychiatrist?[182] Why was he taken to a public asylum instead of Dr Riedel's private sanatorium? Why, when he was ill and dying, were none of his influential Viennese friends alerted? Or were they? Perhaps it is one thing to champion a slightly difficult but brilliant provincial without family ties and another to take an interest in a deranged lunatic, however regrettable his suffering. It was also the holiday season. More than likely Rokitansky was mountain climbing in the Dolomites. Skoda was no doubt in attendance on the Queen-Empress wherever it was her unpredictable whim to travel.

But about the nature of Semmelweis's last illnesses and about the immediate cause of his death no doubt remains. The body was taken to Rokitansky's Institute where Rokitansky's assistant, Schöneberg, performed a careful autopsy followed by the microscopic examination of several organs. The post-mortem protocol still exists. The remains were exhumed and re-examined first in 1887 (when the body was transferred to Budapest) and then again in 1961, when the skeletal remains were subjected to scrutiny and photographed. Semmelweis had certainly been suffering for some years from progressive neurosyphilis. Known also as GPI or general paralysis of the insane, it was extremely common in all countries in Europe, though rarely mentioned in polite society.[183] The immediate cause of death was unrelated to this illness except that the initiating injury might not have occurred outside a lunatic asylum. It was generalised pyaemia with multiple abscesses under the skin, in the lungs, in the peritoneum and in the bones. The lesions were similar to those of his friend, Kolletschka, and of countless women who had died of childbed fever. His unrelieved sufferings during his last fortnight must have been intense.

In his own country Semmelweis's death was followed by a period of 'stunned silence'.[184] A lengthy obituary by von Markusovszky appeared in the *Hungarian Medical Weekly*, delicately hinting that death had spared its victim years of suffering.[185] He was replaced as professor by a nonentity, Johann Diescher, who did not trouble to maintain even in Semmelweis's own clinic his antiseptic regime. The incidence of puerperal fever, less than 0.5 per cent in Semmelweis's last year, soared. It was a memorial of sorts.

Abroad the situation was different. Few had the moral courage of Späth, for long one of Semmelweis's most determined adversaries and recipient of his first vitriolic open letter. Soon after Semmelweis's death he wrote:

> I venture to state as clearly as I can that in my opinion there is no longer a reputable teacher in midwifery who is not in his own heart convinced of the truth of the doctrine of Semmelweis, even when he still professes to be opposed to it ... Let me ask: who today treats his patients not in accordance with the principles of Semmelweis? Why do we all preach that the utmost cleanliness is necessary? Why do we carefully wash our hands in an antiseptic solution? Why do we attend to the ventilation of our wards? Why do we see that all our utensils are perfectly clean? Why do we isolate infected cases? It is all a tribute to Semmelweis.[186]

Perhaps in medicine (as in science) claiming another man's discovery is the most sincere form of flattery. If true, Semmelweis had his share of post-mortem flatterers. Scanzoni and Carl Braun led the way. To numerous self-important professors and fashionable obstetricians, it was perhaps easier to concede that the truculent and uncompromising Hungarian had been right after all now that he was no longer dipping his pen into poison. Perhaps dying when he did, he rendered a last service to 'his mothers'. His? It was another common grouse against him, an offence against polite usage in professional circles. The mothers were obviously not 'his' in a biological sense. So why did he persistently refer to them as if they were? One could never trust a character like that.

The specific cause of puerperal fever was proclaimed and Semmelweis's ideas were finally vindicated 14 years after his death. 'On 11 March 1874,' Emile Roux wrote,

> in a discussion in the [French] Académie one of his [Pasteur's] weightiest opponents was eloquently enlarging upon the 'numerous and varied' causes of puerperal epidemics in lying-in hospitals. Pasteur interrupted him. 'None of those things cause the epidemics. It is the nursing and medical staff who carry the microbe to healthy women.' And when the orator petulantly replied that he feared that the mythical microbe will never be found, Pasteur went to the blackboard and quickly drew a diagram of the chain-like organism. 'There, that is what it is like.'[187]

Eventually even Semmelweis's compatriots emerged from their stupor. During the celebrations of Sir Joseph Lister's visit to Budapest in 1883, he is said to have turned to one of his hosts. Why was the great Hungarian, Semmelweis, not mentioned in any of the welcoming speeches? Whether or not Lister actually made such a remark (and it is doubtful), the theme was taken up by the *Prague Medical Weekly*. 'Last week Professor Sir Lister was feted in Budapest. It struck us [an anonymous Czech correspondent] as odd that no mention was made of Semmelweis in any of the festive addresses.'[188]

Perhaps the provenance of the rebuke as much as the rebuke itself stung some of the country's great and good. A commemorative committee was formed. The committee laboured for years. Funds were slow coming in. Once again, a prod came from abroad. The first monograph of Semmelweis was published in Germany in 1905.[189] The state, in the person of Hungary's Minister of Education, Count Albert Apponyi, stepped in. A fund was voted by Parliament. Semmelweis's remains were reburied in Budapest with solemn pomp. Hungary's leading sculptor, Alajos (Aloys) Strobl, was commissioned to carve a life-size statue of him in Carrara marble. Last-minute difficulties and disagreements, too numerous to mention, were overcome. (Most seriously, the arrival of the pieces of marble coincided with Hungary's first official strike of monumental masons. According to legend the pieces were transported to the plinth and put together by medical students the night before the unveiling.[190]) The statue was first erected in the leafy tranquillity of Pest's Elizabeth Square. In 1946 it was transferred to the square in front of the Rokus hospital where Semmelweis had worked after his return to Pest.

Alajos Strobl was an excellent traditional artist and the statue is a fine work. Semmelweis is shown in a vaguely Hungarian costume, as specified by the commissioning committee. Strobl used his young wife as the model of the mother on the base; she is charming. The unveiling was a grand occasion. In Budapest as elsewhere in Europe, this was the golden age of municipal junketings. At the five-hour banquet the night before, gold, silver and bronze medals (according to rank rather than merit) were distributed among the international celebrities. They included leading obstetricians from nearly every country. The only notable absentee was the much-lauded artist: his young wife was giving birth to their first child at home. Soon after the unveiling ceremony had begun the next day, Budapest's leading obstetrician, Professor Ivan Balla, was called away urgently by a messenger.

'You took your time, Ivan,' Strobl stormed when the professor arrived at his home. 'Not to worry, Alajos,' Balla replied, 'your wife is safe. Let me wash my hands first. Even we Hungarians have at last learnt our lesson from Semmelweis.'

PART III

LISTER AND
ANTISEPTIC SURGERY

Joseph Lister (1827–1912)

Portrait reproduced by permission of Science Photo Library

CHAPTER ONE

FRIENDS

By the end of the eighteenth century the followers of George
Fox, calling themselves Friends but to the outside world
better known as Quakers, were no longer thrown into prison
for blasphemy, executed for treason or transported to distant
and dangerous lands for being a thorn in the flesh of the
establishment.[1] They still had much to contend with. Since
their conscience forbade them to take the oath or to subscribe
to the thirty-nine articles—the codified doctrines of faith of
the established church—they were excluded from the old
universities and therefore from an academic career.[2] They were,
of course, barred from taking holy orders. Firmly maintaining
their Christian testimony against war, they neither could nor
wished to join the navy or the army. Many therefore followed a
career in business or a trade; and, since they were hard working,
frugal and honest, they prospered.

Nevertheless, they were still a people apart. Living without
ostentation or display, they did not indulge in 'vain sports and
idle diversions'. They did not visit the theatre, dance or hunt.
They had no music in their homes. This gave them time to
devote much thought and energy to education and science, and
they excelled in both. It was not uncommon to find a Friend of
modest circumstances but highly respected for his original work
by the scientific community, serving behind the counter of his
shop.

In the early nineteenth century Friends still adopted a
characteristic dress, not that of George Fox any more, but one

that took no notice of the fads of the day. For the men it was a plain black, grey or drab suit, the coat shaped like a court dress with an upstanding collar. The necktie was white and the hat black and broader-brimmed than was generally worn. It was not removed in salutation, nor in places of worship. The women dressed in sober hues with a spotless folded kerchief round their necks and a patternless shawl over their shoulders. They wore a white muslin cap of a distinctive shape, the 'coal-scuttle' bonnet.

Both men and women used the 'plain address' of 'thee' or 'thou', not only among themselves but also when addressing others. They had no use for such prefixes as 'Mr' or 'Mrs' (let alone 'Ms' or 'Esq'). It was plain 'Friend Lister' or 'Friend Hodgkin', even when it was the servant addressing the master, provided that the servant was 'one of us'. Friends could not marry outside the Society without being 'disowned', which meant a good deal of intermarriage and a large number of Friends being more or less distantly related. (To make the amateur genealogist's task even more difficult, first names too tended to run in families.)

Attendance at meetings for worship was central and, since there was no clergy or liturgy of any kind, these were sometimes conducted in virtual silence lasting an hour or more. Many young Quakers at an impressionable age both looked forward to and dreaded the time when they would receive a 'personal call' to 'appear in the ministry' by uttering a few words of exhortation or prayer. It sometimes precipitated a crisis of faith. In addition to twice-weekly meetings of worship, there were business meetings, the so-called Meetings for Discipline, which were held monthly, quarterly and yearly. The last was a kind of parliament of Friends for the whole kingdom and assembled in London for sessions lasting a week or more.

All this might sound dour and inhibited, but the Listers of Upton House were neither. They were a lively and happy family, not particularly judgmental and free from sanctimoniousness. They had their cricket and their bowls, skating in the winter and evening parties with the neighbours. Among their chief recreations were long country walks and the collection of fossils and other interesting natural history specimens. Pets, domestic animals and wildlife merged into one world. On the domestic side they had chickens, horses, a cow, calves and carrier pigeons, but also goldfish, dogs and cats. The doings and occasional misbehaviour of the menagerie formed an important part of their voluminous correspondence. 'Spot is in disgrace because he found a nest of rabbits under the terrace and killed one ...' On the wild side there were deer, rabbits, rats, foxes and silkworms.

The family had its roots in Bingley in Yorkshire, where in 1705 Thomas Lister, maltster and farmer, married Hannah Lister, the daughter of a yeoman. They joined the Society of Friends and some of their descendants are Quakers still. Their grandson, John, migrated to London, married the daughter of a Friend, and in due course acquired the wine business of his father-in-law in the City of London. He lived to the age of 98. Twenty-seven years after the birth of his two daughters, he and his wife were blessed with a son, Joseph Jackson. A promising youth, he attended several Quaker schools. At ten he was capable of writing a respectable letter in French, with only a word or two corrected by the usher.[3] He delighted in Virgil and knew his Tacitus well enough to find him too oracular. He was a good calligrapher. At 59 John Lister wrote to his boy:

Dear Joseph [later known as Joseph Jackson],
As I often think of thee with desires that thou may grow up a sober and industrious Lad, so am also desirous that thou shouldst see a little of what is publishing for th' instruction and benefit of youth of the present Generation and adapted for the capacities and employments of many of them, have therefore sent thee 9 books for the purpose, and I greatly desire that thy principal care may be to discharge thy duty to thy teachers, and to keep a conscience void of Offence to thy Creator from whose bounty we are supplied with every favor that we enjoy ... On enquiring after thee from J. Vully, the usher, I hear that he is satisfied with thine work

generally but that he has to complain of thy being very long in writing 10 Lines in a Copy and learning a little spelling that one and a half hours are often taken up therewith, which am satisfied thou might's easily accomplish in one hour, so that hast but little time for the Latin. This has made me sorry because an hour wasted is a loss thou may have great reason to regret, as well as such a habit continued in idling thy time must prove of bad consequence ... O my Son, there nothing like doing the best thou can to please those who have the care of thy instruction and thy good at heart ... So hoping that I shall hear no more complaints of thee, I remain with love, joined by thy Mother and Sisters, Thy truly affectionate Father, John Lister ...

P.S. We intended to have sent thee a plum pudding cake had we heard a better account but shall now leave it till another time.[4]

Joseph Jackson did eventually get his cake and fulfilled all his father's hopes. Soon he himself would combine travelling on business with visits to Friends' schools scattered all over the country. It was while visiting Ackworth School near Pontefract (intended for the education of the children of Friends 'not in affluent circumstances and for those of the peasant class' of whom there were still many) that he met Isabella Harris, his future wife. She was the younger daughter of the school's superintendent and was to be memorialised in the school's centenary volume published in 1879:

Whilst a temporary cloud rested on the fame of the reading on the boys' side, that of the girls was attaining the highest excellence under the guidence of their young reading mistress, Isabella Harris. While the girls' department was administered by this lady's mother in a manner which ever gave supreme satisfaction to the Committee, the daughter became in 1813 a recognised authority on reading, a position that has become historic in the annals of the

School. Those who have been privileged to listen to her reading have spoken of its grace and force, of its masterly rendering of the author's meaning, and of the delicacy of the reader's intonation and emphasis, excellencies never approached by anybody else in their experience and affording an intellectual feast of the purest quality ... She left the school in 1818 [to be married to Joseph Jackson Lister] when the Committee made her a handsome present in token of their high appreciation ... for her valuable exertions in endeavouring to instruct the children in the paths of virtue and religion and to promote the peace and harmony of the family.[5]

A portrait survives of her attired in the Quaker habit, drawn by her husband six years later: she looks grave and beautiful.[6] By then success in business had enabled Joseph Jackson to purchase (at the recommendation of another Friend, Samuel Gurney, a banker in Lombard Street) Upton House, a spacious Queen Anne mansion with extensive grounds in Essex.[7] In the 1830s the family had a domestic staff of a cook, a nanny, a footman, a coachman and a lady's maid. Upton itself, now a concrete wilderness shivering on the threshold of gentrification, was then barely more than a winding lane leading from Romford Road to Plaistow. A dozen or so comfortable houses were scattered along it. They backed onto pastures and tilled fields.[8] Ham House, the elegant home of the Gurneys, stood opposite, and some of the rare and exotic plants collected by banker Sam found their way into the grounds of Upton.[9] The cedar trees were especially cherished. Hainault and Epping forests were close and the nearby Barking marshes, the haunt of wild fowl and golden plover in the winter, were famous botanising areas. It was in this house that on 5 April 1827 Joseph Lister, the couple's fourth child and second son, was born.[10]

In early potted biographies Lister's ancestry is sometimes described as 'undistinguished'. This can be true only by the most exalted or distorted of social standards. It was certainly not lacking in talent. Isabella Lister was a woman of many domestic accomplishments (apart from her gift of reading as lauded by the governors of Ackworth School); and Joseph Jackson was not only a successful businessman and good amateur artist but also a self-taught scientist. His work on lenses, which he ground himself, and on the construction of microscopes led to his election to the Royal Society in 1832. His circle of friends—they were regularly entertained at Upton—included the eminent palaeontologist James Scott Bowerbank, the astronomer John (later Sir John) Herschel, Herschel's friend, the economist Charles Babbage, and the pioneer comparative anatomist Sir Richard Owen.

Closest perhaps to Joseph Jackson as a friend as well as a Friend and scientist was Dr Thomas Hodgkin, pathologist to Guy's Hospital.[11] In a joint paper they described the improbable but characteristic biconcave shape of the human red blood cell and the tendency of the cells to aggregate in piles or 'rouleaux' when exposed to air.[12] Among regular attendees at the Plaistow meetings on Sundays and Thursdays (or First and Fifth Days, in Quaker parlance) were the prison reformer Elizabeth Fry, Sam Gurney's sister, as well as numerous Barclays, Dimsdales and Shepherds. Already a successful businessman, Joseph Jackson also took lessons in French literature from Camille de Gène, a French émigré, more perhaps to support the teacher than to enlarge his already good knowledge of the French classics. After the abortive revolutions of 1848–49 in most Continental countries, a wave of French, Polish, German, Italian and Hungarian refugees sought asylum in London. While Quakers kept out of day-to-day party politics and were opposed to any armed conflict, once a conflict had been irrevocably lost they were generous in helping its victims. In one of his letters the Hungarian patriot Lajos Kossuth, starting his 38-year exile, mentions 'the wine merchant in the City, Joseph Jackson Lisster [sic]' as one of those offering him 'warm and open-handed hospitality'.

Even by the standards of the time, the Listers were and remained a close-knit family. Three of John Jackson and Isabella's children would eventually settle in houses near Upton, Mary Godlee and her husband only a mile or two away in Plaistow, Arthur in the new suburb of Leytonstone and Jane, after she married the successful Quaker merchant Smith Harrison, in Woodford. Even when he went to live in Scotland, Joseph would regularly return to Upton for Christmas, as did his brothers, sisters and their growing families. Between Christmases they visited each other and carried on a large, intimate and wonderfully literate correspondence. The opening of the railways helped. The Eastern Counties Railways (later known as the Great Eastern) did not start to operate fully till 1839, but the line to Romford, not far from Upton, was in use earlier. The main line from London to Birmingham stopped at Hitchin in Hertfordshire, where the Lucases, another group of relatives, lived. There Joseph witnessed the first recorded derailment. It was spectacular but there were no serious casualties. Steam travel by land and sea also made Continental holidays easier. These too were usually undertaken in family groups. In 1846 Joseph made up a party of six cousins for a trip up the Rhine and a tour of Switzerland, Italy and France.

Of course, even in a close and increasingly prosperous middle class family growing up during the first decades of the Industrial Revolution, all was not sunshine. One of Joseph's summer holidays was interrupted by having to appear as a witness in the trial of two lads, one 12, the other 14, who had stolen two cricket bats from the Quaker school that he attended. On being found guilty, one was sentenced to seven and the other to nine years' transportation. Upton was idyllic but the city was only a few miles away and it was Dickens's London. To reach the nearest public gibbet on which the bodies of cattle thieves and other malefactors were left hanging until they rotted away was less than half an hour's walking distance.

There were private tragedies too. John Lister, the eldest son of Joseph Jackson and Isabella, a gifted and promising youth, died at 19 from a distressing and painful brain tumour.[13] His long suffering affected his parents and siblings deeply. While such deaths were of course inevitable in large mid-Victorian families—

tuberculosis was the commonest but not the only killer—as the Listers' and many other families' correspondences show, there was never a way of taking the losses in one's stride. Joseph Jackson virtually gave up his scientific work after the death of his eldest son.

Joseph, 16 at the time, now became Joseph Jackson's heir and might have been expected to step into his brother's shoes and join the family business. In fact, he had already decided to become a surgeon. No pressure was put on him to change his mind. What had induced him to entertain such an outlandish ambition is hard to guess. He was a handsome and bright young man but shy, an intellectual rather than a physical doer. He had a slight stammer that at times caused him anguish. He was fit but not particularly robust. He was cherished by his parents and sisters, but he was not a natural star player on any stage. Even as a schoolboy he had an inquisitive mind, but this was not regarded as an important attribute for a surgeon; perhaps the reverse. Since John Hunter, surgeons were allowed to ask intelligent questions but were not expected to provide too many clever answers.[14]

Nor was surgery a particularly desirable profession socially or financially. As in France, the status of surgeons in England had improved since 1800, when the Company of Surgeons had become the Royal College of Surgeons,[15] and one or two fellows had already become famous. Nevertheless, they were the exceptions. As Joseph Jackson repeatedly pointed out to his son, it was still easier to make a contribution to the sciences as a physician. There were no charismatic surgeons among the Listers' friends; indeed, the only medical relation was a distant and slightly disreputable cousin who had deserted the Society and had allegedly emigrated. Perhaps, as still occasionally happens, it was his very 'unsuitability'—or apparent unsuitability—that attracted the slightly tongue-tied schoolboy to surgery. Under the charming, compliant, even at times meek surface, there would always be a streak of admirable obstinacy. Medicine

might be an easier or most obvious choice. It would probably be more lucrative and certainly more gentlemanly. But surgery was the greater challenge.

In the London of the 1840s it was a rather fearful challenge too. It was bloody. It was inseparable from physical suffering. Its scope was also severely restricted. As in medicine, tuberculosis loomed large. The incidence of the disease in poor urban populations was at its disastrous peak. In London it accounted for over a quarter of all hospital admissions and was incidentally present in at least another quarter. This was despite the fact that once the diagnosis was made, the patients were declared incurable and promptly discharged. They would not be re-admitted except as acute emergencies or following an accident. Though tuberculosis of the lung, the commonest and ultimately the most killing form of the disease, was outside the scope of surgery, the disease also accounted for at least 20 per cent of all operations. They included drainage of tuberculous abscesses in the neck and elsewhere, the opening of 'Psoas abscesses' in the groin,[16] and amputations of limbs for the 'white swellings' of joints, almost all tuberculous.

Even leaders of the profession like Sir William Fergusson of King's College Hospital rarely operated more than twice a week. One day they would perform operations on two or three hospital patients. Another day they might operate privately in their own or in their patients' homes. Hospitals provided no private beds and there were no private nursing homes in London till the 1850s. Even in the largest teaching hospitals—St Bartholomew's and the London had the most beds—the number of operations rarely exceeded 200 a year. The comparable figure today would be about 10,000. In 1832 the editor of the *Lancet* reported the interesting item of news that four operations were performed at St George's Hospital on 25 April and another three less than a week later. Some of these sessions were still public spectacles and more or less discreetly advertised. The *Times* described how on 6 June 1842 Mr William Fergusson (not yet a knight or a baronet) removed one side of the upper jaw of a child of 12 (without anaesthesia) to the admiration of an audience of 200. Aston Key, nephew of the great Astley, removed a tumour weighing 68 lb from the thigh of a Chinese patient at Guy's Hospital. The patient had travelled from Canton for the operation and the procedure lasted over two hours, a performance witnessed by 680 onlookers. When the patient died a few days later, his demise was generally attributed not to the surgery but to exposure to an atmosphere 'so poisoned by human exhalations that many of the onlookers had also fainted'.

Of the so-called capital operations (and the resonance with capital punishment was apt) by far the commonest were amputations. They carried an overall mortality of about 40 per cent. Tuberculosis once again accounted for about half of those, bone infections (today called osteomyelitis but then called necrosis of bone) and injuries resulting in open fractures for the rest. Road accidents did not start with the internal combustion engine. Heavy drays and carts as well as horses out of control caused at least six deaths every week in London. Most were the result not of the injuries as such but of generalised septicaemia. The dung-strewn streets of the capital were superb culture media for some of the most lethal organisms. Their existence was not even suspected, and had it been suspected nothing could have been done about them. Tetanus, popularly known as lockjaw because of the early painful spasm of the jaw muscles, and gas gangrene were common.[17] When bone was exposed by the injury, amputation offered the only hope of survival.

The variety as well as the number of operations was small. The inevitable sequel of peritonitis, a horrible and painful death, forbade any procedure that involved opening the abdominal cavity. The lungs, the heart and the brain were of course out of bounds. The suffering that attended even minor procedures had to be weighed against potential benefits. One in about four patients died from shock even before the operator got into his stride. Surgeons like Liston or Fergusson were tough—they had to be—but they were not sadists. They rarely operated unless they judged the alternative to be certain death. Children died of appendicitis. Young people died of perforated peptic ulcers. At any age obstruction of the bowel was fatal.[18] On the other hand, the operators were—once again, they had to be—extraordinarily skilful. In that knowledge they sometimes attempted procedures that were almost doomed. Strangulated inguinal or femoral hernias could fall into this category. Every effort was made to reduce them into the abdomen—a rather fearsome procedure called traxis—but if that failed, operation was the patient's best hope of survival. In the hands of a master like Fergusson, as many as a quarter survived. Peritonitis or shock killed the other three-quarters.

Fergusson was in many ways the prototype of the successful and widely admired pre-Listerian surgeon. He was a roaring, rumbustious lion of a man whose inventiveness and manual skill made him a popular celebrity.[19] Like several other leaders of the profession in London, he was a Scotsman, trained in Edinburgh. There the famous anatomist Robert Knox (to whom the 'resurrectionists' Burke and Hare sold their strangely fresh bodies) was one of his teachers. A few superbly executed Fergusson dissections are still treasured by the museum of the Royal College of Surgeons of Edinburgh. In 1840 he was offered the newly created chair at King's College Hospital in London. From that time almost every day he was driven in a magnificent coach, with postillions and two Dalmatians trained to run under the rear axle, from his house in George Street, Hanover Square, through the mean slums surrounding the hospital in the Strand. Street urchins cheered. He became surgeon to the Prince Consort and later to the Queen and the royal household.

More importantly, his casebook over a seven-year period survives and remains a valuable source on the type of surgery he performed.[20] Among spectacular cases, he tackled a girl of nine who had aspirated a plum stone, which had lodged in her trachea or windpipe. After numerous doctors had made fruitless attempts to extract it with a variety of instruments, Fergusson decided on an open operation. He cut through several of the cartilaginous rings of the trachea and eventually managed to recover the stone with one of his fishing hooks. 'Thereupon,' Fergusson recorded, 'the patient leaped from the grasp of her friends and danced around the room, clapping her hands.' Sadly, she did not survive for long. Her parents made her (and the plum stone) into a fairground exhibit and she perished a few weeks later from 'all the continual gadding about'. On another notable occasion Fergusson was confronted with a newborn with a blind dimple where the anal opening should have been.[21] Against the advice of his colleagues, he attempted to reach the blind lower end of the bowel by cutting through the perineum to a depth of an inch and a half. He failed, but was not so easily defeated. After a night spent experimenting on dead bodies, he revisited his patient at dawn and reached the bowel following a metal guide introduced through the bladder. He was gratified 'when plentiful meconium [the faeces of the newborn formed in utero mainly from desquamated cells of the lining of the bowels] gushed forth merrily'. After a slow recovery the child survived for six years. He then died from complications of the measles.

These were of course the highlights. Passing 'bougies' or dilators to overcome strictures of the urethra,[22] opening abscesses, dealing with anal fissures and fistulas, setting broken bones after closed fractures, amputations after open ones, dressing cuts and sprains and crushing stones in the bladder and their extraction were the bread-and-butter stuff. Fergusson's results with harelips and cleft palates were unsurpassed. He claimed 129 successful corrections out of 134 cases; and, for a surgeon, he was not boastful.[23] Such operations were rarely undertaken by lesser practitioners. In the lower reaches of the profession (or trade) attendance at duels was a more common and lucrative by-line. It usually entailed no great display of surgical skill: the prospective patients were either unhurt or dead.

Because the pain of operations could be excruciating, speed was still a key to success. The famous William Cheselden, one of the founders of the Royal College of Surgeons, is said to have removed stones from the bladder by the open operation of lithotomy, cutting through the perineum, in less than a minute.

Astley Cooper in 1824 was the first to amputate a leg at the hip joint. He took 20 minutes over the procedure. James Syme of Edinburgh, Lister's future father-in-law, with a better understanding of the anatomy, claimed to have reduced the time to one minute. Of course, these 'records' involved some cheating. Having removed a leg in 10 or 15 minutes, the operator would often spend another quarter of an hour tying or cauterising the bleeding points and stitching up the wound. But by then the patient was usually in a state of shock and insensible. Even so, two qualities were essential: manual dexterity and the capacity to make instant decisions. There was no time to think or weigh up carefully the pros and cons of the next step, let alone indulge in light-hearted badinage with the anaesthetist. Decisions had to be based on an intimate knowledge of anatomy. All eminent surgeons of the day were outstanding anatomists and many continued to operate on dead bodies for practice, much as a concert pianist continues to practise the scales every day.

Physical strength too was required, though muscular coordination was more important. Robert Liston, professor of surgery at University College Hospital, was said to have combined the 'strength of Hercules with the delicate touch of a miniature artist'. Surgeons had to be ambidextrous, so that they could use the knife with either hand. Liston was reported to have grasped the spurting end of an artery with the fingers of one hand, thrown a ligature around it with the other and tied the knot on the ligature with his teeth. Oddly perhaps, among the new operations introduced during the early years of Lister's career, most would be classified today as 'vascular surgery', generally regarded as a modern development. Damaged or diseased arteries—syphilis rather than atheroma was still the common underlying cause—dilate to form so-called aneurysms. Under the unceasing impact of the heartbeat, transmitted as the pulse, these tend to get steadily bigger; as they get bigger their wall becomes more and more attenuated. Eventually they leak or burst. The result is death. The only available treatment at the time was to expose and tie the artery on the heart side of the dilated segment. The best sites for doing this without causing peripheral gangrene by the total loss of blood supply were fiercely debated.

If the variety of operations performed was small, the range of individual surgeons was wide. Not only were all available operations their province. To make ends meet, many combined general practice with the cutting. The great surgeon Sir Jonathan Hutchinson of the London Hospital was better known as a 'skin doctor' than as an operator.[24] According to its original regulations, the Royal College of Surgeons refused to admit anyone to membership who practised exclusively as a dentist, an eye surgeon, an orthopaedic or bone surgeon or an ear or nose specialist. This was not yet because conservative bodies like royal colleges disapproved of specialisation as such; raising the general surgeon on a pedestal was a later fashion. Rather, the 'odour of charlatanery' surrounded 'excessive specialisation'. In today's parlance, such super-specialists constituted the fringe medicine of the day.

It was this kind of profession that young Joseph Lister chose as his life's vocation; and he chose it without knowing much about it. Or perhaps he did, from hearsay, and wanted to prove to himself that he could do it. In fact, he was immensely lucky. One of the horrors of operations, the pain, would begin to be conquered during his studentship. The other, infection, he himself would defeat. But neither development could have been foreseen.

CHAPTER TWO

THE END OF PAIN

Lister's academic career did not start propitiously. He left home and school in the spring of 1844 aged 17 and entered University College London. This was a new foundation, established specifically for those debarred from the older English universities by religious tests. It was ostentatiously non-sectarian and rather solemn, occupying its present site in Gower Street. It had recently acquired a hospital across the street, the original long pulled down but modern and up-to-date at the time. Lister began his studies with a three-year general course leading to the BA degree of London University. His father thought it was essential even for a surgeon to obtain a 'broad base' of learning. Perhaps he hoped that his son might still be deflected from surgery by having his enthusiasm kindled by a more congenial (and more gentlemanly) discipline. It was not an unreasonable hope.

In his student quarters, gloomy lodgings that he shared with two other Quaker youths, the son seemed unhappy. He missed home. In his letters to his parents, he barely mentioned any specific goal. He appeared to be drifting, intensely preoccupied with religious thoughts and perhaps doubts. Such spiritual perturbations, like undue 'enthusiasms', were uncharacteristic of Quakers. Was he on the right track? An experience, barely remarked at the time, almost certainly helped to steer him back onto his original path.

On 21 December 1846 Lister was a silent witness at a memorable event. He was still completing his general BA course, so why he should have been present in the operating theatre of the hospital on that day is uncertain. If he himself had not confirmed the story many years later, one might have had doubts. Historic events—or rather, events later recognised as historic—are rarely stage-managed so effectively. But Lister was the opposite of a fantasist. His powers of recollection rarely failed him. And he remembered the occasion clearly and in detail. Indeed, he appears on a painting commemorating the event. (The artwork dates from several decades later and if unsupported would be questionable evidence.[25]) It is certain that news that Robert Liston would be demonstrating a new procedure on that day, an exceptionally cold Monday, seems to have spread among medical students during the morning.[26] It is possible, even probable, that Lister, though still on his basic course in the natural sciences, was known to be aiming at surgery. He may therefore have been alerted by a friend. It was not unusual for students from other faculties to attend Liston's famous operating sessions. While they could be gruesome, they were never dull. Several fairly consistent accounts of the day's happenings survive, even to the point that, in view of the bitter weather, a merry fire was ablaze in the operating theatre's huge fireplace. It seems that by the afternoon when the session was scheduled, the atmosphere was 'cosy'.[27]

The immediate antecedent of the event was a letter from Dr Jacob Bigelow of Boston to his old friend Dr Francis Boott, a popular general practitioner in Gower Street, who had spent much of his youth in the United States.[28] In the letter Dr Bigelow, the father of the already famous Boston surgeon Henry Jacob Bigelow, informed Dr Boott of a momentous medical advance. It had been exercising the medical community and indeed the lay newspaper-reading public of Boston for some days. A week earlier a New York dentist by the name of Morton had been invited to attend the operating session of the famous surgeon John Collins Warren, at the Massachusetts General Hospital. Contrary to expectations (after an earlier fiasco by Horace Wells), he had demonstrated the astonishing anaesthetic properties of a preparation based on sulphuric ether. Morton maintained that the solution was a carefully balanced mixture of liquids, the composition of which was known only to him (and would soon be patented). The older Bigelow suspected, rightly as it proved, that this was a 'piece of cheap mystification'.[29] Indeed, at a personal level, all the protagonists of the new discovery were, in Dr Bigelow's judgement, a 'thoroughly rum lot, I would say disreputable, perhaps criminal'. Indeed, who were they exactly?[30] The uncertainty did not detract from the importance of their find—or not much.

Of course the idea—and even the occasional experiment—of a general anaesthetic had been wafting about for some decades.[31] Sulphuric ether was purified to a degree probably capable of producing anaesthesia in the early eighteenth century; and nitrous oxide, today's dentist's 'gas', was prepared in an impure form by Joseph Priestley in 1772 and by the process still used today (from ammonium nitrate) by the French chemist Berthollet in 1797. That remarkable young man Humphrey Davy published the results of three years' research into the gas in 1800 and suggested at the end of his book that 'since nitrous oxide ... appears capable of destroying pain, it could probably be used in surgical operations.'[32] In 1824 Henry Hill Hickman, a surgeon in Shropshire, tried a combination of anoxia and carbon dioxide with some success in animals. And hypnosis, known as 'mesmerism', was once again being seriously advocated.[33] What was lacking was not knowledge but faith. Samuel Taylor Coleridge, Davy's friend, showed a mild interest in ether, but few others did.

In the public mind, and even more in the mind of surgeons, pain was inseparable from surgery. And it was right that it should be so. Suffering was an essential precondition of a cure. Health had to be earned. It was no accident that modern anaesthesia originated in a country little burdened with traditional shibboleths.[34] Sadly perhaps but inevitably, that country also lacked what the old world still regarded as 'professional decorum'. It also had a somewhat exaggerated respect for the dollar. The incentive in the minds of men such as Horace Wells, Gardner Quincey Colton, William Thomas Green Morton and even Professor Charles Jackson of Boston was lucre. Some were amiable scoundrels, but dreams of a happier future for suffering humanity probably rarely crossed their minds. Perhaps the thought of monetary gain or worldly advancement did occur to men like Jenner, Harvey, Laennec, Semmelweis and other earlier medical benefactors too, but none engaged in such a single-minded and in the end tragic fight for patent right and profits.

On receiving Bigelow's letter, Boott at once realised that the news from the United States should be brought to the attention of his eminent colleague Robert Liston of University College Hospital, barely 100 yards up the road. On the other hand, sensational news emanating from across the Atlantic had on more than one occasion in the past turned out to be useless and even dangerous commercial stunts. Not wishing to end up as a target of Liston's biting sarcasm, he decided to try the experiment himself first. He invited a dentist friend, James Robinson, to visit him in his surgery the next morning with a patient who needed a tooth extracted. In the meantime he rigged up an apparatus incorporating his wife's perfume vaporiser. It seemed to resemble the one described by Bigelow. Something of an amateur chemist himself (as was common among medical practitioners of the day), he armed himself with a bottle of purified sulphuric ether and a roll of gauze. Robinson and a young woman, Liza Martin, duly arrived the next morning. After a few whiffs of the ether vapour squirted onto the gauze and pressed to her nose, she relaxed unconscious and Robinson extracted the offending tooth. On removing the gauze, Miss Martin came round within a few seconds and assured Boott and Robinson that she had felt nothing.[35]

In a state of excitement, Boott hurried up the road to see Liston. Fortunately (for Liston might have been hugely offended by being the second to be notified of an important new development in Boston), Liston himself had that morning received a newspaper cutting from Dr Henry Jacob Bigelow, the son of Dr Boott's friend, informing him of Morton's remarkable discovery. Even so, Liston declared himself sceptical and merely told Boott that he might some time in the future give the new gimmick a trial. In fact, he at once drove to Peter Squire's famous pharmacy in Oxford Street. There he took Squire aside and swore him to secrecy. Squire should at once rig up a vaporiser connected to a tube and fill a container with a pure and concentrated solution of sulphuric ether. He should then send the sealed package to University College Hospital, using his nephew as the messenger.

Despite such precautions, the secret of some new experiment being afoot must have leaked out, for a remarkable number of students and a few doctors assembled on the benches ranked around the operating table two days later. After a short and unusual delay—Liston was known for his punctuality and for ejecting latecomers—Liston's assistant William Cadge entered, accompanied by William Squire carrying a mysterious-looking apparatus. With ill-concealed excitement Cadge explained that Professor Liston was about to try a new American invention that purported to dull pain to the point of abolishing it entirely. Cadge himself had doubts, but he had made a preliminary trial the evening before. He had asked his cousin first to let Cadge breathe in the vapour of the preparation and then to stick pins into him. The experiment had been successful. Cadge had fallen into momentary sleep and had felt nothing of the pinpricks. He showed the bleeding points on his forearm. Would any of the audience like to try for themselves? There was no mad rush. Cadge then summoned the male nurse in attendance, a mountainous man by the name of Sheldrake. Sheldrake reluctantly agreed to breathe in the vapour. He had hardly taken a sniff or two when he started to bellow like a wounded animal, pushed Cadge away (who almost dropped the precious bottle) and ran with flailing arm towards the audience. Panic ensued. Fortunately, he had only taken a step or two when he collapsed and seemingly fell asleep.

At the height of the pandemonium Liston entered with a surgical colleague, John Ransome, and his dresser, John Palmer.

Cadge explained what had happened. Sheldrake was still unconscious. Cadge suggested that the experiment should be postponed indefinitely, the method was too unpredictable. Liston decided otherwise: the method would be tried that very afternoon. Let the first patient be brought in. He was Frederick Churchill, a footman in the service of Lord Aberdeen, who had sustained an injury to his left thigh some weeks earlier. The wound had gone septic and Liston had drained the abscess, which had proved ineffective. The patient developed general septicaemia with a swinging temperature and was rapidly going downhill. Liston decided that amputation above the mid-thigh offered the only hope.

Churchill was carried in on a stretcher by two porters and laid on the operating table. He looked moribund, but he was whimpering that he would rather die than lose his leg. There was no chance of that. Liston told Cadge to put the tube attached to the gauze mask and the vaporiser into the patient's mouth and start pumping the ether. At first Churchill had a fit of coughing and Cadge once again suggested giving up. Liston motioned him to continue. Suddenly Churchill went quiet. Cadge whispered: 'Your patient is ready, sir,' a statement to be echoed countless times down the years.

Liston took off his frock coat, rolled up his shirtsleeves and picked up the knife from the tray next to the operating table. 'Keep your hand on the pulse,' he instructed Palmer. Then he turned to his audience: 'Time it, gentlemen.' Some of the students had their watches in their palms already. At lightning speed Liston performed two U-shaped incisions on the front and back of the thigh and fashioned two skin flaps. Palmer handed him the saw. Five or six to-and-fro movements and the detached lower limb was ready to be dropped into the basket of sawdust under the table. Twenty-eight seconds, one student whispered. Liston looked at Churchill. He seemed fast asleep. In deathly silence Liston tied the main bleeding points, stitched up the flaps. Four and a half minutes, the timekeeper announced.

For once, there was no applause. Every eye was on the sleeping patient. At that point, as a rule, patients would lapse from ear-splitting incoherent yelling into a kind of sobbing delirium. As Liston lowered his arms, Cadge removed the tube. A very long two minutes (but no more) later, the patient opened his eyes. 'When will you start?' he suddenly shouted. 'No, no, I will not have my leg taken. Stop it. Let me off. I will rather die.'

Liston motioned one of the porters to lift the amputated limb from the basket of sawdust and show it to Churchill. Churchill closed his eyes in fright, mumbled words of incredulity. There was a long pause. All eyes were now on Liston. Several observers noted tears running down his cheeks. Nobody stirred. Then he seemed to recover, turned to the audience and said: 'Well, gentlemen, this Yankee dodge surely beats Mesmerism hollow.'

The advent of anaesthesia would have a profound effect on Lister's career—but that lay in the future. The immediate chronological sequel was probably unrelated, but was a far from happy one. Though barely mentioned by his first official biographer and by works based on that biography, within a few months of witnessing Liston's historic operation Lister suffered a nervous breakdown.

Such setbacks in apparently happy and fit young people often of exceptional promise, embarking on their studies or on their first jobs carrying unaccustomed responsibility, were no less common in the mid-nineteenth century than they are today.[36] Then as now, they were rarely mentioned by the family at the time or spoken of later. Those who suffered its agonies found the experience impossible to describe; they still do. Lay witnesses often found it incomprehensible; this too has changed little.

In Lister's case the father's affectionate and deeply concerned letters refer to 'phantoms of the dark' and the son's 'general distress' at the state of the world. Dr Thomas Hodgkin, family friend as well as medical counsellor, suggested a deep religious conflict. The relatively recent death of John Lister was mentioned as having had a possible delayed effect. Joseph left his lodgings and rejoined the family in Essex. They were, as they would always remain, fully supportive. So was John Hodgkin, fellow lodger and nephew of Thomas.

In only one respect did such breakdowns differ from what they are today: none of the powerful psychotropic drugs were available then. The suffering must have been far more intense. But perhaps pharmacological poverty carried a small compensation. Recovery when it eventually came may have been more complete than it often is today. Victims sometimes even seemed more serene— or at least in better emotional control—for the rest of their lives than they would have been otherwise. This may have happened to Lister. Even as a famous man he was to suffer his share of tragedies. Success itself imposed certain obligations. He never tried to evade them. Yet nobody ever saw him lose his temper or in a state of terminal exasperation. He was prone to shed tears when moved, but so were Mr Gladstone and Lord Kitchener. His equanimity could indeed be exasperating. Certainly, nobody who met him later would guess at the period of youthful turbulence. To Rickman Godlee, Lister's nephew and official biographer, it was a minor and passing episode, 'probably an after-effect of small-pox'. If young Lister did have smallpox, it must have been extraordinarily mild. In any case, by the time of his recovery his choice of career seemed to be no longer in doubt.

Except for one mention in a letter of total dejection and inability to rise in the morning, the symptoms of the breakdown remain unknown. After the acute phase he was sent with a friend on an extended holiday to the West Country and then to Ireland. In Dublin he stayed with Friends, the Pims. His contemporary, Thomas Pim, would later marry Isabella, his eldest sister. They were extremely kind; but travelling around the country in the grip of the potato famine must have been a devastating experience.

The sights and sounds were not unexpected. Apart from sporadic newspaper reports, none particularly detailed about this ever-so-troublesome island, Joseph Jackson had already visited it and had written to his son: 'It is terrible and heart-rending to see the fragmentary garments and the worn starved look of the poor.'

Like many Quakers, he was in favour of sending government relief to the areas worst hit by the disaster. High-minded ministers and civil servants in Westminster and Whitehall, wedded to the sacred doctrine of laisser-faire, regarded such ideas as bordering on the criminal. Better by far to let tens of thousands of unfortunates die and allow a depopulated country to sink into despair than to offend against the dogmas of free trade. The improvident of this world had to learn their lesson.

In view of Joseph's recent breakdown, the Pims tried to deflect him from a country tour, but his quiet obstinacy prevailed. He wanted to see the suffering for himself, even if he could do nothing about it. There is no mention of it in his letters. After the experience he was ready for a more cheerful tour of Holland and North Germany. His academic record for the year is a blank.

By 1876 Lister was to all appearances restored to normal. His religious uncertainties were things of the past. He resumed his studies. Almost, it seems, inevitably he became president of the student medical society. There was about him already a slightly solemn air that inspired trust and would always make such elevations a foregone conclusion. He was less successful in debating, though he never performed less than creditably. Quick repartee and improvisations were not his forte. He also did well in his examinations.

In one field he excelled. His father had taught him the art of microscopy and he had the best instrument in the College. Still as a student he wrote two papers on the muscular tissue of the skin and the muscles of the iris. Both are remarkable for the author's command of the literature as well as for the accuracy of their observations. The paper on the skin, introducing a technique of cutting thin vertical slices suitable for the microscopic examination of the hair follicles, also showed his exceptional gift for methodological innovation. The one on the iris put him in touch with several eminent Continental surgeons and physiologists. Some of the friendships would last a lifetime.[37]

Yet under the calm and composed surface he still seemed to be drifting; at least one of his teachers so divined. William Sharpey was a Scotsman who had gravitated south as the academic establishment in London expanded. After a stint in Paris, he had been invited to occupy the new chair of physiology at University College. He was physically huge and cultivated a bluff manner. In fact he was a person of great sensitivity and kindness. He sensed not only the promise but also the still lurking confusion in young Lister's mind. He suggested a study tour on the Continent, but that, before departing for France and Germany, the young man should visit Edinburgh. There James Syme, professor of surgery and Sharpey's boyhood friend, might be just the man to allay his uncertainties. Joseph Jackson declared himself ready to support his son financially over a further period of study. A little reluctantly, for Lister was more drawn to Germany, Joseph departed for Scotland to stay for a month. He stayed for nearly two decades. They were to be his most productive years.

CHAPTER THREE

SYME'S PUPIL

Edinburgh was a revelation to the studious young visitor from the South. London was a huge and fast-growing metropolis, the political and commercial hub of a far-flung and dizzily expanding empire. Its hospitals and medical schools were scattered and of no particular importance. The University of London did already exist but it was, as it would remain, something of a paper construct, without a discernible character. Edinburgh, by contrast, had a stable population of just under 200,000 and its medical facilities were geographically concentrated. The university itself was embodied (rather than simply housed) in Robert Adam's majestic edifice. The city was indeed a university town, more common at the time on the Continent of Europe than elsewhere in Britain. The Palladian frontages of the Royal Infirmary and the Royal College of Surgeons were not far from the university; and the university and the medical school enjoyed a sometimes acrimonious but in the long run mutually beneficial relationship.

There were other differences too. As in all Scottish universities, but in contrast to Oxford and Cambridge, the correct religion — or at least its profession—had never been a precondition for admission. Dissent was not encouraged but it was tolerated. Dissenters came from England too, as did the Quaker Thomas Hodgkin, the friend of the Listers. Many came from Northern Ireland. More importantly, at the time of Lister's arrival the student body represented a wider spectrum of the country's population than it did in any of the English universities. In

Scotland universities did not deliberately cater for paupers, but they were never the preserve of the rich either. Student fees and accommodation were comparatively cheap. Crofters' lads worked beside the offspring of lairds. There was a wider age range too. Boys of 12 and 13 attended as well as men with grey hair up to the age of 50 or even 60. In Lister's day in Edinburgh the class of prospective doctors included a 'great stout fellow of fifty-two straight from the plough'. Young men from famous public schools with a polished classical education rubbed shoulders with others who knew not a word of Greek and not much more of Latin.[38] Teaching at all levels was held in higher esteem in Scotland than in England (as it still is) and was correspondingly more dedicated. Professors were addressed as professors and doctors as doctors: none pretended to be huntin' and shootin' country gentlemen in mufti.

In the narrower field of surgery James Syme, to whom Lister carried an introductory letter from Sharpey, was already recognised as one of the leading surgeons of Europe. A small, wiry man, he had given proof that he was a man of ideas even before he took up surgery. In 1818, at the age of 19, still more interested in chemistry than in medicine, he discovered that india rubber could be dissolved in coal tar and that the resulting solution could make clothing waterproof. As a budding member of the medical profession he had scruples about patenting his discovery, so it was a Glaswegian industrialist by the name of Macintosh who made a fortune from it and introduced his name into the language. Ten years later Syme was refused a surgical appointment at the Royal Infirmary, largely because of his quarrel with his cousin, Robert Liston (then still in Edinburgh), so he opened a private hospital known as Minto House. It was a forerunner of the Mayo Clinic and similar establishments in the United States, providing accommodation for thousands of patients a year, short-term training for surgical apprentices and a formal course of surgery for more students than did the Royal Infirmary. In 1833, when Liston removed to London, Syme was appointed professor of clinical surgery, remaining a consultant to Minto House.

'The originator of almost every improvement in surgery this century,' the verdict on him by his pupil Joseph Bell, was an exaggeration but shows the reputation he enjoyed at least in his own country. The amputation of the foot at the ankle, described by him and named after him, is one of the few operations of the period still occasionally performed a century and a half later almost unchanged.[39] Ironically, after many years of comparative poverty—his father, a lawyer, had lost his money speculating when his two sons were still schoolboys—Syme and his brother inherited a fortune from an uncle about the same time as he succeeded to the chair. The inheritance enabled him to purchase a house and small country estate on the south-western outskirts of the city. It was called Millbank and commanded, as it still does, a wonderful view over the gardens towards the Pentland Hills. Here he grew orchids in the conservatory and pineapples and bananas in a greenhouse and entertained friends and foreign visitors. Belying his reputation for taciturnity—it was said of him that he 'never wasted a word, a drop of ink or a drop of blood'—he was a charming and generous host.

Lister arrived in Edinburgh in September 1853, took short-term lodgings in Frederick Street, and presented himself to Syme with Sharpey's letter. A month later, when he was due to leave for the Continent, he wrote to his sister Mary:

> I have decided to postpone my departure by a few weeks or months though it will make my Continental journey rather short ... The Royal Infirmary here has 200 surgical beds and a much greater variety than the 65 beds of University College Hospital ... Mr Syme has his own views on everything based on great experience with a sound judgement and a very original mind.[40]

This was the first expression of Lister's growing admiration for Syme, originally the main reason for prolonging his stay. Though no written testimony survives, the admiration must have been mutual. A month after Lister's arrival, the young Londoner was appointed Syme's 'supernumerary clerk', a post that Syme more or less invented. In January 1854 he became Syme's house surgeon. This was an important post: it meant that he was in charge of five or six 'dressers' who called him 'the chief'. In the past the position had always gone to one of them or at least to an Edinburgh graduate. At 24 Lister was not even a fellow yet of the Royal College of Surgeons of Edinburgh.

The close relationship between the two men, separated in age by 30 years, was not unique. Until the twentieth century the craft of surgery was often handed down from one generation to the next through such apprenticeships. The apprentices were often sons, sons-in-law or nephews. The nepotism was freely acknowledged, not regarded as an aberration. Several decades later one of Lister's house surgeons, Hector Cameron, recorded that Lister's students were used to sudden pauses in a demonstration or discourse. They knew what was coming. After a second or two the professor would say reflectively: 'This is one of the many things I have learned from Mr Syme.' From the start, Lister admired qualities in the older man that he lacked or thought he lacked himself. He shared Syme's originality and independent judgement; but Syme also represented authority, certainty and, above all, decisiveness.

Of course, in middle age Lister too became a *persona* of commanding presence, the very embodiment of professional gravitas. Intellectually, he would be recognised as a creative thinker. Nevertheless, by nature he always remained a man of doubts and uncertainties, a first-class mind but a comparatively slow one. Did he really say 'my indecision is final'? Perhaps not; but he might have done. He was also one of those rare people — or perhaps not so rare — who, without actually trying, could turn such limitations to his advantage. His approval was valued because it was clearly based on careful consideration. His disapproval was feared for the same reason. In a profession better known for its instant enthusiasms and cherished prejudices, these were important assets. They may partly explain Syme's admiration for him. But there were other reasons too.

Syme's past experience with Londoners, the English, and with University College Hospital in particular was not a happy one. After Robert Liston's sudden death in 1847 he had been invited to occupy the chair of surgery there. To be invited rather than to have to apply was a rare honour and Syme was temporarily bedazzled. He recalled other Scotsmen and Scottish surgeons in particular conquering the South. It was probably the only occasion in his life when he yielded to such a bedazzlement. He resigned his posts in Edinburgh, accepted the invitation and moved to London. His career at University College Hospital lasted less than six months. (It happened to be the six months when Lister was away following his nervous breakdown: the two men had never met before their meeting in Edinburgh.) Syme hated it both professionally and privately. Academic bureaucracy, intrigue and politicking were probably no worse in London than they were in Edinburgh; but in Edinburgh Syme knew his way around. In London he was a stranger. He found Londoners devious. Their frivolity irked him. They were unreliable, disrespectful and possessed no sense of values.

The governors of University College Hospital seem to have decided to amalgamate Syme's chair, designated 'of clinical surgery', with another chair, called 'of systematic surgery'. The latter was supposed to be concerned with courses of lectures rather than patients and had become unexpectedly vacant on the resignation of the ailing Samuel Cooper. It was in many ways a non-job. Cooper, an amiable nonentity, had been appointed because he had connections in the profession and in politics. The governors wanted to save money—the student population was declining—and the amalgamation was not unreasonable. Even then, medical schools laboured under the difficulty of fast-changing disciplines (or at least of fashions within and between disciplines). It was difficult to abolish academic posts that were perceived to have outlived their usefulness. Sometimes chairs had been created to accommodate individuals rather than to fill needs; Lister himself would later benefit from such an arrangement. Nevertheless, nobody had thought of consulting Syme. Governing bodies of hospitals are prone to such gaffes. According to another source, the governors had had a long discussion with Syme but had misunderstood his 'impenetrable' Scotch. The incomprehension may have been mutual. Whatever the truth, as soon as Syme read about the decision, he walked out of the hospital, packed his belongings and, with his large family, servants and numerous pets, returned to Edinburgh. Fortunately for him, none of his past posts had yet been filled and, once he had reassured his colleagues that he would reimburse their expenses arising from farewell presents and valedictory banquets, he was reinstated.

After such an experience Syme could not fail to be moved by the rapt attention shown to him by the young Londoner and University College graduate. Nor was this just any young Londoner. Syme had read Lister's papers and he was impressed. None of his students had ever produced anything like them. They were original, mature, meticulously researched and stylishly written. Not for the last time, the qualities in Lister that his father and others had thought 'wasted' in a surgeon stood him in good stead. Many of his surgical contemporaries in Scotland were able young men, skilful with their hands, keen to master their craft and dedicated to perfecting it; but the stylish communicators had chosen medicine (or in some cases obstetrics) as their speciality. Lister stood out.

Soon after his appointment as a house surgeon he started to publish reports of Syme's lectures, first in the *Monthly Journal of the Medical Sciences*, a local publication, and soon in weekly instalments in the *Lancet*. The first dealt with an operation Syme had improvised to remove a bony tumour from the thigh and included microscopic observations on the histology by Lister. A later one, again with added observations by Lister, described the removal of a tumour of the jaw under chloroform anaesthesia. These papers are still a pleasure to read on a long journey; but they would not gladden the heart of a medical editor today. The sentences are long and ponderous. Nothing that could conceivably be regarded as relevant is omitted, least of all an apposite simile or a learned allusion. Every phrase is both weighty and well turned, like a Victorian ornamental vase. They are, in short (but of course the very idea of expressing anything in short was anathema), in the well-upholstered style of contemporary academic discourse or even Gladstonian polemic.

This was true even of the occasional controversy. In March 1854 Lister reported on a case of Syme's amputating a foot at the ankle. In the same issue, Mr Wilfred Adams of the Royal Orthopaedic Hospital in London (to whom the editor had shown the article) declared that the operation was impossible. In the next issue Lister answered:

> If Mr Adams shows so little respect for the veracity of the word of a colleague of international repute like Mr Syme, even when recorded by the inadequate pen of a one comparatively young and inexperienced, then he must not be surprised if some of his own statements, however securely based on experience and therefore to be respected, are not read occasionally without some hesitation.[41]

Such reports could not but please Syme. No house surgeon of his had ever before gone to such trouble to publicise his ideas. He himself was a clear writer, though a stranger to semicolons. Lister was not unaware of this. 'I am doing him some substantial service,' he replied to his father when Joseph Jackson expressed anxiety about the time taken up by the weekly reports, 'but it is in return for much kindness.'

More remarkable in some ways was the affection in which the young Londoner was held by the dressers. These were young men who were his juniors only by a year or two and who were not merely friends but also potential rivals. He had done them no favours. He was an outsider and had many advantages over them. He was extraordinarily good-looking, the favourite of landladies and hospital matrons. Despite his slight stammer, his speech was pleasantly cultivated, southern of course but without any hint of affectation. His allowance from his father was more generous than that of most of his colleagues. He was highly regarded by their chief. Yet neither in later reminiscences nor in contemporary letters and a few surviving photographs is there a hint of resentment. Of course, there could be no doubt about Lister's intellect, his industry and his high moral standards. But even his faults were almost endearing.

He was incorrigibly late. How late depended on the function he was supposed to be attending. He was 15 minutes late for his own lectures, 20 minutes late for dinner parties, and half an hour late for informal social occasions. When friends turned up to fetch him from home to ensure that he was on time, he contrived to delay them all by finding a matter of the utmost urgency that needed his attention before leaving. 'One could set one's watch by his lateness,' Hector Cameron was to recall. 'He would always be late but eventually turn up.' Thirty years later Lister was asked to deliver the Croonian Lectures of the Royal College of Physicians of London, a signal honour for a surgeon. His audience included a bevy of royal physicians, including the President and most of the Council of the College. They had to suffer the statutory quarter of an hour wait in a somewhat strained silence. When the lecturer arrived, he was, as usual, full of self-deprecating apologies. It was impossible to bear him any grudge, though the President in his introductory remarks referred to the 'most important gift in the career of a surgeon: the gift of delaying action'.

Other minor faults already evident during his house surgeoncy were negatives. Most conspicuously, his sense of humour was vestigial. He would smile politely when he perceived that a joke had occurred, even congratulate the joker on the humorousness of his remark, but his understanding of it always remained in doubt and nobody ever saw him rock with laughter.[42] He was easy to 'wind up', a favourite student pastime; too easy, in fact. The effort with one so gullible was rarely worthwhile.

Apart from Syme's personal patronage and the young man's gratifying popularity with his colleagues, there was an advance in surgery itself that affected Lister's plans.

The news of Liston's successful operation on a patient under anaesthesia had spread extraordinarily fast. The earlier events in Boston too had been widely canvassed in Europe. Soon similar operations were being reported from Edinburgh and Glasgow. In France Joseph Magendie and Alfred Velpeau (who earlier had publicly declared that surgical anaesthesia was physically impossible) tried it with success, though both had moral reservations. In Germany interest became so keen that the Royal Bavarian government made a public announcement of successful experiments on animals. These were followed by experiments on men in Munich and Erlangen. They were 'as successful as they were gratifying'. In Vienna public lectures were given in the university 'to accord the public an insight into this medical miracle'. While the Rector objected and the course was discontinued, anaesthesia became the topic of conversation in every Kaffeehaus on the Ringstrasse. Franz von Pitha reported an unbroken series of nine successes from Prague. In St Petersburg the great N.A. Pirogoff reinforced ether inhalation with the injection of the vapour into the rectum. His brilliant results led to the claim, vigorously propagated in Stalin's empire, that anaesthesia was a Russian invention.

Though never before had a medical discovery spread so fast or so widely, ether was not the ideal anaesthetic. It was too irritating for inhalation in comfort and often caused profuse salivation and sickness. Patients vomited; under anaesthesia the aspiration of vomit could be fatal.[43] The purity of the liquid was sometimes in doubt and the consequences could be dire. Untoward reactions started to be published. Nevertheless, the pain barrier had been breached: progress was now unstoppable.

A year after the introduction of ether, while Lister was still completing his medical studies in London, the Edinburgh obstetrician James Young Simpson introduced chloroform as a general anaesthetic into obstetrics.[44] This precipitated a storm of protest from the Kirk as well as from god-fearing laypersons. Was it not both sinful and unnatural to allay—or even to try to allay—the suffering of childbirth? But Simpson, the son of a village baker who had worked his way up to a university chair against fierce opposition, was not easily overawed. Could the Almighty Himself not claim to have been the first obstetric anaesthetist when He caused a deep sleep to descend on Adam while He operated on his chest to create Eve? Ah, thundered more than one cleric, that may have been so *before* the Fall. After the Curse it was 'in sorrow [that Eve] shalt bring forth children'. Yes, Simpson counter-attacked, but sorrow is not pain! He even suggested that the Hebrew text had been mistranslated for centuries. The word should not be 'sorrow' but 'effort'.[45]

The controversy was settled neither by Simpson, nor by Hebrew scholars, but by Queen Victoria. In 1854, before giving birth to her fourth child, the Prince Leopold, future Duke of Albany, she was persuaded by her physicians and obstetricians to try chloroform anaesthesia.[46] She saw that it was good.[47] Then everybody saw that it was good.[48]

By the time Lister arrived in Edinburgh, anaesthesia was widely though not yet universally practised.[49] This was a decisive development. His technical gifts as a surgeon have been much debated. That the greatest surgical benefactor of his time was rather a clumsy operator was too good a story ever to be put to rest. There was probably never any truth in it. The memoirs of numerous assistants and younger surgeons testify that he was exceptionally gentle and efficient. Most persuasively, not only his sister but also several of his colleagues chose him when they or their family needed an operation. However, he did not operate at lightning speed as Liston, Fergusson and other virtuosi of the knife had done. There was no need to. Later, antiseptic practice inevitably slowed down operations. Speed and the spray were incompatible. Success would depend as much on the meticulous and painstaking arrest of bleeding as on killing the germs. But quite probably, even if Lister had tried to emulate the surgical giants of the past, he would have failed. He was a good but slow and deliberate draughtsman and experimenter. People do not change their rhythm of work, at least not easily. Nor was he in the habit of making instant decisions. Only a decade or so earlier such lack of speed at operations would have barred him from the top echelon of the profession. He might even have given up.[50] Ether and chloroform happily intervened.

MARRIAGE

Altogether, after six months in Edinburgh, Lister was well settled. Though he sorely missed the proximity of Upton and his family, he seemed more at ease with himself than he had been at University College in London. While he spent a month in Paris on what appears to have been a working holiday, attending classes of surgical anatomy and dissections,[51] a lengthy Continental tour was no longer planned. Yet there was no hint in his letters that he saw for himself a long-term future in Scotland. The migration of talent had always been in the opposite direction. Scotland was a small country bursting with native genius. Scottish surgery in particular had always produced a surplus of gifted young practitioners. Lister's house-surgeoncy would eventually come to an end. Other things being equal, he would then return to England. But other things are rarely equal. Two circumstances, neither of them foreseeable when he arrived in Edinburgh, changed the course of his life and perhaps the future of surgery. One was an international conundrum, the other a private romance.

The international conundrum had its roots in a squabble (long-standing and smouldering but with unpredictable flare-ups) between the holy monks of the Latin church and the holy monks of the Greek Orthodox Church over the holy keys to the holy sites in the Holy Land. Since the region was still a province of the Turkish Empire, the decision ostensibly rested with the Sublime Porte in Constantinople. To them the matter had always been one of discreet bribes, even-handedly accepted. By the mid-nineteenth century, however, as both the religious revival in Catholic countries and the evangelical movements in Protestant ones gathered force, the question began to exercise the minds and consciences of far-away Christian lands.

The Czar, traditionally the patron of Orthodox Christians under Turkish rule, had no doubt that the keys should be given to the holy monks of the Orthodox Church. To underline his view, he ordered two of his friskiest regiments to the Turkish frontier.[52] In the past such moves had always settled matters to everybody's satisfaction. However, France's new emperor, Napoleon III, was also keen to live up to his somewhat dubious Bonaparte pedigree. He was also courting the Catholic vote. What worthier cause for sabre rattling than the holy keys in the Holy Land? He sent a battleship to the Bosphorus. For a few weeks, common sense seemed to prevail. England, France and Russia, with the participation of Austria and Prussia, held a conference in Vienna and reached a reasonable compromise. The holy keys should be evenly divided between the two groups of holy monks. The diplomats went home, well satisfied with their labours and with traditional Viennese hospitality.

Then the unexpected happened. Turkey, the sick man of Europe, whom none of the powers had bothered to consult, declared war on Russia. The ramshackle Turkish fleet sailed into the Black Sea. It was annihilated by the Russian fleet near the port of Sinope. What came to be known (for no obvious reason) as 'the massacre of Sinope' stirred public opinion in the West.[53] Or it stirred the newspapers and the newspapers stirred public opinion. For the first time the 'media' (not yet so called) assumed an independent and ultimately decisive role in shaping events. This took Britain's prime minister, Lord Aberdeen, by surprise. He was a pacific gentleman of the old school, who could see no merit in a war with Russia and little merit in war with anybody.[54] In this he was right. However, he felt that the best way of preventing war was to ignore the possibility. Such a non-policy had worked admirably in the past; it worked no longer. Public opinion had

been whipped into a frenzy by broadsheets, pamphlets and public meetings. Ever since the bloody suppression of the Hungarian and Polish uprisings, Russia had had an evil reputation in Britain. Even Quakers, firmly opposed to war, regarded the Czar with suspicion. Russia was also encroaching on Britain's natural sphere of civilising influence in Central Asia. The 'Great Game' had begun.

In uneasy partnership with France, war was declared to defend Constantinople. By August 1854 a considerable British and French force had gathered under the walls of the city. Having gathered, they discovered that the city did not need defending. It was not being menaced, except by its regular summer epidemic of cholera. This raised the awkward question, not unusual when wars are begun, of what to do with the assembled armies. Somebody—it is not clear who—suggested taking Sebastopol. This was the base on the Black Sea of the Russian fleet and seemed—indeed was at the time—virtually undefended. The British and French forces landed nearby without difficulty. This was judged to be such a strategic triumph that for some weeks no further moves were contemplated. The delay gave the Russians time to reinforce the port. By the time the British and French did move, the town had become a fortress.

The unpreparedness of the British War Department for a prolonged war in a far-away land now became apparent.[55] Lack of surgical cover was one of the most glaring deficiencies.[56] Appeals for volunteers struck a responsive cord in Scotland. Scottish surgeons had traditionally been the backbone of the medical services of the British army.[57] In Edinburgh the memory of Sir Charles Bell, hero of Waterloo, was still alive.[58] Five surgeons volunteered their services, including Dr Ian Mackenzie, the man next in line to Syme at the Royal Infirmary, and Dr Casimir Munro, his deputy. Both greatly distinguished themselves at the Battle of Alma. Then they contracted cholera. Mackenzie died in Scoutari; Munro perished on the way there.

Mackenzie's course of lectures on surgery had been suspended for the duration of the war (expected, as usual, to last no more than a few months). Lister offered to continue the course. At first Syme seems to have had doubts, then Lister was appointed to take Mackenzie's place. His fellowship of the Royal College of Surgeons of England did not entitle him to practise or even to teach as a surgeon in Scotland. At Syme's prompting, he was elected a fellow of the Edinburgh College on 21 April 1855. Though the assistant surgeoncy at the Royal Infirmary would not be filled for some months, he would be the obvious choice.

In the meantime, there was no reason why Lister should not start in private practice. He took well-appointed lodgings in 3 Rutland Street in the New Town, opposite Syme's consulting rooms. Joseph Jackson, who was paying for it, approved, though the rent was 'very high'. While he was obviously pleased at his son's success, he added: 'Pray remember when thou comst up to bring thy account book with thee.' A few weeks later Lister treated his first private patient, a titled lady with a dislocated ankle. He reduced the joint under chloroform to the patient's satisfaction.

Syme's professional support may have been influenced by private developments. He had had nine children by his first wife, only two of whom, Agnes and Lucy, survived childhood. His wife died soon after the birth of their last child. Syme remarried a year later. He had a second family of five, including a son, James; but Agnes remained the favourite. Several photographs of her survive. She was twenty in 1853 when Lister arrived in Edinburgh, a slightly ungainly young woman with dark, luminous eyes. She dressed plainly and pulled her hair back over her ears in an unflattering chignon. Her plainness was accentuated by the beauty of her sister, Lucy, though to many it was outweighed by qualities of mind and character not revealed in photographs. She was certainly no fragile pre-Raphaelite damsel. Fortunately, Lister had little taste for the arts and none whatever for the pre-Raphaelites. (He later became friends with William Holman Hunt, another first recipient of the Order of Merit, but he admired only the artist's late religious confections.) Agnes had already helped her father in his laboratory work and had assisted him once or twice at operations. She wrote in a beautiful hand and may have acted as his amanuensis. Lister met the family at Millbank soon after his arrival. He seems to have been immediately attracted to Agnes; she certainly was to him. By March 1854 his parents had become aware of his interest. On March 25 Joseph Jackson wrote:

> Thy dear mother tells me she has been persuading thee not to allow thy *other* engagements to absorb thee too entirely to our loss ... I do not know how some apprehensions of hers have been awakened and I try to assure her that they are groundless, that probably no thought has entered thy mind to warrant them ... And what I once said suggested I will venture to repeat—that it may be well to be on thy guard that in the friendly intercourse to which thou are kindly invited, nothing in thy deportment may give any ground for suspicion that thou has an intention beyond it.[59]

Isabella Lister's intuition proved more sensitive than her husband's. Perhaps what exercised her was the religious question. The Symes were members of the Episcopal Church of Scotland, the sister church of the Church of England north of the border, and Agnes was firm in her faith. Lister was by now less so. A few years earlier, before his nervous breakdown, it was his religious enthusiasm that had worried his parents. Now what exercised his mind most were doubts about his father's continued financial support if he were forced to resign from the Society. This was not particularly mercenary: he had to know before he formally approached Agnes's father. By then his courtship was common enough knowledge to inspire a slightly crude student ditty in the traditional no-holds-barred Christmas entertainment. Nevertheless, his worries proved groundless. Joseph Jackson answered promptly:

> Believing from all thou hast told me that thy affections are fixed on a really virtuous and amiable young woman, I

would not allow the circumstances of her not being within our society to affect my pecuniary arrangements for thee or to alter the expectations given thee some time ago.[60]

The doubts were now dispelled. Lister was soon fully though not yet formally committed. He described 'my precious Agnes' in a characteristic style in a letter to Rickman Godlee:

Outward appearances, as I have often said before, are not at all showy, but there is in her countenance an ever varying expression that artlessly displays a peculiarly guileless, honest, unaffected and modest spirit, and a very amiable and at the same time sprightly though sobered disposition, while there is no lack of sound and independent intelligence; and on rare occasions, though to *me* not now so rare as formerly, her eye expresses the deep feeling of a *very* warm heart.[61]

In case this sounded more like a testimonial for a lady's maid than a profession of love, he added:

Therefore to me her face has become dearer than thee might at first sight suppose. But thee will say that I am talking nonsense.

Meanwhile negotiations for a financial settlement between Joseph Jackson and Syme, 'assuming that my son proceeds with his honourable and firm intention and if his suit were accepted', proceeded. Neither parent felt that the other was particularly generous. Though Syme wrote that in his opinion the young couple's income would be 'barely adequate', both sides were prepared to be accommodating. The real value of the sums committed is difficult to assess today, but they were obviously adequate for the young couple to set up house in style.

Joseph Jackson and Lister's sister Mary visited the Symes and stayed for a few days. Isabella was too frail to travel. The visit was entirely successful. Agnes was invited to Upton, though Mrs Syme thought that this would be inappropriate before the wedding. Instead, the elder Symes stayed there for a few days. That visit too was a success. A suitable house was found in the granite splendour of Edinburgh's New Town, 11 Rutland Street. It had three floors and a basement and nine principal rooms. 'The chimneys,' as Lister reported home, 'were happily and after some doubts, found to be in good order and the cupboard space, though not over-generous, is adequate in all parts of the building.' In this light, a formal proposal was deemed appropriate and was accepted. Lister could now write to Rickman Godlee:

> Since the making and acceptance of my offer, I have been from time to time favoured, as I have assuredly believed, with a rather remarkable and to me unexpected sense that I am in my right place in this matter ... Without some measure of this feeling I should I believe be thoroughly miserable, notwithstanding Agnes's love, and what may appear to the World the bright prospect before me ... As it is, however, I feel able at times, and ought I believe do so more constantly, to rejoice with true thankfulness for what I am assured are present services bestowed; and, on the other hand, to look forward with some degree of trustfulness for the future, and to pluck up a little courage with reference to the mass of laborious duty that lies before me, as yet almost untouched as a teacher of surgery, and to hope that, this step being rightly made, the rest of my path through what I perhaps too much anticipate as a very shady and rough world, may be also safely directed.[62]

One has read letters more impassioned than these somewhat convoluted sentences; there was still—and perhaps there would always be—a deep core of anxiety and self-doubt in Lister. To many it mitigated, as did his slight stammer, his sometimes intimidating air of solemnity. Few of Agnes's confidences survive, but there is no doubt that she was much in love. Of course there was no unseemly haste. The wedding date was fixed for 23 April 1856 and was celebrated in the drawing room of the Symes' town house. It was a religious ceremony, a church venue being avoided out of consideration for the bridegroom's family. By then Lister had resigned from the Society and had been received into the Episcopal Church. When he put up his first professional nameplate, he announced himself as *Mr* Joseph Lister, not plain Joseph Lister as he would have done as a member of the Society of Friends.

The honeymoon lasted four months. After a few days staying with one of Agnes's uncles at Kinross and Agnes's first visit to Upton, the couple crossed the Channel to Ostend and went on to Brussels. Travelling for pleasure up the Rhine and around the Swiss lakes of Lucerne and Thun soon merged into a study tour of Continental surgical centres. Carrying letters of recommendation from Syme, Sharpey and Wharton-Jones of University College Hospital, the couple were hospitably received. After Turin, Geneva, Florence, Milan and Padua, they stayed with the Rokitanskys in Vienna.[63] Lister and his host spent 'many diverting hours inspecting the Hofrat's incomparable museum containing more than 27,000 priceless specimens'. In Vienna that was not of course for ladies' eyes, though in Edinburgh Agnes had often helped to mount her father's carefully dissected anatomical preparations. Sadly, it seems that Semmelweis's one-time friend and patron made no mention of the gifted but somewhat troublesome Hungarian obstetrician, now safely back in Pest.[64] Of course, antisepsis was not yet one of Lister's interests and childbed fever was not a surgical problem. The Frau Hofrat had also strongly disapproved of Semmelweis's open letters. To her, a native of Bavaria, the Hungarian frontier was where Asia began and that was where Herr Doktor Semmelweis and his like rightly belonged.[65]

After Vienna the Listers went on to Prague, Würzburg, Dresden, Frankfurt, Berlin, Amsterdam and Paris. Everywhere, but especially in German-speaking cities, they charmed their hosts. To Continental savants Lister was not only a bright young doctor but also the very incarnation of the English gentleman. Above all, he was invariably well informed about the work of their hosts, a sure way to their affection. She, for her part, was modest and, according to Frau Professor Rokitansky, 'cultivated and artistic'. She made no attempt to butt in on the serious business of the *Herren*. On the other hand, she complimented the Frau Professor on her incomparable *Kugelhof*, though in her letters she confessed to being overwhelmed by the sheer quantity of food and drink pressed on them. ('The poor dears must have starved when they stayed with us at Millbank.') Both made gallant attempts to speak the language of the country, while they even more gallantly desisted when their hosts preferred to converse in more or less fluent English.

CHAPTER FIVE

IN JOHN HUNTER'S
FOOTSTEPS

Back in Edinburgh Lister was duly appointed to the assistant surgeoncy at the Royal Infirmary and, in addition to teaching and clinical work, he continued his experimental studies. His private practice inevitably suffered: in one of her letters Agnes referred to 'my poor Joseph and his one patient'. But a reception room on the ground floor was converted into a laboratory and a garden shed served as the animal house. Agnes proved an invaluable assistant and note keeper: many of the experimental protocols, as well as draft papers, still exist in her hand. Like so many Victorian middle-class ladies, she combined refinement and sensibility with astonishing toughness. In later years she and her husband performed lengthy experiments on each other testing the optimal concentrations of chloroform for different degrees and lengths of anaesthesia. Any of these could have ended in disaster. There are hints in Lister's letters to Upton that a few months after the wedding Agnes was expecting a baby. Then the references to the need for her to rest and avoid travel stop. Their childlessness may have been a disappointment—he was fond of children and extremely good with them—but perhaps it also strengthened the conjugal bond.

Lister's papers and lectures of the period, some of the most important ones delivered to the Royal Society, cover an astonishing range of subjects, though his main interests centred on two overlapping topics. In several series of experiments he used the interdigital web of the frog's leg or the bat's wing, both capable of being examined under the microscope in the living, to study the early stages of inflammation. He noted the amazingly coordinated and uniform changes in the blood vessels and blood flow in response to a wide variety of injuries. He provided support to John Hunter's inspired statement that 'inflammation is not in itself a disease but a salutary operation consequent upon some violence or disease'. But not always salutary: it could also be the beginning of a chain of complications, leading to sepsis, gangrene, fever, pyaemia and death. How? Why? When? Lister described the slowing of the circulation and the exudation of fluid from the dilated capillaries. Oddly perhaps, he observed the movement of white cells but did not recognise their scavenging role.[66]

At that stage he still believed that the outcome of the inflammatory response, whether beneficial or harmful, was decided early: that there were in fact two kinds of inflammatory responses. He therefore tended to focus on the immediate changes in the small vessels and capillaries rather than on subsequent developments. Later, he would come to accept a more unitary concept. Even when his interpretations were still tentative or faulty, his experimental observations were accurate. He realised more clearly than most the potential importance of foreign material in a wound. The realisation stimulated his interest in different kinds of surgical ligatures. It led to his exploration of 'catgut' and other absorbable suture material.[67]

Lister then tackled the difficult question of nervous control, difficult because the answer is more complex than a simple yes or no. He showed that the local inflammatory response could proceed even after all connections with the central nervous system had been severed; in other words, that the response depended on autonomous local regulators. On the other hand, nervous control could and did modify the local response. Unlike many experimental scientists, he was open-minded and ready to change his ideas in the light of fresh evidence. It was a characteristic that would remain one of his strengths throughout his career, both in the laboratory and in clinical trials. In his early years in Edinburgh he modified his views on nerve action. For at least a century it had been axiomatic in Britain that nerves had a stimulatory function. In the classical frog's leg preparation, still a standard classroom experiment, excitation of the nerve causes a muscle to contract. But Lister was intrigued by the concept mooted in Germany that nerves could act in the opposite direction too. He conducted a series of experiments on mouse intestines and showed that nervous stimulation could slow as well as enhance peristaltic movements. Eventually he coined the term 'inhibitory' to correspond to the German *Hemmung*.

Lister's second main interest was blood coagulation, then as now one of the most controversial topics of biomedical research. Was blood or blood plasma essentially a liquid that needed some trigger mechanism to make it solidify? Or was it in reality a solid or at least some kind of gel that active principles maintained in an unnatural liquid state? Most importantly, what brought about the change from one to the other? And what could inhibit it? Some 150 years after Lister, the answers are still not entirely clear. Then as now, these were not theoretical problems. From the surgical point of view they were of cardinal importance. Failure of the blood to clot could be disastrous: after septicaemia, haemorrhage was the commonest cause of death during or after operations. The two complications were in fact related; or could be. Bleeding that had been successfully arrested at operation could suddenly and catastrophically start again in an infected wound. Why? What had gone wrong in the clot that seemed solid and clean initially? Failure of the blood to flow could be no less fatal. It was clear that healing depended on the provision of essential nutrients, not least of oxygen, and this depended on the free flow of fresh blood to the wound. How to steer between these two dangers, excessive bleeding and insufficient blood flow, was the key question to be answered.

Lister was not of course alone in the field. Numerous hypotheses were being canvassed and argued about. Was it something in the air that made liquid blood clot? Was cooling the essential trigger? Or was it the cessation of flow? Or all three? Or none? The eminent physician Sir Charles Scudamore had written at length on the liquefying role of carbon dioxide. Benjamin Ward Richardson had won the Astley Cooper Prize of the Royal College of Surgeons with a well-argued essay concluding that blood remained liquid in the circulation because of a small amount of dissolved ammonia. When exposed to air, the ammonia evaporated and blood clotted. Both ideas were still fashionable in the 1850s and both had gathered an astonishing amount of seemingly conclusive experimental support.

In an extensive investigation Lister showed that under certain circumstances in an amputated sheep's leg blood might stay liquid for up to six days. Very politely, he demolished both the carbon dioxide and the ammonia hypotheses. On the other hand, he showed that injuries to the vessel wall could start or at least hasten clot formation even in the living. He studied the effect of silver wires introduced into the vessels of living animals. They could initiate clotting even in the circulation. This was a radical departure from accepted doctrine. His suggestion that the state of the vessel wall was as important in clot formation as the state of the blood was prophetic. Of course, such insights (like successful generalship) are partly, but never entirely, a matter of luck.[68] He drew attention to the layers of clot that often formed in aneurysms where the vessel wall was thinned or damaged and the circulation was sluggish. The observation was to become one of the foundations of Virchow's historic researches on thrombosis 20 years later.[69]

Lister also linked up inflammation with coagulation. Coagulation was an essential step in the normal inflammatory response that led to healing. However, conversely, a clot in the wound could also turn green with putrefaction and could become the starting point of sepsis, pyaemia and gangrene. Many of his findings were summarised in a paper read before the Medico-Chirurgical Society of Edinburgh, entitled 'The Spontaneous Gangrene from Arteritis and the Causes of Coagulation of the Blood in Diseases of the Blood Vessels'. The very title encapsulated not only his own work but also the direction of much future research.

Lister's reputation grew. The influential figures who would promote his career after his early Edinburgh years liked and trusted him as a person; but they were also impressed by his work. He was beginning to be seen as an heir to John Hunter even before the discovery of the antiseptic principle. In 1860 he decided to apply for the fellowship of the Royal Society. His father warned him against disappointment: he would probably be regarded as too young for such an honour. In the event he was one of 14 to be elected out of 450 applicants. Thirty years earlier his father had been one of four candidates, all elected. The change in numbers reflected not only the son's growing fame, but also the staggering growth of interest in matters scientific as the century progressed.

Looking back on it in 1899, Alfred Russell Wallace, the man who had proposed evolution and the survival of the fittest independently from Darwin, published a 'retrospect' under the title 'The Wonderful Century'. He credited 24 fundamental scientific advances to the immediately preceding 100 years against 15 to all the rest of recorded history. The numbers were of course a little fanciful—turns of centuries tend to impair people's sanity—but they were not as far-fetched as they may seem. By the mid-century science, especially applied science, enjoyed a prestige and popularity unparalleled before or since. This prestige and popularity attached to commanding individuals, not the amorphous mishmash of awe, suspicion and queasiness that surrounds science today. And both the prestige and popularity were deserved. Men like Davy, Faraday, Tyndall, Darwin, Huxley, Helmholtz, Liebig, Virchow, Cuvier, Saint-Hilaire, Claude Bernard, Dumas, Pasteur and others addressed the intelligent public as well as their fellow scientists in a language that was simple but also precise and often elegant; no idiot soundbites or portentous oversimplifications by television gurus.

Also, even when the messages they conveyed were controversial, the aim of these men was transparent: it was the betterment of the human condition. Their work and their objectives transcended both class and national frontiers. Davy was honoured in France at a time when England and France were at war.[70] Pasteur was celebrated throughout Europe.[71] Virchow was feted in England. Tyndall's lectures in the Royal Institution were star attractions that drew visitors from the United States. Faraday was well aware of the importance of explaining science to non-scientists and wrote a brilliant essay on the art of lecturing. In 1861 thousands of schoolchildren gave up their Christmas holiday to listen enthralled as he talked to them about the history of the candle.[72]

Lister reached his scientific maturity at this, 'the most shining moment in the history of science'.[73] It is impossible to understand his dedication to his scientific labours at the expense of private comforts and earnings, except in this context. Nor is it possible to recapture the prestige he would soon enjoy with the general public as well as within the medical profession, abroad as well as in his own country.

In the year of his election to the Royal Society, Lister was also appointed professor of surgery in the University of Glasgow. The position, being a regius chair, was in the gift of the Crown, as represented by the home secretary Sir George Lewis, not within the power and patronage of the university senate. It was preceded by intense lobbying in favour of a local or at least a Scottish candidate. When Lister's appointment was announced, he expected to be appointed to the honorary staff of the new Royal Infirmary as a matter of course. He was not. As he began to explain to the Infirmary's Board of Management that, as a teacher of surgery, he wished to illustrate his statements by demonstrating surgical problems on patients in the wards, he was interrupted by the chairman, David Smith, a prosperous boot maker: 'Stop, stop, Mr Lister, that's a real

Edinburgh idea. Our infirmary is a curative, not an educational institution.'

The difference between Edinburgh and Glasgow was in fact clear from the start, not least in the patient population in the wards. (Lister objected to calling it the 'clinical material', just as he objected to the use of the term 'case'.) This excluded anybody who could pay for his or her treatment at home or be accommodated in some special benevolent institution like a workhouse or a lunatic asylum. The rule embraced not only the rising middle classes but also domestic servants and business employees, for whose welfare their masters or employers were morally if not legally responsible. Apart from emergencies, which were admitted without question, the patients were therefore drawn from the newly 'urbanised' industrial masses. The majority were filthy, half-starving factory or dock workers and their families, often sleepless from the vermin that preyed on them, unwashed, half-crazed or disabled by drink. Cholera had struck Glasgow as recently as 1848. The plague, smallpox and venereal diseases were common, tuberculosis almost universal. Many 'febrile contagions', including malaria and typhoid, were not separately identified. Surviving statistics are therefore difficult to interpret.

Unhealing discharging sores, the effects of rickets (either tuberculous or due to vitamin D deficiency or both), injuries, burns, abscesses and a variety of tumours, both benign and malignant, were to make up the bulk of Lister's clinical problems when eventually, a year after his appointment to the chair, he was given his wards at the Infirmary. Many of his patients were children, aged 10 or younger, who had been working in factories for 12 or more hours a day. Most were illiterate. The number of industrial accidents on the shop floor or from transport machinery was increasing at an alarming rate. Except that it did not seem to alarm anybody except perhaps as a distant threat to the available workforce.[74] In 1840 Alexis de Tocqueville wrote of Manchester: 'Here civilisation performs its miracles and civilised men are turned back into a savages.' Twenty years later Glasgow was catching up. Safety regulations against industrial injuries were rudimentary. Guards and other protective devices did not become required by law until the first Factory Act in 1840 and then only in mills. But in the 1860s in a city like Glasgow the supply of manpower still seemed inexhaustible.

All this was a new experience for both Agnes and Joseph, and a challenging one. Of course they had seen destitution in Edinburgh and London, but nothing like the raw poverty of the sprawling and still growing Glasgow slums. Among Agnes's books preserved with her library was one by Mrs Ellen H. Raynard entitled *The Missing Link*. It is a devotional work that addresses itself to the Christian problem of the degradation of poverty in unsparing language (as did many books at the time). It also describes the evangelical labours of the Bible Society in the slums of London. It is inscribed: 'Agnes Lister with JL's dear love, Christmas 1861'. What was the answer? As to most other compassionate Christians of the Listers' background, it was charity and working towards the spiritual and physical betterment of the poor by education and example. Only a handful of exceptionally imaginative (or mad) reformers could conceive of a fundamental change in the Victorian class structure or in the economic laws which sustained it. The Listers were not among them, any more than was Florence Nightingale or 'our dear Queen' herself. Yet the soldiers in Scutari were Florence Nightingale's 'children'; and Lister cared deeply for his patients. This was a side of him that first unfolded in Glasgow. He was now the chief and set the tone. Many of his assistants were to write memoirs in later years.

There is a natural tendency to endow medical benefactors of humanity with the trappings of a compassionate doctor. The two do not necessarily mesh. The attitude to hospital patients of many of the Victorian grandees, still reverently commemorated in the names of instruments, operations, dressings, memorial orations and wards, would be deeply shocking today. Lister's would not be. John Rudd Leeson recounts a telling incident. On one occasion the instrument clerk, whose duty it was to arrange the implements required for an operation on the table beside the patient, brought a trayful into the theatre uncovered.

> Lister instantly threw a towel on the tray and said in sorrowful tones: 'How can you have such a cruel disregard for this poor woman's feelings? Is it not enough for her to be passing through this ordeal without adding unnecessarily to her suffering by the display of all this naked steel? Really, Mr —, I am surprised at you.[75]

Lister never referred to patients in their presence as anything other than 'Mr' or 'Mrs' or sometimes 'this good man' or 'this good woman'. He accompanied serious operative cases back to the ward and took the head of the stretcher when the patients were transferred to their beds.

> He would then arrange sandbags and hot water bottles with the invariable warning that they must be wrapped in flannel. [Anaesthetised patients could be accidentally burnt.] With almost womanly care he would arrange the bedclothes.[76]

During ward rounds he did his own dressings even before this became an essential part of the antiseptic ritual. According to Leeson, he never left a patient without asking: 'Now are you comfortable? Is there anything else you want?' And he would adjust the pillows. While all this may sound mawkish, the cumulative impression is clear. These patients, temporarily in his charge, were to be cosseted as if they were his immediate family. Of course the attitude was wholly paternalistic and politically incorrect, but the vast majority of Lister's charges accepted this. 'When the Professor comes into the ward, I feel as if God Almighty had come in,' one recorded. There were inevitable exceptions. Ward journals mention patients being discharged for repeated misconduct, even for using obscene language. Interference with a dressing was a cardinal sin. But such instances were rare. Lister was a good man and a good doctor.

CHAPTER SIX

THE MOMENT OF TRUTH

One day between March and June 1865 Lister was walking home with Thomas Anderson, professor of chemistry in the university. Anderson, a well-read man and the son of a Leith general practitioner, casually mentioned the work of a French chemist, recently published, on the idea that invisible 'germs' could be responsible for a variety of chemical transformations, including putrefaction. Could this conceivably be of some surgical relevance? Improbable as this must have sounded, Lister expressed a mild interest. The publications were all in French but yes, he could cope with a scientific text in most major European languages. A few days later Anderson sent him a pile of journals. Lister read Pasteur's papers with mounting excitement. He was not given to self-dramatisation; but he told Godlee many years later that, by the time he finished his reading, his mind was alight, seething with ideas. He thought that he knew the cause of 'hospital sepsis'.

What he had realised—or thought he had realised—was that wounds were not infected by malign 'miasmas' wafting about and impossible to track down and dispel. They went septic not because of mysterious but ill-disposed 'radiations' from the sun, the moon, the stars, the Devil or anywhere else. The cause was not even 'dirt' as such. Pasteur had shown that the air, the atmosphere, was teeming with invisible living 'germs', trillions of them. They were of a great variety, more distinct species perhaps than populated the visible world. Though invisible to the naked eye, some at least could be visualised through the microscope. And

even unseen, they could be detected by the extraordinary range of chemical transformations they brought about. They could convert wine to vinegar. They could sour milk. They could destroy the larvae of silkworms. They could bring about the putrefaction of fresh meat. They seemed to thrive on living matter or on dead matter that had once been alive. Surely, they could bring about the actual death of that 'matter'.

Because germs were alive, they could reproduce. They could elaborate poisons. They could spread; or at least they could be carried about by air and water. If by air and water, why not by blood? It was their 'livingness' that crucially distinguished them from mythical miasmas and imaginary radiations. Given the right environment—'milieu', as Pasteur had called it—they could multiply at a fantastic rate. Alighting on the living body they could set up not merely one lesion but hundreds. But not of course any living body. The healthy body, protected by normal skin and mucous membranes, clearly provided them with no portal of entry. There had to be a wound, an open wound. An open fracture. A surgical incision.

If these thoughts did cross Lister's mind—and there is no reason to doubt his word—it was the beginning of modern surgery. To appreciate their full impact one has to consider the meaning of the term 'hospital sepsis'.

Hospital sepsis—or 'hospital disease' as it was known to the lay public—was, and had been for centuries, the main cause of death of surgical patients. In 1859 Thomas Bryant, surgeon to Guy's Hospital in London, published details of a series of 300 deaths following amputations. General pyaemia, just one form of hospital disease, accounted for 42 percent of fatalities.[77] It was characterised by the appearance of abscesses in all parts of the body, including bones and internal organs. It could be harrowingly painful.[78] Three other forms of 'hospital disease' were usually classified separately. They were hospital gangrene, septicaemia and erysipelas. All were usually fatal, though hospital gangrene was perhaps the most feared. It could sweep over wards and hospitals with apocalyptic speed and ferocity. Its aetiology is still uncertain. It may have been the infection known today as gas gangrene, caused by the anaerobic organism *Clostridium welchii*.[79] Some workers, including F.F. Cartwright, have suggested that another organism, unknown today, may have been the cause. If that was so, it first appeared in the 1840s, reached its peak virulence in the 1860s and then slowly disappeared. The gangrene started at the site of the operation and spread rapidly. It was accompanied by a fall in blood pressure, a racing pulse, extreme weakness and a sense of terror, in retrospect all characteristic of some form of bacterial poisoning. Sometimes the urine turned brown or black as in blackwater fever, another name for malignant malaria.[80] The condition was invariably fatal within 48 hours, but often as quickly as an hour or two after the first symptoms. In a gruesome way the gangrene sometimes continued to spread after death: there was no way of stopping it.

Septicaemia would be classified today as a milder or earlier form of pyaemia in which bacteria but not yet clumps of pus circulated in the blood. Hectic fever heralded its onset. Patients often died in a general toxic state before the condition could progress to pyaemia. Delirium—or 'madness'—was common. The ravings of such patients were one of Thackeray's 'eerie noises' that he heard in hospitals at night. Erysipelas was much like septicaemia but it was accompanied by a fiery and painful rash, like a slowly spreading burn. It was the origin of such ancient terms as 'the Rose', 'St Antony's Fire' or 'Ignis sacer'. St Antony, compassionate founder of monastic life in fourth-century Egypt, was known sometimes to intercede on behalf of sufferers. It was their best hope.[81]

Most of these hospital illnesses appeared as epidemics. A ward or an institution might be free from them for months or even years. Then for no obvious reason, there would be an explosive outbreak. Little could be done to prevent it and even less once it had started. Individual patients were treated, if they could swallow, with alcohol, opium and hot broths; with cold compresses, leeches and words of comfort if they could not. Wounds were bathed with a range of 'antiseptic fluids', including chloride of zinc solutions or Condy's famous fluid (hot diluted sodium or potassium permanganate). Many surgeons put their faith, or what faith they had, in private remedies. Le Gros Clark of St Thomas's Hospital in London used lint soaked in spirits of wine. Others favoured an ancient concoction based on alcohol, known as Friar's Balsam, or some other alcoholic tincture. Some preparations, such as potassium or sodium sulphite, were used not only externally but also taken by mouth. According to Professor Polli of Milan, they acted as 'antiputrescent agents'. The multiplicity of regimens testified to their uselessness. Floors were drenched and bedding was soaked in a variety of 'cleansers'. Some hospitals installed expensive apparatus that pumped chlorine gas through the wards. Huge fires were kept burning even in the heat of summer to increase ventilation.

The combined effect of all these was marginal. Wise surgeons closed their wards and stopped operating. When it was judged that the epidemic had burnt itself out, the wards were fumigated with sulphur candles or a mixture of saltpetre and sulphuric acid and the walls and floors were scrubbed, usually with chloride of lime. It was not just for the sake of patients. In such epidemics everybody in the hospital was at risk: nurses, students and doctors as well as inmates. Pricking one's finger when threading a needle could be fatal. Numerous charities catered specifically for the families of doctors and nurses who gave up their lives in the line of duty.

There was a widespread impression during the 1840s and 1850s that the epidemics were becoming more fierce and more common. With increasing overcrowding, the impression was probably correct. Where would it all end? Proposals of closing all hospitals were being seriously canvassed. But what should replace them? Tents in open fields? Single-room huts? The ever-inventive and not-to-be-contradicted Miss Florence Nightingale, whose reputation after the Crimea surpassed that of any doctor, advocated completely separated 'pavilions' dotted around in wooded grounds.[82] Hyde Park perhaps? Or further out in the country? The New Forest was mentioned. As a compromise, Miss Nightingale would accept ward blocks opening from and separated by long open corridors. At her instigation dozens of such blocked hospitals were built from the 1860s onwards. Some still exist, though most open corridors are now glazed.[83] It is doubtful if the design had any effect on the frequency or course of epidemics. By the time the new Nightingale-style hospitals were built antisepsis had made them obsolete.

Bright ideas of what caused the hospital diseases abounded.[84] The standard explanation was drifting invisible 'miasmas' originating in sewers and cesspits, gaining a grip on fresh wounds. Invisible they might have been, but their stench was unmistakable. Sometimes it provided early warning of what was impending. Nobody, of course, knew what the 'miasmas' actually were or what made them lethal.

One counter-measure based on the tarnishing of silver was widely practised during the 1850s. Silver was known to discolour when exposed to the sulphurous atmosphere of Victorian London. In ducal and archiepiscopal households its constant polishing occupied at least one full-time servant. In less affluent establishments frequent washing with clean cold water reduced the need. (The sulphide had less time to form a thick film on the metal.) Based on the notion, wholly unsupported by evidence, that hospital miasmas and the tarnishing of silver spoons depended on a similar chemical mechanism, it was suggested that boiled but then cooled to ice-cold water might prevent hospital disease. Enormous quantities of such water were used to clean operation sites and instruments and to irrigate wounds. The 'cleanliness and cold water school' was adopted by such eminent surgeons as Sir Thomas Spencer Wells of the London Samaritan Hospital, by Robert Lawson Tait of Birmingham and, indeed, for a time, by Lister himself.[85] Good results were claimed for it and in some places perhaps achieved.[86] There is nothing wrong with clean water, but cleanliness was difficult to achieve in a city where, during the month of the Great Stink in the summer of 1858, two million gallons were pumped into the cisterns of houses (and of course hospitals) from the Thames that had shrunk to a narrow, foul-smelling trickle between banks of rotting garbage. While parliament could go into recess (and did), hospitals could not.

The man whose work brought illumination to Lister and through Lister put an end to hospital disease knew nothing about septicaemia, compound fractures and suppurating wounds. He was a chemist, not a doctor, the son of a former sergeant in Napoleon's army. After Waterloo Sergeant Jean-Joseph Pasteur and his family settled in the village of Dôle in the Jura, later moving to Arbois in Eastern France. There the former sergeant opened a small tannery. It was in Dôle that Louis (named after the pious St Louis of Toulouse, not the crusader king) was born, on 27 December 1822, the youngest of four children and the Pasteurs' only son.

Louis Pasteur remained all his life the product of the class of hard-working small tradesmen of rural Catholic France. In the same way Lister remained a child of the rising and prosperous Victorian middle classes of England. Their background and upbringing had little in common at a time when background and upbringing mattered. Lister and all his family spoke passable French. Pasteur spoke not a word of English. The two men met four times, all on formal occasions late in life. Though they held each other in high esteem, there was no scope for an intimate friendship to develop between them. Neither man made friends easily.

And yet, one is struck by the parallels in their lives.[87] The family always remained the centre of Pasteur's universe, as it did for Lister. Jean-Joseph Pasteur had received little formal schooling but devoted his evenings to reading books on history and later, better to understand his son's work, popular works on science. What both Pasteur *père* and Lister's father valued above all and tried to achieve for their sons was a good education. Education, not wealth or rank, was the path to dignity both for the provincial tanner of Arbois and the City wine merchant of Essex.

Pasteur *père et fils* remained in close touch by long letters throughout Jean-Joseph's life. So did the Listers, father and son. The appearance of Isabella Lister is known today through a sensitive drawing by her husband. Mme Pasteur's was commemorated on paper by her son Louis in a splendid pastel, executed when he was 15. Draped in a shawl, she sits on a carved oak chair, serene and a little stiff, the embodiment of the hard-working, devout French provincial housewife.[88]

Louis was sent to school first to Besançon and then to Paris, where he was desperately homesick. He developed a deep interest in science—initially more philosophical and cosmological than experimental—and passed the entrance examination to the select Ecole Normale Supérieure. Here he met his first inspirational master, the great chemist Jean-Baptiste Dumas, 'allumeur d'âme', the man he continued to revere for the rest of his life.[89] He also attracted the attention of Antoine Jérôme Balard, one of the notable eccentrics of the French scientific scene (not short of eccentrics) and of the physicist Jean-Baptiste Biot.[90] It was under their influence that Pasteur became captivated by the mysteries of crystal structure and embarked on his first important investigation, the mirror-image specificity of the two possible crystals of tartaric acid. He showed how the two forms could be distinguished by the way in which they deflected the path of light.[91]

He then began a statutory stint as a schoolteacher in Dijon, instructing 10-year-olds in elementary physics. It was the French equivalent of compulsory military service for science graduates and was widely denounced as a terrible waste. Pasteur thoroughly enjoyed it. This was another trait he shared with Lister. Both were inspired by the young, even by small children, often transmitting their messages and their enthusiasm more effectively than they did to adult audiences. (Hector Cameron, a man not given to sob stories, relates how in Glasgow Lister spent 20 minutes on a ward round, operating on the doll of a patient with a crushed leg, 'under full aseptic precautions'.) Eventually, Pasteur's patrons in Paris obtained exemption for him from the full stretch prescribed by the law by having him appointed assistant professor in the University of Strasbourg.

This was a great opportunity. He took modest quarters in the house of the physicist Pierre Bertin-Mourot, a middle-aged bachelor and bon viveur rather than a dedicated seeker after natural laws. It was a happy choice. Bertin-Mourot would remain one of Pasteur's few close friends, facing the younger man's emotional storms, outbursts of rage and lack of humour with a mildly sceptical but always amiable air.[92] At critical junctions Pasteur would ask for his advice, reject it in baroque prose, then almost invariably act on it.

Soon after his arrival in Strasbourg, he was asking for Bertin-Mourot's views on Marie Laurent, 'that angel in human guise'. For once Bertin-Mourot agreed, or at least was wise enough not to disagree. Marie was the only daughter of the Rector Magnificus of the university. The Rector himself was a remote and august figure, much like Syme must have seemed to Lister when he arrived in Edinburgh. Yet within two months the newly appointed assistant professor was writing home to his father, asking the father to present himself 'in black, as you wear for *Pardons*' to the Rector and to ask for the hand of Marie on behalf of his son. Pasteur also addressed a characteristic epistle to the Rector personally:

Monsieur le Recteur: An offer of the greatest importance to you and your family is to be made to you on my behalf; and it is my duty to put you in possession of the following facts which will help you to determine your refusal or acceptance ... My father is a tanner in the small town of Arbois in the Jura and I have three sisters. One has suffered as a child from cerebral fever which interrupted her development. She is an adult in body but mentally a child. We hope to place her shortly into a convent where the good Sisters of the Sacred Heart are ready to look after her with care and kindness. My two other sisters keep house for my father and help with the books, taking the place of our dear mother whom we had the misfortune to lose last May ... My family has no fortune. I do not value what we possess at more than fifty thousand francs. I have long ago decided to hand over my share to my sisters. My only means are good health, intelligence, courage and my position at the university ... My few works published so far have been well received. As for the future, Monsieur le Recteur, I propose to devote myself entirely to chemical research. I hope to return to Paris after I have acquired some reputation for my scientific studies ... My father himself will come to Strasbourg to present my proposal which, in case you refuse, is not known to anyone else.[93]

To Marie he wrote in a different vein:

I have not cried so much since the death of my dear mother when I woke up last night and thought that you might not love me ... Even my work means little to me. To me, who loved my crystals so much that I used to wish for the nights to be shorter so that I could return to them fresh in mind.[94]

Marie was 22, shy and petite, with a pleasant singing voice. She became the complete and devoted scientist's wife, retaining just enough of her natural gaiety to add a touch of lightness to the home. Despite his ardent professions during their courtship, for Pasteur work would always come before domestic pleasures; indeed, most of the time his immersion in his laboratory projects was total. Marie sustained his dreams and did her best to understand his long and sometimes incoherent ruminations about his current scientific problems. She also accepted his occasional uncouthness, just as she accepted for many years that any income on top of his always modest salary, such as prize money, should be spent on laboratory equipment rather than on repairing the roof or a new pair of boots for one of the children.[95]

On the day of their thirty-fifth wedding anniversary she would write to them:

> Your father is absorbed in his thoughts, talks little, sleeps less, rises at dawn and, in one word, continues the life I began with him happily on this day thirty-five years ago.[96]

Reading Roux's description of Mme Pasteur, writing to her husband's dictation and occasionally asking for clarification or even suggesting a better wording, one thinks of Agnes Lister. Both women, in their different ways, became perfect wives to their not always perfect husbands.

Pasteur's work on the stereospecificity of tartaric acid may sound somewhat esoteric, but it led to one of his first moments of truth. By accident one of his solutions became contaminated with a mould that destroyed the 'right-turning' but not the 'left-turning' isomer.[97] It revealed for the first time the highly selective action of many invisible micro-organisms on a chemical process and turned his attention to the 'germs' that invisibly populate the visible world. And not only populate: the more he probed, the more he realised their supreme importance in actually changing the visible world. At that moment he was appointed dean of science at the new University of Lille, with specific instructions from Emile Joubert, Minister of Public Education, to take an interest in local industrial matters.[98] The one preoccupying the city's brewers was the disastrous spoiling of much of their beer. Soon Mme Pasteur was writing to her father-in-law:

> Louis is now up to his neck in beet juice. He spends all his time in the distilleries. He has to give only one lecture a week which leaves him most days and much of his nights to immerse himself in fermentation. I hear about nothing else.[99]

His immersion led Pasteur not only to formulate but also to prove his revolutionary idea that fermentation was caused by specific living germs. Once a few such germs gained access to a medium that supplied them with their essential nutrient, they multiplied. As they multiplied, they used up more and more of their nutrient. Gradually the medium turned into something chemically different. And alas, a medium that was chemically different tasted different too. No less important, the process could be prevented either by preventing the entry of germs or by destroying them after they had entered. They could never—'jamais, jamais, le grand jamais'—arise 'spontaneously' from non-living matter. Their destruction could be achieved by chemicals. It could also be achieved by prolonged exposure to even moderate heat. The latter process would one day be known as 'pasteurisation'. That would have been sufficient to ensure his fame. In fact, it was the first of many studies into the action of bacteria capable of bringing about an astonishing range of chemical transformations, some beneficial, some harmful. They still provide the foundation of modern dynamic biochemistry.[100]

In 1859 Pasteur was appointed assistant director of the Ecole Normale Supérieure in Paris. His two poky laboratories are now preserved as a museum and marked with a plaque in the rue d'Ulm. He also became involved in the first of those intensely heated controversies that would continue to punctuate his career. He had, he convinced himself and his followers, totally demolished the idea of the spontaneous generation of life,[101] but there still remained a few *chameaux* who needed to be pulverised. (Camels to Pasteur were the equivalent of firefighters or *pompiers* to Monet, the reasoning behind both epithets remaining somewhat obscure.) He was a vigorous, eloquent and sometimes scurrilous debater, a master of the annihilating phrase, always passionately convinced of his rightness. (The conviction was usually—though not invariably—well founded). He was merciless to his opponents even when his opponents were venerable figures of great achievements or even recently dead. But he could also be deeply remorseful and magnanimous when it was pointed out to him (usually by Madame Pasteur) that he had offended against Christian charity. He would then address long and contrite letters to his victims (which had to be toned down by Bertin-Mourot not to sound like a retraction of his actual thesis).

Between 1860 and 1865 he discovered, among other achievements, butyric acid fermentation, the life of certain germs in the absence of oxygen, the role of yeasts and bacteria in various diseases of wine and vinegar, and the decomposition of organic matter by countless different species of bacteria, some requiring oxygen, others inhibited by it. 'Without the infinitely small, life would soon become impossible because decomposition after death would be incomplete' was an observation whose metaphysical overtones appealed to Lister: he quoted it frequently.

Pasteur was an inventive designer of simple experimental tools, most notably perhaps of the 'Pasteur flask'. This was a globular vessel with a curved and drawn-out capillary neck that allowed the entrance of air but not of dust-carrying micro-organisms. It would become Lister's standard experimental container. Long days in the laboratory and heated debates in scientific meetings did not consume all the Frenchman's energy. His curiosity about the density and distribution of germs in the atmosphere took him from the cellars of the Paris Observatoire to Alpine peaks above Chamonix. Some of his investigations on the fermentation of wine were carried out in the vineyards of his native Arbois, where a laboratory was improvised for him at the local *auberge*. His assistants feared that it might be attacked by ignorant rustics, provoked by the encroachments of science on their natural preserve. Pasteur reassured them that, once the purpose of the encroachment was explained to them, the laboratory would become sacred. He was right. He spoke the language of French peasants as naturally as Lister spoke the language of Victorian drawing rooms. He regularly lectured to school children on chemical structure and in 1865 gave a series of field demonstrations to the vinegar manufacturers of Orléans.[102]

In 1865 he yielded to the pleading of his old master Dumas and travelled to the South of France to explore the disease of silkworms that threatened one of France's famous luxury industries. He found the region sunk in despair. 'Everything had been tried,' he was assured. 'The situation is hopeless.' One has to marvel at his self-confidence. He had (by his own account) never seen a silkworm or mulberry tree. The whole complex life cycle of the creature had to be explained to him. He was either astonishingly lucky or the possessor of a creative instinct more common (or more commonly observed) in artists and poets than in scientists. He justified both his self-confidence and Dumas's faith in him. He not only discovered the micro-organism responsible for the epidemic but also designed effective counter-measures.[103] The work provided him with an entrée into the jealously guarded fields of animal and then of human diseases. No non-medical scientist has made the transition with such aplomb. By 1870, when he eventually published the full text of his *Etudes sur les maladies des vers de soie*, he was deep in anthrax, chicken cholera and soon in rabies.

The papers that Armstrong passed on to Lister in November 1865 were probably 'Sur les corpuscules organisés qui existent dans l'atmosphère', published in 1861 and 'Mémoire sur la fermentation appellée lactique', published in 1864. Both are clear but neither is light reading for a non-chemist. Lister was determined to understand the message and he could be extraordinarily persistent. All his life he would acknowledge the debt he owed to Pasteur, almost to the point of exaggeration. At the time Pasteur knew nothing about hospital sepsis and had never envisaged the surgical implications of his researches.[104] Nine years later Lister was to write to him from Edinburgh:

My dear Sir: Allow me to beg your acceptance of a pamphlet which I sent by the same post, containing an account of some investigation into the subject which you have done so much to elucidate, namely the germ theory of fermentative changes. I flatter myself that you may read with some interest what I have written on the organisms which you were the first described ... I do not know whether the records of British Surgery ever meet your eye. If so, you will have seen from time to time notices of the antiseptic system of treatment which I have been labouring for the last nine years to bring to perfection ... Allow me to take this opportunity to tender my most cordial thanks for having, by your brilliant researches, demonstrated to me the truth of the germ theory of putrefaction, and thus furnished me with the principle upon which alone the antiseptic system can be carried out ... I need hardly add that it would afford me the highest gratification to show you personally how greatly surgery is indebted to you ... Forgive the freedom with which a common love of science inspired me.[105]

Lister's was a kind of lateral thinking before the term was invented and became trendy, coupled with a rare 'feel' for clinical problems. Remarkably in the absence of any direct evidence, he convinced himself from the start that germs were not just *a* possible factor in hospital sepsis but *the* long-sought explanation.

Thomas Spencer Wells, apostle of the cold water school of antisepsis, had by then also read reports of Pasteur's work and had speculated that germs might be responsible for some cases of wound infection. It never occurred to him to translate the idea into action. Lister also convinced himself, arguing from the remote evidence of changes brought about by germs in milk and wine, that if these germs were alive, they could also be killed. Killed, that is, in surgical wounds as well as in food and drink. This was a bold jump, not envisaged by Spencer Wells or anybody else. Soon Lister was preoccupied with two practical problems. First, what kind of clinical cases would provide a safe and convincing experimental model to test his hypothesis? And second, what kind of a germ killer should be used to provide conclusive proof?

In answer to the second question, phenol or carbolic acid, a coal tar derivative, had been discovered by Ferdinand Runge of Berlin in 1834; and observations on its antiseptic properties had been published by Jean Lemaire of Paris in 1860.[106] About the same time Frank Crace Calvert, professor of chemistry at the Royal Institution in Manchester, had returned from a trip to Paris where he had read a paper to the Académie des Sciences on the use of coal tar derivatives in medicine. A true Victorian in combining a questioning mind, a sharp business acumen and a large family to feed, a year later he started to distribute samples of his comparatively pure preparation of carbolic acid to Manchester surgeons. One of them, Edward Lund, published a favourable report in the *Lancet*. But it was still little known in England and had therefore been neither tried nor discredited. This was probably one of the reasons Lister chose it.[107]

The answer to the first question took a little longer to crystallise. His first experimental case, a young woman whose tuberculous wrist he had excised and had then cleansed with carbolic acid, was a failure. The wound went septic and never properly healed. Lister worked out an improved technique that would not only cleanse the wound but also protect it from germs after the operation. He also decided to confine his trial to compound, that is open, fractures.[108] This was a brilliant decision and, like most brilliant decisions, perfectly obvious. Compound fractures required an operation for the bones to be aligned and the wound to be cleaned and closed. The operation carried a horrendous mortality as well as a high failure rate. Most cases in fact were regarded as clear indications for immediate amputation. Many of the remainder eventually led to the same treatment under less favourable conditions. Ethically as well as medically, therefore, the trial was more than justified.

On 21 March 1865 Lister used carbolic acid again on Ted Kelly, a youth of 22, to set a compound fracture of the two bones of the leg. This too was a failure: the wound went septic and the limb had to be amputated. Four months passed. On 12 August 1865 an 11-year-old boy was admitted to the Infirmary. He was James Greenlees and he had sustained 'a compound fracture of the left leg caused by the wheel of a cart passing over the limb just below the knee'. Under chloroform anaesthesia 'the wound was washed as thoroughly as possible with carbolic acid in linseed oil'.[109] It was then dressed with a mixture of putty and carbolic acid. The putty would prevent the carbolic acid from being washed out by blood and other discharges. Carbolic acid–putty was also applied widely over the skin around the wound, further to reduce the risk of germs entering. It was then covered by a sheet of tinfoil to prevent the evaporation of the carbolic acid from the putty. The leg was splinted and bandaged. Four days later the dressing was removed. There was much soreness but no smell or other evidence of putrefaction. This was significant, since 'hospital diseases' usually showed themselves between the fourth and fifth days. The leg was dressed again as before and left for five days. The boy's temperature remained normal. When the second dressing was removed, the wound was clear but the skin around it was inflamed. A smaller dressing soaked in carbolic acid and linseed oil was applied to the wound alone for another four days. By the time that dressing was taken off, the wound had begun to heal. Lister judged that the danger of sepsis had passed and applied water dressings to the excoriated skin. Six weeks and two days after the fracture Greenlees was discharged, walking with crutches but on two legs.

While Greenlees was still in hospital, another labourer, Patrick Ferris, was admitted with a compound fracture of the thigh. He was treated in a similar way and seemed to make good progress. Then, while the Listers were on a short holiday in Upton, the leg turned gangrenous and had to be amputated. Lister now had to wait eight months for the next patient. He continued his microscopic experiments trying to culture 'pus corpuscles', presumably white blood cells, in egg white, and repeating some of Pasteur's experiments using urine as a culture medium. A passing note in one of Agnes's letters mentions that, travelling by train from Glasgow to London, she and her husband had to balance two fragile 'culture bottles' on their knees, 'to the amazement and even perhaps the mortification of our fellow passengers'. It conjures up a picture more vivid and perhaps more sympathetic than the formal portraits that would soon proliferate. He also tried the antiseptic treatment on leg ulcers, with variable success.

The third case of compound fracture was admitted on 19 May 1866. John Hainy, a 21-year-old moulder, had his leg broken when a heavy iron box containing sand for the casting of an iron pipe that he was trying to steady slipped and fell on it. The external wound was two inches long and heavily contaminated. Hainy was admitted three hours after the accident. Such a case would normally have been for immediate amputation to save the patient's life. Lister cleaned and dressed the wound antiseptically and then splinted the leg. During changes of dressings he could observe for himself (perhaps the first man in surgical history to do so) the bloody scab covering such a wound being gradually converted into healthy clean 'granulation tissue'.[110] There was, as so often happens, an anxious waiting period. Hainy developed pressure sores on his back that required frequent doses of opium. Two patients in beds on either side of him developed pyaemia following elective amputations. Hainy was transferred to a 'side ward', not a term commonly used at the time. With dedicated nursing, the pressure sores healed. The patient was discharged on 7 August. On 18 December, when he attended again as an outpatient, he was shown to a class of medical students. They cheered.

James Wyllie, aged 10, was admitted on 8 June. He had been working in a steam-powered turner's factory for the past two years. His right arm was drawn in between strap and shaft and it took more than two minutes to stop the machinery. He was admitted in a state of shock two hours later. The Infirmary had been alerted and a few minutes after admission, under chloroform anaesthesia, Lister was pouring carbolic acid into the gaping wound. No attempt was made to close it. He applied a carbolic acid–putty dressing under tinfoil. He then discovered that the upper arm too had been broken. He set and splinted both fractures. After seven weeks the bones had united and both the wounds had healed. Though 'the alignment was not good', the boy was discharged with 'a useful hand'.

Charles Finlay was a 'fine and intelligent boy' of seven when he was knocked down by an omnibus, 'crowded both inside and out.

One or both wheels on one side had passed over his right leg.' He was in deep shock, his pulse racing but barely palpable. Lister saw him three hours later. Under 'light chloroform anaesthesia', undiluted carbolic acid was poured into the huge wound, 'squeezing it repeatedly to induce the liquid to insinuate itself in all the interstices'. Having set the bone fragments as best he could, Lister applied a carbolic acid–putty dressing under tinfoil. The boy was delirious for three days, but on the morning of the fourth 'he became intelligent again'. His pulse and breathing returned to normal. It was then that a small, secondary wound, not originally treated with carbolic acid, became infected. Several more infections developed in superficial wounds. The next few weeks were fraught; but 'the boy conducted himself with exemplary self-discipline'. As the main wound continued to heal satisfactorily, Lister could observe how some of the bone fragments provided starting points for new bone formation. Though the bones and all the wounds were healed after seven weeks, the scarring had drawn the leg up into a severe deformity. The boy was kept in hospital for another two months while the contracture was corrected with splints and a traction apparatus designed by Lister and the hospital carpenter. The end result was satisfactory: the boy could walk and even run with a limp.

A 15-year-old mill worker, Georgina Robb, was admitted on 21 September with a large wound on the back of her hand caused by machinery toppling over. Lister treated it with an antiseptic regime and she was discharged well on 4 October. Three weeks later a 57-year-old labourer, John Campbell, was admitted. While he was working in a stone quarry a large rock fell on him and he suffered a compound fracture of the thigh and a broken collarbone. It took a six-hour journey on a cart over rough tracks to get him to hospital. There was severe blood loss. For three weeks progress was nevertheless satisfactory; then infection set in. Patient and surgeon battled on until February, when a bone fragment pierced an artery and the patient, already enfeebled, died of a massive haemorrhage. It was the only death in the first experimental series.

Four days after Campbell's death William Chambers, a deaf and dumb labourer of 34, was admitted after he had been run over by an omnibus. He had suffered a compound fracture of the tibia. He was treated antiseptically and was discharged six weeks later. Mary Morrison, the only woman in the series, was 62 when she fell and sustained a compound fracture of the forearm. She was treated antiseptically and discharged three weeks later, her fracture on the way to union. Samuel Boyle, a factory worker aged 13, had both legs fractured when he was struck by the governor of a steam engine. Lister was away, but the fractures were treated antiseptically by his house surgeon, A.T. Thompson, and the patient was discharged with two 'stiff but serviceable legs' six weeks later.

The first antiseptic operation to open an abscess was performed on a 12-year-old mill-worker, Mary Phillips. While the result in her case was satisfactory, this would remain a problematic field. A high proportion of chronic abscesses, especially those connected to bones, were tuberculous and would recur sooner or later.[111] The immediate results were nevertheless often spectacular. Pus flowed out as soon as the abscess was lanced; and if the carbolic acid–putty dressing did not cover too large an area of healthy skin, the cavity healed without the dreaded secondary infection. On 24 February 1867 Lister wrote to his father:

> The course run by cases of abscesses treated in this way is so *beautifully* in harmony with the theory of the whole subject of suppuration, and besides, the treatment is now rendered so simple and easy for any one to put into practice, that it really charms me.[112]

While he continued to apply the antiseptic method to abscesses and a few burns, the compound fracture series progressed. Case 10 was Thomas McBride, a dock labourer aged 52. A compound fracture of his leg caused by being run over by a luggage waggon was treated antiseptically; he was discharged, the fracture united and the wound healed, six weeks later. The last case in the historic series was admitted on 4 April. The patient, John Duncan, was 'a calico worker of intemperate habits' who fell, jumped or was pushed out of a window and fell 15 ft, breaking both bones of his lower right leg. The case was interesting, Lister wrote, 'because the pumping action of the fragments of bones had spread air throughout the tissues'; but 'the germs had been caught up by the blood clots near the wound'. Though the comment does not quite make sense, it points to his belief that nature's defence mechanisms tried to eliminate germs. 'It is never Man that heals the disease, it is always Nature: all that man can do is to remove as many obstacles as he can.'[113] This echoes the great Ambroise Paré: 'I dressed him and God healed him.'

CHAPTER SEVEN

THE ANTISEPTIC
PRINCIPLE

The series of compound fractures was in progress when Lister was confronted with the hardest kind of surgical test. In July 1867 his sister, Isabella Pim, consulted him by letter about a lump in her right breast. He advised her to see Sir James Paget in London and then Syme in Edinburgh.[114] She saw both. Both wrote to Lister telling him that in their opinion the disease had advanced too far for surgery. Both counselled against an operation. Isabella then went to see her brother in Glasgow. Lister, like all surgeons of his day, was widely experienced in treating tumours, both benign and malignant. He felt that a radical mastectomy—that is, removal of the breast, together with its main area of lymphatic drainage (or what was at that time thought to be the main area of lymphatic drainage)—offered a chance of a cure.[115] He also hoped that his antiseptic treatment might prevent the most feared complication, infection of the large raw area left behind. He rehearsed the operation on a cadaver. On impulse he also went to consult Syme in Edinburgh. The day before the operation he wrote to his father:

Before this reaches thee, the operation on darling B [Bella] will be over. It was evidently undesirable to delay a day longer than was necessary as soon as it was determined that it was to be: so last evening I made all arrangements and the operation shall be at half past one o'clock

tomorrow morning ... Today I consulted Mr Syme personally and he said 'no one can say that the operation does not afford a chance'. He also alluded to the carbolic-acid treatment (which he himself has been trying with much satisfaction) as depriving the operation of one of its main perils. I felt his true kindness keenly manifest though little expressed in words, and left Edinburgh much relieved ... Not that I do not feel the prospect of operating on my dear sister *very* much; but the degree of legitimate hope that has opened up must have the decisive influence ... She distinctly said to Aggie that she would much rather have the operation performed by me than by anyone else. Darling B seems to have thorough confidence in me.[116]

The operation was performed in the Listers' house in Woodside Place under chloroform anaesthesia, perhaps administered by Agnes. All went smoothly. Next day Lister wrote to his father: 'I may say that the operation was done *at least* as well as if she had not been my sister ... but I would not wish to do such a thing again.'[117] The wound healed rapidly without suppuration and Isabella was back home a month later.[118]

Not long after the operation on his sister, his parents came to visit their son and daughter-in-law in Glasgow, Isabella for the first and last time. She was frail but the Great Eastern Railway had recently installed comfortable invalid compartments where, for a comparatively modest sum, passengers could travel in a bed attended by nurses and, if necessary, a porter with a wheelchair. Medical attention was also on hand. Joseph Jackson expressed his satisfaction over the excellent service. The visit, followed by a few days with the Symeses at Millbank in Edinburgh, was a success, though Lister was puzzled by a 'kind of resignation' in his mother. Formerly a deeply religious woman, she now said to her son: 'Be sure that thou art happy. That is what matters. Life is but a dream.' What did she mean?

Lister was always careful, perhaps over-careful, not to claim statistical significance for his clinical series,[119] but there could be no doubt about the significance of his first 11 cases of compound fractures. It was not just a question of avoiding amputations or saving life. 'None of us, including the professor, have ever seen five cases in a row in which all sign of suppuration and putrefaction was absent,' one of Lister's assistants wrote. However, Lister now faced a task almost as difficult and certainly as critical as the one he had set himself when embarking on the experimental trial. He had to persuade his professional brethren to accept his discovery and his doctrine.

Advances in science depend on the continuous elaboration of a comparatively few ideas. Even the wheel or the fire in their practical applications must have been the products of generations of inventors passing on their knowledge from one to the next. The value of any new scientific insight therefore depends on how successfully it is communicated to other scientists. There is also a time limit on such communications. Anybody discovering Newton's laws of thermodynamics or Einstein's theory of relativity today would have difficulty in having his (or her) discovery published in *Nature*, however independently he may have made his observations. Regrettably perhaps (and unlike great works of art and literature), great creative achievements in science do not keep. This applies to medical science too; indeed, because of the moral dimension of many medical advances, it applies to it with a vengeance.

Some 150 years after his great discovery, Semmelweis is still being castigated by biographers for not widely 'publicising' his ideas or for doing it without the required diplomatic finesse.[120] The criticism might be justified if his discovery had been a new drug or even a new or improved surgical instrument. But it is never easy for a doctor to tell his fellow practitioners, some of them older and more experienced, that their past practices have led to unnecessary suffering and loss of lives.[121] It may be even more difficult to persuade them to change their habits. Sensation seeking may be one of the milder charges innovators may

face. Some degree of animosity and suspicion may be impossible to avoid. Medical practice is—and surely should remain—an inherently conservative pursuit. Original research may be extolled by appointment committees and slightly inebriated after-dinner speakers. In principle, nobody will deny its value. In practice, most doctors who need medical advice for their own ailments seek out colleagues who have never had an original idea in their lives.

Fortunately for Lister, though his ideas about germs causing 'hospital disease' were as revolutionary, or at least as unorthodox, as were Semmelweis's, he had several advantages over the Hungarian doctor. Instead of being an outsider and a junior in a hostile environment, he was a regius professor of surgery. He was surrounded by a small army of assistants, juniors and medical students who would always bear witness to his statements and support him against criticism. This was one of his great assets. He commanded extraordinary loyalty even though, among themselves, his firm sometimes mocked his 'solemnity'. Leading organs of medical literature might not always be behind him, but their columns would always be open to his communications, letters and rebuttals. Volumes of the *Lancet* of the 1870s fairly bristle with them.

Unlike Semmelweis, Lister was too big and too much his own man to be used as a weapon in medico-political infighting. From the start he had some of the most influential figures of the profession on his side. Proponents of new ideas or 'hobbyhorses' may be carried away by their enthusiasm. Nobody could carry away people like Sir James Paget in London or Syme in Edinburgh. Lister's advantages were of course reflections of his personality as much as of his position. Semmelweis was an impatient, temperamental and uncompromising Hungarian with few social skills and a wayward judgement of character. While Lister was often aggrieved by the incomprehension or hostility of his colleagues, he could never be provoked into intemperate or unprofessional pronouncements. When sorely tried, he would raise his eyebrows, turn his eyes to heaven and sigh. (He did this rather often. 'We wilted when he did,' one of his assistants later recalled.) He held firm views on many subjects but never publicly attributed unworthy motives to his adversaries, as Semmelweis often did. His whole being, even his unsmiling countenance, radiated righteousness: it was possible to think him mistaken but not to question his rectitude. Yet, with all these advantages, his path was not as smooth as it might appear in historical retrospect.

The very first written communication relating to the antiseptic principle was linked to failure. During the first trial on compound fractures, the chair of systematic surgery at University College Hospital London fell vacant. Lister was not entirely happy in Glasgow and he remained hopeful that one day he might return to London. It was the family rather than metropolitan bustle that drew him south. In July 1866 he applied for the post. He also wrote to Lord Brougham, President of the College and the Hospital, asking for his support. He enclosed a specially printed notice of a new method of treating compound fractures. It referred to Pasteur's work and described in some detail the carbolic acid regime. It mentioned five consecutive cases in which bony union had been uninterrupted and wound sepsis prevented. He rightly stated that such an outcome was 'almost unheard of in this disastrous condition'. Nevertheless, he lost the election to John Marshall by one vote. It was not a humiliation. Even some of Lister's former patrons voted for Marshall who had served a 'fifteen years apprenticeship' at the hospital, waiting for the chair. Still, Lister was disappointed.

Professional setback was compounded by private grief. His mother's health had been declining since her visit to Scotland. During her last weeks Agnes looked after her with great devotion; her own daughters all had family illnesses on their hands. She died on 3 September 1867.

The publication proper of the compound fracture series began on 16 March 1867 in an article in the *Lancet*, with further instalments on 23 March, 30 March, 27 April and 27 July. On 12 April Joseph Jackson wrote to compliment Lister: 'It reads to me very satisfactorily—supposing Pasteur's observations to be reliable—and thy great success of thy practice based on them tells much in their favour.' In fact, with hindsight, the doctrine of antisepsis could have been better explained. The case histories are vivid and any surgeon who has dealt with compound fractures (as most practising surgeons must have done) could not fail to be impressed. But the emphasis on carbolic acid was excessive and may have left the impression that what Lister was describing was no more than a new antiseptic agent. The crucial statement that 'when using the expression "dressed antiseptically", I do not mean merely "dressed with an antiseptic" but "dressed so as to ensure the absence of putrefaction" appears only in a footnote. Unlike Pasteur or even his eminent Victorian contemporaries in England like Darwin, Huxley or Galton, Lister was not a natural persuader. On cursory reading, it is easy to conclude that all will be well if only a sufficient amount of carbolic acid is sloshed around the wound. Fortunately, his lectures and verbal contributions to medical discussions were clear; surprisingly perhaps since he always completed them at the very last minute, sometimes in the carriage in which he was driven to the venue. He was also convincing and unequivocal (if sometimes a little long-winded) when answering questions.

Lister was aware of the potential dangers of carbolic acid and changed and perfected his method of applying it with almost every case. Without actually realising it, his aim was the *prevention* of sepsis—that is, *asepsis*—not the effective *combating* of sepsis already established—that is, *antisepsis*—though many years later the word asepsis became anathema to him. He was also essentially a practical surgeon, not a theorist, and his continued emphasis was on technical details, even minutiae. Not surprisingly perhaps, his revolutionary doctrine, based on Pasteur's concept of ubiquitous germs but transplanted into an entirely new context, sometimes got submerged if not actually drowned. However, he never gave up and his persistence won through.

It is always difficult to trace the spread of a new and practical idea simply by following exchanges in the literature. Professional conferences were still something of a novelty and therefore important. On 9 August 1867 Lister addressed the annual meeting of the British Medical Association in Dublin. The title of his talk was 'On the Antiseptic Principle in the Practice of Surgery' and it provoked a lively discussion. He concluded his paper, generally understated rather than sensational, with the statement:

> Because they are unfortunately placed with respect of the supply of fresh air, the two large wards in which most of my cases of accidents and operations are treated are among the unhealthiest in the Royal Infirmary. Yet ... during the last nine months not a single case of pyaemia, hospital gangrene or erysipelas has occurred in them.[122]

And if any visiting personage cared to buttonhole one of the professor's juniors (as visiting personages still occasionally do), they would hear an unreserved confirmation of this statement. A few weeks later Syme published an article on the treatment of incised wounds and compound fractures by the antiseptic method. The method, he claimed, 'made it unnecessary to keep the wound open for drainage for no infection occurred'. A leader in the *Lancet* was enthusiastic. William MacCormack, later president of the Royal College of Surgeons, travelled north from London to observe Lister in his habitat and became one of his proselytisers. Lister's cousin Marcus Beck, now on the staff of University College Hospital, spent some weeks in Glasgow and became a disciple. So did Joseph Bell of Edinburgh.

Of course there was dissent. Sir James Young Simpson, perennial rival and opponent of Syme (and, by extension, of Lister), thinly disguised as 'Chirurgicus', published a strongly worded attack on the method, claiming that it was both unsafe and a mere rehashing of something 'extensively tried' by the French.[123] It was not much more than a shot fired in the guerrilla war between Syme and Simpson that had kept the Edinburgh medical establishment enthralled for decades (and did not stop Sir James consulting Syme about his own ailments or Mrs Syme regularly consulting Sir James). A lengthy and not particularly edifying correspondence ensued and rumbled on. At least it kept the topic alive.

By 1868 foreign visitors began to arrive in Glasgow. In April 'a very gentlemanly man from the Southern States of N. America came to observe my practice,' Lister wrote to his father, 'and declared himself after a short stay to be a complete convert to "the system".' George Derby, the 'gentlemanly man', carried the message to Boston. One of Lister's house surgeons, Alexander Malloch, returned to Halifax, Ontario and preached the antiseptic gospel to Canada. From the Continent German and Scandinavian surgeons came in increasing numbers and became Lister's most enthusiastic disciples. Carl Thiersch of Leipzig read Lister's paper in the *Lancet* and tried the method at once on six patients. He was so impressed that he dispatched his assistant, Herman Georg Joseph, to Glasgow for two months to study the method in depth and at first hand.[124] Professor Saxthorpe of Copenhagen also came in person and was conquered. 'Not a single case of pyaemia occurred in my wards over the past three months,' he reported back after his return. Surgical visitors arrived from St Petersburg led by Professor Bunin and a group of young surgeons came from Vienna. The wonderfully flamboyant Professor Danzani of Milan charmed all the ladies (with hardly more than a dozen words of English at his command) while seemingly being absorbed in and perhaps patchily even absorbing Lister's explanations. All left full of praise. The French were generally less impressed, though Just Lucas-Championnière of Paris spent some weeks in Glasgow and became a convert.

Friedrich von Esmarch, professor of surgery in Kiel, was among the first to realise the potential importance of the antiseptic principle in war surgery.[125] And almost providentially, the Franco-Prussian War of 1870–71 would vindicate the antiseptic method in the treatment of war wounds. In a strange reversal since Napoleonic days, field surgery in the Prussian Army proved vastly superior to that in the French. On the French side bottles of carbolic acid ordered by William MacCormack and Marion Sims of the Anglo-American ambulance team working with Bazaine's army were summarily sent back on the order of General Dufrais; and Lucas-Championnière was commanded not to use his *système idiot* by Bazaine personally. (For this alone the marshal deserved to be court-martialled at the end of his disastrous war.) On the other side, von Esmarch, now a temporary major general and loving it, was rearing to put Lister's (and his own) ideas to the test. This meant that wounded French soldiers were more inclined to surrender to the Prussians than the other way round: they knew that they would get better treatment from the enemy than in their own over-worked and under-equipped ambulance stations.[126] Corporal Jean-Baptiste Pasteur may have been one of the willing captives.

In February 1869 Mrs Syme died and a few months later Syme himself suffered a stroke. He resigned from his chair and Lister was elected to replace him without serious opposition. His move from Glasgow to Edinburgh was delayed by the illness of his own father. He and Agnes travelled to Upton and, with most of the family, were at Joseph Jackson's bedside when he died. The bond between father and son had been exceptional. Probably not even Agnes quite perceived the uncertainty, even the occasional confusion in Joseph's mind in the way Joseph Jackson did. The son's long letters convey not only information but also confessions, doubts, pleas for understanding and the need for love. To these Joseph Jackson responded without fail. At the same time the son was fulfilling the father's most cherished hopes. In his last letter Joseph Jackson wrote:

> However slowly and imperfectly the improvements suggested by thee may be adopted, and however thy claims may be slighted or disputed, it is a great blessing to have been permitted to be the means of introducing so great a blessing as the antiseptic treatment to thy fellow men, and thou hast abundant cause to persevere.[127]

Upton was sold and eventually demolished, but the family remained close. With his younger brother, Arthur, Lister jointly purchased a holiday home in Lyme Regis in Dorset. High Cliff, as the house was called, was without modern amenities and the nearest railway station, Axminster, was seven miles away; but it commanded a superb view over Portland Bill to the south-east and along the white undercliff stretching to the mouth of the Axe and the village of Beer to the west. It was a rambler's, botanist's, bird-watcher's, painter's and fossil-hunter's paradise; and for almost 30 years the family gathered there for a few weeks every summer and virtually always for Christmas. Their number steadily increased. Childless themselves, Joseph and Agnes watched with affection their nephews and nieces grow to adulthood.

A fortnight after Joseph Jackson's death Lister delivered his inaugural lecture in Edinburgh. His opening remarks were addressed to Syme, who was present though partly paralysed:

> First and foremost let us rejoice that our master is still among us, to cheer us by his presence and aid us by his counsel; and it is a source of great satisfaction to myself that, as I have the privilege of free access to his inexhaustible store of wisdom and experience, he will, in some sense and through me be still be your teacher.[128]

On such occasions Lister's gift for the resonant phrase and noble sentiment could make a formality memorable. Syme died in his sleep five months later. Lucy Syme, Agnes's still beautiful but unmarried younger sister, came to live with the Listers.

CHAPTER EIGHT

EDINBURGH

The Edinburgh years were probably Lister's happiest, perhaps his only ones unclouded by secret tribulations. He and Agnes took up residence in Syme's old town house in Charlotte Square. They entertained at dinner parties once a week. There was room for Lister to continue his experiments. He was popular with students and felt relaxed with his Edinburgh classes. Relaxed did not mean familiar; except with his closest family, he would never be on terms of familiarity with anyone. Lack of constraints constrained him. One of his most devoted disciples and collaborators, Hector Cameron, after 30 years would still address him in his letters as 'my dear Professor'. Social life in Edinburgh's upper strata was itself measured and formal. Disputes and disagreements were sometimes fierce but, by and large, they were settled behind closed doors. One such controversy would continue to engage and stimulate Lister's powers of persuasion to no great effect.

Miss Sophia Jex-Blake, a tempestuous but entirely respectable young lady, the sister of the distinguished divine Thomas Jex-Blake, had taken it into her head some years earlier to become a doctor. Since the medical schools of Britain were closed to women, she travelled to Boston where she qualified MD in 1868. She then returned to Britain and, a year before Lister's move from Glasgow back to Edinburgh, somehow or other—the details are still unclear—obtained her matriculation in the medical faculty of the university. This was a kind of formal recognition of her qualification and enabled her not only to set up in general practice but also to launch a formidable one-woman campaign for the admission of women as medical students. The campaign did not stay one-woman for long; change was in the air. Sophia was brilliantly persuasive, finding the most promisingly sensitive spot in the armour of crusty Scottish academics. She contrasted the traditional obscurantism and hypocrisy of the English universities with the equally traditional liberalism of Scottish academia. Forget John Knox and there was a granule of truth in this. Learning was a basic human right in Scotland, regardless of wealth and faith. Now gender was to be added. The prospect of scandalising the medical establishment south of the border was delicious. When, in the autumn of 1872, the matter was put to the vote, all faculty members except two voted for the reform. Both opponents were English. One was John Hughes Bennett, ironically Lister's most determined opponent on the subject of germs; the other was Lister himself.[129] The latter put forward his views in a well-argued memorandum, inevitably dictated to Agnes and preserved in her hand:

> The reasons which generally make it inexpedient for ladies to attend lectures on medical subjects along with male students in the College class-rooms apply with tenfold force against such a mixed attendance in the wards of an hospital where the treatment of the living human body takes the place of theoretical discussion and inanimate illustration, and where students ... may be crowded together and somewhat withdrawn from their teacher's control.[130]

There were other insuperable difficulties to which he felt it 'needful to allude'.

> If ladies were admitted as students, they would have to be allowed to hold hospital offices without which no studentship can be regarded as complete ... Thus we would have not only female Dressers and Clerks, but female House Surgeons and House Physicians, on whom would devolve the charge of the patients in the absence of their superior

officers. And it must be a serious concern for Management whether they would be prepared to entrust to young ladies duties which often tax to the utmost the energies of man ... Young people of one sex thrown into intimate association with the opposite sex would, I fear, on the long run, lead to great inconvenience and scandal.

Lister's opposition to woman doctors was still the reason why, 30 years later, he withheld permission to have the chair of surgery in Glasgow named after him. The attitude was of course coupled with exquisite courtesy shown towards the ladies, even, once they were qualified, to women doctors. Mary Scharlieb, the first woman to win the London University Gold Medal in Medicine and the first to be awarded the MD London degree, recalled how, after a guest lecture by Lister at the Royal Free Hospital, she quakingly addressed a question to him.

I expected him to bite my head off ... or to ignore me. But he answered at length and with the utmost tact, making sure that I fully understood the answer. I felt like the Queen conversing with Mr Gladstone about the Constitution.[131]

But he would later never allow women to attend his own lectures at King's College Hospital, whether medically qualified or not.

Such controversies rarely if ever led to private animosities, not at least on the surface. In contrast to Glasgow, Lister got on well with the Academic Board and even with the lay and often cantankerous management of the Royal Infirmary. Yet he was no model employee. To improve hospital hygiene and overcrowding generally, Syme's 70 beds were reduced to 54 when Lister took over. Lister heartily approved of the management's objectives, but not of the means. The solution was to accept the former in principle and ignore the latter in practice. He often had 70 patients in his wards, two or three children sharing one bed and 'comparatively fit patients' on improvised pallets on the floor. Management addressed respectful memoranda to him: could he see his way to restricting the number of patients to *approximately* the number of beds allotted to him? Lister (Agnes, as usual, acting as his scribe) replied at length and with mingled contrition and distress. Then he continued as before.

Another source of 'some mighty concern' to management (as it had been in Glasgow) was the increasing length of stay of patients in Lister's wards. There were several reasons for this. First, the application of the antiseptic principle was inherently time-consuming. Patients with compound fractures subjected to immediate amputation could often be discharged within a fortnight, sometimes sooner. If they could not be discharged, they were probably dead. Similar patients treated antiseptically and without amputation might survive but remain in hospital for months. Second and no less time-consuming, Lister liked to keep patients under his eye until he was sure that they could be properly looked after at home or look after themselves. As early as June 1871 management 'respectfully drew Professor Lister's attention' to 'the growing number of patients who had stayed in the Infirmary *for over a hundred days'*. Six months later they again addressed a memorandum, concerning 'the apparently growing expense of the antiseptic treatment'. Lister reassured them and management expressed themselves satisfied. In October 1873, however, management once again wondered if the Professor 'would have the goodness to meet the Board regarding four patients who had been in his ward for *over a year'*. Lister did of course meet the Board and gave a detailed account of the four cases.

The first, John Wright, had a diseased foot that would formerly have been amputated but that Lister tried to treat conservatively. After 11 months every effort to save the foot (which was probably tuberculous) failed and the foot was lost. The patient would 'soon' be discharged. The second, Annie McCanna, had been in hospital with multiple lumbar abscesses for 568 days. 'Because of her weak constitution, as soon as one abscess healed, another appeared.' (Once again tuberculosis was almost certainly the cause.[132]) The third, Jane Maid, had a chronic suppurating condition of several tendon sheaths of both her hands. She could not be discharged 'because she lived in Arbroath and local medical care there left something to be desired'. Nor, of course, could she afford or be expected to afford to travel regularly to Edinburgh. Nevertheless, the matter would be dealt with in due course. The fourth patient was the poet William E. Henley who, at 24, had already lost one leg because of tuberculosis and who had been recommended to Lister 'by a Lady in the South of England ... of the highest social standing ... frequently seen at Court'. Henley had been in the ward for 565 days but 'a substantial donation had already been made on his behalf and had been passed on to Management, so that the Infirmary would not incur any expenses'.[133] To clinch matters, one of Lister's assistants submitted a lengthy memorandum, arguing with remarkably modern-sounding statistical acrobatics that 'although antiseptic treatment had led to the retention of some patients for longer than was formerly necessary, this was commonly because some patients were kept alive who would have formerly died ... and that, on the other hand, the antiseptic treatment also led to the earlier discharge of many patients.'[134] Whatever the fiscal merits of the case, management expressed themselves reassured and congratulated Professor Lister on his 'praiseworthy efforts'.[135]

It helped to allay the doubts of management that Lister's prestige, already high, continued to rise. There had not been such a stream of distinguished medical and academic visitors to the city in living memory; and they came not only from Russia, the United States and Portugal but even from England. To put a seal on his recognition as a leader of the profession, in July 1870, at the recommendation of Sir William Jenner Bart, president of the Royal College of Physicians of London, the Queen was pleased to appoint him surgeon-in-ordinary to Her Majesty in Scotland. Since Balmoral was at the time Her Majesty's favourite residence, this was no sinecure.

Within a month Lister was summoned to examine Princess Louise, the Queen's youngest daughter, who may have had an infection of her leg. (Details of royal ailments were never disclosed, though the comings and goings of royal physicians and surgeons were given with exact times in the Court Circulars.) Lister advised masterly inactivity—that is, tonics and wholesome food—and the Princess recovered. A few months later he was summoned again by telegram from holiday in Ambleside by the Queen's resident physician in Balmoral, Dr Marshall. It was now the Queen herself who had developed an abscess in her axilla, 'both painful and undignified'. He found a bevy of medical knights at the Castle who had been called from London, including Sir William Jenner himself. The Queen recorded in her letter to her eldest daughter, the Princess Victoria:

> Dr Lister thought the swelling should be cut ... I felt dreadfully nervous as I bear pain so badly. I shall be given chloroform but not very much, as I am far from well otherwise, so I asked for the part to be frozen ... This was agreed. Sir William gave me some whiffs of chloroform and Mr Lister froze the place, Dr Marshall holding my arm and Sir John Foreman steadying my shoulder. The abscess which was six inches in diameter was very quickly cut and I hardly felt anything excepting the last touch when I was given a little more chloroform ... In an instant there was relief.[136]

The next day she wrote in her journal:

> Had a cup of coffee before the terribly long dressing of the wound took place. Dr Marshall assisted Dr Lister whose great invention, a 'carbolic spray' to destroy all organic germs, was used before the bandages were removed and during the dressing.[137]

The carbolic spray mentioned by the Queen was to become an essential ingredient of the Lister legend and would appear on the Lister centenary stamps in 1965.[138] It was in fact based on a theoretical misconception, the idea that most microbial invaders were airborne. While this may have been true of organisms contaminating wine and beer in Pasteur's experiment, it was comparatively rare in surgery. At least, it was comparatively rare compared to contamination by instruments, the surgeon's or assistant's hands, ligatures, swabs, dressings, sweat dripping from the surgeon's brow or coughs and sneezes. Nevertheless, the spray was spectacular and imposed a certain amount of heroic hardship on the operating team, enough to catch the imagination of both contemporaries and later generations. Its objective was admirable: it was to help defeat the enemy whose size and invisibility made them formidable.

Its introduction was preceded by long and exacting experiments. Using mostly normal urine as a culture medium, Lister showed (as had Pasteur) that the only certain way of preventing germs from multiplying in a natural nutrient medium was heat, a method inapplicable to patients.[139] Lister had already used a syringe occasionally to create a fine carbolic spray when changing dressings. It seems to have been his house surgeon, John Chiene, who had overheard two students discussing the Richardson 'spray', an anaesthetic device. He suggested it to his chief. Lister at once adopted what was in fact a slightly modified scent bottle and described its use in a paper published on the last day of 1870. From then on he was constantly modifying and widening the scope of his 'unconscious caretaker'. Soon the surgeon, his assistants as well as the patient were enveloped in a cloud of yellowish mist with the pungent carbolic acid odour. Many found it exceedingly unpleasant and it was difficult to get rid of. Wives and girlfriends—but not Agnes—complained. A constant and irritating hiss indicated that the spray was in action. At least it killed idle chit-chat during operations (of which Lister disapproved).

In 1873 a modification known as 'Dr Siegle's Patent Spray Producer' was described in Agnes's Commonplace book, accompanied by a fine drawing by her husband. In its final form the instrument, widely known as the 'donkey', was a large copper atomiser that had to be worked by a foot treadle. The carbolic solution was placed beneath it in a large flask. The whole weighed about 10 lb and sat on a tripod about 3 ft high. A long handle could direct the spray to the spot indicated by the surgeon— or not. On one occasion the jet caught Queen Victoria full in the face. Fortunately, she kept her eyes tightly shut during all surgical procedures. She bore the experience with exemplary stoicism. So bulky was the contraption that Listerian surgeons could always be spotted as they drove in their carriages to operations in private houses by part of the machine sticking out of the carriage window. Eventually there were two sizes (both continually modified and improved). A smaller 'hand spray' was used mainly for changing dressings, and a larger one for operations. The latter could throw a jet of carbolic 'cloud' for a distance of 12 ft. It would quickly fill the operating theatre with carbolic vapour.

The spray to some extent distracted attention (as it still does) from the astonishing amount of original experimental work that Lister, unfailingly assisted by Agnes, accomplished during his Edinburgh years. The whole field of bacteriology was new; and some of the excitement of fresh discoveries still emanates from entries in the Commonplace book. There are notes for almost every day, including holidays at High Cliff and visits to Arthur's family in Leystonstone, even for Christmas Day 1872. Some are eloquent in their brevity, like 'subculture in Flask B-6-339 started at 3 a.m. on 25, 12 72'. The extraordinary diversity of germs gradually unfolded and replaced the idea of pleomorphism that Lister had initially envisaged.[140] Some were airborne, others not; some required oxygen, others seemed to be inhibited by it. Even before the new methods of staining, fixing and, above all, pure cultures came into use, different and characteristic morphologies emerged.[141]

The work would have done credit to a full-time laboratory investigator. But Lister always remained a busy practising surgeon; indeed, the absence—or relative absence—of post-operative infection made it possible continually to expand his operative repertory. In this respect he was not in the class of the stars of the operating theatre who were emerging on the

Continent, mainly in Germany, and who would make the next decades the most exciting period in the history of surgery. He would also be surpassed by some of the next generation of surgeons in Britain. Yet he described new operations for kidney stones, varicose veins, harelips, the exploration of joints and skin grafting. Replying to his letter (in French), Pasteur rightly marvelled at the English surgeon's achievement:

> It is an enigma to me that you can devote yourself to researches which demand so much care, time and unceasing attention and, at the same time, pursue the profession of surgery and to be the chief surgeon of a great hospital.[142]

He asked Lister to send him a detailed account of his antiseptic system that he, Pasteur, would communicate to the Académie des Sciences in Paris. He also wanted to read all of Lister's earlier papers, 'which would be translated to me by a veritable expert in your language'.

Many of the foreign visitors who flocked to Edinburgh as well as some of Lister's assistants left detailed accounts of his ward rounds. If a dressing showed traces of a discharge, a clerk would at once be dispatched for two basins of carbolic acid solutions, one for the instruments and one for hands. The dresser looking after the patient would then

> fall on his knees at the bedside ... and start the hand spray. Lister gently lifted off the outer dressing which was solemnly handed round each distinguished foreign visitor to smell. Having satisfied themselves that there was no putrefaction, the deeper layer of gauze ... was passed round to show that there was no pus either ... Then came the *pièce de résistance*. In cases where it had been impossible to bring together the edges of the wound, Lister usually covered it with a 'carbolic protective dressing'. Now this was carefully peeled off with forceps ... and, as a rule, a gasp of surprise would emanate from the distinguished foreigners. There was no sign of

suppuration. The gasp was often followed by an outburst of violent chatter and gesticulation, so that one became alarmed lest the peace of the nations was being endangered.[143]

In addition to such grand teaching rounds, Lister did a quick 'private round' every evening and an extended one, lasting sometimes five or six hours, on Sunday afternoons, accompanied only by his house surgeon. (In the mornings he and Agnes attended the church of the Trinity in Princes Street Gardens.) 'These visits were arduous,' his house surgeon John Stewart wrote later, 'but they are among my happiest memories.' (As so often, following Victorian greats on their daily round of activity, whether in Parliament, at their studies or in the African jungle, their timetable leaves one breathless.)

In May 1875 Lister asked for and was granted extended study leave to visit Continental hospitals. He had accumulated a pile of pressing invitations whose acceptance he had regularly postponed. He liked travelling, but his experimental work could not be delegated. Now he felt that it was essential to embark on a 'missionary voyage' to spread his doctrine in Italy, Germany and France. The 'missionary voyage' turned into what the *Lancet* described as a 'triumphal march'. After an interesting and enjoyable spell of two weeks in Italy, travelling as far as Naples and visiting all the obligatory historic and artistic sites, the 'surgical leg' of the journey began in Munich at 11 o'clock in the morning on 9 June. At the station a large welcoming party, attired in morning dress and armed with bouquets, was led by Professor von Nussbaum and the Bavarian Minister of Culture, Adalbert von Feuer. For the first time Lister and Agnes realised that antiseptic surgery had become one of the sensations of the age in Germany. All able-bodied professors of the university attended the festive dinner, '11 substantial courses discounting an unbelievable selection of nibbles,' Agnes reported in a letter to Lucy. The university's student body formed a thanksgiving deputation, Lister was decorated by the King (presumably in one of his saner moments) with the Order of the Wittelsbach Lion, and a gala performance at the Hofoper was attended by the cream of Munich society. Among those celebrating was a junior professor, Theodor Billroth from Zurich, soon to transfer to the chair of surgery in Vienna.[144]

Even the Munich reception was eclipsed by Leipzig, where Herr and Frau Professor Thiersch acted as the Listers' hosts.[145] Some 200 of Germany's most eminent academics attended the *Lister-Bankett* at the Schützenhaus (with the ladies being served separately and somewhat intermittently in the gallery). There was 'festive music' by Mendelssohn—the Wedding March, perhaps—and a student choir sang part-songs especially composed for the occasion. Professor Thiersch's speech 'in faultless English' was both complimentary and witty. Great discoveries, like Professor Lister's, usually pass through three stages, he said. First, the world smiles and shakes its head and says: 'It's all a piece of nonsense.' Second, it shrugs its shoulders and says with distaste: 'It's all the merest humbug.' Finally, it looks bored and says: 'Oh, that's an old story, we knew that all along.' But nobody looked bored in Leipzig. Lister replied in German.

The day after the banquet he was introduced to the young King of Saxony, who had made a special journey from Dresden to demonstrate his interest in science. Both he and Lister attended Thiersch's operating session, which included an exploration of the knee joint and the removal of a tumour from the thigh. Neither operation, Thiersch explained to his Majesty, would have been possible without Professor Lister's discovery.[146] More medals, more banquets, another gala opera ('not Lohengrin this time: Herr Wagner is still not persona grata in Saxony'[147]). In Halle the Listers were welcomed by Professor Richard von Volkmann, third of four generations of medical professors and one of Lister's earliest champions in Germany.[148] An allegedly funny student song composed for the occasion (to be sung to a lugubrious tune by Brahms), entitled 'Carbolsaure Tingel-Tangel', was performed to general acclaim.[149]

In Berlin the Listers were received at the Charité by Professor Bardeleben and attended the venerable Professor von Langenbeck performing his first 'antiseptic operation' in their honour at the age of 73. Both patient and professor survived. In Bonn they were welcomed by Professor Bush and his assistant Dr Madelung, both of whom had already spent some time in Edinburgh and now more than repaid the hospitality they had received. The reception in Köln and Heidelberg was similar. 'Mountains, truly mountains of food! How do these kind people cope with it?', Agnes wondered. At last, at the end of August, they were back in Edinburgh, where Lister presided over the surgical section of the annual meeting of the British Medical Association.

The next year the couple, together with Arthur Lister and his wife Susan, embarked on another tour, less memorable surgically but privately even more interesting. In 1876 the United States celebrated its centenary with, among other festivities, an International Medical Congress in Philadelphia. Lister was invited to preside over the surgical sessions. He had always wanted to travel to America. The party of four crossed the Atlantic on the *Cynthia*, the last Cunarder to be equipped with full sails as well as steam. As the most distinguished foreign visitor he was seated next to President Ulysses Grant at the conference dinner. (Not many participants came from Europe, but South America provided a Spanish-speaking contingent and Agnes reported that 'every language of the Tower of Babel' could be heard among the native American delegates.)

Following the meeting the party travelled by the first transcontinental railway to San Francisco. The city's cheerfully lawless cosmopolitan bustle and incomparable situation enchanted them; and the local produce of fruit and grapes was 'the most scrumptious we had ever tasted'. While the gold rush and the age of vigilantes were over, the Frontier was still open. Only a few weeks earlier the Sioux, under Sitting Bull and Crazy Horse, had slaughtered General George Custer's regiment at the bend of the Little Big Horn river. 'History is here still raw and in the making,' Agnes wrote home, 'everything seems to be changing all the time.' Salt Lake City, where the party stopped for a night, was still ruled by the Mormon leader Brigham Young. In Chicago, a thriving meat-packing centre and Great Lakes port, the overwhelming reception was organised by a meat tycoon's wife who, as an injured mill girl in Glasgow ten years earlier, had been one of Lister's patients.[150] It was characteristic of Lister that, when they met—unexpectedly for him—he remembered the exact nature of her injuries and even recalled that her friends called her Trixie and that she was a great one for slightly rude Scottish ditties.

After Chicago Lister gave well-attended lectures in Boston and New York; but, while the personal welcome was always warm, his audience by and large remained sceptical. 'The finickiness of the antiseptic principle,' Henry Welch was to recall many years later, 'went against the American grain'; and it took another 20 years before the idea began to percolate through the surgical hierarchy of the United States.[151]

CHAPTER NINE

KING'S

On 10 February 1877 the mighty Sir William Fergusson died.[152] He had been professor of surgery at London's King's College Hospital for 30 years and departed while still in harness.[153] Who could succeed this giant figure? On the world stage, or what counted then as the world stage, one British surgeon stood out. Lister was 50, famous and known to be receptive to the idea of moving back to London. His reputation never stood higher in Scotland; but his roots, as well as all his remaining siblings and their families, were in the South. Many expected him to be invited at once.

It was not quite so simple. In Edinburgh his staff, students as well as his personal friends urged him to stay. There were public meetings. Resolutions were passed. Agnes and Lucy were at home in Scotland and would have preferred to remain there. Lister was also aware that he would face problems in London. The number of students at King's would be minute compared to his class in Edinburgh. His income from private practice might plummet. While he would never be a small fish, the London pond was significantly bigger; nor would its waters be necessarily friendly. In contrast to his unchallenged position in Scotland, the London surgical world was, by and large, sceptical and exclusive. It was also resolutely philistine. Lister's scientific attainments would be a matter for concern, not an attraction. Battle was joined at every level as soon as his interest became known. The *Times* as well as the *British Medical Journal* and the *Lancet* burst into editorials of staggering prolixity and irrelevance. Correspondence columns

sizzled. 'It is only a question of time before the antiseptic bubble bursts,' one anonymous colleague wrote. 'We shall all be the better for its demise.' Several correspondents stressed the French origin of the doctrine. Need one say more?

Antagonism was particularly strong at King's. The College and Hospital had been founded 30 years earlier as a counterblast to the godless venture in Gower Street, Lister's own alma mater. Both College and Hospital were dedicated to religious and political orthodoxy. Lister was known by now to be a high Tory; but once a Quaker, always a Quaker (or, as one musical wit put it, at least a semi-Quaker or even a semi-demi-Quaker). His surgical ideas and practice were certainly far from orthodox. Eventually it was the College Council that settled the matter—or so they thought. They unanimously appointed an old King's man, John Wood, to the chair. However, that was not the end. Wood's partisans maintained that Lister had been offered another chair but had rejected it. This was strictly untrue; not that the strict truth matters on such occasions. Such an offer had never been made. More importantly, Lister's supporters in London, including such powerful figures as John Ericson at University College Hospital and Sir James Paget at Bart's, were roused to fury.

In May Lister attended a meeting of the General Medical Council on which he represented the University of Edinburgh. He let it be known that he would accept another chair at King's if one were offered. This was a signal for new motions, counter-motions, amendments and counter-amendments and presumably much arm-twisting and decorous academic blackmail. Lister had made it clear that he would continue to practise antiseptic surgery and would require all the necessary facilities. He had also specified the number of students and staff that would have to be allotted to him and the manner of the division of fees between his and Wood's department. London was already far more expensive than Edinburgh; and he had no intention of repeating Syme's mistake. From his share of Joseph Jackson's fortune, he was a wealthy man, not dependent on his income from private practice; but, like Joseph Jackson, he was careful with money and circumspect about spending capital. His conditions were difficult for the College Council to fulfil, the more so since Lister made no secret of his dislike of 'London's slapdash teaching methods'. It was not in fact the teaching. What he deplored was the custom of students being examined by surgeons other than their teachers.[154] However, in the 1870s the London medical schools were still fiercely competing for custom. Student fees not only brought in the funds: students would also spread the fame of the teaching staff and, after qualifying and setting up in practice, become the source of private patients.

King's College Hospital was a latecomer in the race but had already acquired the reputation of a somewhat backward institution. It had resisted the reforms of Miss Nightingale at St Thomas's Hospital across the River.[155] It could boast a few illustrious names on its staff, but teaching was not their top priority. The student intake was sinking, a matter of some concern. To many young people Lister's name would be a draw. And he was, after all, despite his unwholesome preoccupation with germs, perfectly acceptable socially. He was a dignified figure, irreproachable in his private life. Indeed, he was already a member of the Royal Household, if only in Scotland. The importation of such a personage would dispel the impression of fustiness without endangering the tone of the senior staff dining room. While no categorical assurances were given in response to his demands, the College Council at last resolved to invite him to a new chair of clinical surgery (as distinct from Fergusson's and Wood's chair of surgery plain). By then Lister was committed to the move if invited; and, without further quibbles, he accepted.

It was nevertheless a wrench. Despite his roots in Essex and the welcome proximity of his family, Lister would probably never feel as relaxed in London as he had been in Edinburgh. He took a long lease on an elegant Nash house, 12 Park Crescent, facing Regent's Park. It was somewhat outside the medical hub of the West End, still centred on the lower end of Harley Street; but he had recently added bird-watching to his long-standing relaxation of botanising, and the ponds of Regent's Park were still home to many strange and wonderful species. The delightfully stuccoed cream-coloured façade of the Crescent obscured its jerry-built interior. Poor John Nash had never had enough funds to look after both the inside and outside of his lovely terraces. (Perhaps he was not particularly interested in the inside: he never expected to live there.) The leaking roofs and draughty windows were almost symbolically different from the granite solidity of Edinburgh's Charlotte Square. Still, after relining several rooms with oak panelling, furnishing the windows with heavy brocade curtains, covering the floors with layers of Turkish carpets and installing suitably immovable mahogany furniture, the place was ready to receive the household. It now included Lucy Syme and a domestic staff of 12, with horses and two carriages to occupy the mews. They moved in on 11 September 1877. The upheaval was not allowed to interrupt the experiments in progress. Flasks containing bacterial cultures had already been installed in two rooms converted into a laboratory at the back of the building. The Commonplace book for 11 September 1877 records that the boiled milk in Flask No 14 was still fluid at noon.

London was different not only architecturally. The number of students at King's was not only small: contrary to expectations, for some time it dwindled rather than increased. Lister's teaching was not lacking in interest but it was 'unsafe' in terms of passing examinations. Often no more than a dozen students would turn up for lectures and fewer for teaching rounds. That was a contrast to the 300 or more who would crowd into the operating theatre twice a week in Edinburgh. On 4 January 1878 one of Lister's assistants noted: 'Prof just returned from holiday. He was ready for his lecture but found no audience.' Nor was the behaviour of those who did attend above reproach.

Lister got a foretaste of what was to come when he delivered his inaugural oration. He had prepared it with care. It would not only inform: it would cast a shaft of light into the future; it would illuminate the 'scientific foundations' of modern surgery. He had brought his favourite backroom boy, Watson Cheyne, with him from Edinburgh.[156] They, as well as Godlee and Cameron, arrived equipped with test-tubes and flasks, illustrating lactic fermentation. Large-scale pictures showed the appearance of newly discovered microbes. There were graphs and even, horror of horrors, a 'numerical table'. Most of Lister's colleagues looked bemused, then dozed off. The students, about 50 in number, were less passive. What they had expected was a discourse about new operations, possibly the display of one or two clever instruments, a few gory illustrations and an amusing quip or two (teetering perhaps on the edge of the improper). Instead the talk was about acidification, the spoiling of milk, atmospheric pollution and the antiseptic properties of obscure chemicals: all utterly useless.

> We first showed our boredom by shuffling our feet. Then, whenever Lister referred to a cow, we moo-ed loud in unison. When he mentioned 'germs' we buzzed like flies. Each time he spoke of a dairy maid we went oooh and aaah. When he referred to contamination, we said 'tut-tut-tut'. When five o'clock struck, we reminded him, slurping audibly, that it was tea-time.[157]

Nor was the behaviour of King's students in the operating theatre significantly more mature. As the professor and his retinue processed in to begin an operation, followed by dressers rolling in the carbolic acid spray, all in grave silence, somebody in the students' gallery would invariably intone: 'Let us s-s-s-s-pray!' The professor would turn his eyes to heaven and sigh deeply. Many of the nursing staff were frankly hostile, every hospital doctor's nightmare. Though Lister himself commanded a measure of respect, his juniors from Edinburgh suffered.

Yet many years later, such events and attitudes would be remembered as teething troubles. Matters were bound to improve and they did. John Wood, Lister's former rival, was an early convert. He was a Yorkshireman of few words who disliked show and what he described as playing to the gallery. About antiseptic surgery he had heard only from others, though what he had heard he mistrusted. But fair's fair: now he came to watch Lister at work and observe Lister's results. He was impressed and was honest enough to admit it. Only some two months after Lister's arrival he announced that antisepsis would rule in his wards too. He would remain one of Lister's staunchest allies. Lister also invited general practitioners to his operating sessions and ward rounds. Few claimed to understand the fancy rigmarole about germs, but all could tell a healing wound from a gangrenous one. Patients got better after outrageously risky operations. Antisepsis was more than a gimmick.

The new professor's personality also pleased. Far from being a puffed-up celebrity, he was polite with the ignorant and gentle with the sick. He addressed his seniors (in years) with respect. While he could be sorrowful with his juniors, he was never rude. His integrity was transparent. To ease tension on one occasion he even essayed a joke, his only such alarming venture. After a suitable pause he turned to his new house surgeon, Arthur Cheatle: 'Cheatle, you ought to be a very honest man.' After another pause Cheatle asked apprehensively: 'Why, sir?' 'Because you cheat ill!' came the reply. Such a man was impossible to demonise.

Seemingly small incidents helped. Though Lister was not an inventive operator, a few weeks after his arrival at King's he had the chance of performing a landmark operation. One of his patients, a young city messenger called Smith, had suffered a simple broken kneecap. Immobilisation had been tried for months but the fracture would not unite. Smith's livelihood was at stake. Lister decided to cut down on the fracture site and join the two fragments with a silver wire. This broke the strictest rule of the pre-Listerian surgeon: it converted a closed fracture into a compound or open one. This was universally recognised as carrying a grave risk of amputation or even death from septicaemia. If the patient had died, Lister might have had to face a charge of manslaughter. However, the patient did not die. By modern standards the end result was far from brilliant; but, after a fortnight, Smith could walk with a limp.

Wood too had a patient with an unhealing kneecap and he asked Lister to operate. Lister insisted that the operation should be performed by Wood, though he offered to assist. Carbolic acid trays, buckets and sprays were in evidence. All the antiseptic ritual was observed. The operation was a success. Over the next six years Lister repeated the procedure six times without a single patient being lost or needing an amputation. Fractures of the kneecap were common not only among city messengers but also among the fox-hunting fraternity. More than anything else, the series convinced the London surgical establishment that antisepsis might be worth trying.

Looking at surgery from a narrow, nationalist point of view, the recognition came a little late. During the post-Napoleonic decades French surgery had led the field. Then material circumstances as well as a few outstanding practitioners—Syme, Simpson, Liston, Fergusson and young Lister himself—had made Britain a place of pilgrimage. In the late 1870s the role of trail blazer passed back to the Continent, especially to Germany. Perhaps it helped that the country had to start from a level far below that of pre-Listerian Britain. By British standards German hospitals before the 1870s were filthy, sometimes no better than medieval pesthouses. While the Franco-Prussian war was not won by antisepsis, it did teach German surgeons that clean wounds heal more quickly than dirty ones. The surgeon majors and surgeon major generals returned to civilian life determined to change bad old habits. It is not in the German character to do things by half. German hospitals soon outshone hospitals elsewhere—almost literally. Wards and theatres in Berlin, Heidelberg, Vienna, Munich and even in small provincial centres became models of cleanliness, Not a pool of vomit or soiled dressing in site. The stench of putrescence was replaced by the welcoming smell of disinfectant. Lister's triumphal tour in Germany could now be seen as more than a personal homage. It had marked the beginning of German dominance in most branches of surgery.

In Berlin the elderly Professor von Langenbeck was succeeded by Ernst von Bergmann. A Baltic Prussian born in Riga, he barked his orders and expected them to be obeyed; they generally were. Bergmann quickly realised—as did Lister himself a few years later—that the spray was fighting non-existent enemies. Noxious germs were real, but they did not, on the whole, descend from the air. So 'Fort mit dem Spray!' But this did not mean 'Fort mit Antisepsis': it meant the replacement of antisepsis with asepsis. Instead of the spray there would be scrubbed hands, sterilised instruments, gowns, caps, masks, boots; all the paraphernalia familiar from soap operas today. This did not of course happen from one day to the next and Lister was right to urge caution. A readiness to admit his own mistakes was one of his endearing qualities. When he realised that the spray was an unnecessary encumbrance, he abandoned it and expressed his regret. As sprays went out of use, the beautifully crafted 'donkeys'—or 'caretakers', as Lister preferred to call them—found their way to junkshops. After the Second World War they could still be purchased for a pittance in London's Petticoat Lane market. Nevertheless, Lister maintained that the abandonment of the caretaker, which had been designed to deal with airborne germs, should lead to a redoubling of effort to kill germs from other sources. To him the alternative approach of never letting germs get anywhere near a wound from any source—that is, asepsis instead of antisepsis—remained anathema.

Both Lister's own and Von Bergmann's reforms were only a means to an end. Organs and body cavities that had been forbidden territory since time immemorial became accessible to surgeons. It happened over a matter of a few decades. The excitement of new operations is almost palpable reading the surgical literature of these years. Vaginal hysterectomies had been performed or at least attempted from time to time for 100 years. Now in Heidelberg Vincenz Czerny (a nephew of the composer) approached the uterus through an abdominal incision and successfully removed two large fibroids. In Königsberg the German-Pole Johann von Mikulicz-Radetzky devised not only the operation still known by his name for the two-stage removal of cancer of the large bowel, but also several other ingenious intestinal manoeuvres. Some worked. In Munich Johann von Nussbaum transformed the city's Allgemeines Krankenhaus, formerly known as the 'Tor zum Friedhof' ('door to the graveyard'), into a model hospital and pioneered operations on the biliary system. Instead of scooping out a few gallstones, whole gall bladders were removed. In Zurich Theodor Kocher tackled some spectacular goitres. (They were endemic in Switzerland before the introduction of iodinated salt.) Not all the clever procedures have stood the test of time. 'Drooping kidneys' are no longer hitched up and 'kinks' in the bowel are no longer straightened out. But even comparatively small provincial towns contributed their quota of advances or at least novelties. Anton Wölfler of Graz was the first to report the famous operation of gastroenterostomy, mentioning that two such procedures had already been performed though not yet reported by his eminent colleague, Professor Theodor Billroth of Vienna.[158] That was a gilt-edged guarantee.

Billroth remains the most impressive figure in this gallery. Not only did he devise and first perform an astonishing number of new operations, most famously perhaps the partial removal of the stomach, but he also carried out important studies in applied anatomy, outlining the blood supply and lymphatic drainage of many organs. It provided the basis for critically revising operations for cancer. He also devoted almost as much care to the long-term follow-up of his patients as to the original operations, a startling new concept at the time. The now common criteria of 'one-year-survival', 'two-year-survival' and even 'five-year survival' were his brainchildren. Their introduction permitted for the first time to assess the value of operations to patients as well as to surgeons, a revolutionary concept. Ironically, while he followed Lister's teaching in practice and demonstrated more convincingly than anyone else its value, he was never quite converted to the idea of germs. Or perhaps he was merely teasing his French colleague, Antoine Lembert, an ardent Listerian and disciple of Pasteur as well as the originator of a still widely used surgical stitch. This would have been in character. Billroth also enjoyed pretending that he regarded surgery as a terrible 'Umfall' after his youthful dreams of becoming a composer of symphonies and concertos. His good friend Johannes Brahms, by contrast, was probably honest when recalling that he would have become a surgeon had poverty not forced him to earn his living playing the piano in Hamburg brothels after leaving school at 15.[159] Pretence or not, from the larynx to the rectum Billroth made almost every formerly forbidden anatomical region accessible[160]—and often successfully accessible. If Lister made surgery safe, Billroth showed what safe surgery could accomplish.

Of course, despite the undoubted German dominance, Listerian surgery advanced worldwide. The first textbook of antiseptic surgery in any language was written by Lister's French disciple, Just Lucas-Champonnière; and Lucas-Champonnière's colleague, Paul Broca, was a pioneer neurosurgeon using the antiseptic method. Two French Listerians, Jean-Claude Guyon and Jean Albarran, made the Hôpital Necker, the place where Laennec had first demonstrated the stethoscope, a world centre for urology. By the 1880s even the United States was catching up, the first American treatise on antisepsis appearing in 1888. Its author was Árpád Gerster, a Hungarian immigrant.

In this revolution Britain took some part, though young surgeons from the Continent and the United States no longer flocked to London or Edinburgh to see surgical history being made. The one figure who remained universally recognised as the fountainhead of all recent advances was Lister. In fact, antisepsis was only the first of the basic scientific developments that would continue to transform surgery over the next 100 years; and it is perhaps the true measure of Lister's greatness that his mind remained open to them. This may seem to contradict the oft-repeated charge (implied earlier by the present writer) that, having devised antisepsis, he would not tolerate moves away from it. That was true. Even towards the end of his surgical career, when more and more of the younger surgeons began to cultivate the 'theatrical affectations' of asepsis, Lister would enter the operating theatre in his frock coat, turn up his collar to protect his shirt and cravat, roll up his sleeves, dip his hands into carbolic and start operating. What he felt was that the old and well-tried should not be jettisoned in favour of passing fads; and that asepsis improperly enforced was more dangerous than old-fashioned antisepsis. (Billroth usually entered the operating theatre with a large Havana cigar in his mouth and often continued to smoke it while operating. At his command, a well-trained nurse would remove and reinsert it in the gap between the great man's moustache and beard if his hands were otherwise occupied.) In the wider field of the basic sciences Lister remained alert to every new advance and felt personally called upon by Providence to explore how they could be applied to clinical practice. There were several such advances during his last years at King's.

Pasteur was still active when the next heroic scientific figure, this time a medical man, emerged. Robert Koch was born in Clausthal in the Harz mountains in 1843, the third of thirteen children of a mining engineer. He trained as a doctor at the University of Göttingen, one of the smaller of Germany's numerous medical schools. He was slightly built, studious, bearded and extremely short-sighted. Under the unassuming exterior he harboured a well-concealed romantic streak: he would later recall his boyhood dreams of exploring the South Seas and winning the Iron Cross in battle. But the realisation of those could wait: there were other goals in sight. At the not unreasonable insistence of his newly wed wife, he settled down after qualifying to earn a modest living as a general practitioner in the Prussian town of Wollstein. But that too was appearance only.

In between attending (conscientiously by all accounts) to the ailments of local farmers, their wives, their brood and often their cats, dogs and livestock as well, Koch spent his time poring over a microscope, Frau Emmy's wedding present. It was an instrument so rudimentary that an Oxfam shop would hesitate to accept it today as an educational toy. He did not mind. He taught himself the basics of microbiological research, not yet available in textbooks let alone DIY manuals. He made many of his own instruments. He built his own cages. He paid out of his modest salary for the experimental rats and guinea pigs he needed. He had nothing in common with his great and already famous contemporary Pasteur except his priorities. The rats and guinea pigs came first; wife, family, friends and other interests nowhere. Frau Emmy accepted this, as did Mme Pasteur.[161] After six years the country doctor had not only identified the organism that causes anthrax but showed that anthrax spores could survive almost indefinitely under extremely adverse conditions (as in dead and buried carcasses) and revive and start to grow, multiply and kill when transferred into a living host.[162] This was and remains one of the great and unvarnished romances of medical research; and it was only the beginning.

Koch was fortunate in his choice of authorities to whom, after six years in the wilderness, he decided to reveal his discoveries. Ferdinand Cohn and Julius Cohnheim were both professors at the comparatively unimportant university of Breslau (today's Wroclaw), products and victims of the Jewish emancipation in Wilhelmine Germany.[163] Both realised not only the significance of Koch's findings but also the genius in the shabbily dressed country doctor, and set out to persuade the great Virchow to start taking microbes seriously.[164] It took them two years of assiduous lobbying before Koch was transferred to a modest laboratory in the Imperial Health Office in Berlin.

It was there, even before his momentous work on the tubercle bacillus, that occurred the incident of the baked potato. One of his assistants, identity unknown, was either exceedingly sloppy or desperately over-worked, probably the latter in Koch's laboratory. He not only consumed his supper of baked potatoes at the laboratory bench but left an uneaten half-potato in the incubator (or warm cupboard, as the erratic receptacle available at the time was called). The next morning Koch discovered both the deed and its unexpected consequences. The cut surface of the potato was dotted with pearly 'colonies' of various sizes and shades, all superbly regular half-spheres. He suspected at once that each 'colony' arose from the multiplication of a single organism: in other words, that they were pure homogeneous cultures. So it proved. Today the procedure is so elementary that it is difficult to appreciate its significance. It represented the path through the inspired chaos of Pasteur's, Lister's and even Koch's own past microbiological researches.

The date was 1880 and the next International World Congress of Medicine was scheduled to meet in London the following year. 'Meet' is perhaps too casual a word to describe these events. The half-century between the Franco-Prussian War of 1870–71 and the First World War saw the apogee of international medical gatherings. Steam travel had put an end to the informal, often impromptu meetings of a handful of savants to exchange views and experiences over the kitchen table. Air travel and tax dodges had not yet spawned the multibillion-dollar industry of jamborees that now infest the world's former beauty spots.[165] The international medical conferences of the Long Peace were solemn and uplifting occasions, not unlike imperial durbars or state funerals. They took place at appropriately spaced intervals in the world's medical centres, where the top representatives of international science and medicine with their carefully selected retinues were expected to and did exchange their latest and most momentous discoveries. They unfolded majestically under high royal patronage.

Their first half-day was invariably devoted to an unhurried opening ceremony. No paparazzi were admitted to ask moronic questions. No pushy professors (and would-be professors) jostled for an orgasmic television soundbite. Later the event would be commemorated by an internationally acclaimed academician on a canvas of gigantic proportions. National anthems were played by military bands as national delegations paraded forward and backward in morning suits or uniforms. Vast bouquets, both floral and verbal, were handed out right and left. During the following week each half-day session consisted of two or three substantial papers at the most, each followed by a discussion as meaningful as it was decorous. There were leisurely private luncheons and dinner parties to supplement the formal proceedings, culminating in a conference banquet and ball (and an opera performance of never less than three and a half hours' duration in German-speaking countries). Decorations were distributed, Gallic kisses exchanged, honorary doctorates bestowed. Every junior usher was aware of the historic import of the event. The printed account of the lectures would point the way to further advances for years to come.

Some 3000 doctors and scientists, an unprecedented number, gathered for the London conference. To avoid even the semblance of international discord, it took place under the joint patronage of the Prince of Wales, the future Edward VII, and his cousin, the German Crown Prince, the future Emperor Frederick I. Sir James Paget was president and Lister secretary general. Yet, impressive though the plenary sessions were, the most poignant moment came at a private meeting organised by Lister at King's College Hospital. He had invited Koch, still a comparatively insignificant member of the German contingent led by Virchow, to give an account of his new methodological discoveries at a private demonstration.

Unbeknown to Koch, Lister had also invited the French delegation, which included Pasteur. He and Koch had never met. Until then a minor blemish on the conference had been the smouldering hostility between the French and the German delegations, acceptable so long as it was only smouldering, but serious when the two groups threatened to walk out during the opposite side's national anthems. Pasteur in particular was known to be an ardent advocate of *La Revanche*: for him and for Madame Pasteur, a native of Strasbourg, it could not come soon enough.[166] The two parties still did not speak to each other when they met at King's; and Watson Cheyne had some difficulty in keeping them at arm's length. Koch eventually gave a demonstration of single cultures on solid media. In his

understated way he was as impressive a performer as Pasteur, and Lister himself acted as the interpreter. At the end of the performance Lister turned directly to Pasteur, asking him to comment. Pasteur walked up to Koch and extended his hand. 'C'est un grand progrès, monsieur,' he said.

CHAPTER TEN

THE GREAT AND THE GOOD

After the Congress Lister and Agnes took a three-week holiday in the Tyrol.[167] In the mornings he worked on papers as usual; but the afternoons were devoted to walks, 'usually about five miles or so' in the mountains. On arrival back in London, 'much refreshed as usual', a letter was waiting for him from Mr Gladstone, offering him a recommendation for a knighthood.[168] The tribute was distinctly belated, though it would soon be followed by elevation to the baronetcy. In the ward books at King's references to 'J.L.' or 'Prof L' changed to 'Sir Joseph Lister', always in full. He had already been elected to the Council of the Royal College of Surgeons and of the Royal Society and the Presidency of the Clinical Society (as well as to the Athenaeum). He was becoming not merely a public man but a pillar of what was not yet called the Establishment, and the most admired representative of his profession. His and Lady Lister's formal dinner parties once a month at Park Crescent were coveted marks of distinction among the international medical and scientific community. They were also cherished but dreaded occasions for the junior staff of King's, one of whom Sir Joseph invariably invited and seated next to Lady Lister.[169] (Those careless enough to admit that they recognised a keyboard would be asked to accompany one of the distinguished guests after the meal in a recital of ballads or romances.)

While the antisepsis–asepsis controversy rumbled on, it was really about words rather than about actions, and the tone of the controversy became muted. Rubber gloves were patented in 1878.[170] Koch's assistant, Georg Wolfhügel, devised a system of steam sterilisation of laboratory equipment, a method quickly adopted by surgeons. Georg Neuber introduced sterilisation by boiling of operation gowns and masks.[171] Somebody coined the phrase 'no-touch technique': it was too snappy to miss. The crucial importance of bacterial contamination had been established beyond doubt. In 1890 a German surgeon, Friedrick Ruf, was convicted for malpractice when he operated on a child without antiseptic/aseptic precautions and the child died of septicaemia. Lister wrote a generous letter in his defence.[172]

Success and universal recognition did not mean that Lister was abandoning research. He went on experimenting with antiseptic agents, perfected catgut and re-investigated the importance of dust as a vehicle of germs. Throughout the 1880s the number of his publications actually increased; and he rarely put pen to paper unless he had something to say. He lectured widely to learned societies, universities and to the Woolwich Military School on the antiseptic treatment of war wounds. Some of these lectures required a good deal of experimental as well as literary preparation. He never improvised. Even his course to undergraduates (now well attended) was brought up to date and rehearsed every year. Inescapably, matters of public health and policy began to be thrust on him. He only rarely refused such requests, though there is nothing to suggest that power gave him particular pleasure. The year 1886 brought a notable example.

In July of the previous year an Alsatian peasant boy was bitten by a rabid dog. His parents rushed him to Paris. They consulted Pasteur. Pasteur in turn consulted his medically qualified assistant, Emile Roux, and other medical colleagues. For once — he did not as a rule mix science with religion — he even consulted the Abbé Bolestin, his spiritual adviser and a notable naturalist in his own right. After brief but intense soul searching, he decided to treat the boy, Joseph Meister by name, with a course of inoculations of the attenuated rabies virus. It was a breathtaking decision. The preparation had never been tested in humans.[173] The injections were (and continued to be) painful. Recipients would often develop a mild feverish illness which might have presaged—but fortunately never did—full-blown rabies. The experiment was taking place in the glare of publicity. For the first time bulletins about the progress of an otherwise unimportant patient were telegraphed to distant lands. Encamped reporters in the Hôtel Dieu were chatting up the Sisters of Mercy, hoping to catch the first news of the latest up or down of young Joseph's temperature chart. After a mild influenza-like illness, Meister recovered. It was a sensation comparable to an important political or military event.

Patients began to descend on Paris from all parts of Europe. Nineteen moujiks arrived from Smolensk in Russia after being mauled by a rabid wolf.[174] It happened while the Grand Duke Cyril Alexandrovitch was hosting a shooting party in the region. He telegraphed his cousin, the Czar. The Czar ordered one of the imperial trains to pick up the victims and transport them to Paris. All this took rather longer than might seem from a written account. The moujiks arrived in Paris 20 days after sustaining their injuries. They were all ill already, at least so far as one could tell. The only word in French they knew was Pasteur. A week was the time limit that Pasteur had arbitrarily set for the vaccine to be worth trying. After that it might even aggravate the illness. Reluctantly, he took another terrible risk. He condensed the fourteen-day course of one injection a day into a seven-day course of two daily injections. Two of the patients died within 48 hours, probably from septicaemia rather than from rabies. Pasteur and Roux estimated that another 14 or 15 would die. In fact, all the remaining 17 recovered.

Once again, the news echoed round the world. The Czar sent Pasteur the diamond cross of St Anne and, more usefully, a gift of 100,000 francs. It was a colossal sum at the time—and timely. Pasteur and his small team at the Hôtel Dieu could no longer cope with the demand. More donations were asked for and arrived. The French State guaranteed the future of what was soon to be known as the Institut Pasteur. Within three years seven 'rabies institutes' (all soon to be called Pasteur institutes) were established in Russia, five in Italy, and one each in Vienna, Budapest, Barcelona, Bucharest, Rio de Janeiro, Havana, Buenos Aires, Chicago (the first of many in the United States) and Malta.

Such headlong action was of course alien to the British tradition. In Britain rabies was less common than on the Continent; but at least 50 people every year were known to die a horribly painful death from it. Around 200 suspected cases had been rushed to Paris during the year following the saving of the Russian peasants. A select committee and later a commission were established by the House of Lords under Lister's chairmanship to investigate what (if anything) needed to be done. At Lister's insistence, the commission carried out its own extensive tests on dogs and bats with the new vaccine.[175] The material was first sent by courier from Paris, later manufactured locally in the laboratories at King's. The commission then travelled to Jamaica (where rabies was common) to test the preparation on natives. Some became sick, though none actually developed the illness. Eventually the commissioners reported favourably on the need for action.[176] (A minority disagreed.)

In the course of the investigation it became apparent that a more permanent body and indeed an institute was necessary to cope with problems created by the welcome but expensive advances in the new science of bacteriology. The problem of what to do about diphtheria antitoxin and the revolutionary possibility of compulsory inoculation of all children were pressing. (George Bernard Shaw had already written a devastating pamphlet deploring the idea.) The Duke of Westminster donated a plot of land in Chelsea. The Prince of Wales bestowed on the commission his generous patronage: it could henceforward display (free of charge) the princely ostrich feathers on its letterhead. The plan eventually grew into the Lister Institute of Preventive Medicine.[177]

The next international conference of medicine to which Lister was invited as an opening speaker was scheduled to be held in Berlin in August 1890. By now Koch had become a world figure for his greatest discovery. On a cold and cheerless evening on 24 March 1882 he had reported to the Berlin Physiological Society—or to the 30 or so members who had foregathered in the reading room of the Physiological Institute[178]—that he had identified and isolated the bacillus responsible for the most dreaded disease of the age, tuberculosis.[179] It was by any standard a colossal achievement; and the first reaction to it was one of stunned incredulity.[180] But Koch's evidence was cast iron and the doubters quickly lost ground.[181] Only in the light of the terrible prevalence of the disease can the reaction to the discovery be appreciated. Starting as a plague of the urban poor (which it remained) during the early Industrial Revolution, the illness had long broken through the class barrier as it did through all natural and political frontiers. In England there was probably no middle-class family without at least one young member being affected and almost certainly doomed to an early and heartbreaking death.[182] The Listers were no exception. The victim among them was one of Joseph's nieces, Elizabeth Harrison, the youngest daughter of Joseph's sister Jane Harrison.[183].

While the discovery of the specific cause was of immense scientific significance, what made it a world-class sensation was the expected sequel. In several, indeed most, bacterial diseases whose causative organism had recently been identified, a way of dealing with the disease had followed within a few years or even months. Ordinary people did not quite understand the link, but there was now an anthrax vaccine, a diphtheria antitoxin and, of course, the anti-rabies course of injections, in addition to a number of animal diseases that had become treatable or preventable. The same would surely happen to the one most dreaded of all. The number of those looking forward to that blessed day probably ran into the hundreds of thousands if not millions, from starving workers' families in industrial slums to grand dukes dying on the Riviera. Many were immured in sanatoria in some of the most remote parts of the world.

However, for some years there was silence. It was rumoured that Koch, the dragon-slayer, and his select troupe of helpers were working on some kind of an antidote day and night, most likely on some attenuated organism like the attenuated rabies virus; but, in answer to regular and sometimes despairing enquiries by newspapers and scientific bodies, nothing of practical significance emerged. (Koch and his team were not alone. Watson Cheyne in England spent all his spare time experimenting.) Then the news was leaked, nobody knows by whom, that a momentous announcement would be made in Berlin, appropriately at the first World Medical Congress to be held in the imperial capital.

The opening speech to the plenary session was delivered by the president of the Congress, Rudolf Virchow—'the Pope', as he was already known in his own country—and he was followed by Lister's review of antiseptic surgery. For once, it is doubtful if he commanded much attention, since the next speaker was to be Koch. Expectations were not disappointed. After some slight hedging, Koch announced that he and his colleagues had at last discovered a substance that 'in some cases' would protect and 'in certain circumstances' even cure the disease. As Dr Arthur Conan Doyle, present on the occasion, perceptively noted in his report (but nobody took much notice), such tantalising equivocations were quite out of character. Pasteur, had often been accused of rushing into print or, more characteristically, staging dramatic and slightly preposterous public announcements before he had gathered solid evidence, and his detractors never ceased to predict that sooner or later he would land himself in trouble. He never did. Koch, by contrast, was known for his caution bordering on pedantry: Even with the verbal provisos, he had never before made such claims without the matter being thoroughly tested and found to be foolproof.

It still remains a mystery what induced him to make his unwarranted announcement. The claim was untested and would prove to be untrue. It was bound to cause an explosive upsurge of hope. Of course, he did not know that hope would be followed not only by disappointment but also by much unnecessary suffering.[184] Did he really believe that an injection of his 'lymph', a laboratory preparation of altered and killed tubercle bacilli named 'tuberculin', was or could be curative? It is almost impossible to think so. He is thought to have tried the injections on himself and had an unpleasant week of prostration as a result of the experiment. However, there had been no preliminary tests on animals, no trials with gradually increasing doses in humans, no standardised technique of preparing the material that could be duplicated in other laboratories. It is unlikely that there ever will be a satisfactory explanation.

An unsigned editorial in the *Lancet* a few months after the announcement hinted at a possible scenario:

> Professor Koch has never yet rushed into print with a discovery until he has been sure of his facts; and those who are in any way acquainted with the circumstances know that he was practically compelled by his government superiors and his colleagues to make a premature statement.

A paragraph later there followed the baffling sentence: 'Everybody will sympathise most deeply with Dr Koch that he was compelled to break through his customary reticence ...' Sympathise why? Compelled by whom? Wilhelmine Germany was a swaggering sycophancy and its academic establishment, one of the most intellectually brilliant in the world, was monolithic in its political servility; but nobody sent uncooperative scientists to concentration camps or a Gulag or even threatened them with the loss of their jobs if they did not toe the patriotic line. One has to assume (until contrary evidence emerges) that Koch himself was, for once, blinded by his wish to bring glory to the Vaterland. Who then wrote the editorial in the *Lancet*? Could it have been Lister? The style could be his and he was certainly bowled over (as were most of Koch's audience) by Koch's claim. Not only would he spread the good news: he at once announced that he would bring his much-loved niece to Berlin to undergo a course of injections. This proved to be a calamitous decision.[185]

Within a week of the end of the conference Lister was back in Berlin with the mortally ill but at the time virtually symptom-free Betty. She was given her first injection and then a second. The immediate effect was encouraging, though there was an alarming febrile reaction after each inoculation. Betty's cough seemed to abate, her sputum became less viscid and less blood-stained. Nevertheless, she was frightened and homesick in a strange hotel room in Berlin, even with two English nurses in attendance, and Lister took her home with a supply of two dozen further injections given to him by Koch.

She never had the chance to test the whole course. Within a few days back in Woodford she became desperately ill. She developed severe chest pain, a feeling of suffocation and cramps in her limbs. Her last few days were agony, unresponsive even to morphine. It was a death more cruel than was usual in tuberculosis, though terminal laryngitis and enteritis could be devastating.[186] During Betty's last two days Lister was away, giving a lecture to a conference in Manchester. It was not callousness: he was unaware of the seriousness of Betty's condition. By the time he returned to Park Crescent Betty was dead. He and Agnes were asked *not* to attend the funeral. It became the one rift in the Lister family. It was never healed, though Jane eventually became Joseph's only surviving sibling. Soon after her daughter's death she wrote a letter to Rickman Godlee:

> It is strange to look back to the day when we met last—at Park Crescent, when we were going away! ... I was full of foreboding but I should most certainly have blamed myself if I had used my influence against the visit to Berlin. Now I cannot help wondering why it was that the doctors could not see that the treatment was making her very ill. I cannot tell thee how we miss her! Our one tiny comfort is that she herself was entirely satisfied with the result of her stay in Berlin.[187]

No further correspondence took place between Lister and any member of the Harrison family, not even a formal exchange of Christmas or birthday cards. Ten of Lister's nieces and nephews inscribed the huge and embossed copy of the *Great Rift Valley* presented to their uncle in 1900; but none of the Harrison nieces and nephews was among them.

If tuberculin was a cruel fiasco, there were other spectacular advances to take people's mind off it. A thousand scientists and doctors gathered in London for the International Congress of Hygiene in the autumn of 1891 under the chairmanship of Lister. The list still reads like a roll call of honour. Charles Louis Alphonse Laveran, professor of medicine at the Val-de-Grâce Military Hospital in Paris, gave an account of his discovery of the plasmodium parasite that causes malaria.[188] Dr Albert Hueppe of Prague spoke about the cholera toxin. Koch had discovered the causative vibrio five years earlier.[189] Emile Roux, Pasteur's former lieutenant and now director of the Paris Pasteur Institute, gave an account of the diphtheria toxin and the laborious preparation and miraculous efficiency of an antitoxin. It was not simply a new drug: it was a new concept in medical treatment.[190] Heinrich Büchner of Munich and Almroth Wright of St Mary's Hospital, London introduced a debate on the topic of the decade, immunity. That too was a new word.[191] The fact that nobody could quite understand the long and rambling paper read by Elie Metchnikoff about 'the brave little phagocytes' and 'their heroic deeds' did not detract from the enthusiasm that rewarded his lecture.[192] Both Dr Paul Ehrlich, already searching for his 'magic bullet', and his Japanese colleague Shibasaburo Kitasato of Berlin contributed to the debate. Among the guests at a private dinner party given by the Listers in Park Crescent was Emil von Behring, the young Charles Sherrington and Victor Clarence Vaughan from Michigan.[193] Scientific medicine had crossed the Atlantic.

The following year brought Pasteur's seventy-fifth birthday celebration. He had suffered a series of strokes in recent years and was unable to speak himself, which added to the poignancy of the occasion. While he was leaning on the arms of the President of the Republic, Jean Baptiste read his father's speech. It referred to Lister with admiration. Lister was of course present in the front row, representing the Royal Societies both of England and of Edinburgh. He had a lengthy response prepared, replete with lofty sentiments and vibrant phrases about the benefits of medicine and science. In the event, whether overcome with emotion or accurately sensing the mood of the audience, he threw his hands in the air and merely exclaimed: 'Vive Pasteur.' He stepped onto the platform and embraced the great Frenchman. As if in response, the band of the Garde Republicaine intoned the Marseillaise and the cheers of the crowd raised the roof. To find the right gesture and words for such an occasion there had never been anybody like Lister and there probably never will be.

Later in the year Lister delivered his last lecture at King's, but was asked to stay on as a surgeon for another year. By now he was as highly regarded by physicians as he was by surgeons. He had also become an international emblem of the universality of science. Early in 1893 Jean-Martin Charcot of the Salpêtrière in Paris proposed him for the foreign membership of the Académie des Sciences in succession to Sir Richard Owen, Joseph Jackson's old friend.[194] Lister attended the ceremony and was given a rousing ovation.

After these exertions he and Agnes took their holiday a little earlier than usual and, instead of Swanage, went to Italy. In Rapallo Agnes caught a chill. She was a strong woman and only 57. She had never been seriously ill since childhood, but her condition rapidly deteriorated. On 10 April she died. Lister described the illness to Hector Cameron. Concluding his letter he wrote:

My grief, bitter though it is, is sweetened by the extremely beautiful frame of mind in which Agnes was when & after I told her of her danger yesterday afternoon. I never saw her character so beautiful before, full of love for all, thinking almost more of others than herself, and, though very humble, relying in undoubted confidence in our Saviour. So I do not sorrow as those that have no hope! But oh how different life will be for me in the future.[195]

Lister still had almost 20 years to live and much of that time his mind remained alert even while his body was ailing. Lucy Syme, always addressed by him in public as 'Miss Syme', stayed on as housekeeper and was to preside over the formal dinner parties at Park Crescent. A year after Agnes's death he was elected first foreign secretary and then president of the Royal Society.[196] It gave him the chance to bestow the foreign fellowship of the Society on Metchnikoff and a year later to introduce Rudolf Virchow, who delivered the second Huxley lecture.[197] He had his portrait painted for the Royal College of Surgeons and received honorary doctorates from Glasgow, Oxford and Cambridge. Of greater interest to him (perhaps) was news of the last great medical advance of the century.

On the evening of 8 November 1895 Wilhelm Conrad Röntgen, professor of physics in the University of Würzburg, was investigating the effects of passing an electric current through a vacuum tube. The laboratory was in darkness and the tube was enveloped in black cardboard. Since this was supposed to make it impervious to light, Röntgen was startled by a few crystals left some distance away in the dark becoming brilliantly illuminated. He placed various objects between the tube and the crystals. Most seemed transparent to the mysterious rays. Then he placed his own hand in their path and became the first man to see the moving bones of a living hand.[198] He announced his discovery to the Würzburg Medical Society on 28 December 1895. Within a year it was headline news in Germany and abroad.[199]

Lister was among the first to grasp its potential surgical significance. While Miss Marie Lloyd immortally apostrophised the 'naughty naughty Röntgen rays' at the London Alhambra,[200] he gave one of the first lectures on the subject in Britain to the British Association's Annual Meeting in Liverpool.[201] There was nothing wrong with his mind, even if he was beginning to look his age. At the festive banquet to mark the closure of the conference, the Lord Mayor, the Earl of Derby, with inimitable wit remarked that his toast to one of the greatest benefactors of humanity would be received with enthusiasm by any audience in Europe unless it was an audience of bacilli. In the Honours List to mark the Queen's Golden Jubilee Lister was created a baron, the first surgeon to be so honoured.[202] The widowed Madame Pasteur was among those who sent congratulatory telegrams.[203]

In June 1898 it was Edinburgh's turn to celebrate. Together with Lord Wolseley, commander in chief of the Army, Lister received the Freedom of the City. Did he invent the awful cliché about surgeons and military commanders having much in common, removing malignant tumours and malignant enemies of the state respectively? One hopes not. More convivially, he was toasted by his old students and house surgeons at a festive but intimate dinner. Next year, on the occasion of being given an honorary degree by Liverpool University, he praised the work of Ronald Ross. Two years earlier, on 'mosquito day', 20 August 1897, Ross had made the observation at the army medical laboratory in Scunderabad that established the role of the mosquito both as a vector and as the intermediate host of the *plasmodum malariae*.[204] Lister's interest in malaria research was comparatively recent though well informed: his presidential address to the Royal Society in 1900 remains one of the best reviews of the subject at that time and was reprinted in full in the *British Medical Journal*. In June the Royal Institute of Public Health bestowed on him its Harben Medal and on his next and last visit to Paris in February 1899 he was feted at a dinner in his honour by the Académie de Médicine.

In January 1901 Queen Victoria died: 'What a terrible blow!' As her late Majesty's Sergeant Surgeon ('the only person who had ever plunged a knife into Her Majesty's Sacred Body'), Lister was present at the funeral service in St George's Chapel, Windsor, and moved the loyal address to the new king of the Royal Society and of the Royal Medical and Chirurgical Society. Next it was

Glasgow University, which, in the mixed company of Lord Kelvin (formerly William Thomson, the great physicist) and Andrew Carnegie (the Scottish-born philanthropist, steel magnate and mass murderer of strikers), bestowed its degree of Doctor of Laws on him. He must have been by then the recipient of more honorary degrees than anybody in the kingdom other than sprigs of the House of Hanover and Saxe-Coburg.

Nevertheless, he remained more than a ceremonial clothes horse. Later in the year he presided over the Tuberculosis Conference in London at which Koch announced his 'opinion' that bovine tuberculosis was not only caused by a distinct mycobacterium but that it was not transmissible to humans. He was right on the first count but grievously wrong on the second, a severe blow to those who were agitating for the compulsory pasteurisation of milk. Lister led a delegation to Koch in his hotel room, trying to persuade him to change the wording of his pronouncement and emphasise that he was merely expressing a personal opinion, unsupported by evidence. Koch readily obliged.[205]

In mid-October Lister represented the Royal Society and several other scientific bodies in Berlin at the celebration of Virchow's eightieth birthday. These journeyings, however gratifying in some respects, began to tire him. He fell ill in January 1902. A sea voyage was proposed to South Africa and Madeira, and Isabella, Arthur's eldest daughter, offered to accompany him.[206] Uncle and niece read a chapter of the New Testament, an ode of Horace (in Latin) and a Canto of Dante's *Divina Commedia* (in translation) every morning. Later in the day he would umpire deck games and distribute prizes. They arrived back in London on the day that peace in South Africa was declared. He felt refreshed and was ready to face his last notable medical task.

A few weeks before the coronation the new king went down with acute appendicitis. His doctors were reluctant to operate and the king himself was insistent that the coronation, scheduled for June, should not be postponed. However, he developed a swinging temperature and, on 24 June, Sir Frederick

Treves, one of the royal surgeons, decided that operation offered the only hope of saving his elderly and far from fit patient. By now the king was ready, but Treves insisted on summoning both the king's physicians, Francis Laking and Thomas Barlow, and the two other two royal surgeons, Sir Thomas Smith and Lord Lister. All were awaiting the summons and came at once. All briefly examined the king. The much put-upon royal appendix had obviously burst but, fortunately, it had formed a local abscess rather than precipitate general peritonitis. Nevertheless, the abscess itself would burst unless it was drained. Lister expressed his concern because he could percuss a band of resonance over the swelling and he felt that a loop of bowel might be overlying the abscess. Nevertheless, he deferred to Treves' opinion; and, as the most senior and, by common consent, 'the most reassuring' of the royal doctors present, conveyed their unanimous decision to the patient.

The operation was later described as an appendectomy, though it was in fact no more than an incision, the pushing aside of a loop of bowel (which Lister had percussed) and the drainage of the still walled off abscess.[207] It was a complete success and a few months later Berty, now Edward, was duly crowned King of Great Britain, Ireland and the Dominions Overseas and Emperor of India. To mark the occasion, the Order of Merit (closely modelled on a similar Prussian Order) was instituted to reward those most distinguished in the arts, the sciences and public life. Its membership was limited to 24 and Lister was among the first batch of 12 to be selected. He was also sworn of the Privy Council.

However, the Christmas of 1902 was his last in Lyme: the excitement and noise generated by his growing number of young nieces and nephews, however joyful, did not quite suit him any more. To recuperate, he and Lucy spent some time in Buxton. On retiring from the presidency of the Royal Society he himself received the Copley Medal and the *British Medical Journal* devoted an issue to commemorating the fiftieth anniversary of his election to the fellowship of the Royal College of Surgeons. He advised his one-time student Watson Cheyne, whose knighthood had been announced, that 'Miss Syme much prefers Sir Watson to Sir William: far more distinctive'. But Sir William it would be. He continued to read the medical literature and commented on various new developments either in private correspondence or in published letters.

In 1907 the City of London made Lord Lister a Freeman, the last of such ceremonies that he attended in person and the occasion of his last photograph. His face had become thin, his mouth drawn. He now had a full beard instead of whiskers, completely white. It is not a happy face.

He suffered an attack of the shingles that left him enfeebled. In the summer of 1908 he and Lucy moved to Brook Cottage in Walmer in Kent, hoping that the sea air might do him good. His coach stood ready in Park Crescent to go and fetch him should he be needed in London; he never was. His brother Arthur, closest to him of all his siblings, died in June. On receiving Arthur's biography written by his daughters, Isabella and Guilielma, he wrote to them in characteristic style: 'I send, as usual, a most unworthy response which I know thee will excuse ...' The nieces were the last to whom he used the Quaker pronoun.

Lister declined the chancellorship of the University of Glasgow but accepted the last of the prodigious array of honours heaped on him. The County Borough of West Ham, within whose boundaries Upton Park had once stood, elected him Honorary Freeman. In 1910 he wrote to Cameron mentioning his fast deteriorating vision: 'but happily, I can still see the sunset'. A little later he wrote to comment on the news of the death of Edward VII, 'a terrible blow to the country'. His hearing too was getting worse.

Apart from Lucy, the Godlees, the servants, his physician, Richard Powell of the Middlesex Hospital, few saw him in his last years. He died on 10 February 1912. In his will he expressed the wish not to be buried in Westminster Abbey, preferring to rest next to Agnes in the cemetery in West Hampstead; but a crowded memorial service was held in the Abbey and a marble

plaque was later unveiled. Otherwise a bust in Great Portland Street, not far from Park Crescent, a microbiological species particularly feared in pregnant women and a patent antiseptic mouthwash enshrine his memory.

PART IV

REED AND THE
CONTROL OF EPIDEMICS

Walter Reed (1851–1902)

Portrait reproduced by permission of Science Photo Library

CHAPTER ONE

A Young Christian Gentleman from Virginia

The scandal broke in Paris on 2 November 1892 with an article by Edouard Drumond in Maurice Barrès's disreputable *La Libre Parole*. The word 'panama' would soon pass into several European languages to describe fraud and political corruption on a grandiose scale. There had been rumours of bribery, mismanagement and cover-up ever since the Panama Canal Company had been forced into liquidation with an estimated debt of about 10 billion francs. Now it was out in the open.

For five years, under the guidance of France's national hero, Ferdinand de Lesseps, the builder of the Suez Canal, the Panama Canal Company had been engaged in digging a waterway to join the Atlantic Ocean with the Pacific across the Isthmus of Panama.[1] The surveys had begun in 1881 and soon de Lesseps was able to reduce the originally estimated cost of £33,000 to £28,000. He assured his backers that the project presented far fewer difficulties than did the Suez Canal. In purely geographical terms it did. In all the voluminous and beautifully printed and bound sales literature there was no mention of yellow fever. (Malaria was considered a 'somewhat unpredictable hazard'; a generous allocation was made for quinine.) The venture was to be financed by a privately owned but government-backed company whose shares went through the ceiling within a month of being officially launched on the Bourse. Even after three years of rumours of mistakes and even disaster, the share prices were rising. By then the cost had passed the £10 million mark. Nevertheless, the project could not fail. Among the guarantors and major shareholders, besides numerous titled but shadowy characters, was the political elite of the Third Republic. They included the Minister of Finance, Rouvier, the President of the Chamber, Floquet and the *franc-tireur* of the left, Georges Clemenceau.

After the first salvo it took less than a month for the shocking story to unravel. During all the years of waiting, and to the sound of relentlessly upbeat bulletins emanating from the company's headquarters in the Rue d'Alma, virtually nothing had been built. Worse (though not for the shareholders), about 100,000 workers, imported from Central and South America, the West Indies, French Africa and even the United States, to clear the jungle, drain the swamps and start digging, had perished. They had been the victims of a multiplicity of unforeseen hazards, most of all of a fever of which few people in metropolitan France had heard. Because jaundice was an invariable feature, it was known to experts in tropical medicine as *la fièvre jaune* or *la fièvre ictérique*.[2] By November 1892 the campsites were ghost towns and the rainforest was fast reclaiming the first clearings. The few surviving European engineers, who had been evacuated to hospitals in the United States, were being threatened with death and ruin to their families if they spoke up in public. The great Monsieur de Lesseps himself, beacon of the whole enterprise, was being treated in hospital in a state of nervous collapse and was soon to be transferred to prison.[3]

The scandal swept through French public life, ruined millions of thrifty citizens, and almost buried the Third Republic.[4] However, as had happened before in such crises and would happen again, the Third Republic survived.[5] What seemed to have been irretrievably buried was the dream of a canal linking the world's two greatest oceans.

But the burial was not irretrievable. The realisation that from San Francisco the S.S. *Oregon* had to travel round South America and Cape Horn to reach the Caribbean struck the strategic planners of the United States War Department with surprising force during the brief Spanish-American War of 1898. (The force was surprising because, as Mr Asquith was heard to remark to a lady friend, the fact might have been gleaned from a brief perusal of a terrestrial globe.) Negotiations were set on foot at once with what remained of the French Panama Canal Company, and despite strong opposition from Colombia (which led to the people living on a strip of a few miles on either side of the projected canal suddenly discovering their ancestral wish—and indeed right—for independence under United States patronage), the Treaty of Herran Hay transferred all the French company's dubious rights and non-existent assets to the United States.[6] Digging began in 1905 and, though the canal was not officially declared open by President Wilson until 1920, the colossal enterprise proceeded at a brisk pace, with no major technical hitch and, above all, with virtually no loss of life to disease.[7]

So what happened between 1890 and 1905 to transform France's costly failure into an engineering triumph for the United States? While simplistic answers are always to be distrusted in medical as well as in international history, one is tempted to answer: Major Walter Reed of the United States Army Medical Corps and his Yellow Fever Commission.[8]

It has been suggested that, sadly perhaps, great doctors are mostly remembered, if at all, by having some more or less unpleasant ailment named after them. Walter Reed was a little more fortunate. His worldwide fame today rests on his name being attached to the Washington hospital, medical centre and home of the United States Army Medical Corps, where presidents, secretaries of state, generals, as well as ordinary privates with interesting diseases have their health checked, confirmed, denied, foretold and occasionally rectified. He would probably find the posthumous honour pleasing but excessive. He was born, bred, looked like and in fact *was* a Christian gentleman of the South, a breed not entirely extinct even today. Gentleman in his case meant not a plantation owner, judge, colonel, banker or local politician. He was the youngest of the five children—four sons and one daughter—of a Methodist Minister, the Reverend Lemuel Reed, and he was born in a four-roomed cottage in Gloucester County, Virginia, on 13 September 1851.

The Reeds were a close-knit family who moved, as directed by the Methodist Conference, between parsonages in small Southern towns like Gatesville, Murbreesboro and some, like Belroi, that have since disappeared. The children were brought up on a wholesome diet of cornbread and local farming produce. They benefited from daily readings from the Bible, but also from Sir Walter Scott's wonderfully meandering romances.[9] They enjoyed an abundance of unfussy parental affection. Their domestic chores were easily combined with enjoyable outdoor pursuits. The family circle was not broken until the marriage of Laura, the eldest, to the Reverend James Bilcoe, a Methodist minister, in 1859; the siblings and their offspring always remained close.

Walter was 10 when a crowd of abolitionists and Negroes seized the United States arsenal at Harper's Ferry, Virginia. The state government sent forces under Colonel Robert E. Lee and J.E.B.S. Stuart. The leader of the attack, John Brown of Pottawatomie, a man of limited intelligence but great dignity, was captured and hanged. The drift towards secession from the Union of the Southern, slave-owning states accelerated. It had been foreshadowed by speeches, pamphlets, riots, Acts of Congress, uncertain compromises and the canvassing and collapse of geographical, ideological and political mirages. Every new development in a country that was changing at a breathtaking pace seemed to bring the catastrophe closer.[10]

The presidential campaign of 1860 ended with the election of Abraham Lincoln on a platform that declared slavery an evil and denied Congress the right to declare it legal in any territory. Even before the new President was inaugurated, South Carolina held a conference and on 20 December formally seceded from the Union. It was followed by Mississippi, Florida, Alabama, Georgia, Louisiana and Texas. The seven states held a joint convention in Montgomery, Alabama, and elected Jefferson Davis as *their* president. As state after state declared for secession, their senators and congressmen withdrew from Congress; and forts, arsenals and munitions supplies in the South, the property of the national government, were taken over by Southerners. The first shots were fired by the shore batteries of Charleston, South Carolina, at the warship *Star of the West*, dispatched by President Buchanan to bring supplies to the beleaguered regular army garrison in Fort Sumter. The ship was driven away. 'Like a wounded bird', the Stars and Stripes over Fort Sumter fluttered down. The Civil War had begun.

Few Methodist ministers were affluent enough to own slaves and the Reverend Lemuel was a Whig who disapproved of the 'peculiar institution'; but there was no question of where the Reeds' loyalty lay. The two oldest sons, Tom and James, joined the Confederate army, James leaving his classes at Randolph-Macon College to join the Liberty Light Artillery. He lost a hand at Antietam.[11] While Walter was too young to fight, had teenagerhood been invented in the 1860s his generation would have missed it. The dangers, tribulations and sufferings of the Civil War touched even a modest parsonage. When Sheridan's marauding men requisitioned their horses, the family was left with no means of transport. A week after Lee's surrender ex-sergeant James arrived home. 'Well, my son, it's all over now,' the Reverend Lemuel greeted him. The son's diary records himself replying: 'No, sir: we will rest up awhile and then we will ... lick them out of their boots.' But that was bravado. After the bloodiest war for centuries, the South was irrevocably beaten. Worse, perhaps, after it was beaten it was beaten down. Would Lincoln have been able to prevent or at least mitigate the excesses of the 'Reconstruction Act': the horde of carpetbaggers and scallywags, the robbery, corruption and humiliations? His successor, Andrew Johnson, probably tried but failed. The dispute still rumbles on. If the war left the South prostrate for years, 'Reconstruction' left it aggrieved for generations.

The Reeds were too poor and politically too insignificant to feel its full impact—they were also too truly Christian to bear a grudge—though it left its mark. There would always be a gravity about Walter Reed, a streak of resigned, slightly melancholic pessimism, which made him respected rather than loved. All who knew him well esteemed him highly—to Jefferson Randolph Kean he was the 'the perfect Christian gentleman'—but to others he often seemed aloof, even austere. Even in unbuttoned mood his jocularity was perhaps a little forced: in convivial company he would never be quite one of the boys. Perhaps it was a hidden obstacle to his more spectacular advancement in the army, where good cheer was highly valued.

Despite the disarray of the post-war years the Methodist Conference was able to grant the Reverend Lemuel Reed's urgent request for a transfer to Charlottesville, where the University of Virginia offered the only available opportunity for the education of his four sons. The parsonage on Ridge Street was near the railroad tracks where for four years cheering young men had travelled to the battlefields of Chancellorsville, Manasses and Wilderness. There also the shattered bodies of many had returned to the improvised Confederate Military Hospital, a warehouse on the site of the present Union Station. Within a few weeks of the move, Mrs Reed, a self-effacing women worn out physically by the anxieties of the war, died at the age of 48. Perhaps to keep a promise to her, Walter and his brother Christopher officially joined the Methodist Church on the day of the funeral. Walter and later his family would always remain practising, churchgoing Christians, though he distrusted fundamentalist Christianity. He would pass his mother's grave in the churchyard on his daily walk to school, an establishment run by a Confederate war veteran, William Richardson Abbot, and his wife.[12] The Abbots were excellent teachers. 'Telling is not teaching and hearing is not learning' was an Abbotism Reed would quote later in life. A parson and senior elder of a district needed a wife; and within a year the Reverend Lemuel married again, a rich and generous Harrisonburg widow, Mary Catherine Byrd Kyle. The children came to love her.

The University of Virginia, 50 years old when Reed entered it, had been founded by Thomas Jefferson. It consisted of eight schools: Latin, Greek, Natural Philosophy, Natural History, Mathematics, Rhetoric and Written Language, History and Medicine. Students could enter at 16 but exceptions were made where younger brothers could lodge with an elder sibling, as Walter did at 15 with his 16-year-old brother Christopher. To obtain a master's degree candidates had to complete all eight schools, sometimes taking ten years. Oddly perhaps to modern minds, it took only a year or two to obtain an MD, a much less demanding course. Jefferson had included Medicine among his schools because he felt (quite properly) that a well-rounded gentleman should have sufficient medical knowledge to get by without needing the ministrations of a physician or surgeon in most disturbances of health. The only distinction between such a gentleman and an MD was that the former had to obtain only grade 75, whereas the latter was expected to obtain 80 in the specialist school.

Reed did not see a clinical thermometer at the university[13] nor a microscope, but he was taught by the first full-time professor of medicine in the United States. In 1825 Robert Dunglison, then 25, had been persuaded by Francis Gilmer, Jefferson's roving agent in England, to come to Charlottesville. He had been offered $1500 a year and a fee of $25 from each student, and was allocated a handsome porticoed red-brick house on the Lawn.[14] Strictly speaking, Reed was a medical student for exactly nine months, from October 1868 to July 1869; but into that period the course managed to cram a remarkable amount of what nowadays would be called the basic sciences. Theology was included, as it was at Harvard and Columbia, and anatomy loomed large. The school was lucky to have the services of a resourceful resurrectionist, a Negro janitor by the name of Tom, the son of one of the founder's slaves, who could always be relied on to produce the more or less fresh body of an executed criminal or an unclaimed pauper.

The apparently full academic programme still left time for fun, even high jinks. In the 1860s at least one professor, the distinguished lawyer John Staige Davis, was accidentally shot dead by an inebriated undergraduate; and the Rotunda clock, an irresistible pistol target, had to be protected by a bullet-proof face, at some cost. It was the former event that, against much opposition, led to the introduction of an Honor Code.[15] Its modest restrictions (by modern standards) seemed in no way to restrict the sober and serious Reed boys. Before embarking on medicine, Walter earned his intermediate honours in four schools in one year.

Since the curriculum, though more comprehensive than that of most American medical schools, did not provide for work with patients, new MDs were expected to proceed for further study to one of the large teaching hospitals in Baltimore, Philadelphia, New York or Boston. (This was not compulsory or a condition for being granted a licence to practise.) Christopher wanted to study law in New York, so the two young men, who might save on sharing their lodgings, travelled there together. The train took them through still ravaged, terribly silent countryside. It arrived in a loud, brash, rowdy, fast-moving, cosmopolitan metropolis to which neither would ever get entirely acclimatised.

New York was already not only America's largest and most exciting but also its most corrupt city. The talk in the streets, in the shops, in eateries, in lodging houses, in the university, in the law courts and even in church was of the dollar. It was counted in millions. Four of the great western railroads had just been completed with government aid in cash and land amounting to approximately 130,000,000 acres, three times the area of New England. Not content with this stupendous loot, the promoters had watered the stock on an innovative scale, insiders organising their vast profits before passing on the risks to the feverishly speculating public. This kind of selective but amazing prosperity depended on a close alliance between criminals who called themselves financiers and elected confidence tricksters who called themselves politicians. Some successfully combined the two. Oakes Ames, leading figure of the colossal Union Pacific scam and member of Congress for Massachusetts, distributed shares in his little goldmine to fellow members, senators and judges 'where it will do us most good', on the splendidly altruistic principle 'that it will educate our fellow citizens to look after their property'.[16]

But by and large the American businessman, meaning broadly the entire electorate above the poverty level, had clearly adopted the method of allowing the government and much of the judiciary, whether state or municipal, to be run by hired men, leaving himself free to pursue more lucrative callings. As the profits soared, the politicians and their servants wanted their share and by and large got it.[17] The Reed brothers arrived in the city just about the time the Tweed Ring came into malodorous flower. Boss Tweed had been elected to City Hall in 1869 and by the autumn of 1871 he had carried off loot from the Treasury variously estimated at the time between $45 and 200 million (equivalent of about the same number of billions today). When Walter was shown by Dr Jeremiah Croaker, his friend and guide to the city, the plot assigned for the new fever hospital with no sign of a building on it, Croaker explained that the cost, originally estimated at $2 million, had notched up $8 million before the first brick could be laid. The project was then temporarily shelved.

Yet after devoting six hours to the examination of the city's books, such upright citizens as John Jacob Astor, Moses Taylor and Marshall O. Roberts declared the financial administration of New York to be sound and indeed prudent.[18] The scale and openness of municipal stealing—enthusiastically copied in other cities though nowhere realised on the scale of New York—left the innocents from Virginia gasping. It also left them with a depressing sense of inadequacy that would never rub off. Walter would never openly admit it; but he continued to regard his (and most of the Reeds's) chronic penury and spectacular lack of success in business ventures as slightly embarrassing if not exactly shameful. Whatever was true of the founding fathers, by the last quarter of the nineteenth century poverty was no longer an American virtue.

On the wider stage, what saved the American Dream during those decades was the almost immeasurable magnitude of the country's natural resources (still at the time largely unexplored), a fast-growing market and the seemingly never-ending supply of cheap labour. There was still no restriction on immigration and more than a million people a year were flooding in from the Old World, mainly by way of New York.[19] Sadly, some of the masses yearning to be free arrived only to suffer and to perish, the hopelessness of their plight providing the foundation of mind-boggling wealth.[20]

Bellevue, where Reed enrolled, was the country's oldest public hospital. It had originated in 1658 when five workshops of the Dutch East Indies Company in New Amsterdam had been set aside for hospital use. In the late 1860s it occupied a grand five-storey stone structure in a pleasantly verdant setting and had 1200 beds divided into speciality wards. The medical staff included some of the most prestigious names in American medicine. The two Austin Flints, father and son, taught medicine, Alexander Mott, Frank Hamilton and W.J. Van Buren taught surgery, R. Ogden Dorremus taught chemistry and toxicology, Jeanneret looked after the chest ward, mainly of course tuberculous patients, and Fordyce Baker was professor of midwifery.[21] They were unpaid or paid very little, earning a good living by their private practice.

The hospital had other claims to fame too, notably a 24-hour hospital-based ambulance service.[22] This had been organised by Dr William Hammond, surgeon general of the tiny Medical Corps when the Civil War began, and reflected his experience in the Union Army. Ten ambulances and horses stood on the alert in the hospital stables and set out (and sometimes arrived) at a

gallop on receiving notice by telegraph of any disaster. A medical officer would go out with the driver, who had been chosen for his intimate knowledge of the city's fast-expanding geography. The hospital's teaching facilities and the clinical material—about 12,000 admissions and 500 deliveries a year—were impressive. Apart from regular lectures, students could buy tickets for special classes such as medical chemistry; and private instruction was offered to those who felt the need and could afford it. Contagious patients were sent to the old Smallpox Hospital on Blackwell's Island where the Charity Hospital also housed about 1000 chronically ill.

In short, the institution looked splendid on the pages of its lavishly produced yearbook—as it still misleadingly does. In fact in the early 1870s, under the malign influence of Tammany Hall, headquarters of the Tweed Ring, it was a pit of filth, infection, uncontrolled bleeding and, even by the standards of the time, a dreadfully high mortality.[23] Hygiene was appalling, the food poisonous and large-scale pilfering of everything movable, including drugs, equipment and food, the norm. Although crudely administered anaesthesia mercifully reduced suffering at operations, it also widened the scope for infection and bleeding. Lister's ideas had not yet penetrated; or, if they had, nobody acted on them. Puerperal fever was rampant, with a mortality of 20–25 percent of admissions. How could some of the country's most eminent physicians, surgeons and obstetricians tolerate this? One searches for an answer in vain, as no doubt did young Reed. But he had come to learn and learn he would.

Since he got credit for his basic science courses at Virginia, he could concentrate on his clinical studies; in December 1869, aged just 18, he passed a highly competitive examination for the position of assistant physician at a Bellevue dependency, the Nursery Hospital on Randall's Island.[24] This had been founded by wealthy and charitable matrons concerned about the infants of mothers who served as wet nurses; dreadful tales were being told about their plight. They were not exaggerated. While officially the hospital had 450 beds, many beds held two or three patients, most of them suffering from tuberculosis, congenital syphilis, starvation, fits, meningitis and rashes of various kinds. The death rate, so far as it could be ascertained, hovered around one in two admissions. Here too, as at Bellevue, a large volume of cheap spirit was used, some no doubt to sedate and quietly to ease the passing of the hopelessly sick; but more to cajole workers to stay on at a job where their pay was derisory or non-existent. The unemployed of the city (or those who were unwise enough to register) were still compulsorily used for looking after the hospital sick, a state of affairs that outraged the hospital's resident physician, Dr Dunster. He begged the Commissioners of Public Charities and Corrections to stop

> staffing my hospital with society's derelicts ... I believe that the whole system of caring for orphans and foundling infants by relying on free labour is vicious ... that we should pay at least as freely for the care of these little ones as we now pay for the care of our domestic animals ... If such a system could be introduced the neglect of duty and sullenness of disposition which now prevails would at once disappear.[25]

Dunster was dismissed as an amiable eccentric even though he was not asking for much. Doctors at the hospital were paid $8 a week and nurses the same amount per month. He raged and petitioned in vain.

Reed's next appointment could hardly have lifted his spirits. King's County Hospital, Brooklyn, was connected with County Farm, a municipal 'resource' for the penniless sick and old. It housed about a thousand inmates, 'the bottom of abdication of human dignity,' as Reed wrote home. At least 80 percent were fresh or first-generation immigrants, speaking (if they spoke at all: many had literally lost the power of speech) a variety of languages nobody understood. About half were designated by numbers rather than by names; in the records, their chief symptom on admission (paralysis, confusion, diarrhoea, sores, ulcers, gangrene) stood for the diagnosis. No progress notes

were kept, presumably because no progress was made. The approximate number of dead over the preceding week was entered into a ledger every Saturday. It remained unnaturally constant over the months and the seasons.

From 'The Farm' Reed rotated to a residency at Brooklyn City Hospital. It is possible that it was here that his interest in public health was kindled. His chief, Dr A.N. Bell, was an opinionated but clever man with a burning interest, fuelled by unquenchable anger, in sanitation. At the time of Reed's residency he was particularly concerned with the need to sterilise rags. These were being imported from every part of the world, partly to be used as dressings in hospitals and partly for the manufacture of paper. Bell regarded them as the source of a variety of pestilences and perhaps he was right. Right or wrong, his agitation struck a responsive chord with the press (who used paper more than most), which in turn galvanised the politicians. Bell was also something of an authority on yellow fever, which he regarded as infectious but not contagious.[26]

Somewhat to his own surprise, Reed was then appointed Assistant Sanitary Officer of the Brooklyn Board of Health, responsible for the general health of about quarter of a million people. He was 22. He also became a member of the local Medical Society, which was campaigning for a mandatory drainage law. But despite the grand title, the move was not really an advance. Nor could he see any prospect of advancement. After his first few years in New York he was beginning to realise that without influential backing—which meant either pleasing venal municipal officers or flattering the financiers who controlled them—he would get nowhere in the public service. He had neither the inclination nor the talent for either. Nor was he any good at self-advertising, essential if he wanted to build up a private practice.

What discouraged him most was observing what passed for medicine around him. Cuppers and bleeders, men appallingly ignorant of the rudiments of their trade, waxed prosperous, while ordinary, hard-working doctors like himself went unpaid and starving. In a letter home, Christopher Reed described finding his brother with tears in his eyes after the visit of a fashionable doctor who had reported the death of a child. 'This first-class quack,' one of the leading physicians in Brooklyn,

> had arrived in a splendid carriage with a coachman and footman in attendance and spoke to Walter condescendingly without alighting. 'He was so ignorant that I could hardly believe it,' Walter later related. 'He located the pancreas in the neck and the kidneys in the chest and misused every Latin name he pronounced. Oh, I shall quit the profession.'[27]

Christopher usually managed to calm his brother, but a few days later he found Walter once again staring out of the window of their shared lodgings, utterly dejected. He had just returned from a municipal meeting that had vetoed medical and sanitary expenses. It was soon after one of the financial scandals that had added a few more millions to Jay Gould's fortune but had virtually bankrupted the city.

> Walter was muttering to himself: 'Woe unto thee, Chorazin, woe unto thee Bethsaida, for if the mighty works which were done in you had been done in Tyre and Sidon, they would long ago have been repented in sackcloth and ashes.' Then he knelt by his bed and said the Lord's Prayer with great feeling.[28]

There was one glimmer of light, though even that caused anxiety as well as joy. On a visit home to Murbreesboro a young woman caught Walter's eye in church. Though Emily Lawrence (who had just begun to spell her name more elegantly as Emilie) had been born across the street from the Reeds when Walter was six, Walter had hardly noticed her before. Now he fell in love 'for the first time in my life'. 'She would be,' he wrote, 'my eternal and only love.' This was almost certainly true, both for the past and for the future. In matters sexual, as in matters financial, he was a deeply moral person.

From now on, almost every day during their many long separations, he would write to her in tones of ardour and, later, with deep concern and tenderness, even if in a childishly jocular manner. Sometimes he referred to her letters to him; so she too must have written, but few of her letters survive. (Emilie usually asked him to destroy them, though sometimes he could not bear to do so. Nevertheless, she kept his side of their correspondence. It was in one of his early letters, after sharing with her his painful awareness of being 'young and unsponsored and therefore unlikely ever to advance in my profession in this city', that he first mentioned the possibility of joining the Army Medical Corps.

CHAPTER TWO

OFFICER

R eed was not the only young doctor drifting in this direction. In the autumn of 1873 500 candidates sat the Army Medical Corps entrance examination to fill 30 vacancies. The tests lasted for five hours a day for six days, covering Greek, Latin, French, mathematics and history besides medicine; but members of the examining board could, if they wished, venture further afield and ask candidates to discourse about Shakespeare, engineering, anthropology or the stars. Even ignoring how little time Reed could have devoted to his studies—he was in full-time employment and had in fact just drafted a good (though fruitless) report on drainage and related problems to the City Health Officer—his still extant examination papers are humbling. His access to libraries was limited; the libraries themselves were inadequately stocked and often chaotic. He had no private tuition. His contact with fellow students was slight. Yet his illustrated description of the anatomy of the throat would almost certainly surpass in detail anything the average lecturer (let alone professor) in anatomy could write and draw today, unless he or she was a specialist in the region; and his essay on yellow fever (which made up most of the hygiene paper) seems almost prophetic in its depth of understanding.

Of course his speculations were mostly wrong (as he himself would later show), but they faithfully represented accepted doctrines; and he got his facts right. He wrote learnedly about the fever being endemic in Cuba, British Guyana, Louisiana, Santa Domingo, Haiti and the coast of Peru and 'hazarded a guess', almost completely accurate, at the incidence of the disease in Havana, Demerara and New Orleans. He considered it transmissible 'either by germs clinging to the clothing or in the cargo of a ship' or by a person 'who, at the time of being sick, is transported to another place'. The last, he noted, was dependent on the temperature, moisture and sanitary conditions of the new locality. He was aware that the fever seldom appeared above 40° north and that a cold spell usually brought the epidemic to an end. He pointed with satisfaction to the reduction of the disease in New Orleans (where he had never been) when the city was under military government. He quoted the generally accepted view (which he himself would disprove later in life) that quarantine helped to prevent the introduction of the disease into a new place, especially the quarantine of ships, and that the disinfection of clothing was useful. Answering another question on typhoid (five years before Eberth discovered the typhoid bacillus), he speculated about the 'close connection between the pollution of water with faecal matter and the outbreak of typhoid fever'.

Such a wealth of information might lead one to believe that he stunned his examiners. This is disproved by a note from the president of the examining board appended to the letter informing him that he had passed. It 'respectfully informed' the candidate that, 'while he was deemed generally satisfactory, his acquaintance with foreign literature was not up to the expected standard'. Perhaps it was this criticism that prompted Reed's life-long efforts, entirely futile, to master French or Spanish.

Soon after his examination he dispatched a characteristic letter to Emilie, nearly but not quite proposing to her:

During the past six years I have seen something of the affection which men and women can bear to each other, though, God knows, I have witnessed its absence far more often ... and I have given much thought to this subject. Living in the largest city in America I have seen and met some of the most fascinating women of the world; and yet (need I tell you?) that you and you alone are the *only* woman whom I truly admire.[29]

During the customary formal visits to members of both families, Reed could wear his smart new uniform, complete with ceremonial sword,[30] but he was acutely aware of his uncertain financial prospects. He agonised at length over the choice of an engagement ring that he could afford and yet did not look too paltry. At one point Emilie too may have become slightly frightened by what she was hearing about military life; or perhaps she was gently prodding her future betrothed to declare himself. In several letters she hinted at another wealthy suitor (vaguely 'from Baltimore'), provoking from Reed the exclamation: 'What a miserable mortal I am ... to have been born so poor!' However, after her next letter, reproving him for suggesting that she may have developed an interest in anybody else, Reed declared her to be 'my only happiness in life'.

Such convulsions almost proved academic when, 'with immediate effect', he was posted to Yuma in Arizona. That was the Frontier, already legendary and fearsome. It was also almost infinitely far from either Virginia or New York. Could he have a short leave to get married first? 'Young man,' the answer came from his commanding officer, 'if you do not want to go to Arizona, resign from the Service.' In a more helpful vein the general suggested that he might wish to delay getting married until the need to escort a mad soldier personally from Arizona to the East might give him a happy chance to be reunited with his betrothed and consummate his troth.[31] The only alternative was to forget about the financial uncertainty and the customary protracted engagement and get married at once. They did so with parental blessing on 26 April 1876. A few days later the groom set out for his first posting in the West, promising to make all 'necessary arrangements' for the arrival of his bride.

Since recruitment was no problem to the small Medical Corps, there was no need to raise expectations. (Nor were public relations yet invented.) Before every new posting officers were handed a written briefing on the conditions they might expect to find as well as on their duties. About Yuma Reed was sent a copy of the Surgeon General's report of a few years earlier, which described the place as

> well chosen for defence against the Indians but about as uninviting a hell-hole as it would be possible to find on earth ... The air is so dry that sweat evaporates before it dries, furniture and travelling chests fall to pieces and dehydration causes eggs to dry out within twenty-four hours ... The water is drinkable but unsuitable for ablutions since it will dissolve soap only with difficulty.[32]

The journey itself by rail, stage coach and army waggon took a month. Almost as soon as he arrived, Reed was dispatched to Camp Lowell on the outskirts of Tucson where the mean temperature slightly exceeded even that of Yuma. This was Apache country and Geronimo's name was beginning to be known and feared. However, the Surgeon General was reassuring on that particular point: the Apache who 'regularly murder and plunder travellers and especially army personnel prefer to operate in the more northern mountain ranges'. The Papano Indians, who were more numerous locally, were described as friendly. That was true. They were occupied mainly in raising corn and melons. The report also referred to the production of excellent vegetables in season 'provided artificial irrigation is painstakingly maintained'. This was important, since the cost of imported food (like butter and eggs) was beyond the purse of a junior army officer on a regular basis.[33] But the Surgeon General seemed to believe that the cost of alcohol kept drunkenness and acute alcoholic intoxication at bay. This proved to be naïve. Locally distilled spirits were cheap and easily available in Tucson; and, despite the fact that they often caused temporary or permanent blindness (among other unpleasant and antisocial effects), they were consumed in large quantities. Though they were prohibited in the army camp, the prohibition was treated rather like a biblical commandment. Together with venereal disease—both gonorrhoea and syphilis—'alcohol-related illnesses' were the main causes of sickness and almost impossible to treat.

Tucson, the territory's capital with about 3200 inhabitants, was three miles away. It had been known as a mean, ugly and violent town, mostly Spanish speaking, for 100 years. Would it survive? Some of the frontier towns did; others did not. It would be no great loss if it went under. Only the innumerable flies would miss the human debris on which they fed. Main Street was lined with unpainted, shabby houses. The town's prosperity, such as it was, depended on stirring up sufficient 'Indian trouble' to goad Washington into sending in troops and starting a little local war. The 'Tucson ring' was rather good at that.

There was to contemporaries like Reed nothing romantic and beautiful about the frontier. Everything was harsh, restless, impermanent and uncertain. In the long dry months the dust was everywhere. It stung the eyes, seeped through windows and covered furniture and household implements an hour after they had been dusted. It got into the hair and stayed there. The water was too hard for washing with soap either objects or bodies. It showed. Women who would clean their windows every day in the East let the dust settle for months. There was a kind of mental famine too. Anything would make talk for weeks: a few Indians skirting through, a dog fight, a swearing quarrel between two drunks, good men, bad men, a roof falling down, a change in the weather, tittle-tattle. The mail came twice a week by way of San Diego and Yuma. Sometimes it was plundered by Indians or mail gangs.

Emilie's girlhood had been comfortable and sheltered and to set out from Virginia first to San Francisco and then for the frontier was an act of courage. By now she had heard much of the 'horrows' (sic) of Army life and indeed of life in the West. Perhaps it was no less brave on the part of Reed to ask her to join him. He was blessed, for his confidence was not misplaced. But the fierce moustache he grew while waiting for her was perhaps an unconscious act of defiance. They met among the electroplated nymphs and aspidistras of the Palace Hotel in San Francisco. They spent two weeks there. It was their honeymoon and they would often reminisce about it in later years. They then went by steamer to San Diego. The journey introduced Reed to a new and horrible experience. He was violently seasick; it would be a life-long curse.

Then they embarked on a 500-mile journey in an army ambulance. This was a slow but sturdy structure drawn by two mules: it covered about 15 to 20 miles a day. After sundown Reed usually had to walk the team. By seven in the evening on the first night it was cold and completely dark. 'Emilie showed exquisite bravery,' Reed wrote to his sister Laura, 'but had there been a stone wall nearby I should have brought my head in violent contact with it.' Nevertheless, they plodded on through the dark over a road so rough that at times it seemed that the ambulance would break in two. At about 11 they came to a small encampment of suspicious-looking prospectors, where they were told that the army station that was their destination was still two miles away 'over the worst road in California'. The trail lay between steep hills that they felt rather than saw. The mules balked at picking their way through the rocks in the dark.

Fortunately the driver had a lantern and part of a candle. This we lit and taking the soldier with me who rode with the driver, I started ahead to light the way. By keeping immediately in front of the team and continually hulloeing ... we managed to make some progress. But poor Emilie was calling out continually ... 'Where are you Dr Reed? Please come back and let the soldier carry the lantern.' But I had to tell her that I could trust no man living to get us out of this horrible canyon; and on I went in sand nearly up to my knees, calling out to the driver. Excellent as he was, every fifty yards or so we would find a wheel stopped by a boulder.[34]

They eventually reached the station, a small house, about ten feet square and a stable; and as soon as Emilie was indoors 'her spirits rose and when tea was ready all her sprightliness returned. She took a glance at the room and laughed heartily, declaring that she wouldn't take anything for the experience.'[35]

By the time the Reeds undertook their next ambulance journey six months later, from Fort Lowell to Fort Apache, no less hazardous though a little shorter than the first, Emilie was pregnant. Unrest among the Indian tribes was now an added hazard; but, though they traversed recent camp sites and saw signs of skirmishes, they did not encounter any. The Indians always buried their dead. Once they had settled in Fort Apache, Reed's Indian patients became a much-needed source of sustenance. The always meagre appropriations by Congress for the army fell to zero in 1877 and for nine months all ranks depended on family dole, loans from usurers and money earned by moonlighting. 'Reconstruction' and the vain hope of Southern congressmen that the occupying army might be starved out from the South formed one reason for this low point in the history of the US Army, graft and corruption in high places another.

Reed's Indian patients, by contrast, though they usually summoned the medicine man to back up the counsel of the white doctor, were grateful for any help he could give. Painkillers were welcome. They often brought a haunch of venison as a present to show their gratitude. Emilie later recorded:

> If no one was in the house or I was in the back garden, they would stealthily find their way into our bedroom and lay the meat, often still dripping with blood, on my white musslin dressing table or take a picture from the wall and hang it there. They never waited for me to come back and thank them.[36]

Reed delivered his own son: he was the only doctor over a radius of 400 miles. Labour must have been difficult. Recalling the event in the stilted third-person style that reticence dictated when describing private or delicate matters, Reed recorded that

> Papa remembers how sick his poor sweet wife was and how patiently she bore it all, and, remembering this he could never see his precious brought to bed again except if it should be her own wish![37]

The baby was christened Lawrence. Soon there was another addition to the family, a five-year-old Indian girl they named Susie. She had been badly burnt in an Indian fracas and left on the battlefield for dead. After Reed treated her burns she remained with the family for fifteen years.[38] She helped to look after Lawrence and, four years later, after the Reeds' second child, a little girl named after her mother but always known in the family as Blossom. A year after Lawrence's birth, Emilie with the baby returned to Virginia, expecting to be reunited with her husband (due for a posting to the East) in a few months. In the event the couple did not see each other again till May 1880, when at last Reed was posted to Richmond.

Apart from his one year of postgraduate studies at Johns Hopkins in 1890–91—a seminal experience that at the time seemed to lead nowhere—the next 12 years in Reed's life consisted of a humdrum and often frustrating series of moves from one remote posting to another. Soon after the family reunion at Richmond, he was promoted to captain and they enjoyed a few pleasant months in Fort McHenry in Baltimore. Then it was back to the West, where army medical officers were always urgently needed and often pushed around to meet emergencies. Yet their efforts were rarely appreciated by their regimental commanding officers, especially if, like Reed, they took their jobs as sanitary officers as well as doctors seriously. They were outsiders and often troublemakers. Sometimes they entertained wild humanitarian notions about the Indians and even the bison. It did nothing for either discipline or good fellowship. It is impossible to believe that Reed's honesty and high moral standards (which included an intense dislike of swear words and cursing) did not win him respect even in raucous officers' messes, but at times he must have cut an awkward figure. Northerners and Southerners were still ill at ease with each other and slavery remained a divisive issue. What puzzled Reed was that those most vocal in denouncing the oppression of the Negro often regarded the extermination of the Indians (or 'savages') as a virtuous necessity.

Financial and family worries too weighed heavily on him. His brother Tom was hurt in an accident and lost a hand. He and his family needed at least moral support: it was all Reed had to give. Laura's husband, the Reverend James Blincoe, died in his forties, probably of tuberculosis, leaving her with 10 children and a woefully inadequate pension. Yet Reed himself was always short of money and had none to give away. When eventually he could visit his sister, he found her pale, despairing and exhausted. He listened to her chest and suspected that she too was tuberculous. It was an alarming thought. What would happen to her family, aged between two and fourteen, if she died or was completely disabled? Fortunately she recovered, though her financial worries remained.

Reed's posting from Nebraska to Mount Vernon Barracks in Alabama seemed to come as a long-overdue relief. Emilie liked the South, and after several years in an unfriendly climate the balmy sunshine and exquisite flora of the region promised a few years of pleasant existence. The barracks also had a good medical reputation. But if he thought that here at last he would be free of the 'Indian problem', often a point of friction between himself and his brother officers, he was wrong. Indeed, it was at Mount Vernon that he first encountered not the greed and bigotry of a few locals but the viciousness of official policy. In a recent agreement between General George Crook and the Apaches, they had been promised 'by the Great White Father himself' that they would be dispersed to live out their lives in peace in the Arizona mountains. Then most of them were herded together and forcibly transported by the government to what in effect were concentration camps in the South. General Crook was outraged, especially since the deportees included some of his own faithful scouts. His protestations were of no avail, though his rages were terrifying to behold. Nevertheless, he did not resign.

When Reed arrived in Mount Vernon Barracks, the Indians—men, women and children—were camped outside its walls. Discipline among them was breaking down. There were rapes and deadly fights. Many were already suffering from tuberculosis. All were numbingly homesick for the mountains from which they had been spirited away. Though medical facilities and sanitary conditions in the army barracks were exceptionally good, they were of no use to the Indians outside it. Fear of tuberculosis was all-pervasive and displaced Indians were known to be particularly susceptible to it. (The incidence of the disease in their homelands was apparently low: no exact statistics exist.) They were also suffering from scarlet fever and other more or less obscure ailments, perhaps nutritional deficiencies. The climate the Reeds enjoyed was drastically different from the dry cold of their homeland to which they had been acclimatised. Within a month of sending his first report, Reed had to report the death from 'pulmonary disease'—tuberculosis was a taboo word—of three previously strong young women who had been fit when he arrived. He knew that it was tuberculosis and foresaw the spread of the illness both within the Indian encampment and beyond it. The answer from Washington could not have been more explicit: he was to do everything possible to prevent contact between the Indians and the army barracks; but so far as the Indian prisoners were concerned, their health was not his responsibility. It was government policy for these redundant people to be 'annihilated'.[39]

How far trying to minister to the doomed Apaches contributed to Reed's bitterness is impossible to say, but by midsummer 1890 he was convinced that his career, such as it had been, was over. He was almost 40, and in the army this was well past middle age. While Mount Vernon was not an unpleasant posting, it was a stagnant backwater at a time when medicine was moving ahead faster than ever before. There was no possibility of keeping up with these advances. A sound all-round doctor, Reed could not consider himself an expert in any field. This meant that he was and would always remain at the mercy of whoever happened to be (often for purely political reasons) his superior officers. He had been unsuccessful financially in the few ventures he had tried, and he and his family were as poor as when he and Emilie got married. Then at least there was hope. Now, it seemed, there were only ever-mounting responsibilities.

He applied for four months' leave 'to enable me to avail myself of the opportunity of pursuing certain special studies in my profession'. It was a hopeless application. Only a year earlier he had been told that for any leave lasting more than a month he would have to find a replacement and pay him. That was of course out of the question. Then what Reed always described as a stroke of kindly providence changed the course of his life.

In the week when Reed's application arrived in Washington, Jedediah Hyde Baxter was made Surgeon General. His was to be the shortest tenure of the top post in the history of the Medical Corps. Baxter was already ailing when he took up his appointment and within six months, at the age of 53, he was dead from a stroke. Nevertheless, he made a lasting impression. Throughout his career he had been advocating in a stream of memoranda the need for the continuing education of medical officers in the army; his brief on being made Surgeon General was to implement his ideas, 'provided they constituted no further drain on the Treasury'. Baxter had always maintained that there was a lively demand among junior officers to broaden their professional education; he was to be quickly disillusioned. On taking up his post he wrote to 14 recently promoted majors in the corps, suggesting that they took advantage of a new scheme of bursaries amounting to about half pay to attend three-month postgraduate courses in some medical or surgical speciality. All expressed their appreciation, but pointed out that they were indispensable wherever they happened to be and that they considered their education to have been both complete and adequate for the discharge of their duties. They were usually backed up by their regimental commanding officer. A medical officer they knew, even if drunk, difficult and disorderly, was better than a new high-powered boffin.

It was at this awkward moment that Baxter was presented with Captain Reed's unusual application. The scheme was originally designed for majors, but at a pinch an ambitious captain would do. He approved at once. There remained two difficulties. The course in pathology and bacteriology at Johns Hopkins Hospital in Baltimore that Reed hoped to attend lasted seven months. The original bursaries were only for three. Johns Hopkins was also planning to charge a fee. At the command of the Surgeon General the difficulties dissolved. Johns Hopkins waived the fee in return for unspecified favours. And an essential job was found for the captain. He was to examine the mental fitness of new applicants to the Medical Corps. They were few and mental fitness was usually the least of their problems. When it was a problem, it was generally insurmountable. When Reed eventually left, the essential post was never filled again.

Johns Hopkins had been founded only a year earlier under the will of a Baltimore millionaire. John Shaw Billings had been entrusted to recruit the academic staff. He was not a modest man, but he succeeded beyond his own expectations. His catches were all bold young men on their way up, not prestigious names with established reputations to husband. William Stewart Halsted, who became head of surgery, was a thinking as well as a skilled surgeon. He introduced Lister's ideas and methods to the United States, exploited rapid advances in anaesthesia, and devised new operations based on current pathological doctrines.[40] William Osler came from Canada, the son of English parents. He would end his almost impossibly distinguished career as a knight, Regius Professor of Medicine in Oxford and an oracle on all matters relating to medical ethics and clinical conduct. When he arrived in Baltimore he was already working on his classic *The*

Principles and Practice of Medicine. For decades it would be the doctors' bible.[41] Howard Atwood Kelly from New Jersey became head of gynaecology and obstetrics; but he never allowed his title to limit his activities to the female pelvis. Among his surgical publications was the first standard monograph on acute appendicitis, then still a rare disease;[42] and some of his surgical instruments are still in use.[43] To preside over such a team of towering egos a man of exceptional stature was needed; Billings found him in the slight and quiet figure of William Henry Welch.

Welch had been born in Norfolk, Connecticut, in 1850, the son, grandson and great-grandson of successful New England physicians. Like his father before him, he embarked immediately after graduating on a tour of Europe. The 1870s and 1880s were the most exciting so far in the history of western medicine. Among other advances, they witnessed the beginning of bacteriology, immunology and virology. These in turn exploded seemingly indestructible concepts of disease. In the past dramatic advances in the basic sciences—the revision of anatomy by Vesalius in the sixteenth century, Harvey's discovery of the circulation of the blood 100 years later, the invention of the microscope and the diagnostic revolution between 1800 and 1820—took decades to bear practical fruit. Now, within an astonishingly short space of time, the new ideas transformed clinical practice in every branch of medicine and surgery.[44]

Of course living organisms had been suspected and vaguely hinted at before as causes of illnesses; and of course the impact of Pasteur's discoveries owed something to his brilliant improvisations and occasional showmanship. Neither fact can dim the fireworks, even in retrospect. Inspired largely by Pasteur's achievements but benefiting most from Koch's new experimental methods, the causative organisms of such important and for centuries mysterious diseases as tuberculosis, cholera, leprosy, glanders, erysipelas, diphtheria, cerebrospinal meningitis, pneumonia, typhoid fever, puerperal fever, anthrax and wound infection were established beyond reasonable doubt.[45] Some microbiological diseases like rabies were shown to be transmissible and indeed preventable, even though the organism was too small to be visualised even under the most powerful microscopes of the age.[46] The idea that defensive reactions against organisms could themselves under certain conditions cause disease was aired for the first time.[47] Proof was published that many microbiological diseases left 'markers' that could be used for diagnosis even in healthy subjects and without demonstrating the organism itself.[48] The fact that some bacteria or bacterial toxins could be 'attenuated' and used in the prevention and treatment of diseases opened up the vast therapeutic horizons pioneered but never quite envisaged by Edward Jenner 100 years earlier.[49]

Not surprisingly Welch, though a clinician by family tradition and perhaps by intention when he had set sail for Europe, was irresistibly drawn to the new sciences. He met Pasteur and his associates as well as Fernand Widal in Paris; he worked in Koch's new institute in Berlin for some months; and he attended the lectures of Max Gruber in Vienna. He also accompanied Gruber's brilliant young English assistant, H.E. Durham, to the Staatsoper. It is inconceivable that they did not discuss what later became autoimmunity in the intervals of *Tristan*.[50] His personality helped. The bearded giants of European science in its golden age tended to patronise American visitors as 'open-minded', 'refreshing' and 'enthusiastic', but often regarded them as incapable of assimilating European ideas at their more complex, sophisticated and adult. It was impossible to patronise William Henry Welch. Sporting only a neat Van Dyke beard instead of a bushy excrescence, he was personable and modest; but of his intelligence, mental capacity and adulthood there could be no doubt. (He was also, of course, extremely rich by the standard of a Pasteur or a Koch.) Returning to New York in 1879 he was made Professor of Pathology at Bellevue and helped in the recovery of that institution without being bribed or shot. Then he moved to Johns Hopkins as professor of pathology and bacteriology as well as dean of the medical school. His authority was never to be challenged.[51]

Welch left an account of Reed's time at Johns Hopkins. Written after Reed's death it is slightly obituaristic in tone; but Welch, an acute talent spotter and free from any trace of jealousy, undoubtedly recognised the qualities of intellect and character behind the humdrum appearance of the middle-aged army doctor. Reed started work on the clinical side of the hospital, though he was soon allowed to

> follow his own inclination and enter the regular courses in pathology and bacteriology ... These new fields of scientific medicine became the centre of his interests and activity ... and one felt at once that he had found his true vocation ... They were fields which he was destined to cultivate with signal benefit to medical science and to the welfare of all mankind.[52]

Reed himself always looked on his year at Johns Hopkins as a turning point in his life. He ran a series of experiments clarifying the pathology of typhoid fever. He helped Welch to identify the hog cholera bacillus. These were useful achievements. More importantly, they gave him the confidence later to stand his ground against Sanarelli and other seasoned but often mistaken professional bacteriologists. He also made friends with other juniors working in the department, including Simon Flexner who went on to discover the causative organism of dysentery, the *Shigella dysenteriae*, in the Philippines 20 years later.

But Reed was still in uniform and, even before he settled in at Johns Hopkins, in early December 1891 he was ordered to go to Fort Keogh in Montana. Once again Indian unrest was feared and, according to the War Department, medical officers were needed. Over the next few weeks Reed was to witness one of the indelible tragedies in the history of the American Indian.

On 15 December 1890, Sitting Bull, chief of the Sioux, who had led his people at Little Big Horn, was murdered.[53] He had protested against the sale of 11,000,000 acres of Sioux land at 50 cents an acre, which had convinced Washington that the savages were an unwarranted nuisance and had to be eliminated once and for all. (The Seventh Cavalry was in any case rearing to avenge Custer; and who in Washington was prepared to argue with or try to restrain such noble soldierly sentiments?) Not surprisingly perhaps in view of their experience with the white man, the Sioux put their faith increasingly in the ghosts of their ancestors. Once that faith was kindled, hope was rapidly transformed into belief. Their 'Ghost Dance Religion', which alternately puzzled, enraged and frightened white observers, was in fact a deeply pacific movement, in many respects akin to fundamental Christianity. So strongly did it strengthen their belief that 'with the next greening of the Grass' their ancestors and dead relations would reappear and that the white man would disappear from their lands that their chief, Big Foot, offered no resistance when he and what remained of his tribe were taken prisoner.

They were led by the US Cavalry to Wounded Knee Creek, where they were carefully counted. They were 120 men and 230 women and children, not counting babies in arms. They were given tents for the night and blankets against the cold. Major Samuel Whitside, a man of compassion, ordered a stove to be placed in Big Foot's tent: the chief was in the terminal stages of tuberculosis and coughing up blood. Troops of cavalry were posted around the encampment and two and later another two Hotchkiss guns were placed on top of a rise overlooking it. Later in the evening the remainder of Seventh Regiment marched in and Colonel James W. Forsyth took charge. He was untroubled by Whitside's concerns. The officers settled down with a keg of whiskey to celebrate the capture of Big Foot.

Next morning the Indians were disarmed. The soldiers searched the tents and removed everything that could be used as weapons. At some point in the proceedings a shot was fired. The immediate and exact sequence of events after that remains unclear. In panic, the Indians tried to flee; there was nowhere for them to go. At Forsyth's command, the Hotchkiss guns went into action, firing a shell a second. By the end of the 'battle' 300 of the

Indians—men, women, infants and children—lay dead. The soldiers lost 25 dead and 39 wounded from friendly fire. There was no other.[54] Reed, one of three medical officers at or near the scene, was soon operating on them. He successfully removed a bullet, together with a timepiece that buffered its impact, from Lieutenant Hawthorne's abdomen.

Few of the savages who were still alive after the massacre survived. Most of those left lying on the campsite for the next 12 hours froze in the blizzard that followed the shooting. There must have been a keen photographer among the soldiers, since a picture of Big Foot frozen into a grotesque shape survives in the Smithsonian Institution in Washington. The few Indians still breathing 12 hours later were carried in a wagon to Pine Ridge. Since the local hospital was full of wounded or exhausted soldiers, they were moved on and accommodated in the hall of the Episcopalian Mission. Reed himself never described the experience but he must have been among the three army doctors who were ordered to inspect the consignment. There was not much they could do. Most were dead, including all the children. It was four days to Christmas and the hall was already decorated for the festive season. Perhaps the dying took comfort from a banner strung up across the chancel: 'PEACE ON EARTH AND GOOD WILL TO ALL MEN.'

After Reed's year at Johns Hopkins, he must once again have asked himself whether the experience had made his life better or worse. He had learnt much, acquiring practical knowledge as well as 'high-powered notions' about health, sanitation and disease; but he was firmly told that regiments needed sound medical officers, not scientists or academics. His appeal for help to John Shaw Billings to find him a posting where he could use his skills and newly gained knowledge was turned down.

Instead he was sent to Fort Snelling in Minnesota, another wilderness outpost. He fully expected to remain there for the customary two to four years and then perhaps be dispatched to another similar posting before retiring as a major. His depression could not have been lightened by the first 'fitness report' from his commanding officer, a Colonel Mason. It stated that his new medical officer had no special attainments to offer and had displayed no desire to go beyond the daily routine of duty. In fulfilling those he could not be seriously faulted. It was as insulting a testimonial as a commanding officer could write without turning a fitness into an unfitness report. The colonel did not like 'health boffins'.

Other worries crowded in on Reed. His household expenses were mounting. He was troubled by the Methodist revival of the fire-and-brimstone variety that had gripped Randolph-Macon Academy where Lawrence had been sent to school. They were filling his 'loving and tenderhearted boy with tormenting ideas of sin'. Reed was seriously thinking of 'giving it all up' (whatever that meant) and 'escaping to the South Seas'. Then, once again, a development in Washington changed the course of his life.

Contrary to expectation, in May 1893 the post of Surgeon General was offered to George Miller Sternberg, an internationally recognised scientist aged 55. He was later to be described as America's first bacteriologist, not an army politician. Perhaps the War Department had had its fill of politicking medics and was actually hoping for an elderly and other-worldly academic. He would no doubt occupy his time writing elegant reports about louse control and the bacterial flora of latrines, rather than lobbying congressmen, buttonholing newspaper editors and dining and wining senators in pursuit of a larger staff, better accommodation and such-like nuisances. Sternberg accepted and quickly proved that other-worldly elderly academics, given the chance, usually make the most cunning politicians. In Reed's own words, 'suddenly, when least expected, the fossil age has passed'.

CHAPTER THREE

ACADEMIC

The new Surgeon General's first move was to ignore the parsimonious mood of Congress (aggravated by the financial panic of 1893) and establish an army medical school. On the face of it, this was an unexceptionable reform. Schools as a concept were laudable; provided, of course, that they did not cost money. There was no reason why they should. Those with knowledge to impart should be allowed to do so in the army as well as in civilian life. Nevertheless, this was not what George Miller Sternberg had in mind. His was not to be a poor man's night school. Yet he had assured the War Department that he would use 'existing manpower'; and where such manpower did exist, he certainly used it. On Welch's personal recommendation—the new medical sciences were still a cosy club where everybody knew everybody else—he invited Captain Reed (now to be Major) to become professor of pathology and assistant curator of the Army Medical Museum. Of the two appointments, the latter was by far the more important.

On both sides of the Atlantic pathological museums were still the hub of medical education, just as morbid anatomy had been worshipped for the previous 100 years as the bedrock of scientific medicine. Every medical school had its museum and every museum proudly displayed its serried ranks of 'pots'. What the pots contained were literally tens of thousands of beautifully dissected hearts, lungs, stomachs, bones, testicles, brains and every other organ imbedded in formaline and hermetically sealed and numbered. They displayed 'lesions', ranging from common varicose ulcer and gangrenous toes to gigantic cysts of the ovary and feet swollen to elephantine proportions. Their preparation (often involving the insertion of coloured 'sondes' to guide the viewer to hidden communications) was a craft requiring great skill and knowledge. The pots were lovingly turned and dusted daily by specially trained 'specimen technicians'. It was not all gloom. Gallstones, sometimes 100 or 200 removed from one gall bladder, could be arranged in fanciful patterns. The corresponding case histories and post-mortem findings bound into little booklets were usually found hanging by chains at the sides of the shelves.[55] Two-headed monsters and other rarities were particularly prized. The skeletons and other remains of giants, dwarfs and conjoined twins in the best-endowed collections were objects of pilgrimage to visiting doctors and others of an enquiring cast of mind. No medical examination was complete without a session with 'pots', candidates being expected to talk learnedly about the organs nestling in their bed of formaldehyde. To be in charge of such a treasure, including in the case of the Army Medical Museum hallowed remains from famous battlefields, was a signal honour as well as an onerous responsibility.[56]

To help Reed in his laboratory and museum work and with the preparation of lectures and demonstrations, he acquired his first assistant. He remembered James Carroll from his days at Johns Hopkins and specifically requested his transfer to Washington. According to Welch, Carroll had helped Reed at Johns Hopkins, showing 'peculiar aptitude' for laboratory work. He was an Irish working-class man who, by his own account, had drifted across the Atlantic in search of a better life (or at least food), first to Canada and then to the United States. He drifted into the army after being a blacksmith's apprentice, a railroad labourer and a lumberjack. He made it to sergeant and, while serving as a hospital steward (what in England today would be called a male charge nurse), attended medical lectures at St Paul and, after being posted to the East, at the University of the City of New York. Nobody ever quite knew how he managed to complete his medical course, but he surfaced with a medical degree from the University of Maryland in 1891. He was now married with four children.

Reed and he got on well. It was of course a 'working relationship' rather than a friendship; but it worked. At Johns Hopkins they had attended lectures together and Carroll had been allowed to assist Reed in his experiments. Now they were reunited. To Reed Carroll was 'something of a rough diamond but loyal and hard-working when he feels like it'. While Carroll was the older of the two, he was outranked and outclassed by Reed. For some years he probably felt gratified at being chosen as Reed's right-hand man; at times he also felt slighted. In his publications after Reed's death, he tended to imply that his contribution to their joint labours had been unfairly neglected. He may have been right. It was nevertheless a memorable partnership while it lasted.[57]

With the new appointments went a lifestyle such as the Reeds had never enjoyed before. They lived in a house in Georgetown, not yet the chic suburb it is today but a quiet, respectable neighbourhood where Blossom could play in the street with her friends. She would meet Papa on the corner as he alighted from the streetcar in the evenings. Lawrence went to high school in Washington. Emilie could go to the theatre, entertain her neighbours for tea and work on charitable committees.[58]

What mattered to Reed personally was that scientifically he was becoming an insider. He had become a member of the Columbia Medical Society. He was lecturing, examining, arguing and discussing with other scientists such topical questions as the diphtheria antiserum, the tuberculin fiasco, rabies, the bacteriological flora of the Potomac and the spread of typhoid.[59]

Much passion was aroused by the question of painful and unnecessary experiments on animals (at a time when the experimental immunisation of 'unclaimed' children in orphanages was common and freely described in medical articles). Reed, who would later authorise life-threatening experiment on his friends, was appointed a member of the Government's Joint Commission on Vivisection. A paper in the *British Medical Journal* published on 18 December 1897 was also widely discussed. An Indian army surgeon by the name of Ross, working in the Far East, had found that the malaria parasite, the plasmodium, underwent critical changes inside the anopheles mosquito. This made it possible, indeed likely, that the parasite was conveyed by the insect and by no other means after a requisite incubation period; and that the parasite entered the victim's blood as the mosquito bit.[60]

Reed was among the first in the United States to demonstrate the parasite in human red blood cells. Then he was sent to Florida to study a suspected smallpox epidemic. Though the epidemic had happily fizzled out, he met Jefferson Randolph Kean, a Virginian of impeccably aristocratic ancestry who would remain his closest friend and staunchest defender. Smallpox was still important, as were typhoid and malaria. But one disease above all exercised not only Reed's mind but the minds of all medical scientists in the United States.

At a time when many pestilences rarely if ever seen today were common, yellow fever was the single most dreaded disease in the Americas.[61] Its statistical mortality tended to be high, but its psychological impact was out of proportion to its death rate. Like no other illness, it concentrated deaths within the span of a few weeks and its course was rapid and horrific. Before the turn of the nineteenth century, every American family knew its symptoms. They knew that it might strike suddenly at any time in the summer and autumn, but would withdraw in the cold of the winter. (What was not realised was the reason: frost killed the mosquitoes.) Hundreds of thousands died horribly of the haemorrhagic 'black vomit', and more hundreds of thousands were sickened and terrified to the point of madness. The epidemic came in irregular surges to one area after another, sometimes withdrawing and then returning just as people were beginning to sigh with relief. Often it started at the waterfront and in the port, then jumped to dockside taverns and later to districts further inland. It ate its way through towns 'as larvae eat

through corn', plunging whole communities into hysterical fear. In some years it would stay away completely. In others it would creep up the West Coast of the United States, appearing as far north as Philadelphia, New York and Boston.

Though it tends to be neglected by non-medical historians, the disease was inextricably bound up with the history of the American Continent. Horror stories were passed on from generation to generation and sometimes surpassed by fresh outbreaks. In Santa Lucia in 1604 the disease killed 1441 out of 1500 soldiers. It was thought that more than 100,000 people were sacrificed to the disease in Spain's attempt in the early nineteenth century to hold on to Cuba. The island was already known to have the fever at its most severe. A particularly horrific epidemic also spread up the Mississippi Valley in 1878, causing an estimated 120,000 cases with a mortality of about 30 per cent. The irrational hope persisted in the Southern states that if the geographical source of the pestilence could somehow be controlled, such visitations could be prevented. There were no grounds for this belief—except that it eventually and unexpectedly came true, though for reasons that could not be foreseen. In the Americas the news of the costly French Panama Canal fiasco came as no surprise. It simply confirmed what most people had expected to happen. It also served as a warning for European colonial powers to keep out of the western hemisphere. If the canal would ever be built, it would be by the United States, and it would happen after the conquest of yellow fever. Sadly, of such a conquest there was as yet no sign.

Loss of human life was bound up with loss of business and revenue. The fever not only frightened customers and paralysed enterprise: it also stopped trains, bottled up ports, kept cotton from reaching the mills and prevented the distribution of perishable merchandise. It caused endless futile but heated arguments about quarantine laws. They were widely regarded as essential—but they were also ruinous. Even without the quarantine laws the unpredictable threat of outbreaks made business with the South a risky proposition. This was one of the less obvious but most important causes for poor investment in the region and for the slowness of its commercial growth compared to the North. Much of the South's foreign trade consisted of fruit, coffee and other seasonal produce. Quarantine laws, enforced with desperation, paralysed their onward movement and ruined businesses.[62] President Rutherford Hayes in his annual message to the nation reckoned that 'loss to the country through yellow fever had to be counted in billions of dollars every year'.

Clinically the disease tended to come on rapidly, most often heralded by a rigor or chill. It affected women and men equally. The victim might sense a strange excitement, not yet unpleasant. Then he might start to feel dizzy and light-headed. Or he might be wakened from his sleep by a headache, violent enough to jerk him, retching, out of bed. His temperature would climb swiftly. Some patients were spared the 'second stage', which usually lasted about three days. The temperature would rise even faster, the skin grew flushed, the headaches become excruciating and muscles and joints felt as if compressed in a vice. There were nausea and bleeding from the mouth and nose. A frightening sort of excitement could make patients seem mad or drunk: sometimes they were difficult to restrain. About the fifth day the symptoms would deceptively abate. Pain and fever would subside, the churning of the stomach ease and the vice relax. The patient might fall asleep and awake weak but refreshed enough to assume that the worst was over. This was well known as 'the eye of the hurricane', giving false hope. In fact, the respite was only the prelude to the final stage. Toxic necrosis of the liver would then become clinically manifest. First the jaundice deepened. There would then be massive bleeding under the skin, into the joints, from the nose but mainly into the gastrointestinal tract.[63] The last led to the black vomiting, red haemoglobin being changed to a black pigment by the digestive enzymes. Death was now only a few hours away, but often the patient remained conscious, even alert, to the end.

Individual experiences can convey such horrors better than generalised descriptions 'Lucille died at Ten O'Clock Tuesday night, after such suffering as I hope never to witness again,' wrote a Memphis resident during the 1897 epidemic to a friend.

> Once or twice my nerve almost failed me, but I managed to stay. The poor girl's screams might be heard across the square; and at times I had to exert my utmost strength to hold her in bed. Jaundice was marked; the skin being of a bright yellow hue: tongue and lips dark, cracked, and blood oozing from the nose and mouth ... Then came the black vomit which I never before witnessed, the most terrible and terrifying feature ... By Tuesday evening it would be like ink and ejected with terrific force. I had my face and hand spattered but had to stay and hold her. It was too terrible to write more about it.[64]

It was an experience shared by thousands of households during some of the summer epidemics.

> When whole cities were stricken, gloom and despair hung over the place. At night the town was silent like a grave but pierced sometimes by the sound of wailing ... by day it was desolate as the desert. The solemn oppression of universal death bore upon the human mind, as if the Day of Judgement was about to dawn. Not a sound was to be heard. Death prevailed everywhere. The poor were reduced to beggary and even the rich gladly accepted alms ... A family of four was found dead on a street corner, the bodies partly decomposed. Nobody would move them. Then men, women and children started to pour out of the city by every possible avenue. A few steamboats were filled but mostly shunned by those who had the means for railroad travel and had minds sufficient to envisage that the boats might become charnel houses. They quite often did. Out by the country road to the little hamlets and plantations, out by every possible conveyance ... hacks, carriages, wagons, furniture vans and drays ... bateaux, anything that could float on the river. The trains were packed literally to suffocation.[65]

There were many puzzling features about the illness. In antebellum New Orleans it was widely known as the 'stranger's disease'. Since childhood cases were often mild—no more sometimes than 'colds on the liver' with transient jaundice—and because they seemed to confer immunity, those who had grown up in the town seemed to be less at risk than the waves of Italian and Irish immigrants who came as young adults. But in cities less often visited by the illness, cohorts of natives could grow up uninfected and therefore without immunity. Though an attack did confer immunity for life, it was not always easy to tell whether a person had had the illness in childhood. Filth was always felt to be a principal breeding ground and blame for outbreaks fell heavily on government officials charged with the collection of rubbish and municipal sanitation. On the other hand, in contrast to many other nineteenth-century pestilences, lack of personal cleanliness and morality were not held responsible and the patients were therefore treated as innocent victims. Rarely mentioned in early treatises, it was widely believed that Negroes had a significant degree of immunity. Indeed, the knowledge was one of the justifications for slavery by the South: labour under southern conditions tended to kill whites, so blacks were the 'natural' choice for the plantations.[66] Sanitary regulations also tended to engender vicious witch-hunts against those accused or found to have breached them. Vigilantes were active and often received official support: none was ever prosecuted. In Mississippi and Louisiana some offences against quarantine laws carried the death penalty.

The cause of the disease was unknown, despite an unmanageably large literature on the subject. Under the influence of discoveries reported from Europe, by the late 1870s most physicians in the South (but not in the North) felt confident that the disease was caused by some kind of a germ; even before the germ was identified, strenuous and expensive efforts were made to eradicate it.[67] While Guiseppe Sanarelli's claim to have found the yellow fever bacillus later became famous because he clashed with Sternberg and Reed on the subject, at least 20 such claims were made in the 1880s.[68] Abraham Jacobi, president of the New York Academy of Medicine in 1884, coined the phrase 'bacteriomania' to describe an 'unwholesome trend' that was 'sweeping through the medical profession'.[69] While he praised the careful researches of Koch 'and his peers', he deplored the sloppy methods, over-enthusiasm and tendency to premature claims of many of his American followers.

> Also, the American physician is too ready to accept every announcement ... The theory that almost all diseases have their own bacillus is so beguiling that its resistance requires a certain courage.

At least one medical editor expressed similar misgivings.

> We have earnestly tried to keep up with the times and to escape the reproach of old-fogeyism. But while each year we have proclaimed the bacterial causation of various diseases, we have had to retract most of the announcement the next year.[70]

Such counsels are rarely heeded and by the mid-1880s the germ theory without the germ was widely accepted. The president of the Louisiana Board of Health wrote:

> It is generally admitted that the chief danger to a city lies in the transportation of yellow fever bacillus in holds of ships, cargoes and baggage but that the disease is rarely if ever propagated from person to person.[71]

Actual evidence for this (or the reverse) was non-existent. The issue of personal contagion remained disputed, but most public health officials acted on the assumption that infected people 'might be' dangerous.

Whatever the source and mode of transmission, most doctors believed that the mythical germ entered the body through the respiratory tract in a cloud of vapour or droplets. The 'evidence' was analogy with the human strain of the tubercle bacillus. The wafting of the germ by air currents was thought to account for the ability of the disease to jump from house to house without the occupants ever meeting and explained simultaneous outbreaks at several remote points in one city. An extension of this belief was that air, particularly air heavy with potentially unhealthy vapours, such as emanations from garbage heaps or mounds of putrefying food, provided a particularly hospitable environment for the microbe. By contrast, it was widely believed that the microbe could not survive in a clean environment.

Though like every other doctor, especially those coming from the South, Reed was deeply interested in yellow fever, he would probably never have become a leading figure in its pursuit but for the outbreak of one of history's least bloody but most unnecessary wars. It was also, until the present century, one of the most mindlessly popular. The psychological roots of the Spanish-American conflict remain somewhat problematical; but perhaps the closure of the frontier in the 1890s had something to do with it. While throughout the nineteenth century European powers scrambled in a competitive madness for colonial possessions in the 'backward' continents, the United States of America expanded into virgin territory—the Indians did not count—that must have seemed limitless. But it was not. When the frontier closed in the 1890s, eyes turned elsewhere; and many in the United States showed themselves no less captivated by the idea of colonial conquest than their imperialist cousins in Europe. Even the rhetoric was the same. 'God has not been preparing the English-speaking and Teutonic people for nothing but vain and idle self-contemplation and self-admiration,' one senator declared. 'No! He has made us adepts in government that we may administer government among savages and senile people.'

The rich and beautiful island of Cuba, only 100 miles from the southern tip of Florida and under Spanish misrule for four centuries, seemed to qualify under both headings: it suddenly became an object of desire. The desire was not of course openly expressed. At the beginning of the conflict Congress passed a self-denying ordinance, proposed by Senator Henry M. Teller, proclaiming to the world that the United States had no designs to exercise 'any kind of sovereignty, jurisdiction or control over Cuba, Puerto Rico or the Philippines'.[72] Its own constitution explicitly forbade the annexation of territories inhabited by alien people who had expressed no wish to be annexed. Would they be colonies? Or states? Self-denying ordinances tend to be broken; this one was breached even before it had a chance of coming into effect.[73]

The population of Cuba consisted of Scottish and English planters of sugar and coffee, some pure-blooded Spaniards and a mass of mixed bloods of Spanish, British, French, American-Indian and African ancestry. In 1895 its more or less chronic state of rebellion against Spanish authority flared up once again and Spain named as governor the hard-boiled General Valeriano Weyler. Weyler adopted the unstatesmanlike policy of brute repression, which, to start with, was not without effect. The more effective it was, the more public sympathy in the United States was stirred. As de Tocqueville observed, Americans are prone to display the 'under-dog complex' (except perhaps when the creature is whimpering in their own backyard). The outrage was fanned by lurid newspaper reports. Though mostly penned in New York and Washington, some of these turned out to be approximately true as well as chilling. Weyler noted that most resistance to the government had always been in the countryside. This he proposed to remedy by 'redistributing the population'. The town of Guines was one designated by him as a 'centre of reconcentration'. The population of the region was rounded up and herded into the urban area. The area was surrounded by barbed wire. Since no arrangement had been made to feed the *reconcentrados*, most of them perished from starvation or a galloping form of tuberculosis. The atrocities were not all on one side, nevertheless. A Spanish ship carrying conscripts as well as prospective emigrants was captured by the patriots when it sought refuge from a tornado in a bay. It was set on fire with crew and men aboard. Those trying to escape were shot in the water.

The truth was that Cuba had been chronically misgoverned and was no longer profitable to the government in Madrid. The governor and his staff had been traditionally both corrupt and incompetent. But to those with first-hand experience of the island, the scales of injustice were rather more evenly balanced than was portrayed by the press. The patriots, most effectively represented by the rebel army of General Máximo Gomez, were not the reincarnation of the American Colonists of 1776. The extortion rate under the guise of protection levied by the two sides on American business interests and European planters rose and fell more or less in parallel. Unfortunately, in the last days of 1897, an official in the War Department in Washington —his identity and his motives have never been established— ordered the battleship *Maine* to Havana harbour 'to watch over American interests'. How this was to be accomplished was never disclosed. On 15 February 1898, while at anchor there, the battleship was blown up by an explosion, killing 260 American servicemen. The cause of the explosion has remained a mystery to this day.[74]

Immediate investigation by an impartial tribunal offered by Spain was declined, though only a few months earlier the United States had firmly committed itself to such a procedure in cases of international disputes. Inflamed by the yellow press of Joseph Pulitzer of the *New York World* and Randolph Hearst of the *New York Journal*, the public went into a patriotic frenzy. One of the last great discoveries of the century of great discoveries was that patriotic frenzies sell newspapers. 'Remember the *Maine*, To hell with Spain' was one of Hearst's poetic inspirations. Not to be outsmarted, Pulitzer furthered his anti-Spanish campaign by 'intercepted and leaked' telegrams. Most but not all were fakes. The Spanish ambassador, in a perceptive but badly encoded message, did describe President McKinley as 'weak and a bidder for the admiration of the crowd'.[75] Theodore Roosevelt, Assistant Secretary of the Navy and always bellicose—without the war he would never have had the chance to take his 'rough riders' for the 'charge of San Juan Hill' and would probably never have become

President—demanded that the Spaniards should be driven from the New World once and for all.

President McKinley was for peace but irresolute. He particularly feared that trying to stem the tide of jingoism would disrupt the Republican Party and interfere with his tariff reform and other interesting functions of government. When he sent an ultimatum to Spain, General Woodford, the US envoy, cabled back within 24 hours that Spain was ready to make any concession to avoid war. The offer included the annexation of Cuba by the United States. As a starting gesture Weyler was recalled. Compensation would be paid wherever judged to be fair by independent observers. Nothing more could conceivably be asked from another power, even a decrepit one like Spain.[76] McKinley expressed himself satisfied and made pacific noises. Roosevelt remarked that the President 'had no more backbone than a chocolate éclair'. McKinley proved the negative with a positive by asking Congress to declare war the next day.

The war took the armed forces by surprise, as wars usually do. No part of it was more unprepared than the Medical Corps. Its 177 commissioned officers and 750 enlisted men were adequate to cope with the peacetime army of 25,000, but inadequate for the voluntary army that promised to reach 100,000 within a week. Nor was any machinery in place for an emergency increase of the peacetime complement. The hasty recall of 15 physicians, dismissed over the previous years ostensibly as an economy measure but also for varying degrees of incompetence, brought the numbers up to 192. The War Department then hit on the ingenious idea of instructing the newly appointed colonels of the new regiments to recruit their own medical officers. This was quickly accomplished, though at some cost. Volunteer doctors for the duration were plentiful but their appointments usually owed more to their being good fellows who could hold their liquor than to their competence in sanitation. The outcome was not altogether surprising.

Militarily the war was a picnic, though a rowdy one. Some of the rowdiness was provided by every victory being greeted with wild enthusiasm in the press and by the public. An unusual number of bungling commanders were elevated to the status of national heroes for a few months. This obscured the futility of the enterprise, bad planning, obsolete equipment, gross mismanagement of supplies, poor leadership and, above all, the grave death toll. This was only fractionally due to military action. The number of those killed in actual combat was less than 1000.[77] Far more deaths were the result of disease, many of them theoretically preventable. Despite more zealous doctoring of statistics than of patients, 20,739 cases of typhoid fever were recorded among the first 171,000 American soldiers enlisted. The death rate was 7.6 per cent.

But the real menace was yellow fever. The War Department had overlooked its seasonal incidence (known for 300 years) and had planned the Santiago Campaign, the centrepiece of its strategy, for July and August. The fever invaded the American camp immediately after the victory of Santiago at the beginning of July and infected nearly 2000 soldiers. The mortality approached 80 percent. General William R. Shafter, supported by the ubiquitous Colonel Theodore Roosevelt, urged the Secretary for War, Russel Alger, to allow the army to move away from the city of Santiago to higher and presumably healthier ground. Alger pointed out that holding Santiago had been the primary object of the war (at least as sold to the newspaper-reading public). In a letter purposely leaked to the Associated Press to stir Alger to action, Roosevelt wrote: 'If we are kept here it will mean an appalling disaster: the surgeons estimate that over half the army will die.' He was only slightly exaggerating. Alger still dithered. Fortunately on 17 July Spain sued for peace; the army might not have survived another wave of the infection.[78] By 18 August 1898 Shafter's entire corps (and, happily, Colonel Roosevelt) were back in the United States.

This was not the end of the story. For weeks after the signing of the Peace Treaty, recruits were still streaming into the camps in the scorching summer heat and many were still dying from a variety of fevers. Cuba, moreover, would have to be held and governed 'until deemed ready for independence'. This meant that about 50,000 men would continue to be stationed on the island. It was, in the opinion of the Secretary for War, time to appoint a commission—indeed, several commissions—to deal as expeditiously as possible with the health problems that were expected to arise during the war that had just ended. Top priority—simply because it was much publicised and might be amenable to sanitary measures—was typhoid. A Typhoid Commission was quickly assembled by Sternberg. Its members, under the chairmanship of Major Walter Reed, were Victor C. Vaughan, dean of Ann Arbor's Medical School, and E.O. Shakespeare, a distinguished epidemiologist.[79] It would provide Reed with his first chance to visit Cuba and come face to face with yellow fever.

CHAPTER FOUR

CUBA

For about 10 weeks the Typhoid Commission travelled widely and in some comfort. The more appalling the sanitary conditions, the warmer the hospitality offered by the camp commanders. Reed was enough of a soldier to make it clear even to senior officers that non-cooperation would not be tolerated and might cut short a promising career. The first camp they investigated, Camp Alger on the Potomac, revealed the complete lack of laboratory equipment. The medical officer had never in his life looked down a microscope. Reed doubted if he had ever seen one. The Commission decided to investigate every patient in every camp they visited and inspect every well and kitchen. They would then determine the extent of typhoid throughout each camp, using a new kind of grid that they designed specifically for that purpose. In almost every camp they visited they were informed that 'typhomalaria' was rife but not typhoid.

Typhomalaria did not and does not exist. It was a comforting figment created in 1863 by the bible of American military medicine, Woodward's *Outline of the Chief Camp Diseases in the United States Armies*, perhaps for the specific purpose of obscuring the incidence of typhoid. Even before the discovery of the typhoid bacillus and the establishment of the aetiology of malaria, typhoid was associated in people's mind with poor sanitation and negligent hygiene, whereas malaria was accepted as an act of God. To perform a Widal reaction for the diagnosis of typhoid as well to confirm malaria by identifying the parasite in a blood film under the microscope, basic equipment was needed

that most army camps did not possess. Even so, it was surprising that the differential response to quinine did not provide a clue. Or perhaps it did but nobody rushed to interpret it. 'Typhomalaria', like malaria, was supposed to respond to quinine; none of the typhoid cases did.

In Camp Cuba Libre the commissioners found faecal matter of several weeks disposed in open tubs around the camp or scattered near the company roads. There were 2092 cases of 'typhomalaria' (or 'acute typhoidal indigestion', an alternative face-saving diagnosis). Forty-two enlisted solders had died over the previous two weeks. In Jacksonville the Commission were shown with some pride a local speciality, a device for sprinkling faecal matter with lime. Within an hour at lunch in the officers' mess Reed was able to demonstrate the delicate white lines left by flies on the food they were eating. At Camp Chickamauga the unyielding soil made it 'impossible' to build latrines. 'I have never seen so large an area of faecal-stained soil,' Vaughan was to write in his memoirs.

> The woody lands were smeared with discharges ... one could not walk under the trees anywhere inside or around the camp without soiling one's shoes with human excrement. The occasional rain would sink the pollution just below the surface where typhoid bacilli are known to retain their vitality almost indefinitely.[80]

At Chickamauga the Commission also availed themselves of the opportunity to establish the incubation period of the disease. Three days before their arrival a group of 50 volunteer nurses had arrived from Chicago to help in the camp hospital. The first came down with typhoid ten days later and another eight sickened within the next three days. This implied an incubation period of 10 to 14 days. The suggestion was incorporated in the Commission's final report and has stood the test of time. Even more important was the first clear delineation of the 'carrier state'. Before then transmission of bacterial disease by asymptomatic carriers had been considered only in diphtheria.

Now it was shown that a similar mechanism could start an epidemic of typhoid. It could also account for the repeated flare-ups of the disease in one locality where an asymptomatic carrier had regular access to food. Hopefully, the days of Typhoid Marys were numbered.[81]

Apart from the major problems of demolishing the myths of typhomalaria and typhoidal indigestion and writing recommendations about sanitation and diagnostic facilities, there were the usual irritants of army soldiering. Just as Reed was embarking on the analysis of the typhoid charts with Vaughan and Shakespeare, he was ordered to investigate and report immediately on the efficacy of 'cholera bands'. Should 50,000 be issued to the army in Cuba as a matter of high priority? These bands were itchy and smelly adhesive plaster bandages recommended to be wound around the abdomen of cholera patients. Whose invention they were nobody knew: they had never been described in the medical literature. Presumably somebody wanted to get rid of a stock of unwanted appliances in a state of advanced decay. That somebody had access to a newspaper reporter or was prepared to pay for the news item. Whatever the background, one of Hearst's newspapers had run a headline deploring the scandal that such life-saving devices, 'often curative and essential for the prevention of contagion', had not already been issued to all members of 'our seriously handicapped Armed Forces'. By the time Reed submitted his report—it took him six weeks to establish the total uselessness of the bands—they had been forgotten. More and more, as the Typhoid Commission laboured on their final report, it was yellow fever that claimed their attention.

Hostilities with Spain had hardly in fact begun when the Surgeon General lobbed his opening salvo across international boundaries. A few weeks earlier Giuseppe Sanarelli had made a sarcastic reference to Sternberg's negative but well-founded conclusions about the causation of yellow fever, referring to them as the 'most rich and methodical negative contribution so far published about the disease'. Sanarelli regarded anybody who questioned his *idée fixe*, the *Bacillus icteroides*, as a murderer; in the prevailing uncertainty many were anxious to accept his ill-founded but positive assertions. Taking up Sanarelli's challenge in the *Transactions of the Association of American Physicians*, Sternberg re-stated that not one single organism 'has been shown so far to be present indisputably in every case of yellow fever, including the organism *devised* by Dr Sanarelli' [author's italics]. He bristled at being misquoted, but was quite able to respond in kind. 'The misrepresentation by Dr Sanarelli of what I said in my published report is unworthy of a scientific man.' He then promised that, nevertheless, 'all resources of the United States Army Medical Corps will be utilised to investigate Dr Sanarelli's claims, however dubious'. A month later he reported that this had been done and the claims had been found to be 'entirely without foundation': Sanarelli's *Bacillus icteroides* or an organism like it was present in only a small proportion of cases of yellow fever: they were clearly contaminants.

In fairness, he should have waited a little longer. Sanarelli now counter-attacked and showed that 'grievously insufficient time has elapsed for such a claim' to be credible. He was right. He also half-openly hinted that Sternberg 'or one of his uniformed underlings' had lost the specimens he had sent them. There he was wrong. The specimens had been discarded as soon as they had arrived. Scientific differences apart, it was a clash of styles of conducting a medical argument. Sanarelli was eventually proved to be comprehensively wrong—though never to his own satisfaction—but not by Sternberg's magisterial dismissals. In fact, Sternberg too was wrong (despite his vigorous assertions to the contrary a few years later, endorsed by his official biographers) in dismissing the 'mosquito idea' when it reached his ears as 'lunatic'. Perhaps, by luck or intuition, the man who got nearest to the truth was a young and relative outsider, George Frederick Novy, who had just started his long career at the University of Michigan.

It seems to me that the most likely germ of yellow fever may be similar to those of small-pox, hydrophobia, measles, etc., belonging to a group of organisms smaller than bacteria and still awaiting discovery. The recent work of Roux and Nocard [in Paris] proves the existence of organisms smaller than the 'infinitely small' bacteria.[82]

What seemed at the time a side issue also attracted attention. In one of his papers Sanarelli referred to a toxin being 'injected into patients in the hope of identifying the specific germ of yellow fever'. 'At least I suppose they were patients because they were in a hospital,' wrote Victor Vaughan. 'If so, such a practice is ridiculous.'[83] This in turn elicited a sharp comment from the great William Osler.

Ridiculous is not the term, I beg to submit, which I would use. The limits of human experimentation should be clearly defined in our minds. From the clinical point of view almost every dose of medicine we give is an experiment. Who knows what may result from giving a 2-grain dose of quinine to a child? It may die, as did recently one of my friend McKittrick's patients. But to deliberately inject a poison of known high degree of virulence into a human being is not ridiculous, it is criminal.[84]

Reed was not at the time involved in the controversy, but soon the exchanges would become relevant to his own mission.

By the spring of 1899 it was obvious that the United States would have to retain responsibility for Cuba for some time to come. True, the island was to be independent at an undisclosed future date; but until then it was to be administered by its liberating army. In the light of this Sternberg secured from a reluctant Secretary for War the appointment of another medical board to pursue 'scientific investigations of acute infections prevalent on the island of Cuba'.[85]

The Surgeon General had, until now, firmly refused Reed's requests to join the army on active Duty (the last word always capitalised in Reed's writings). The major, though relatively junior in rank, was too valuable a trouble-shooter when some scandal threatened or some delicate and unpleasant task (like the Typhoid Commission or cholera bands) needed a cool and meticulous if at times somewhat plodding approach. Whatever his shortcomings, and a few years later Sternberg would be willing to enlarge on them, Reed was so patently incorruptible (either by money or any other underhand favour) that his conclusions were never questioned. But now matters seemed to be settling down on the home front and, almost as a matter of course, Sternberg appointed Reed as the Board's (later changed to Commission's) presiding officer. This would inevitably mean his departure for Cuba, though he could always be recalled at short notice. (This was to happen more than once, much to Reed's chagrin. He was desperately seasick even over relatively short journeys, losing 5 lb of weight that he could ill afford at every crossing.) Reed suggested James Carroll as a member. The other two were selected for him and were already on the island.

Jesse Lazear came from a southern professional family—his father was a judge—and became an outstanding student at Johns Hopkins. Inevitably his talent and intelligence were spotted by Welch, who arranged for him to go on a two-year tour studying bacteriology and pathology in Germany. (He had already spent a year in Edinburgh attending Sir William Turner's widely acclaimed course of anatomy.) On his return he became Osler's assistant and first head of the new clinical laboratory; from there, on the outbreak of the Spanish-American War, he volunteered for the Army Medical Corps for the duration. At 33 he was, by all accounts, even those written in his lifetime, a wonderfully agreeable man: 'we could not have had a more modest, pleasant and intelligent fellow,' Reed himself wrote. Lazear in turn loved Cuba, 'the first place where I was not pressed to play golf'. When he went there he left behind his young wife, expecting their second baby.

The other Commission member, Aristides Agramonte, had been born in Porto Principe and was a member of the Cuban Spanish aristocracy: his father, General Eduardo Agramonte, a leader of the insurrection against Spain of 1868–78, was killed in battle. After the defeat of the uprising the family moved to the United States, but Aristides was thought to have suffered a comparatively mild attack of yellow fever before their departure. He certainly regarded himself as—and probably was—immune. This was perhaps one of the reasons why he was appointed to the Commission: he was to do all the post-mortem work. The Commission also needed a native Spanish speaker who spoke fluent English. He had other qualifications as well. In the United States Aristides received a sound medical education and qualified in 1892 with high honours from the College of Physicians and Surgeons of New York.

At a personal level people differed in their response to him. Some were offended by his aloofness and his seeming indifference to the opinion of his colleagues and indeed of anybody outside his own social circle. Alva Sherman Pinto, a man who was later to volunteer for one of Reed's experiments, considered him 'about the lamest excuse of a doctor I ever associated with ... he could not care less about his patients and just bluffed his way through'. But this was not Reed's opinion. Reed admitted that Agramonte 'could be offensive, even outrageously so, but he often had reason to be', that 'he did not suffer fools gladly or indeed at all', but that he was 'an exceedingly hard worker without making a song and dance about it'. Reed's favourable opinion was reciprocated. Carroll too thought of him 'as a bit of a peacock but all right'.[86]

In appointing a commission to study fevers, there was of course a hidden agenda. To the fury of the Surgeon General, just as the bacterium idea seemed to be well and truly buried, Eugene Wasdin and E.D. Geddings of the 'rival' Marine Hospital Service (later the United States Public Health Service) published a report in which they professed to be convinced that the 'infection was caused by the yellow fever bacterium isolated by Dr Sanarelli. [The infection] takes place by way of the respiratory tract' and 'colonisation by the organism of the lung followed by secondary infection'.[87] The rest of their booklet was a compilation of acute observations and extraordinarily bizarre notions. Discussing diagnosis, they suggested (on what grounds is not clear) that a disproportionate swelling of the patient's upper lip was a useful differential diagnostic sign, as were 'waves of jaundice' of the face; 'presumably a kind of yellow aurora borealis', Sternberg acidly commented. Their recommendations for treatment were no less eclectic in their confusion. They included high colonic enemas, 'sometimes warm, sometimes cold' (but which when was not stated), the use of turpentine, cocaine, oil catharsis and dietary modifications (without going into detail). This section concluded with the statement that 'therapeutic treatment was desirable' without indicating what 'non-therapeutic treatment' might mean and whether it would presumably be undesirable.

Yet Wasdin and Geddings were reputable scientists who could not be dismissed as Sanarelli's hirelings. It was clear to Reed that they were motivated—how consciously it was impossible to say—by their dislike of the Surgeon General and the Army Medical Corps. This was heartily reciprocated. According to Sternberg, the Marine Hospital Service had no business to poke their noses into a matter that was traditionally the province of the Corps. The Report (probably written in haste to pre-empt any similar pronouncement from the Surgeon General) was therefore presumptuous as well as preposterous. Any statement by Wasdin and Geddings, even their occasional shrewd observation, was to be disproved by the Surgeon General's Commission. By contrast, it is at least possible that the Report's contemptuous reference to Dr Finlay's 'wholly imaginary idea relating to mosquitoes' was one reason Reed was determined to look into it.

Dr Carlos Finlay, the son of a Scottish expatriate father and a Parisian mother, was past 60 when Reed first landed on the island. Born in Cuba, he had been sent to France for his early schooling and spoke both English and Spanish fluently but with an engaging and (according to Agramonte) totally spurious French accent. He graduated as a doctor from Jefferson Medical College in 1855 and received more than one pressing invitation to settle in New York. Without question, whatever his clinical skills, his bedside manner and verbal fluency would have made him the darling of the city's upper crust. He preferred to return to Havana and become a general physician and specialist in ophthalmology. He lived with a married Spanish lady of aristocratic descent in a dilapidated baroque mansion in the heart of Havana, dyed his hair an improbable gold and was, by all contemporary accounts, loved by the poorer sections of the city's polyglot population.[88]

In the 1870s, some years before Manson and Ross but perhaps not before Laveran,[89] Finlay's mind was 'bitten by the mosquito bug', and he convinced both himself and his faithful disciple, Juan Guitéras, that the common household mosquito, then called *Culex fasciatus* but now *Aedes aegypti*, was the agent that caused and spread yellow fever. To prove this he conducted between 1881 and 1898 104 experiments (he kept careful notes in a literary style with lengthy digressions that embraced the nature of human love and the paradoxes of life) in which mosquitoes were first encouraged to bite yellow fever victims and then emigrant 'volunteers'.[90] Exactly how he recruited his volunteers was never clearly explained, but it is possible, as Finlay maintained, that all immigrants to Cuba expected to and usually did catch yellow fever within a year or two of their landing; and that the generous 'bounty' he paid them either helped them to set up in business or provided a dowry for their widows to remarry. How many actually did die was never recorded or at least never published; mortality in new immigrants in most epidemics in Cuba varied between 30 and 70 per cent.

Though Finlay was right about the key role of the mosquito—a belief he continued to proclaim despite the ridicule heaped on him by visiting experts—he got most of the details wrong. He was convinced that the poison—he was vague about viruses—was injected by the mosquito's bill much as a dirty hypodermic needle conveys hepatitis (or nowadays AIDS). He thought that only very sick patients were likely to transmit the disease. He was convinced that maximum infectiousness was towards the end of the illness or near or even after the patient's death. He did not appreciate that a critical time interval had to elapse between the mosquito biting a sufferer and being able to infect another victim. In the light of these misconceptions—and perhaps fortunately—many of his experiments proved negative: how many was never disclosed.

However, he was delighted to receive Carroll and Lazear, whom Reed had dispatched for a preliminary talk. It was, to Finlay's mind, the first belated recognition of his insights and labours and he went to great trouble to charm as well as to instruct. He showed his esteemed visitors his clusters of tiny, cigar-shaped mosquito eggs in a bowl with some water at the bottom. The eggs clung to the bowl's side slightly out of the water. While the position was essential for maturation, Finlay had found that the eggs could be dried, frozen or shaken around for up to three months and still hatch into larvae and then pupae once they were re-moistened and warmed. Then, a few days later, 'my pretty little children would emerge. Ah, but they were naughty as well as pretty.' He was certain that they spread the disease, but he readily admitted that, after all his experimentation, he was still not certain how. Did the female (the only one that bit for blood) insert tiny eggs into her victim? Did she pass the infection to her offspring as ticks did in Mexican cattle fever? Or could the mosquito be actually poisoned by the imbibed blood and fall into the water and poison that in turn? Finlay's speculations tended to go off on imaginative tangents. Lazear was exquisitely polite but deeply sceptical; Carroll was gruff as usual but more ready to be persuaded.

There was one other investigator who had something to teach Reed and whose personality as well as scientific thinking chimed in with his. Henry Rose Carter was an impecunious southern gentleman like Reed who had originally joined the army as a civil engineer. When he found that a leg injury suffered in the Civil War might interfere with his engineering, he moved to medicine and joined the Marine Hospital Service. (He was thus an enemy but an honourable exception to the rule promulgated by the Surgeon General that the rival service was 'thoroughly corrupt and scientifically negligible'.) Yellow fever had been his main preoccupation for years. Unlike Finlay, who had a plausible but wildly incorrect explanation for everything, Carter was acutely conscious of his and everybody else's ignorance. But there seemed to be enough facts available to convince him that current theories of quarantine and contagion were deeply flawed.

Two observations in particular puzzled him. 'Fomites' were articles of clothing and other personal belongings of patients with yellow fever.[91] In one way or another, they were almost universally held responsible for at least potentially spreading the disease. However, on 11 June 1888 a Norwegian boat docked in Ships Island, having sailed from Rio de Janeiro on 20 May. It had left behind several crew members who had already shown signs of yellow fever; another crew member got the fever within a day of leaving port, as did the ship's master. Both died. Then nothing untoward happened for 13 days, after which about half the crew members began to complain of headaches, turned yellow, started to vomit and died. Having once seen the pattern, Carter saw it repeated time and again. There would be a primary case or two around the departure of a ship, then a period of quiet for two or three weeks. Then other crew members would start falling ill. It happened not only on ships. A man would come down with yellow fever in a house. He might die or get better or move away. But after two or three weeks a cluster of other cases would appear in the same house. There were the odd jumps in space as well as in time. A man in 102 Real Street would come down with the fever. Then the fever would skip round the corner to 20 General Lee Street. From there it would hop across the road to No. 83. Yet none of these families had anything to do with each other; indeed, they swore that they had never met.

The other observation that, to Carter's mind, made nonsense of the fomites idea was the apparent immunity of baggage handlers and customs inspectors. He—and soon Reed as well—kept returning to this strange phenomenon. No group of individuals should have been more exposed to infection than the men who daily rummaged around clothing and personal possessions that, in the light of later events, must have been impregnated with the lethal yellow fever toxin. Yet not in 100 years had a baggage handler or customs inspector gone down with the disease. At least, nobody could recall a single case. The jobs were certainly not regarded as particularly hazardous. This anomaly would eventually lead to one of Reed's most horrific but most conclusive human experiments.

Reed was impressed by Carter, perhaps because Carter's ideas were similar to his own.[92] Both men had clear, precise minds that reacted like seismographs to inconsistencies and internal contradictions. And both were incapable of brushing them aside or 'fitting them into a larger picture'. There was, so far as Carter and Reed were concerned, no larger picture, only countless minute but incontrovertible facts. At times this could be exasperating. Finlay later complained to Agramonte (in confidence) that the excellent major's attention seemed to wander as soon as he, Finlay, got into his 'expository stride'. But that characteristic can also be a more useful asset facing the challenge of a medical (or scientific) mystery than a brilliantly soaring imagination.

The infective—or potentially infective—material from patients clearly had to undergo some kind of a change in the environment, lasting about two weeks, before it was capable of infecting another person. And more and more, against his initial inclinations, Reed became convinced that 'environment' meant mosquito. Nevertheless, the mosquito could not be a simple carrier as Finlay had suggested. The infective material sucked up by the female from a sick person had to undergo changes inside the insect before it could transmit the disease. In other words, there had to be 'external incubation'. The 'infective material' could not be a parasite, as it was in malaria, since that would surely have been seen by now in blood films and tissue sections. Agramonte, who had performed hundreds of post-mortem examinations on yellow fever victims and had meticulously examined their livers, lungs, intestines, bone marrows and brains under the microscope, was firmly of the opinion that there was no specific bacterium or plasmodium that was invariably present and might account for the disease. 'How can you be so sure?', Reed taxed him time and again. Agramonte shrugged his elegant shoulders. A Cuban gentleman was not in the habit of making categorical statements unless they were true. (In this respect he was also a fairly typical morbid anatomist of the old school.)

Reed eventually accepted this. There was no bacterium. There was no parasite. This meant that the infective agent had to be a virus, something undetectable with a microscope. It had to be transmitted by a mosquito. This was unprecedented. In malaria Laveran had demonstrated the parasite, a comparatively large and striking creature, well before the mosquito came buzzing into the picture. And, to complicate matters, the presumed yellow fever virus attacked only humans. Numerous attempts to give yellow fever to a wide range of experimental animals had all failed. Such species specificity was not unusual with virus infections: rabies and smallpox were available examples. But it was an infernal nuisance. It meant that the mechanism of the infection could be demonstrated in only one way. While the moment of truth was drawing near, it had not yet quite arrived.

From all these labours and speculations there was the occasional respite. Within a week of his arrival Reed went to visit his son Lawrence in Camp Vedado. He described their reunion in a characteristic letter to Emilie:

> He [the bibulous Captain Shenek, the commanding officer of the camp] was the same old drunken S. I remembered and was delighted to see me. Yelled for 'Serg't Reed like a bull roaring. Here came the dear boy, smiling and looking the very picture of health. The Captain gave him a 24 hour pass so down to the town we went and had a nice lunch together of chicken salad, beefsteak, etc, etc. You ought to have seen him eat! Appetite? Stand off! Then we went down Obispo Street & got something for Mother and Little

Sister, & then came down to the dock and took the steam launch 7 over to the Missouri [Reed's boat]. He will spend the night with me—is now Battery Quartermaster Sergeant —ranks next to the 1st Sergeant & is perfectly happy ... Dearboy [Lawrence] sends you & dear little Sister all manner of love—I never saw him looking so well & he has enjoyed talking and strolling with his daddie more than I can tell you ... I got your letter written on Friday. Hope this will find you in good health back at home. Love & kisses for my Precious babies. Must go back on deck now to talk to the dear boy—am very well—Devotedly, 'Papa'.[93]

But private finances were frustrating as usual. 'When I looked at my bank account,' he reported to Laura in the spring of 1899, 'it was less than $10. But who ever knew a Reed to have any 'spare change'? Not I, not you. And yet I never worked so hard in all my life.'[94]

Continually, as Reed and his fellow commissioners were groping their way to the conclusion to 'try the experiment', there were setbacks and interruptions. Sanarelli was by no means beaten. Most recently he had produced a 'yellow-fever prophylactic serum' prepared from his *Bacillus icteroides*. He suggested that it would stamp out the disease. It was everybody's dream: dreams generate hope; hope begets faith. The trouble with such sera, as with all prophylactic measures, including house burning and quarantine, was that their efficacy was difficult to *disprove*. If nothing happened, they worked. Fortunately for Reed and his Commission, less so for the victims, Sanarelli's serum patently did not. In a trial run most 'volunteers' (whoever they were) fell ill with an influenza-like illness and one subsequently went down with yellow fever. None, happily, died; but enthusiasm for the serum rapidly abated.

More serious was the fluctuating support the Commission received both from their home base and from the local military. While, as a rule, good news is no news for the popular press, there are times when the prescription for sales needs to be reversed. This is especially so during a particularly wet holiday season and after an unduly long spell of gloom. In April 1900 Leonard Wood was appointed Governor General of Cuba, the first doctor and former officer of the US Army Medical Corps to achieve such eminence. While still in the army, his quick intelligence had attracted the attention of such political leaders as Nelson A. Miles and Theodore Roosevelt, and they persuaded him to set aside, 'temporarily at least', his medical aspirations for political and military pursuits. He was 38 when he was appointed to command Theodore Roosevelt's 'rough riders'. This was a swashbuckling voluntary cavalry regiment. Its exploits had no effect on the war, but it made him a war hero. After the war he was promoted to general.[95] Despite such glittering prizes outside his original profession, he professed to be 'a doctor at heart'. He would transform the health of Cuba. June 1900 seemed a good opportunity to make a start by winning the support of the popular press. The *Medical Record* quoted him as saying while on a visit to Washington:

> There is no yellow fever in Cuba and no other contagious disease. Santiago is all right. All we want down there is a chance to earn an honest living and for our kids an opportunity to go to school. [An odd choice of a phrase for a childless bachelor.] ... There is no illness in the province. The death rate there is lower than in New York or Philadelphia ... about 14 in 1000. Yellow fever is virtually stamped out and there is no indication that it will return. This is the first summer when there has not been some.[96]

The reason for this welcome development was obvious. It was attributed by the General to

> my insistence that people, even locals, should take a bath now and then, that their vaults should be white-washed, that their houses should be kept clean ... and that the streets should be drained and the drainage carried away.[97]

After all the 'disaster-mongering' from officers who 'relished the limelight', this was a refreshing confirmation of middle America's faith in soap, water, clean living and a simple mind. For a short time even Sternberg, anything but simple, was bitten by the optimism bug. In his contribution to the *Report of the Commission Appointed by the President to Investigate the Conduct of the War Department in the War with Spain*, he expressed the view that

> Under United States supervision yellow fever, as it prevails in Cuba, will be fairly easily controlled. It is of a mild type with a low mortality. The recent outbreak might have been prevented by burning all the houses of Siboney and the more complete isolation of Spanish and Cuban refugees ... That the dread disease was kept out of our local cities was due to the watchfulness of our local and national quarantine officers and to the establishment and mainten-ance of a detention camp at Montauk.[98]

The last was of course the Surgeon General's brainchild.

Fortunately for the ultimate outcome of Reed's quest, the period of idiot optimism, entirely due to the short-term natural fluctuations of the disease, did not last. By 12 July Wood was writing to a friend in New York in consternation about 'another outbreak confined entirely to the American residents in Havana'. Though he hinted at an 'uncouth and flotsam element among those who had come to Cuba in the wake of our Army', the death rate among the military was especially heavy: it seemed to be fatal among all those who went down with the disease. Yet he still thought that the outbreak was essentially an affliction of the unclean and attributed it to 'damned bureaucratic delays in the implementation of my orders. Tying the whole place up with cast-iron military discipline was going to cause a great deal of kicking'; but it would work. The orders went out from General George Andrews's headquarters in Havana to close bars, restaurants and brothels (but not churches and schools), and for an all-out effort to be made to 'clean up the ship' from top to bottom.

Cubans watched with tolerant bemusement as the *Norte Americanos* toiled away with their scrubbing and fumigating. This, in their opinion, was not the way to face a terrible illness or indeed death. And if any proof was needed that a clean body and pure mind were *not* the answer, there was the case of poor Colonel Kean. Kean thought that the Cuban custom of washing many garments successively in the same liquid to save water and soap and failure to boil the laundry were two of the root causes of the illness. He was busy formulating orders to remedy this. The third cause was the decidedly insanitary habits prevalent in the numerous unlicensed brothels whose business always boomed during epidemics. With Wood's approval, he accordingly withdrew all night passes from headquarters staff. This was a popular move with the natives: the going rates immediately plummeted. However, his own habit of visiting soldiers taken ill worried both General Andrews and General Wood, whose medical right-hand man he had become. He was therefore ordered to stop visiting yellow fever victims so long as he remained on the staff of headquarters and was messing with senior officers.

Kean at first obeyed; but when his close friends, Major John Edmunds and his wife, fell ill and their condition became alarming, he was too worried to stay away. Of course he did not want to disobey orders either, not too flagrantly anyway.

So I arose at daybreak on 16 June and went over to his house. Mindful of the General's orders, I did not enter but sat on the open porch and talked to the poor man through a window which was well protected by an iron grill.

The iron grill did not deter the mosquito, though. Five days later he was feverish. He fortunately recovered (though Major Edmunds and his wife did not), but suffered an unusually long period of 'mental prostration and depression' afterwards. Reed recorded later that Kean was the first yellow fever patient he actually saw in a crisis and 'it was not a pretty sight'.[99]

For a time the public relations exercise back home and the epidemic in Cuba ran in uneasy parallel. On 23 June the

Army and Navy Journal stated that

> the yellow fever outlook in Havana is one to give entire satisfaction to those who have been administering the affairs of Cuba and comfort to those who have relatives or friends on the Island. Thanks to our stringent sanitary measures, enforced not without opposition, Havana is now in a very good sanitary condition as a whole with little liability to any visitation of yellow fever or other disease.[100]

This may have been strictly true on that day of Havana itself (whence the dispatch had been date-marked), but it was already out of date in the near-by village of Quemados. Though much of Cuba had been laid waste first by Weyler's atrocities and then by the war, this was still a charming and picturesque habitation, its pastel-coloured houses nestling among brilliant green hills splashed with the scarlet and purple of hibiscus and bougainvillaea. In this tropical paradise a sergeant from the Seventh Cavalry who lived in General Lee Street among other army personnel had fallen ill a few days earlier. It turned out that his wife had been unwell for some days, shivering, feeling week and bleeding; like many others, she was terrified of reporting her symptoms lest she be taken to the hospital where everybody seemed to die almost at once. Instead she died at home, and by the time of her funeral her husband was in bed with fever and blinding headaches and, within a few days, so was her daughter. The sergeant died; the daughter recovered.

By then the disease was flitting about rapidly and unpredictably. From Quemados it spread to Havana. Severe quarantine measures were applied to all incoming ships. They proved futile. Yellow fever patients were isolated in a secluded hospital. The response was a steady increase in the disease. The city's military governor, General William Ludlow, died within a few days of developing the first symptoms. The chief commissary officer, Major Patterson, a popular man, went down with it. His wife was summoned from Cincinnati by telegram, but by the time she arrived her husband was dying. To the horror of those who witnessed the scene, Mrs Patterson threw herself on her husband, covering herself with his *vomito negro*. Clasping the major in her arms, she begged him to ask God to take her too, and soon. Conscious to the end, he prayed for this. When their prayer went unanswered, Mrs Patterson shot herself. Husband and wife were buried together on the following day in Campo Colombo's fast-spreading military cemetery. A member of the Commanding Officer's staff who attended the funeral found himself shivering as the coffins were lowered into the ground. Within 48 hours he was dead.

On the same day the American superintendent of the San José Asylum died. A mess of eight men organised by the chief quartermaster, Chancey B. Baker, had begun using at meals the old English toast: 'To those who are gone and here's to the next to go.'[101] Before long only Baker and the general's aide de camps were left. They stopped the toast. Both survived. But between 1 June and 19 October there were 789 *reported* cases of American dead in the fiercely sanitised city of Havana. The true figure was almost certainly much higher.

CHAPTER FIVE

THE MOMENT OF TRUTH

When Finlay's eggs were hatched, Reed sent some of the mosquitoes to Washington to the eminent entomologist, Leland Howard, for identification. This was a correspondence that was to blossom over the next year. Leland was delighted to help in identification and provide information in return for a few choice specimens to add to his unrivalled collection. For 50 years he had carried on an impassioned correspondence with the other great insect collector of the age, Professor Heinz Fallheim-Wartburg of Freiburg in Breisgau in Germany—the two men never met— about the correct nomenclature of the species *Aedes*. In some way comprehensible only to the two experts, Reed's specimens might just tilt the balance in favour of the system proposed by Howard.

Reed for his part was an avid and quick-learning pupil, much to the merriment of his messmates. From now on he was never without some learned tome on entomology; and in his rooms he had a case full of journals, pamphlets and periodicals. As Lieutenant Truby later recorded,

> Usually on the taciturn side, he became quite voluble on the subject of insects. Soon he had us all collecting mosquitoes with large-mouthed cyanide bottles. These specimens he and indeed all of us would study with strong hand lenses. Any specimen we could not identify, off it would go by mail to Howard in Washington. He must have been in seventh heaven or wherever entomologists go as a reward for their labours.[102]

There was indeed a great deal to learn. *Aedes aegypti* is a supremely beautiful but vulnerable insect, all gossamer wings with fragile legs and slim, gracefully curved antennae. Though incapable of a long flight, the female can nevertheless move with great agility at 600 wing-beats per minute. She likes human smells and can hover until the sensors in her legs and antennae signal to her to alight. Apparently it is the carbon dioxide exuded by humans through the skin in low concentrations that attracts her, though she seems to respond in a choosy, idiosyncratic way. She does not stab her victims but delicately introduces into the skin her proboscis, which is finer than any human hair. The insertion would almost certainly not be noticed if she did not drool a tiny amount of anticoagulant into the wound. It is this that causes the itching. After sucking blood she departs, seeks a moist spot and lays her eggs. Her eggs can survive for as long as five years and still mature under the right conditions. The male insect is no danger to humans.

All the females that came from Finlay's stock of eggs were kept in Lazear's care in individual glass tubes stopped with cotton wool and carefully labelled. Some were allowed to bite yellow fever patients at Las Animas Hospital. Before leaving for another short visit to Washington, Reed wrote: 'Personally I feel that only experimentation on humans can serve to clear the field for further effective work.' And before he left it was agreed between members of the Commission 'in a rather informal way' (as Carroll later recorded) that 'they would themselves be bitten and subject themselves to the same risk that necessity would compel them to impose on others'.[103] One of their messmates, Alva Sherman Pinto, knew about this and insisted on being included. On 11 August Lazear and Pinto deliberately let themselves be bitten by a mosquito that had just fed on a severely ill yellow fever patient. The patient died the next day, but nothing happened to Lazear and Pinto. Consternation overshadowed relief. Finlay, who was kept in the picture, was crestfallen. He suggested that patients after two to three days of illness might not be infective; and that some time might have to elapse between the mosquito biting an infected patient and becoming infective itself. Reed had been thinking along similar lines.

On 27 August Lazear spent the entire morning at the hospital, coaxing his 'little birds' to light on and take blood from yellow fever patients. There was one reluctant insect, originally XYA34 now renamed LAZY, who had bitten a patient 12 days earlier but now resisted all blandishments to bite again. As noon approached Lazear gathered her up in a special container and took her back to Campo Columbo. He was beginning to lose faith—and respect—for his insects as pathogens, but was enough of a scientist to continue the meticulous labelling and feeding of his charges. By now both he and Carroll were more concerned with the survival of the mosquitoes than with any possible risk to themselves. The latter they regarded as regrettably negligible. Agramonte was later to recall that LAZY had been hatched in the laboratory 14 days earlier. At that time no particular significance was attached to time relations. Working in the laboratory in the afternoon, Carroll suggested that they should try once more to feed the indolent and infuriating creature. Otherwise it might die by the next day. First Lazear and then Carroll held it for minute after minute on their forearms. Eventually the mosquito seemed to perk up and discreetly introduced its proboscis under Carroll's skin.

Two days later, while swimming in the pool in the hospital grounds late in the afternoon, Carroll developed a headache. Pinto looked at him and declared that he must have yellow fever. 'Don't be a damn fool, I have no such thing,' Carroll retorted. By eight o'clock he was in the yellow fever ward. He was obstinate and obstreperous at first, but soon became delirious. In Medical Corps jargon he was 'in a bad shape'. In plain English he was dying. He first 'died' on the fifth day when his breathing seemed to stop. (This was a familiar feature of the illness.) Again on the seventh day all hope was given up. The hospital padre was repeatedly summoned, the saintly Father Matteo, a Spanish Jesuit who claimed to be immune but later died of the fever.

Agramonte and Lazear were in a turmoil. They had persuaded themselves that Reed was leading them on a wild goose chase. They frantically searched for possibilities other than LAZY that might be blamed for Carroll's suffering and what seemed like his imminent death. When they found none, it placed them in another agonising no-win situation. On the fourth day of the illness Carroll was clear-headed enough to answer questions and he reluctantly admitted that, unwisely and contrary to their agreement, between being bitten by the mosquito and his sickening he had ventured into the yellow fever ward, the autopsy room and for 'just a little airing' into Havana. He was sure that it was LAZY that had 'done it'; but, while Lazear and Agramonte did their best to reassure him, they agreed between themselves that they could not regard Carroll's illness as experimental proof. There remained an outside chance that he had been infected by another mosquito or another infective agent somewhere else.

While still hoping that Carroll would recover, they decided that, without waiting for Reed, they would get an infective mosquito to bite another volunteer, the first to come forward, under strictly controlled conditions. When rumour of this seeped out—nothing could be kept secret for long among the cooped-up patients in the hospital and Truby's Medical Corps detachment looking after them—it was treated as a joke. But within a few hours

> Jesse [Lazear] was standing in the door of his laboratory, trying to coax one of his 'little birdies' from one test-tube into another. A soldier came walking by and saluted; but since Jesse had both hands engaged, he answered with a pleasant 'Good afternoon'. The man stopped. 'You still fooling about with mosquitoes, doctor?' 'Yes,' Jesse replied laughing. 'Will you take a bite?' 'Sure, I ain't scared of them.'[104]

The man was William E. Dean of Oklahoma, a member of Troop B, Seventh Cavalry, 23 years of age. He had never been in

the tropics before and had not left the military reservation for a month. The conditions for a test case were near ideal. Private Dean could be the first indubitable case of yellow fever produced experimentally. Reed was in Washington on one of his flying visits, and Agramonte later confessed to 'great trepidation'. But, trepidation or not, he and Lazear agreed to press ahead. They induced an infected mosquito to bite Dean's forearm before putting him into strict quarantine. Three days later Dean duly fell ill. Agramonte and Lazear were now, in Agramonte's words, 'on the verge of complete distraction'.

Carroll's condition was still alarming. When Captain William Gorgas visited him, Gorgas was shocked by the appearance of his colleague. Carroll was 'lying in a state of prostration, his face flushed a deep red, his eyes blood-shot, his body tossing and turning and he muttering and shouting about a mosquito'. Gorgas was convinced that Carroll was delirious and so was the nurse who was looking after him. 'He keeps babbling about some mosquito,' she told Gorgas. Gorgas had not heard of the mosquito theory before and was to remain unconvinced for some time even after Reed's first communication. He agreed with the nurse that Carroll was raving.

Reed in Washington was kept informed by daily cablegrams. 'I cannot begin to describe to you my mental distress and depression over this unfortunate turn of events,' he wrote to Kean, and implored his friend to make sure that the whole dreadful business should remain strictly confidential. By 7 September he was able to inform Jenny Carroll that her husband was 'better but not yet out of danger'. He then wrote to Carroll a solicitous message that was interrupted by more news from Cuba: 'C. much better: prognosis now regarded as fair.' Reed's reaction was added to his letter:

> Hip! Hip! Hurrah! God be praised. I shall simply go out and get BOILING DRUNK! I can never recall such a sense of relief all my life.[105]

But on the back on the envelope he scribbled: 'Did the mosquito actually DO IT?'

To add to the relief of those in Cuba, Dean's attack proved to be unusually mild, though the diagnosis was not in doubt. He too was recovering by the time Agramonte wrote his first detailed account of the two cases to Reed. He added:

> After Dean's case I agreed with Lazear not to tempt fate again by trying the mosquito on ourselves. Even I determined that no mosquito would bite me if I could help it, since even my own immunity could not be taken for granted.[106]

However, it was not for Agramonte and Lazear or even for Reed to 'determine' events. As Lazear was holding a test-tube over a patient's abdomen to capture a mosquito that had landed there, 'an insect of some sort' landed on his own arm. At first he wanted to frighten it away—mosquitoes usually took a few seconds to meditate before starting to bite—but he did not want to lose the mosquito on the patient by moving too abruptly. So 'the insect' had all the time in the world to fill itself with Lazear's blood and fly away. Nevertheless, Lazear attached so little importance to this that he did not mention the incident to Agramonte until he started to feel unwell five days later. Within 24 hours he was delirious and in such pain that he had to be restrained by two soldiers. A week later he was dead.

On the day of Lazear's death Sternberg cabled to Kean asking him to secure Lazear's notes about the experiments. The first Lazear's wife knew about her husband's illness and death was a telegram from Kean relating to the funeral; he thought that she had already been notified. She was alone with her little boy and a baby daughter Lazear had never seen when Kean's telegram arrived.[107] Reed hurried back to Cuba, but missed Carroll who had left for sick leave a day earlier. He was physically on the mend but not perhaps without some long-term emotional damage. 'My friend [meaning Reed] will return in a few days and be as brave as a lion now that the yellow fever season is over,' he wrote to Jenny before departing. The comment augured ill for their friendship. Agramonte, devastated by Lazear's death, was prevailed on to take a short leave. Reed was therefore the only one of the Commission left in Cuba. Immediately on arrival, accompanied by Kean, he went to see Wood. Kean later described the meeting.

Reed spoke to the general with 'earnest but emotional eloquence'. Apart from Carroll's near-fatal illness and Lazear's death, the month had been the worst in Havana for yellow fever for years. Reed assured Wood that he knew the answer. 'You know it or you think you know it?' Wood wanted to know.

'I am as certain as a man, sceptical by nature, can be,' Reed replied. 'But knowing is not enough.'

'No, sir, it is not.'

On behalf of the Commission and naming also Finlay and the entomologist Howard, Reed said that he could give a preliminary communication to the American Health Association Meeting in Indianapolis in October. But he would not be believed unless he could provide clear, incontrovertible evidence. There would be too many people there who had a personal stake in the bacterium and other aetiologies, some who had spent a lifetime propagating their ideas. The old controls and quarantine laws provided the livelihood of many, but it was prestige more than anything else. And of course, a genuine concern for the victims of any mistake. Wood wanted to know what Reed needed to prove his theory.

'More human experiments under strictly controlled conditions,' Reed answered.

Wood 'did not bat an eyelid'. What was necessary for such experiments, he wanted to know.

For the first time Reed hesitated. Then he said in a calm, controlled voice. 'I need a small custom-built camp, sir.'

Reed had always been on easy, friendly terms with Wood, whose incisive mind he admired; but he fully expected to be bawled out. This was the army, after all, and Reed had spent years battling and often battling in vain for essential resources and the funding of piffling projects. But Wood responded without a moment's hesitation.

'Go ahead, Reed. You can have $10,000 at once to finance the construction work.' Then he added after a short pause: 'If that is not enough, I will give you another $10,000. Don't waste any more time. Goodbye.' The birth of Camp Lazear was assured.

By 9 November Reed had found a suitable campsite about two miles from Quemados and put Dr William Ames in charge. He warned Wood 'in confidence' that 'whether we will be able to carry out the experiment before the end of the winter depended on finding enough immigrant volunteers ... willing to undertake the risk of being bitten'.[108] In the meantime Emilie had got wind of Lazear's death and was writing a succession of increasingly agitated notes. Reed assured her that he would be doing laboratory work only: she had no reason to worry over him. She was not reassured and nor was Jenny Carroll when her husband insisted on returning to Cuba.

A few days later Reed was reporting to Sternberg that so far 'three candidates had offered themselves to have themselves inoculated' and he anticipated no difficulty in getting volunteers for the 'fomites experiments'. Sternberg expressed himself gratified, especially since he too felt that 'the profession generally will not be disposed to accept the experiments so far published as definitely settling the question'. This was putting it mildly. Eugene Wasdin had just published a statement in the *Philadelphia Medical Journal* pointing with scorn at the 'inutility and folly of the experiments conducted by Dr Reed'. Nothing had been proved to justify them. Reed's 'feeble claim' that he had not been able to find Sanarelli's *Bacillus icteroides* in the blood of yellow fever victims was 'beneath notice'. The theme was taken up by other medical journals and then by the lay press. It did nothing for Emilie's morale or to reassure Lazear's deeply distressed widow when the *Washington Post* carried a prominent article about 'the pathetic fumbling of medical amateurs seeking information about the causes, conditions, symptoms and treatment of yellow fever'. Its editorial described the mosquito hypothesis as 'silly beyond compare ... whoever may have invented this idiot concept'. For some reason

Major William Gorgas was singled out for attack, the more unjust since the poor man was at that time still highly critical of Reed's work.

The weather did not help. About the middle of November a storm hit Cuba. It uprooted trees, destroyed buildings and, most grievously, blew mosquitoes, already getting sparse and listless, out to the sea. Reed was frantic, but with some difficulty persuaded some of his colleagues to go mosquito hunting. 'A few mosquitoes were seen,' Truby recalled many years later,

> as we pulled out empty cans from a rubbish heap. After several hours we came across a galvanised container ... that held some water. Carefully extracting it, we saw some of the few beautiful lyre-marked *A. aegypti* escape. Reed, Neale and Andrus secured the 'wrigglers' and picked out the eggs with great glee ... The richest yield came from cans which had been used for toilets before the installation of the sewage system.[109]

On 18 November Reed could write to Emilie that the houses for his experiments were approaching completion and that 'eight men were willing and anxious to undergo any experiments that we desire to subject them to'. They were dispatched to the camp a week in advance of the projected start of the study. From the moment of their entry they were not allowed to leave and no unauthorised person was allowed to visit them. The camp was as closely guarded as a high-security prison.

A few days later the Spanish-language *Discussion*, Cuba's leading newspaper, exploded a bomb. It carried a headline with the impact of the Spanish double exclamation marks: '¡HORRIBLE IF TRUE!' The article did not pull its punches.

> A rumour has reached us of a happening so horrible, so repulsive and so monstrous that, resisting to believe it and almost daring to deny it, we feel compelled to publish it ... solely as a rumour ... in our columns. Here is what is being said ... To those immigrants who remain for a short

446

time in Tricornia is offered work in an American Camp in Quemados, promising them one dollar a day, being taken in groups of thirty or forty men ... And here begins the horrible part. At night ... they are shut up in special habitations ... in which are released large numbers of mosquitoes which have bitten individuals with yellow fever. The object of this is to study on humans if the contagion is due or may be due to the inoculation from these bites. If the workman is taken sick and dies, the experiment has *successfully* demonstrated that the disease is indeed due to such an inoculation.[110]

The article continued to inveigh against 'this monstrous case of human ... savagery'. When all is said and done, while an impartial judge or jury might object to the emotional language, there is not a word in it that it would not sustain. And a great deal *has* been said and done, both immediately after the appearance of the article and during the next months, years and decades. It was immediately pointed out and printed in *Discussion* that so far only one person had died, possibly as a result of the experiments, and he was an American doctor. This was true but irrelevant. Later it was claimed that not one Spanish-speaking volunteer worker (or American volunteer) actually died from yellow fever, though 23 of the former did get the disease as a result of the mosquito bite. It is certainly a fact that none was ever named and in no case has a claim for compensation been put forward or at any rate preserved. This has now become rock solid evidence.

Yet it is worth recalling that on purely statistical grounds and in the light of known Cuban epidemics over the previous 20 years, a mortality of less than 5 percent in susceptible adults of no immunity would almost amount to a miracle. Miracles of sorts— that is, events contradicting medical predictions and later reconstructions—do of course happen; but even if this were such a case, it would not alter the most salient fact. Such an outcome—if it *was* the outcome—could not have been predicted. *The expectation on the basis of existing knowledge had to be that some of the volunteers would die.* This has to be said even ignoring any short-term suffering and long-term damage in those who survived. Only in the light of such a statement can some 'mitigating circumstances'—insofar as they do mitigate—be mentioned.

Reed discussed his plans with the Spanish consul in Havana and the consul assured him that all that was required was a simple explanation by a Spanish-speaking officer to the immigrant workers that the experiments entailed considerable risk. Reed was not satisfied with this. He had a written contract drawn up in Spanish, which read:

> At the completion of these experiments, within two months of the date, the undersigned will receive the sum of $100 in American gold and in case of his contracting yellow fever ... during his residence in this camp, he will receive in addition to that sum a further $100 in American gold; upon his recovery and in case of his death because of the disease, the Commission will transmit the said sum ... to the person whom the undersigned shall designate at his convenience.[111]

Reed also worked out what many years later was to be described as the first 'informed consent' form.

> The undersigned understands perfectly well that in the case of development of yellow fever in him, that he endangers his life *to a certain extent* but it being entirely impossible for him to avoid infection during his stay on this island he prefers to take the chance of contracting it intentionally in the belief that he will receive from the said Commission the greatest care and the most skilful medical service.[112]

Kean reported later—and there is no reason to doubt it—that immigrants who failed to qualify because they were under 24 'almost wept' when denied the chance to earn so much gold so easily. There is today a small bag containing some heavy material in the Walter Reed Army Institute for Research that, according to a note in Emilie Reed's handwriting, held the gold pieces with which the men who offered themselves to be bitten by mosquitoes were paid. Agramonte wrote in his reminiscences that the Spaniards in the camp told him they had never had so much to eat or been treated so kindly in all their lives. 'They expected to get yellow fever anyway when they emigrated to Havana.'

Reed did not ask any of the enlisted men to 'serve'; but, to his surprise, Private John E. Kissinger, not previously known to any of the Commission, said he would like to volunteer. It was, as Albert E. Truby was later to write, 'a stirring and unforgettable event', the more so 'since [Reed] was experiencing some difficulties with the Spaniards'. (What were the difficulties? Truby did not say.) When Kissinger insisted that he did not wish to be paid for participating but only to advance science, 'Reed saluted him, too overcome to say anything'. According to another version he uttered something suitably uplifting. Whatever he said, he was surely moved and expressed his sentiments in a suitably military language. A day or two later, Reed 'was fairly beaming when he told us that John J. Moran, a civilian clerk at General Fitzhugh Lee's Headquarters, had also volunteered. He too insisted that he did not want to be paid. Other members of the detachment ... soon followed.'[113] The last is probably a slight error of recollection. The only two Americans to volunteer for the mosquito experiments at this stage were Kissinger and Moran. Neither ever went on record giving any specific reason (if there was one). Reed was asked on one occasion two years later. He is said to have answered: 'I didn't ask. I'd have done the same.'

The other three volunteers to take part in what Reed described as the 'fomites' experiment were no less brave; but Reed explained to them that in his and his colleagues' opinion they were not likely to catch yellow fever though they would have a tough time. This was no overstatement. When Camp Lazear went into operation, it consisted of two kinds of accommodation. There were seven properly floored, spacious and comfortably furnished hospital tents, 20 ft apart. The only danger in these would be the mosquitoes deliberately introduced. Building designated 'No 1', by contrast, was a deliberately constructed horror pit, 14 by 20 ft, with a capacity of 2800 ft^3. Two tiny windows facing south were heavily shuttered to keep out the sun from the dark and humid chamber. A triple door served as a barrier against mosquitoes.

On the evening of 3 November 1900 Robert Page Cooke, a contract surgeon, Private Levi Everett Falk and Private Warren S. Jernegan entered the chamber. Of the three, only Cooke was personally known to Reed. Inside they began unpacking three large boxes of bedding and other linen stained with the vomit, blood, urine, faeces, sweat and tears of yellow fever patients, either alive and still in hospital or already dead and awaiting their post-mortem in the morgue. After making up the beds with the soiled linen, the men hung up the rest into festoons to allow the vapours to permeate their cell. Then they 'gingerly crept between the encrusted sheets and tried to sleep'. Each morning they packed the linen away and each night they unpacked it, adding new shipments as they made up their beds. Their assignment never grew easier. On 12 December, when a particularly foul shipment splashed wet filth onto them, they lost control and rushed into the air struggling with nausea, their surviving fastidiousness forbidding them to add their own vomit to what already surrounded them. They were of the generation newly shocked by the revelation of germs and bacteria 'everywhere'. All the time they awaited their first chill that would signal their destruction. (Indeed, it is a near-miracle but a well documented one that they did not catch some pestilence, even if they escaped yellow fever.) Cooke noted that 'we felt like we were all coming down with yellow fever every day'. At times the prospect seemed almost like a relief. However, they were even more frightened when they heard of Kissinger falling ill. If a mosquito's tiny bill could carry enough infection to convey the disease, what would the masses of contaminated material around them do? 'Our squad, with one accord, developed chills every morning and we greeted each other with gestures of farewell,' Cooke wrote later, 'convinced that there was no chance of us escaping.'

There were two reasons for hoping that these forebodings should prove groundless. First, Reed cared about his victims, whom he could observe through a specially constructed 'window'. He was himself a clean and fastidious person and he regarded their undertaking as 'heroic', perhaps more so than the volunteering of those who had declared themselves ready to be bitten by the mosquito. Second, it was essential for establishing the pathogenesis of the disease to show that fomites without the mosquitoes did *not* convey it. He must also have felt anxiety for the mental state of his 'guinea pigs'. The fomite experiments were enough to break down anyone's psychological defences and great care was taken not to allow the inmates to secrete away knives, forks or any potentially lethal implement after meals. (But of course, they could easily have strangled or suffocated each other or themselves.) What must strike the modern observer is that none had been subjected to any preliminary psychological testing, let alone advanced training or counselling.[114]

Cooke later recalled that each day they were served the best meals the mess could provide: fresh fruit, freshly baked bread and cakes, Cuban coffee, anything they fancied. But they did not fancy anything, even though they were allowed to eat outside in the sunshine, surrounded by mosquito nets. All rapidly lost weight and became emaciated, though all tried to keep up a minimal food intake. Two lost all body hair. All three suffered from painful constipation, despite being given massive doses of laxatives. They tried to play cards but after the first day they could not concentrate; nor could they read. 'We just lived in a kind of phantasy world,' Cooke wrote, 'we barely moved off our beds.'[115] He had vivid religious visions. The group never washed. For a week two wore garments previously worn by yellow fever patients throughout their illness without changing. All suffered violent weeping fits during the first few days. Then apathy took over.

Their time was up on 19 December. They sobbed uncontrollably when released, but none showed any sign of yellow

fever. They were nevertheless kept in strict quarantine for five days in case they harboured the infection. After a few hours most of them fell into a deep sleep helped by some medicinal concoction. They did not fully wake up for 36 hours. They did not approach their normal selves until Christmas Day.

In the meantime both Kissinger and Moran spent their day immured in beautifully salubrious surroundings but being bitten by mosquitoes. Kissinger was first bitten on 20 November by a mosquito that had fed on an extremely sick yellow fever patient on the fifth day of the attack eleven days earlier. Nothing happened. When Kissinger stayed well after a second bite from the same insect and three bites from other insects, the possibility that he was for some reason immune had to be considered. But, as Reed wrote to Truby on 10 December,

> I knew that the theory was alright! And yesterday Kissinger came down with a *beautiful* case, just eighty-four hours after being bitten on the fifth day by two twenty-one-day birds and three birds of nineteen, sixteen and twelve days.

Kissinger's condition deteriorated comparatively slowly, though by 20 December he was deeply jaundiced and delirious. He began to vomit altered blood on 22 December.

John Moran did not fall ill until 23 December. Reed and colleagues watched the mosquitoes settling down on his arms and face through the screened partition that afforded them a good view of the 'mosquito room'. Moran himself observed the mosquitoes on his arm through a magnifying glass. Later he would write an account of his experience for the *Public Health Journal*, commenting that it was getting a rather 'tedious and monotonous vigil'. Nothing happened for three weeks. Then on the evening of the 23rd he had his first chill and the aches and pains started in his limbs. However, he had made a wager with a messmate that he would attend a festive lunch in the mess the next day and did not report his symptoms until he was shivering. He was not confined to the yellow fever ward until next morning. He was by then very ill indeed. On

Christmas Day, he would later recall, the pains 'were too intense for description—not in any particular part of my body but everywhere. I prayed to die.'[116] His prayer was very nearly answered.

CHAPTER SIX

CHRISTMAS AND AFTER

Throughout this trying period Reed kept up his usual cheerful daily correspondence with Emilie. She had hoped that they would be together for Christmas (as Jenny Carroll had hoped to see her husband) and Reed was doing his best to pacify her. When she complained of 'pains in her foot', he commiserated with her over 'the nasty gout in her footsey and toseys'; but he also explained to her the importance of the experiments his group was conducting. On 9 December when Kissinger at last contracted the infection, he wrote:

> Rejoice with me, sweetheart, as, aside from the diphtheria antitoxin and Koch's discovery of the tubercle bacillus, this will be regarded as the most important work scientifically this century. I do not exaggerate, and I could shout for very joy that Heaven has permitted me to establish this wonderful way of propagating Yellow Fever. It was Finlay's theory and he deserves much credit, but he did nothing to prove it and it was rejected by all including General Sternberg ... Its importance to Cuba and the United States cannot be estimated. Kean says that the discovery is worth more than the cost of the Spanish war, including lives lost and money expended.[117]

And on another occasion:

> I know you wanted to spend Christmas together. Perhaps you are a little cross. But you will change your mind when

you are 'Mrs Surgeon General ... holding big receptions on K Street! [The headquarters of the Corps.][118]

It was the only time he mentioned what may have been a shared dream.

In a different style, Carroll too tried to comfort his wife.

Reed is very much elated because we have obtained a true case of yellow fever from the bite of his experimental mosquito. He wants to read another paper before the Pan American Congress here in February. He thinks the US Government should award us some money. This should be our consolation for spending a lonely Christmas.[119]

The friendship had lost its warmth. Was it a legacy of his illness? Old medical books on yellow fever—there are no new ones based on recent experience—often mention long periods of depression and 'character changes', but they seem to suggest that survivors ultimately return to normal. Reed did write to the Surgeon General recommending that Carroll be advanced in rank, though not perhaps as warmly as he might have done. In any case, his intervention was ineffective. Carroll was soon writing to Jenny:

I send you today's Havana paper in which I have marked an editorial paragraph referring to our work in which great credit is given to Drs Reed and Agramonte and I am not even mentioned. A newspaper man was out to interview R. That and the times General Wood's name was mentioned gives the game away. I think I shall forward the paper to General Sternberg so that he can see which way things are going.[120]

But he did not. He would wait until the Army Bill, see if he would be made a major. 'Nothing better will ever come to me.'

Pinto was another slightly disgruntled participant. Perhaps he was disappointed that he was not being honoured for volunteering to contract yellow fever, even if he did not catch it.

He had not realised that he was probably immune. Nevertheless, his disgruntlement was not directed at Reed personally. Later he would recall Reed as 'a very austere man ... not easy to get to know ... very much impressed with his own superior knowledge. But honourable.'

There was nothing austere about Reed's letters home over his memorable last Christmas in Cuba. This was a Latin country and, the sufferings of the war forgotten, there were convivial gatherings everywhere. One of the first and most resplendent was arranged by General Wood at Delmonico's Restaurant to honour Finlay. Everybody came to what Reed described as 'a very recherché affair'.

> All those who had for years turned impatiently away from the old gaffer with the obsession about mosquitoes, what a terrible bore the man was, were now eulogising him in impassioned Cuban Spanish with dear old Agramonte in the lead. The speech was almost drowned by the popping of champagne corks.

He was still able to convey the highlights with approval:

> 'For many years,' according to Agramonte, 'we on this island have fumbled in the darkness of our ignorance for a means of controlling this awful malady.' He regretted 'the fruitless search for useless remedies and costly disinfection ...' He was especially scathing about 'supposed means of immunisation, such a rich source of revenue and acclaim for some well-known scientific humbugs'. Then, in case his message was not clear enough, he singled out Sanarelli and his 'corps of so-called experts'. But their behaviour and failure was no surprise because their work was 'not instigated by the holy sentiments of humanity, nor by the natural thirst for knowledge and truth, as was ours', but 'by a bastard feeling of commercialism and a hope for early and abundant lucre, regardless of consequences'.[121]

The climax of the evening was the presentation to Finlay of a bronze statuette of a nude lady brandishing a wreath and representing the goddess of science or truth (or something), attended by two draped but voluptuous female acolytes and a mythical beast. Reed was gratified that not only Agramonte but also Guitéras, the master of ceremonies for the occasion, gave full credit to the United States Commission for vindicating Finlay's ideas. And General Wood went on record comparing their discovery to Jenner's discovery of vaccination. Only Carroll had stayed away because 'I had neither evening dress ... nor blue uniform. Nor was I really invited. And I was still suffering from my neuralgias.' Nobody, it seems, missed him much.

There were other festive gatherings. The officers of the German man of war, *Veneta*, were invited for a gala luncheon followed by a review of troops. There had been a certain frostiness during the Spanish War between Germany and the United States (and a passing wave of cousinly love towards Great Britain) when Admiral Chichester of the Royal Navy tactfully but firmly warned off the German Admiral Diedrich from interfering with Dewey's clumsy manoeuvres around Manila Bay. Now, in true Christmas spirit and in the glow of scientific cooperation, all that was forgotten. 'It was rather a swell affair,' Reed reported home, 'with several Cuban ladies and leading hostesses present after luncheon, speaking, as usual, almost incomprehensible but charming English.'

In more homely style, a celebration was arranged for United States officers and men and their families by two army wives, Mrs Stark and Mrs Kean. They trimmed a guava bush to resemble a Christmas tree and had gifts for everyone. Those for adults were 'pointed and fun'. A bibulous officer was given a miniature water waggon. Another very thin one got a cake of 'obesity soap'. Reed was given a small object with wiry appendages sticking out in all directions. It brought the house down. There was a verse attached to it that was recited among great hilarity:

Over the plains of Cuba
Roams the mosquito wild

No one can catch or tame her
For she is Nature's child.
With Yellow Jack she fills herself,
And none her pleasure mar,
Till Major Reed does capture her,
And puts her in a jar.

Reed was sorry that Emilie could not see 'the colourful style and dress of the Cuban ladies at the Governor General's Ball which a thousand people attended'. Music was furnished by a military band in the park: 'It was just like summer.' To round off the season: 'I feel as if I had not slept for a month—the entire garrison assembled at Captain Waterman's for a progressive euchre party, where we laughed, played and ate good things till after midnight.'

It was a pity that Moran, approaching the crisis of his illness and in almost unbearable pain, could not be there to participate in the jollification. No doubt he was remembered between the jokes.

Even the best things must come to an end and, by the last days of December, there was the Pan American Congress of Medicine to prepare for. It had originally been planned for Mexico, but the venue had been changed to Havana to celebrate the liberation of the island and the unshakeable solidarity of all the Americas. Reed was gratified that Sternberg had made him an official United States delegate, though he suspected that the Surgeon General may have had more than one reason for keeping him away from Washington.

It seems that the more Sternberg pondered the matter, the clearer it became to him that, without wishing to diminish Reed's merit as the executive arm, both the idea of appointing a commission to investigate the spread of yellow fever and the strong possibility of the mosquito being culpable were originally his. Although the document establishing a commission did not mention yellow fever at all, this was always the prime target in the Surgeon General's mind; and, although the Surgeon General's repeated dismissals of the mosquito theory as 'lunatic', 'garbage' and a 'Latin American figment' might lead one to believe that his faith in it was less than total, it was he who had really implanted the idea in Reed's mind. The matter was the more urgent since Sternberg's term of office was coming to an end within the next year, and it was important to fix his record for the benefit of history as well as perhaps influence the choice of his successor.[122]

Such myths, when nurtured by a manipulator of Sternberg's skill, tend to gather weight. Even Leland Howard, an admirer and by now almost a friend of Reed's, inadvertently added his part to it. In a book published in 1900 he repeatedly suggested that Reed had been sent to Cuba by Sternberg specifically to investigate the role of the mosquito in yellow fever. Howard, better versed in the doings of mosquitoes than in the wiles of surgeons general, was mortified when his error was pointed out to him: he explained that Sternberg had talked so often and at such length about the transmission of yellow fever by the mosquito at Washington's select Cosmos Club (after Reed's first report, but how was Howard to know about that?) that Howard had made the assumption that it had all been Sternberg's inspiration.

These were 'trivial matters of personalities' (as Mrs Sternberg was to describe them in her reverential biography of her husband).[123] Even before the Pan American Congress the campaign against the mosquito had began in Cuba. Gorgas, now Havana's chief health officer, had held out against Reed's ideas almost to the last. To Finlay he would hardly speak, regarding him as a simpering queen (without foundation: Finlay was a rampant heterosexual), a bore and a charlatan. Now he threw himself into the work with extraordinary energy. Of course, he had the not inconsiderable advantage of martial law to give weight to his orders; they were impressive nonetheless. Even more useful was Kean's discovery that the breeding of mosquitoes could be prevented by covering all open barrels and other containers of drinking water and stagnant pools with a thin layer of oil. Not surprisingly, this seemingly absurd decree was fiercely resisted by the population, fearing that their water supply would be permanently polluted; but General Wood imposed a penalty of $10 for any violation of the order. It worked. In time Gorgas's measures would not only free Havana from yellow fever for the first time in 150 years, but would carry him to Panama and then to the Surgeon Generalship.[124]

Carroll continued to be a problem. He kept pointing to the gaps in their knowledge. There was, of course, still much to learn. Could the larvae of an infected mosquito retain the poison when they became adults? Could the injection of blood from one person with yellow fever transmit the disease to another? Could an ultrafiltrate of plasma do so?[125] This was a crucial question. It was to be a year later that Carroll would write to Reed and Sternberg proposing another human experiment. He was back in Cuba and perhaps anxious to establish his personal credentials as an independent investigator. Though he was firmly denied permission, he certainly carried out at least one such experiment. The details were never published; but the virus aetiology was confirmed.[126] He never got any credit for it.

Before then, the Pan American Congress itself, when it came, was the usual mixture of backslapping, backstabbing, backbiting, eulogies and outrage. Reed's paper was undoubtedly the highlight of the conference—the hall was crowded, even the doors were packed with listeners—and the elderly Brazilian president of the session, Professor Vergas (chosen presumably for his impartial lack of command of both English and Spanish), was unable to stem the tide of the discussion. H.B. Horlbeck of Charleston rejoiced that the mystery of 200 years was about to be solved by none other then a fellow alumnus of the University of Virginia. (On such occasions the relevance of such matters tends to go unchallenged.) Luis Perna from Cienfuegos in Bolivia could not be expected to share this particular sentiment. He found the mosquito hypothesis neither new nor interesting and wished to go on record protesting against the disgusting idea of human experimentation. Dr Emilia Martinez of Colombia seems to have disagreed with everything that had been said and then sat down. Dr Manuel Guitéras of Mexico, by contrast, accepted Reed's results as incontrovertible, 'though they reversed all that he [Guitéras] had hitherto believed in'. Finlay spoke at length in a mixture of Spanish and English that nobody understood. When the chairman tried to sum up for the benefit of journalists present, Finlay protested that the summary was a 'travestia'. Several speakers emphasised the immense economic significance not only of the positive discovery of the mosquito, but of showing up the ineffectiveness of costly and vexatious quarantine regulations.

In reply, Reed thanked the contributors and added that: 'in regard of the moral aspects of the case, he did not think anybody appreciated the dilemma which I faced'. It was not perhaps very enlightening. Then he recalled that the members of the Commission had themselves volunteered and that the first pale survivor of the pestilence, James Carroll, was sitting in the audience at that very moment. Carroll was thereupon given a rousing ovation, an incident that may have temporarily lifted his gloom. It also served to bring the discussion on human experimentation to a dignified if not a notably illuminating close. Reed himself (as he was to write to Emilie) 'received a dozen of the warmest of handshakes from Cuban, Spanish, Mexican, South American and North American delegates, men whom I had not even met'.

The *Washington Post* was somewhat less enthusiastic, ending its editorial:

> We should like to offer the suggestion that since the controversy has now been finally resolved the yellow fever board and the Pan-American Medicals generally can well afford to cease experimenting upon inoffensive persons ... if these gifted scientists are now convinced that the mosquito is the one and only means of infection, why not devote themselves to the eradication of the medium instead of killing people by way of academic demonstration.[127]

Whether the editor was aware of it or not, his lofty counsel had already been disregarded. Gorgas and Guitéras had somehow persuaded themselves that more experiments on human volunteers were needed. Finlay was of course enthusiastic, as was the director of Los Animas hospital, Dr William Ross. They had come to believe that Reed's volunteers had survived because the fever had been promptly diagnosed and treated effectively. They decided accordingly to keep an eagle eye day and night on their potential victims and admit them to what today would be described as 'intensive care' as soon as they showed the first sign of sickening. In fact, all that was established about the disease was against such an idea. Treatment, whether early or late, had never had any effect on the outcome of the illness; and they should have known. The affair has always been murky and nobody has made much effort to clear the murk. Perhaps the reverse.

Reed was no longer on the island. Indeed. so far as he was kept in the picture, the evidence suggests that he strongly advised Sternberg against allowing further work on human volunteers. Sternberg certainly gave no encouragement. But Wood was still Governor General and must have given Gorgas the go-ahead. Eight volunteers were allowed to be bitten by mosquitoes fed on yellow-fever blood. Among them was a newly arrived nurse from Tennessee, Clara Louise Maass. Three of the volunteers, including Nurse Maass, died after the usual horrible suffering. There was a local outcry. Almost certainly, the news at home was vigorously manipulated. There was no inquiry. Nobody was held accountable. All the originators and perpetrators of the experiment went on to greater glory. The *Washington News* carried a short obituary of the 'plucky' nurse who had 'volunteered to nurse yellow fever patients, knowing about the danger'. The nursing and the danger had of course nothing to do with each other. Perhaps it was the old story of the genie let out of the bottle.

By then, Reed in Washington was grappling with tiresome administrative tasks and trying to cope with public relations. He was aware that Sternberg was taking more and more credit for the yellow fever work, but was unable to do much about it. He warned Gorgas about being careful not to let 'Old Moses' take credit for the rapid public health improvements in Havana.[128] He also asked Gorgas to 'warn Dr Finlay to look to his laurels as the proposer of the mosquito theory, since Dr Sternberg in an article in the July *Popular Science Monthly* is putting his own name forward without any reservation'. His need for money put him quickly back into harness, teaching night classes at Columbia, giving extra tutorials and examining.

He was confirmed as the next Director General of the Army Corps Pathology Museum. This was a post he had once coveted, but now looked forward with dread. (He was to fill it for exactly 23 days.) The museum was already taking up too much of his time: it was under-financed and the butt of widespread criticism. Nevertheless, there were compensations. In April Reed spoke at Johns Hopkins where his old mentor, Dean Welch, warmly praised his work, comparing it in importance to the discovery of anaesthesia. He received an LLD from the University of Michigan and an honorary MA from Harvard.

But the prospect of the Surgeon Generalship was fast slipping away. Reed probably felt genuinely ambivalent about it. 'I should be less than candid,' he wrote to Kean, 'if I said that the thought had never crossed my mind ... but, *Commandante mio*, when you and others ask me to enter into a bitter struggle ... you ask me to do something that my better sense tells me to avoid.' Kean was not so easily swept aside; and Wood undoubtedly did everything in his power to promote Reed's chances, including a word in the President's ear. Kean also warned his friend that he must not be 'too finicky' in putting out his hand for the palm.

Throughout the cold spring of 1902 the matter seemed to hang fire, though Reed's candidacy was endorsed by Osler, Welch and the presidents of Harvard and Michigan. But Sternberg wondered whether Reed, 'upright and hard-working man though he is', had the right 'political skills'. Perhaps he was right. Eventually the post was 'temporarily' filled with Colonel William H. Forwood

until his retirement. A permanent appointment would then be made. On the confidential list of those to be considered Reed was not even mentioned. In a letter to the Secretary for War, Sternberg also noted that Reed might no longer possess the 'robust physique' necessary for the job: his splendid achievements in Cuba seem to have left him in a rather indifferent state of health. Sternberg wondered if Reed needed a lengthy period of rest.

This seems to be the first reference to Reed's physical decline: whatever his shortcomings, Sternberg was an acute clinical observer. But soon Emilie and friends too noted Reed's listlessness and tired look. Kean at first attributed it to depression over the Surgeon Generalship, though such a response was not in character. Reed himself was aware that he was out of sorts, unable to cope effectively with routine daily tasks. He could no longer give his lectures without notes. He told friends that he could not even remember having written them only a few months ago. When his old friend, Louis Flexner, invited him to receive a medal and to speak at the University of Pennsylvania, he declined. 'I have hardly thought of yellow fever for a year, being engaged in nothing but humdrum duties which have reduced me to a state of helpless idiocy.' Emilie wrote to Lawrence, saying that she thought that each day took a year's toll. Her husband was losing his appetite and he was losing weight. He developed severe abdominal pain on Friday, 12 November, and his surgeon friend, William Borden, suspected a 'grumbling appendix'. He got better and then, on Sunday evening, worse again. Borden and Kean in consultation decided to operate. Emilie left an account of their last night together: 'I was not brave enough to speak to him and ask, and if he was in pain, he gave no indication of it.'

Reed refused a stretcher when he went to the Army Hospital in Washington Barracks. He even stopped on his way out of the house to write a cheque to settle a household bill. Before going under the anaesthetic he told Kean: 'I am not afraid of the knife but if anything should happen, I am leaving my wife and daughter so little.' His last words were: 'so little, so little, so little'.

Borden later said that the patient's symptoms in no way indicated the gravity of the illness. It appeared to be some kind of an appendix abscess, perhaps amoebic rather than bacterial. Borden removed the appendix, tried to 'wall off the area' and left a drain in.[129] Reed never regained consciousness, though he lingered on for another three days. On 22 November he developed signs of general peritonitis. He died on 23 November 1902. He was 51 and just missed being promoted to colonel. While Kean brought Blossom to his bedside, Emilie refused to come.

The large gathering at the graveside in Arlington Military Cemetery included many of Reed's mentors as well as friends and admirers. William Henry Welch, William Osler and Simon Flexner came. Elihu Root, Secretary of State for War, made a short speech. The epitaph read: 'He gave man control over the dreadful scourge of yellow fever.'

Emilie was left with an inadequate pension. A fund was set up in Reed's memory to which a long list of officers and academic luminaries as well as personal friends and some charitable foundations contributed. Even so, it was slow to reach its target. Emilie eventually received much-needed help from this fund until she died in 1950, aged 96. Blossom was supported until her death 14 years later. A memorial bust to Reed was then commissioned and eventually dedicated in the grounds of the Walter Reed Medical Centre in Washington on 21 November 1966. The fund and the Cuban government also arranged the restoration and preservation of Camp Lazear in memory of the first volunteer doctor to give up his life. It is still well maintained.

Carroll, still only a captain, was offered a posting to the Philippines but declined. According to Jenny, he never fully recovered from his attack of yellow fever. She was probably right. But he did succeed Reed as professor of bacteriology and pathology at the Army Medical College in Washington and received honorary doctorates from the Universities of Maryland and Nebraska. Eventually, a few months before his death in 1907, aged 53, he was promoted to the rank of major by special

Act of Congress. It helped Jenny and the children to subsist on his meagre pension.

Private Kissinger, the first non-medical volunteer to develop what Reed at the time described as a 'beautiful' case and to survive, never recovered sufficiently to return to duty. He was discharged with a commendation and a gold watch. He remained an invalid for many years, supported by his wife who took in washing. Their straits were reported to Congress on 2 March 1907, when he was given a pension of $12 a month. Within a few days this was rescinded on the grounds that it might set a 'vexatious precedent'. No doubt the 'thin end of the wedge' had its customary airing. Three years later a bill was offered to the Senate to allow him a pension; this time it passed. None of the other volunteers or their descendants was rewarded or officially commemorated.

In 1944 John J. Moran, a fit 76, had the pleasure of taking Dr Philip Hench on a conducted tour of the then still neglected site of Camp Lazear in Cuba when Hench was gathering material for his collection of Reed memorabilia. That happy occasion is still commemorated by a slightly faded photograph in the University of Virginia Library in Charlottesville.

EPILOGUE

Medicine did not stop advancing with Lister's death or even with that bloody watershed, the First World War. People today live longer and healthier lives than they did before 1914. But the character of medical progress has changed. After the First World War the formerly clear outline of individual great doctors becomes fuzzy. In this respect medical science is no different from other sciences. Neil Armstrong, the first man on the moon, never claimed to be a great scientist. Who, then, was responsible for the most spectacular scientific feat of the century? Similarly, who really deserves the credit for the antibiotic revolution? Sir Alexander Fleming had many excellent qualities—his silences were especially memorable—and his observation in 1928 that the mould penicillium inhibited the growth of some pathogenic bacteria on culture plates proved seminal. Nevertheless, he was not a man of soaring imagination, and he was as surprised as anybody to learn 10 years later that his discovery could be of therapeutic significance. Perhaps credit should go to some unnamed civil servant or politician who, in a moment of illumination under wartime stress, saw the potential of the mould and shipped a brilliant research team to the United States. Without the shipment penicillin might still be a troublesome contaminant to be kept out of a modern hospital at all cost.

Individual heroes of medicine are increasingly difficult to identify. Teamwork has become the politically correct cliché. It is, of course, what Edward Lear would have called a 'great big jumblie'. Great scientific discoveries are not made by teams any more than great pictures are painted by cohorts of artists or great poems written by writers' cooperatives. To make matters more complicated, the team delusion must accommodate the seemingly opposite trend, the ever more mindless public craving for celebrities. Medical Nobel Prizes must not only be announced: the laureates must actually be seen on the television screen, popping bottles of champagne. Is their messy skill at bottle popping what got them the prize? The station's house scientist is trundled out to explain it all. He seems to be as bemused as his viewers.

With Laennec, Semmelweis, Lister and Walter Reed there was no mystery. They wrote their own papers and books single-handedly and signed them without equivocation. This was true even of Reed, who usually included all members of the 'Reed Commission' among the authors of his reports. Nobody had any doubt who was the boss and the inspiration. Medical papers today are almost never signed by a single author. If they were, editorial eyes would scan them with suspicion. 'That chap Lister (or Laennec or Koch or Pasteur) must be a pathological loner. Odd that. Better be careful. Reject. The next paper has 25 authors. That's more like it.' The list may indeed read like the board of a multinational conglomerate. Except for insiders, it is usually impossible to apportion credit or blame. When it is done, mistakes often become apparent years later. Nobel Prizes for literature may seem eccentric; but at least one can be reasonably certain that the laureates wrote their own books. Nobel Prizes for medicine have been for years distributed to important *fields* of advance (or what the assessors hope will prove important fields), representatives being plucked from a crowd of tillers.

The scene has been changing ever since the end of Wallace's 'Wonderful Century'. Banting and Best, a young Canadian doctor and medical student respectively, shared their Nobel Prize for discovering insulin with their head of department, J.J. Macleod. Macleod was a popular teacher and a charming host, but he had spent the time of the crucial experiment hunting in the Rockies, unaware that anything out of the ordinary was afoot in his laboratory. Following a still widespread convention, his name was included in the historic paper for providing 'facilities' and 'encouragement'. Conversely, all the benchwork that led to the discovery of streptomycin was carried out by Alfred Schatz, S.E. Waksman's post-doctoral student. While Schatz may not have been a genius, his kind of benchwork needed more than an industrious plodder. Yet he never got a mention in the citation or a share of the prize money. At least one player in the DNA saga was airbrushed out of the picture by her longer-lived male colleagues. In countless similar instances, who had the original ideas? The professor or his incoherent PhD student? Nobody knows any more.

And yet, the lone medical hero or heroine experiencing a moment of truth in the laboratory, at the bedside or in the small hours of the morning cannot be wholly extinct. Indeed, one must assume that he and she still exist. Medicine may be advancing more slowly than it did 50 years ago, but it is still advancing. Without the moments of truth the advance would have stopped. Of course, not all advances prove unmixed blessings. The creative moments cannot be blamed for that. The Laennecs, Semmelweises, Listers and Reeds of today may no longer be celebrities. They may not even be execrated. Indeed, they may be—and they may remain—unrecognisable. Let that not deter them. Long long, long may they flourish.

NOTES

INTRODUCTION

1. It is, to be fair, a mouthful. The Latin *Ars longa, vita brevis est* is more manageable.
2. Both the single-serpent and the double-serpent variety have been used as medical emblems since the sixteenth century. The Royal Army Medical Corps chose the former while the United Stated Army Medical Corps opted for the latter.
3. And the minds of animals? Perhaps. The fact that old elephants find their way to graveyard sites at the premonition of death has been advanced for centuries as evidence that animals too are aware of death. The 'fact' is a legend: what animals think remains a mystery.
4. And in those that are spiritually deprived, like much of Western Europe and the United States of America.
5. Increased intracranial pressure, causing headache, blunting of consciousness, progressing to coma and death, can be the result of bleeding inside the unyielding skull. This can follow a trivial-seeming injury. When the source of the bleeding is a vein rather than an artery, the progression of symptoms and signs (including bizarre behaviour and mental changes) can extend over months, even years. In such cases the trephining of the skull may have allowed the slowly growing semi-fluid blood clot to escape and may have restored the prehistoric patient to prehistoric health.
6. The school's first named principal, the Benedictine monk Alphanus from the nearby monastery of Monte Cassino, travelled to Constantinople in 1086 and became acquainted with Greek and Latin medical texts, although most of the school's sources were Arabic translations rather than the Graeco-Roman originals. Great Arab physicians like Avenzoar (Abu Merwan Ibn Zohr, 1113–1162) and learned Persian doctors like the great Avicenna (Ibn Sina, 980–1037) added their own wisdom and experience. Students came from as far as Poland and Scotland and of course from the Norman homeland in today's France.
7. However, there was no named doctor among their ancestors.
8. Aureolus Theophrastus Bombastus von Hohenheim (1493–1541), a celebrated physician from Basel in Switzerland, is said to have coined the name Paracelsus to indicate his superiority to the great Roman physician, Celsus. (As he put it himself more pithily: 'All the universities and all the old writers put together are less knowledgeable than my arsehole.') He attacked superstition and witchcraft and introduced a form of chemotherapy. He also formulated a secret remedy named laudanum, but it is unlikely to have contained opium.

    Ambroise Paré (1510–1590) began his career as a barber surgeon and became first an army surgeon then surgeon to France's royal family. He benefited from Vesalius's anatomical discoveries and applied some of them with astonishing success to gunshot and other wounds. He reinvented many forms of surgical ligatures and introduced trusses for hernias.

Jacobus Sylvius was a French anatomist (Jacques Dubois, 1478–1555) who took up medicine at the age of 51, studied in Montpellier and became a famous professor of anatomy in Paris. He described the Aqueduct of Sylvius, a fine passage leading from the cerebral ventricles to the central spinal canal, but not the Sylvian fissure of the brain, which was named after another later anatomist (Francis de la Boë, 1614–1672) also confusingly known as Sylvius.

Sir Thomas Browne (1605–1682) was an English writer and physician who, after studying at Pembroke College, Cambridge, travelled extensively and eventually settled in Norwich. While the civil war raged, he was serenely absorbed in metaphysical speculation on the meaning of life. His scorn expressed in his majestic work, *Religio Medici*, for 'the trivial and vulgar' union between the sexes did not imperil his long and happy marriage to his wife, Dorothy.

9. In his book on gunshot wounds Paré modestly concluded his case histories with 'I dressed him, God healed him'.

10. Andreas Vesalius's *De humani corporis fabrica* was based mainly on dissections carried out on executed criminals in Padua, where the author was a teacher at the university, although it was published in Basel in 1543 by the pioneering printer Joannes Oporinus. Vesalius (Wesal) himself was born in today's Belgium in 1514 and studied in Louvain; his mother was English. His great work dispelled many misconceptions that had been copied from textbook to textbook since the days of Galen. The masterly woodcut illustrations were added by Ian Stephan van Calcar (1459–1546), from the Netherlands.

11. William Harvey (1578–1657) made his great announcement of the circulation of the blood in 1628 in a treatise entitled *Exercitatio anatomica de motu cordis et sanguinis in animalibus*. A festive oration was instituted in his memory a year before he died.

12. John Hunter (1728–1793) served in the army before he became surgeon to St George's Hospital in London. He wrote on a wide range of anatomical and pathological subjects and bequeathed his collection of animal and human specimens to the Royal College of Surgeons of England.

13. Since the works of Harvey and Hunter are voluminous and well annotated, this is not usually arduous and takes no more than a few minutes.

14. This is true of most sciences, but is in sharp contrast to works of art, music and literature. Only a few dedicated scholars actually read Harvey today, but every schoolchild reads Shakespeare; and millions still enjoy listening to Mozart while nobody would want to listen to a lecture by John Hunter. The sciences are the path to individual oblivion.

15. Edward Jenner, a Gloucestershire country doctor, discovered the protection given by cowpox inoculation against smallpox. His historic paper, 'Inquiry into the Cause and Effects of the Variolae Vaccinae', was published in 1798. His experiments almost certainly included injecting hopefully protected—i.e. vaccinated—individuals with smallpox. He died in 1823, aged 74.

William Withering, a practitioner in Cheshire and an ardent amateur botanist (as were many eighteenth-century doctors), discovered the extraordinary and still mysterious cardiotonic properties of infusion of foxglove leaves (digitalis). He recorded his observations in *An Account of the Foxglove*, published in 1785. Digitalis preparations are still widely used but have occasional toxic effects. It is unlikely that a licence would be granted to Withering's preparation today. He died in 1779, aged 58.

16. Thomas Sydenham, 'the English Hippocrates', gave classic descriptions of many diseases, including gout, measles and scarlet fever (which he named), as well as introducing the chinchona plant (quinine) to England. He was a captain of the horse in the Puritan army in the Civil Wars before turning to medicine. He died in 1689, aged 65.

17. Hermann Boerhaave was undoubtedly a charismatic teacher and great writer of letters and textbooks. His *Institutones Medicae* became the doctors' bible in the eighteenth century. He died in 1738, aged 70.

18. 'Clinical' literally means bedside, from κλινή meaning bed in Greek.

19. Hence the surgical style 'Mr' in Britain, though nowhere else.

20. In pregnancy the urine sometimes contains traces of albumin and may become slightly turbid. The test is far from foolproof, but if the inspection had other uses early physicians kept the secret to themselves.

21. Laboratory tests, X-rays and similar investigations were introduced as extensions of the patient's physical examinations. None existed before the mid-nineteenth century.

22. Regular temperature charts were unknown until Carl Wunderlich published his monumental *Medical Thermometry* in 1858 and 1868 based on tens of thousands of measurements.

23. The problem is compounded by a special brand of medical Latin that even classical scholars find difficult to understand.

24. The name of Friedrich Anton Mesmer, a German physician, has passed into the language in 'mesmerism'. He was born in 1734, the son of a factor on the estate of the Prince Archbishop of Constance on the German side of the lake, and, under ecclesiastical patronage, received a good education at various Jesuit colleges and universities. Eventually he qualified as a doctor in Vienna in 1766, his doctoral thesis expounding the influence of heavenly bodies diffusing a subtle fluid throughout the universe. This, he suggested, acted on the nervous system of all living creatures, including humans. He called the effect 'animal magnetism'. Essentially, he was an immensely accomplished hypnotist and this ensured him an intermittently glittering if scandalous career, first in Vienna, where he became a close friend of the Mozarts, and then in pre-revolutionary Paris. His mumbo jumbo and his steadfast refusal to impart his 'secret' to anybody (or perhaps his success) got him expelled from most European capitals. He died in 1815 in apparently contented obscurity, reconciled to his church and tending his patients, in the village of his birth, aged 81.

25. See Part I, Laennec.

26. This is how they were described in the 1950s by an eminent chest physician, renowned for his wizardry with the stethoscope but outclassed by junior radiologists in the detection of early tuberculosis.

27. This as much as 'fresh air' was the reason that sanatoria were so often on mountain tops or in remote and inaccessible parts of the country.

28. See Part II, Semmelweis.

29. See Part III, Lister.

30. Lytton Strachey's *Eminent Victorians* was published in 1918. It examined the Victorian age through four individual lives. The chosen four were Florence Nightingale, General Gordon, Dr Arnold of Rugby and Cardinal Manning.

31. See Part IV, Reed.

32. The valves are so shaped and disposed that they prevent the backward flow of blood in the veins. (Varicose veins result from incompetent valves.) The valves had been described before Harvey but their significance was not appreciated. Harvey recognised that they meant that blood could flow only in one direction, that is *circulate*, rather than moving in a kind of ebb-and-flow motion.

33. Antonj van Leeuwenhoek (1632–1723), a Delft draper and amateur lens grinder, communicated his discovery of the microscope to the Royal Society of London in 1677. Microscopy became his lifetime hobby, but it was not put to medical use for another hundred years.

34. The real significance of the discovery of Johann Gregor Mendel (1822–1884), an Augustinian monk working in Brno in what is today the Czech Republic, is still often misunderstood. Of course, the inheritance of traits and characteristics had been known before him and its importance was appreciated by breeders of royalty and race horses alike. But before him inheritance was regarded as a kind of amorphous soup, a mixture of paternal and maternal soups. Mendel realised that individual traits (which were not called genes for another 50 years) were inherited individually and independently of each other and that each individually obeyed certain laws. Like the recognition of individual elements in chemistry, individual traits made inheritance capable of being studied scientifically. Mendel's results with his peas were in fact almost too good to be true—there was virtually no scatter around a mean—and may have been at least partly worked out in advance on paper.

35. See Part IV, Reed.

36. The term was coined by Paul de Kruif and was the title of his bestseller published in 1936. The book's relentlessly upbeat and jolly tone is hard to take today, but de Kruif undoubtedly created the prototype of the hero medical researcher.

37. See Part III, Lister.

38. See Epilogue (but without skipping the book in between).

39. Phthisis was the medical name for tuberculosis. The lay term was consumption.

40. The late Roy Porter, not a doctor himself, called his massive and far-ranging history of medicine *The Greatest Benefit to Mankind*. Unsurprisingly the title pleased doctors; but was it meant in all seriousness? (Porter's tragic and untimely death prevented the present writer from probing the truth.) Great, perhaps; but greatest? Even discounting the contribution of the great spiritual teachers (and artists, composers and poets) to the happiness of mankind, and forgetting such momentous material discoveries as the wheel, fire, speech and even (dare one say it?) the printing press and television, medicine has surely been responsible for both harm and good. This is probably still true, and true of individual doctors as well as of medicine as a whole. To the present writer, good doctors are good doctors because they are good people; and bad doctors are bad doctors because they are bad people. There is of course a moral dimension to medicine as such, but no more so than there is to any other pursuit.

41. The condition is called retrolental fibroplasia and involves the formation of opaque scar tissue behind the lens. Its mechanism is still incompletely understood.

42. Taken early in pregnancy the drug caused thousands of babies to be born with missing digits, missing limbs, with other serious deformities or dead. It continued to be advertised by the makers in Germany and the United Kingdom long after the first alarming reports began to appear. Nobody was ever charged for the mass murder. The United States was saved from disaster by a middle-ranking employee of the Food and Drug Administration who was dissatisfied with the safety checks and was almost driven from her job by irate pressure groups.

43. See Part II, Semmelweis.

44. Here as elsewhere in the book, medicine and medical are used to embrace all branches of medicine, including surgery, pathology and other specialities.

45. The composer set great store by the opinion of the two gifted Fräulein Auenbrugger and dedicated a sparkling group of his middle-period clavier sonatas to them.

46. The opinion attributed by Horace Walpole to Charles II when referring to a bad preacher popular in his own parish.

47. Clark, a walking medical disaster, later became Queen Victoria's physician and presided over the death of the Prince Consort. He was duly knighted.

48. A prolific conflator of popular histories has identified the decade after Waterloo as the time when 'the Modern' was born. He has filled 1000 pages describing it. It was certainly the decade of the diagnostic revolution, of Laennec and of the stethoscope. Health is rarely a matter of total indifference to people. The practice of medicine is not entirely unrelated to health. Yet Laennec and the stethoscope get no mention, and tuberculosis, a transforming influence on the arts, music, literature and way of life of the next century, is dismissed in a cursory page and a half. Bizarre.

PART I: LAENNEC

1. It was not geographical configuration. Both during the Revolution and during the Second World War and German occupation the centres of resistance were France's flattest and most hilly regions, the Vendée and Savoie.

2. The latter was Beaufranchet d'Ayat, son of Fragonard's favourite model, the lovely Mademoiselle O'Murphy.

3. The word 'esclave' was never used in France, 'ebony' being the socially acceptable euphemism understood by all. The institution was formally abolished by the Revolution in 1792 but re-legalised (under the influence, it is said, of Josephine, a Créole herself from the West Indies) by Bonaparte in 1802.

4. The butchery in the Vendée by the Republican armies was almost on a modern scale. At the end of the 'campaign' the Republican general, François-Joseph Westerman, proudly reported back to the Committee of Public Safety: 'There is no more Vendée, citizens. It has perished under

our free swords along with its women and children. I have buried thousands [and he meant it literally and often alive] in the marshes and mud of Savenay. Following the orders you gave me I have crushed the children under the feet of our horses and massacred women who at least will engender no more brigands. I have no prisoners with which to reproach myself.' There have been French historians, justly proud of some achievements of the Revolution, who have denied or at least tried to tone down these events, just as there are so-called historians who assert that the Holocaust is a myth.

5. He had had an adventurous youth, qualifying in Montpellier and spending some months in London as an assistant to John Hunter, surgeon to St George's Hospital. He had to re-qualify before he was allowed to settle and start practising in Nantes.

6. What across the Channel became Cornwall.

7. The name is often spelt Laënnec to indicate that the two vowels are pronounced separately, but the family themselves never did so. The word is of somewhat uncertain Celtic origin. The eminent Celtic scholar Joseph Loth discovered an old Breton word, *laennoc*, which means man with a lance (*llain* in middle Welsh). From lance to lancet is but a short step, providing a pleasingly prophetic etymology.

8. An interesting early work on Laennec is a *Thèse de Doctorat* by M.H. Saintignon, *Laennec, sa vie et son oeuvre* (Paris, 1904). Much of Laennec's early work and letters were collected and reprinted by his devoted biographer and Guillaume Laennec's successor as professor of medicine in the University of Nantes in two authoritative volumes: A. Rouxeau, *Laennec avant 1806* and *Laennec après 1806* (Paris, 1912). Previously unpublished works were collected in a centenary volume published by the Editions Masson (Paris, 1926). His early *Fable* and translations from Latin dating from his schoolboy days are reprinted in an affectionate volume, E. Rist, *La Jeunesse de Laennec* (Paris, 1955). A more up-to-date and sympathetic biography by Roger Kervran, himself a Breton chest physician, with a good bibliography, has been published in an excellent translation by D.C. Abrahams-Curiel, *Laennec, His Life and Times* (Oxford, 1960).

9. Most women in both the Laennec and Guesdon families (aunts and cousins of Théo) seem to have died young and R. Kervran suggest that the illness was tuberculosis. Yet in later life Laennec always praised the climate and air of Brittany and returned there himself. But *la phthisie* was certainly becoming common in France during the last decade of the eighteenth century.

10. The Collège had been recently re-organised by its young principal, Father Fouché de Rouzerolles, later member of the Convention, regicide and 'butcher of Lyon', even later imperial minister of the police, created Duc d'Otranto by Napoleon.

11. See Note 8.

12. It was perhaps not quite his invention. A form of guillotine had been used on the Continent and in England since the Middle Ages, and an early model called the 'Maiden' is preserved in Edinburgh. Dr Joseph-Ignace Guillotine was born in Saintes in 1738 and in 1789 put forward two proposals. First, that all criminals sentenced to death, regardless of their station in society, should be executed in the same way; and second, that the act should be swift and painless. The propositions were adopted by the Convention and a German piano maker called Schmidt was commissioned to build and furnish a machine for each département of France. 'Executions' were first

carried out on dead bodies. The first live criminal to be executed was a highwayman called Genie. Contrary to legend Dr Guillotine was not killed by his own machine, though he was imprisoned during the Terror and was in line to perish when he was saved by Robespierre's fall. He returned to practice and died in 1814.

13. The instantaneousness of death by guillotine has been argued about from early days and certainly since the execution of Charlotte Corday, murderer of Marat. Nervous reflex arcs confined to the head and upper neck may continue to function for some minutes after the head has been severed from the body, including reflexes responsible for moving the lower jaw and even lips and cheeks. When the head of Charlotte Corday was held up, onlookers swore that it was addressing the crowd and even quoted what it said. A similar story was told later of Queen Marie Antoinette.

14. In contrast to Dr Guillotine, whose intentions were plainly humanitarian, Dr Jean-Paul Marat, whose name was adopted by Carrier's special constables and similar scum elsewhere, was a doctor (an MD of the University of St Andrews) whose gutter journalism during the early days of the Terror was partly at least responsible for many innocent deaths, including that of the great chemist Lavoisier.

15. G. Le Notre, *Les Noyades de Nantes* (Paris, 1947).

16. Even today most villages in Brittany have their particular patron saints whose feast days are celebrated by solemn *Pardons*. The events inspired Gauguin, Van Gogh and many other artists of the Pont Avon group. See also Note 89.

17. The romantic ballads and epic stories, claimed to have been discovered and translated but actually written by the Scottish tutor James Macpherson, made an even greater impression on the Continent than in Britain. Goethe was an admirer as were Pushkin and Arany, and Schubert set some of the words to music.

18. In Paris the corresponding Supreme Being was called Vertu and was crowned by Robespierre.

19. As happens after wars and other terrible upheavals, the end of the Terror was marked in France by a wave of festivities and the collapse of public morality and decorum. The Directory was its public face.

20. On the death of his older brother, Louis XVIII, Artois was to become king of France, the last to be crowned in the Cathedral of Rheims, under the name Charles X in 1824. He was monarch when Laennec died.

21. The plotters planning to overthrow the Directory were intent on using the 'hero of the hour', General Bonaparte, as their dumb instrument. As was to happen again with future dictators, the instrument took charge of the plot.

22. It was in Paris's Notre Dame to break with the royal tradition of the Sacré in Rheims.

23. The transformation of Consulate to Empire (which so enraged Beethoven that he changed the dedication of his Third Symphony from 'To Bonaparte' to 'For a Hero') was endorsed by 3,572,329 votes to 2,579. Nobody questioned the genuineness of the result.

24. Even dictating his memoirs in St Helena, Napoleon seemed puzzled by the outcry that had greeted the abduction and execution of the Duc d'Enghien. There had been several royalist plots on Napoleon's life (still as Bonaparte, First Consul) and the killing of Enghien was in the venerable tradition of Corsican vendettas.

25. In 1803. The plot to assassinate the First Consul was discovered before it could be put into effect. Of Cadoudal's fellow conspirators, Pichegru was 'found strangled' in the Temple and Moreau was allowed to go into exile in England.

26. R.-T.-H. Laennec, *La Guerre des Vénètes* (Masson, 1931). The manuscript was discovered in old family archives by Laennec's biographer, A. Rouxeau, and published in a lavish format. The Venetes (without the accents) were a genuine Gallic tribe mentioned by Julius Caesar.

27. The Farmers General were the tax collectors of the Ancien Régime. They became immensely rich (and immensely hated), though not all were corrupt. The great chemist Lavoisier and his father-in-law were among the honourable ones. The toll was reimposed by the Bourbon Restoration; hence the setting of Act II of *La Bohème*. It was finally abolished by the Third Republic, but the names of the tollgates or *Portes* were resurrected in naming the directions of the Métro.

28. Out of France's total urban population of less than 2 million. About 95 percent of the country's total population of 26 million still lived in isolated farms, hamlets, villages and small country towns. Young people tended to migrate to Paris to study (like the Laennec brothers) or to make their fortune. Their dream of a contented old age was to retire to the country, and many did.

29. Benoit, the landlord in *La Bohème*, climbs up from the ground floor to knock on the door of the Bohemians, living under the roof. But where was Mimi going when her candle went out?

30. In contrast to the monsters and buffoons who sometimes seemed like Bonaparte clones in the twentieth century, the prototype had a great respect for true expertise in every field—he himself was an expert in the art of war—and surrounded himself with the best talents available to him. He created the Council of State to advise and educate him; it was and remained after him the most powerful body in the French state. The modern French school and university system was largely its creation.

31. Almost every eminent French physician or surgeon over the next 100 years whose name is eponymously enshrined in modern medical parlance was a *practicien*, from Jean Guillaume Lugol (of Lugol's solution for thyroid deficiency) to Prosper Ménière (of Ménière's disease of tinnitus and giddiness) and Jean-Martin Charcot (of syphilitic Charcot's joints).

32. The coat of arms displayed a bird, perhaps a *corbeau* or raven; hence the name.

33. Born in 1769, the future Emperor was six years Corvisart's senior. After a false start as a Corsican freedom fighter against the French, he so distinguished himself as a French artillery officer at the recapture of Toulon from the Anglo-Royalists in 1793 that he was made a brigadier general. Besides Goethe's *The Sorrows of Young Werther*, he already carried Plutarch in his greatcoat pocket. There was to be no stopping him.

34. The seat of the soul was still the pineal gland, a comparatively unimportant and vestigial structure. It was located there by no lesser man than Descartes, who was fascinated by its shape and central position between the two hemispheres of the brain.

35. It is often said that life expectancy was short in the eighteenth and nineteenth century. Unqualified, the statement is nonsense. Because of the high infant and childhood mortality, life expectancy was indeed short *at birth* compared to the twenty-first century. But because only the fittest

survived until late middle age, life expectancy at 60 was probably as high as it is today and at 70 it may have been higher.

36. Georges Léopold Chrétien Frédéric Dagobert Cuvier was born in Montbélard, then under the rule of the king of Würtenberg. He was a prodigy as a student in Stuttgart. After a spell of private tutoring he was called to Paris to preside over the Jardin des Plantes. He began to publish papers on the fossil bones of Montmartre, which eventually led to his great work, *Recherches sur les ossements fossiles des quadrupèds*. Under Napoleon he re-organised the scientific education of most of Europe and became president of the Council of State. Louis XVIII revered him. His books transformed anatomy, comparative anatomy and embryology; he was widely regarded as the greatest naturalist of his age. He died in 1832 aged 63. The main venous channels in the embryo (the 'Ducts of Cuvier') are named after him.

37. Later professor of surgery and great-grandfather of the painter Gustave.

38. On and off for ten years before the Revolution the Protestant Genovese banker and millionaire was hailed as France's financial saviour. He did institute a few minor useful reforms in running the country's chaotic finances, but his real achievement was to borrow huge sums rather than raise taxes or curb the Court's extravagance. On balance, like most such saviours, he probably hastened rather than delayed the *déluge*. Madame Necker (née Suzanne Cuchod, Edward Gibbon's early love) used her husband's vast fortune and her own exceedingly modest literary talent to found a salon and indulge in fashionable charities like endowing hospitals. The celebrated writer and bluestocking Madame de Staël was their daughter.

39. It did not save him from the guillotine under Robespierre.

40. The Treaty ended the war with Austria that had been decided by Bonaparte's near-defeat-turned-into-victory at Marengo and Moreau's victory at Hohenlinden.

41. Aphorisms were the craze of the age: everybody with any pretension to academic excellence wrote a set for the edification of his students and friends. Corvisart wrote some himself around 1805, which are staggering in their cynicism. (Number I reads: 'Medicine is *not* the art of healing. That happens occasionally but it is rare.') The collection was not published until 1929 (collected by F.-V. Mérat, Masson, Paris).

42. Since he died in 1787 aged 54, Corvisart could not have met him personally.

43. Franz-Joseph Gall preached that the brain was the organ of character; and that individual characteristics were governed by specific localised areas or 'bumps'. These could be recognised and from their size character profiles could be deducted. Phrenology was fashionable for a time in most European countries and in the United States. It was also important, since it could be used to underpin the moral therapy of mental illnesses pioneered by Pinel. Apparently criminal and anti-social behaviour could be explained by the inborn anatomical configuration of an individual's brain. With political reaction in the ascendant, Gall was hounded out of Vienna in 1805 for his 'materialistic' views. He died in poverty in 1828, aged 70.

44. It was—and remains—a brilliant technique, though it has now been superseded by X-rays and other more expensive and cumbersome imaging techniques. Auenbrugger sometimes followed his patients over weeks or

even months, keeping careful notes of changes in the sounds he elicited and eventually correlating his findings with post-mortem appearances.

45. It was entitled, a little forbiddingly to modern readers, *Inventum novum in percussione thoracis humani ut signo abstrusos interim pectoris morbos detegendi*, but in fact is extremely clear and readable as well as astonishingly comprehensive. It was translated into English by John Forbes in 1824 under the title: *A New Invention for Percussing the Human Chest to Detect Hidden Signs of Disease*. M. Neuburger published a useful biographical note to a facsimile edition of the work (see Bibliography).

46. Percussion as Auenbrugger described it was direct tapping of the chest with the tip of a crooked finger, but it was soon modified by having a slither of wood placed on the chest and tapping on the wood. This in turn led to the present practice of laying on the chest the middle finger of the left hand instead of the slither of wood.

47. Sadly, both the music and the text of *The Little Sweep* are now lost. Auenbrugger was also an accomplished player of the harpsichord and chamber organ. Musical evenings in his house on the Mehlmarkt were popular social events.

48. A day after Auenbrugger's death Napoleon took up residence in Schönbrunn for the second time, soon to be joined by Corvisart.

49. There had been one previous translation by Rosière de Chassagne of Montpellier, but the translator clearly misunderstood the Latin text and admitted that he had never himself tried the technique.

50. The translation was far more than a rendering into French. It clearly distinguished (for the first time so far as one can tell) dilatation of the heart from hypertrophy. The former reflects a terminal failure to cope with the workload. The latter is a compensatory increase of the size of the heart muscle comparable to the increased musculature of an athlete. In both the size of the heart enlarges; but the significance of the two kinds of enlargements is entirely different.

51. For this alone he deserved to have a Métro station named after him, the only doctor to be so honoured. (Clemenceau was honoured because of his attainments as a statesmen, not as a general practitioner in Montmartre.)

52. In every creative field they illuminated the first half of the nineteenth century: Keats, Shelley, the Brontës, Schiller, Petöfi in literature, Chopin, Weber, Pergolesi in music ... the list could be continued.

53. *La vie fulgurente d'un génie* is the apt subtitle given to a biography by Dobo and Ruel (see Bibliography).

54. Said to have been founded by Saint Landry in 651, there was a hospital of sorts on the present site in the Cité by the eighth century. Unlike the present edifice (opened in 1877) the old hospital was vast, spanning the Seine, the two sections connected by an internal bridge, itself a ward. In 1788 it had 1100 beds, each bed holding two to five patients. In emergencies patients were placed atop the canopies of the *charniers* or on heaps of straw on the floor. The largest wards might accommodate up to 800 patients. The average patient population at the outbreak of the Revolution was of the order of 3500. As in other Hôtels Dieu throughout the country and in several other hospitals in Paris, the medieval tradition was still alive: the patients included not only the sick but also many of the city's homeless, vagrants, insane, foundlings and cripples. (The Hôtel Dieu probably had more inmates than the whole hospital population of London at the time.) Voltaire wrote in 1768: 'You have in Paris a Hôtel-Dieu where eternal

contagion reigns, where patients are piled on top of each other and where they bring to each other pestilence and death.' It had not changed much by 1789 when Desault was appointed chief of surgery and started to improve his own service. The air was so foul that most doctors and visitors pressed sponges soaked in vinegar to their noses as soon as they entered. (A similar image is shown in Gros's monumental painting of the plague hospital visited by Bonaparte in Jaffa.) The wards and corridors resounded with the screams of women in labour, of patients undergoing operations, of the sick in pain and of the violently insane. The estimated mortality rate of those admitted was 30–35 per cent.

55. Pierre Joseph Desault was an impressive representative of surgery in the process of transformation. He died aged 51 in 1795.

56. He is also commemorated on the pediment of the Panthéon, by a small museum in his native Thourette and by annual medical meetings in Paris named in his honour *Entretiens de Bichat*.

57. Sydenham was sometimes labelled 'the English Hippocrates'. To those who like such labels Hippocrates was presumably the 'Greek Hippocrates'.

58. If histologists crave paternity, this can be more appropriately bestowed on Marcello Malpighi (1628–1694), professor of anatomy and a popular teacher in Bologna, who gave an excellent description of the microscopic structure of the skin and the excretory apparatus of the kidney.

59. The concept of connective tissue diseases like rheumatoid arthritis was a significant medical advance of the first half of the twentieth century. Steroids have been particularly useful in their management.

60. Hannah K. Barsky, *Guillaume Dupuytren, a Surgeon in his Place and Time* (New York, 1984), also provides a valuable survey of the emancipation of surgery in France.

61. Paré's great innovation as a military surgeon was to cauterise infected or potentially infected wounds. He undoubtedly saved many lives (though he modestly claimed to have merely dressed wounds while God healed them). He also operated unsuccessfully on Henri II after the king suffered a fatal head injury in a friendly joust. To 'practise', he asked and was given permission to operate on three imprisoned villains first. He died in 1590, aged 80.

62. If the absence of registration did not noticeably affect mortality, Dr Guillotin's invention coincidentally did. In England too anybody can practise medicine and surgery, but they must not pretend to be qualified to do so. The French decree was among the first to be revoked by Bonaparte. The changes in the regulation and status of the profession are well described in M. Ramsey, *Professional and Popular Medicine in France, 1770–1830: The Social World of Medical Practice* (Cambridge, 1988).

63. He realised that after complicated open fractures a wounded man's only hope of survival was instant amputation. He must have saved thousands of life. He died in 1820 aged 70.

64. Larrey taught and wrote a great deal in addition to taking part in 22 military campaigns. He died in 1842 aged 78.

65. Dufriche-Desgenette accepted the first but declined the second. He died in 1826 aged 68.

66. The Emperor had many faults, but Alfred Cobban's assertion (in his majestic and immensely readable *History of Modern France*) that, unlike Marlborough or Wellington, he cared not at all for the lives of his men is unfair. The surgical care of the wounded in and after battle was infinitely

superior in the French army to that in the English, Prussian, Austrian or Russian armies. Whether or not this expressed genuine concern or was calculated to raise the soldiers' morale is anybody's guess.

67. He is still revered in French surgery, with a street named after him near the Ecole de Médicine. Internationally his name is linked to the thickening and contracture of the connective-tissue sheath under the skin of the palms (the so-called palmar fascia), leading to the progressive bunching together of the fingers. Dupuytren first observed it in his coachmen and attributed it to the long-continued holding of the reins. This was not implausible at a time when coaches and coachmen were common, though it hardly explains the frequency of the condition today. The cause remains unknown and treatment is less than satisfactory, but the deformity is still called Dupuytren's contracture. He died in 1835 aged 58.

68. Sir Astley, who had just retired from his post at Guy's Hospital, was showing his visitor from Paris round the park of his palatial country mansion. 'Beautiful trees,' Dupuytren commented. 'Yes. And every morning I keep wondering which one I should choose to hang myself on,' his host replied. Dupuytren made an instant diagnosis. 'You must go back to London at once and resume your work,' he advised. Sir Astley did and died happily in harness in 1871, aged 78.

69. See note 8. Bayle's nephew, A.-L.-J. Bayle, a distinguished physician himself and the first to establish that general paralysis of the insane (GPI) is a late sequel of syphilis, became Gaspard-Laurent's first and best biographer in 1834.

70. He was born in Saint André in 1745, studied medicine in Toulouse and became chief of medicine at the Salpetrière in Paris in 1779. During the Revolutionary Terror a tailor expressed subversive views about the trial of Louis XVI. Realising that he had been overheard, he became obsessed with the idea that he was about to be executed. He was confined to the lunatic asylum in the Salpetrière under Pinel's care. Pinel first arranged for the tailor a kind of occupational therapy, letting the patient repair some of his fellow inmates' clothing for a token fee. When this resulted in only temporary improvement, Pinel arranged a charade of a mock trial where the patient was formally acquitted of any treasonable views. As a result, Pinel noted, the man's symptoms disappeared (though they later returned 'in a milder form'). In his great work, *Traité médicophilosophique sur l'aliénation mentale* (quickly translated into English, German and Spanish), Pinel argued with great force about the moral causes and treatment of certain mental disorders and pleaded eloquently for reformed asylums and for new approaches to the treatment of the insane. He was admired by Laennec as a man rather than as a doctor. In England his views were first adopted by the Quaker Retreat in York. He died in 1826, aged 81.

71. Today, sadly, such a remark would disqualify an examiner for life.

72. The history of tuberculosis is discussed in more detail in T. Dormandy, *The White Death* (London, 1999).

73. Struma and phyma were some.

74. In English-speaking countries tuberculosis of the spine is still called Pott's disease. Pott, a surgeon to St Bartholomew's Hospital, died in 1738, aged 75.

75. They were spotted on wall paintings in ancient tombs by Auguste Darrell, an army surgeon and amateur archaeologist who accompanied

Bonaparte's expedition to Egypt in 1798. Later, evidence of Pott's disease was found in mummies and in pre-Columbian ossuaries in the Americas. It is reasonable to assume that the *Mycobacterium tuberculosis* antedates *Homo sapiens* and will probably outlive it.

76. Some cases were almost certainly tuberculous, but there are other causes of enlarged cervical lymph nodes. The condition was extremely common and it was widely believed that it could be cured by the touch of a king. Philip-Auguste of France (1180–1223) is credited with 1500 touches in a single ceremony. Queen Anne was the last English monarch to touch, the future Dr Johnson as a child being one of her successes.

77. The Goncourt brothers became his ardent champions in the 1860s.

78. Tuberculous laryngitis, a complication of pulmonary tuberculosis, was one of the most painful and intractable forms of the illness. It made both speech and swallowing a torment and was usually treated with large doses of opium. Pulmonary tuberculosis was otherwise characteristically painless though physically enfeebling. This was one reason for its extraordinary association with artistic and literary creativity.

79. In 1673, aged 51. He may have contracted the illness in the debtors' prison as a young man.

80. She died in 1764, aged 43.

81. None of the current explanations for why tuberculosis suddenly becomes common and then less common fits all the facts. Its upsurge towards the end of the eighteenth century was almost certainly related to the overcrowding, poverty and malnourishment of the Industrial Revolution, but this cannot be the whole answer. Conversely, its decline began long before the introduction of effective antituberculous therapy around 1950. See Note 72.

82. Post-mortems on suspected tuberculous bodies were performed in Italian hospitals and medical schools too, but they were directed by the pathologist from a safe distance, often a raised balcony, with a pointer. The actual handling of the bodies was usually left to prisoners from the local jails, who thereby earned remission of their sentences.

83. Quoted by Kervran, *Laennec*, p. 87.

84. See Part II, Semmelweis.

85. They are diagnostic and just visible with a good magnifying glass. They form a 'crown' around the anterior end of the scolex or 'head' of the parasite.

86. After the Bourbon Restoration he would adapt those without much damage to the metre to exalt 'our beloved king and sun', Louis XVIII.

87. Through its first years, while Laennec took an active part in its affairs, it was a purely religious organisation. It was dissolved by Napoleon in 1809 and not re-established till 1816. Under the Bourbons it became increasingly politicised. From then on Laennec took no part in its activities.

88. Ernest Renan, whose *La vie de Jésus* (published in 1862) became an anti-Catholic and anti-Christian manifesto during the second half of the nineteenth century, was born in Tréguier in Brittany. He was in fact a deeply religious person, though an enemy of all institutionalised religions.

89. Registered or not, those seeking heavenly intercession and prepared to visit some of the friendliest shrines of Europe may find the following abridged list useful. The dates indicate the day of the *Pardons*. For illnesses affecting the head: Saint Yvertin in Liverin and Everzin (5 May); Saint Bieuzy in Sant-Bilui (24 November); Sainte Eugenie and Saint

Eutrope in Tujane (25 December); St Germain l'Auxerrois (also for gastrointestinal complaints) in Plogastel-Saint-Germain (31 July); Saint Maturin in Montcontour (1 November); Saint Noyala (or Nolwenn) in Pontivy (6 July); Saint Gurloes in Quimperlé (much venerated by Mme Laennec; 7 November); and Saint Tremeur in Carlot (7 November). For ailments of the mouth and teeth: Saint Mauron in Kernec (15 January); Saint Apolline in Mordelle (9 February); Saint Gwaltaz in Cast (5 October); Saint Moris in Genolguen (5 October); and Saint Tujen in Primelin (26 January). For ailments threatening the eyes: Sainte Anna in Betton (26 July); Sainte Katell in Ploiré (31 January); Saint Guenhael in Batz-sur-Mer (3 November); Saint Hervé in Saint-Brieuc (17 June); Saint Jacut in Saint-Venée (8 February); Saint Juien in Brioude (28 August); Saint Lunaire in Loscouet-sur-Meu (1 July); and Sainte Nonne in Dirinon (3 March). For diseases of the ears: Saint Diboan (in extreme desperation) and Saint Egarec in Kerlouan (4 March); Saint Mériadec (particularly venerated by the Guillaume Laennecs) in Conech (9 September). For diseases of the throat: Saint Theonnec in Douaoult (September); Saint Blaise and Saint Opportune in Plouarzel (22nd April). For neurological ailments: Sainte C'hloda in Plougastel (6 June); Saint Columban in Saint-Modan (21 November). For epilepsy: Saint Briac in Kerdrogouen (17 December). For paralysis: Saint Ildut in Sizun (6 November). For disorders of speech: Saint Gili in Lauidut (1 September). For diseases of the stomach and intestines: Saint Cyr and Sainte Juliette in Molac (16 July); Sainte Emerence in Loudeac (23 January); and Sainte Ediltrude in Treflet (23 June). For 'furies and rages': Saint Barne in Fougisse (4 December). For haemorrhoids: Saint Fiacre in Brandineuf (30 August) and Saint Mamert in Tredaniel (11 May). For contagious maladies: Saint Kado in Guesnac's (6 August); Sainte Petronille in Ploudaniel (23 March); and Saint Efflan in Kervignac (near Laennec's estate and frequently visited by him; 6 November) For disorders of the skin: Saint Aignan in Ille-et-Villaine (5 July); and Saint Armel in Vieux-Bourg (16 August). For sickness and vomiting: Sainte Armel in Voudrine (23 January); and Saint Guénole in Finistèrre (3 March). For burns: Saint Laorens in Boquého (10 August). For rickets: Sainte Brigitte in Merdignac (6 May). For rheumatism: Saint Aubyn in Bré (1 March); Saint Armel in Pluneret (6 August); Saint Ivy in Trolimon (3 July); and Saint Lubin in Posier (8 September). For backache: Saint Ildut in Izart (6 November); and Saint Ronan in Fuseau (3 March). For complications of pregnancy: Saint Urfol in Languidic (15 August). In desperate illnesses: Saint Diboan in Côte-d'Armor (22 May) and Saint Meven in Saint-Quay-Perros (21 June). For a more complete and detailed list, map and photographs, see H. Gancel's indispensable two-volume guide (see Bibliography).

90. The name was applied to everybody who had voted for the King's execution in the Convention in 1793.

91. No papal bull was to be published and no papal representative was to be active in France without the permission of the government. The bishops were placed under the close control of the prefects. The agreement was bound to break down and did so in 1809.

92. Ironically perhaps, the ultimate result was to strengthen the influence of the Vatican in the Catholic Church in France. The intermittent struggle between Church and State that was to bedevil French politics for at least 100 years was its main legacy.

93. 'I don't believe in medicine but I believe in Corvisart,' was Napoleon's recorded judgement. The Emperor lived in constant dread of being poisoned and literally rolled on the ground 'in agony' at the slightest indigestion. Corvisart had no patience with such imperial histrionics: 'Get up at once, Sire! What would be said if the master of the world were seen crushed by fear?' Corvisart also attended Napoleon's sister, Pauline, Queen of Naples, his step-daughter, Hortense, Queen of Spain, his first empress Josephine, and his most faithful mistress, Marie Walevska. Eventually he also looked after Marie Louise, the Emperor's second wife, a remarkable hat trick.

94. Hugues Felicité Robert de Lamennais was horrified at the anti-religious policy of the Revolution. Returning from exile in London during the Hundred Days he took holy orders. The first volume of his great work, *Essai sur l'indifférence en matière de religion*, published in 1817, stirred Europe by its violent denunciation of religious tolerance. He died in 1854, aged 72, disillusioned by a deeply reactionary Papacy and disappointed by the accession of a second Bonaparte emperor.

95. François René Vicomte de Chateaubriand was born in St Malo and spent his childhood in Combourg Castle, the family seat in Brittany. After a brief sojourn in America he returned, married, and joined the ranks of the émigrés during the Revolution. Returning to France in 1808 he became the leader of the Romantic movement in literature and one of France's great poets. For a brief period he was foreign minister under the Bourbons. One of literature's great hypochondriacs, he died in 1848, aged 80.

96. Recounted by Rouxeau, *Laennec après 1806*, p. 237.

97. During the early years of the Revolution republicans who wanted to avoid any reference to the king or the monarchy often referred to the 'French Empire'. To distance himself from the kings of France, Napoleon called himself Emperor of the French rather than Emperor of France. Only gradually did he start to ape Europe's old dynasties, creating titles, orders and all their idiot trappings.

98. The Condés were a cadet branch of the Bourbons: Louis XIV's famous marshal was the son of a Duke of Bourbon.

99. Fever is now recognised as part of the systemic inflammatory response. The inflammatory response can sometimes be 'inappropriate'—that is, excessive—but it is essentially part of the body's defence mechanism.

100. The choice between Latin and French remained optional until 1810.

101. Quoted by Rouxeau, *Laennec après 1806*, p. 231.

102. Quoted by Rouxeau, *Laennec après 1806*, p. 246.

103. Quoted by Rouxeau, *Laennec après 1806*, p. 247.

104. If Rouxeau was as good and dedicated a doctor as he was a biographer (and why not?), he must have been the Breton Hippocrates.

105. Quoted by Rouxeau, *Laennec après 1806*, p. 250.

106. Madame de Chateaubriand does not say what he was eminent in or about.

107. Isabel de Chateaubriand, *Cahiers Rouges* (Paris, 1852), p. 78.

108. The Cardinal was an odd mixture of the Corsican showman and the religious ascetic. His home, the Hôtel Hocquart (in the rue St Lazare, now pulled down), housed one of France's great art collections. He and Laennec became friends. When the Cardinal had to depart for Rome in 1811, after quarrelling with his nephew, he presented Laennec with a beautifully worked Italian Renaissance crucifix. Laennec passed it on to his friend Bruté de Rémur when Bruté departed for Baltimore to found

a mission and a seminary. The crucifix is still in the Roman Catholic Cathedral there.

109. With Joseph Black, Adam Smith and David Hume, he was a leading light of the Scottish Enlightenment. He held, it seems, every available medical chair in Edinburgh either simultaneously or in succession (anatomy, pathology, physiology, chemistry and medicine among them). His fundamental universal doctrine was that life was a state of continuous nervous excitement produced and modulated by environmental stimuli. Though he admitted that he could not clearly identify the source of the nervous excitement, he tended to identify it with an aethereal fluid that was also the basis of light, heat, magnetism and electricity. He constructed an elaborate disease classification, modelled, like that of Boissier de Sauvage of Montpellier, on Linné's great *Systema naturae*. He was saved from Boissier de Sauvage's more extreme absurdities by his Scottish good sense, but half the time it is still difficult to know what he is talking about. He died in 1790, aged 80.

110. The epithets are Napoleon's.

111. Napoleon himself was keen to march on St Petersburg, but for once he gave in to the urgings of his marshals. Perhaps he should have followed his instinct.

112. The best modern account is probably Nigel Nicolson's *Napoleon 1812* (London, 1985).

113. This was untrue. Unlike the exceptionally severe winter of 1942–43, which contributed to the defeat of Hitler's *Wehrmacht*, the winter of 1812–13 was comparatively mild.

114. This, he stated in St Helena, was a mistake. Murat was a dashing cavalryman, not a strategist. The statement was true, though Napoleon always blamed others for his mistakes. There was little anyone could have done differently: the *Grande Armée* was doomed.

115. Kutuzov is brilliantly portrayed in *War and Peace* and he remains a Russian folk hero, though it is possible that he could have inflicted a final bloody and spectacular defeat on the totally demoralised French. It was hardly necessary, but the Czar would have preferred the war to end with a bang, preferably delivered by himself.

116. Heine's *Die Beiden Grenadiere*, set to music by Schumann, is not quite historical though it wonderfully evokes the power of the Napoleonic legend. A few Grenadiers returned with the straggling remains of the *Grande Armée*, but no Grenadier taken prisoner ever returned.

117. R.E.P. de Fézensac, *Journal de la campagne de Russie en 1812* (Paris, 1824), p. 269.

118. Both were dead.

119. Bayle had been to Spain and was horrified by the atrocities of the Civil War. They were not Goya's fevered imaginings. Although Bayle was to be appointed physician to Louis XVIII after the first Bourbon Restoration, his health was already fast declining.

120. In St Helena he described this as his greatest single mistake, though the faithful Bertrand meekly pointed out that he had thus described several errors already.

121. The first European coalition tried to extinguish the Revolution and rescue the King and Queen, but its commander-in-chief, the elderly and mentally decrepit Duke of Brunswick, was so mortified to meet any resistance at all from the revolutionary army near Valmy that, after a token cannonade,

he ordered a general retreat. Dysentery turned the retreat into a rout and saved the Revolution. Goethe, present at the Duke's headquarters, commented that it was the dawn of a new age.

122. The linguistic divide ran north to south just west of St Brieuc, separating Breton-speaking 'Lower Brittany' in the west from French-speaking 'Upper Brittany' in the east. The dialects in Lower Brittany, all related to Cornish and mid-Welsh, were still markedly different from each other.

123. Quoted by Rouxeau, *Laennec après 1806*, p. 213.

124. Quoted by Rouxeau, *Laennec après 1806*, p. 215.

125. Napoleon's son and heir by Marie Louise was created King of Rome in 1810 as soon as he was dangled in the air and shown to be a boy by Dubois, imperial obstetrician, after a difficult labour. Napoleon entrusted his wife and son to Corvisart, who accompanied them as far as Munich. The news of Napoleon's abdication reached him in Switzerland. He was devastated.

126. It was assumed that Louis XVI's older son, the Dauphin, who had been given into the care of a 'patriotic tailor' by the Revolutionary Convention and had subsequently disappeared, had nevertheless survived his father. He had therefore been, for however long, Louis XVII, by the Grace of God King of France. Louis XVI had two younger brothers, the elder known as the Comte de Provence and the younger as the Comte d'Artois. After Napoleon's fall, Provence reigned as Louis XVIII and Artois as Charles X. Of the latter, Talleyrand (ending his career as France's ambassador in London) said that his royal master's stupidity gave one a conceptual inkling of the infinite.

127. T.-R.-H. Laennec, *Oeuvres inédits* (Masson, Paris, 1926), p. 54. Henri IV had been the first and most popular of the Bourbon kings.

128. According to Talleyrand, the Bourbons in exile had forgotten nothing and had learnt nothing. Nevertheless, many felt that they had learnt many new tricks of misrule.

129. They are both clearly written, but illustrate the difficulty of interpreting old medical texts. To Laennec the difference between 'dégénerescence' and 'dégéneration' seems to have been largely one of degree, the latter being more severe. But 'dégéneration' is hardly used in French medical parlance today, whereas 'dégénerescence' has no English equivalent. To confuse the modern medical reader even more (if they exist apart from the present writer), Laennec regarded malignant change as a form of degeneration whereas the outcome of ischaemia was a form of 'dégénerescence'. Senile degenerative changes, the most common use of the word today, is hardly mentioned in either article.

130. Laennec, *Oeuvres inédits*, p. 321.

131. Despite new holiday resorts like Benodet, much of this part of Brittany is still barely touched by tourism and industrial developments. It is easy to retrace Laennec's explorations.

132. It is still there and still worth a visit.

133. The boat barely escaped a patrolling English frigate that mistook it for a fishing vessel.

134. He wisely avoided the staunchly royalist Provence in favour of the more difficult route over the Alps.

135. Ney, one of Napoleon's best and most trusted marshals, had been welcomed by Louis XVIII and had taken the oath to the King.

136. The garrison was hostile. They crossed the frontier near Ghent.

137. Ney was shot, though he was given the chance to escape. The second Treaty of Paris was much more severe than the first, imposing a large indemnity on the country.

138. His last years on his country estate in Courbevoie near Paris were miserable. His marriage had broken up many years earlier. He had been something of a philanderer but popular with stars of the theatre, opera and ballet. Now he was alone. His only son had died in his twenties in obscure circumstances. In 1817 Corvisart had a stroke that left him partly paralysed. Laennec is known to have visited him at least once. The 'patron' died after a final stroke in 1821.

139. See Part II, Semmelweis.

140. As Charles X, who tried precisely this, learnt to his cost. He succeeded his elder brother in 1824. Six years later, after three days of street fighting in Paris, les trois glorieuses, he abdicated in favour of his infant grandson and fled to England.

141. The influx of foreign students to Paris is described in E.H. Ackerknecht, *Medicine at the Paris Hospitals, 1794–1848* (Baltimore, 1967). American students began to abandon Britain for Paris after 1814. By 1844 there were 50 of them and soon they had their own club in the rue St André des Arts. Thomas Hodgkin, John Forbes and James Clark were among Laennec's British students. Future leaders of the Second Viennese School like Skoda, Rokitansky and Schuh all visited Paris. (See Part II.)

142. Quoted by R. Porter, *The Greatest Benefit to Mankind* (London, 1997), p. 316. The abysmal state of teaching did not seem to worry Paget. 'I am not sure,' he added, 'that being well disposed to work myself, I was any the worse for it.' (This is the trouble with exceptional youths who manage to cope with a pernicious system: later in life and in a position of power they feel less compelled to try to alter it.)

   Sir James Paget was the youngest of the nine surviving children of seventeen born to Samuel Paget, a brewer and provisioner of the Navy, and his wife, in Great Yarmouth in Norfolk. During the peace and economic depression following the Napoleonic wars there was no money left to send James to Charterhouse where his brothers had been and he was apprenticed to a local surgeon for five years. In 1834, aged 20, he managed to enter St Bartholomew's Hospital in London but, despite winning all the prizes, he had a hard slog, eking out a living by tutoring and by cataloguing the vast Hunterian collection of pathological specimens of the Royal College of Surgeons. Eventually, in 1847, he was elected to the surgical staff of his hospital; and from then on his rise was rapid: fellow of the Royal Society in 1851, sergeant surgeon to the Queen in 1858, baronet, and president of the Royal College of Surgeons in 1871. He was a patron and later a staunch friend of Lister's (see Part III), a brilliant teacher and public orator—according to Mr Gladstone 'the greatest public speaker in the land'—and a man of immense industry and dignity. Two diseases are still eponymously linked to him: a comparatively rare cancer of the nipple, and the increasingly common and often painful deformity of the bones of the elderly. The cause of the latter is still unknown; but Paget's description of its varied manifestation could not be bettered. (Repeatedly ill-fitting dentures are, however, a more common presenting feature today than repeatedly ill-fitting top hats.) In his seventies he still travelled in Europe in consultation and at 80 he gave a memorable address to the Abernethian

Society. He died in his eighty-fifth year on the last day of the century he adorned.

143. The first medical licensing body in England was the Society of Apothecaries, whose licence to practice became compulsory in 1815. London University was founded as a purely examining body in 1835. It acquired two medical colleges and teaching hospitals, University College Hospital and King's College Hospital, in 1837 and 1840 respectively.

144. See Part II, Semmelweis.

145. The word is Laennec's own coinage, a surprisingly poor one for a classical scholar since the chest (στέθος) is not the only organ that can be auscultated and seeing (σκοπέω) does not come into it.

146. Listening to the approaching horses of a tribe in this way was a staple of boys' stories of cowboys and indians.

147. Until the matter was cleared up by Corvisart, 'succussion' and 'percussion' were not infrequently confused. Normally the closed space between the two layers of the pleurae (one closed double sheath enveloping each lung) is virtual, accommodating only a few drops of lubricating mucus to allow the layers to glide over each other. In inflammation of the pleura, usually secondary to some underlying pathology in the lung, the two layers become separated by an inflammatory effusion. When the effusion becomes infected and turns to pus, it becomes an 'empyaema'.

148. R.-T.-H. Laennec, *Traité de l'Auscultation mediate* (Paris, 1926), vol. I, p. 87. The more complete and updated second edition was reprinted to mark the centenary of Laennec's death.

149. Laennec, *Traité de l'Auscultation mediate* (Paris, 1926), vol. I, p. 110.

150. Quoted by Rouxeau, *Laennec après 1806* (Paris, 1921), p. 156.

151. The combined surfaces are about the size of a tennis court.

152. See Dormandy, *The White Death*, p. 37. Keats was a doctor as well as a poet and knew what he was talking about.

153. Laennec himself mentioned whooping cough as a possible cause.

154. In chronic inflammation the specialised ciliated lining is replaced by a less specialised one resembling the skin. This may later undergo malignant transformation.

155. The grain was named millet from the Latin *mille*, thousand, because of its fertility. In 1697 Bonetus observed a lung 'seeded with minute tubercles'. His book, *Sepulchretum*, was republished in 1700 by Jean-Jacques Manget and it was Manget who compared these tubercles to millet seeds.

156. Bailley was the son of a professor of divinity in Glasgow and the nephew of John and William Hunter. In 1787, at the age of 27, he was appointed physician to St George's Hospital in London. He described caseation in his textbook, *The Morbid Anatomy of Some of the Most Important Parts of the Human Body*. The fatty capsules of the tubercle bacilli may be responsible for the cheese-like consistency of what is in effect tuberculous pus.

157. In the artificial pneumothorax (AP), for half a century a standard treatment of tuberculosis, air was deliberately introduced into the pleural space to allow the underlying segment of lung containing the cavity to collapse on itself.

158. J. Forbes, Introduction to Laennec's *Treatise on Auscultation* (London, 1828).

159. In the writer's experience, at least one lecturer in the basic sciences has been known to sport a stethoscope around his neck at all times though he never went nearer to a patient than the occasional visit to a sick relative in hospital.

160. The idea of a 'biaural' or 'binaural' stethoscope appears to have been introduced in 1829 by Nicholas Comins, but only sketches exist of his multi-jointed instrument. The first commercially available model was apparently marketed by a Dr Marsh in Cincinnati in 1851; it was also equipped with a diaphragm. A usable and recognisable binaural instrument was made by Dr G. Cammann of New York in 1855. From then on models multiplied, including one with duplicate earpieces to allow two people—presumably teacher and student—to auscultate at the same time. By 1880 most of the main components of the modern stethoscope were in existence, including a tension mechanism to hold the earpieces in place, heavy rubber tubing, longer tubes, the Ford's bell chest piece, various folding mechanisms and—inevitably—a lively and still flourishing market in antique instruments.

161. They would prove to be eminently incompetent. For many years Laennec was bombarded with letters from colleagues who were trying to obtain the book but were told that it was unavailable. The second edition was entrusted to another firm, MM Chaudé, booksellers at 56 rue de la Harpe, and they did it proud.

162. Dying in 1847, aged 76.

163. Sanatoria have had a bad press over the past 50 years (including in *The White Death* by the present writer) and many were indeed terrible. Nevertheless, there can be no doubt that thousands of tuberculous found that they could function almost normally in a certain place and environment but relapsed as soon as they moved away from it. Ckekhov wrote his greatest plays in Yalta in the Crimea, though he became desperately ill as soon as he returned to Moscow. There is still no satisfactory explanation, especially since the ideal environment varied from patient to patient. Laennec remains a classic example. Until his terminal illness, however ill he was in Paris, he recovered within days of returning to his native Brittany.

164. Quoted by Rouxeau, *Laennec après 1806*, p. 231.

165. Hodgkin graduated in Edinburgh in 1823 and went to Paris in the same year. A Quaker of deep faith, his admiration for Laennec was reciprocated: despite their religious differences, Laennec mentions the young Englishman in at least one of his letters. Hodgkin later became curator of the pathology museum at Guy's Hospital in London (where he described the disease of the lymph nodes named after him), though he was never appointed to the clinical staff. He died in 1866, aged 68, a man of great nobility like the Frenchman he had visited in his youth. (See also Part III, Lister).

166. He was largely responsible for the only successful foreign intervention of the Holy Alliance. A French army was sent to Spain to rescue and reinstate Ferdinand VII, by common consent the worst king that unhappy country had had since the imbecile Charles II. In sharp and surprising contrast to Napoleon's foray into the Peninsula, the expedition was an easy success. But Chateaubriand was not a politician and Villèle, the chief minister, soon got rid of him.

167. She was the wife of the Duc de Berry, the future Charles X's only son and heir. The duke was assassinated but she gave birth to his son eight months later. After Charles X's abdication in 1830, 'l'enfant du miracle' became the pretender to the French throne (as the Comte de Chambord). He remained a pretender only for 60 years mainly because he never wavered in demanding that the Tricoleur should be replaced by the white flag of the

Bourbons. When the duchess became pregnant again two years later, the faith even of the most devout faltered.

168. A good and balanced account of the Broussais doctrine is given by F.H. Ackerman, *Medicine at the Paris Hospital 1794–1848* (Baltimore, 1967), p. 70.

169. A wall painting in an Egyptian tomb shows a doctor or slave holding a vessel that looks suspiciously like a bleeding bowl to the arm of a reclining figure. The history of blood-letting is briefly but well reviewed in D. Starr, *Blood, an Epic History of Medicine and Commerce* (London, 1998).

170. Quoted by Starr, *Blood*, p. 43. A more detailed account of blood-letting is given in F.H. Garrison, *An Introduction to the History of Medicine* (Philadelphia, 1929).

171. One of its secretions, hirudin, is the most potent natural anti-coagulant (anti-clotting agent) known.

172. Leechcraft is reviewed in an article by K. Codell Carter, 'Leechcraft in nineteenth century British medicine', *Journal of the Royal Society of Medicine*, vol. 94 (2001), p. 38, and the correspondence in following issues.

173. Leeches went out of fashion towards the end of the nineteenth century, though they were still occasionally used in the 1950s in Britain and were sometimes life saving.

174. In 1807 Wordsworth wrote: 'He told, that to these waters he had come/To gather leeches, being old and poor:/Employment hazardous and wearisome!'

175. While it is often done, it is fatuous to dismiss blood-letting, a treatment that has prevailed for thousands of years, as a total aberration. It provided instant (though rarely lasting) relief in acute pulmonary oedema, a highly distressing and often fatal condition, for which no other treatment was available. The condition occasionally complicated a variety of comparatively common cardiac and pulmonary conditions, including tuberculosis. However, there was more to blood-letting than relief in an emergency. After a moderate bleed the body quickly restores the total volume of blood while it replaces the lost red blood cells more slowly. During the transitional period blood flow is much easier; the 'thickness' or 'viscosity' of the blood—which depends largely on the proportion of cells to plasma—is diminished; and that may more than compensate for the decline in oxygen-carrying capacity, the specific function of the red blood cells. In other words, fewer cells may be delivered more efficiently. This may also explain why regular blood donors often feel buoyed up after giving a pint of blood and miss it when for some reason they are not wanted. When the lost red blood cells *are* replaced, which in a normal person may take only a few days, the overall population of red cells is younger and perhaps more efficient than it was before. There are other reasons too why blood-letting may have been more effective than is often implied today. (See also S. Chien, J.A. Dormandy, E. Ernst, and A. Matrai, *Clinical Haematology*, Dordrecht, 1987.)

176. He had all the mannerisms of the old Napoleonic soldier, the *grognard*, and he united behind himself all the opposition parties of the Restoration. The Revolution of 1830 was—or should have been—his moment of triumph. Under the Orléans Monarchy he was given a chair in the Faculty of Medicine, a seat in the Academy and the rank of inspector general in the Service de Santé Militaire. But his doctrine proved catastrophically wrong

when he became chief government medical adviser during the 1832 cholera epidemic and his regime of purgation and blood-letting probably trebled the number of casualties. He retired from the Val-de-Grâce two years later and died from cancer in 1838, aged 66.

177. He was born in 1787, the son of a wine grower in Champagne. He went to Russia as part of the retinue of the Comte de St Priest, France's ambassador.

178. Including Andral, Barty, Nélaton, Grosvelly and the young Armand Trousseau, future professor and great clinical teacher.

179. He became particularly popular in the United States and remained so even after he was virtually forgotten in France. When in 1905 William Osler visited Paris and wished to lay a posy of flowers on Louis's tomb, nobody could tell the visitor where the Frenchman had been buried. (He lies at the northern end of La Père Lachaise, in case anybody wants to follow Osler's example.)

180. Louis's only son, Armand, died of tuberculosis in 1853. It was a blow from which Louis never recovered, though he lived on as a recluse till 1873.

181. The château and indeed Couvrelle no longer exist. This was a region of France that was fiercely fought over in 1870–71 and again during the First World War; and it seems uncertain when the building and the hamlet disappeared.

182. Close to the frontier, Bordeaux was the haven of wave after wave of Spanish refugees. (They included the painter Goya, who died there.) All hated the tyrannical and inefficient regime of Ferdinand VII. Who Laennec's patient was is still uncertain, but he may have been a former Bonapartist minister who escaped after the collapse of Joseph Bonaparte's reign with part of the national treasury.

183. Quoted by Kervran, *Laennec*, p. 162.

184. C.A. Sainte-Beuve, *Premiers Lundis* (Paris, 1827), p. 65. Towards the end of his life Laennec's interest embraced other Celtic languages besides Breton. He corresponded with Forbes about Cornish and with Lloyd and Throgmorton about Welsh. Scholars often sought his advice, 'though [he wrote] I am completely fluent in only two of the four dialects of Armorica'.

185. Quoted by Rouxeau, *Laennec après 1806*, p. 356.

PART II: SEMMELWEIS

1. For the best part of 1000 years it was the western rim of the kingdom of Hungary. Having escaped the devastation of Turkish occupation in the sixteenth and seventeenth century, it remained part of civilised Mitteleuropa. Part of it was handed over to Austria for no very good reason by the Treaty of Trianon in 1919. No natural boundary separates Hungary and Austria here.

2. In the service of the Princes Eszterházy Haydn spent some of his most productive years here, either in Fertöd (Eszterháza), now on the Hungarian side of the frontier, or in the provincial capital, Eisenstadt, now in Austria. Both places stage summer festivals in his honour. Fittingly, he was Semmelweis's favourite composer.

3. The frontier bisects the lake when it can find it.

4. The family tree was lovingly researched by a distant relation of Ignác, Karl Semmelweis, municipal librarian in Eisenstadt. He published his findings in the *Burgenländische Heimatsblätter*, 3 (1967). Semmelweis's first and admiring biographer was the gynaecologist Alfred Hegar, *Ignaz Philipp Semmelweis, sein Leben und seine Lehre* (Freiburg-Tübingen, 1882). A well-researched and more detailed life was written by the Austrian general practitioner Fritz Schürer von Waldheim, *Ignaz Philipp Semmelweis: Sein Leben* (Vienna, 1905). His first biography in English was Sir William Sinclair's *Semmelweis: His Life and his Doctrine* (Manchester, 1909). An extremely readable if rather flamboyantly entitled biography in English is that by F.G. Slaughter, *Immortal Magyar* (New York, 1940), and an excellent biographical article was published by S.W.B. Newsom in *Journal of Hospital Infection*, 23 (1993), p. 175. A perceptive biography in Hungarian is by Imre Domány, *Semmelweis küzdelmes élete* (Budapest, 1918). Embodying nearly all recent research, a scholarly and detailed study of Semmelweis's life and times is I. Benedek, *Semmelweis és Kora* (Budapest, 1967).

5. Buda did not unite with Pest to become Budapest until 1886. The first stone bridge, the Chain Bridge, an engineering *tour-de-force* designed by the Scotsman Adam Clark, was opened in 1852, shortly after Semmelweis's return.

6. Before then it was the seat of Matthias Corvinus (1443–1490), Renaissance prince and collector of one of Europe's great libraries, the Corvina.

7. The university had been founded by Cardinal Péter Pázmány in 1656 in the western Hungarian City of Nagyszombat, at a time when Buda was still under Turkish rule. The medical faculty was added by Maria Theresa.

8. The district is still known by its old Turkish name of Tabán.

9. Almost all had more resplendent town residences in Vienna and usually in Prague.

10. It was certainly enough to make him thoroughly unpopular at Court in Vienna.

11. In 1597 by St Joseph of Calasance; it was the first free grammar school in Europe. Whether or not to charge fees still intermittently exercises the Order.

12. The University of Vienna, the second such institution (after the Charles University in Prague) in Central Europe, had been founded by the first Habsburg emperor, Rudolf, in 1365, though it did not acquire a medical faculty until the reign of Maria Theresa in 1753. The moving spirit behind the venture and its presiding genius was Gerhard van Swieten, a Dutchman who began his career as physician to Marianne, wife of Charles of Lorraine and Maria Theresa's much-loved sister, and ended it as the confidant and medical factotum of the Empress. The medical faculty was modelled on that of the famous Dutch school of Leyden: its first professor of medicine was the Dutchman, de Haen, a pupil of Boerhaave's. Beside his contribution to medicine, van Swieten was also a music lover, Haydn's librettist for *The Creation* and the dedicatee of Beethoven's first symphony.

13. Paris was its only rival. The Dutch and Italian medical schools, famous in past centuries, were all in decline by the early decades of the nineteenth century. Berlin and the other German medical schools had not yet risen to international fame. London had teaching hospitals but no university; Oxford and Cambridge had universities but no teaching hospitals. Dublin

was a famous medical centre but geographically on the periphery. The Rotunda, its obstetric hospital, was nevertheless on the itinerary of every travelling obstetrician.

14. The other was Rudolf Virchow (1821–1902), in the 1840s still a medical student voicing brilliantly subversive revolutionary sentiments. See Note 164 to Part III, Lister.

15. Morgagni was professor of anatomy in Padua for 59 years. His great work, *De sedibus et causis morborum*, was published in Venice in 1761. Numerous anatomical structures eponymously commemorate him. He died in 1761, aged 89.

16. The microscope in various rudimentary forms has a history going back to antiquity, but it is the Dutch draper and amateur lens grinder, Anton Leeuwenhoek, who is widely acknowledged as the inventor of the modern instrument. He discovered his 'little animalcules' in tooth scrapings (and later in blood) in 1683 and communicated his findings in lengthy letters to the Royal Society in London. Many others contributed improvement and refinements until the monocular microscope acquired its basic modern form in the early twentieth century. Biopsies did not become widely used till the 1920s.

17. There was (as is true of many scientific fantasies of clever people) a grain of truth in Rokitansky's doctrine. A change in the chemical properties of blood plasma is the final common pathway of many and widely different disease processes. Virchow's counter-arguments, on the other hand, were effective but later proved to be nonsense.

18. See also Part III, Lister. His reputation grew despite the fact that he was a monumentally boring lecturer. A casual remark of his own would sidetrack him on a long and nearly incomprehensible monologue or inspire him to lapse into meditative silence, sometimes lasting a quarter of an hour. By the end of the intermission both he and most of his listeners had forgotten what he had been talking about.

19. At least this was so until comparatively recently. That microscopic appearances, especially the appearances of cells, can be as misleading as any other clinical sign did not become apparent until cytological screening for cancer became common and proved to be as uncertain a diagnostic tool as any other. Centuries of past (and probably false) reputation for infallibility now haunt the speciality.

20. He was right, of course. The palatial new Institut where the department moved in the 1860s soon became a citadel of blinkered traditionalism. He died in 1878, aged 74.

21. Only just. Skodaic resonance is the drum-like sound that can be elicited by percussing the chest over a strip adjacent to an area of consolidation—that is, disease—in the lungs. But percussion is a lost art: X-rays and other modern imaging techniques can provide the same information more painlessly (to the doctor). Few medical students, let alone doctors, familiar enough with Skoda cars, would recognise Skodaic resonance today.

22. See Part I, Laennec.

23. It was almost an accident. The princeling's personal physician, Vaclav Porges of Prague, needed a translator. (Porges was one of the few patriotic eccentrics who continued to use Czech rather than German or Latin in his medical practice.) Skoda was sent for and, instead of tremulously translating the great man's utterances, proceeded to examine the patient for himself. All but von Türkheim were flabbergasted.

24. Today aneurysms of the aorta are usually in the abdomen and the result of degenerative arterial disease. In Skoda's time syphilitic aneurysms were comparatively common and almost invariably affected the arch of the aorta in the chest.

25. At least this was so until the advent of more powerful drugs such as steroids.

26. Among the many skin diseases he described (and many of which he named) were eczema, erythema, impetigo, lichen, lupus, pityriasis and syphilitic rashes.

27. The son, Hans von Hebra, became a notable dermatologist himself; and his daughter, Elise, married another, Moritz Kaposi, who described Kaposi's sarcoma. Seventy years after Kaposi's death (1902) the disease named after him was recognised as a comparatively common complication of AIDS.

28. Joseph II was Maria Theresa's eldest son. Born in 1741, he became Holy Roman Emperor on the death of his father, Maria Theresa's husband Francis of Lorraine, but this was an almost meaningless title. He became effective ruler of the Habsburg lands only on his mother's death in 1780. He died ten years later, in 1790. It is not known how Boër, whose earlier career had not been particularly distinguished, came to the Emperor's notice; but perhaps his efforts on behalf of Vienna's poor attracted the Emperor's attention. Looking after the destitute in his realm was every enlightened despot's pride.

29. Joseph fell deeply in love with his first wife, the Infanta Isabella of Bourbon-Parma, a noted beauty, after her arrival in Vienna; but she never recovered from seeing her lover murdered in front of her at her father's command on the eve of her departure from Parma. She may also have suffered from tuberculosis. She died in childbirth (as did the baby) three years after their marriage. Her first daughter died three years later, perhaps from smallpox. Joseph's second wife, Princess Josefa of Bavaria, chosen by the Empress Maria Theresa for her son, suffered from an incurable skin disease, perhaps congenital syphilis, and proved barren. Unhappy and humiliated, she died two years after the wedding, which was probably never consummated. After that Josef refused to marry but had numerous more or less passing affairs with working-class and peasant girls that he or one of his aides-de-camp picked up in the Prater or on his country estates. The offspring of these liaisons were awarded a regular annuity of 50 Kronen, a not ungenerous sum, which was continued by all of Joseph's successors until the collapse of the Monarchy in 1918. The Emperor also had a succession of aristocratic lady friends in whose company he found relaxation. It was late in life that he developed a deep paternal love for the 17-year-old bride of his nephew, Francis (the future Emperor), the Princess Elizabeth of Würtenberg.

30. A remark attributed to the Archduchess Sophie, mother of the Emperor Francis Joseph.

31. The law was eventually promulgated 150 years later by the republic of Austria in 1924.

32. He was never popular with the archduchesses at court—at one time there were 18—but they had no choice in the matter.

33. Hooks and other extracting instruments were probably used in obstetrics since antiquity—the word itself (probably a contraction of *ferriceps*, the iron for seizing anything hot) was certainly used by Celsus—but the

modern obstetric forceps was invented by the Chamberlens, a Huguenot family of the seventeenth century, who fled from France to England after the Revocation of the Edict of Nantes. The actual inventor was probably Peter Chamberlen (1560–1631), but the secret was kept in the family and perhaps modified for over 100 years. It was eventually revealed by Peter's grandson, Hugh Chamberlen. Once the secret was out, numerous developments followed. Dusse crossed the arms of his forceps in the 1730s; Levret changed the shape and introduced the 'pelvic curve'; Smellie added the English lock in 1752; and there were several early attempts at incorporating the axis-traction feature (so called because it allows the direction of the necessary pull to coincide with the axis of the pelvic canal) before it was given its more or less current form by Tarnier in the mid-nineteenth century.

34. What Boër's motivation was is unclear, but perhaps he half-intuitively anticipated Semmelweis's discovery.

35. Despite having accepted lavish bribes and having made even more lavish promises. As soon as the Emperor Charles was dead the King of Prussia, Frederick II (not yet the Great), opportunistically seized Silesia, a French army invaded Bohemia and occupied Prague, and a non-Habsburg, the Elector of Bavaria, was elected Emperor. In a situation that many might have given up as hopeless, Maria Theresa used the traditional weapons of the Habsburgs: patience, obstinacy, a professional army and temporary (previously unthinkable) alliances. She appeared before the Hungarian Diet (with her baby son in her arms) and extracted the ambiguous promise that the country's nobles would willingly shed their blood and give their lives for their queen but would not pay taxes. She prevailed against all the odds and during her long reign succeeded in creating an administrative unity of her disparate lands.

36. Even discounting Hungary, never officially part of the 'Austrian Empire', German-speaking people were a minority in Francis's limp brainchild.

37. They had also promoted the Counter-Reformation in Central Europe.

38. One of the spoils of victory Napoleon extracted from Austria in 1809 was the hand of a Habsburg archduchess, the later Empress Marie-Louise.

39. 'The empire was being administered rather than governed,' as Franz Hartig, one of Metternich's colleagues, put it.

40. He had no 'patriotic' feelings for Austria. His entry into Austrian service was prompted by his marriage to the daughter of Maria Theresa's chancellor, Prince Kaunitz, and a generous offer of a salary from the Emperor.

41. It was an astonishingly persuasive mirage that would last till 1918. Some still regret its passing.

42. In fact, the choice of a more suitable successor was limited. Francis Charles, Ferdinand's younger brother and husband of the Archduchess Sophie, though not actually a half-wit, was almost as ill-fitted to rule as Ferdinand; and the youngest sibling, Ludwig, was obtuse to say the least. Some of Francis's younger brothers were still alive, including the Archduke Rudolf, Beethoven's pupil and patron, but they were getting elderly and were more interested in music and their mistresses than in the throne. The only two capable members of the August House, the Archduke Charles (Napoleon's victor at Aspern) and the Archduke John, had excluded themselves by openly criticising Metternich. The Archduke John had also married a postmaster's daughter and was therefore banished from Court.

43. He was also twenty-first King of Jerusalem, but even the Habsburgs did not take that literally.

44. This may be a little unfair. After Metternich's resignation and flight in 1848 his only contribution to a panicky family conclave was 'Nur nicht schiessen' (only no shooting). This was leaked to the crowd milling around the Hofburg and, when he emerged for his daily constitutional, he received a few cheers for the first and last time in his reign. The remark also made the family — or the Archduchess Sophie, 'the only man at Court' according to the Saxon ambassador — decide that he must be dumped.

45. Like so many art-historical names invented to mock or to castigate (e.g. Impressionism or Fauves), the term 'Biedermeyer' was invented to ridicule. Wieland Gottlieb Biedermeyer was a fictitious character invented by two young German poets, Ludwig Eichrodt and Adolf Kussmaul, who collaborated to create the Biedermeyer *oeuvre* with some assistance from like-minded friends. The poems appeared from 1854 onwards in *Fliegende Blätter*, Munich's satirical magazine. The name was chosen carefully. *Bieder* means upright, virtuous and respectable (there is no exact English equivalent) and *Meier* is the German equivalent of Smith. The poems proved so popular that several volumes were later published. There was in fact a true model for 'bieder Meier'. Eichrodt and Kussmaul had by chance discovered a weighty publication of 500 pages entitled *The Complete Poems of the Old Village Schoolmaster Friedrich Sauter*, printed at the author's expense in Karlsruhe in 1845. Eichrodt and Kussmaul were entranced by the naïve simplicity merging into the fatuous of the schoolmaster's work and indeed republished some of Sauter's own poems in their collection. The concepts of Biedermeyer art as well as of a Biedermeyer 'age' were the products of the turn-of-the-century nostalgia for a pre-industrial, more simple and, above all, more *gemütlich* society. The best and most sympathetic book on Biedermeyer art is probably G. Norman's *Biedermeyer Painting* (London, 1987).

46. The Imperial Academy of the Fine Arts in Vienna had a succession of professors of flower painting.

47. He had died in 1828 at the age of 30 when Semmelweis was still a schoolboy.

48. The booklet is now preserved in the library of the Semmelweis Museum in Budapest.

49. Robert Schumann (1810–1856) was probably infected in about 1836 during his enforced separation from his beloved Clara. Most old textbooks state (rightly or wrongly) that long-delayed neurosyphilis tended to be more severe in cases where the primary stage (a genital sore) and the secondary stage (a general rash accompanying a flu-like illness) were mild or even unnoticed.

50. Mercurial ointments were particularly valued in genital sores recognised as venereal in origin. Mercury in all forms was almost certainly vastly over-used. In such cases the delayed cause of death was most often kidney failure.

51. For a time Metternich had to give way to Kolovrat, an immensely rich Bohemian aristocrat of vaguely reformist leanings. It proved a blip. More significantly, in Hungary the fiery patriot, Lajos (Louis) Kossuth who would have no truck with the Habsburgs, was increasingly replacing the more moderate Count István (Stephen) Széchenyi as leader of the reform movement.

52. Quoted by Benedek, *Semmelweis és Kora*, p. 234.

53. Latin was still widely used in Hungary in scientific communications, whereas in Austria German had virtually replaced it. Plants remained Semmelweis's hobby all his life.

54. *Collected Works of Semmelweis*, edited by T. Györi (Budapest, 1905), p. 59.

55. *Collected Works of Semmelweis*, p. 73.

56. Quoted by T. Györy, 'Semmelweis Irodalmi Hagyateka' (Semmelweis's literary legacy), *Orvosi Hetilap* (Budapest, 1906), p. 1.

57. Joseph Semmelweis survived his wife by only two years: he died while his eldest son was an assistant in Klein's clinic and could not return for the funeral.

58. T. Györy, 'Semmelweis Ignác családfája' (Semmelweis's family tree), *Budapesti Orvosi Ujsag*, 1906, p. 2.

59. Benedek, *Semmelweiss és Kora*, p. 235.

60. *Klinik* meant and still means a university hospital in German-speaking countries and in Hungary, not an outpatient department (clinic) as it does in England and the United States. It is in the former sense that the term is retained here, though spelt in the English way. (See Note 18 to Introduction.) It appears that the first regular 'clinical' bedside instruction began in Venice, where in 1579 the council ordered two teachers of practical medicine to be present at stated times at the hospital to teach students at the bedside.

61. I.P. Semmelweis, *Die Aetiologie der Begriff und die Prophylaxis des Kindbettfiebers* (Pest, 1861), p. 45. The quotations from this key work have been translated by the writer. An excellent (but not quite complete) translation with a perceptive introduction by K. Codell Carter was published by Wisconsin Publications in the History of Science and Medicine Series (1983). Translations of key sections by F.P. Murphy were also published in *Medical Classics* (Philadelphia, 1954), v, nos 5–8. The P in Semmelweis's publications stands for Philipp, the Christian name of his paternal grandfather. He never used the name outside publications.

62. Benedek, *Semmelweis és Kora*, p. 142.

63. The term 'epidemic' (from δέμος, meaning populace) was used by Hippocrates to describe a disease that was common or prevalent. He also applied it to diseases that were periodically or seasonally common in certain places. (One of the Hippocratic books is devoted to this kind of illness.) The term later fell into disuse, but was revived in the sixteenth century. In Semmelweis's day it referred to outbreaks of a disease in a certain place at a certain time, almost always due to some *external* influence. (Had the aetiology of puerperal fever been known, it would *not* have been classed as an epidemic.) Bacteria or viruses were not of course envisaged, but 'miasmata' were often blamed. 'Epidemic' was not synonymous with 'contagion' (a medieval coinage that appears in Chaucer), where the spread of the disease was ascribed to physical contact between individuals.

64. The section on the pre-Semmelweis history of puerperal fever is heavily indebted to the excellent chapter by I. Loudon, 'Puerperal Fever' in *Death in Childbirth*, edited by I. Loudon (Oxford, 1991), and on Loudon's more recent *The Tragedy of Childbirth* (Oxford, 2000). The author's dislike of Semmelweis is perhaps an over-reaction to earlier somewhat adulatory works.

65. C.D. Meigs, *Females and Their Diseases: A Series of Letters to his Class* (Philadelphia, 1848), p. 587.

66. J.-F.-E. Hervieux, *Traité clinique et pratique des maladies puerpérales* (Paris, 1880). Translated by I. Loudon.

67. They are 'benign' in the sense of not infiltrating the surrounding normal tissues and not metastasising; but they can cause serious blood loss and mechanical complications. The word is a bad hybrid term from the Latin *fibra* (fibre, scar) and ἔιδος (meaning 'like') to describe such benign tumours arising in the uterine muscle. Benign tumours of fibrous tissue elsewhere are called fibromas.

68. Semmelweis, *Die Aetiologie*, p. 134.

69. Meigs, *Females and Their Diseases*, p. 590.

70. A. Gordon, *A Treatise on the Epidemic of Puerperal Fever in Aberdeen* (London, 1795), p. 68.

71. W. Leishman, *A System of Midwifery* (Glasgow, 1876), p. 762.

72. Quoted by Benedek, *Semmelweis és Kora*, p. 151.

73. A. von Mouralt, *Handbuch der Frauenheilkunde und Geburtshilfe* (Leipzig, 1828).

74. C. White, *A Treatise on the Management of Pregnant and Lying-in Women* (London, 1773), p. 420.

75. White, *A Treatise on the Management of Pregnant and Lying-in Women*, p. 128.

76. A. Hirsch, *Handbook of Geographical and Historical Pathology* (London, 1885), ii, p. 450.

77. Gordon, *A Treatise on the Epidemic of Puerperal Fever in Aberdeen*, p. 62.

78. It is now known that the causative organism of erysipelas, the haemolytic Streptococcus, is (or was) also by far the commonest organism causing puerperal fever. Erysipelas (from ἔρυθρος meaning red and πέλλα meaning skin), sometimes referred to in the past as St Anthony's Fire or the Rose, is in fact a wound infection, like puerperal fever, though the breach in the skin that provides the entry for the organism may be minute.

79. I.H. Porter, *Alexander Gordon, MD, of Aberdeen*, Aberdeen Studies, 139 (Edinburgh, 1958).

80. J. Armstrong, 'Additional Facts and Observations Relative to Puerperal Fever which appeared in Sunderland and Several Places in 1813', *Edinburgh Medical and Surgical Journal*, 10 (1814), p. 440.

81. J. Roberton, 'Is Puerperal Fever Infectious?', *Medical Gazette*, 9 (1831–2), p. 503.

82. E. Blackmore, 'Observations on Puerperal Fever', *Provincial Medical and Surgical Journal*, 173–74 (1845), p. 210.

83. T. West, 'Observations on Some Diseases, Particularly Puerperal Fever in Abingdon and its Vicinity in 1813 and 1814', *London Medical Repository*, 2 (1815), p. 103.

84. R. Lee, *Researches on the Pathology and Treatment of Some of the Most Important Diseases of Women* (London, 1833).

85. W. Campbell, 'On Puerperal Fever', *Medical Gazette*, 9 (1831), p. 354.

86. Quoted in Slaughter, *Immortal Magyar*, p. 81.

87. Quoted in J. Berger, *Orvostörténelem*, (Pecs, Hungary, 1832), p. 58.

88. *Transactions of the College of Physicians of Philadelphia*, 1 (1801–6), p. 50.

89. J.S. Parry, 'Description of a Form of Puerperal Fever', *Journal of American Medical Sciences*, 69 (1875), p. 46.

90. O.W. Holmes, 'On the Contagiousness of Puerperal Fever', *New England Quarterly Journal of Medicine*, 1 (1842), p. 503.

91. B. Cullingworth, *Oliver Wendell Holmes and the Contagiousness of Puerperal Fever* (London, 1906).

92. O.W. Holmes, *Puerperal Fever as a Private Pestilence* (Boston, 1855), p. 69.

93. Among the treasures of the Semmelweis Museum Archives in Budapest is a textbook specially written for the instruction of midwives by Heinrich Johannes von Nepomuk Krantz, professor of obstetrics in the University of Vienna, at the express command of the Empress Maria Theresa, and published in translation into Hungarian by Istvan Veszprémi in Debrecen, Hungary, in 1766. This must be among the first textbooks of its kind in Europe and is extraordinarily detailed and modern. Fifteen years later regulations governing the training of midwives in the Habsburg Empire were embodied in a book by Anton Stoerck, imperial physician and one of the outstanding figures of the first Vienna School of Medicine. He was partly inspired by the practice in Leyden in Holland, though he further developed it. As a result, both in Hungary and Austria by the early nineteenth century the training of midwives was rigorous. For some reason (obscure after the lapse of two centuries) midwives, but not apparently doctors, received detailed training on how to baptise newborn parts as they emerged from the mother in case the child might not survive.

94. In retrospect the reason was almost certainly the routine participation of student midwives in post-mortem examinations, one of the achievements of the Napoleonic reforms. Osiander of Göttingen visited the place on his travels as a young doctor and described the 'party atmosphere' that prevailed in the garden shed set aside for autopsies, 'young women giggling and prancing around with their forearms covered in blood to their elbows, digging into the bodies, chatting and laughing'. Quoted by Benedek, *Semmelweis és Kora*, p. 91.

95. Semmelweis, *Die Aetiologie*, p. 65.

96. They nowadays fetch silly prices at auction. Some artistic specimens are preserved in the Semmelweis Museum in Budapest.

97. This of course was nonsense. The Vienna Krankenhaus and its Lying-in Hospital became a mecca for postgraduate students from all over Europe because of its vast patient material. Klein had never published a scientific paper and even if his later detractors were a little too ready to paint him as the epitome of the ignorant, selfish, vain and tyrannical medical boss, he had no international reputation.

98. Twenty-five pages in the *Midwives' Vademecum* were devoted to the proper rites and wordings required by canon law when an infant was suspected or feared to be dead or dying (see Note 93). The question of baptism of actually dead infants in utero had been the subject of lengthy discussions at the Council of Trent, but had never been fully resolved. Men and women were obviously 'conceived in sin' and there was similarly no doctrinal question (as there still is not) that embryos are living human beings from a very early stage of their development. Did they therefore need to be absolved of their inherited sins through the sacrament of baptism? In practice, infants were baptised as soon as they or any of their parts were *visible* during delivery, but not before. A special service of baptism existed in cases of abortion or stillbirth. It is not known how far Semmelweis practised these rites or indeed if he himself was a regular churchgoer, but he had certainly been baptised and confirmed, and the Austrian variant of the Hippocratic Oath included a commitment to upholding the teachings of the Holy Catholic Church. (An oath of loyalty to the August House of Habsburg was also

a requirement.) Many years later Semmelweis was married in a church in Pest and all his children were baptised; though he never, so far as is known, received the absolution of the last sacrament.

99. Semmelweis, *Die Aetiologie*, p. 124.
100. Semmelweis, *Die Aetiologie*, p. 153.
101. Mary Wollstonecraft (1759–1797), the brilliant radical writer, had an uncomplicated first delivery in France and had no truck with the fashion of well-bred ladies keeping to their room for weeks before labour was expected. Her second delivery also began smoothly, but the placenta would not separate spontaneously. After a day of suffering, Dr Poignard of the Westminster Lying-in Hospital was called in and removed the placenta manually. Despite the loss of blood, for a day or two she felt better but then developed puerperal fever and died. Her daughter, Mary, survived to become Shelley's second wife and the creator of Frankenstein.
102. Semmelweis, *Die Aetiologie*, p. 165.
103. Semmelweis, *Die Aetiologie*, p. 201.
104. One of the main reasons for the collapse of the revolutionary movements of 1848–49 was the incompatibility of the declared aims of the revolutionary leaders in different parts of the Empire. The Hungarian leader, Lajos Kossuth, proclaimed the aim of establishing an independent Kingdom of Hungary to embrace all the lands of the Crown of St Stephen, which included the northern *tót* regions, now the Slovak Republic. The aspiration of the Czech patriots, on the other hand, Kossuth's natural allies, would not allow them to abandon their 'Slovak brethren' (however backward and lamentably bigoted in their Catholic religion) to the mercy of their Magyar lords. Of course, the differences were not unbridgeable but their exploitation allowed the dynasty to re-establish its rule. The incompatibilities did not operate at an individual level. Kolletschka as a Slovak and Semmelweis as a Hungarian, both stranded in the German-speaking (though cosmopolitan) city of Vienna, may have had a shared sense of being expatriates.
105. As a political and economic power it was still near its nadir. Having emerged from the Congress of Vienna in 1815 as a picturesque appendage of the Austrian Empire, it had been deliberately neglected by the bureaucracy in Vienna. Its once-great port was allowed to shrivel in the shadow of the cosseted imperial city of Trieste; its famous luxury industries (with the exception of Murano glass, in which several archdukes had a financial interest) were taxed out of existence to protect the products of the Austrian homelands; its palaces and churches were allowed to crumble into the canals. Between 1815 and 1840 the city's population actually declined. With hindsight, of course, this saved it from being turned into a pompous Austrian provincial city with neo-Baroque monstrosities replacing the palazzi on the Canale Grande. However, even its incomparable natural beauty and art treasures were not appreciated north of the Alps until Byron's *Childe Harold* (as widely read on the Continent as in England) opened people's eyes to them. When visited by Semmelweis (soon after Turner's last visit), it was not yet overrun with tourists and must have been at its most entrancing.
106. Quoted by Benedek, *Semmelweis és Kora*, p. 321.
107. Quoted from fallible memory. Two later Hungarian biopics, one made in 1939 and other in 1952, were romanticised and slanted to suit the ruling political ideology of the day, though both were distinguished by some fine acting.

108. Known since Galen as the 'inflammatory response' or simply as 'inflammation'.

109. These outlined the lymphatic vessels by which the infection often spread initially. The lymph drains into a vein and thus into the general circulation.

110. The reason was not known until Roux, Behring and others showed that the absence of oxygen in dead tissue favours the growth and multiplication of some of the most lethal pathogenic micro-organisms.

111. Semmelweis, *Die Aetiologie*, p. 256.

112. Davy realised and demonstrated that chlorine was an element in its own right rather than a mixture. By convention, newly discovered elements were given a name that reflected one of their specific properties. In the case of chlorine this was the greenish tinge of the gas, from χλόρος meaning green.

113. Von Liebig was professor of chemistry in Giessen at the time, having been appointed in 1826 at the age of 23. Whether or not he actually carried out any experiments with 'cadaveric particles' is uncertain, but he was in no doubt that chlorine would 'digest' them.

114. In the 1880s and 1890s the eminent professor of dermatology, Hans von Hebra, is said to have started his annual course of lectures by telling his students that they had better take notice of what he was saying because they were listening to the 'first infant delivered by the immortal Semmelweis after his great discovery'.

115. One of these notices is preserved in the Medical Historical Library of the Semmelweis Museum in Budapest.

116. It is possible that Klein has been excessively blackened in the Semmelweis literature. Like countless professors and heads of departments before him and since, he was offended in his vanity when a discovery was made by one of his juniors without his 'signal contribution and support', let alone 'constructive criticism'. It even contradicted his own traditional teaching. He resented Semmelweis's lack of polish, a quality always highly valued in Vienna. For his part, Semmelweis could undoubtedly be tactless both then and later, which his friends, but not necessarily his enemies, readily overlooked. Klein was an insignificant plodder and a natural sycophant; but his venomous dislike for Semmelweis probably only developed after 1849 as a result of Skoda's intervention.

117. Semmelweis, *Die Aetiologie*, p. 243.

118. His own epithet.

119. 'For once, Klein did not try to undermine me,' Semmelweis wrote later.

120. Semmelweis, *Die Aetiologie*, p. 265.

121. In his monograph *The Tragedy of Childbed Fever*, Loudon suggests that many misunderstandings 'were entirely Semmelweis's fault and no one else's' (p. 100); in particular, they were the result of Semmelweis's unwillingness to publish. With great respect for Loudon's profound scholarship, this seems to the present writer a quite unjustified interpretation of the historic facts as well as of Semmelweis's character.

122. Kussmaul became successively professor of medicine in Heidelberg, Erlangen, Freiburg and Strassburg (as it then was as part of the Second German Reich). In clinical practice his name is still associated today with 'Kussmaul breathing', a periodic type of abnormal respiration in which a few seconds of total apnoea (cessation of breathing) are followed by a crescendo and then a diminuendo of hyperpnoea (overbreathing). It is usually a sign of advanced heart failure and is of ominous prognostic

significance. Kussmaul published his delightful book (Strassburg, 1890) when he was 68 and died in 1902 aged 80.

123. Franz Karl Naegele published several important books on obstetrics, including *The Obliquely Contracted and Pathological Pelvis* (Heidelberg, 1839). This particular bony deformity is still associated with his name. He died in 1871, aged 73.

124. Kussmaul, *Jugenderinnerungen eines alten Arztes*, p. 65.

125. F. Hebra, Editorial, *Übertragungen der Kaiserlichen and Königlichen Gesellschaft der Ärzte zu Wien*, 10 (1 December 1847). This important association, the forum of many significant medical advances in Vienna and elsewhere in the Empire, was formed in Baron Türkheim's flat in 1836; and in the 1840s its journal was probably the most widely read medical publication in German-speaking countries. Hebra's editorials were reprinted in Hebra's *Collected Works* and are quoted by E. Lesky in *Die Wiener Medizinische Schule* (Graz-Köln, 1965), p. 265.

126. Even at this early stage of the Hungarian Liberation Struggle of 1848–49 there were some who felt that Kossuth was going too far. Among them was Ferenc Deák, a respected small landowner, who felt that 'the Diet was getting drunk on rhetoric and there is no point in trying to argue with a drunk'. During the years of oppression following the defeat in 1849, he became the leader of Hungarian passive resistance and then of the gradual rapprochement with the dynasty. He was the effective architect of the Compromise Treaty of 1867, but declined the premiership in favour of his lieutenant, Count Julius Andrássy.

Some may find the term 'Liberation Struggle' over-dramatic to describe a historical event. There is in fact no accurate translation for the Hungarian *Szabadságharc*, nor is there an English technical term to describe it. The 'struggle' was more than an 'uprising': it lasted for about 18 months and was fought between two (later three) regular armies with regular command structures. There were several formal battles and sieges. However, it was not a war that was ever declared; nor, in any sense, was it a 'civil war'.

127. Once again, Paris sneezed and Europe caught a cold.

128. He died in Claremont in Surrey two years later.

129. The 1848 uprisings in the Habsburg Empire all started in cities of more than 100,000 inhabitants (Milan and Venice in Italy, Vienna in Austria, Pest in Hungary and Prague in Bohemia.) They were fuelled by their growth over the previous decades through migration from the countryside and the lack of industrial employment for the new urban proletariat. They were the products not of the Industrial Revolution but of its delay.

130. The *robot* was the peasantry's main grievance: it was an often crippling labour tax that peasants owed to their landlords. The hero of the 15 March uprising in Pest was the brilliant consumptive poet Alexander Petöfi, whose poem 'Arise Magyar' enthused his audience. A year and a half later Petöfi disappeared in the battle of Segesvár; his body was never found. Semmelweis loved his poetry and quoted two lines in one of his letters to his future wife.

131. The archduke was banned from Court for the rest of his life.

132. Hebra was an ardent revolutionary too at the time.

133. Baron Joseph Jelačić was a scion of the Croatian lesser nobility and an Austrian army officer. After 1848–49 he commanded Croatian troops against Montenegro. In the time he could spare from being a national hero, he wrote and published poems. He died in 1858, aged 57.

134. 'We are one people with the Serbs,' the Croat Diet declared and Jelačić spoke of the Serbs as 'our brothers in race and blood'.

135. Radetzky was of Bohemian extraction and joined the Austrian army in 1785. He 'did his job' despite his openly expressed contempt for the endless manoeuvrings and intrigues of the Habsburg Court. His dislike was heartily reciprocated. He died in 1858 aged 92, after which Austria never won a battle or a war.

136. Italian claims to Trieste and South Tyrol stirred Austrian patriotism (perhaps for the first and last time) and revolutionary students left the barricades that they had erected against imperial forces in Vienna to serve in the same forces in Italy. This bizarre event is still commemorated every year in Vienna's New Year's Concert, when the Radetzky March is handclapped through by a well-heeled audience.

137. Kossuth's Hungarian army under the leadership of General Arthur Görgey had won a number of victories over the Austrians. Instead of marching on Vienna, which might have saved the revolution there and might have ended the Liberation Struggle with a Hungarian victory, Görgey, under pressure from Kossuth, turned back to free Buda from the Austrians instead. An 'Academic Legion' formed in Vienna to meet and join Kossuth's army was easily turned back by imperial troops near the frontier. Contrary to what has been written in some biographies, Semmelweis did not join the legion. His sympathies were probably there; but Klein promptly withdrew to his villa on the Wolfgangsee as soon as there was any 'disorder' in the streets and somebody had to look after the patients.

138. Only once did Ferdinand re-emerge. He had been told about the outbreak of hostilities between Austria and Prussia in 1866. A fortnight later he observed the victorious Prussian troops marching under his window in Prague. 'Well, even I could have achieved that,' he is said have remarked. Perhaps he was not quite the *Trottel* he was made out to be.

139. He died in 1916 at a critical moment in the First World War. The writing for the dynasty was already on the wall.

140. Quoted by Benedek, *Semmelweis és Kora*, p. 348. Benedek also gives a good and well-documented account of the bureaucratic machinations that led to Semmelweis's departure from Vienna.

141. Quoted by Benedek, *Semmelweis és Kora*, p. 158.

142. Lesky, *Die Wiener Medizinische Schule*, and Benedek, *Semmelweis és Kora*, p. 196.

143. Quoted by Benedek, *Semmelweis és Kora*, p. 247.

144. See also Part III, Lister. Sir James Young Simpson was 38 in 1849 and had already contributed numerous papers (on cellulitis, uterine cancer and hermaphroditism, among others) to the obstetric literature. Today his main claim to fame is his introduction to Great Britain of chloroform anaesthesia. Traditionally, he was testing various chemicals when one of his assistants upset the bottle of chloroform. When Mrs Simpson brought in the dinner, he found the assembled company asleep. Simpson tried half a teaspoonful on a rag applied to the nose of a woman in labour and it worked. He was also a noted archaeologist. He died in 1870, aged 58.

145. Franz Hektor von Arneth was born in the same year as Semmelweis but lived until 1907. He remained his friend's staunch supporter after his appointment to the chair of obstetrics in St Petersburg in 1850.

146. Semmelweis, *Die Aetiologie*, p. 153.

503

147. Quoted by T. Györy (ed.), *Collected Works of Semmelweis* (Budapest, 1905), p. 132.

148. Not only by the mad Rudolf II but also by Leopold I and Joseph II. Most of the Austrian-Viennese aristocracy had their second (and usually much prettier) town residence in Prague, still one of the attractions of that lovely city. It was in Prague that Mozart enjoyed one of his relatively few great successes with the first performance of *The Marriage of Figaro* in the presence of Joseph II (who liked the opera but thought that it contained too many notes).

149. There was some substance to this.

150. In 1851 aged 38.

151. He was three years younger than Semmelweis: he died in 1891, aged 70. The family came from South Tyrol, hence the Italian name.

152. In so far as Scanzoni had any original ideas about puerperal fever, he seemed to subscribe to Rokitansky's 'Krasis' theory long after Rokitansky himself had quietly dropped it.

   Seyfert's assistant, August Breisky, was another who publicly and with great vigour attacked Semmelweis, attributing puerperal fever to a substance he named 'divinum aliquid', which would always remain inexplicable and therefore incurable. But Breisky was a man of honour and in the late 1860s he publicly confessed his error and, as professor first in Prague and later in Vienna, became one of Semmelweis's posthumous admirers.

153. Among those who did much of their ground-breaking work on cadavers was Leopold Auenbrugger (1729–1809), the inventor of percussion as an aid to diagnosis.

154. What worried the Czar, Nicolas I, was not so much the impending humiliation of Austria as the number of Polish generals who served in Kossuth's army. 'We shall surprise the world with our ingratitude,' Metternich is said to have commented on hearing about Russia's intervention on Austria's side. His prophecy was correct.

155. Kossuth and many of those closest to him fled. Görgey surrendered at Világos in Transylvania to the Russian, not to the Austrian, commander, though this did not save his generals from being tried by an Austrian military tribunal. Görgey himself had not been an army officer and was allowed simply to retire.

156. Battyányi, a man of nobility (and an illegitimate descendant of Prince Eugène of Savoy), had been constitutionally appointed by Ferdinand and had refused to follow Kossuth's extremism. His execution was the most openly outrageous act of the Haynau terror. (He seems to have been particularly hated by the Archduchess Sophie, Francis Joseph's mother, perhaps a spurned mistress of his youth.)

157. These were solemn ceremonies where the name and crime of the traitor were nailed to the gallows and a volley was fired by an execution squad. Among these 'hanged' in this way was Count Gyula (Julius) Andrassy, future prime minister of Hungary and foreign minister of the Dual Monarchy. Queen-Empress Elizabeth, perhaps more than a little in love with him, addressed him playfully in her letters as 'mon beau pendu'.

158. Today Budapest's town hall.

159. He took his revenge on being told of his dismissal by immediately pardoning and setting free all prisoners still in the New Building, including those

awaiting execution the next morning. Among them was Semmelweis's friend, the surgeon Janos Balassa.

160. Hungarians called them the 'Bach hussars'. Throughout his long reign Francis Joseph dismissed his loyal and sometimes long-suffering ministers when they had served their purpose without a moment's hesitation or any token of gratitude or even appreciation. But Bach, the perfect bureaucrat, was a kindred spirit; and, when the events of 1859 made his dismissal necessary, he was sent to Rome as Austria's ambassador to the Holy See and remained there for the rest of his life.

161. Semmelweis learnt to ride to be able to join: unlike most Hungarian professors (like von Markusovszky) he was a townie who had never ridden a horse before. He fell off on the second occasion and broke his arm.

162. Austria's first major defeat came in 1859 when Sardinia was provoked into war by a senseless ultimatum summoning it to disarm. But Radetzky had died in 1857 and his incompetent successor, Gyulay, who owed his position to court intrigue, could not be provoked into action even by a telegram from the Emperor's adjutant: 'Surely you can do as well as that old ass Radetzky.' The French under Napoleon III's personal command (or dither) had time to come to the aid of the Piedmontese. Two months later, attempting to repeat Radetzky's victory at Custoza, the Austrian army blundered into the French at Solferino. The two antiquated war machines competed in incompetence but the French, mostly by accident, held the field. The event shook Francis Joseph's faith in his army for the rest of his life, which did not stop Austria from suffering a more decisive defeat by Prussia seven years later. Each time political concessions followed.

163. Most of them had spent some weeks or months in prison, Balassa acquiring tuberculosis there, which eventually killed him. Korányi was banished to the provinces.

164. Its street facade on the Rákoczy Street has not changed much. Rokus, Saint Roche or San Rocco was the patron saint of those suffering from the plague and is usually represented pointing to a bubo (abscess) in his groin.

165. T. Györy, *Orvosi Hetilap*, 1 (1905), p. 12.

166. All professorial appointments in the empire were signed by the Emperor and appointees were expected to appear for a two-minute audience at the Hofburg or Schönbrunn (much as recipients of British decorations are herded through Buckingham Palace today). Semmelweis declined, claiming ill-health.

167. Austria's foreign minister, Buol, there on sufferance since Austria had remained neutral in the war, had naïvely hoped to win a French guarantee for Austria's Italian possessions. Instead, he had to sit through Cavour's impassioned denunciation of Austrian rule, warmly applauded by delegates from both sides.

168. von Waldheim, *Ignaz Philip Semmelweis*, p. 68. Semmelweis's wife has been criticised by historians for her apparent 'desertion' and for changing her 'illustrious name' (by Györy). She was by all contemporary accounts a rather simple but kindly person who had much hardship to endure.

169. But he did apply for the chair of obstetrics in Vienna after Klein's death in 1856; and, contrary to earlier biographies, he received much support from Skoda, Rokitansky and others. Considering the way he left Vienna, this was not ungenerous treatment.

170. The boy, Béla, committed suicide when he was 23. He was known as something of a gambler, but the reason for killing himself has remained

a mystery. The elder daughter, Margit, never married and supported herself as a private language teacher. She repeatedly applied for a state pension, citing her father's achievements, but was turned down each time. She died in 1928. The younger daughter, Antonia, a charming and witty person, married a circuit judge, Kálmán Lehoczky. Their two sons changed their name to Lehoczky-Semmelweis and one of them became a successful gynaecologist-obstetrician in Budapest. He died in a mental hospital in 1962. The other became a soldier: his descendants now live in Germany. Antonia died in 1942.

171. The number of complimentary copies sent remains uncertain.

172. Joseph Späth was professor at the Josephinum, Vienna University's prestigious postgraduate institute founded by Joseph II.

173. I.P. Semmelweiss, *Magyar Orvosi Hetilap*, 10 (1862), supplement 1. It is inconceivable that a professor of medicine should pen such a letter today to another professor and even more inconceivable that a reputable medical journal would print it. Yet the occasional grounds for such letters have surely not disappeared.

174. I.P. Semmelweis, *Magyar Orvosi Hetilap*, 11 (1863), supplement 1.

175. I.P. Semmelweis, *Magyar Orvosi Hetilap*, 11 (1863), supplement 2.

176. I.P. Semmelweis, *Magyar Orvosi Hetilap*, 11 (1863), supplement 4.

177. Quoted by Benedek, *Semmelweis és Kora*, p. 413.

178. Quoted by Benedek, *Semmelweis és Kora*, p. 415.

179. Quoted by Benedek, *Semmelweis és Kora*, p. 418.

180. Quoted by Slaughter, *Immortal Magyar*, p. 200.

181. Semmelweis seems to have been unaware of Pasteur's microbiological discoveries, the first of which were published in the early 1860s. Though he was of course an assiduous morbid anatomist, there is no evidence that he ever looked down a microscope. In some respects this makes his observations even more remarkable.

182. There were several outstanding neurologists and neuropsychiatrists working there at the time.

183. Among Semmelweis's own compatriots and contemporaries it caused the death of one of the country's greatest poets, M. Vörösmarty, greatest painters, M. Munkácsi, greatest scientists, J. Bolyay and greatest political thinkers, Count I. Széchenyi. (The last committed suicide in the mental home, a not uncommon ending.) Until recently these deaths were referred to in history books as being the result of grief over their country's misfortune. Semmelweis did not of course actually die of the disease, but he might never have sustained the injury that caused his death outside a mental hospital. For how long the illness may have clouded his judgement is impossible to say. It could explain the intemperate tone of his open letters. On the other hand, he was active in clinical practice until two or three months before his collapse. Both in its onset and course GPI has always been recognised as an unpredictable disease. Some notable sufferers in the arts (like Manet and Gauguin), in literature (like Baudelaire, Maupassant and Oscar Wilde), and in music (like Schumann, Wolf and Delius) continued to create great works while the disease was physically far advanced. One of the last works of the artist M. Munkácsi was a portrait of Liszt. It is an excellent painting, but the dedication with its duplication of syllables ('To Feferenc Liliszt') is a well-established manifestation of GPI. Sufferers' handwriting often deteriorated before their poetic or musical impulse or scientific creativity waned. This was true of Semmelweis.

184. Benedek's expression.
185. But it also spared the country's medical fraternity years of embarrassment.
186. Quoted by Benedek, *Semmelweis és Kora*, p. 432.
187. G. Marais, *Emile Roux, médecin français* (Paris, 1938), p. 43. What Pasteur drew was the characteristic garland-like appearance of the *streptococcus* (from στρέπτος meaning chain or garland and Latin coccus, meaning berry, another bit of hybrid kitchen Latin-Greek), the haemolytic variety of which was the commonest cause of puerperal fever. The term coccus, still widely used, was introduced by the great Viennese surgeon Theodor Billroth (see Part III, Lister) in 1874 to describe small round bacterial forms. Pasteur recognised the organism as the common pathogen in childbed fever in the early 1870s: he called it 'microbe en chapelet de grains'. It was first cultured by Rosenbach in 1884.
188. Quoted by Benedek, *Semmelweis és Kora*, p. 427.
189. See notes 4 and 168. Fritz Schürer von Waldheim was a Viennese doctor who spent many years researching Semmelweis's life with admirable thoroughness and sympathy. All Semmelweis's biographers (including the present writer) owe him a great debt.
190. But medical students are surely too lazy a breed to make this story credible.

Part III: Lister

1. George Fox, founder of the Society of Friends or Quakers, died in 1691, aged 67. Between 1653 and 1673 he was imprisoned on six different occasions. In 1654 he and nearly 1000 of his followers were in jail.
2. Medicine did not require an academic degree, but Thomas Hodgkin's faith was probably the main reason why, despite his MD degree from Edinburgh (which did not ban Quakers), he was never elected to the clinical staff of Guy's Hospital. However, several Quaker physicians had already achieved fame and fortune in England, most notably John Coakley Lettsom, tireless philanthropist and pamphleteer in good causes (the care of prostitutes, cheap porridge for the poor, the evils of tea drinking, Sunday Schools, free dispensaries, sea-bathing infirmaries for consumptives, the virtues of smallpox vaccination, the care of deaf-mutes and many more) as well as a highly sought-after and remunerated physician. Lettsom had had a long apprenticeship with Abraham Sutcliff in Yorkshire and then at St Thomas's Hospital, but he had to go to Leyden in Holland to obtain his MD degree. His publications, some remarkably prescient (especially those relating to public health), earned him the fellowship of the Royal Society. Sadly and un-Quaker-like, his many admirable qualities did not embrace financial prudence; and, despite inheriting a fortune, marrying an heiress and being reputedly the highest-earning doctor in London, his charitable and educational ventures frequently led him into dire financial straits. He died in 1816, aged 72, remaining a role model for young Quakers contemplating medicine as a career.
3. Usher was (and is) the name of the teacher in Quaker schools.
4. Quoted by Sir Rickman J. Godlee, *Lord Lister* (London, 1917), p. 4.
5. Quoted by Godlee, *Lord Lister*, p. 6.

6. Joseph Jackson was an adept user of the camera lucida as well as an accomplished silhouette artist.

7. Mary Lister painted a charming watercolour of the porticoed back of the house and part of the garden, reproduced in Godlee's book.

8. A particularly hideous block of flats more or less on the site of Upton House now bears the name of Lister Court.

9. The Ham House opposite Upton was not the Ham House that was the seat of the Lauderdales in Surrey and is now a National Trust property. The prison reformer Elizabeth Fry was Samuel Gurney's sister.

10. Lister's earliest and authorised biographer was his nephew, Sir Rickman J. Godlee, Bart, himself a distinguished surgeon. The book focuses on Lister's professional career rather than on his private life, but it is written with insight and genuine sympathy. Several other biographies based on this book are listed in the Bibliography, as are the more important memoirs written by Lister's colleagues and juniors. The best and most up-to-date biography based on fresh and original research of letters, Lister's Commonplace books, ward journals and other personal documents is R.B. Fisher, *Joseph Lister, 1827–1912* (London, 1977). It is an indispensable source. Lister is set into context in an excellent but more general work: F.F. Cartwright, *The Development of Modern Surgery* (London, 1967).

    Between 1820 and 1832 Isabella Lister had seven children, six of whom survived into adult life and three of whom had descendants. The last child was Jane. By then her health was declining; but even in her last years of ill-health her grandson remembered her as a 'dear dignified old lady'.

11. See also Note XX to Part I, Laennec.

12. T. Hodgkin and J.K. Lister, 'Notice of some Microscopic Observations of the Blood and Animal Tissues', *Philosophical Magazine*, 2 (1827), p. 130. Their observations have been extended but never superseded.

13. Though it is impossible to make a firm retrospective diagnosis, the progressive symptoms over a period of nearly two years are consistent with a brain tumour. Even a slowly growing and essentially 'benign' tumour like a meningioma would kill in those days.

14. John Hunter migrated from Glasgow to London with his brother William and became surgeon to St George's Hospital and a celebrated teacher. He was inquisitive and industrious and wrote extensively on a prodigious range of subjects. He is still widely regarded (for no clearly discernible reason) as the founder of scientific surgery. He often asked penetrating questions, though he rarely provided the correct answers. He died after a tempestuous hospital board meeting in 1793, aged 65.

15. Physicians could acquire a mark of distinction by obtaining a doctorate in medicine offered by universities. The only such distinction open to surgeons was the membership of the Royal College of Surgeons. However, membership of the College was not at first necessary to practise as a surgeon (as was the licence of the Apothecaries); nor did a higher surgical qualification find much favour with practitioners. Fellowship examinations were first introduced in 1836, but only six candidates presented themselves during the next four years and the scheme fizzled out. Eventually the College acquired a new charter in 1843 (changing its name from Royal College of Surgeons of London to Royal College of Surgeons of England) and elected 300 distinguished members to become foundation fellows. Fellowship examinations were soon instituted.

16. This was the classical complication of tuberculosis of the spine. As vertebrae became diseased and collapsed, their contents were squeezed out as semi-liquid tuberculous pus. The pus tracked from the back to the groin along the sheath of the Psoas muscle, which stretches from the spine to below the hip and is the main flexor muscle of the joint. The abscess usually pointed just below the inguinal crease and was sometimes difficult to distinguish from an inflamed lymph node or even a hernia. It could be lanced and drained, but this had no effect on the underlying disease of the spine.

17. The causative organisms, now known as the *Clostridium tetani* and *Clostridium welchii* respectively, can be members of the normal bacterial flora of the large bowel of horses and sometimes of humans. They were not identified and described until the 1880s.

18. Many of these emergencies are treatable today without operation, but that has become possible only since the advent of antibiotics and intravenous therapy. They were almost invariably fatal at the time Lister embarked on surgery.

19. Sir James Paget of the next generation of great surgeons (and a very different character) described him as 'the greatest practical surgeon of our time'. He actually made as well as designed many of the new instruments still named after him. Among them are the aptly named Fergusson's lion forceps.

20. Extensively quoted in Cartwright, *The Development of Modern Surgery*.

21. The condition known as 'imperforate anus' is not uncommon and varies from a delicate membrane easily pierced to more severe forms in which the bowel ends blind some centimetres from the skin.

22. These were most commonly the result of sexually transmitted gonococcal infection.

23. Sir W. Fergusson, *A System of Practical Surgery* (London, 1842), p. 342.

24. Like Lister, he came from Quaker stock and became a highly successful practitioner. He is eponymously known for the abnormally notched 'Hutchinson's teeth', one of a triad of manifestations of congenital syphilis. The other two are interstitial keratitis (a form of scarring of the cornea of the eye) and deafness.

25. The picture is now in the possession of University College Hospital, London.

26. Like his rival Fergusson, Liston was a Scotsman, born in Ecclesmachen in Linlithgowshire, the son of the manse. After completing his studies in Edinburgh, he helped his cousin, James Syme, to run a private course of anatomy (severely hampered by lack of bodies). His success as a surgeon, though without beds or an appointment at the Royal Infirmary, aroused much jealousy; on being offered the chair of clinical surgery at University College Hospital in London, he migrated south. He was a tall, powerful and handsome man, something of a dandy, and a brilliant operator. He died suddenly almost exactly a year after the event described in the text, aged 53, from an aortic aneurysm. He is buried in Highgate Cemetery.

27. The most dramatic is the account, perhaps slightly fictionalised, by H.S. Hartman, published by his grandson Jürgen Thorwald (see Bibliography).

28. The Bigelows were a medical dynasty in Boston. Jacob Bigelow was born in 1818 but, after studying at Harvard, spent several years in England and on the Continent of Europe. His name became linked with an ingenious device for crushing stones in the bladder and then evacuating the fragments by suction. It had in fact been invented by a French urologist, Jean Civiale, in 1824. Bigelow died in 1890, aged 72.

29. Morton had added a scented substance and a dye (fortunately harmless) that coloured the ether pink.
30. Priority had been much disputed, but probably belongs to the dentist Horace Wells, of Hartford, Connecticut. He was impressed by the effect of nitrous oxide on pain, the liquid being hawked at fairs by an itinerant showman, Gardner Quincey Colton. Wells was a clever but somewhat unstable character and had the misfortune that his first and much-heralded demonstration of general anaesthesia at the Massachusetts General Hospital misfired. In the middle of the operation the patient leapt from the chair screaming, though he later professed to have felt no pain. Thereafter Wells fought a desperate losing battle against Morton, Jackson and other medical entrepreneurs. He visited France where he had some success; but, returning to New York, he got into trouble with the law and committed suicide in Tombs prison. The background is murky. Colton, the only person of a generous nature involved in the saga (he always acknowledged Wells's priority) later founded the Colton Painless Extraction Company and administered gas to 67,455 patients without a fatality and making a fortune. (If his results were as good as he claimed, the fortune was not undeserved.) In the meantime William Thomas Green Morton, Wells's one-time friend and partner, attended the chemistry classes of Professor Charles Jackson and it was apparently Jackson who drew Morton's attention to the possible anaesthetic properties of sulphuric ether (already described by both Davy and Faraday). He also explained Morton's early failure by pointing out the need to use a highly purified preparation: most preparations were dilute and often heavily contaminated.

Eventually, Morton demonstrated ether anaesthesia successfully at a historic operating session by the surgeon John Collins Warren, at the Massachusetts General Hospital on 14 October 1846. Thereafter he and Jackson engaged in a pitched legal battle for patent rights and glory that lasted for years, joining forces occasionally to fight off Wells's claims (and later the claims of Wells's widow) and to discredit him. There were endless lawsuits and congressional hearings, complete with vast bribes to congressmen, senators and judges, the parading of false witnesses and the production of piles of forged documents on a grandiose scale. On the whole, the medical profession turned against Morton at an early stage when he refused to disclose the composition of his 'magic fluid' without being paid a huge sum for patent rights; this stance he maintained till his death. Meanwhile, Jackson concocted a story that pictured Morton as a mere executor of instructions given to him by Jackson. The rights of Wells's widow were defended free of charge by the great lawyer Truman Smith; they were eventually recognised. Morton suffered a mental breakdown and died in St Luke's Hospital in New York in 1868, aged 48. Five years later Jackson too went mad and spent the last seven years of his life (until his death in 1880) in the mental illnesses wing of the Massachusetts General Hospital. It is not one of the heart-warming stories of medical progress and never attracted the attention of Dr Paul de Kruif in his brave search for medical heroes. However, some years after Morton's death a pretty memorial was erected over his grave by the citizens of Boston with a tribute in verse by Dr Jacob Bigelow, reproduced in H. Ellis, *History of Surgery* (London, 2000).
31. Opium and alcohol had been used since time immemorial and various herbal preparations of uncertain nature had been hawked about since at

least the early seventeenth century. F.F. Cartwright's *The English Pioneers of Anaesthesia* (Bristol, 1852) is a valuable study.

Lister stated in 1870 that he had never seen any adverse effect from opiates—opium or morphine—and used both freely, though their addictive nature was suspected. At King's he used *Cannabis indica* to relieve headaches. If it did not work, quinine was often effective. He successfully injected atropine to ease severe muscular spasm and used belladonna freely. Chloral hydrate, one of the first of the synthetic drugs, was used regularly and often in combination with morphine to induce sleep. Patients with cough from acute bronchitis were given chloroform, sometimes in combination with tincture of camphor and ammonia. Calabar bean was given in tetanus, a strange choice since it is supposed to be a muscle stimulant rather than a relaxant, but, like other strange choices, it often worked, at least symptomatically.

32. Between 1798 and 1800 the future discoverer of sodium, potassium and of the miner's safety lamp worked closely with the eccentric medical genius Dr Thomas Beddoes in Bristol. Beddoes published some of Davy's findings in his *Notice of Some Observations Made at the Medical Pneumatic Institution* (Bristol, 1799). He was surrounded by a remarkable circle of friends that included Southey, Wordsworth, Coleridge, James Watt, Roget (of the *Thesaurus*), Maria Edgeworth and Josiah and Thomas Wedgwood.

33. See Note 24 to Introduction. Mesmerism seemed to die a natural death after the death of Mesmer in 1815, though it was resurrected in the 1830s in England by no less a figure than John Elliotson, professor of medicine at University College Hospital, Lumleyan lecturer and Harveyan orator of the Royal College of Physicians, reputed to be one of the ablest doctors in London. Having seen mesmerism work in a number of patients, he conceived it his duty to persuade his surgical colleagues to use it. His demonstrations at first aroused great interest—Dickens attended one and was 'bowled over'—but soon embroiled him in bitter controversies. The Council of University College Hospital eventually resolved to ban mesmerism within the hospital, whereupon Elliotson resigned. In 1843 he founded a journal, *The Zoist: A Journal of Cerebral Physiology and Mesmerism and their Application to Human Welfare*, which continued publication for 12 years and reported numerous surgical operations, mostly minor, performed under hypnosis. Its converts included James Esdaile, surgeon in charge of the Native Hospital at Hooghly in India, who later reported an impressive series of major operations like mastectomies and amputations performed painlessly under mesmerism. In 1840 James Braid, an enlightened Edinburgh graduate working in Manchester, developed a more rational theory than animal magnetism to account for hypnotic effects and expounded it in an astonishingly modern book, *Neurypnology* (London, 1835). He performed many minor procedures like tooth extractions under hypnosis. Though Elliotson continued his advocacy until his death in 1868, the advent of ether and chloroform, both more effective and more widely applicable, put an end to hypnosis as a surgical anaesthetic.

34. The term 'anaesthesia' was to be coined by Oliver Wendell Holmes, professor of anatomy and physiology at Harvard, in November 1846 (see Part II, Semmelweis).

35. The event is commemorated today by a blue plaque on Boott's house in Gower Street. It is one of London's meanest memorials, mentioning neither Boott, his anaesthetist, nor the patient by name.

36. Sir Francis Galton, the great geneticist, had his nervous breakdown as a student about the same time as Lister.

37. One enthusiastic recipient of the paper was Rudolf Kölliker, professor of physiology in Würzburg. Thirty-five years later Lister, then president of the Royal Society, would bestow on him the Society's Copley Medal.

38. But a smattering of Latin was a prerequisite of entry, just as a 'basic knowledge' of the Scriptures was required at Oxford, Cambridge or London's King's College. The former could be acquired in two weeks, the latter was reputed to take an afternoon.

39. The usual indication was tuberculosis of the foot. The heel, turned by 90 degrees, could be fashioned into a useful stump. Syme also designed a short-bladed knife that is still in use.

40. Quoted by Godlee, *Lord Lister*, p. 89.

41. Quoted by Fisher, *Joseph Lister*, p. 87.

42. This may be a fairly general (though certainly not universal) minor deficiency of great creative minds. 'How could anybody accomplish anything immortal/If stopping all the time to make people chortle?', Ogden Nash wondered in *Don't Grin or You'll Have to Bear It*.

43. A ritual eight-hour fast before a general anaesthetic, still in force in many hospitals, was not introduced till the mid-1860s when several fatal cases of aspiration pneumonia were reported.

44. See also Part II, Semmelweis. The name chloroform derives from a muddled combination of chlorine and formyl (the hypothetical radical of formic acid). It was described under different names more or less simultaneously in 1832 by Soubeiran in France and von Liebig in Germany. Its composition was first accurately determined by Pasteur's patron and master, Dumas, in 1834; and its anaesthetic properties in animals were noted but not described in any detail by Flourens in 1847. Amazingly perhaps, a verbal account by a student who knew another student who had met a third student who had heard about Flourens's experiments was enough to persuade Simpson to try the vapour first on his family, friends and himself and then on his patients. Chloroform was far more pleasant to patients than ether but probably more dangerous in the long run. Its toxic effects on the liver, heralded by the onset of jaundice, could be delayed by weeks, but when they did occur they tended to be untreatable and irreversible.

45. The Hebrew word in fact means sadness or sorrow.

46. The anaesthetic was administered by Dr John Snow, who had made a private study of anaesthetic gases and who can be regarded as the first specialist in the field. Modest and unassertive, he was also to become something of a role model. He was also tuberculous and died soon after anaesthetising the Queen for a second time during her next delivery.

47. 'The effect was soothing, quieting & delightful beyond measure,' the Queen recorded in her diary.

48. But not everybody *everywhere*. While anaesthesia spread with extra-ordinary speed in Britain and on the Continent, on its home ground in the United States it continued to arouse fierce controversy. Objections to it were raised not only on moral and religious grounds (as in Scotland) but also for medical and scientific reasons. 'Anaesthesia is not safe and never will be, even when administered in the most cautious manner,' thundered the editor of the *New York Journal of Medicine*; and Chief Army Surgeon John B Porter had no doubt that 'by inhaling ether

... even in the most cautious way ... the blood is poisoned, nervous regulation is destroyed, muscular function is ruined and healing is delayed or completely abolished'. There were other harmful effects. Infection was promoted and 'shock was made more likely' (rather than the reverse). Several prominent practitioners raised the awful spectre, sometimes regarded as the product of the age of curare and other muscle relaxants, that ether merely erased the memory of pain, not pain itself. 'Anaesthesia is death,' declared John P. Harrison, Vice President of the American Medical Association, 'deeply mistaken philanthropy. Pain is intrinsically an essential component of the cure.' Some of the objections verged on the bizarre. 'How is the anaesthetised patient to protect himself or herself not only against rape, theft and other injuries inflicted by aggressive or deranged surgeons but also against the surgeon amputating the wrong limb or extracting the wrong tooth?' (All these do happen on rare occasions, but are no longer regarded as powerful contraindications of anaesthesia as such.) 'A satanic invention ... not to be countenanced,' William Henry Atkins, first president of the American Dental Association, announced. Anaesthesia was fiercely resisted by the majority of elderly and respectable obstetricians: it removed 'the essential reflexes mediated by pain which alone would ensure a smooth delivery and a satisfactory return to normal'.

No less acrimonious were debates about the careful selection of patients requiring painkillers: gender, age, social class, unsocial habits (like alcoholism) and of course race were all to be taken into account. That anaesthesia should be available to everyone, even to debauched alcoholics, coloured people or criminals, was barely considered. Ten years after Morton demonstrated ether anaesthesia, a third of amputations at the Pennsylvania Hospital were still performed without anaesthesia and death from shock continued to be high; see M.S. Pernick, *A Calculus of Suffering* (New York, 1895).

49. It was of course far from the modern anaesthetic, which can keep patients under for hours with safety. Often it gave the surgeon a 'window' of a few minutes to perform the most painful part of the operation. This was nevertheless enough to make possible operations like Syme's amputation of the foot at the ankle (which inevitably took some minutes).

50. This may have been true also of other outstanding British surgeons of his generation, like Benjamin Collins Brodie of St George's Hospital and Sir James Paget. Neither of them were particularly speedy.

51. The provision of bodies, regulated by Napoleonic legislation, was always easier in France than it was in England.

52. Among the friskiest subalterns under Prince Gortchakoff's command was Count Leo Tolstoy.

53. The Turkish ships were all sunk but human casualties were small.

54. Gladstone, a political opponent, said 30 years later that in all his public life there was nobody he had loved more as a person.

55. Aberdeen was swept away by a rebellion of his ministers (less single-mindedly dedicated to office than they are today) and a vote of censure in the House of Commons.

56. Lack of nursing was even more glaring but not perceived as such. Florence Nightingale had to fight to be given permission to take her troupe of young ladies to the front or at least near it.

57. The Royal Army Medical Corps was not established till 1892.

58. Bell did not actually participate in the battle, but arrived a few hours late to operate without rest for three successive nights and days in the improvised military hospital in Brussels. He bequeathed a series of vivid oil sketches of the wounded to the Royal College of Surgeons of Edinburgh. In 1835, after 30 years' successful practice in London, he became professor of surgery in his native city, and died in 1842, aged 68. He discovered the separate identity of sensory and motor nerves and described 'Bell's palsy', the common facial deformity (usually transient) resulting from paralysis of the facial nerve on one side. He was an excellent original investigator as well as an outstanding surgeon, much revered by both Syme and Lister.

59. Quoted by Fisher, *Joseph Lister*, p. 126.

60. Quoted by Fischer, *Joseph Lister*, p. 128.

61. Quoted by Godlee, *Lord Lister*, p. 67.

62. Quoted by Godlee, *Lord Lister*, p. 69.

63. The Rokitanskys had already visited Edinburgh and had stayed with the Symeses in Millbank. They had also spent a day with the Listers in Upton. The world of European science was still small.

64. See Part II, Semmelweis.

65. The legend was apparently started by Hueppe at the International Congress of Obstetrics in Budapest in 1894 that 'Lister acknowledged his great debt to Semmelweis in initiating antiseptic surgery'. The notion was later endorsed by the eminent Semmelweis scholar Tibor de Györy. This does credit to de Györy's patriotism but not to his otherwise impeccable scholarship. Almost certainly Lister's attention was first drawn to Semmelweis's work only in the late 1880s by Theodore Duka, a Hungarian obstetrician who had fled Hungary with Kossuth in 1849 and had settled in London (see Part II, Semmelweis). By the 1880s Duka was a successful obstetrician and a prominent fellow of the Royal Obstetrical Society, but he still cherished his links with Hungary. In 1894 Lister wrote to Weckerling, a Vienna obstetrician, that he was much impressed by what he had learnt about Semmelweis's achievement but that he had come across it only two or three years earlier. There is no reason to doubt this.

66. They had been discovered and named 'white cells' (to distinguish them from the much more numerous red blood cells) by Littré and Robin in 1705; their amoeboid motion was noted by Wharton-Jones, one of Lister's teachers at University College Hospital; and their purposeful migration was described by Cohnheim. Their essential scavenging action was discovered by Elie Metchnikoff in 1884: it is he who named the cells 'phagocytes'.

67. Catgut, still widely used, is prepared from the intestine of the sheep, not of the cat. The word should properly be 'kitgut', where 'kit' stands for fiddle, the material having been used for centuries for the strings of musical instruments. It can be sterilised and is gradually absorbed by the tissues. Lister introduced it to surgery in an article in the *British Medical Journal* on 3 April 1869.

68. 'Is he lucky?' was the first thing (and sometimes the last) Napoleon wanted to know about an officer before he promoted him to general.

69. Virchow established the three groups of factors that influence the onset of thrombosis—that is, clot formation in the living—alterations in the composition of blood, alterations in the flow of blood, and alterations in the vessel wall. They are still known as Virchow's Triad and are still valid.

70. Following a visit to Paris by Volta in 1807, Napoleon founded a scientific prize of 3000 francs; and, despite the fact that France and England were at

war, the first medal was awarded to Davy. In 1813, the two countries still at war, Napoleon gave Davy permission to visit the volcanoes in the Auvergne and the English party was entertained by French chemists and at Court.

71. Though Pasteur was an ardent patriot and refused the Prussian Order Pour la Mérite bestowed on him by Kaiser Wilhelm I, he backed Koch at a critical moment in Koch's career and proposed him for election to the French Académie.

72. In 1872–73, during one of the most severe winters in living memory, packed audiences in New York, Boston and Philadelphia earned him $13,000 in entrance fees when he lectured on light.

73. Wallace's phrase. It was certainly the most shining in terms of public interest and esteem. The first edition of Darwin's *On the Origin of Species* was sold out on its day of publication (24 November 1851) and even the first edition of his distinctly less eye-catching *Formation of the Vegetable Mould through the Action of Worms* sold out within a couple of years and is now a collector's item. More than 1000 people attended the famous debate on evolution between Thomas Huxley and Bishop Wilberforce in Oxford in 1860. (It was not yet famous and the attendance was not exceptional.) The First International Exhibition of Scientific Instruments in London in 1876 was visited by 11,000 people on the day of opening. They included Queen Victoria, who listened 'with lively interest' (according to the *Times*) to James Clerk Maxwell explaining to her the working of an air pump and the secrets of the Magdeburg hemispheres. (If true, this was more than she was prepared to devote to Mr Gladstone's expositions of constitutional matters.) This was not an English phenomenon. In Germany von Liebig's *Familiar Letters on Chemistry* was a bestseller; and lay as well as scientific audiences flocked to hear Helmholtz (a linear descendant of William Penn) lecture in Heidelberg and Berlin on topics that easily embraced physics, physiology, religion and aesthetics. In France Claude Bernard published some of his seminal papers on the physiology of the blood in the widely read *Revue des Deux Mondes*; and Alexandre Dumas *père*, George Sand, Victor Duruy and the Emperor's cousin, the Princesse Mathilde, attended Pasteur's lectures at the Institut and were thrilled.

74. What Karl Marx (unbeknown to the Listers but at about the same time) described as 'the reserve army of labour'.

75. J.R. Leeson, *Lister as I Knew Him* (London, 1927), p. 243.

76. Sir H.C. Cameron, *Reminiscences of Lister and of His Work in the Wards of the Glasgow Royal Infirmary* (Glasgow, 1927), p. 46.

77. T. Bryant, 'Three hundred deaths from amputations', *Medico-Chirurgical Transactions*, 42 (1850), p. 67.

78. See Part II, Semmelweis.

79. This was different from ordinary gangrene, caused by the cutting off of the blood supply to the part. In gas gangrene the organism flourishes in dead tissue and characteristically produces minute gas bubbles that 'crepitate' on palpating the area (it is not a pleasant sound). Gas gangrene also produces profound toxaemia and heart failure. The causative organism was described by William Henry Welch (see Part IV, Reed).

80. This is caused by the large-scale sudden destruction of red blood cells. The freed red pigment, haemoglobin, turns brown and then black.

81. See Part II, Semmelweis.

82. A few such hospitals were in fact built in Germany, where Miss Nightingale was revered as much as she was in England.

83. Before glazing in cold weather the journey of surgical patients from the 'theatre block' back to the ward on a trolley could be as lethal as any operation (or so it seemed to the theatre party of nurses, porters, doctors and medical students who made up the procession).

84. See Part II, Semmelweis.

85. Thomas Spencer Wells was born in St Albans, the son of a builder. He served in the Navy and in the Military Hospital in Isnik during the Crimean war; his war experience made him 'less frightened [than were other surgeons] by the thought of opening the abdomen'. Returning to London, he performed and perfected the operation of ovariotomy (removal of cysts, sometimes huge, of the ovary). His fame today rests on the invention of the 'Spencer Wells forceps', the still standard tool for stopping bleeding preliminary to tying a bleeding vessel. (Before then this was done with the surgeon's or assistant's two fingers.) He became one of the surgical grandees of the London scene with a palatial residence in Golders Hill Park, president of the Royal College of Surgeons and a baronet. He died in 1897, aged 79, in Cannes.

Robert Lawson Tait was born and trained in Edinburgh but spent his surgical life in Birmingham. He was a faun-like little man with a leonine head and was a brilliant operator. William Mayo called him the 'father of abdominal surgery'. As part of the 'cold water regime' he washed his hands thoroughly with soap and water before each operation, and both the operation site and the simple operating theatre had to be spotlessly clean. He rejected Lister's ideas of germs as nonsense but was, in a sense, one of the originators of 'aseptic' (as distinct from antiseptic) surgery. His results were astonishingly good. After seeing two women die from a ruptured ectopic pregnancy—an occurrence invariably fatal at the time—he decided to operate on the third. He removed the tube and saved the woman's life. He was a dedicated womaniser and died in 1899, aged 54, from a not unrelated cause.

86. Some surgeons (like Lawson Tait) refused to operate in large hospitals and performed surgery in small nursing homes that were kept scrupulously scrubbed and clean. This was purely empirical but successful.

87. Pasteur's is perhaps the best documented of all the great scientists' lives, mainly thanks to the labours of his son-in-law and grandson who wrote his biography, collected his letters and published work, and even produced an elegant volume of his drawings (see Bibliography). The most sympathetic and perceptive short biography was written by another scientist, René Dubos: *Louis Pasteur: Free Lance of Science* (London, 1951).

88. Pasteur was an accomplished pastellist, especially good at portraits. He might have made a name for himself as an artist (see Pasteur-Valléry-Radot, Bibliography).

89. Like many other great nineteenth-century scientists, Liebig and Claude Bernard among them, Dumas began his career as an apprentice pharmacist. He moved from his native Alais in the South of France to study first in Geneva and then in Paris. There he became one of the founders and leaders of the new science of organic chemistry, a charismatic teacher and an influential figure in public life during the Second Empire and Third Republic. He was probably the first to guess how much young Pasteur might contribute to science and promoted and protected him (as he protected Daguerre, inventor of photography, during Daguerre's struggle for recognition). Pasteur in turn revered him above all his other teachers. It was in answer

to Dumas's entreaties that Pasteur undertook to study the disease of silkworms that was devastating the economy of Dumas's home province. Dumas died in 1878, aged 78.

90. Balard lived like a Bohemian in an unheated garret or in his laboratory, where he cooked for himself and slept on a bench (when he did not entertain one of his lady friends) even after becoming professor at the Institut and then at the Sorbonne and one of the leading chemists of France. Starting, like Dumas, as a pharmacist, he discovered bromine at the age of 24. He continued all his life to travel with one change of underwear and socks wrapped in a newspaper that he stuffed into the pocket of his enormous overcoat. When he heard that his pupil Pasteur was to be sent to a small secondary school by the ministry of education, Balard unleashed a one-man campaign that left the ministry reeling. Eventually Pasteur was allowed to remain for an extra year at the Ecole Normale. Balard died in 1874, aged 69.

Biot was in his seventies, a man of high reputation for scientific rigour, when Pasteur approached him. He was initially sceptical about the optical experiments Pasteur had carried out on self-made instruments, but was able fully to verify Pasteur's results. He became a 'second father' to Pasteur. His letters to Pasteur are moving documents. In 1847 Jean-Joseph Pasteur visited the old man (who lived in austere simplicity in a room in the Collège de France) to thank him for the support he had given to Louis. 'I deeply appreciated your father's visit, the rectitude of his judgement, his calm reasoning, and the enlightened love he bears you,' Biot wrote to the son a few days later. During his last illness Biot sent his young friend a photograph with the injunction: 'If you place this portrait near to that of your father, you will unite the pictures of two men who have loved you very much in the same way.' Biot died in 1856, aged 82.

91. The properties of the two acids, mirror images of each other, differ significantly. Pasteur showed that para-tartaric acid was an equal mixture of the two isomers. The chemical and industrial implications were considerable. Eight years later the Royal Society of London awarded him the Rumford Medal in recognition of his work on crystallography.

92. Pasteur's work on the fermentation of beer and wine was fundamental, but he was not a beer drinker and not much of a connoisseur of wine. To judge the quality of both drinks after various types of 'pasteurisation', he relied on Bertin-Mourot's infallible palate.

93. Quoted by Dubos, *Louis Pasteur*, p. 37.

94. Quoted by Dubos, *Louis Pasteur*, p. 38.

95. The Pasteurs had five children: Jeanne, born in 1850, Jean-Baptiste, born in 1851, Cécile, born in 1853, Marie-Louise, born in 1858, and Camille, born in 1863. Jeanne died of scarlet fever, aged nine; and Camille died of a fever of some kind in 1865, aged two. Both deaths affected Pasteur deeply. Jean-Baptiste was taken prisoner at Sedan in 1870. Pasteur scoured the battlefields and prisoner-of-war camps trying to locate him.

96. Quoted by Dubos, *Louis Pasteur*, p. 75.

97. A reference to the deflection of the path of light.

98. Pasteur's scientific idols were the great thinker-scientists like Pascal, Newton and Galileo, whose impact on philosophical, cosmological and religious thought was even greater than their influence on practical or applied science; but he accepted the task of improving French industry as a patriotic duty.

99. Quoted by Dubos, *Louis Pasteur*, p. 100.

100. Dynamic, as distinct from the purely descriptive, biochemistry is the science of enzyme activity. The term 'enzyme', meaning 'in yeast' (ἐν ζύμη) was proposed by Wilhelm Kühne of Breslau in 1876. Repeating Pasteur's experiments on fermentation he showed that extracts from yeast could act like yeast even after the destruction of the cells, but not after boiling the extract. Pasteur immediately saw the importance of this discovery and adopted and popularised the term, always referring to Kühne.

101. Pasteur was a religious man and a devout Roman Catholic, but he never allowed his religious convictions to influence his scientific researches. He repeatedly affirmed that if his experimental studies had supported spontaneous biogenesis—that is, the generation of living cells from non-living material—he would have, without hesitation affirmed, its validity. Like many other great scientists, he separated religious from scientific truth, the former being 'not susceptible to being discovered by our feeble instruments'.

102. He was also a natural showman who made sure that such occasions were well attended by representatives of the press.

103. 1865 was a year of scientific triumph in Pasteur's career, but also one of personal grief. His letter home on the occasion of his father's death illuminates the emotional side of his complex personality:

> Dear Marie and dear Children:
> Grandfather is no more: we have taken him this morning to his last resting place, close to our little Jeanne's. In the midst of my grief I have been thankful that our little girl has been buried there ... He died on the day of your first communion, dear Cécile: those two memories will stay together in your heart ... I had a presentiment and I asked you to pray for Grandfather in Arbois. Your prayers will have been acceptable to God, and perhaps dear Grandfather himself knew of them and rejoiced with dear little Jeanne over your prayer ... I have been thinking of all the marks of affection I have had from my father. For thirty years I have been his constant care. I owe everything to him. When I was young, he kept me from bad company and instilled in me the habit of working and the example of a loyal and well-filled life. He was far above his position both in mind and in character ... The touching part of his affection for me was that it was never filled with excessive ambition. Remember that he would have been pleased to see me headmaster of Arbois school? ... And yet I am sure that some of the success that came my way in my profession must have filled him with joy and pride: his son! his name! the child he had guided and cherished. Dear father, how thankful I am that I could give you some satisfaction ... Farewell, dear Marie and children! We shall talk often of Grandfather. I long to see you but must get back to Alais to continue my studies. (Quoted by Dubos, *Louis Pasteur*, p. 231.)

104. However, by 1878 his interest in surgical problems was well and truly awakened. In his *La théorie des germes et ses applications à la médicine et à la chirurgie* he quoted Lister extensively and acknowledged the English professor's 'luminous insights'. Yet Pasteur's work that would arouse the greatest popular acclaim and lead to the many Pasteur Institutes around the world, his studies on rabies and its preventive inoculation, was still to come.

105. Quoted by Fisher, *Joseph Lister*, p. 215.
106. Lister was later accused anonymously of getting his ideas from Lemaire without acknowledgement. The accusation is still sometimes trotted out. In fact, Lister was meticulous in acknowledging his sources and never claimed that he had discovered carbolic acid or phenol. Nor was the nature of the antibacterial agent important: what mattered was the technique of applying it and its rationale.
107. It was not an entirely happy choice. Used undiluted and in large quantities it often gave rise to toxic symptoms (like green urine, more alarming than dangerous, headaches and gastrointestinal upsets). Lister was not unaware of this and went on experimenting with other, possibly less toxic or corrosive agents until his retirement. In October 1878 Darwin wrote to him and suggested benzoic acid, which Darwin had found had killed some plants. Neither benzoic acid nor any other antiseptic tried was entirely free from side effects and dangers, one reason why asepsis gained ground as a replacement for antisepsis after 1890.

    Grace Calvert later opened the Tower Chemical Works in Bradford to manufacture 'pure' carbolic acid and made a fortune from it.
108. Any fracture was deemed to be 'open' or 'compound' if the skin was broken. But the degree of 'openness' varied widely, which made statistical evaluation difficult. R.B. Fisher's biography of Lister is particularly informative on this series.
109. Only absolutely pure phenol or carbolic acid is soluble in water. Lister's preparations did not reach this degree of purity till the 1880s.
110. Granulation tissue used to be called 'proud flesh': it is the bright red, extremely friable and seemingly fragile tissue that forms in clean wounds and covers raw but clean areas. In fact, though fragile and vulnerable to mechanical injury, it is highly resistant to infection: the perfect dressing devised by nature. To the naked eye it sometimes looks like a blood clot, but microscopically it is a network of fresh capillary channels sprouting from existing capillaries at the edge of the wound and replacing the original blood clot. They bring oxygen and nutrition to the area as well as white blood cells to scavenge organisms and dead material. It is along this network of capillaries that fibroblasts begin to appear to lay down fibres that will eventually form a permanent scar.
111. The tuberculous nature of many abscesses connected to bone was not appreciated until the work of Koch and others in the 1890s. Bone tuberculosis was often caused by the milk-borne bovine organism and was always especially common in Scotland.
112. Quoted by Fisher, *Joseph Lister*, p. 128.
113. Quoted by Fisher, *Joseph Lister*, p. 134.
114. For Paget see Note 142 to Part I, Laennec.
115. Mastectomies have been performed fairly regularly at least since the eighteenth century. Fanny Burney gave a vivid and gruesome description of such an operation in her wonderful *Diaries*. The classical operation called radical mastectomy, which held undisputed sway in the treatment of breast cancer for at least half a century, was described in 1890 by William Stewart Halsted of Johns Hopkins Hospital (see Part IV, Reed); but attempts to remove the lymphatic drainage area of the breast together with the tumour had been tried earlier, notably by Richard von Volkman of Halle. Since the mid-twentieth century the tendency has been to limit surgery

to the tumour itself and combine the operation with radiotherapy or chemotherapy or both.

116. Quoted by Fisher, *Joseph Lister*, p. 148
117. Quoted by Fisher, *Joseph Lister*, p. 150.
118. She remained symptom free for about three years. Then the cancer recurred and she died three and a half years after the operation.
119. Re-examining his results and subjecting them to modern statistical analysis, many were undoubtedly statistically highly significant (see Acknowledgements).
120. See Part II, Semmelweis.
121. This is not of course true of a minority of doctors who delight in publicising their regular 'breakthroughs', preferably on television. One would not describe them as the cream of the profession.
122. Quoted by Fisher, *Joseph Lister*, p. 157.
123. Simpson was referring to Lemaire's enormous tome, 750 pages, in which every conceivable use of 'acid phénique' (carbolic acid) was discussed at great length but often rather unconvincingly. Lemaire considered its use as an antiseptic in the last chapter and based it purely on a priori considerations. Lister never read the book, nor was it available in the university library in Glasgow. He nevertheless procured a copy and, after struggling through it, wrote a letter to the *Lancet*, acknowledging its 'insights'. The accusation kept resurfacing.
124. Thiersch was a pioneer of plastic surgery and described a type of thin skin graft still known by his name. He died in 1895, aged 78.
125. Johann Friedrich August von Esmarch became one of the commanding figures of German surgery and invented the elastic bandage linked to his name and still used in orthopaedic surgery. (Wound round the limb from the extremity upward, it ensures a bloodless field for operations on the knee, elbow and other peripheral joints.) By his second marriage to Henrietta von Schleswig-Holstein, he became an uncle by marriage to Kaiser Wilhelm II. He died in 1908, aged 81.
126. As usual, such medical matters are rarely mentioned in general histories: even Sir Michael Howard's masterly tome on the Franco-Prussian War does not refer to it. Yet as the reminiscences of many combatants testify, the standard of field-surgical care had a discernible effect on morale.

    The Russo-Turkish War of 1877–78 provided a further field test for the antiseptic principle. The Russian surgeon general, Karl Reyher, had visited Lister in Edinburgh and applied Lister's methods to the treatment of the wounded with remarkable success. British colonial wars repeated the experience. T.B. Moriarty reported two successful cases treated with the 'spray' in the Afghan War of 1878; and Edgar Cruikshank, one of Lister's former house surgeons, described the successful application of the 'antiseptic principle' in the Egyptian Campaign of 1882. During the Boer War the Commander in Chief, Lord Wolseley, declared: 'Medical advice is welcome when I ask for it and I have not asked for it.' In response to critical newspaper articles he agreed nevertheless that soldiers should be equipped with antiseptic dressings and base hospitals with requirements for antiseptic surgery. Results with wounded casualties were comparatively good, though Godlee attributed it largely to the dry fresh air of the Veldt. Dysentery and typhoid, on the other hand, took more lives than did the Boers.
127. Quoted by Fisher, *Joseph Lister*, p. 168.

128. Quoted by Fisher, *Joseph Lister*, p. 234.
129. Sophia Jex-Blake got her way, of course. Later she became one of the founders of the London School of Medicine for Women (still later to become the Royal Free Hospital School of Medicine), as well as of a school of medicine in Edinburgh and of numerous charitable institutions concerned with the health of women and children. She died in 1912, aged 72, an admirable nuisance to the medical and political establishment. She denied saying 'When God created Adam, He was merely testing', but sometimes claimed 'I was in sympathy with the sentiment expressed'. Her brother, the Rev. Thomas, became headmaster of Rugby; though a kindly man, he did not approve of this.
130. Quoted by Fisher, *Joseph Lister*, p. 189–90.
131. Dr, later Dame, Mary Scharlieb, died full of honours in 1930, aged 75.
132. Lister would never say so since tuberculous long-stay patients, widely regarded as incurable, were not supposed to be in the Infirmary. However, it was as difficult to prove tuberculosis as was the opposite.
133. Henley showed his gratitude in a poem, 'The Chief', which his friend and patron, Leslie Stephen, published in *The Cornhill* magazine in May 1875:

> His brow spreads large and placid and his eye
> Is deep and bright, with steady looks that still.
> Soft lines of tranquil though his face fulfil
> His face at once benign and proud and shy.
> If envy scouts and ignorance deny,
> His faultless patience, his unyielding will,
> Beautiful gentleness and splendid skill,
> Innumerable gratitudes reply,
> His wise, rare smile is sweet with certainties,
> And seems in all his patients to compel
> Such love and faith that failure cannot quell.
> We hold him for another Herakles,
> Battling with custom, prejudice, disease,
> At once the son of Zeus with Death and Hell.

Not many surgeons can boast such a testimonial. Henley's generous patron was probably Lady Randolph Churchill. After losing a leg, Henley more or less recovered, moved to London and became an important medical and political figure in the 1890s, best known perhaps as the poet of muscular Christianity. He died in 1903, aged 54.
134. Quoted by Fisher, *Joseph Lister*, p. 236.
135. Later, when Lister moved to King's College Hospital in London, he transferred six of his long-stay Edinburgh patients to a private nursing home at his own expense and one to a ward at King's. The nurses at King's objected, but Lister had his way. The long-stay problem remained with him in London, but ultimately management at King's proved to be as sensible and cooperative as they were in Edinburgh. Neither body would get brownie points let alone a star from the Department of Health today. Lister of course would have been sacked long before he arrived at King's.
136. *The Letters of Queen Victoria*, Second Series, Vol. II, 1870–78. Edited by G.E. Buckle. (London, 1926), p. 432.
137. Quoted by Fisher, *Joseph Lister*, p. 236.
138. What exactly 1965 was the centenary of must remain a secret of the Post Office: the spray was introduced only several years later.

139. But not as inapplicable as Lister thought. In the early years of the next century Julius Wagner Jauregg of Vienna introduced malaria therapy—the induction of spikes of high temperature—into the treatment of neurosyphilis, based on the idea that the fever would kill the spirochete. It was not always wholly ineffective.

140. In other words, he believed at first that a comparatively small number of germs could exist in a wide variety of forms.

141. Bacillus lactis, the organism responsible for the souring of milk, was first clearly described by Lister. *Listeria monocytogenes*, the causative organism of listerosis, a rare but often fatal cause of septicaemia, meningitis, encephalitis, uterine infections and stillbirth, was named in honour of Lister, not discovered by him.

142. Quoted by Fisher, *Joseph Lister*, p. 328.

143. Sir W.W. Cheyne, *Lister and His Achievement* (London, 1925), p. 138.

144. Born in Bergen and qualified in Berlin, Billroth had already made a name for himself as an army surgeon in the Franco-Prussian War of 1870–71. In Zurich, still not a particularly prestigious university, he doubled as professor of surgery and the splenetic music critic of the *Neue Zürcher Zeitung*. Typically: 'The Finale of this dreadful work [*Lohengrin*] was rendered inaudible by the knights pointlessly but in this case mercifully belabouring their shields with their swords.'

145. Frau Professor Thiersch was the daughter of the great chemist Justus von Liebig.

146. 'The young King bore the operation very well but his adjutant, Colonel Friebitz, had to leave the theatre to be sick in the corridor. It made Joseph wonder how much use he might be on a battlefield.'

147. His participation in the 1848 Dresden uprising was still not quite forgiven.

148. He was accompanied by his father who, at 84, was still a formidable and much-feared professor of anatomy in the university. In Richard von Volkman's clinic carbolic acid was regularly sprayed around from a gardener's watering can in wards and corridors. 'If dirt cannot be entirely avoided, at least it should be antiseptic dirt,' was the professor's dictum. Today his name is associated with a disabling contracture of the hand that can follow too tight a plaster of Paris applied to the forearm following a fracture of the wrist.

149. The text has happily been lost.

150. She made a good recovery from terrible injuries but was no longer capable of manual work. Lister persuaded her employers to give her a job in the design department, where she proved so efficient that, when the firm sent its wares to an international fair in Chicago, she was put in charge of the consignment. In Chicago she met a young American textile man who, as befitted young American textile men at the time, became both her husband and a millionaire.

151. See Part IV, Reed.

152. He died of kidney failure, already called Bright's disease, in London, but was buried in West Linton, near his much-loved Scottish home of Spittlehaugh.

153. See Note 19.

154. Operative surgery on models was an important part of the surgical examination and a student persuaded by Lister to follow an antiseptic routine risked failure if he encountered a more hidebound examiner.

155. King's College Hospital was then still in the Strand, next to the College.

156. William Watson Cheyne was the son of a sea captain and was born off the

coast of Tasmania in 1852. He was brought up by his grandfather, a vicar in the Shetland Islands. After graduating from Edinburgh and inheriting £150, he decided to follow his inclination and study the exciting new science of bacteriology in Germany. He returned fired with enthusiasm and for two years acted as Lister's backroom boy, carrying out micro-biological researches in 'a little blind passage behind the operating theatre of the Infirmary, with no benches, no incubator, no staining facilities and only one rickety microscope abandoned by the histologists as useless'. At that point he could have been Britain's answer to Koch; but, when his money ran out and he was about to enter general practice, Lister, about to move to London, offered him the post of a house surgeon. At King's his surgical career prospered—professor in 1880, baronet in 1908, president of the Royal College of Surgeons in 1912—but, though he carried out valuable trials with Koch's tuberculin, he was lost to microbiology.

157. Quoted by Fisher, *Joseph Lister*, p. 224.

158. For many years before the introduction of effective acid-neutralising drugs, gastroenterostomy was a standard operation for duodenal ulcers. The communication established between a loop of small intestine and the stomach introduced sufficient alkaline intestinal fluid into the stomach to bring about a temporary healing of the acid-dependent ulcer. Unfortunately, late complications were comparatively common and difficult to treat.

159. Most of Brahms' late chamber music received its first performance in Billroth's grand villa, the surgeon sometimes playing the viola. As he had wished, Billroth was buried near the grave of his beloved Schubert, Beethoven and the unmarked pauper's resting place of Mozart.

160. The chest was a notable exception and remained so until the introduction of the 'negative-pressure chamber' by Sauerbruch in the 1920s.

161. But the Koch marriage did not last 'till death us do part'. In about the 1890s Koch met and fell in love with the gifted young artist Hedwig Freiberg, 40 years his junior and some years younger than Trudy, his youngest daughter by Frau Emmy. He and Frau Emmy divorced, the potential scandal being ruthlessly suppressed by the Imperial authorities. (Some letters of Robert to Hedwig had fallen into the hands of a newspaper man, who was threatened with ruin and imprisonment if he published them.) Robert married Hedwig and they set out on a round-the-world honeymoon. He was by then regarded as a national treasure (like Pasteur was in France); on their return, the Kaiser personally decorated him with the Order of the Crown and Star. He became director of the Institute of Infectious Diseases, soon to be named after him, and made many more important contributions to microbiology. The tuberculin fiasco and perhaps his divorce may have militated against him being awarded the first Nobel Prize in Medicine in 1901, though he received the prize in 1905. He died in 1910, aged 67. Hedwig survived him by 45 years, becoming an expert in oriental religions while living in Japan.

162. Spores, meaning seed in Greek, was an ancient term, but it was Koch who demonstrated their importance for the survival of certain organisms. Because of their survival potential, they are today the number one weapon in threatened bacteriological warfare.

163. Jews were still effectively (if usually tacitly) barred from holding university chairs in Berlin and most other prestigious universities in Germany; hence the flowering of formerly insignificant medical schools like Breslau, which could not afford to be anti-Semitic. Ferdinand Cohn was the founder of

modern plant physiology who did not pretend to know anything about human diseases, but he immediately appreciated the significance of Koch's work. He died in 1898, aged 70. Julius Cohnheim was head of pathology and already famous for his *Lectures on General Pathology*. These gave a classic account of the events of acute inflammation. Though he was a pupil of Virchow, he maintained an open and well-ventilated mind and at once accepted Koch's evidence. He died in 1884, aged 45.

164. Virchow was at that time—and and for some time to come—totally opposed to the idea of microbiological diseases, which seemed to contradict his own grand concept of cellular pathology. (Both are true and not of course incompatible.) After youthful years as a politically and scientifically active radical, he became head of the department of pathology at La Charité Hospital in Berlin and gradually became something of a universal medical oracle. He also entered the Reichstag and turned into one of the few academic politicians on the Opposition benches whom Bismarck, the Iron Chancellor, learnt to respect. ('But the Herr Professor sees imperial politics entirely and exclusively as an extension of the public drainage system in Berlin.') Apart from his monumental *Cellular Pathology*, published in 1843, while he was still professor in Würzburg and regarded as a dangerous agitator in Berlin, he edited for 50 years the most prestigious journal of pathology, the *Archives*, organised the world's first and best public health statistical service in Berlin, wrote two awful historical novels and made useful archaeological contributions. He died in 1802, aged 81.

165. One awaits with bated breath the first International Congress of International Medical Congress Organisers.

166. He clearly saw and deplored the growing German dominance in scientific matters as well as in European politics and agitated for greater public support for the sciences in France.

167. Though Lucy Syme lived with them, she never accompanied them on their holidays. Often she and Agnes went away separately later in the summer, usually to German spas to take the waters.

168. It was a somewhat belated tribute, but Mr Gladstone did not hold with the elevation of Tories and did not particularly like Lister as a person.

169. Etiquette forbade talking shop (in which Agnes was deeply interested) and she had no small talk. The Listers rarely went to the theatre, never to the opera or concerts, and read little outside medical and scientific works. There was not much to chat about once the vagaries of the London weather were exhausted. (In Edinburgh, where everybody knew everybody else, one could chat about people; but London was too big and anonymous.)

170. See Part IV, Reed.

171. The modern autoclave—that is, sterilisation by superheated steam under pressure—is quite ancient in concept but did not become routine until the 1920s. It is misnamed since the term means—and has meant for centuries—a self-locking device, which the modern surgical autoclave is not. A complete change of attire for operations was first popularised by Berkeley Moynihan of Leeds, later Lord Moynihan, the second surgical peer and an accomplished showman.

172. There were, he wrote, many surgeons in his own country who had still not adopted antisepsis and Ruf's unfortunate case was as much a testimony to the advanced state of surgery in Germany in general as it was to his own error. The letter probably helped to persuade the Bavarian judge to impose a merely nominal fine.

173. The inoculations had been tested only in a comparatively small number of dogs, in whom the preliminary injection of an attenuated preparation of the virus did have a protective effect. The attenuation had been carried out purely by hunch by removing the spinal cords of rabbits who had been given and had died of rabies and letting the organs dry in warm air for 14 days. The procedure was the more experimental since no organism could be seen under the microscope and the idea of submicroscopic viruses was still unformed. It is inconceivable that such inoculations could be carried out today—except by very rich drug companies in darkest Africa or South America.

174. For reasons not clear, being bitten by rabid wolves (rather than by dogs or bats) is still regarded as a particularly dangerous form of the disease. (Perhaps the injuries are more severe.) Rabies was sometimes referred to as 'hydrophobia' because attempts to drink set up immediate spasms and convulsions spreading from the throat to the rest of the body. It looked as if the animal/patient was frightened of water. Reality was the reverse: thirst and dehydration formed the immediate cause of death. It was a ghastly spectacle, once seen never forgotten. Perhaps the transmission of the disease from wolf to man accounts for the role of 'big bad wolves' as incarnations of menace and evil, from Dante (at least) to Grimm and Walt Disney. (The she-wolf who nursed Romulus and Remus is an honourable and perhaps more realistic exception, as are the wolves of Kipling.)

175. Pasteur called it 'vaccine' to honour 'that great Englishman', Edward Jenner, discoverer of vaccination against smallpox. The rabies, anthrax, BCG and other later vaccines had of course nothing to do with *vacca* (cows in Latin).

176. Fortunately, in the meantime Pasteur and his collaborators had established that healthy dogs did not need a course of injections but only one to protect them from acquiring rabies. This was soon made compulsory in most European countries.

177. Originally the establishment was to be called the Jenner Institute. It then transpired that a privately owned Jenner Institute of Calf Lymph of a somewhat dubious reputation already existed in South London, and the name had to be changed. Lister became nominal head (and remained so until 1911), but never himself did any work there. After a period of important research into microbiological and haematological problems, the Institute was killed off comparatively painlessly by selling the site and building and converting it into research fellowships. Not everybody approved of this very British kind of euthanasia, described by its perpetrators (but not by anybody else) as a 'phoenix-like resurrection'.

178. They included several notable names, like Helmholz, Löffler and Ehrlich; but, contrary to Hollywood legend, Virchow, the Pope, was absent. He learnt about the demonstration two days later and, despite his total opposition to the idea of a microbial cause of tuberculosis, at once sent a congratulatory note to Koch.

179. The writer is grateful to Professor Douglas E. Eveleigh of Ruttgers University, New Jersey (where Waksman and Schatz discovered streptomycin) for kindly correcting an error in *The White Death*, his previous book on the history of tuberculosis. John Tyndall in London received a copy of Koch's *talk*, not a copy of Koch's slightly later publication, and was able to arrange the publication of the text in the *London Times* on Saturday, 22 April 1882.

180. The *Mycobacterium tuberculosis*, a distant cousin of the organism that causes leprosy, is still a difficult pathogenic organism to visualise and isolate in pure culture. Koch's original material came from a 32-year-old labourer, Heinrich Günther. Previously a strong and fit man, he was suddenly struck down by the illness and, atypically, died within a fortnight. Post-mortem examination revealed almost every organ to be riddled with tuberculosis. Koch began to inject material from him first into guinea pigs and then into rabbits, using a method he had learnt from Cohnheim. Within three months he and Löffler caught their first glimpse of the small, slender and seemingly fragile rod they instantly suspected of being the cause of the disease. It took them another year before they were certain that, by Koch's own rigid criteria, they had isolated the organism responsible for tuberculosis. The first man to diagnose tuberculosis by detecting the organism in his own sputum was Paul Ehrlich, later the discoverer of salvarsan (the first effective antisyphilitic drug) and apostle of chemotherapy. He went to Egypt and recovered. Perhaps his diagnosis was mistaken.

181. Some of the opposition sprang from ignorance but some, especially in England, was fuelled by humane sentiments. Dr Henry Bennett, advocate of the 'dry climate school of therapy', argued that the acceptance of Koch's ideas would 'increase a thousandfold the sufferings of patients and their families ... who would now be treated like medieval lepers, separated from their beloved, isolated, shut up, refused admission to hospitals.' But all this had already been happening in thousands of sanatoria round the world, some famous and luxurious but others not much better than prisons.

182. It stamped its mark on the social and cultural life of the age like no other illness, yet it is still barely mentioned (if at all) in standard social histories of England.

183. She had already been to Davos in Switzerland for two years with no improvement in her condition. She was deeply unhappy there and her parents brought her home to die.

184. The effect of Koch's announcement was electrifying. The *Lancet* welcomed it with a special editorial in its next issue—'glad tidings of great joy'—as did the *British Medical Journal*: 'In the Middle Ages the discovery of a new wonder-working shrine often led to a rush of the sick and the lame to God's chosen spot. It was a similar rush which took place over the last month to Berlin.' Conan Doyle, already a celebrated writer but not yet a knight and still in medical practice, wrote in the *Review of Reviews*: 'On the Riviera, the last ditch of the consumptive, the news sounded like the advent of Christ must have sounded in the villages of Judea ... The consumptives of Europe stamped for dear life to the capital of Germany.' There 'an atmosphere of adulation built up around Koch ... a veiled prophet ... unseen to any eyes save his immediate coworkers'.

185. This initial favourable reaction could last some months and was one reason why a treatment so cruel and malign—it almost certainly shortened life as well as causing much suffering—survived for several decades after being condemned as useless by Koch himself. One of thousands given a course of injections was Franz Kafka in Prague in 1920; and Sir Robert Philip, Edinburgh's famous and influential professor of tuberculosis, continued to advocate it throughout the 1920s. (See R. & J. Dubos and T. Dormandy in Bibliography.)

186. Tuberculosis was unique among the great killing diseases since physical pain, the great destroyer of creativity and character, was often absent till the last stages of the disease. Chopin created some of his most marvellous works dying, as did Schiller, Weber, Keats, Shelley, Emily Brontë, Beardsley, Chekhov, Katharine Mansfield, Modigliani and many others.

187. Godlee, *Lord Lister*, p. 243.

188. He did so while he was an army surgeon in Algiers, a brilliant piece of research with a microscope even more primitive than Koch's. He reported it to the Académie de Médicine in 1880. His paper was published the following year. He died in 1922, aged 77.

189. The search for the identity of the cholera bacillus or *vibrio* was a race between a French team led by Roux and Thuillier and the Germans led by Koch and Gaffky. All were shocked when in Cairo Thuillier fell victim to the disease. The race was eventually won by Koch, who demonstrated the organism in more than 50 victims of an outbreak in Calcutta. He returned to Berlin in triumph. It was this that prompted the aged Professor Max Pettenkofer of Munich, a fervent sceptic, to ask for a test-tube of a pure culture of virulent cholera bacilli from Koch and then to swallow the contents at a public lecture. He did not turn a hair, though the culture should have been enough to extinguish a regiment. The explanation is still not known, but Pettenkofer's survival did not discredit Koch's discovery. Hueppe did useful work on isolating the toxin of the bacillus.

190. The diphtheria bacillus was discovered by Albrecht Klebs, a pupil of Virchow's, in 1883 and was shown by Friedrich Löffler, a Koch disciple, to be the cause of the disease a year later. The antitoxin, developed by Roux and Alexandre Yersin in Paris and Emil von Behring and Shibasaburo Kitasato in Koch's laboratory, represented a new concept of treating a bacterial disease, an early fruit of the developing new science of immunology. The first injection of diphtheria antitoxin was given to a moribund child in Berlin's Children's Hospital on Christmas Day, 1891. The child survived and many have followed her since. Klebs died in 1913, aged 70; Löffler died in 1915, aged 62; von Behring died in 1917, aged 69; Yersin died in Paris in 1843, aged 80; and Kitasato died in Japan in 1931, aged 69. Prophylactic diphtheria immunisation was introduced by the Hungarian Bela Schick, who died in the United States, an exile from Nazi Europe, in 1967, aged 90.

191. The original Latin term meant exemption from military service. In 1888 Büchner of Munich described specific protective substances in the blood that he called 'alexins'. Where the modern usage of the term originates is uncertain. It was certainly used by Richard Pfeiffer and Jean Bordet in their ground-breaking studies in the 1890s. The concept of potentially harmful 'autoimmunity' and its possible role in such diseases as tuberculosis was mooted in the 1890s and developed by H.E. Durham of Cambridge.

192. Elie Metchnikoff was born of Jewish parents in the Ukraine and studied biology at the University of Kharkoff, though he was largely self-taught. His first wife died of tuberculosis. Eventually, from a professorship in Odessa he migrated with his second wife, Olga, to the new Pasteur Institute in Paris, where he described the process known as phagocytosis, the ingestion and destruction of potentially harmful organisms by white blood cells, a natural defence mechanism against infections. The excitement caused by the discovery is perfectly conveyed in *Doctor's Dilemma* by G.B. Shaw, first staged in London in 1905. Shaw had heard

about it from his friend, Almroth Wright of St Mary's Hospital, a pioneer immunologist and probably the model for Sir Colenso Ridgeon in Shaw's play. Lister too developed a lively interest in the topic and emphasised the importance of natural defences by white cells and 'specific chemical agents'. Metchnikoff spent his last years chasing the secret of longevity and claimed to have found it in the lactobacillus present in natural yoghurt. He died in 1916, aged 71.

193. Von Behring beat Koch to the post, becoming the first Nobel laureate in medicine in 1901. Sherrington became a founder of modern neuro-physiology and (with A.D. Adrian) Nobel laureate in 1932. For V.C. Vaughan, see Note 79 to Part IV, Reed.

194. A Napoleonic figure, Charcot and his eight-volume textbook dominated French medicine during the last decades of the nineteenth century. Although he was a general physician, he took a special interest in neurological and mental diseases and is revered today as a founder of neurology. He described the disorganised joints of patients who had lost their response to joint pain, a common feature of neurosyphilis in his day. As an ardent anglophile he presented some of his specimens to English pathological museums, who started to call the condition 'Charcot's joints'. His Sunday morning demonstrations at the Salpetrière were open to the public and were attended by a vast audience. Among them in the late 1880s was the young Dr Sigmund Freud from Vienna. Charcot died in 1893, aged 68.

195. Quoted by Godlee, *Lord Lister*, p. 356.

196. The first surgeon to occupy that office was Sir Benjamin Brodie of St George's Hospital, London, one of the great surgeon pathologists of his day. His name is still associated with a now rare chronic abscess of the tibia, sometimes tuberculous or syphilitic, and with a rare form of cancer of the breast. An exceptionally modest and learned man, he died in 1862, aged 78.

197. Thomas Huxley, the great evolutionist, had died in 1885. The first lecture instituted in his memory was delivered by his friend Michael Foster, eminent physiologist at University College, London, and soon to be knighted. The third was to be delivered by Lister. In his capacity as President of the Royal Society Lister also successfully lobbied the India Office to allow Alexandre Yersin of the Paris Pasteur Institute to carry out experiments in Bombay on plague victims.

198. A few months later he paid 25 Marks to a market porter to stand in front of his machine and become the first living person to have his whole skeleton (as well as his belt buckles and gaiters) revealed. The picture, reproduced in *The Ascent of Man* by J. Bronowski, was seen by a consultant chest physician, Dr Peter Ormerod, 100 years later. He immediately diagnosed bilateral apical tuberculosis.

199. The *Frankfurter Allgemeine Zeitung* carried the sensational news of the Würzburg meeting on its front page the next day and students of the university organised a torchlight procession. Within a few months Röntgen's paper was translated into several languages and rightly hailed as a historic discovery. Röntgen himself, a modest man, declined numerous honours, including a barony offered by the King of Bavaria; but he was the first laureate of the Nobel Prize for Physics in 1901. He died in despair in 1915, aged 69, during the First World War, which he had valiantly opposed. He rightly feared its outcome, whichever side should win.

200. 'I am full of daze/Shock and amaze/For nowadays/I hear they'll gaze/ Through cloak and gown and even stayes/Those naughty, naughty Röntgen rays.' Several clothing firms advertised X-ray-proof ladies' underwear.

201. Even earlier, at a Conversazione of the Royal Society, he showed a Röntgen-ray picture of a bullet embedded in a patient's hand sent to him by Oliver Lodge, professor of physics at University College; and he speculated whether the new invention might herald a new era in surgical diagnosis. Even more presciently, he wondered if too much use of the new rays might cause internal damage from a kind of 'excessive sunburn'. This was some years before the first harmful effects of irradiation were reported in the medical press, observed in a shop assistant in the shoe department of Bloomingdale Brothers' Department Store in New York (where X-rays were first used to check the fit of shoes, a tremendously successful gimmick) after a particularly busy pre-Christmas rush.

202. Sir Benjamin Brodie had been offered a barony but declined because he did not feel that he was wealthy enough to maintain a station appropriate to such a rank.

Lister chose the title Lister of Lyme. He made four speeches in the House of Lords, only one of them noteworthy. He supported prison reform, in which he had developed an interest in his last years. Perhaps the subject stirred childhood memories of meeting Elizabeth Fry and her circle.

203. Her husband had died within a year of his seventy-fifth birthday · celebration. Madame Pasteur survived for another 12 years.

204. See Part IV, Reed.

205. Nevertheless, Britain was one of the last countries to introduce the compulsory pasteurisation of milk.

206. He was of course accompanied by Burns, his valet, and Isabella by her lady's maid.

207. Treves was a notable character and the principal of hundreds of anecdotes. Most memorably, perhaps, he addressed the anaesthetist apparently bending over the mask applied to the face of a restless patient: 'If the patient can stay awake during the operation, Mr Anaesthetist, so, surely, can you'. He died in 1923, aged 70.

Part IV: Reed

1. Such a waterway had been proposed in the sixteenth century by the Portuguese Gomera and a number of routes were discussed at the time. The concession actually to build a canal was eventually granted by the Republic of Colombia to the French Panama Canal Company in 1878. The eventual cost before the work was abandoned and the company went into liquidation was approximately £20 million, of which only about £1 million could be accounted for.

2. The name had been given to the fever by Griffith Hughes in his *Natural History of Barbados*, published in 1750; but under various other names there had been numerous accounts of it in the sixteenth and seventeenth centuries. It was first recorded in North America (in Philadelphia) in 1699.

The disease was known to be prevalent in Central America and it is still a mystery how it could have been ignored by the French surveys.

3. Ferdinand de Lesseps (and his son Charles) were exceedingly naïve but had not actively participated in or benefited from the huge fraud: Ferdinand was indeed a man of courage and nobility. Criminal charges against them were eventually dropped and Ferdinand took refuge in England, where he had been feted and created an honorary Knight of the Bath after Suez. A little disappointingly, none of his royal and aristocratic friends now remembered him. He later returned to France where he died in 1894, aged 89.

4. It took the discredited Clemenceau 10 years and several more crises, both national and international, to claw his way back into public life, eventually to become *Père Victoire* in November 1918.

5. Panama erupted only a few years after the Boulanger *affaire*, a half-baked but nearly successful attempt by a right-wing general to topple the Republic; and the Dreyfus case was already simmering when the Panama Canal Company collapsed.

6. It was as disreputable a transaction (masterminded by President Theodore Roosevelt) as any blot on European colonialism—and it was basically unnecessary. Colombia was ready to sell the future Canal Zone for a reasonable price had diplomatic niceties been observed; and it eventually obtained three times the sum originally offered.

7. The engineer who did most to convert a moral and physical swamp into one of the healthiest and most profitable spots on earth was Colonel (later Major General) George W. Goethals; but what made his triumph possible was a 10-year campaign to eradicate yellow fever and malaria. This was led by Walter Reed's former adversary and later friend, Colonel (later Major General) William C. Gorgas, and Henry Rose Carter.

8. In 1940 Dr Philip Hench (a future Nobel Prize winner for his work on cortisone) was called on to address a dedication ceremony to open the Jesse Lazear Chemistry Building at Washington and Jefferson College, Washington, Pennsylvania. Lazear's memory was being honoured for his work and death as a member of the Walter Reed Yellow Fever Commission; but Hench, like many others called on to deliver similar orations, found the honour unexpectedly onerous. Not only did he himself have only a vague idea who Jesse Lazear was or why his name was being commemorated, it was also extremely difficult to find out anything about the Commission of which Lazear had apparently been a member. Thereafter and until his death in 1965, Hench corresponded with and visited the survivors and the families of all those who had participated in the work of or had been involved with the Commission. He amassed a superb and superbly annotated collection of letters, diaries, photographs, newspaper reports and other memorabilia that his widow presented to the University of Virginia, Charlottesville, and is now known as a Hench–Reed Collection. The collection was shown at an exhibition in 1997 and is available for study in the University Library.

Extensive use was made of the Hench–Reed Collection by the distinguished physician Dr William B. Bean in writing his biography of Reed: *Walter Reed* (Charlottesville, Virginia, 1982). Bean himself also interviewed many of Reed's family and descendants. His book is highly enjoyably as well as an invaluable source of information (except for the absence of a bibliography) and has been extensively used by the present writer.

Bean was not the first eminent doctor to write a biography of Reed. A few years after Reed's death, Howard Atwood Kelly, professor of gynaecology and obstetrics at Johns Hopkins University for 30 years and still revered as one of the ornaments of American medicine, wrote an elegant, informative and sympathetic life, *Walter Reed and Yellow Fever* (New York, 1906), marred irredeemably by one or two crudely racist remarks. (They are said to have been omitted from the third edition, published in 1926.) Kelly had known Reed during the latter's postgraduate studies in Baltimore and had a personal interest in yellow fever. Both his paternal grandparents had contracted the fever during the great Philadelphia epidemic of 1793 and his grandfather had succumbed. As a boy his great-grandmother used to recall the grim days when, twice a day, a waggon was driven through the streets of the city, the driver calling out on every street corner: 'Bring out your dead! Bring out your dead!'

A.E. Truby, retiring from the U.S. Army Medical Corps as a brigadier-general in 1943, wrote a pleasing memoir of the Yellow Fever Commission's work in Cuba in which he himself had participated: *Memoirs: The Yellow Fever Episode* (New York, 1943).

Some of the main publications arising from and some letters and documents relating to the Yellow Fever Commission were collected into a useful official publication, *Yellow Fever: A Compilation of Various Publications, Results of the Work of Major Walter Reed and the Yellow Fever Commission*, presented by 'Mr Owen' (no other identification given; Washington, Government Printing Office, 1911).

9. Did they influence some of the extraordinary acts of chivalry that characterised the first years of the Civil War and were not entirely the invention of Hollywood?

10. In 1849 there were no railways of importance to the West. By 1860 the northern West had nearly a third of the 30,000 miles in the whole country and was not only covered with a network that made marketing of its produce easy, but was also well connected by trunk lines with the East. Had the West joined the South, the break-up of the Union would have been inevitable. As it was, the railways made it possible for the West to join the North, which it marginally (but only marginally) preferred because of its opposition to slavery. Once joined to the North, however, coercion of the South became vital because of the geographical unity of the Mississippi Valley. In fairness, half a dozen such scenarios could be plausibly constructed to explain the inevitable drift to the bloodshed and even its eventual outcome. 'The witches' cauldron had long been brewing, and more ingredients than can easily be analysed had gone into the unholy broth which we were all, North and South, West and Far West forced to drink' (J.T. Adams, *The Epic of America* (New York, 1931), p. 264).

11. One of the bloodiest of the Civil War battles, fought on 17 September 1862, between Lee, trying to carry the war into Maryland, and McClellan. It left 26,000 dead on the battlefield and was essentially a draw. After James Reed's shattered hand had been amputated in a crudely improvised field hospital, he is said to have addressed the surgeon with a bow: 'Thank you, Doctor, for leaving me enough to hang the girls on.' He saw further active service and was outraged by Lee's surrender.

12. The grave is still there and being cared for.

13. They were first introduced by William Dabney during the 1874–75 academic session.

14. He ministered to four Presidents and taught Jefferson to catheterise himself in the latter's final illness.
15. Alcohol was not forbidden, but Edgar Allan Poe, an undergraduate in 1826, was often held up as a deterrent example of where the evil might lead.
16. The Union Pacific appears to have been built entirely at the expense of the government and the first-mortgage bondholders at a total cost of about $50 million, while the promoters got about $23 million through a private subsidiary corporation, the Crédit Mobilier.
17. The US Minister at the Court of St James at the time left a lasting impression for using his official position to market the stock in a non-existent goldmine to the social élite of the country of his accreditation. Several ministers, members of parliament and royalty were stung; arguably not enough.
18. Unlike the gangsters, robber barons and mass murderers of the next generation who died in the odour of sanctity as benefactors of hospitals, universities, libraries and other philanthropic foundations, Boss (William Macy) Tweed was eventually brought down by a reform coalition that included the intrepid cartoonist Thomas Nast and was led by the wealthy lawyer Samuel J. Tilden. Asked on entering the prison to state his occupation, Tweed replied 'statesman'. And, compared to socially better-placed politicians in the Grant administration, there was a granule of truth in this: some of Tweed's massive stealing at least provided funds for a welfare system that embraced Catholic parochial schools and the occasional distribution of food and fuel to the poor.
19. The population of the United States was about 38 million in 1870, 50 million in 1880 and 63 million in 1890.
20. In November 1871 the Guardian Savings Bank, of which Tweed was president, and then a series of other banks (including the National, where newly arrived immigrants were officially advised to deposit what little money they had)—but not of course their boards of directors—failed. Business, as well as payment for public services, was paralysed for weeks. The classic (or notorious) battles between 'Commodore' Vanderbilt, Jay Gould, Daniel Drew and a few other financiers, leading to the first Black Friday', plunged thousands of small firms and tens of thousands of individuals into bankruptcy. The network of corruption involved senators, congressmen and judges; and the slimy trail led perilously close to the President. Grant was probably not personally in league with Gould, but he was certainly 'painfully blunt in his ethical perceptions'; and his sheltering in high office of some of the most corrupt helped to debauch public life for decades.
21. Though still only in his early thirties, Edward Gamaliel Jeanneret (who later diagnosed his friend Trudeau's tuberculosis) was already recognised as the country's greatest authority on diseases of the chest. Fordyce Baker was professor of clinical midwifery, but his predecessor, Isaac Taylor, still gave lectures.
22. At the time London and Paris had a few municipal ambulances, but they were not hospital based and the service was intermittent and inefficient. New York and Roosevelt hospitals followed Bellevue about 10 years later.
23. Compared (as much as such comparisons are possible) with similar hospitals in London, Paris or Vienna.
24. Bellevue did not award him its MD till the ripe old age of 21.
25. Quoted by Bean, *Walter Reed*, p. 42.

26. Many years later the paths of Reed and Bell crossed again, not entirely happily. After Reed's brilliant presentation at the 1901 meeting of the American Public Health Association, Bell, quite crotchety by then, attacked Reed's 'phantasmagorical' ideas on the spread of yellow fever, reiterating his own discredited theory of transmission by contaminated material.

27. Quoted by Bean, *Walter Reed*, p. 52.

28. Quoted by Bean, *Walter Reed*, p. 53.

29. Quoted by Bean, *Walter Reed*, p. 55.

30. Senior officers could more or less design their own, but up to the rank of colonel uniformity was strictly enforced: a light blue coat with trousers of a lighter shade of blue, trimmed with emerald green piping. The emblem of the corps was a Maltese Cross. The uniform was smart, but did not adapt well to hot climates and there was no summer uniform. The last became one of the many more or less hushed-up scandals of the Spanish-American War.

31. Such a duty did in fact come Reed's way, though not for 13 years.

32. Quoted by Bean, *Walter Reed*, p. 58.

33. Butter was $2 a pound and a dozen eggs $3. Reed's pay was in the region of $600 a year.

34. Conforming to the custom of the time, she always called him Dr Reed when anyone else was present as well as in her correspondence. Reed called her Mrs Reed in public but not in his letters.

35. Quoted by H.A. Kelly, *Walter Reed and Yellow Fever* (New York, 1926), p. 65.

36. Despite several attempts by individual congressmen and senators to have the law changed, officers of the Army Medical Corps were not allowed to accept any payment for professional services rendered to Indians. The resistance came from civilian medical associations, not the War Department.

37. Reed Papers, Hench–Reed Collection, University of Virginia, Charlottesville.

38. Reed also taught Susie reading, writing and arithmetic, but she had otherwise no schooling. One day, while the Reeds were living in Washington, she disappeared without a trace and was never heard of again, 'thus giving ample evidence of the cruel and deceitful character of her race', according to Kelly.

39. It was from Fort Apache that Reed contributed his first publication to medical literature: an account of the obstetric practices of the Apaches published in the *Transactions of the American Gynaecological Society*.

40. He also introduced the surgical rubber glove, initially to protect the sensitive skin of his theatre sister, whom he later married. He was a brilliant intellect but almost painfully shy—or aloof or arrogant, depending on who was being questioned about him. His formal teaching invariably made a great impression on his students, though outside the lecture theatre he avoided all contact with them. While he and his wife met for breakfast, they otherwise lived virtually independent lives. Inspired by the studies of Virchow and others, showing how cancers spread by lymphatic channels to the nearest lymph nodes that seemed to act as some kind of filtre, he also advocated and described the massive resections in one 'block' of primary malignancies together with their lymphatic drainage areas. These mutilating operations, especially 'radical mastectomy' (removal of the breast together with all lymph nodes in the axilla), held undisputed sway until the 1960s; and any medical student

expressing reservations about them would face severe reprimand and certain failure in examinations. They are now out of favour and indeed regarded by most surgeons as unnecessary and barbarous with a fervour similar to their advocacy 50 years ago.

Halsted died in 1922, aged 70, an unwitting martyr to medical progress. Local anaesthesia with cocaine was introduced by a young Viennese ophthalmologist, Carl Koller, in the 1880s, perhaps at the suggestion of his friend Sigmund Freud. Characteristically, Halsted started to investigate the drug on himself and three assistants, without consulting anybody and without realising its potentially addictive nature. All four 'guinea pigs' became addicts and hopeless psychiatric cases. (Halsted was at first 'successfully weaned' by a course of morphine, but became a morphine addict instead.) By 1905 several other non-addictive local anaesthetic agents were introduced. It was too late to save Halsted and several other investigators who had become cocaine addicts. Koller died in 1944, aged 87.

41. He also published readable though not particularly profound essays on the ethics and the history of medicine. He died in 1919, aged 70.

42. Rare (and perhaps new) in the sense that the diagnosis and the operation for it did not become common till the introduction of anaesthesia and antisepsis. As a post-mortem finding and named 'perityphlitis', it was known in the eighteenth century and in 1759 Mestivier operated for it. (The patient died.) The term 'appendicitis' was introduced by Reginald Heber Fitz of Boston in 1886. In 1902 Sir Frederick Treves operated on Edward VII draining an appendix abscess just before the king's coronation (see Part II, Lister). Until the 1960s it was by far the most common acute abdominal emergency. It then, for no accountable reason, virtually disappeared. It may be coming back.

43. Like Kelly's proctoscope, an instrument for the examination of the rectum. Kelly died in 1948, aged 90. (See also Note 8.)

44. Only psychiatry has so far remained relatively immune.

45. The list is by no means complete and does not include many animal and plant diseases of great importance. The last 'great' organism to be identified during this heroic period of microbiology was the *Spirochaeta pallida*, the causative organism of syphilis, by the German biologist Fritz Schaudinn in 1905.

46. The description of such organisms by the ancient term 'virus' (meaning poisonous fluids or venom) was first suggested by Beijerinek to denote the cause of mosaic diseases in plants in 1889. Later Loeffler demonstrated that foot and mouth disease was caused by a filterable virus. This proved to be a decisive advance in Reed's later search for the yellow fever virus. Viruses were eventually visualised by electron microscopy in the 1950s.

47. The concept was probably launched by Richard Pfeiffer, Robert Koch's 35-year-old assistant, in 1889. It proved particularly applicable to tuberculosis.

48. Fernand Widal of Paris described the serological test for typhoid fever (still named after him) in 1896. The test was in fact pioneered by Max Gruber of Vienna and his English assistant H.E. Durham.

49. Jenner, a country practitioner in Gloucestershire, published his epoch-making article on cow-pox inoculation conferring protection against smallpox in 1796.

50. H.E. Durham published his paper in the *Proceedings of the Royal Society* in 1896. He later became professor in Cambridge and died in 1945, aged 79.

51. In his own field he is eponymously known today for describing Bacillus Welchii (properly *Bacillus aerogenes capsulatus*), the cause of gas gangrene in contaminated wounds. In his seventies and eighties he was sometimes referred to (at least in after-dinner speeches) as 'the Dean of American Medicine', accepting at 76 the newly created Chair of History of Medicine at Johns Hopkins. He died in 1934, aged 84.

52. W.H. Welch, *Journal of the American Medical Association*, 32 (1920), p. 69.

53. The background to this remains murky. The assassin was another Sioux, Red Tomahawk, but the scenario may have been arranged by the Indian Police acting on instructions (or hints) from The Great White Father in Washington.

54. The events leading up to Wounded Knee and the actual slaughter are described evocatively and with eloquent restraint in Dee Brown's *Bury My Head at Wounded Knee: An Indian History of the American West* (London, 1971). Until the 1960s there was virtually no Indian history of America (except of course in fiction, mostly terrible films and when electioneering politicians and presidents were being elected 'chiefs' by happily grinning stage Indians). In standard histories and school books the Indians were barely mentioned and, when mentioned, they were usually coupled with the bison. As so often, this attitude was brilliantly encapsulated by a *New Yorker* cartoon by Barney Tobey in the 1950s. A well-heeled lady tourist visiting an Indian reservation pokes her head into a shack where an Indian family are having their frugal meal. 'Oh, I *beg* your pardon!' she says, 'I thought you were extinct.'

55. One cannot but wonder what happened to the millions of these specimens when they ceased to be objects of veneration in the 1960s and 1970s. In London some came to adorn 'atmospheric' East End pubs; but that cannot account for more than a handful.

56. Much controversy was aroused in the first years of the present century by the 'news' of organs having been removed from the dead (and sometimes at operations from the living) for 'teaching' and 'research' purposes without permission: in fact to be preserved in the museum. Until recently no permission was ever sought for what was universally regarded by pathologists as a 'normal' procedure. Yet the problem is not new. One of Reed's predecessors as curator of the Army Museum, the distinguished pathologist J.H. Brinton of Philadelphia, recalled that specific permission was granted to the Surgeon General's Department by the War Department during the Civil War to 'secure specimens accruing from action in the field'. These specimens were packed in barrels and forwarded to Washington. Specimen 1335 came from a leg crushed by a 12 lb shot at Gettysburg and had been forwarded in a makeshift coffin to which was affixed a visiting card reading: 'With the compliments of Major General D.E.S., U.S. Volunteers.' A few months later the original owner of the limb, a man from the ranks, limped into the Museum and demanded its return. He was told that under no circumstances would the specimen be surrendered. 'But it's mine,' the man insisted, 'part of myself.' The Museum Assistant, a captain in the Medical Corps, asked the claimant the length of his enlistment. When the man replied that he had signed up for three years or the war, the Captain pointed out that the contract had not yet expired. 'Come back at the end of the war and you can have your limb. In the meantime most of yourself will be posted wherever necessary; but one detachment of you has

been stationed in this Museum on Government duty. Such is the opinion of the US Attorney General.'

57. When, at Reed's request, Sternberg assigned Carroll to what was later to be known as the Yellow Fever Commission in 1900, he was appointed 'Acting Assistant Surgeon'. He never got beyond this during Reed's lifetime.

58. Neither Reed's background nor his character disposed him to engage in the social game of the capital for professional advancement. Emilie and the formidable Mrs Sternberg only met once.

59. Koch's premature and false claim that his laboratory's more or less secret preparation, 'tuberculin', made from live tubercle bacilli, might act as a cure for tuberculosis (see Part III, Lister) engendered much suspicion against other similar but effective preparations. In advocating the often life-saving diphtheria antiserum for children, Reed had to devote several lectures to the difference between 'toxoids' (like tuberculin) and 'antisera' (like the diphtheria antidote).

60. This was a crucial extension of the earlier work of Patrick Manson, whose pioneering contribution Ronald Ross could have ignored but was always careful to acknowledge. Both men received the Nobel Prize. Reed was among the first in the United States to appreciate the importance of Ross's discovery, though at the time he did not link it with yellow fever. When told by an elderly professor that what he saw under the microscope was 'cellular debris', he replied that anybody who could mistake the malaria parasite for 'cellular debris' would confuse the 'Capitol with an army tent'.

61. The popular jokey name of 'Yellow Jack' was a kind of whistling in the dark.

62. Vigilantes reckoned to have shot 23 people trying to escape from 'infected' to 'clean' areas in one epidemic in New Orleans.

63. The cause of the bleeding in liver failure is the inability of the liver to synthetise prothrombin, an essential clotting factor. It is often the terminal complication in liver disease. The false hope kindled for a few days before the last stage is not specific to yellow fever, but can still be seen today in other forms of massive chemical liver necrosis such as may occur in paracetamol overdose.

64. W.E. George, *Letters to a Friend* (Memphis, 1897), quoted by M. Humphries, *Yellow Fever and the South* (New Jersey, 1992), p. 4.

65. Humphries, *Yellow Fever and the South*, p. 35.

66. This was a terrible myth, though it is possible that slave babies and infants were more likely than whites to catch the disease and either die or acquire immunity. But this was no longer true at the time of the Spanish-American War and when the Twenty-Fourth Infantry, an African-American regiment, was sent to look after the sick in the Siboney Yellow Fever Hospital in 1898, because of their supposed immunity, more than a third of the regiment's 460 men died of yellow fever or malignant malaria in 40 days. The episode would have been suppressed but for Theophilus G. Steward, chaplain of the Twenty-Fifth infantry, who in 1904 described it in his book, *Colored Regulars in the US Army*. He was cashiered and died in poverty in 1925.

67. M. Warner (Humphries), 'Hunting the Yellow Fever Germ', *Bulletin of the History of Medicine*, 59 (1985), p. 361.

68. From the American literature describing the yellow fever controversy Sanarelli tends to emerge as something of an unprincipled villain or, charitably, a clown. The exchanges were certainly vitriolic and there is

no doubt that Sanarelli's *Bacillus icteroides* was a moderately common harmless contaminant and not the cause of the disease. One can also sympathise with Sternberg for not wanting to waste time and precious manpower disproving a theory that he regarded as absurd from the start, though not with his categorical but untrue assertion that he had done so. Sanarelli was in fact a man of many parts and undoubted scientific attainments. Born near Sienna in Italy and a graduate of the university there, he worked for some years at the Pasteur Institute in Paris before being appointed professor of bacteriology in Sienna, the first occupant of such a chair. Driven and adventurous, he gave up the chair two years later to go to Uruguay at the request of the government there and set up an institute of hygiene and public health, still flourishing. This was the time of his clashes with Sternberg and Reed in which he was vehemently supported by all Latin-American scientists. In 1899 he returned to Rome as professor of microbiology and there described myxomatosis and the first malignant tumours in animals caused by a transmissible and filterable virus. He died in 1940, aged 76.

69. A. Jacobi, 'Bacteriomania', *Medical Records*, 27 (1885), p. 172.
70. 'Yellow Fever Microbe', editorial, *The Alkaloidal Clinic*, 4 (1897), p. 549.
71. Quoted by Humphries, *Yellow Fever and the South*, p. 36.
72. J.T. Adams, *The Epic of America* (New York, 1931), p. 383.
73. The Platt Amendment gave the United States the right to coaling stations on the island, the right to intervene in its affairs for the preservation of order and a veto over financial and diplomatic relations with any foreign power. Other rights soon followed. 'Otherwise', Cuba was to remain a sovereign independent state.
74. An American Board of Investigation announced that the ship had been blown up from the outside. A Spanish board that was not permitted to visit the ship announced that it had been blown up by an internal explosion. Subsequently the United States Government had it towed out to sea and sunk so deep that no commission will ever be able to investigate the question.
75. This was more or less true, though tactless. McKinley later went on record as saying that, left alone, he could have avoided the war. Unfortunately, one of the few things not in the power of Presidents of the United States is to be left alone. (Nevertheless, John Adams stood alone when he saved the United States from war with France.) McKinley, a kindly and popular man, was assassinated by a Polish anarchist in 1901, aged 58.
76. The scenario was replayed in 1914 when Austria's foreign minister, Count Berchtold, determined to go to war with Serbia., win an easy victory and stir patriotic feelings in the somewhat lethargic Habsburg Monarchy, rejected every offer Serbia made in a succession of ultimata. (His efforts led to the First World War.) The scenario has arguably been replayed since.
77. The Spanish navy was old and decrepit and its leadership utterly defeatist: despite deficiencies on the American side, it was easily overcome both in Manila Bay in the Philippines and while trying to make an escape from Santiago in Cuba. Most Americans thoroughly enjoyed the first few weeks of the war. There was no draft, and there were 223,000 volunteers out of a population of 76 million. (Among them was Lawrence Reed.) For the first time Virginians and men from Massachusetts fought shoulder to shoulder. In the flush of victory it was easily overlooked that, because of the poor quality of the army rifles and incompetent planning, it took 6500

Americans six hours to subdue 600 Spaniards at El Caney. Morale only began to sag after the war was over and repatriation lagged while diseases went on the rampage.

The war left the United States with two large territories the status of which was never to be properly resolved. Subduing a subsequent insurrection in Cuba against American rule (which did not exist on paper) cost more lives than did the expulsion of the Spaniards.

78. By the Peace Treaty of Paris Cuba received a somewhat shadowy independence and Puerto Rico, Guam, Wake Island, the Hawaiian Islands and the Philippines were annexed. The United States paid $20,000,000 for the last, or about $2 per Filipino. By slave trade standards this was a bargain.

79. The report of the commission, *The Origin and Spread of Typhoid in the United States Military Camps*, was eventually published by Vaughan in 1904 in two volumes and became a public health classic.

Vaughan, the descendant of poor Welsh immigrants, had travelled to Europe with F.G. Novy after qualifying and had spent two years in Koch's institute in Berlin. Back in Michigan he became a formative influence on American bacteriology, public health and medical education, publishing works on tuberculosis, vaccination and a wide range of other topics. Placid and genial to distinguished visitors, he was revered but also feared in his own university. He was also a popular visitor at international gatherings and a regular visitor at the Listers' house in Park Crescent. In 1926 he published his informal and benign memoirs recounting his work with Reed on the Typhoid Commission: V.C. Vaughan, *A Doctor's Memoirs* (New York, 1926). (His fellow commissioners appear as somewhat shadowy figures and Vaughan was not averse to referring to the publication as the 'Vaughan Report'.) He died in 1929, aged 78.

80. Vaughan, *A Doctor's Memoirs*, p. 65.

81. This lady was a popular kitchen hand in a fashionable New York restaurant for 15 years and was later supposed to have been responsible for more than 15 outbreaks of typhoid (as well as unconfirmed individual cases) among the clientele. She was wholly symptomless but had a chronic typhoid focus in her gall bladder and went on excreting virulent typhoid bacilli in her faeces. She was cured from her carrier state by the surgical removal of her gall bladder, but had some difficulty in finding re-employment.

82. F.G. Novy, 'The Aetiology of Yellow Fever', *Medical News*, 73 (1898), p. 36.

83. V.C. Vaughan, 'Experiments on Patients', *American Journal of Experimental Medicine*, 12 (1898), p. 21.

84. W. Osler, 'Human Experimentation', *American Journal of Experimental Medicine*, 12 (1898), p. 78.

85. It was later suggested by Martha Sternberg, Sternberg's widow, in her biography of her husband, that the Commission had been set up by her late husband specifically to study yellow fever; and Sternberg himself had more than once referred to it as 'my yellow fever commission'. In fact, yellow fever was not specifically mentioned in Reed's remit.

86. In later years Agramonte felt somewhat slighted by official accounts of the Commission's work and produced his own version under the somewhat florid title of 'The Inside History of a Great Medical Discovery' (*Medical Monthly*, 12 (1915), p. 34. This was critical of most of the individuals involved (Carroll being especially singled out as 'very surly' and 'ill-bred'),

though not of Reed. Reed, so far as Agramonte recollected, was 'a charming personality, honest and above-board, someone everybody loved and confided in ... a polished gentleman and a scientist of the highest order'. Like most Cubans of pure Spanish blood, Agramonte was an ardent Cuban patriot. He died in 1931, aged 63.

87. *Yellow Fever: A Compilation* (Washington, 1911), p. 342.

88. F. Delaporte, *The History of Yellow Fever* (Cambridge, Massachusetts, 1991), p. 69.

89. Charles Louis Laveran, a graduate of Strasbourg University, became an army surgeon in 1867, and, while stationed in Algiers, discovered the protozoon, later called Plasmodium, as the cause of malaria two years later. He also hinted at the possibility that it might be spread by the mosquito, but did not pursue his inspired guess. A brilliant investigator, he ended his career as professor of medicine at Val-de-Grâce in Paris and died in 1922, aged 77.

90. C. Finlay, 'Inoculation for Yellow Fever by Means of Contaminated Mosquitoes', *American Journal of Medical Sciences*, 102 (1891), p. 254.

91. Pronounced fo-my-tees.

92. *Yellow Fever: A Compilation*, p. 432. Reed always gave Carter credit for his pioneering observations and Carter grieved over Reed's premature death. Later Carter went on to a distinguished career in the Marine Hospital Service, serving on the Panama Canal Commission in 1904 that ensured the eradication of yellow fever from the future Canal Zone. He was then loaned to Peru and other South American governments, helping them to combat the disease. He retired as Assistant Surgeon General and died in 1925, aged 73, leaving his magnum opus on yellow fever unfinished.

93. Quoted by Bean, *Walter Reed*, p. 267. Eventually Lawrence got his commission and retired from the United States Army in 1938 as a major general.

94. Quoted by Bean, *Walter Reed*, p. 142.

95. In 1920 he almost won the Republican nomination for president, which, in all likelihood, would have carried him to the White House. He died in 1927, aged 57.

96. *Yellow Fever: A Compilation*, p. 145.

97. *Yellow Fever: A Compilation*, p. 156.

98. *Yellow Fever: A Compilation*, p. 142.

99. Kean retired a colonel in 1910, but rejoined the Army in 1916 and served with distinction on the Western Front, retiring for a second time as a Brigadier General in 1920. He received many honours and decorations, including the Order of Carlos Finlay, instituted by the Cuban Government in 1926. He died in 1950, aged 90, and was buried in Moticello, near his illustrious forebear, the Third President.

100. *Yellow Fever: A Compilation*, p. 23.

101. The toast was revived in 1940, during the Second World War, by Battle of Britain pilots.

102. A.E. Truby, 'Walter Reed in Cuba', *Journal of American Pathology*, 43 (1912), p. 21.

103. J. Carroll, 'A Brief Review of the Aetiology of Yellow Fever', *New York Medical Journal*, 79 (1904), p. 244.

104. J. Carroll, 'Yellow Fever: A Popular Lecture', *American Medicine*, 9 (1905), p. 212.

105. Quoted by Bean, *Walter Reed*, p. 265.

106. A. Agramonte, *Medical Monthly*, 12 (1915), p. 17.

107. From the point of view of Lazear's life insurance, it was essential that any suggestion of Lazear volunteering for dangerous experiments and of exposing himself to unnecessary risks should be suppressed. This partly accounts for his part being 'downplayed' in official publications.

108. *Yellow Fever: A Compilation*, p. 54.

109. A.E. Truby, 'Walter Reed in Cuba', p. 23.

110. *Yellow Fever: A Compilation*, p. 276.

111. *Yellow Fever: A Compilation*, p. 268.

112. *Yellow Fever: A Compilation*, p. 289.

113. Quoted by Bean, *Walter Reed*, p. 234.

114. *Yellow Fever: A Compilation*, p. 120.

115. J.J. Moran, 'My experience with Yellow Fever', *Public Health Journal*, 23 (1911), p. 45.

116. Quoted by Bean, *Walter Reed*, p. 243.

117. Quoted by Bean, *Walter Reed*, p. 245.

118. Quoted by Bean, *Walter Reed*, p. 245.

119. Quoted by Bean, *Walter Reed*, p. 247.

120. Quoted by Bean, *Walter Reed*, p. 250.

121. *Yellow Fever: A Compilation*, p. 138.

122. J.M. Gibson, *Soldier in White: The Life of General George Miller Sternberg* (Durham, North Carolina, 1958).

123. M. Sternberg, *George Miller Sternberg: A Biography* (Chicago, 1920).

124. Finlay, Reed, Gorgas, Carroll and Keen cleared the path for many later students of yellow fever. It is now known, for example, that several species of *Aedes*, besides *aegypti*, can carry the disease. Another kind of mosquito, the *Haemagogus*, is also known to transmit yellow fever to humans and monkeys in the jungles of Central and South America.

125. An 'ultrafiltre' will allow the passage of viruses, which are single large molecules, but not of cells or multicellular organisms.

126. Carroll's work led eventually to the isolation of the virus in the early 1930s and to the development of the very effective anti-yellow-fever vaccine, 17D. It has saved many thousands of lives around the world, though the recent unexpected resurgence of the disease in Africa points to the need for the continued control of the mosquito population, the wider dissemination of the vaccine and perhaps the development of new ones.

127. *Yellow Fever: A Compilation*, p. 100.

128. This was a reference to Sternberg's occasional pose as an all-knowing prophet, not a snide and wholly out-of-character racist remark. Sternberg's forebears were in fact German immigrants: both his father and his maternal grandmother were Lutheran pastors. After a busy and active retirement Sternberg died in 1915, aged 77. He is described on his memorial plaque in Arlington Military Cemetery (not far from Reed's final resting place) as 'America's pioneer bacteriologist'.

129. Reed's appendix in a pot was preserved in the Pathology Museum (soon to be named after him) in Washington until the Depression years of the mid-1930s when, with many other pots, it was discarded as an economy measure.

BIBLIOGRAPHY

This bibliography is largely confined to books: only a few key papers published in learned journals are listed.

J.J. Abraham, *Lettsom: His Life, Times, Friends and Descendants* (London, 1933). Admiring biography of the most important Quaker physician of the generation before Lister.

K.B. Absolon, *The Belle Epoque of Surgery: The Life and Times of Theodore Billroth* (Rockville, Madison, 1985). An abridged and highly readable version of the author's massive four-volume biography of the great surgeon.

E.H. Ackerknecht, 'Broussais or a Forgotten Medical Revolution', *Bulletins of the History of Medicine*, 27 (1953), p. 320.

E.H. Ackerknecht, 'Laennec und die Psychiatrie', *Gesnerus*, 19 (1962), p. 93.

E.H. Ackerknecht, 'Laennec und sein Vorlesungsmanuskript, 1822', *Gesnerus*, 21 (1964), p. 142.

E.H. Ackerknecht, *History and Geography of the Most Important Diseases* (New York, 1965).

E.H. Ackerknecht, *Medicine at the Paris Hospitals, 1794–1848* (Baltimore, 1967). A key source book by one of the authorities on medical history of the period, embellished with brilliant drawings by Daumier.

E.H. Ackerknecht, *A Short History of Medicine* (Baltimore, 1968).

J.T. Adams, *The Epic of America* (New York, 1941).

A. Agramonte, 'The Yellow Fever Commission', *Medical Monthly*, 12 (1915), p. 17.

E. Andrews, 'The Oxygen Mixture, a New Anaesthetic Combination', *Chicago Medical Examiner*, 9 (1868), p. 656. The addition of pure oxygen to nitrous oxide made prolonged anaesthesia safe.

J. Antall (ed.) *Pictures from the Past of the Healing Arts, Semmelweis Medical Historical Museum, Library and Archives* (Budapest, 1972). Contains several valuable essays in English by Hungarian scholars on Semmelweis and his times.

J. Antall, V. R. Harko & T. Vida, 'Semmelweis összegyüjtott kéziratai' ('Complete Manuscripts of Semmelweis'), *Communicationes Historiae Artis Medicinae*, 51–53 (1968), p. 261.

P. Astruc, *Gabriel Andral* (Paris, 1955). A good biography of one of Laennec's contemporaries.

L. Auenbrugger, *Nouvelle méthode pour reconnaître les maladies internes de la poitrine, traduit et commenté par Jean Nicholas Corvisart* (Paris, 1808; reprinted Paris, 1855). Something unique: a great long book spawned by a great short one.

L. Auenbrugger, *Inventum novum in percussione thoracis humani ut signo abstrusos interim pectoris morbos detegendi*, reprinted and edited with a biographical note by M. Neuberger (Vienna, 1922). One of medicine's classics: the title is long but the book is short.

H. Bailey & W.J. Bishop, *Notable Names in Medicine and Surgery* (London, 1946).

Idiosyncratic and charming vignettes, entirely admiring, of some of the greats in medicine and surgery.

W. Bainbridge, *Remarks on Chloroform in Alleviating Human Suffering* (London, 1848). A neglected pioneering work.

L.G. Ballaster, R. French, J. Arrizabalaga & A. Cunningham, *Practical Medicine from Salerno to the Black Death* (New York, 1994).

B. Barker Beeson, 'Corvisart, His Life and Work', *Annals of Medical History*, 24 (1929), p. 197.

D.S. Barnes, *The Making of a Social Disease: Tuberculosis in Nineteenth-Century France* (Los Angeles, 1995).

H.K. Barski, *Guillaume Dupuytren, a Surgeon in his Place and Time* (New York, 1984). A good and sympathetic biography of one of Laennec's friends/enemies/rivals.

A.-.L.-J. Bayle, *Notice historique sur la vie et les oeuvres de G.-L. Bayle* (Paris, 1834). An excellent biography by the nephew of G.-L. Bayle, himself a notable physician who gave a classic account of general paralysis of the insane.

G-L. Bayle, *Idée générale de la thérapeutique* (Paris, 1805; reprinted Paris, 1855).

G.-L. Bayle, *Recherches sur la phthisie pulmonaire* (Paris, 1810; reprinted Paris. 1855). A pioneering book in its day, but no longer easy to understand.

W. Bean, *Walter Reed* (Charlottesville, Virginia, 1982). The most perceptive and best-researched biography of Reed available, written by a distinguished physician. A key source book.

I. Benedek, *Semmelweis és Kora* (Semmelweis and his times) (Budapest, 1967). The most up-to-date and sympathetic (but not adulatory) biography of Semmelweis at present, which, sadly, remains encoded in Hungarian.

R.F. Berkhofer, Jr, *The White Man's Indian: Images of the American Indian from Columbus to the Present* (New York, 1978). A great eye-opener.

J.D. Bernal, *The Social Function of Science* (London, 1839).

C. Bernard, *Introduction à l'étude de la médicine expérimentale* (Paris, 1865). A medical classic, brilliantly written and still enlightening.

M.F.X. Bichat, *Recherches physiologiques sur la vie et la mort* (Paris, 1800). A sparkling book in the tradition of French natural philosophy by one of the consumptive geniuses of the age.

M.F.X. Bichat, *Traité des membranes en générale, et de diverse membranes en particulier* (Paris, 1802). The beginning of the study of tissues as the basis of pathology.

H.J. Bigelow, *Surgical Anaesthesia: Addresses and Other Papers* (Boston, 1900).

W.J. Bishop, *The Early History of Surgery* (London, 1960).

M.D. Blaufox, *An Ear to the Chest: An Illustrated History of the Evolution of the Stethoscope* (London, 2002). An enthusiast's guide to the history of an instrument that changed the course of medicine, with a vast bibliography and a profusion of pictures.

G. Bloch, *Mesmerism: A Translation of the Original Scientific and Medical Writings of F.A. Mesmer* (Los Altos, California). The writings of Mesmer (containing much deliberate obfuscation) were never as influential as his personal teaching, but this is an excellent translation of his works.

J.L. Boer, *Sieben Bücher über natürliche Geburtshilfe* (Wien, 1834). A collection revered by Semmelweis.

T.N. Bonner, *American Doctors and German Universities: A Chapter in International Intellectual Relations, 1870–1914* (Lincoln, Nebraska, 1963).

T.N. Bonner, *Becoming a Physician: Medical Education in Britain, France, Germany and the United States, 1750–1945* (Oxford, 1995). An important and authoritative book on a neglected subject.

P. Bouillaud, *Eloge de Laennec* (Paris, 1869).

B.A. Boyd, *Rudolf Virchow: The Scientist as Citizen* (New York, 1991). An excellent and sympathetic biography.

S. Bradbury, *The Evolution of the Microscope* (Oxford, 1967).

B. Braid, *Neurypnology or the Rationale of Nervous Sleep Considered in Relation to Animal Magnetism* (London, 1835) A serious and practical examination of the potential use of hypnotism in surgery. It came too late: 'the Yankee dodge' of ether, quickly followed by chloroform, 'beat mesmerism hollow'.

R.C. Brock, *The Life and Work of Astley Cooper* (Edinburgh, 1952). A master surgeon's tribute to another.

T.D. Brock, *Robert Koch: A Life in Medicine and Bacteriology* (Madison, Wisconsin, 1988). The best monograph currently available; but the character was more complex (and more interesting) than the simple genius that emerges from most biographical writings.

F.J.V. Broussais, *Histoire des phlegmasies ou inflammations chroniques*, 2 vols (Paris, 1822). Almost completely incomprehensible to a modern medical mind, though worth dipping into.

F.J.V. Broussais, *De l'irritation et de la folie* (Paris, 1828). The *folie* is right.

F.J.V. Broussais, *Examen des doctrines médicales et des systèmes de nosologie*, 4 vols (Paris 1829–1834). Broussais is much more credible in demolishing doctrines propounded by others than in creating his own. His flamboyant style is at the opposite extreme from Laennec's.

D. Brown, *Bury my Head at Wounded Knee: An Indian History of the American West* (London, 1971). A ground-breaking work, beautifully written.

J. Bruck, *Ignaz Philip Semmelweis* (Vienna, 1887). A readable early biography that contains little original material.

W. Bulloch, *The History of Bacteriology* (London, 1938).

P. Busquet, *Le Baron Guillaume Dupuytren* (Paris, 1929).

A. Cabanès, *Dans l'intimité de l'Empereur* (Paris, 1924). Excellent on the remarkable relationship between two seemingly incompatible characters, Napoleon and Corvisart.

P.J.G. Cabanis, *Rapports du physiques et du moral de l'homme*, 2 vols (Paris, 1824). An influential book propounding an early humanist outlook on life and medicine. For a time the author was important politically too: he drafted the proclamation issued by Bonaparte on 18 Brumaire, 1799. He died a spiritualist believer.

H.C. Cameron, *Joseph Lister: The Friend of Man* (Glasgow, 1927). A sympathetic biography by the son of Lister's closest friend in old age, himself a surgeon.

J. Carroll, 'A Brief Review of the Activities of the Yellow Fever Commission', *New York Medical Journal and Philadelphia Medical Journal*, 2, February (1904), p. 13.

J. Carroll, 'Yellow Fever', *American Medicine*, 9 (1905), p. 212.

F.F. Cartwright, *The English Pioneers of Anaesthesia* (Bristol, 1952).

F.F. Cartwright, *Joseph Lister* (London, 1963).

F.F. Cartwright, *The Development of Modern Surgery* (New York, 1968). An excellent introduction to the subject that splendidly conveys the excitement of new surgical developments and the personalities of the pioneers.

J.H. Cassedy, *Medicine in America: A Short History* (Baltimore, 1991). Excellent background to Reed.

D. Caton, *What a Blessing She Had Anaesthesia* (London, 1999).

R. de Chateaubriand, *Le Génie du Christianisme* (Paris, 1802). The most influential book of Laennec's friend, patron and patient and one of

Laennec's favourites. It is a brilliant (though of course highly biased) apologia for the author's faith, not on theological but on cultural, literary and aesthetic grounds.

A.M. Chesney, *The Johns Hopkins Hospital and the Johns Hopkins University School of Medicine*, vol. I (Baltimore, 1948). Covers the time when Reed was seconded there.

W.W. Cheyne, *Antiseptic Surgery* (London, 1882).

W.W. Cheyne, *Lister and His Achievement* (London, 1925). An affectionate memoir by one of Lister's devoted pupils and friends. (Lister never quite forgave him, though, for embracing asepsis.)

H. Chick, M. Hume & M. Macfarlane, *War on Disease: A History of the Lister Institute* (London, 1871).

S. Chien, J.A. Dormandy, E. Ernst & A. Matrai, *Clinical Haematology* (Dordrecht, 1987).

A. Cobban, *A History of Modern France* (London, 1964). Vol. 2 still provides the best overall historical background to Laennec. But, as in other general histories, medicine does not get a mention.

Communicationes de Historia Artis Medicinae, *Semmelweis Memorial Volumes*, Vol. 46–47 and Vol. 55–56 (Budapest, 1968 and 1970). Apart from the two memorial volumes dedicated to Semmelweis, this official quarterly publication of the Semmelweis Historical Library in Budapest contains numerous scholarly papers dealing with the life and work of Semmelweis and the Vienna and Pest medical schools during his life.

J.D. Comrie, *History of Scottish Medicine*, 2 vols, 2nd edn (London, 1932). An important source book, but not an easy read.

L. Conrad, M. Neve, V. Nutton, R. Porter & A. Wear, *A Western Medical Tradition: 800 BC to AD 1800* (Cambridge, 1995).

B. Cooper, *The Life of Sir Astley Cooper, Bart*, 2 vols (London, 1843).

J.N. Corvisart, *Essai sur les maladies et les lésions organiques du coeur et des gros vaisseaux* (Paris, 1818; reprinted Paris, 1855). A cardiological classic in elegant French.

J.N. Corvisart, *Aphorismes de la médicine clinique, par le baron Corvisart, receuillit par F.V. Merat* (Paris, 1929). Some of the most stunningly cynical observations uttered by a great doctor. It was never meant for publication.

A. Crabtree, *From Mesmer to Freud* (London, 1993).

P. Crampton, 'On the application of leeches to internal surfaces', *Dublin Hospital Reports*, 3 (1822), p. 223.

E. Crankshaw, *The Fall of the House of Habsburg* (London, 1963). An unfashionably sympathetic but beautifully written account of the Habsburg Empire in Semmelweis's day and after.

V. Cronin, *Napoleon* (London, 1971). As background to Laennec, still the best popular short biography of Napoleon.

G. Crook, *Autobiography*, edited by M.F. Schmitt (Norman, Oklahoma, 1946).

B. Cullingworth, *Oliver Wendell Holmes and the Contagiousness of Puerperal Fever* (London, 1906).

P.D. Curtin, *Death by Migration: Europe's Encounter with the Tropical World in the Nineteenth Century* (Cambridge, 1989).

W.C.D. Dampier, *A History of Science and its Relation with Philosophy and Religion* (New York, 1930). An interesting and in its time pioneering work.

G. Daremberg, *Les grands médecins du XIXe siècle* (Paris, 1905).

H. Davy, *Researches, Chemical and Physiological* (London, 1800). This volume by one of the few wunderkinder of science contains the passage speculating about the possible use of nitrous oxide in surgical operations. It elicited practically no interest.

F. Delaporte, *The History of Yellow Fever* (Cambridge, Massachusetts, 1991). The essential background to Reed.

P. Delauney, *Le monde médical parisien du XVIIIe siècle*, 2nd edn (Paris, 1946). An excellent general survey.

P. Delauney, *D'une revolution á l'autre* (Paris, 1949).

P. Delauney, *Louis and the Numerical Method in Science, Medicine and History* (London, 1953). The birth of medical statistics.

L. Delhoume, *Dupuytren*, 3rd edn (Paris, 1935). A well-written if somewhat uncritical work.

L. Delhoume, *Cruveilhier* (Paris, 1937).

P.J. Desault, *Oeuvres chirurgicales*, edited by Xavier Bichat, 2 vols (Paris, 1789).

J. Deveze, *An Inquiry into and Observations upon the Causes of Yellow Fever and the Effects of the Epidemic which Raged in Philadelphia from August to the Middle of December, 1793* (Philadelphia, 1794). A thoughtful account of one of the most memorable outbreaks of yellow fever in the United States, reviewing in detail all the possible causes and mechanisms of spread. The mosquito is not mentioned; ignorance of the real mechanism of spread was complete.

I. Dobo & B. Ruel, *Bichat, la vie fulgurente d'un génie* (Paris, 1987). An excellent biography: *fulgurente* is right.

I. Domány, *Semmelweis küzdelmes élete* (Semmelweis's life and fight) (Budapest, 1958). A sympathetic biography by a medical compatriot.

T. Dormandy, 'Fort mit dem Spray', *Lancet*, 1 (1956), p. 846. The Teutonic bark is Von Bergmann's, ordering antisepsis to give way to asepsis (see Part III, Lister). The decade after the Second World War saw a bonanza of miraculous new antibiotics; and some otherwise sane surgeons began to advocate 'routine antibiotic cover' for all surgical admissions to replace the 'the time-wasting aseptic ritual'. The challenge was taken up Sir Theodore Fox, great editor of the *Lancet*, who caused his most bumptious and barely qualified leader writer to draw a parallel between the Listerian spray and the indiscriminate use of antibiotics. 'Fort' with both! The call proved less than effective.

T. Dormandy, *The White Death: A History of Tuberculosis* (London, 1999).

R. Druitt, *The Surgeon's Vade Mecum* (London, 1851). One of the books in Lister's library.

R. Dubos, *Louis Pasteur: Free Lance of Science* (London, 1951). A perceptive and beautifully written biography by a scientist.

R. & J. Dubos, *The White Plague: Tuberculosis, Man and Society* (London, 1953). A pioneering book on the social history of tuberculosis.

E. Duclaux, *Pasteur: Histoire d'un esprit* (Sceaux, 1896). Well-informed hagiography.

E. Duclaux, *Le Laboratoire de M. Pasteur* (Paris, 1922). Published to mark the centenary of Pasteur's birth by his successor at the Pasteur Institute.

J. Duffy, *The Sword of Pestilence: The New Orleans Yellow Fever Epidemic of 1853* (Baton Rouge, 1966). A vivid evocation of the disease as it must have appeared to Reed when he took up the challenge.

N. Duin, *A History of Medicine: From Prehistory to the Year 2020* (London, 1992).

J. Duns, *Memoir of Sir James Y. Simpson, Bart* (Edinburgh, 1873).

A. Dupic, *Antoine Dubois, chirurgien et accoucheur* (Paris, 1907).

E. & L. Edelstein, *Asclepius: A Collection and Interpretation of the Testimonies* (Baltimore, 1945). Speculative but interesting.

J. Elliotson, *Numerous Cases of Surgical Operations without Pain* (London, 1843). The last attempt to resurrect mesmerism as a surgical anaesthetic by a professor of medicine of high repute.

H. Ellis, *A History of Surgery* (London, 2000). An excellent and lavishly illustrated introduction for a primarily medical readership.

J. Erichsen, *The Science and Art of Surgery* (London, 1853). One of the textbooks used and admired by Lister.

O.B. Falk, *The Geronimo Campaign* (New York, 1969).

J. Fayet, *La Revolution Française et la science* (Paris, 1960).

S. Fekete, 'Semmelweis, Pasteur, Lister', *Présse Médicale*, 76 (1968), p. 1082. One of numerous articles by an eminent Hungarian Semmelweis scholar.

R.B. Fisher, *Joseph Lister, 1827–1912* (London, 1977). This remains *the* Lister biography: sympathetic, judicious and thoroughly and independently researched, using primary sources. It has a good index and bibliography.

A. Folsing, *Wilhelm Conrad Röntgen* (Vienna, 1995). A deservedly sympathetic biography.

W.D. Foster, *A History of Medical Bacteriology and Immunology* (London, 1970).

M.J.P. Foucault, *Histoire de la folie à l'âge classique: folie et déraison* (Paris, 1961).

M.J.P. Foucault, *Naissance de la clinique* (Paris, 1963). Excellent on Bichat.

J. de Fourmestraux, *Histoire de la chirurgie française, 1790–1920* (Paris, 1934).

P.F. & P. Frankland, *Pasteur* (New York, 1898).

R. Fülöp-Miller, *Triumph over Pain* (New York, 1938). A much criticised but readable history of anaesthesia.

F.J. Gall, *Anatomie et physiologie du système nerveux en générale, et du cerveau en particulier*, 2 vols (Paris, 1810). A highly influential book reviewed (and demolished) by Laennec.

H. Gancel, *Les Saints qui guérissent en Bretagne*, 2 vols (Paris, 2000). A beautifully illustrated guide to more than 60 healing saints and shrines in Brittany. A treasure.

P. Ganière, *Corvisart* (Paris, 1951). A good biography, focused on the doctor rather than on the man.

F.H. Garrison, 'The History of Bloodletting', *New York Medical Journal*, 97 (1913), pp. 432, 498.

F.H. Garrison, *An Introduction to the History of Medicine*, 4th edn (Philadelphia, 1966). Still a standard work of reference.

G. Gask, *Essays in the History of Medicine* (London, 1950).

G.L. Geison, *The Private Science of Louis Pasteur* (Princeton, 1995).

J. Gelis, *History of Childbirth* (Oxford, 1991).

J.M. Gibson, *Soldier in White: The Life of General George Miller Sternberg* (Durham, North Carolina, 1985). A somewhat uncritical but well-written authorised life.

L. Glendenning, *Sourcebook of Medical History* (New York, 1942).

Sir R.J. Godlee, *Lord Lister*, 3rd edn (Oxford, 1924). The only important Lister biography before Fisher's by Lister's nephew, himself an eminent surgeon. It is weighted on the professional side and extremely discreet, but it is beautifully written and a valuable first-hand source.

N.G. Goodman, *Benjamin Rush, Physician and Citizen* (Philadelphia, 1934). A great citizen, one of the signatories of the Declaration of Independence, but a medical calamity.

A. Gordon, *A Treatise on the Epidemic of Puerperal Fever in Aberdeen* (London, 1795). An important and pioneering book that anticipated Semmelweis's discovery by 50 years but whose message was largely ignored.

H.L. Gordon, *Sir James Young Simpson and Chloroform* (London, 1896). The source of many anaesthetic legends, some perhaps true.

G. Gortvay & Z. Imre, *Semmelweis élete es munkássága* (Semmelweis: His Life and Achievement) (Budapest, 1965).

G. de Grandmaison, *La Congrégation* (Paris, 1889). The work of a not uncritical believer.

M. Greenwood, *The Medical Dictator and other Biographical Studies* (London, 1986). Contains good short biographies of P.C.A. Louis and other pioneers of medical statistics.

G.B. Gruber, *Einführung in die Geschichte und Geist der Medizin*, 4th edn (Stuttgart, 1952). A perceptive general history.

J. Guiart, *Histoire de la médicine française* (Lyon, 1947).

E.J. Gurlt, *Geschichte der Chirurgie*, 3 vols (Berlin, 1981). An excellent and comprehensive history of surgery up to the date of publication, particularly good on the impact of Listerism and the advent of anaesthesia.

D. Guthrie, *A History of Medicine* (Nelson, 1960). Short, civilised and readable.

T. Györy (ed.), *Collected Works of Semmelweis* (Budapest, 1905). The labour of love of a great and patriotic medical historian.

E. Haigh, 'Xavier Bichat and the Medical Thought of the Eighteenth Century', *Medical History*, Supplement 4 (1984).

H. Hale Bellot, *University College Hospital, 1826–1926* (London, 1929).

R. Hare, *The Birth of Penicillin* (London, 1970).

G.A. Harrison, *Mosquitoes, Malaria and Man* (New York, 1978).

W. Harvey, *Exercitatio anatomica de motu cordis et sanguinis in animalibus*, translated by G. Whitteridge (Oxford, 1976). A medical landmark, still a pleasure to read for the unanswerable simplicity of its logic.

L. Héchemann, *Corvisart* (Paris, 1906). A somewhat pedestrian biography.

A. Hegar, *Ignaz Philip Semmelweis: Sein Leben und seine Lehre, zugleich ein Beitrag zur Lehre der fieberhaften Wundkrankheiten* (Freiburg, 1882). The first biography of Semmelweis, vindicating his work. Alfred Hegar was for 30 years professor of gynaecology in the University of Freiburg in Breisgau, which he made into a centre of gynaecological research. He described the cervical dilators still known by his name. He died in 1914, aged 84.

C. Helman, *Culture, Health and Illness* (Bristol, 1984).

J. Hemlow (ed.), *The Journals and Letters of Fanny Burney (Madame d'Arblay)*, vol. 6 (Oxford, 1975). Contains a vivid and gruesome account of a pre-anaesthetic mastectomy.

R.M. Hodges, *A Narrative of Events Connected with the Introduction of Sulphuric Ether* (reprinted Boston, 1981). Probably the most reliable contemporary account of this long and discreditable controversy.

O.W. Holmes, *Medical Essays, 1842–1882* (Boston, 1891). A brilliant read.

O.W. Holmes, 'The Contagiousness of Puerperal Fever' (1843) and 'Puerperal Fever as a Private Pestilence' (1855), *Medical Classics*, vol. 1 (Baltimore, 1936).

H.H. Hueben *Der Gefesselte Biedermeyer: Literatur, Kultur, Zensur in der Guten Alten Zeit* (Leipzig, 1924). The not so gemütlich Biedermeyer age: a useful corrective.

M. Humphries, *Yellow Fever and the South* (New Brunswick, New Jersey, 1992). An important book on a comparatively poorly documented subject.

R. Jackson, *Doctors and Diseases in the Roman Empire* (Norman, Oklahoma, 1988).

J.H. James, *On the Causes of Mortality after Amputations of the Limbs* (Worcester, 1850). The state of the art a few years before Lister.

J.M. Keating, *History of the Yellow Fever Epidemic of 1878* (Philadelphia, 1879). A vivid and gruesome first-hand account.

H.A. Kelly, *Walter Reed and Yellow Fever* (New York, 1906). The first biography of Reed written by an eminent contemporary; but see Note 8 to Part IV, Reed.

R. Kertész, *Wenn Semmelweis ein Tagebuch Geführt Hätte ...* (Budapest, 1957). An imaginative reconstruction.

R. Kervran, *Laennec, His Life and Times*, translated by D.C. Abrahams-Curiel (Oxford, 1960). The author, a Breton chest physician like Laennec, had real empathy for his subject.

K.F. Kiple, *The Caribbean Slave: A Biological History* (Cambridge, 1984) Important background to Reed's work.

R. Knoett, *Herman Boerhaave: Calvinist Chemist and Physician* (Amsterdam, 2002). A useful update on Boerhaave set in his time.

C. Koller, 'Über die Verwendung des Cocain zur Anaesthetisierung am Auge', *Wiener Medizinische Wochenschrift*, 34 (1884), p. 1309. The discovery of local anaesthesia.

E. Kratzman, *Die neuere Medizin in Frankreich, Theorie und Praxis* (Leipzig, 1846). Laennec as seen by a francophile German patriot.

P. de Kruif, *Microbe Hunter* (London, 1930). The bestseller of the 1930s that created the character of the medical hero, now almost unbearably upbeat and 'readers' digested'. Walter Reed is one of the hunters.

T. Kuhn, *The Structure of Scientific Revolutions*, 2nd edn (Chicago, 1970).

R.-T.-H. Laennec, *Propositions sur la doctrine d'Hippocrate*, Thèse de Paris (Paris, 1804).

R.-T.-H. Laennec, *Traité de l'auscultation mediate et des maladies du coeur et les poumons*, 2nd edn (Paris, 1826). A great and still highly readable landmark in the history of medicine.

R.-T.-H. Laennec, *Documents inédits* (Centennaire), (Paris, 1926). A useful collection of primary material.

R.-T.-H. Laennec, *La Guerre des Vénètes* (Paris, 1931). A witty youthful indiscretion: like Semmelweis (but not Lister or Reed), Laennec was a poet as well as a doctor.

E. Lafrange, *Monsieur Roux* (Brussels, 1954). An affectionate memorial.

M.F.R. de Lamennais, *Essai sur l'indifférence en matière de religion* (Paris, 1817). The literary flagship of the Catholic revival in France during the first decades of the nineteenth century. Laennec was a supporter and an admirer of Lamennais's but he disapproved of the increasing involvement of the Church in the reactionary politics of Charles X.

C. Lawrence, *Medicine in the Making of Modern Britain, 1700–1920* (London, 1994). A penetrating study of a neglected aspect of social history.

J.R. Leeson, *Lister as I Knew Him* (London, 1927). Memoir by one of Lister's Edinburgh house surgeons.

J. Le Fanu, *The Rise and Fall of Modern Medicine* (London, 1999). On a timescale this brilliant book starts where the present work ends. What happened to modern medicine once created?

W. Leibrand, *Die spekulative Medizin der Romantik* (Hamburg, 1956). An unusual and provocative approach to the medicine of the romantic age.

A.T. Leitich, *Wiener Biedermeier* (Bielefeld, 1941).

G. Le Notre, *Les Noyades de Nantes* (Paris, 1947). The history of Carrière's reign of terror in Nantes.

A. Le Pelletier de la Sarthe, *Histoire de la revolution médicale du XIXe siècle* (Paris, 1854). An almost contemporary account of the diagnostic revolution.

E. Lesky, *Österreichische Gesundheitswesen im Zeitalter des aufgeklärtes Absolutismus* (Vienna, 1959).

E. Lesky, *Carl von Rokitansky* (Vienna, 1960). The author was a historian rather than a biographer.

E. Lesky, *Ignaz Philipp Semmelweis und die Wiener medizinische Schule* (Vienna, 1964). The unedifying intrigues and politicking surrounding Semmelweis's departure from Vienna.

E. Lesky, *Die Wiener Medizinische Schule im 19. Jahrhundert* (Graz, 1965). An indispensable source book.

M. Lindemann, *Health and Healing in Eighteenth-Century Germany* (Baltimore, 1996).

G.A. Lindenboom, *Herman Boerhaave, The Man and His Work* (London, 1968).

Lord Lister, *Collected Papers* (Oxford, 1909). An astonishing range of interests.

R. Liston, *Lectures on the Operations of Surgery* (Philadelphia, 1846). A pre-Listerian classic.

G.E.R. Lloyd (ed.), *Hippocratic Writings* (London, 1978).

E.R. Long, *A History of Pathology* (New York, 1965).

I. Loudon, *Medical Care and the General Practitioner, 1750–1850* (Oxford, 1986).

I. Loudon (ed.), *Death in Childbirth: An International Study of Maternal Care and Maternal Mortality, 1800–1950* (Oxford, 1992). An essential source book with a brilliant chapter on childbed fever.

I. Loudon (ed.), *Western Medicine* (Oxford, 1997).

I. Loudon, *The Tragedy of Childbed Fever* (Oxford, 2001). A masterly monograph, but in the present writer's opinion the author misjudges Semmelweis.

P.C.A. Louis, *Researches on the Effect of Blood Letting* (Boston, 1836). This ground-breaking book in medical statistics should have put an end to indiscriminate blood-letting but did not. Today it is revered rather than read.

F. Loux, *Pratique et savoirs populaires: Le corps dans la société traditionale* (Paris, 1979).

L. McAuliffe, *La Révolution et les hôpitaux de Paris* (Paris, 1901). An interesting and important subject that still awaits its inspired chronicler.

W.G. MacCallum, *William Stewart Halsted, Surgeon* (Baltimore, 1954). A brilliant but enigmatic figure not fully revealed.

J.H. McGregor, *The Wounded Knee Massacre from the Viewpoint of the Survivors* (Baltimore, 1940).

W.H. McNeill, *Plagues and People* (Oxford, 1976).

B. MacQuitty, *The Battle for Oblivion: The Discovery of Anaesthesia* (London, 1969).

R.H. Major, *A History of Medicine*, 2 vols (Springfield, 1954).

F.O. Matthiessen, *American Renaissance: Art and Expression in the Age of Emerson and Whitman* (London, 1941). This was also the age of Reed, though he gets no mention.

R.C. Maulitz, *Morbid Appearances: The Anatomy of Pathology in the Early Nineteenth Century* (Cambridge, 1987). An excellent book.

P.M.H. Mazumdar, *Species and Specificity: An Interpretation of the History of Immunology* (Cambridge, 1994). A brilliant interpretation of immunology in a wider context.

C.D. Meigs, *Females and Their Diseases: A Series of Letters to his Class* (Philadelphia, 1848). The standard textbook of its time, more or less contemporary with Semmelweis's discovery. Meigs was a highly regarded doctor and teacher who never accepted Semmelweis's doctrine and strongly disapproved of obstetric anaesthesia. He became a sadly isolated figure in old age.

R. Melzack and P.D. Wall, *The Challenge of Pain*, 2nd edn (London, 1888). An exposition for the general reader of the 'gate control' theory of pain, the impetus behind much recent research in this field.

M.J. Menage & G. Wright, 'Use of leeches in a case of severe periorbital haematoma', *British Journal of Ophthalmology*, 75 (1991), p. 755.

J.T. Merz, *A History of European Thought in the Nineteenth Century*, 4th edn (London, 1923–28).

P. Mevel, *Hommage à Laennec* (Paris, 1926). The French do this kind of thing rather well.

A. Miles, *The Edinburgh School of Surgery before Lister* (London, 1918).

A. Miquel, *Eloge de Xavier Bichat* (Paris, 1923).

H. Mondor, *Dupuytren*, 2nd edn (Paris, 1945).

H.M. Morais, *The History of the Negro in Medicine* (New York, 1967).

S. Müller, *Antoine Laurent Bayle* (Zurich, 1965).

R.H. Murray, *Science and Scientists in the Nineteenth Century* (New York, 1925).

H. Neal, *The Politics of Pain* (New York, 1968).

C. Newman, *The Evolution of Medical Education in the Nineteenth Century* (London, 1957). An interesting if rather dry account.

N. Nicolson, *Napoleon 1812* (London, 1985). As background to Laennec, the best modern account of Napoleon's Russian campaign.

F. Nightingale, *Notes on Hospitals* (London, 1859). An immensely influential book that should have been rendered obsolete by Lister's discovery of antisepsis but was not.

G. Norman, *Biedermeyer Painting, 1815–1848* (London, 1987). Semmelweis's Vienna reflected in its art.

S.B. Nuland, *Doctors* (New York, 1988).

G.G.F. Nuttall, 'On the Role of Insects, Arachnids and Myriapods as Possible Carriers of Bacterial and Parasitic Diseases', *Johns Hopkins Hospital Reports*, 8 (1899), p. 1. Early speculation about the possibility of spread of epidemics by the mosquito.

E.R. Nye & M.E. Gibson, *Ronald Ross, Malariologist and Polymath* (London, 1997). Probably the best biography at present of this astonishing man.

A. Oakley, *The Captured Womb: A History of Medical Care of Pregnant Women* (Oxford, 1984).

J.M.D. Olmstead, *Claude Bernard, Physiologist* (New York, 1938).

W. Osler, *An Alabama Student and Other Essays* (New York, 1908). Includes an admirable essay on the influence of Louis and his statistical method in the United States.

F.R. Packard, 'Guy Patin and the Medical Profession in Paris in the Seventeenth Century', *Annals of Medical History*, 14 (1922), p. 366.

W. Pagel, *New Light on William Harvey* (Basel, 1976). One of the author's several important contributions to medical history.

Sir J. Paget, *Studies of Old Case Books* (London, 1891). Vivid and humane recollections of one of the great surgeons of his day and a patron and later friend of Lister's.

A. Paré, *Ten Books of Surgery*, translated by R.W. Linker & N. Womack (Athens, Georgia, 1969). A surgical classic made almost comprehensible.

L. Pasteur, *Oeuvres réunis par Pasteur Valléry-Radot* (Paris, 1933–1939) Collected works in seven volumes, the record of an astonishing life. Surprisingly little of what Pasteur wrote was dross.

L. Pasteur, *Quelque refléxions sur la science en France*, reprinted collected works, vol. 7 (Paris, 1939).

E.E. Pauls, *Der Beginn der bürgerlichen Zeit: Biedermeyerschicksale* (Lübeck, 1927). The society that Semmelweis knew and confronted in Vienna.

L. Payer, *Medicine and Culture: Notions of Health and Sickness in Britain, the US,*

France and West Germany (London, 1989). The exploration of a neglected theme, the differing national traits of medical care. These are as important for the understanding of the history of medicine as for examining current practices.

L. Peisse, *Les médecins français contemporains* (Paris, 1827). A gossipy contemporary account of Laennec and his friends. Even the somewhat malicious author cannot find anything seriously discreditable to say about Laennec, but he tries.

M.S. Pernick, *A Calculus of Suffering: Pain, Professionalism and Anaesthesia in Nineteenth-Century America* (New York, 1895). A brilliant social survey of attitudes to anaesthesia, mainly in the United States.

M.S. Pernick, 'Politics, Parties and Pestilence: Epidemic Yellow Fever in Philadelphia and the Rise of the First Party System', *William and Mary Quarterly*, 3rd Series, 29 (1972), p. 559.

M.J. Peterson, *The Medical Profession in Mid-Victorian London* (Berkeley, California, 1978).

P. Pinel, *Traité médicophilosophique sur l'aliénation mentale*, 2nd edn (Paris, 1800). A ground-breaking book that changed the treatment of the insane, still readable and deeply disturbing.

P. Pinel, *Nosographie philosophique*, 3 vols (Paris, 1818). An important but almost wholly unreadable classic.

I.H. Porter, *Alexander Gordon, MD of Aberdeen* (Edinburgh, 1958). The troubled and tragic life of an important precursor of Semmelweis.

R. Porter, *The Greatest Benefit to Mankind, a Medical History of Humanity from Antiquity to the Present* (London, 1977). A monument that almost begins to fulfil its impossible self-set task. To be taken in small divided doses. It has a good exhaustive bibliography.

R. Porter (ed.), *Medicine in the Enlightenment* (Amsterdam, 1995).

J.H. Powell, *Bring out Your Dead: The Great Plague of Yellow Fever in Philadelphia in 1793* (New York, 1965). A brilliantly vivid account of a historic outbreak of yellow fever and of the role of Benjamin Rush in trying to combat it with blood-letting and purgation.

F.N.L. Poynter (ed.), *The Evolution of Hospitals in Britain* (London, 1964).

G. Qvist, *John Hunter, 1728–1793* (London, 1981). A sympathetic account that does not quite explain Hunter's enduring charisma.

M. Ramsey, *Professional and Popular Medicine in France, 1770–1830: The Social World of Medical Practice* (Cambridge, 1988). A valuable source book.

T. Ranger & P. Slack (eds), *Epidemics and Ideas* (Cambridge, 1992).

P.H.L. Reis, *Etude sur Broussais et sur son oeuvre* (Paris, 1869).

E. Rist, *La Jeunesse de Laennec* (Paris, 1955). An affectionate memoir by a distinguished French doctor.

S. Roberts, *Sophia Jex-Blake* (London, 1999). A more up-to-date and balanced account than M. Todd's.

S. Roberts, *Sir James Paget: The Rise in Clinical Surgery* (London, 2000). The readable and attractive memoir of an eminent Victorian.

V. Robinson, *Victory over Pain. A History of Anaesthesia* (London, 1947). An outstanding and indispensable history with a critical bibliography.

G. Rosen, 'An American Doctor in Paris in 1828', *Journal of the History of Medicine*, 6 (1951), p. 116.

S.M. Rothman, *Woman's Proper Place: A History of Changing Ideals and Practices, 1870 to the Present* (New York, 1978).

E. Roux, *L'Oeuvre Médicale de Pasteur* (Paris, 1922). Roux was for many years

Pasteur's assistant and became director of the Institut Pasteur in Paris in 1904. A great bacteriologist, he was a frail, sickly man, supposedly tuberculous, who was always expected to die any minute, but who lived to the age of 82, dying in 1934.

A. Rouxeau, *Laennec avant 1806* (Paris, 1912).

A. Rouxeau, *Laennec après 1806* (Paris, 1920). A lifetime's labour of love by the successor to Guillaume Laennec in Nantes. The two volumes are indispensable to anyone interested in Laennec, the man and the doctor.

C.A. Sainte-Beuve, *Premiers Lundis* (Paris, 1827). Jottings of one of the luminaries of the French literary scene, recalling Laennec the Breton scholar rather than the physician.

H. Saintignon, *Laennec, sa vie et son oeuvre* (Paris, 1904).

L. Sauve, *Le Docteur Récamier, 1774–1832: Sa famille et ses amies* (Paris, 1938). A charming biography of one of Laennec's closest friends and a leading surgeon of his day, quoting in full a letter from Jacquette written immediately after her husband's death.

J. Savina, *Autour de T.-R. Laennec: Lettres inédites de son père et de ses oncles* (Quimper, 1925).

L. Schönbauer, *Das medizinische Wien*, 2nd edn (Vienna, 1947).

F. Schürer von Waldheim, *Ignaz Philipp Semmelweis. Sein Leben und Wirken. Urteile der Mit- und Nachwelt* (Vienna, 1905). The first fully researched and documented Semmelweis biography by an Austrian general practitioner: a landmark in the recognition of Semmelweis's achievement.

B. Seeman, *Man against Pain* (Philadelphia, 1962).

I.P. Semmelweiss, *Die Aetiologie, der Begriff und die Prophylaxis des Kinderbettfiebers* (Pest, 1861). Semmelweis's magnum opus, published simultaneously in Pest (Budapest today), Vienna and Leipzig. A terrible but fascinating book.

I.P. Semmelweis, *Offener Brief an sämtlichen Professoren der Geburtshilfe* (Buda/Ofen, 1862). The tragic document of a 'deeply hurt but noble mind'.

J. Shepherd, *Spencer Wells: The Life and Work of a Victorian Surgeon* (Edinburgh, 1965).

R.H. Shryock, *The Development of Modern Medicine* (New York, 1947).

G.R. Siegworth, 'Bloodletting over the Centuries', *New York State Journal of Medicine*, 12 (1980), p. 2024.

H.E. Sigerist, *Great Doctors* (London, 1951).

Sir W. J. Sinclair, *Semmelweis. His Life and Doctrine* (Manchester, 1909). The first full Semmelweis biography in English.

C. Singer, *A Short History of Medicine* (New York, 1928).

N.G. Siraisi, *Medieval and Renaissance Medicine: An Introduction to Knowledge and Practice* (Chicago, 1990).

F.G. Slaughter, *Immortal Magyar. Semmelweis, Conqueror of Childbed Fever* (New York, 1950).

F.B. Smith, *The People's Health, 1830–1910* (London, 1979). An important and revealing book.

F.B. Smith, *Florence Nightingale: Reputation and Power* (London, 1982).

J. Snow, *On Chloroform and Other Anaesthetic Agents*, edited by B. Ward Richardson (London, 1858). A posthumous collection of historic papers by one of the most admirable of the great Victorians.

P. Stanley, *For Fear of Pain: British Surgery, 1790–1850* (Amsterdam, 2003). An outstanding work and profoundly thoughtful study of British surgery over the half-century before anaesthesia and antisepsis.

D. Starr, *Blood: An Epic History of Medicine and Commerce* (London, 1998). The book concentrates on recent history but also surveys the history of blood-letting.

P. Starr, *The Social Transformation of American Medicine* (New York, 1982).

M.S. Staum, *Cabanis: Enlightenment and Medical Philosophy in the French Revolution* (Princeton, 1980).

M. Sternberg, *George Miller Sternberg: A Biography* (Chicago, 1920). A widow's homage to her late husband.

M. Sternberg, *Josef Skoda* (Vienna, 1924). The only currently available biography of a remarkable doctor.

S.T.G. Steward, *Colored Regulars in the US Army* (New York, 1904). A book of great bravery by the Chaplain of the Twenty-Fifth Infantry Regiment in Cuba, which cost the author his career in the US Army.

F.C. Stewart, *Hospitals and Surgeons of Paris* (New York, 1843).

A.I. Tauber & L. Chernyak, *Metchnikoff and the Origins of Immunology* (New York, 1991).

A.J.P. Taylor, *The Habsburg Monarchy* (London, 1948). A characteristically brilliant and waspish background to the political events in the Habsburg Monarchy in 1848–49.

O. Temkin, 'Gall and the Phrenological Movement', *Bulletin of the History of Medicine*, 25 (1951), p. 248.

O. Temkin, *Galenism: Rise and Decline of a Medical Philosophy* (Ithaca, New York, 1973).

J.D. Thomson & G. Goldin, *The Hospital, a Social and Architectural History* (New Haven, 1975). An excellent book on a neglected topic.

A. de Tocqueville, *Democracy in America*, 2 vols (New York, 1945). Still a wonderful read.

M. Todd, *The Life of Sophia Jex-Blake* (London, 1910). A reverential life by a lifelong friend and companion.

A.E. Truby, 'Walter Reed in Cuba', *Journal of American Pathology*, 43 (1912), p. 21.

A.E. Truby, *Memoirs: The Yellow Fever Episode* (New York, 1943). A nicely illustrated and admiring memoir of Reed's work in Cuba. (See Note 8 to Part IV, Reed.)

J. Tyndall, *Fragments of Science* (New York, 1896). Reflections from an age of scientific optimism.

J. Tyndall, *New Fragments* (New York, 1896).

F.E. Udwada, *Man and Medicine* (Oxford, 2000). A fresh, readable and up-to-date general history of medicine.

R.M. Utley, *The Last Days of the Sioux Nation* (New Haven, 1963).

R.P. Valléry-Radot, *Pasteur, Dessinateur et Pastelliste* (Paris, 1912). Pasteur was an excellent artist in the tradition of the great French pastellists like Quintin de la Tour and Chardin. A. Edelfeld, the fashionable and accomplished portraitist who in 1885 painted 'Pasteur in his Laboratory', probably the best-known iconic likeness of the scientist, became a friend and was privileged to be shown the youthful pastels of his sitter. He was 'boulversé' by their excellence and maintained (perhaps with some justice) that his sitter was a better artist than he was himself.

R.P. Valléry-Radot, *La vie de Pasteur* (Paris, 1924). An important but exceedingly long and solemn book.

R.P. Valléry-Radot, *Deux siècles d'histoires hospitalière* (Paris, 1947). An important source book.

V.C. Vaughan (ed.), *The Origin and Spread of Typhoid in the United States Military*

Camps (Washington, 1904). The report of the Commission of which Reed was a member.

V.C. Vaughan, *A Doctor's Memoirs* (New York, 1926). Benign recollections that include memories of Reed and of visiting the Listers.

D. Vess, *Medical Revolution in France, 1789–1796* (Gainsville, 1975).

R. Virchow, *Gesammelte Abhandlungen zur Wissentschaftlicher Medizin* (Frankfurt, 1896). When did these great Victorians (not only in England) have time to breathe?

J. Waddington, *The Medical Profession in the Industrial Revolution* (Dublin, 1994).

R. Waissenberger, *Vienna, 1815–1848* (Fribourg, 1985). Semmelweis's Vienna.

A.R. Wallace, *The Wonderful Century: Its Successes and Its Failures* (New York, 1899). A wonderful monument to an optimistic age that now seems as remote as the Dark Ages.

J. Walzer Leavitt, *Typhoid Mary: Captive to the Public Health* (Boston, 1996). A memorable episode in the history of public health, memorably written.

J.H. Warner, 'Therapeutics and the Edinburgh Blood Letting Controversy', *Medical History*, 24 (1980), p. 241.

M. Warner (Humphries), 'Hunting the Yellow Fever Germ', *Bulletin of the History of Medicine*, 59 (1985), p. 361.

D. Weatherall, *Science and the Quiet Art: Medical Research and Patient Care* (Oxford, 1995).

G.B. Webb, *René Théophile Hyacinthe Laennec* (Oxford, 1928).

D. Weiner, *The Citizen Patient in Revolutionary and Imperial Paris* (Baltimore, 1993). The clientele of Corvisart and Laennec.

C. White, *A Treatise on the Management of Pregnant and Lying-in Women* (London, 1773). An influential and in many respects pioneering textbook that was translated into German and may have been read by Semmelweis, but that made comparatively little impact in German-speaking Europe.

A.N. Whitehead, *Science and the Modern World* (New York, 1925). A profound examination of the relationship, still relevant today.

C.E. Winslow, *The Conquest of Epidemic Disease* (Princeton, 1943).

E.J. Wollez, *Le Docteur P.C.A. Louis, son oeuvre et sa vie* (Paris, 1873). An affectionate and informative memoir by a friend.

G.S. Woodward, *The Man who Conquered Surgical Pain: A Biography of William Thomas Green Morton* (Boston, 1962). A rather indulgent life.

K.R.A. Wunderlich, *Wien und Paris* (Stuttgart, 1841; reprinted Berne, 1974). The two centres of the diagnostic revolution of the first half of the nineteenth century.

K.R.A. Wunderlich, *Geschichte der Medizin* (Stuttgart, 1859). An excellent history, now itself part of it.

Yellow Fever: A Compilation of Various Publications of the Work of Major Walter Reed and the Yellow Fever Commission (Washington, 1911). A useful collection and source book.

Sir J. Young Simpson, *Collected Works*, 3 vols (Edinburgh, 1872). Vol. 2 contains the passage on the introduction of chloroform.

A.J. Youngson, *The Scientific Revolution in Victorian Medicine* (New York, 1979). The backdrop to Lister's work and public persona.

L.M. Zimmerman & I. Veith, *Great Ideas in the History of Surgery*, 2nd edn (New York, 1967).

INDEX

A thought-provoking exploration of the nature of humanity

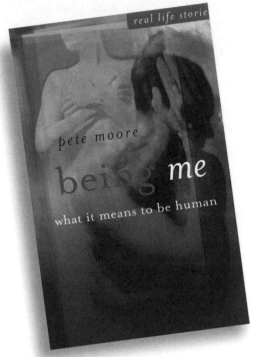

Addressing issues that will shape the future of the human race from a scientific, historical, moral and philosophical viewpoint, bestselling author Pete Moore examines the issue at the very core of our existence – what it means to be human...

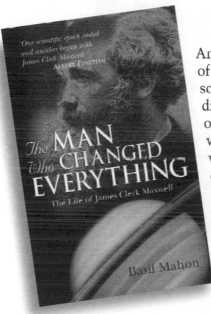

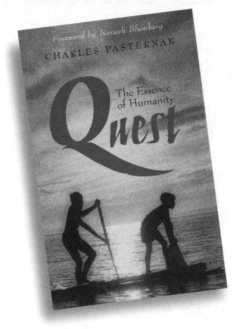